CW00405778

WORLD SOCCER®

EUROPEAN FOOTBALL
WHO'S WHO
2000/2001

WORLD SOCCER

EUROPEAN FOOTBALL
WHO'S WHO
2000/2001

THE ULTIMATE A-Z OF BRITISH
AND EUROPEAN FOOTBALL

Edited by **Gavin Hamilton**

CollinsWillow
An Imprint of HarperCollinsPublishers

First published in 2000 by CollinsWillow
an imprint of HarperCollins*Publishers*

© Gavin Hamilton 2000

1   3   5   7   9   8   6   4   2

All rights reserved. No part of this publication may be reproduced,
stored in a retrieval system, or transmitted, in any form or by any means,
electronic, mechanical, photocopying or otherwise, without the prior written permission of the publishers

The Author asserts the moral right to be identified as the author of this work

A CIP catalogue record for this book is available from the British Library

ISBN 0 00 710681 5

Printed and bound in Great Britain by Omnia Books Limited, Glasgow

All photographs courtesy of Empics

INTRODUCTION

This book originally began as a project for worldsoccer.com, the online version of World Soccer, the leading international football magazine – the UK's oldest football title – of which I am proud to be the Editor. We soon realised the potential for a book, and after months of painful research and hard work, here it is.

It would be wrong to suggest that a magical scientific formula was used to decide upon the final 3000 names featured. There are bound to be people who will disagree with some of our inclusions and argue that we made some serious errors of omission.

We set out to include the major personalities from each European League and national team, placing the emphasis on those people who are set to make an impact on European football in the near future. So there was no place for Paul Gascoigne, who is unlikely to play for England again and has not played in European club competitions for almost three years. But we have included youngsters such as West Ham's Michael Carrick and Bayer Leverkusen's American teenager Landon Donovan.

Players make up the bulk of the book, but we have also included around 300 of the Continent's leading, active coaches, and a smattering of business people, politicians and assorted movers and shakers. I made a conscious decision not to include any journalists for fear of reprisals from colleagues who were not included.

It must be stressed that the opinions expressed are personal, and are mine or those of the contributors.

I would like to thank the following people for their help and contributions: Nick Bidwell, Daniel Fein, Domenico Aquilina, Sam Beckwith, Rab Christie, Alberto da Silva, Klaas-Jan Droppert, Lou Economopoulos, Alan Fairley, Miron Goihman, Victor Gusev, Pentti Hietanen, Dariusz Kurowski, Ori Lewis, Vladimir Novak, Sigurd Odegaard, Michel Stojmanovski, Duncan Shaw, Ivar von Rulach, Oleg Zadernovsky, Paddy Agnew, Dominique Antognoni, Oliver Butler, Jim Holden, David Hamilton, Duncan Bond, Colin Halliday, Mike Hughes, Gary Payne.

I would particularly like to thank Tom Whiting at HarperCollins for believing in the concept and pushing me all the way.

Thanks most of all to Debbie for her love and support. This book is especially for Lola and Ruby. The next 600 pages are the reason they have not seen much of their dad recently. It's payback time.

Gavin Hamilton, London, August 2000

NOTES AND ABBREVIATIONS

Countries

A&B . . . . Antigua & Barbuda
Afg . . . . . Afghanistan
Agl . . . . . Anguilla
Alb . . . . . Albania
Alg . . . . . Algeria
AmS . . . . American Samoa
And . . . . Andorra
Ang . . . . Angola
Arg . . . . . Argentina
Arm . . . . Armenia
Aru . . . . . Aruba
Aus . . . . Australia
Aut . . . . . Austria
Aze . . . . Azerbaijan
Ban . . . . Bangladesh
Bar . . . . . Barbados
Bel . . . . . Belgium
Ben . . . . Benin
Ber . . . . . Bermuda
Bhm . . . . Bahamas
Bhn . . . . Bahrain
Bls . . . . . Belarus
Blz . . . . . Belize
Bol . . . . . Bolivia
Bos . . . . Bosnia-Herzegovina
Bot . . . . . Botswana
Bra . . . . . Brazil
Brd . . . . . Burundi
Bru . . . . . Brunei
BuF . . . . Burkina Faso
Bul . . . . . Bulgaria
BVI . . . . . British Virgin Islands
Cam . . . . Cameroon
Can . . . . Canada
CAR . . . . Central African Rep

Cay . . . . Cayman Islands
Chd . . . . Chad
Chl . . . . . Chile
Chn . . . . China
Cmb . . . . Cambodia
Col . . . . . Colombia
Con . . . . Congo
Coo . . . . Cook Islands
CR . . . . . Costa Rica
Cro . . . . . Croatia
Cub . . . . Cuba
CVI . . . . . Cape Verde Islands
Cyp . . . . Cyprus
Cze . . . . Czech Republic
DAn . . . . Dutch Antilles
Den . . . . Denmark
Dji . . . . . Djibouti
Dom . . . . Dominica
DoR . . . . Dominican Republic
DRC . . . . DR Congo
Ecu . . . . Ecuador
Egy . . . . Egypt
EIS . . . . . El Salvador
Eng . . . . England
EqG . . . . Equatorial Guinea
Eri . . . . . Eritrea
Est . . . . . Estonia
Eth . . . . . Ethiopia
Far . . . . . Faroe Islands
Fij . . . . . Fiji
Fin . . . . . Finland
Fra . . . . . France
Gab . . . . Gabon
Gam . . . . Gambia
Gdp . . . . Guadeloupe
Geo . . . . Georgia

Ger . . . . . Germany
Gha . . . . Ghana
Gre . . . . . Greece
Grn . . . . . Grenada
Gtm . . . . Guatemala
GuB . . . . Guinea-Bissau
Gui . . . . . Guinea
Gum . . . . Guam
Guy . . . . Guyana
Hai . . . . . Haiti
HK . . . . . Hong Kong
Hnd . . . . Honduras
Hol . . . . . Holland
Hun . . . . Hungary
Ice . . . . . Iceland
Ind . . . . . India
Ins . . . . . Indonesia
Ire . . . . . Ireland, Republic
Irn . . . . . Iran
Irq . . . . . Iraq
Isr . . . . . Israel
Ita . . . . . Italy
IvC . . . . . Ivory Coast
Jam . . . . Jamaica
Jap . . . . Japan
Jor . . . . . Jordan
Kaz . . . . . Kazakhstan
Ken . . . . Kenya
Kuw . . . . Kuwait
Kyr . . . . . Kyrgyzstan
Lao . . . . Laos
Lat . . . . . Latvia
Lbr . . . . . Liberia
Lby . . . . . Libya
Leb . . . . Lebanon
Les . . . . . Lesotho

NOTES AND ABBREVIATIONS

Lie . . . . . Liechtenstein
Lit . . . . . Lithuania
Lux. . . . . Luxembourg
Mac . . . . Macedonia
Mad . . . . Madagascar
Mar . . . . Martinique
Mco . . . . Macao
Mdv . . . . Maldives
Mex . . . . Mexico
Mli . . . . . Mali
Mlt . . . . . Malta
Mly. . . . . Malaysia
Mol . . . . Moldova
Mon . . . . Mongolia
Mor . . . . Morocco
Moz . . . . Mozambique
Mra . . . . Mauritania
Mrs . . . . Mauritius
Mst . . . . Montserrat
Mwi . . . . Malawi
Mya . . . . Myanmar
Nam. . . . Namibia
Nep . . . . Nepal
Ngr . . . . Niger
NI. . . . . . Northern Ireland
Nic . . . . . Nicaragua
Nig. . . . . Nigeria
NKo . . . . North Korea
Nor. . . . . Norway
NZ . . . . . New Zealand
Oma. . . . Oman
Pak . . . . Pakistan
Pal . . . . . Palestine
Pan . . . . Panama
Par. . . . . Paraguay

Per. . . . . Peru
Phi . . . . . Philippines
PNG . . . . Papua New Guinea
Pol . . . . . Poland
Por. . . . . Portugal
PR . . . . . Puerto Rico
Qat. . . . . Qatar
Reu . . . . Reunion
Rom. . . . Romania
Rus . . . . Russia
Rwa . . . . Rwanda
SAf. . . . . South Africa
SaM . . . . San Marino
Sau . . . . Saudi Arabia
Sco . . . . Scotland
Sen . . . . Senegal
Sey . . . . Seychelles
Sin . . . . . Singapore
SKo . . . . South Korea
SLe . . . . Sierra Leone
Slk . . . . . Slovakia
Sln . . . . . Slovenia
Sol . . . . . Solomon Islands
Som . . . . Somalia
Spa . . . . Spain
Sri . . . . . Sri Lanka
StK. . . . . St Kitts & Nevis
StL. . . . . St Lucia
STP . . . . San Tome e Principe
StV. . . . . St Vincent & The
. . . . Grenadines
Sud . . . . Sudan
Sur. . . . . Surinam
Swa . . . . Swaziland
Swe . . . . Sweden

Swi. . . . . Switzerland
Syr . . . . . Syria
T&T . . . . Trinidad & Tobago
Tah. . . . . Tahiti
Tai . . . . . Taiwan
Taj . . . . . Tajikistan
Tan. . . . . Tanzania
TCI. . . . . Turks & Caicos
Islands
Tha . . . . Thailand
Tkm . . . . Turkmenistan
Tog. . . . . Togo
Ton. . . . . Tonga
Tun. . . . . Tunisia
Tur . . . . . Turkey
UAE . . . . United Arab Emirates
Uga . . . . Uganda
Ukr. . . . . Ukraine
Uru. . . . . Uruguay
USA . . . . United States
UVI. . . . . US Virgin Islands
Uzb . . . . Uzbekistan
Van . . . . Vanuatu
Ven . . . . Venezuela
Vie . . . . . Vietnam
Wal . . . . Wales
WSa . . . . Western Samoa
Yem . . . . Yemen
Yug . . . . Yugoslavia
Zam . . . . Zambia
Zim . . . . Zimbabwe

NOTES AND ABBREVIATIONS

• All caps records are correct up until July 2, 2000, the Final of Euro 2000 (ie the official end of the 1999-2000 European season). Records for non-European players have not been included.

• In player entries, the nationality of a club has only been included when the club is a foreign club (eg Juventus (Ita) for Zinedine Zidane, Juventus for Alessandro Del Piero).

• Most entries are listed under the conventional European surname, followed by the Christian name. Spanish and Portuguese enties are listed under their most familiar name, family name or nickname, with the full name spelt out below. Turkish entries are listed under the first name rather than last name.

• In accordance with the house style of *World Soccer* magazine, no accents have been used. Where possible, we have tried to give phonetic spellings of names.

A

PLAYER
AASE, Gunnar
Midfielder, Norwegian, 179cm, 79kg
Born: 29.09.71, Norway
Clubs: Viking Stavangar (1994-)
Full international (Norway) 4 caps/1 goal
• Winger who is Viking Stavangar's main weapon down the right flank. Was on the verge of an international career some years ago but has not fullfilled his true potential.

PLAYER
ABBIATI, Christian
Goalkeeper, Italian, 190cm, 90kg
Born: 08.07.77, Abbiategreasso, Italy
Clubs: Monza (1994-98), Borgosesia (1995-96), Milan (1998-)
• One of the stars of Milan's 1998-99 title-winning season, who began the campaign as an unknown and ended it as a key figure.
• Took advantage of a six-match suspension to **Sebastiano Rossi** to take the number one spot at Milan, coming on for Rossi when he was sent off against Perugia in January 1999 and staying on for an 18-match unbeaten run.
• Called into Italy's Euro 2000 squad as a late replacement for the injured **Gianluigi Buffon**, but did not play.

PLAYER
ABDULLAH Ercan
Midfielder, Turkish, 184cm, 76kg
Born: 12.08.71, Istanbul, Turkey
Clubs: Trabzonspor (1993-99), Fenerbahce (1999-)
Full international (Turkey) 54 caps/0 goals
• Blond-haired winger whose crosses from the left are a key attacking weapon for the Turkish national side.

• Started out at Trabzonspor, before moving to Fenerbahce in a high-profile deal with **Ogun** in summer 1999.
• Broke into the national side under **Fatih Terim** and stayed in favour under **Mustapha Denizli.**
• Played for Turkey at Euro 96 and Euro 2000, but was criticised by the Turkish press for his role in the defeat by Italy, and was dropped.

PLAYER
ABEL XAVIER
Full name: Abel Luis da Costa Silva Xavier
Defender, Portuguese, 189cm, 81kg
Born: 20.11.72, Nampula, Mozambique
Clubs: Estrela Amadora (1991-93), Benfica (1993-95), Bari (Ita) (1995-96), Oviedo (Spa) (1996-98), PSV (Hol) (1998-99), Everton (Eng) (1999-)
Full international (Portugal) 15 caps/2 goals
• Much travelled right-back who started out in Portugal but was born in Mozambique.
• Known for his flamboyant haircuts.
• International debut 31.03.93, v Switzerland (1-1).
• Was banned for nine months from UEFA competitions after his protests following Portugal's Golden Goal defeat by France in the semi-final of Euro 2000. His handball, spotted by the linesman but not the referee, had led to France being awarded an extra-time penalty.

PLAYER
ABELARDO
Full name: Abelardo Fernandez Antuna
Defender, Spanish, 180cm, 77kg
Born: 19.03.79, Gijon, Spain
Clubs: Sporting Gijon (1988-94), Barcelona (1994-)
Full international (Spain) 47 caps/3 goals
• Accomplished centre-back who is tough in the tackle and dominating in the air, though has been criticised for his poor reading of the game.
• A product of Sporting Gijon's famous youth school, but was discarded for not being tall enough.

• Joined Barcelona for £1.3million in 1994 and has since become one of the most charismatic players in the Barça dressing room.
• A member of Spain's 1992 Olympic-winning side and one of only two Spanish players to play the full 90 minutes of all of Spain's matches at USA 94.
• Keeps a complete video collection of all of his matches.
• Played in one of Spain's matches at France 98 and in three of their four games at Euro 2000.

PLAYER
ACIMOVIC, Milenko
Midfielder, Slovenian, 186cm, 80kg
Born: 15.02.77, Ljubljana, Slovenia
Clubs: Olimpia Ljubljana, Red Star Belgrade
Full international (Slovenia) 25 caps/6 goals
• Talented and promising young midfielder, but not yet complete player, due to a lack of work-rate. Most effective as a supersub, where his pace and eye for goal come to the fore.
• Became an instant national hero when he scored Slovenia's historic winner, from 50m, in the EURO 2000 play-offs against Ukraine.
• Made his international debut against Cyprus in April 1998 and was the youngest member of Slovenia's Euro 2000 squad.
• Married to the sister of **Dejan Stakovic**.

PLAYER
ACOSTA, Alberto
Full name: Alberto Frederico Acosta
Forward, Argentinian, 178cm, 79kg
Born: 23.080.66, Santa Fe, Argentina
Clubs: Union Sante Fe (1986-87), San Lorenzo (1987-90), Touluose (Fra) (1990-92), San Lorenzo (1992-93), Boca Juniors (1993-94) Univ. Catolica (Chi) (1994-95), Yokohama Marinos (Jap) (1996), Univ. Catolica (Chi) (1997), San Lorenzo (1997-98) Sporting Lisbon (Por) (1999-)
• Much-travelled Argentinian striker whose goals were crucial in Sporting Lisbon winning the 1999-2000 Portuguese League title.

Tony Adams

PLAYER
ACUNA, Roberto

Full name: Roberto Miguel Acuna Cabello
Midfielder, Paraguayan, 175cm, 78kg
Born: 25.03.72, Avellaneda, Argentina
Clubs: Argentinos Juniors (Arg) (1993-94), Boca Juniors (Arg) (1994-95), Independiente (Arg) (1995-97), Real Zaragoza (Spa) (1997-)
Full international (Paraguay)
• Paraguayan midfielder, captain of his national side and arguably his country's best attacking midfielder.
• Born in Argentina of Paraguayan parents. Made his name at Boca Juniors and then Indendiente.
• Joined Spain's Zaragoza in 1997 for a club record £3million.
• A hard worker with plenty of spirit, he is nicknamed 'El Toro' (The Bull) for his domineering approach in midfield.
• Played for Paraguay in the 1998 World Cup.

PLAYER
ADAILTON

Forward, Brazilian, 172cm, 65kg
Born: 24.01.77, Caxias do Sul, Brazil
Clubs: Juventude (1995-96), Guarani (1997), Parma (Ita) (1997-98), Paris Saint-Germain (Fra) (1998-99, loan), Verona (Ita) (1999-2000, loan).
• Young striker who has yet to fulfill the huge potential he showed when finishing as the top scorer at the 1997 World Youth Cup in Malaysia.
• After scoring six goals for Brazil, impressing everybody with his pace and technique, he was hailed as the new Bebeto and earned a transfer to Parma.
• Injuries did not help, but he failed to settle in Serie A, was loaned out to PSG and then back to Italy, to Verona, and was set to move on again during the summer of 2000.

COACH
ADAMEC, Josef

Slovakian
Born: 26.02.42
• National coach of Slovakia since March 1999.
• As a player, he starred for Spartak Trnava (1959-61, 1963-64 and 1966-76), Dukla Prague (1961-63) and Slovan Bratislava (1964-66, 1977-80), scoring 170 goals in 383 matches. Also won 44 caps for Czechoslovakia, scoring 14 goals.
• Gained coaching experience as an assistant at Spartak Trnava, before taking charge of Dukla Banska Bystrica between 1981 and 1985. Then had spells at Vorwarts Steyr (1985-88), Inter Bratislava (1989-91, 1992-94, 1995), Dukla Banska Bystrica (1991), Bohemians (1992), Svit Zlin (1995) and Tatran Presov (1997).

PLAYER
ADAMS, Tony

Defender, English, 190cm, 87kg
Born: 10.10.66, Romford, England
Clubs: Arsenal (1984-)
Full international (England) 64 caps/5 goals
• Joined Arsenal as a trainee in the summer of 1982 and has since become a stalwart centre-back for club and country and a seminal figure in Arsenal's legendary defence.
• Spent six months in jail in 1990 following his conviction on drink-driving charges and went public as an alcoholic in 1997, talking frankly about his additions in an acclaimed best-selling autobiography.
• Continues to defy injury problems, but missed Euro 2000 through injury. Has enjoyed a new lease of life under of **Arsene Wenger**.
• Captain of Arsenal's 1994 European Cup-winners Cup-winning side, and the 1998 double-winning side, scoring a memorable goal on the last day of the season against Everton.
• Capped five times at under-21 level.
• International debut 18.02.87, v Spain (won 4-2).

PLAYER
ADANI, Daniele
Defender, Italian, 181cm, 76kg
Born: 10.07.74, Correggio, Italy
Clubs: Modena (1991-94), Lazio (1994), Brescia (1994-99), Fiorentina (1999-).
• Defender who has developed into a useful campaigner after a number of years up and down the divisions between Serie A and Serie B.
• Started out at Serie B side Modena, before a move to Lazio failed to work out. Did not play any games for the Roman club and instead moved on to Brescia in November 1994.
• Experienced relegation from Serie A twice with Brescia, but did enough to impress Fiorentina, who signed him in the summer of 1999.

COACH
ADELAAR, Frans
Dutch
Born: 05.12.60
• Coach of Utrecht since the departure of Mark Wotte to Den Bosch in March 2000. Was previously assistant coach.

PLAYER
ADEPOJU, Mutiu
Midfielder, Nigerian, 180cm, 73kg
Born: 22.12.70, Ibadan, Nigeria
Clubs: Shooting Stars, Julius Berger, Real Madrid B (1990-92), Racing Santander (1992-96), Real Sociedad (1996-)
Full international (Nigeria)
• Quick and versatile midfielder with subtle ball control and a busy work-rate. Can play anywhere from full-back to attacker.
• Made his name at the World Under-20 Youth Cup in Saudi Arabia in 1989, playing for the Nigerian team which lost to Portugal in the Final. Was signed by Real Madrid but failed to break into the first team.
• Moved to Racing Santander, helping them win promotion and then joining Real Sociedad in

1996 for £1million.
• Played for Nigeria at the 1998 World Cup finals in France, scoring against Spain in the first round.
• Made his international debut aged 19 against Togo in 1990.
• Devout muslim who is nicknamed 'The Headmaster' because of the number of goals scored early in his career with his head.

PLAYER
ADRIAANSE, Co
Dutch
Born: 21.07.47
• Coach of Ajax from the start of the 2000-2001 season, having previously spent three seasons at Willem II.
• Director of the renowned Ajax youth system from 1992 to 97 and before that was in charge of Den Haag for four seasons. Won promotion to the Dutch first division in 1986 with FC Zwolle.
• A modest player whose best spell was with Utrecht between 1980 and 1986, he has earned a reputation as a coach who plays attacking football. But he also is a strict disciplinarian – at Willem II he was nicknamed the Tilburg Tyrant and once made his squad run 26km as a punishment for a poor performance in a friendly.

PLAYER
ADRIANO
Full name: Adriano Felix Texeira
Defender, Brazilian, 182cm, 82kg
Born: 07.04.73, Fortaleza, Brazil
Clubs: Sporte Recife (1990-96), Celta Vigo (Spa) (1996-97), Fluminense (1997-99), Celta Vigo (Spa) (1998-)
• Central defender who has never managed to hold down a regular first-team place in Spain with Celta, returning home on loan to Brazil's Fluminense for the 1997-98 and 1998-99 seasons.
• Not to be confused with the Brazilian striker, also known as Adriano, who was linked with a move to Marseille from Atletico Parana in summer 2000.

COACH
ADVOCAAT, Dick
Dutch
Born: 27.09.47
• The former PSV Eindhoven coach made an immediate impact when joining Rangers in 1998, leading the Ibrox club to the domestic treble during his first season in charge. Some inspired signings by Advocaat have provided Rangers with a sophisticated European dimension and the gap between the club and nearest rivals Celtic has grown appreciably since the Dutchman took over. Acknowledged as a clever tactician, Advocaat is now looking to take Rangers one step further and achieve long awaited credibility in Europe.
• Previously in charge of Haarlem (1987-89), SVV (1989-91), Dordrecht 90 (1991), the Dutch national side (1992-1994) and PSV (1994-98)

PLAYER
AFANOU, Kodjo
Defender, French/Togo, 180cm, 76kg
Born: 21.11.77, Lome, Togo
Clubs: Bordeaux (1995-)
• The number of Italian and English clubs keeping tabs on him of late testify to his quality. Has served Bordeaux well at right-back and defensive midfield, but is now well ensconced at centre-back, his best position. Although born in the African state of Togo, he has adopted French nationality and has played for *Les Bleus* at Under-21 level.

PLAYER
AGALI, Victor
Forward, Nigerian, 193cm, 82kg
Born: 29.12.78, Lagos, Nigeria
Clubs: FC Nitel, Marseille (Fra) (1996-97), Toulon (Fra) (1997-98), Hansa Rostock (Ger) (1998-)
• Fast-improving Nigerian striker signed from French Third Division club Toulon two years ago and has won a lot of praise for his ability to serve as an attacking pivot, strong running with the ball and heading ability. However, he must score more goals; in the last two seasons he has only managed six per campaign.
• Says his role model is Wolfsburg's Nigerian hitman **Jonathan Akpoborie.**

PLAYER
AGBOH, Kuam
Midfielder, French, 176cm, 70kg
Born: 28.12.77 Tsevik, Togo
Clubs: Auxerre (1997-)
• Product of the famed Auxerre youth system who is only now starting to establish himself in the Auxerre first team.
• A defensive midfielder whose team-mates benefit from his hard work and tough tackling.

ADMINISTRATOR
AGNELLI, Giovanni
• Dominating, patriachal figure at Juventus, where he is honorary president and the representative of the interests of the Agnelli family, owners of FIAT and Juventus.
• A hugely influential figure in the Italian political economy.
• Nicknamed 'L'avoccate' (The Lawyer).

PLAYER
AGOSTINHO
Full name: Joaquim Agostinho da Silva Ribeiro
Forward, Portuguese, 179cm, 78kg
Born: 15.10.75, Pacos da Farreira, Portugal
Clubs: Vitoria Guimaraes (1993-95), Real Madrid (Spa) (1995), Sevilla (Spa) (1995-96), Salamanca (Spa) (1996-97), Las Palmas (Spa) (1997-98), Malaga (Spa) (1998-)
• Left-sided midfielder or forward who has revived his career at Malaga after failing to make the grade at Real Madrid.
• An important member of Malaga's promotion-winning side in 1998-99, where his crosses were one of the team's most important sources of goals.

PLAYER
AGUADO, Xavier
Full name: Xavier Aguado Companys
Defender, Spanish, 186cm, 80kg
Born: 05.06.68, Barcelona, Spain
Clubs: Sabadell (1988-90), Zaragoza (1990-)
• Solid but unspectacular central defender who is approaching the end of a career spent almost exclusively with Zaragoza.
• Member of Zaragoza's 1994 Spanish Cup and 1995 European Cup-winners Cup-winning sides.

PLAYER
AGUILERA, Carlos
Full name: Carlos Aguilera Martin
Defender, Spanish, 174cm, 76kg
Born: 22.05.69, Madrid, Spain
Clubs: Atletico Madrid (1986-93), Tenerife (1993-96), Atletico Madrid (1996-)
Full international (Spain) 9 caps/0 goals
• Attacking right-back who won a belated international call-up, making his debut against Slovakia in September 1997.
• Described by former national coach Javier Clemente as 'a clueless footballer'.
• Made his Spanish Liga debut as a winger for Atletico aged 18, but then left for Tenerife, returning after three seasons in 1996 when Atletico had won the Spanish League and Cup double.
• Played for Spain at the 1998 World Cup.

ADMINISTRATOR
AHLSTROM, Fritz
• Danish media director of UEFA who is responsible for overseeing the public relations of European football's governing body.

PLAYER
AHMET Dursun
Forward, Turkish, 175cm, 71kg
Born: 25.01.78, Germany
Clubs: Besiktas

Full international (Turkey) 1 cap/0 goals
• Striker whose crucial goals for Besiktas (21 goals in the 1999-2000 season) took him to the brink of Turkey's squad for Euro 2000.
• A sharp goal poacher who has been likened to **Hakan Sukur**.
• Turkish Under-21 international.
• Brought up in Germany, but made his name at Kocaelispor.

ADMINISTRATOR
AIGNER, Gerhard
Born: 01.09.43
• General secretary of UEFA, European football's governing body and the man responsible for the day-to-day running of the organisation.
• Born and educated in Regensburg, Germany.
• Began working for UEFA in 1969, rising to the post of general secretary in 1989.
• An amateur player with Regensburg, Moutier and Muri-Guligen.

PLAYER
AILTON
Full name: Ailton Goncalves da Silva
Forward, Brazilian, 177cm, 74kg
Born: 19.07.73, Brazil
Clubs: Recife, Santa Cruz, Guarani, Univ Nuevo Leon (Mex) (1997-98), Werder Bremen (Ger) (1998-)
• In the 1998-99 season, the Brazilian striker was a huge flop, contributing little as Werder only narrowly managed to avoid relegation. But in the 1999-2000 season the transformation was dramatic. No more whingeing about life in Germany and instead he concentrated on what he does best – provoking panic in a defence. An attacker of pace, dribbling ability and explosive left-footed shooting power, he scored a dozen goals last term and made 10 more.

AKERS, Chris

- Founder of the Sports Internet group which runs the planetfootball and Premier League club websites and the Carling Opta statistics system.
- Investment banker before taking over Leeds United in 1996. Tried to persuade Time Warner to buy Manchester United five years before BSkyB's attempt in 1999.
- Left Leeds in 1999 to concentrate on his Internet interests.

AKPOBORIE, Jonathan

Forward, Nigerian, 175cm, 69kg
Born: 20.10.68, Lagos, Nigeria
Clubs: Julius Berger, Brooklyn College (USA), Saarbrucken (Ger) (1990-92), Carl Jeiss Jena (Ger) (1992-94), Stuttgarter Kickers (Ger) (1994-95), Waldhof Mannheim (Ger) (1995), Hansa Rostock (Ger) (1996-97), Stuttgart (Ger) (1997-99), Wolfsburg (Ger) (1999-)
Full international (Nigeria)

- Nigerian striker who was Wolfsburg's top scorer in 1999-2000 with 12 goals. A sleek and powerful frontrunner with good finishing skills on either foot and a threatening aerial game.
- Started out with the Julius Berger club in Lagos, and played for Nigeria at the 1987 World Youth Cup in Chile, before spending a year studying and playing soccer at Brooklyn College in New York.
- Headed to Germany to try his luck in the Second Division in 1990, starting with Saarbrucken and moving on to Carl Zeiss Jena and Stuttgarter Kickers.
- Scored 37 goals for Stuttgart's second side in 1994-95, earning a transfer to Waldhof Mannheim and then to Hansa Rostock in January 1996.
- Earned comparisons to **George Weah** while with Hansa, but struggled at Stuttgart, before resurrecting his career at Wolfsburg.
- International debut for Nigeria against Ghana in April 1991.

AKONNOR, Charles

Midfielder, Ghanaian, 182cm, 72kg
Born: 12.03.74, Accra, Ghana
Clubs: Young Hearts, Okwahu United, Goldfields, Fortuna Koln (Ger) (1992-98), Wolfsburg (Ger) (1998-)
Full international (Ghana)

- Athletic and skilful Ghanaian international right-sided or central midfielder. A good team man, a neat passer and packs a mighty shot from distance. Set-piece specialist.
- Captain of the Ghana national side since the retirement of Abedi Pele.
- Started out Okwahu United, where he was known as 'CK'.

AKOTO, Eric

Defender, Ghanaian, 189cm, 74kg
Born: 20.07.80, Ghana
Clubs: Liberty Professionals, Grazer AK (Aut) (1998-)
Full international (Ghana)

- Powerful but impetuous young central defender, who was taken to Austria by then GAK coach **Klaus Augenthaler** and is seen as having a strong future.
- Particularly effective in the air, but can over-elaborate in the penalty area.

AKWUEGBU, Benedict

Forward, Nigerian, 184cm, 80kg
Born: 20.12.78, Jos, Nigeria
Clubs: Lens (1998-99), SW Bregenz (Aut) (1999-)

- Nigerian striker who has been one of the most effective forwards in the Austrian League over the past two seasons.
- Younger brother Emmanuel also plays in Austria.

Demetrio Albertini

PLAYER
ALBERTINI, Demetrio
Midfielder, Italian, 180cm, 75kg
Born: 23.08.71, Besana Brianza, Italy
Clubs: Milan (1988-), Padova (1990-1, loan)
Full international (Italy) 71 caps/2 goals
• The mainstay of the Italian national team midfield for more than eight seasons.
• A European Cup-winner with Milan in 1994.
• A midfield 'Metronome' who dictates the tempo of the game with his thoughtful, intuitive passing.
• Made his Serie A debut aged 17 in January 1989.
• His place at Euro 2000 had been in doubt after a loss of form for Milan, but he had an excellent tournament and was one of Italy's best players as they upset the form book to reach the Final.
• Brother is a catholic priest.
• International debut 21.12.91, v Cyprus.
• Former coach **Arrigo Sacchi** on Albertini: 'He makes the side tick over.'

PLAYER
ALBERTO
Full name: Alberto Lopez Fernandez
Goalkeeper, Spanish, 182cm, 77kg
Born: 20.05.69, San Sebastian, Spain
Clubs: Real Sociedad (1991-)
• Solid and entirely dependable keeper.
• Now in his ninth season with hometown club Sociedad.

PLAYER
ALBERTO
Full name: Alberto Lopez Moreno
Forward, Spanish, 183cm, 83kg
Born: 25.02.67, Madrid, Spain
Clubs: Burgos (1987-88), Valladolid (1988-95), Racing Santander (1995-98), Valladolid (1998-)
• Veteran striker with a strong physical presence and a keen eye for goal.
• Returned to Valladolid to end his career following a spell at Racing Santander

PLAYER
ALBERTZ, Jorg
Midfielder, German, 184cm, 83kg
Born: 29.01.71, Monchengladbach, Germany
Clubs: Fortuna Dusseldorf (1990-93), Hamburg
(1993-96), Rangers (Sco) (1996-)
Full international (Germany) 3 caps/0 goals
• Powerful and versatile midfielder whose
penchant for scoring against arch rivals Celtic
has made him a legend with Rangers fans during
four years in Glasgow.

PLAYER
ALBELDA, David
Midfielder, Spanish, 181cm, 75kg
Born: 01.09.77, Valencia, Spain
Clubs: Valencia (1995-98), Villarreal (1998-99),
Valencia (1999-)
• Returned to Valencia after a two-year spell at
Villarreal and was used as a holding midfielder
by **Hector Cuper**, before breaking a leg in
December 1999.
• Has an unfounded reputation as a hard man
after a tackle which seriously injured **Juninho**.

PLAYER
ALBRECHTSEN, Martin
Defender, Danish, 185cm, 79kg
Born: 31.03.80, Denmark
Clubs: AB (1998-)
• Promising, pacy left-back who likes to get forward
and is strong in the air. Has made great progress
in the past year, establishing himself in AB's first
team and attracting interest from English clubs.

PLAYER
ALDAIR
Full name: Aldair Nascimento dos Santos
Defender, Brazilian, 183cm, 76kg
Born: 30.11.65, Iheus, Brazil
Clubs: Flamengo (1986-89), Benfica (Por) (1989-
90), Roma (Ita) (1990-)
Full international (Brazil) 81 caps/3 goals

• Experienced centre-back who is the longest-
serving foreigner at Roma, having joined from
Benfica in 1990.
• At the heart of the Brazilian defence which won
the World Cup in 1994, and a member of the
team in 1990 in Italy and in 1998 in France.
• Nicknamed 'Pluto' for his languid style.
• Pronounced Al-die-ear

PLAYER
ALEKSIC, Mirko
Midfielder, Yugoslav, 170cm
Born: 26.09.77, Serbia
Clubs: Vojvodina Novi Sad, Obilic
• Promising right-sided wing-back who recently
moved to Belgrade club Obilic.

PLAYER
ALEKSIDZE, Rati
Forward, Georgian, 187cm, 74kg
Born: 03.08.78, Tbilisi, Georgia
Clubs: Dinamo Tbilisi, Chelsea (Eng) (1999-)
Full international (Georgia)
• Oustanding prospect who was Georgian player
of the year in 1999, having captained Dinamo
Tbilisi aged 20.

PLAYER
ALENITCHEV, Dmitri
Midfielder, Russian, 173cm, 67kg
Born: 27.10.72, Velike Luki, Russia
Clubs: Lokomotiv Moscow (1991-93), Spartak
Moscow (1993-98), Roma (Ita) (1998-99), Perugia
(Ita) (2000-)
Full international (Russia) 28 caps/4 goals
• Midfielder who signed for Roma in the summer
of 1998 after catching the eye while playing for
Spartak Moscow against Internazionale in the
UEFA Cup.
• Won Russian title with Spartak in 1994 and made
his international debut against Iceland in 1996.
• Russian player of the year in 1997 and a key
member of the Russian national side.

PLAYER
ALESSANDRO
Full name: Alessandro Andrade de Oliveira
Forward, Brazilian, 170cm, 73kg
Born: 27.05.73, Bahia, Brazil
Clubs: Vasco da Gama (1995), Santos (1996-97), Jubilo Iwata (Jap) (1997-98), Santos (1998-99), FC Porto (Por) (1999-)
• Talented forward whose undoubtable qualities have yet to be put to good use at Porto.

PLAYER
ALEX
Full name: Alex Dias de Almeida
Forward, Brazilian, 174cm, 70kg
26.06.72, Rio Brihante, Brazil
Clubs: Goias, St Etienne (Fra) (1999-)
• Explosive, technically-gifted Brazilian striker who enjoyed a superlative first season in Europe following a move from Goias to Saint-Etienne a year ago. He quickly showed French fans just why he had been dubbed 'The Little Romario' in his homeland, scoring a total of 15 French League goals, including four in one game against Marseille.
• In February 2000, he also had the honour of scoring Saint-Etienne's 3,000th goal in the top flight.
• Not to be confused with international midfielder Alex (De Souza Alexsandro) of Palmeiras.

PLAYER
ALEXANDERSSON, Niclas
Midfielder, Swedish, 181cm, 73kg
Born: 29.12.71, Halmstad, Sweden
Clubs: Halmstad (1989-96), IFK Gothenburg (1996-1997), Sheffield Wednesday (Eng) (1997-2000), Everton (Eng) (2000-)
Full international (Sweden) 39 caps/5 goals
• Industrious, skilful right-sided midfielder who has become a regular first-choice for Sweden.
• Recommended to then Sheffield Wednesday manager Ron Atkinson by **Roland Nilsson**.
• Suffered relegation with Wednesday in May

2000, and was looking for a move to a Premier League club for the 2000-2001 season.
• International debut 10.11.93, v Austria (1-1)

PLAYER
ALEXANDRIS, Alexios
Forward, Greek, 178cm, 75kg
Born: 21.10.68, Kiaton, Greece
Clubs: Veria (1986-91), AEK Athens (1991-94), Olympiakos (1994-)
Full international (Greece) 35 caps/8 goals
• Hugely accomplished striker in the Greek League, winning the League title with AEK and Olympiakos and finishing as the top scorer in 1997 with 23 goals.
• Voted best Greek player in the league by players, coaches and presidents of clubs.
• Played once for Greece at the 1994 World Cup.

PLAYER
ALEXIS
Full name: Alexis Trujillo Oromes
Midfielder, Spanish, 176cm, 76kg
Born: 30.07.65, Gran Canaria, Spain
Clubs: Las Palmas (1985-92), Tenerife (1992-93), Real Betis (1993-)
• Hard-working midfielder with skill and vision.
• Started with his native Las Palmas, moving to Tenerife in 1992 and Betis a year later after playing only four League games.
• Excellent performances for Betis led to his appointment as club captain.
• Future at Betis was uncertain after relegation at the end of the 1999-2000 season.

PLAYER
ALFONSO
Full name: Alfonso Perez Munoz
Forward, Spanish, 178cm, 69kg
Born: 26.09.72, Madrid, Spain
Clubs: Real Madrid (1989-95), Real Betis (1995-)
Full international (Spain) 38 caps/11 goals
• Striker who played a starring role in Spain's

1992 Olympic triumph, and was hailed as the next big thing at Real Madrid, only to suffer a cruciate ligament injury which ruled him out of the 1994 World Cup. Returned to appear in all of Spain's games at Euro 96.
• A talented, two-footed striker who likes to run at defenders. Started out as a goalkeeper.
• Known for his trademark white boots.
• Played for Spain at Euro 2000 and became a national hero when he scored the winner in injury time against Yugoslavia which took Spain into the quarter-finals.

PLAYER
ALGERINO, Jimmy
Defender, French, 174cm, 72kg
Born: 28.10.71, Toulouse, France
Clubs: Niort, Monaco, Epinal, Chateauroux, Paris Saint-Germain (1996-)
• Attack-conscious right-back who loves to get forward in support of the attack, hit the bye-line and deliver an accurate pull-back to onrushing teammates. His defensive work is not quite so noteworthy, but he remains one of France's most underrated full-backs, a consistent performer of no little purpose and grit.
• Surname pronounced Al jay ree no

PLAYER
ALI Eren
Defender, Turkish, 184cm, 688kg
Born: 25.10.75, Ankara, Turkey
Clubs: Genclerbirligi, Besiktas
Full international (Turkey) 6 caps/0 goals
• Strong, physical man-marking defender who has been in and out of the Turkish national team in recent seasons.
• Started out at Genclerbirligi, but made his name at Besiktas.
• Missed out on Turkey's squad for Euro 2000.
• Fell out with Besiktas coach Hans-Peter Briegel during the second half of the 1999-2000 season, and was set to move on in summer 2000.

PLAYER
ALICARTE, Herve
Defender, French, 185cm, 82kg
Born: 07.10.74, Perpignan, France
Clubs: Montpellier (1994-98), Bordeaux (1998-)
• Improving central defender, who is both a good marker and assured on the ball. Sometimes takes penalties.
• Brother Bruno played for Montpellier, Martigues and Bastia.

PLAYER
ALKIZA, Bitor
Full name: Bitor Alkiza Fernandez
Midfielder, Spanish, 169cm, 67kg
Born: 26.10.70, San Sebastian, Spain
Clubs: Real Sociedad (1991-94), Athletic Bilbao (1994-)
Full international (Spain) 3 caps/1 goal
• Ball-playing midfielder and a hero with fans at Bilbao after he left rivals Sociedad, where his father was club president, in a £1million transfer.
• Broke into the Spanish national team after Jose Camacho was appointed national coach.

PLAYER
ALKORTA, Rafael
Full name: Rafael Alkorta Martinez
Defender, Spanish, 179cm, 74kg
Born: 16.09.68, Bilbao, Spain
Clubs: Althletic Bilbao (1985-93), Real Madrid (1993-97), Athletic Bilbao (1997-)
Full international (Spain) 54 caps/0 goals
• Hugely experienced centre-back who returned home to Bilbao after spending four seasons at Real, winning the Spanish League in 1995 and 1997.
• Played only 10 games for Real between 1994 and 1996 while appearing 13 times for Spain.
• The £1.9million transfer to Madrid caused uproar in Bilbao because the Basque club had previously announced that all local talent would be retained.
• Formed a strong central defensive partnership at Real Madrid with Fernando Hierro, but returned

to Bilbao, reportedly to be near his sick brother.
• Insists on wearing the letter 'M' after Alkorta on his shirt in memory of his mother.

PLAYER
ALLBACK, Marcus
Forward, Swedish, 180cm, 77kg
Born: 05.07.73, Gothenburg, Sweden
Clubs: Orgryte (1995-97), Lyngby (Den) (1997-98, loan), Bari (Ita) (1998), Orgryte (1998-)
Full international (Sweden) 3 caps/1 goal
• Sharp penalty-box operator who stayed true to Orgryte despite offers from abroad, having returned to Sweden after a difficult time in Italy with Bari.
• Father Stefan is a club director and former player at Orgyte, while uncle Dan also played for the first team.
• Made his mark at Orgryte in the 1997 season, scoring nine goals and going on loan to Lyngby of Denmark for the winter months. There then followed a shock move to Serie A, but he failed to score in 16 outings for Bari.
• Returned to Sweden in 1999, and won an international debut, v South Africa in November 1999.

PLAYER
ALMEYDA, Matias
Midfielder, Argentinian, 174cm, 72kg
Born: 21.12.73, Buenos Aires, Argentina.
Clubs: River Plate (1991-96), Sevilla (Spa) (1996-97), Lazio (Ita) (1997-2000), Parma (Ita) (2000-)
Full international (Argentina)
• Talented young midfielder who combines hard work with creative tendencies. Plays the '**Redondo**' role in front of the defence to perfection.
• Established himself as key influence in Lazio's midfield in 1998-99, despite heavy competition.
• Hailed, inevitably, as the new Maradona when signed by Sevilla in 1996 after winning the Libertadores Cup with River Plate.
• A member of Argentina's silver medal-winning side at the 1996 Atlanta Olympics.
• Moved to Parma in the summer of 2000 as a

makeweight in Lazio's signing of striker **Hernan Crespo**. The deal valued him at £15million.
• Surname pronounced Al may da.

PLAYER
ALOISIO da Silva
Forward, Brazilian, 185cm, 83kg
Born: 27.01.75, Atalia, Brazil
Clubs: Goias, St Etienne
• Although he did not perform as spectacularly as **Alex**, he has proved himself a fine maker and taker of chances for St Etienne.
• Skilful, mobile and combative, Aloisio represented a headache for the majority of French defenders.
• Pronounced Al loy see oh

PLAYER
ALOISIO Pires Alves
Defender, Brazilian, 185cm, 85kg
Born: 16.08.63, Pelotas, Brazil
Clubs: Internacional Porto Alegre (1983-88), Barcelona (Spa) (1988-90), FC Porto (Por) (1990-)
• Brazilian central defender who is approaching the end of an outstanding career in Portugal.

PLAYER
ALPAY Ozalan
Defender, Turkish, 188cm, 81kg
Born: 29.05.73, Izmir, Turkey
Clubs: Soma Linyitspor, Altay, Besiktas, Fenerbahce, Aston Villa (Eng) (2000-)
Full international (Turkey) 49 caps/1 goal
• Uncompromising central defender who is first choice in the Turkish national side as a man-marker
• Strong in the air and quick on the ground, he won a special UEFA fair play award for his decision at Euro 96 not to bring down Croatia's **Goran Vlaovic** when the striker was through on goal. However, four years later at Euro 2000, he was sent off for clashing with Portugal's **Fernando Couto** in the quarter-final in Amsterdam.
• Joined Aston Villa after Euro 2000.

COACH
ALVARO MAGALHAES
Portuguese
Born: 03.01.61
• One of Portugal's brightest young coaches, a forward-thinking strategist and a strong organiser of teams.
• As a player, he starred for Benfica as a full-back.
• Took Santa Clara into the top flight and then had a brief, less successful spell at Chaves, before taking charge of Gil Vicente for the 1998-99 season.

PLAYER
AMANTIDIS, Giorgos
Defender, Greek, 182cm, 75kg
Born: 21.10.68, Greece
Clubs: Apollon, Olympiakos (1993-)
Full international (Greece) 8 caps/1 goal
• The most consistent player for Olympiakos and the main reason why the team had the best defensive record (18 goals conceded).

PLAYER
AMAVISCA, Jose
Full name: Jose Emilio Amavisca Garate
Midfielder, Spanish, 181cm, 68kg
Born: 19.06.71, Laredo, Spain
Clubs: Valladolid (1989-91), Lleida (1991-92), Valladolid (1992-94), Real Madrid (1994-98), Racing Santander (1998-)
Full international (Spain) 15 caps/1 goal
• Left-sided attacker who was voted player of the season in Spain for his contribution to Real Madrid's 1994-95 title-winning campaign.
• A member of Spain's 1992 Olympic-winning side, appearing in the Final against Poland when they were 1-0 down and helping to turn things around.
• Signed by Racing in January 1999.
• International debut against Cyprus in 1994.

Matias Almeyda

Emmanuel Ammunike

PLAYER
AMBROSETTI, Gabriele
Midfielder, Italian, 180cm, 72kg
Born: 07.08.73, Varese, Italy
Clubs: Varese (1990-93), Brescia (1993-96), Venezia (1994-95, loan), Vicenza (1996-99), Chelsea (Eng) (1999-)
• Surprise signing for Chelsea in August 1999 after modest success with Vicenza (1998 Cup-winners Cup semi-finals).

PLAYER
AMBROSINI, Massimo
Midfielder, Italian, 180cm, 67kg
Born: 29.05.77, Pesaro, Italy
Clubs: Cesana (1993-95), Milan (1995-), Vicenza (1997-98, loan)
Full international (Italy) 8 caps/0 goals
• Midfield workhorse whose form for Milan in 1999-2000 brought him into contention for a Euro 2000 squad place.
• Spent 1997-98 on loan at Vicenza, returning to Milan and winning a regular spot in the first team.
• A member of Italy's squad at Euro 2000, appearing as a substitute in the Final.

PLAYER
AMERHAUSER Martin
Midfielder, Austrian, 180cm, 73kg
Born: 23.07.74, Salzburg, Austria
Clubs: Salzburg (1993-95), Grazer AK (1995-96), Salzburg (1996-1999), Grazer AK (1999-)
Full international (Austria) 6 caps/2 goals
• Useful left-sided midfielder on the fringes of the Austrian national side in recent years, travelling to France for the 1998 World Cup but not playing.

PLAYER
AMMUNIKE, Emmanuel
Forward, Nigerian, 170cm, 69kg
Born: 25.12.70, Ezebado, Nigeria
Clubs: Zamalek (Egy) (1992-94), Sporting Lisbon (Por) (1994-97), Barcelona (Spa) (1996-2000)

Full international (Nigeria)

• Experienced striker who has struggled with a career-threatening knee injury in recent seasons, sidelining him at Barcelona.

• Scored on his international debut for Nigeria against Sudan in 1993 and scored the two goals in the Final of of the 1994 African Nations Cup. Also scored at the 1994 World Cup and the 1996 Atlanta Olympics.

• Won club honours in Egypt with Zamalek before a disputed transfer to Sporting Lisbon, after having signed a contract with Duisburg of Germany.

• Signed by for Barcelona in 1996, but did not play in the 1997-98 and 1998-99 seasons and played only a handful of games at the end of the 1999-2000 season.

AMOAH, Charles
Forward, Ghanaian, 175cm, 70kg
Born: 28.02.75, Ghana
Clubs: Wil (Swi) (1998-99, St Gallen (1999-)
Full international (Ghana)

• Burly striker with tantalising dribble and lethal strike rate. Swiss top scorer in 1999-2000 (25 goals).

• Deeply religious family man who was upset at being dropped from Ghana's squad for the 2000 African Nations Cup. Suspicion is that his request not to be considered for national duties during Swiss championship play-offs could have played a role.

AMOAH, Matthew
Forward, Ghanaian, 172cm, 61kg
Born: 24.10.80, Thema, Ghana
Clubs: The Great Ambassadors, Vitesse Arnhem (Hol) (1998-), Fortuna Sittard (Hol) (1999-2000, loan)

• Dangerous striker who learned his football at Vitesse but couldn't make the first team. Was loaned to Fortuna, where he became a regular scorer. **Ronald Koeman** says he will now give him another chance at Vitesse.

AMOKACHI, Daniel
Forward, Nigerian,
Born: 20.12.72, Nigeria
Clubs: Club Brugge (Bel), Everton (Eng), Besiktas (Tur)
Full international (Nigeria)

• Striker who provided one of the most memorable images of the 1994 World Cup in the USA when he scored for Nigeria against Grece, ran into the goal, and shook the net vigorously.

• One of the three over-age players in Nigeria's side which won gold at the 1996 Olympics.

• Won Belgian League honours with Club Brugge and then moved to Everton after USA 94, but had an unhappy time, although he did score in the FA Cup semi-final, and was on the winning side in the Final.

AMOR, Guillermo
Midfielder, Spanish, 174cm, 73kg
Born: 04.12.67, Benidorm, Spain
Clubs: Barcelona (1986-98), Fiorentina (Ita) (1998-2000), Villarreal (2000-)
Full international (Spain) 40 caps/4 goals

• Product of the Barcelona youth system who became a fixture in their side after replacing Diego Maradona.

• Was suspended and missed two European Finals with Barcelona, against Manchester United in the 1991 Cup-winners Cup Final, and against Sampdoria in the 1992 European Cup Final.

• A member of the Spanish squad at Euro 96.

• Made the surprise move to Italy in 1998, but was not a regular in the Fiorentina first team and returned to Spain in summer 2000.

AMOROSO, Cristian
Midfielder, Italian, 176cm, 64kg
Born: 22.09.76, Pisa, Italy
Clubs: Fiorentina (1994-96), Empoli (1996-97, loan), Fiorentina (1997-)

• Product of Fiorentina's youth system who enjoyed an impressive first season in Serie A on loan to Empoli before being called back to Florence and keeping **Guillermo Amor** out of the team.
• An excellent prospect with good vision, tactical discipline and and a powerful shot.
• Likened by fans to Claudio Merlo, a key member of the last Fiorentina side to win the Italian title, in 1969.

PLAYER
AMORUSO, Lorenzo
Defender, Italian, 179cm, 71kg
Born: 28.06.71, Bari, Italy
Clubs: Bari (1988-95), Mantova (1991-92), Pescavo (1992-93), Fiorentina (1995-97), Rangers (Sco) (1997-99)
• Powerful central defender who spent several months on the sidelines at Ibrox due to injury following his transfer from Fiorentina but has emerged as an inspirational captain and has led Rangers to two successive Scottish League titles.
• Former Under-21 international who won the Coppa Italia and Italian Supercup with Fiorentina.

PLAYER
AMOROSO, Marcio
Full name: Amoroso, Marcio dos Santos
Forward, Brazilian, 179cm, 69kg
Born: 05.07.74, Brasilia, Brazil
Clubs: Guarani (1992), Verdy Kawasaki (Jap) (1992-93), Guarani (1994-95), Flamengo (1996), Udinese (Ita) (1996-99), Parma (Ita) (1999-)
Full international (Brazil) 14 caps/9 goals
• Quicksilver attacker whose career has been ruled by inconsistency and injuries, but on his day is one of the best forwards in the world.
• Made his debut aged 17 for Guarani, but was sold to Japan, only to return 18 months later and would have won a place in Brazil's 1994 World Cup squad had he not injured his right knee.
• Recovered his form following a move to Udinese, where he scored 22 goals in the 1998-

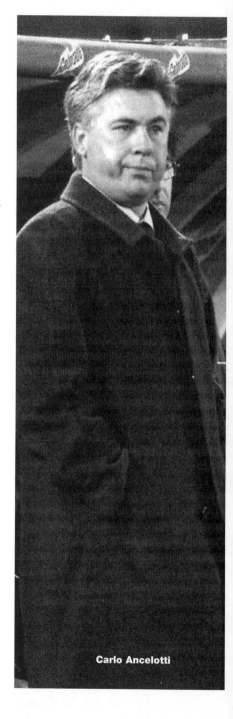

Carlo Ancelotti

99 season to finish as the leading scorer in Serie A, earning a £21 million transfer to Parma to replace **Enrico Chiesa.**
• Partnered **Ronaldo** when Brazil won the 1999 Copa America in Paraguay, scoring four goals.

PLAYER
AMORUSO, Nicola
Forward, Italian, 186cm, 78kg
Born: 29.08.74, Cerignola, Italy
Clubs: Sampdoria (1991-94), Fidelis Andrria (1994-95), Padova (1995-96), Juventus (1996-), Perugia (1999-2000, loan)
• Striker who is a skilful opportunist in the penalty area and is getting back to the form which saw him burst onto the scene in 1997, when his goals helped Juventus win the Italian League and reach the Champions League Final.
• Signed by Juventus after scoring 14 goals in 1995-96 for relegated Padova, having been released as a youngster by Sampdoria.
• Failed to make the breakthrough and establish himself in the Juventus first team thanks to a combination of injuries and loss of form but revived his career on loan to Perugia.

PLAYER
ANASTASIOU, Yannis
Forward, Greece, 187cm, 82kg
Born: 05.03.73, Greece
Clubs: OFI Crete (1996-99), Anderlecht (Bel) (1999-)
Full international (Greece) 4 caps/0 goals
• Greek striker who has been in and out of the Anderlecht side and has been on the fringes of the Greek national team since making his debut as a late substitute against Croatia in March 1999.

PLAYER
ANATOLAKIS, Giorgos
Defender, Greek, 185cm, 79kg
Born: 16.03.74, Greece
Clubs: Iraklis (1992-96), Olympiakos (1996-)
Full international (Greece) 10 caps/0 goals

• Central defender who performed a crucial role for Olympiakos in their recent title successes, leading their rearguard and helping to maintain the best defensive record in the Greek League.
• Made his international debut for Greece against Portugal in Lisbon on March 27, 1996.

COACH
ANCELOTTI, Carlo
Italian
Born: 10.05.69
• Coach of Juventus since 1999, when he replaced **Marcello Lippi.**
• A tough midfielder with Roma and Milan as a player, he won the 1983 Italian League title with his home town club and then a host of honours under **Arrigo Sacchi** and **Fabio Capello** at Milan.
• Started coaching at Reggiana in the 1995-96 season, but made his name at Parma, taking them to second place in the Italian League in the 1996-97 season.
• At Juventus, he struggled to be accepted because of his Milan connections, but he coached them to the brink of the Serie A title in the 1999-2000 season, when they lost the title race on the last day.
• Solid 4-4-2 man who likes his teams to work hard.

PLAYER
ANDERSEN, Erik Bo
Forward, Danish, 190cm, 80kg
Born: 14.11.70, Randers, Denmark
Clubs: AaB (1991-96), Rangers (Sco) (1995-97), OB (1997-98), Duisburg (Ger) (1998-99, loan) OB (2000-)
Full international (Denmark) 6 caps/0 goals
• Tall, rangy striker who returned to form with OB Odense after a disapppointing time in Scotland with Rangers.
• Late starter who was spotted in non-league by Aalborg aged 21. Worked as a clerk in a plumbing firm before a £1.5million transfer to Rangers.
• Went on loan to German side Duisburg, but was set to return to Denmark in the summer of 2000.

ANDERSEN, Soren

Forward, Danish, 183cm, 85kg
Born: 13.02.66, Denmark
Clubs: Hvidovre (1996-97), AB (1997-)
Full international (Denmark) 15 caps/1 goal
• Versatile striker who can perform up front or out on the wing and will always give 100 per cent.
• Made his international debut for Denmark against the United States in January 1993.
• Missed out on Euro 2000, with Danish coach **Bo Johansson** preferring **Mikkel Beck** and **Miklos Molnar.**

AGENT
ANDERSON, Jerome

• London-based agent of, among others, **Tony Adams, Thierry Henry, Francis Jeffers, Niclas Alexandersson,** and **Marian Pahars.**
• Contact: 248 Station Rd, Edgware, Middlesex, HA8 7AU (tel 0044 (0)20 8958 7799).

AGENT
ANDERSON, Rachel

• Represents a number of UK lower division players but most notable as the first female agent in the UK.
• Earned notoriety when she was invited by Julian Dicks to attend the Professional Footballers Association dinner, traditionally an all-male affair.
• Represents **Don Hutchison** and **Michael Hughes**.
• Contact: 362 Suthbourne Grove, Westcliff, Essex SS0 0AQ (tel 0044 (0) 1702 345 111.

PLAYER
ANDERSON, Russell

Defender, Scottish, 183c, 74kg
Born: 25.10.78, Aberdeen, Scotland
Clubs: Aberdeen (1996)
• Central defender and local boy who joined Aberdeen in 1996 from Dyce juniors. He is well established himself in the Pittodrie first team and is greatly admired by national coach **Craig Brown**.

PLAYER
ANDERSON, Sonny

Full name: Anderson 'Sonny' da Silva
Forward, Brazilian, 181cm, 72kg
Born: 19.09.70, Goiatuba, Brazil
Clubs: Vasca da Gama (1988-91), Guarani (1991-92), Servette (Swi) (1992-93), Marseille (Fra) (1993-94), Monaco (Fra) (1994-97), Barcelona (Spa) (1997-99), Lyon (Fra) (1999-)
Full international (Brazil)
• Lithe, explosive striker who became the most expensive player in French football history when he moved in a £12million deal from Barcelona to Lyon in the summer of 1999 and fully justified the outlay by finishing the 1999- 2000 season as the country's top scorer with 23 goals.
• Under-achieved during his two years at Barça, but France has always been a happy hunting ground for him; he was a cult hero at Marseille (scoring 16 goals in 23 games in 1993-94), was the First Division's top scorer in 1995-96 and helped Monaco to the league title in 1997.
• Barred by the likes of **Ronaldo**, Romario, Edmundo and Bebeto from a more fruitful international career.

PLAYER
ANDERSSON, Anders

Midfielder, Swedish, 174cm, 75kg
Born 15.03.74, Tomelilla, Sweden
Clubs Malmo (1991-97), Blackburn (Eng) (1997), Aab Aalborg (Den) (1997-)
Full international (Sweden) 14 caps/2 goals
• Hard-working right-side or central midfielder who is a big threat at deadball situations. Good passer of the ball, with an excellent shot.
• Revived his career in Denmark after failing to make the grade at Blackburn.
• International debut 25.02.94, v Mexico (lost 2-1).
• Non-playing member of Sweden's squad at Euro 2000.

Kennet
Andersson

PLAYER
ANDERSSON, Andreas
Forward, Swedish, 185cm, 77kg
Born: 10.04.74, Sweden
Clubs: Degerfors, IFK Gothenburg, Milan (Ita)
(1997-98), Newcastle (Eng) (1998-99), AIK
Stockholm (1999-)
Full international (Sweden) 28 caps/5 goals
• Striker who returned to the Swedish Allsvenskan
after unlucky spells with Milan and Newcastle.
• The most expensive player in Swedish football
after his £2million move to AIK in July 1999.
• A fast, hard-working forward, who made his
name with Degerfors and IFK Gothenburg, where
he once scored hat-tricks in consecutive games.
• Scored twice on his international debut against
Australia in February 1996. Missed Euro 2000
with a knee injury.

PLAYER
ANDERSSON, Bengt
Goalkeeper, Swedish, 191cm, 92kg
Born: 11.08.66, Gothenburg, Sweden
Clubs: Brage (1986-92), Orgryte (1993-96),
Tenerife (Spa) (1996-98), IFK Gothenburg (1998-)
Full international (Sweden) 11 caps/0 goals
• Seasoned keeper signed from Spain's Tenerife
in 1998, having previously starred for local rivals
Orgryte.

PLAYER
ANDERSSON, Daniel
Midfielder, Swedish, 178cm, 79kg
Born: 28.08.77, Borgeby, Sweden
Clubs: Malmo (1995-98), Bari (Ita) (1998-)
Full international (Sweden) 21 caps/0 goals
• Midfielder with bags of skill and vision, if a little
one-paced and lacking in physical presence.
• Younger brother of **Patrik Andersson** and one
of the emerging talents of Swedish football.
• Joined Bari from Malmo in a £2.5million deal
which also took **Ysel Osmanovski** to Italy.
• International debut v Thailand in February 1997.

29

Nicolas Anelka

PLAYER
ANDERSSON, Kennet

Forward, Swedish, 193cm, 92kg
Born: 06.10.67, Eskilstuna, Sweden.
Clubs: Eskilstuna (1985-88), IFK Gothenburg (1988-91), Mechelen (Bel) (1991-93), IFK Norrkoping (1993), Lille (Fra) (1993-94), Caen (Fra) (1994-95), Bari (Ita) (1995-95), Bologna (Ita) (1996-99), Lazio (Ita) (1999), Bologna (Ita) (2000), Fenerbahce (Tur) (2000-)
Full international (Sweden) 78 caps/31 goals
• Sweden's leading striker who has been performing at the highest level in Italy for the past five seasons. Main strength is his height and aerial ability. But he is also comfortable on the ball and a selfless provider for others.
• International debut against United Arab Emirates in February 1990. Scored five goals when Sweden finished third at the 1994 World Cup in the USA.
• Left Bologna in summer 1999 for Lazio, but returned within two months.
• 'My time in Italy has definitely made me a better player. I've become more aware, and my technique and movement off the ball are better.'

PLAYER
ANDERSSON, Ola

Midfielder, Swedish, 174cm, 71kg
Born: 01.07.66, Sweden
Clubs: Brommapojkarna (1987-89), IK Sirius (1990-94), AIK Stockholm (1995-)
Full international (Sweden) 2 caps/0 goals
• A late developer, who was already 29 when he joined AIK and made his Sweden debut. A constructive midfielder, but his career has been hit by injuries.

PLAYER
ANDERSSON, Patrik

Defender, Swedish, 185cm, 81kg
Born: 18.08.71, Borgeby, Sweden
Clubs: Bjarreds, Malmo (1989-92), Blackburn Rovers (Eng) (1992-93), Monchengladbach (Ger)

(1994-99), Bayern Munich (Ger) (1999-)
Full international (Sweden) 78 caps/2 goals
• The stylish, experienced Swedish international centre-back did not start regularly in his first season with Bayern. But he remains a throughly class act, a wonderful reader of the game, superb in the air and an intimidating tackler. Statistics prove just how effective the Swede has been in German football. For each of the five seasons between 1995 and 1999, no one won more tackles or aerial duels than Andersson, who was starring for Monchengladbach at that time.
• Captain of Sweden at Euro 2000.

PLAYER
ANDERSSON, Sven
Goalkeeper, Swedish, 193cm, 95kg
Born: 06.10.63, Stromstad, Sweden
Clubs: Orgryte (1980-91), Stromstad (1992), Helsingborg (1993-)
Full international (Sweden) 1 cap/0 goals
• Physically imposing keeper who is close to playing his 400th match for Helsingborg, where he is a cult figure for the fans, who feel he should have won more international caps.

PLAYER
ANDERSSON, Trond
Defender, Norwegian, 188cm, 80kg
Born: 06.01.75, Norway
Clubs: Molde (1995-1999), Wimbledon (Eng) (1999-)
Full international (Norway) 5 caps/0 goals
• Versatile defender who moved to England in the winter of 1999 and quickly adapted to life in the Premier League, but suffered relegation in May 2000.
• International debut 20.05.99, v Jamaica.

PLAYER
ANDERTON, Darren
Midfielder, English, 185cm, 78kg
Born: 03.03.72, Southampton, England
Clubs: Portsmouth (1990-92), Tottenham (1992-)

Full international (England) 27 caps/7 goals)
• Talented but injury-striken, nicknamed 'Sicknote' because of his familiarity with the medical profession.
• Made his name in Portsmouth's run to the 1992 FA Cup semi-final, then joined Spurs for £1.75million.
• International debut against Denmark in 1994.

PLAYER
ANDRE CRUZ
Full name: Andre Alves da Cruz
Defender, Brazilian, 182cm, 83kg
Born: 20.09.68, Piracicaba, Brazil
Clubs: Ponte Preta (1986-88), Flamengo (1989), Standard Liege (Bel) (1990-94), Napoli (Ita) (1994-97), Milan (Ita) (1997-98), Standard Liege (Bel) (1999), Torino (Ita) (1999), Sporting Lisbon (Por) (2000)
Full international (Brazil) 29 caps/1 goal
• Central defender with a powerful left foot which he uses to great effect at free-kicks.

PLAYER
ANDRESEN, Martin
Midfielder, Norwegian, 178cm, 75kg
Born: 02.02.77, Norway
Clubs: Krakstad, Ski, Moss, Viking Stavanger, Stabaek, Wimbledon (Eng) (2000-)
• Hard-running, skilful midfielder who was signed by **Egil Olsen** for Wimbledon.
• Former Norway Under-21 international who was voted 'Norway's Sexiest Man'.

PLAYER
ANEGRUND, Johan
Defender, Swedish, 182cm, 80kg
Born: 01.03.73, Sweden
Clubs: Skiljebo (1989-90), IFK Gothenburg (1991-99), Vastra Frolunda (1998, loan), Orgryte (1999-)
• Stylish stopper, who established himself in the Swedish top flight while on loan with Vastra Frolunda. But a move back to Gothenburg did not work out, and he moved on to Orgryte.

Radomir Antic

PLAYER
ANELKA, Nicolas
Forward, French, 184cm, 77kg
Born: 14.03.79, Paris, France
Clubs: Paris Saint-Germain (1995-97), Arsenal
(Eng) (1997-99), Real Madrid (Spa) (1999-2000),
Paris Saint-Germain (2000-)
Full international (France) 16 caps/4 goals
• Controversial and temperamental striker,
dubbed 'The Eternal Malcontent' because of his
failure to settle wherever he has played.
• Left PSG while still a teenager in protest at not
being given a regular first-team spot. Left Arsenal
for Real in a £23million deal amid accusations
that his brothers Claude and Didier had
engineered a transfer.
• Had numerous problems settling in Madrid, com-
plaining about his treatment by the Spanish press
and the club's players and coaches towards him,
leading the club to suspend him for 40 days after
he went on unofficial strike. Returned to favour in
time to play in the Champions League Final against
Valencia 2000.
• When on form, he is a hugely exciting striker,
with pace, technique and a sharp eye for goal.
• Despite all his problems, he has already won
the League and FA Cup double with Arsenal and
the Champions League with Real Madrid.
• Rejoined PSG in a £22million transfer in July 2000.
• **Vicente Del Bosque**: 'He never really identified
with what it means to play in a club like ours.
Overall he took very little part in the season.'

PLAYER
ANDRADE, Luis Filipe
Defender, Portuguese, 177cm, 73kg
Born: 30.09.73, Lisbon, Portugal
Clubs: Sporting Lisbon (1991-92), Estoril (1992-
95), Estrela Amadora (1995-96), Sporting Lisbon
(1996), Belenenses (1997-98), Benfica (1998-)
• Right-sided defender who made his mark at
Benfica under Graeme Souness, impressing many
with his courage and commitment.

PLAYER
ANGIBAUD, Didier
Midfielder, Cameroonian, 183cm, 75kg
Born: 08.10.74, Douala, Cameroon
Clubs: Le Havre (Fra) (1993-94), Istres (Fra) (1994-96), Toulon (Fra) (1996-97) Nice (Fra) (1997-98), Sturm Graz (Aut) (1998-)
Full international (Cameroon)
• Won the Austrian League title in 1999 after a career spent mostly in the French second division.
• Played all three games for Cameroon at France 98.

PLAYER
ANGLOMA, Jocelyn
Defender, French, 180cm, 70kg
Born: 07.08.65, Abymes, Guadaloupe
Clubs: Rennes (1985-87), Lille (1987-90), Paris Saint-Germain (1990-91), Marseille (1991-94), Torino (Ita) (1994- 96), Internazionale (Ita) (1996-97), Valencia (Spa) (1997-)
Full international (France) 37 caps/1 goal
• Right-back who is approaching the end of his career, but still plays with energy and commitment.
• A member of the Marseille team which won the 1993 European Cup, before moving to Italy after Marseille were relegated in 1994.
• Was thought to be past his best when signed by Valencia in 1997, but played a key role in Valencia's run to the 2000 Champions League Final.

PLAYER
ANGULO, Miguel Angel
Midfielder, Spanish, 180cm, 74kg
Born: 23.06.77, Gijon, Spain
Clubs: Valencia (1995-), Villarreal (1996-97)
• Spanish Under-21 midfielder who impressed during Valencia's run to the 2000 Champions League Final.
• Product of the famous Sporting Gijon youth system who failed to make the grade during his first spell at Valencia. Was sold to Villarreal, where his form was good enough to warrant a transfer back to Valencia.

COACH
ANTHUENIS, Aime
Belgian
Born: 21.12.43
• Coach of Anderlecht since 1999 who guided the Brussels club to their 25th Belgian League title, a year after overseeing Genk's remarkable League and Cup double.
• Spent most of his playing career at hometown club Lokeren, where he also began his coaching career with the youth section in 1980. Had a brief spell at Charleroi before returning to coach Lokeren from 1988 to 1993.

COACH
ANTIC, Radomir
Yugoslav
Born: 22.11.48
• Clever motivator who has carved out a useful career for himself in Spain, mostly at Atletico Madrid, where he was sacked by **Jesus Gil** for the third time at the end of the 1999-2000 season, only to be snapped up by Oviedo, where he did well between 1993 and 1995.
• Was previously at Zaragoza and Real Madrid.
• Had a spell as a player in England with Luton.
• Known universally as Raddy.

COACH
ANTONETTI, Frederic
French
Born: 19.08.61
• Coach of Bastia since 1995 who has kept the Corsican side in the French top flight against the odds every season.
• A player with Bastia, Beziers and Puy.

ADMINISTRATOR
ANTOGNONI, Giancarlo
• General manager of Fiorentina and the man responsible for the day-to-day running of the club on behalf of owner **Vittorio Cecchi Gori.**

PLAYER
ANTONIO CARLOS Zago
Defender, Brazilian, 185cm, 73kg
Born: 18.05.69, Presidente Prudente, Brazil
Clubs: Sao Paulo (1990-92), Albacete (Spa)
(1992-93), Palmeiras (1993-95), Kashima Reysol
(Jap) (1996), Corinthians (1997-98), Roma (1998-)
Full international (Brazil)
• Brazilian international central defender who has
twice been voted 'Brazilian defender of the year'.
• Joined Roma in February 1998 and quickly
established himself in the team. Is popular with
Roma fans because of his similarity to former
Brazilian hero Falcao.

PLAYER
ANTONIOLI, Francesco
Goalkeeper, Italian, 188cm, 79kg
Born: 14.09.6, Monza, Italy
Clubs: Monza (1986-88), Milan (1988-90), Cesana
(1990), Modena (1990-91), Milan (1991-93), Pisa
(1993-94), Reggiana (1994-95), Bologna (1995-99),
Roma (1999-)
• Keeper who was called up to Italy's squad for
Euro 2000 at the last minute after **Angelo
Peruzzi** refused to be the third-choice keeper.
• Won 29 caps for Italy at Under-21 level.
• Reserve keeper at Milan when they won the
Italian League title in 1992 and 1993. Signed by
Fabio Cappelo when he became Roma coach.

PLAYER
APOLLONI, Luigi
Defender, Italian, 185cm, 79kg
Born: 02.05.67, Frascati, Italy
Clubs: Lodigiani (1983-84), Pistoiese (1984-86),
Reggiana (1986-87), Parma (1987-99), Verona (1999-)
Full international (Italy) 15 caps/1 goal
• Influential figure in the rise of Parma in the 1990s,
a tough, uncompromising defender in the classic
Italian mould. Rarely crosses the halfway line.
• Played the last 30 minutes of the 1994 World
Cup Final against Brazil.

PLAYER
APPIAH, Stephen
Midfielder, Ghanaian, 178cm, 77kg
Born: 24.12.80, Accra, Ghana
Clubs: Hearts of Oak (1996-97), Udinese (Ita)
(1997-2000), Parma (Ita) (2000-)
Full international (Ghana)
• Promising young striker who joined Udinese
from leading Accra club Heats of Oak and has
slowly established himself in Serie A.
• Made his international debut for Ghana's Black
Stars against Benin on his 16th birthday.

PLAYER
ARAGON, Santiago
Midfielder, Spanish, 178cm, 73kg
Born: 03.04.68, Malaga, Spain
Clubs: Castilla (1987-88), Real Madrid (1988),
Castilla (1988-89), Espanyol (1989), Logrones
(1989-90), Real Madrid (1990-91), Valladolid
(1991-92), Zaragoza (1992-)
• Much travelled midfield all-rounder who won
the Cup-winners Cup with Zaragoza in 1995.
• A product of Real Madrid's youth system, but
failed to make the grade in Madrid.

COACH
ARAGONES, Luis
Spanish
Born: 28.07.38
• The grandfather of Spanish coaches, with a
record number of first division matches.
• In summer 2000, signed a contract to coach
Mallorca, after a poor season at Oviedo. Turned
down the Spain job when **Javier Clemente** resigned.
• Has previously been in charge at Atletico
Madrid (four times), Betis (twice), Barcelona,
Sevilla and Valencia.

PLAYER
ARANZABAL, Augusti
Full name: Agustin Aranzabal Alkorta
Defender, Spanish, 186cm, 78kg

Clubs: Real Sociedad (1996-)
Full international (Spain) 21 caps/0 goals
• Left-back who came through the ranks at Sociedad as a defensive midfielder.
• Powerful player who uses his pace and strength up and down the entire left flank.
• Now well established as the Spanish national team's first-team left-back ahead of **Sergi**.
• International debut against Armenia in June 1995.

PLAYER
ARASON, Arni Gautar
Goalkeeper, Icelandic, 187cm, 85kg
Born: 07.05.75, Iceland
Clubs: IA (1994-96), Stjarman (1997), Rosenborg (Nor) (1998-)
• Ever-improving keeper and hot favourite to succeed Birkir Kristinsson as Iceland's No. 1.

COACH
ARCHONTIDIS, Christos
Greek
• Former national coach of Greece, in charge between 1982 and 1984, who saved Panahaiki from relegation in the 1999-2000 season.

PLAYER
ARIF Erdem
Forward, Turkish, 179cm, 72kg
Born: 01.02.72, Istanbul, Turkey
Clubs: Zeytinburnuspor, Galatasaray, Real Sociedad (Spa) (2000-)
Full international (Turkey) 37 caps/6 goals
• Began as a right-winger but now operates more as a second striker. Can play on either flank.
• Began with Zeytinburnuspor, moving in 1991 to Galatasaray, where he has won five Turkish League titles and the 2000 UEFA Cup. Moved to Real Sociedad in Spain for £2million.
• Has formed a prolific partnership with **Hakan Sukur** for club and country.
• Scored a hat-trick in four minutes against Northern Ireland in the qualifiers for Euro 2000.

PLAYER
ARIFULLIN, Alexei
Midfielder, Russian, 187cm, 85kg
Born: 13.10.70, Russia
Clubs: Lokomotiv Moscow (1989-)
Full international (Russia) 1 cap/0 goals
• Reliable and efficient servant on Lokomotiv Moscow's right flank for more than a decade.

PLAYER
ARILSON Gilberto da Costa
Forward, Brazilian, 177cm, 76kg
Born: 11.06.73, Bento Goncalves, Brazil
Clubs: Gremio (1993-95), Kaiserslautern (Ger) (1995-96), Internacional (1996-97), Palmeiras (1998), Gremio (1999), Valladolid (Spa) (1999-)
• Brazilian forward whose future in Spain is under a massive cloud after a fatal car accident. Has failed to appear in court three times now.

PLAYER
ARMSTRONG, Chris
Forward, English, 182cm, 82kg
Born: 19.06.71, Newcastle, England
Clubs: Wrexham (1989-91), Millwall (1991-92), Crystal Palace (1992-95), Tottenham (1995-96)
• Striker and one-time goalkeeper who made a name for himself at Crystal Palace, earning a £4.5million transfer to Spurs in June 1995.
• Tested positive for cannabis in 1995.
• Pacy, strong in the air, but recently troubled by injury.

COACH
ARMSTRONG, Keith
English
• Born in Newcastle, England, but went to Finland to play as a striker, winning the Finnish League in 1979.
• Coached Rovaniemi and Seinajoki before taking over at FC Haka, leading them to consecutive League victories in 1998 and 1999.
• Popular in Finland as a TV commentator.

ARNAU
Full name: Francesc Arnau Grabulosa
Goalkeeper, Spanish, 185cm, 78kg
Born: 23.03.75, Les Planes, Spain
Clubs: Barcelona (1994-)
• Home-grown keeper who established himself in the Barcelona first-team, after being promoted ahead of **Vitor Baia** to understudy Dutchman **Ruud Hesp**.
• A former Spanish Under-21 international who famously made his Barcelona debut when still in the Barça B team when all three first-choice keepers were injured or on international duty. The match, a League meeting in November 1996 against then champions Atletico Madrid at Camp Nou, ended 3-3.

ARST, Ole Martin
Forward, Norwegian, 190cm, 83kg
Born: 19.07.74, Bergen, Norway
Clubs: Skarp, Tromso (1995-97), Anderlecht (Bel) (1997-99), Gent (Bel) (1999-2000), Standard Liege (Bel) (2000)
Full international (Norway) 2 caps/0 goals
• Striker who came to the fore in the 1999-2000 season, finishing as top scorer in the Belgian League after failing to make the grade at Anderlecht.
• Made his international debut for Norway in January 2000, against Iceland.
• Linked with a move to Tottenhem in England, but eventually joined Standard in summer of 2000.

ARTEAGA
Full name: Moises Garcia Fernandez
Midfielder, Spanish, 185cm, 78kg
Born: 01.09.69, Cadiz, Spain
Clubs: Cadiz (1988-93), Espanyol (1993-)
• Highly effective all-rounder who has been a big success at Espanyol since joining from Cadiz.
• Versatile but most effective in central midfield.

ARTS, Arno
Midfielder, Dutch, 187cm, 81kg
Born: 26.06.69, Groesbeek, Holland
Clubs: NEC (1986-91), Lucerne (Swi) (1991-92), Twente (1992-94), Cambuur (1994-97), Willem II (1997-99), NEC (2000-)
• Skillful playmaker who joined NEC from Willem II after a disagreement with **Co Adriaanse**. Should be playing at a much bigger team.

ARVELADZE, Archil
Forward, Georgian, 180cm, 69kg
Born: 22.02.73, Tbilisi, Georgia
Clubs: Iberia Tbilisi (1991-92), Dynamo Tbilisi (1992-94), Trabzonspor (Tur) (1994-97), NAC (Hol) (1997-2000), FC Koln (Ger) (2000-)
Full international (Georgia)
• Twin brother of **Shota** and as gifted as the Ajax striker. But hasn't had the same recognition as his brother by playing at NAC Breda.
• Can play upfront or as a playmaker. Relegated with NAC in the 1998-99 season but stayed at the club, leading them to promotion before leaving for Koln.

ARVELADZE, Shota
Forward, Georgian, 180cm, 72kg
Born: 22.02.73, Tbilisi, Georgia
Clubs: Iberia Tbilisi (1991-92), Dynamo Tbilisi (1992-94), Trabzonspor (Tur) (1994-97), Ajax Amsterdam (Hol) (1997-)
Full international (Georgia)
• Striker who who was signed as a replacement for the Milan-bound **Patrick Kluivert** at Ajax in summer 1997. Finished his first season in Holland with an impressive 25 goals in 31 games.
• Twin brother of **Archil Arveladze**.
• International debut, Georgia v Slovenia, February 1994.

PLAYER
ARVIDSSON, Magnus
Forward, Swedish, 175cm, 72kg
Born: 12.02.73, Sweden
Clubs: Helsingborg, Forslov, IFK Hassleholm, Trelleborg, Hansa Rostock (Ger) (1999-)
• Swedish attacker who settled in well at Rostock following a move from Trelleborg in 1999. Makes excellent runs off the ball, is resourceful and tough and is a steady finisher with his right foot.

PLAYER
ARZENO, Claudio
Defender, Argentinian, 180cm, 77kg
Born: 16.10.77, Cordoba, Argentina
Clubs: Independiente (1992-98), Santander (Spa) (1998-)
• Powerful defender who is strong in the air.
• Moved to Spain's Santander from Independiente, where he won the South American Supercup.

PLAYER
ASAMOUH, Gerald
Forward, Ghanaian/German, 180cm, 85kg
Born: 03.10.78, Ghana
Clubs: Werder Hannover, Hannover 96 (1998-99), Schalke (1999-)
• Ghana-born but applied for German citizenship despite call-ups to Ghanaian national squad.
• Moved to Germany aged nine and came through at second division Hannover 96. Recovered from a life-threatening heart condition to earn a £1million transfer to Schalke in summer 1999. Scored only four goals in his first season but showed a great deal of promise with his speed, strength and never-flagging spirit.

PLAYER
ASPER, Mattias
Goalkeeper, Swedish, 197cm, 93kg
Born: 12.05.77, Sweden
Clubs: Mjallby (1996-97), AIK Stockholm (1998-2000), Real Sociedad (Spa) (2000-)
Full international (Sweden) 2 caps/0 goals
• Imposing keeper with good reflexes who won a Swedish League title in his debut season in 1998 after moving from Mjallby.
• Attracted attention of the big European club with his performances for AIK in the 1999-2000 Champions League.
• Set a Swedish League record in 1999 after going 797 minutes unbeaten.
• International debut: 27.11.99, v South Africa.

PLAYER
ASSATI, Eric
Defender, French, 171cm, 67kg
Born: 20.09.74, Saint-Joseph, France
Clubs: Auxerre (1996-)
• Product of the Auxerre youth system, a pacy left-back who can also play in central defence.

PLAYER
ASTUDILLO, Martin Mauricio
Midfielder, Argentinian, 173cm, 70kg
Born: 10.07.77, Mendoza, Argentina
Clubs: Godoy Cruz (1995-96), Gimnasia Jujay (1997-99), Alaves (Spa) (1999-)
• Versatile midfielder who can fill a number of positions and combines good technique with excellent positional sense.

PLAYER
ATHIRSON
Full name: Athirson Mazolli de Oliveira
Defender, Brazilian,
Born: 16.01.77, Brazil
Clubs: Flamengo, Santos (loan), Juventus (Ita) (2001-)
Full international (Brazil) 3 caps/0 goals
• Hugely promising left-back who has been touted as the rightful successor to **Roberto Carlos** in the Brazilian national side.
• Signed a pre-contract with Juventus to join them in January 2001, though the Italians were keen for him to move to Europe earlier.

AUGENTHALER, Klaus

German
Born: 26.09.57
• Former German international libero and a World Cup winner in 1990.
• Took charge of second division Nurnberg in March 2000 after a sudden exit from Grazer AK in Austria.

PLAYER
AYALA, Celso

Defender, Paraguayan, 176cm, 74kg
Born: 20.08.70, Asuncion, Paraguay
Clubs: River Plate (Arg) (1994-98), Real Betis (1998-99), Atletico Madrid (Spa) (1999-)
Full international (Paraguay)
• Stylish centre-back who has yet to settle in Spain.
• Suffered relegation with Atletico in May 2000 despite forming a strong central defensive partnership with Paraguayan international team-mate **Carlos Gamarra**.
• Played at the 1998 World Cup for Paraguay.

PLAYER
AYALA, Roberto

Defender, Argentinian, 178cm, 86kg
Born: 12.04.74, Parana, Argentina
Clubs: Ferro Caril Oeste (1991-93), River Plate (1993-95), Napoli (Ita) (1995-98), Milan (Ita) (1998-)
Full international (Argentina) 60caps/3 goals
• Talented libero, strong in the air, who played all of Argentina's five matches at France 98.
• Won a silver medal at the 1996 Olympics.
• Joined Milan in 1998 after Napoli were relegated.

PLAYER
AYBUNN, Jeffrey

Forward, Swedish, 181cm, 75kg
Born: 12.05.77, Sweden
Clubs: Bayern Munich (Ger) (1997-98), Halmstad (1998-)
• Highly-promising left-sided forward who was on Bayern's books as a youngster but did not play.

PLAYER
AYEW, Kwame

Forward, Ghanaian, 178cm, 72kg
Born: 28.12.73, Accra Ghana
Clubs: Al Ahly (Sau) (1992-93), Lecce (Ita) (1993-95) Uniao Leiria (Por) (1995-96), Vitoria Setubal (Por) (1996-97), Boavista (Por) (1997-)
Full international (Ghana)
• Ghanaian forward who starred in Sporting Lisbon's 1999-2000 Portuguese League title victory after making a name for himself in Portuguese football with Boavista.
• A member of Ghana's bronze medal-winning squad at the 1992 Olympics.
• Younger brother of former African Footballer of the year Abedi Pele Ayew. Has been accused of hanging on to his brother's coat-tails, with allegations that Abedi engineered a place for him in the national team.
• Like his brother, he first came to prominence playing in the Arabian Gulf, having failed to make the grade at Metz. He then moved to Italy's Lecce for two seasons, scoring seven Serie A goals but suffering relegation to Serie B.
• Made a disastrous international debut for Ghana, losing to tiny Burundi in a World Cup qualifier in October 1992.

PLAYER
AYHAN Akman

Midfielder, Turkish, 177cm, 68kg
Born: 23.02.77, Istanbul, Turkey
Clubs: Besiktas
Full international (Turkey) 6 caps/0 goals
• Young midfielder who has tremendous pace when running with the ball and is particularly effective when running directly at defenders.
• Broke into the Turkish national side after a series of impressive displays for the Under-21 team, making his full international debut against Israel in February 1998.
• Non-playing member of Turkey's squad at Euro 2000.

B

BA, Ibrahim
Midfielder, French, 180cm, 70kg
Born: 12.11.73, Dakar, Senegal
Clubs: Le Havre (1991-96), Bordeaux (1996-97), Milan (Ita) (1997-99), Perugia (Ita) (1999-)
Full international (France) 8 caps/2 goals
• Headline-writer's dream who burst on to the international in June 1997 at Le Tournoi, the four-nation friendly tournament featuring France, England, Italy and Brazil.
• Known throughout Europe for his distinctive bleached cropped hair, which he dyes in assorted colours in tribute to basketball player Dennis Rodman.
• Born in Senegal but opted to play for France, scoring on his international debut against Portugal in January 1997.
• His father Eusebio Ba played at left-back for Senegal and Le Havre.
• Was on Paris Saint-Germain's books as a teenager, but was released and moved on to Le Havre, where he made his First Division debut.
• Form for France and Bordeaux on the right side of midfield, where he loves to attack defenders, earned a transfer to Milan in summer 1997.
• Failed to win a first-team place at San Siro and was omitted from France's 1998 World Cup squad. Went on loan to Perugia, where he has tried to rebuild his career.
• Had the consolation of being voted 'Italy's sexiest footballer' in a poll of Italian women.

PLAYER
BA, Ismael
Forward, Senegal, 182cm, 74kg
Born: 22.05.74, Senegal
Clubs: Skoda Xanthi (Gre) (1998-)
• Senegal-born striker who had been a regular rather prolific scorer during two seasons in Greece.

PLAYER
BABANGIDA, Haruna
Forward, Nigerian, 166cm, 66kg
Born: 01.10.82, Kaduna, Nigeria
Clubs: Barcelona B (1998-)
• Teenage younger brother of **Tijani Babangida** and an outstanding prospect. Much hyped when he scored prolifically for Barcelona B a few years back as a 16-year-old, but has since been wrapped in cotton wool by the club.
• Nigerian Under-21 international.

PLAYER
BABANGIDA, Tijani
Forward, Nigerian, 169cm, 69kg
Born: 25.09.73, Kaduna, Nigeria
Clubs: Arewa Textiles, Niger Tornadoes, VVV (Hol) (1991-93), Roda JC (Hol) (1993-96), Ajax Amsterdam (Hol) (1996-)
Full international (Nigeria)
• Pacy winger who made his name at Roda and was signed by Ajax as a replacement for the Betis-bound **Finidi George**.
• Scored 16 goals in the 1992-93 season to help VVV win promotion to the Dutch First Division, then played a key role in Roda's emergence in the 1990s as a growing force in Dutch football.
• Played for Nigeria's gold medal-winning team at the 1996 Atlanta Olympics.
• Won the Dutch League title with Ajax in 1998 and the 1998 and 1999 Dutch Cups.
• **Frank Rijkaard** on Babangida: 'I saw him play well for Ajax against Milan. For 20 minutes or so, he tormented **Paolo Maldini** and anyone who can do that, believe me, has a lot going for him.'
• 'Atlanta has to be the greatest thrill of my career. Memories of our celebrations at the end of the Final and the moment we received our gold medals will always be with me. Completely unforgettable.'

BABAYARO, Celestine
Defender, Nigerian, 172cm, 66kg
Born: 29.08.78, Kaduna, Nigeria
Clubs: Anderlecht (Bel) (1994-97), Chelsea (Eng) (1997-)
Full international (Nigeria)
• Left-back or left-sided midfielder who was a teenage prodigy at Anderlecht before a move to Chelsea, where he broke a left foot during a goal celebration but recovered to win a regular first-team place and play at France 98.
• Olympic gold-medal winner in 1996 and played in Nigeria's world under-17 title win in 1993.
• International debut: 1995, v Uzbekistan.

PLAYER
BABBEL, Markus
Defender, German, 190cm, 81kg
Born: 08.09.72, Munich, Germany
Clubs: Gilchin-Agelsried, Bayern Munich, Hamburg, Bayern Munich (1994-2000), Liverpool (Eng) (2000-)
Full international (Germany) 51 caps/1 goal
• Accomplished right-back or central defensive marker whose improved distribution and crossing ability in recent years has led to him being sometimes used on the right side of midfield for the German national team.
• Considered one of the fairest players in Germany.
• The Bavarian-born and raised player used to be adamant that he did not want to move abroad and once famously said: 'I don't want to play for a foreign club. I've already played for one at Hamburg.' But he is not such a homelover these days; he is now at Liverpool.

PLAYER
BABEU, Kuzman
Defender, Yugoslav, 189cm, 89kg
Born: 4.11.71, Belgrade, Yugoslavia
Clubs: Obilic Belgrade
• Reliable centre-back and a great fighter. One of the best in the air in the Yugoslav League.

PLAYER
BACHINI, Jonathan
Midfielder, Italian, 175cm, 68kg
Born: 05.06.75, Livorno, Italy
Clubs: Udinese (1993-99), Alessandria (1994-95, loan), Juve Stabia (1995-96, loan), Lecce (1996-97, loan), Juventus (1999-)
Full international (Italy) 2 caps
• Former Italian Under-21 international who joined Juventus from Udinese for £5million in summer 1999.
• Most effective on the left side of midfield, where he likes to run at defenders.

PLAYER
BACHEV, Georgi
Forward, Bulgarian, 176cm, 68kg
Born: 18.04.77 Bulgaria
Clubs: Pirin Blagoevgrad, Slavia Sofia, Levski Sofia
Full international (Bulgaria)
• Attacking left-footed midfielder who is seen by many in Bulgaria as the long-term successor to **Hristo Stoichkov**.
• Made his name with Slavia Sofia before switching across town to Levski.
• International debut v Macedonia in March 1998.

COACH
BACKE, Hans
Swedish
Born: 14.02.52
• One of Scandinavia's most experienced coaches, who has coached AIK, Dujrgardens and Osters in his native Sweden, Molde and Stabaek in Norway, and currently (until 2000) AaB in the Danish League.

PLAYER
BADIR, Walid
Midfielder, Israeli, 183cm, 74kg
Born: 12.3.74, Israel
Clubs: Hapoel Petach (1992-99), Wimbledon (Eng) (1999-2000), Maccabi Haifa (2000-)

Full international (Israel) 23 caps/4 goals
• One of the few big men in the Israel national side. His transfer to the English premiership, where he played for Wimbledon, served to improve his fitness and toughness on the pitch.
• Is one of the most reliable players in the Israel national squad and is always a danger man. Has scored four times in national team colours.

PLAYER
BAGGER, Ruben
Forward, Danish, 184cm, 88kg
Born: 16.01.72, Denmark
Clubs: Roskilde (1987-90), Jyllinge (1990), Roskilde (19901-93), Brondby (1993-)
• Left-footed attacker who likes to play behind the main strikers and has been involved in Brondby's success in recent years, winning three Danish League titles.

PLAYER
BAGGIO, Dino
Midfielder, Italian, 188cm, 83kg
Born: 24.07.71, Campsampiero, Italy
Clubs: Torino (1989-91), Internazionale (1991-92), Juventus (1992-94), Parma (1994-)
Full international (Italy) 59 caps/7 goals
• Highly experienced central midfielder who can construct and destruct, win ball and distribute it, close down an opponent and get forward to score.
• A regular for the Italian national side since making his international debut against Cyprus in December 1991. But missed out on the squad for Euro 2000.
• No relation of **Roberto Baggio**, but his contribution to Italy's cause in the 1990s was arguably as important.
• Scored important goals against Norway and Spain in the 1994 World Cup finals.
• Turned down a move from Juventus to Parma in summer 1994, then thought better of it.
• Three times a winner of the UEFA Cup with Juventus in 1993, and Parma in 1995 and 1999.

Roberto Baggio

BAGGIO, Roberto
Forward, Italian, 174cm, 73kg
Born: 18.02.67, Caldogno, Italy
Clubs: Vicenza (1982-85), Fiorentina (1985-90), Juventus (1990-95), Milan (1995-97), Bologna (1997-98), Internazionale (1998-)
Full international (Italy) 55 caps/27 goals
• Little Prince of Italian soccer and arguably the greatest Italian player of the past decade.
• Made his name at Fiorentina, where he was such a phenomenon that his then world-record transfer to Juventus (£8million, 1990) provoked riots in Florence.
• Scored one of the goals of the 1990 World Cup against Czechoslovakia.
• Won the UEFA Cup with Juve in 1993, scoring twice in the Final against Dortmund.
• Steered Italy almost single-handedly to the 1994 World Cup Final in Los Angeles, where a hamstring injury restricted his movement, and he missed the crucial penalty kick in the shoot-out against Brazil.
• His star was eclipsed by the emergence of **Alessandro Del Piero** at Juventus, and he moved to Milan for £8million in 1997.
• Nicknamed the Divine Ponytail and famous for his Buddhist beliefs, which do not prevent him spending each summer holiday hunting in Argentina.

BAGHERI, Karim
Midfielder, Iranian, 186cm, 78kg
Born: 20.02.74, Tehran, Iran
Clubs: Teraktor Sazi, Keshavarz, Pirouzi Tehran, Arminia Bielefeld (Ger) (1997-2000), Charlton (Eng) (2000-)
Full international (Iran)
• Goalscoring midfielder who was the leading scorer in the 1998 World Cup qualifiers with 17 goals, thanks largely to his seven strikes in Iran's 17-0 mauling of the Maldives, a World Cup record.
• Although an impressive goalscorer, he can also operate as a ball-winner. Is physically imposing in the air and has a powerful shot.
• Struggled initially in the Bundesliga, where he played with international team-mate **Ali Daei**.

BAH, Thierno
Midfielder, Guinea,
Born: 10.05.82, Guinea
Clubs: Servette
• Attacking midfielder from Guinea. Bags of energy, spirit and technically competent.

BAIDOO, Stephen
Defender, Ghanaian
Born: 25.09.76, Takoradi, Ghana
Clubs: Kayserispor (Tur), Anakaragucu (Tur)
Full international (Ghana)
• Pacy defender or midfielder who has played his club football in Turkey, firstly for Kayserispor and then Ankaragucu.
• Played for Ghana at the 1996 Olympics and the African National Cup finals in South Africa before falling out of favour. Recalled by new national coach Giuseppe Dossena.
• Won the League title in Ghana with Goldfields before moving to Turkey.

BAJEVIC, Dusan
Yugoslav
Born: 10.12.48
• Coach of Greek side PAOK Thessaloniki after a highly successful coaching career at AEK Athens (1988-96) and Olympiakos (1996-spring 2000). Helped struggling PAOK finish fifth in the 1999-2000 season.
• A prolific scorer for Yugoslavia, scoring 38 goals in 40 internationals. Spent most of his playing career with Velez Mostar between 1963 and 83, broken only by four seasons at AEK Athens.

BAK, Arkadiusz
Midfielder, Polish, 176cm, 76kg
Born: 6.10.74
Clubs: Polonia Warsaw
Full international (Poland) 1 cap/0 goals
• Started his career with lower division Blekitni Stargard Szczecinski. Then played for four clubs before joined Polonia in 1997. A versatile midfielder who can also be used as a striker.
• A free-kick specialist who is also dangerous in the air.

BAK, Jacek
Defender, Polish, 188cm, 81kg
Born: 24.03.73, Poznan, Poland
Clubs: Motor Lubin, Lech Poznan, Lyon (Fra)
Full international (Poland) 27 caps/1 goal
• While this versatile Polish international can operate anywhere in defence or in a midfield holding role, he is at his most effective at libero. Reliable, unassuming character.
• Name pronounced Ya sek Bak.

BAK, Lennart
Midfielder, Danish
Born: 13.09.72
Clubs: AGF Aarhus
• Midfielder who is getting his career back on track after a terribly frustrating time in Italy, where a move from Foggia to Salernitana was put on hold after a medical showed up an injury. Salernitana claimed that the player had hidden the injury, his wages were frozen and the dispute went to legal arbitration. Matters were finally settled late in 1999, and Bak, now a free agent, re-signed for AGF.

BAKAYOKO, Ibrahima
Forward, Ivory Coast, 182cm, 79kg
Born: 31.12.76, Seguela, Ivory Coast
Clubs: Stade Abidjan, Montpellier (Fra) (1995-98), Everton (Eng) (1998-99), Marseille (Fra) (1999-
Full international (Ivory Coast)
• Striker with a surfeit of muscle, speed and athleticism, who, when firing on all cylinders, can unlock most defences. However, he can be profligate in front of goal and suffers more off-days than most.
• Returned to France in summer 1999 after a frustrating time in England at Everton (four goals in 23 League matches).

BAKIRCIOGLU, Kennedy
Forward, Swedish, 181cm, 71kg
Born: 02.11.80, Sweden
Clubs: Assyriska (1996-98), Hammerby (1999-)
• Skilful winger and huge favourite with fans at Hammerby's noisy Soderstadion. Signed in 1999 from Assyriska, a Stockholm club with strong links to the immigrant communities, after having trials with Manchester United.

BAKKE Eirik
Midfielder, Norwegian, 189cm, 80kg
Born: 13.09.77, Norway
Clubs: Sogndal (1994-99), Leeds (Eng) (1999-)
Full international (Norway) 9 caps/0 goals
• Signed by Leeds for £1.75million from Sogndal in summer 1999 and established himself in the Leeds midfield despite plenty of competition.
• Former Norway Under-21 captain after playing first game for Sogndal aged 15.
• Son of Svein, also a former Sogndal player who now works for Wimbledon as a business consultant.
• International debut: Norway v Israel, 20 January 1999, in Tel Aviv.

BAKKE, Morten
Goalkeeper, Norwegian, 190cm, 89kg
Born: 16.12.68, Norway
Clubs: Molde
• Long-serving keeper who is in his 10th season with Molde. Has grown into a highly reliable player and is a very good shot stopper. Agile and strong.

BALAKOV, Krassimir
Midfielder, Bulgarian, 176cm, 74kg
Born: 29.03.66, Veliko Trnava, Bulgaria
Clubs: Etar Veliko Tamovo, Sporting Lisbon (Por), Stuttgart (Ger) (1995-)
Full international (Bulgaria) 71 caps/12 goals
• Although at the age of 34, the Bulgarian playmaker's best days are behind him, he is not quite ready for the scrapheap either. On his day, he still has the ability to be a matchwinner thanks to his delicate left-footed passing, dribbling ability and free-kick prowess.

BALBO, Abel
Forward, Argentinian, 180cm, 78kg
Born: 01.06.66, Villa Constitucion, Argentina
Clubs: Newell's Old Boys (1987-88), River Plate (1988-89), Udinese (Ita) (1989-93), Roma (Ita) (1993-98), Parma (Ita) (1998-99), Fiorentina (Ita) (1999-2000), Roma (Ita) (2000-)
Full international (Argentina)
• Intelligent and experienced striker who is nearing the end of a distinguished goalscoring career in Serie A.
• Winner of the Copa America in 1991 and 1993 and a member of the Argentina squad at the 1990, 1994 and 1998 World Cups.
• Won the UEFA Cup with Parma in 1999, and joined Fiorentina to provide cover for their 1999-2000 Champions League campaign.
• A devout catholic.

BALJIC, Elvir
Forward, Bosnian, 182cm, 79kg
Born: 08.07.74, Sarajevo, Bosnia
Clubs: FK Sarajevo (1994-95), Bursaspor (Tur) (1995-98), Fenerbahce (Tur) (1998-99), Real Madrid (Spa) (1999-), Fenerbahce (Tur) (2000-, loan)
Full international (Bosnia)
• Attacking midfielder signed by **John Toshack** for Real Madrid in summer 1999 for £10milllion having enjoyed a hugely successful season in Turkey with Fenerbahce.
• Seriously injured his knee early on in his first season in Madrid, and returned to Turkey on loan for the 2000-2001 season.

BALLACK, Michael
Midfielder, German, 189cm, 80kg
Born: 20.09.76, Chemnitz, Germany.
Clubs: Motor Karl-Marx Stadt, Chemnitzer (1995-97), Kaiserslautern (1997-99), Bayer Leverkusen (1999-2000)
Full international (Germany) 9 caps/0 goals
• One of Germany's brightest prospects and a brilliant all-rounder. Can play libero, stopper, as a defensive or attacking midfielder and even up front.
• Looks set to be a pillar of the German national team for some time and such is his talent that he has been dubbed the 'new Beckenbauer'.
• A tragic figure on the final day of the 1999-2000 season, conceding an own goal in Leverkusen's defeat at Unterhaching, a loss which cost his team the Bundesliga title.

BALLERI, David
Defender, Italian, 181cm, 74kg
Born: 28.03.69, Livorno, Italy
Clubs: Cuoio Pelli (1986-87), Cerretese (1987-89), Cuoio Pelli (1989-90), Siracua (1990-92), Cosenza (1992-93), Parma (1993-94), Padova (1994-95), Sampdoria (1995-99), Lecce (1999-)

- Right-back who moved to Lecce after Sampdoria were relegated in 1999.
- European Supercup winner with Parma in 1993.

PLAYER
BANIN, Tal
Midfielder, Israeli, 172cm, 69kg
Born: 07.03.71, Haifa, Israel
Clubs: Brescia (Ita)
Full international (Israel) 62 caps/11 goals
- A committed and influential midfielder, Banin is the natural leader in the Israel national squad and was the obvious choice for captain. He has improved greatly since going to the Italian league, to second division Brescia.
- Unquestionably the most fearless player in the Israeli national side, and is a crunching tackler who plays fair, but very tough.

PLAYER
BARAJA, Ruben
Full name: Ruben Baraja Vegas
Midfielder, Spanish, 180cm, 77kg
Born: 11.07.75, Valladolid, Spain
Clubs: Valladolid (1993-96), Atletico Madrid (1996-2000), Valencia (2000-)
- Hugely promising midfiedler whose career has been blighted by injuries, in particular his knee.
- Joined Valencia in a club record £8million transfer in summer 2000.

PLAYER
BARANEK, Miroslav
Midfielder, Czech, 179cm, 73kg
Born: 01.11.73, Czech Republic
Clubs: Sparta Prague, Koln (Ger) (2000-)
Full international (Czech Rep) 12 caps/2 goals
- Creative midfielder who featured prominently in the Czechs' Euro 2000 qualifying campaign but who was one of the four players axed from the initial 26 players selected by national coach **Jozef Chovanec**.
- Moved to the Bundesliga with newly-promoted

Elviir Baljic

45

FC Koln in 2000-2001.

PLAYER
BARANOV, Vasily
Midfielder, Belarus, 182cm, 80kg
Born: 05.10.72, Belarus
Clubs: Gomel (1993-95), Vedrich (1995), Baltika (Rus) (1996-98), Moscow Spartak (Rus) (1998-)
Full international (Belarus) 11 caps/0 goals
• Belarus international with powerful shot, who has grown in influence in the Spartak team over the past two seasons.

PLAYER
BARBAREZ, Sergej
Midfielder, Bosnian, 188cm, 80kg
Born: 17.09.71, Mostar, Bosnia
Clubs: Velez Mostar, Union Berlin (Ger), Hansa Rostock (Ger) (1996-98), Borussia Dortmund (Ger) (1998-2000), Hamburg (Ger) (2000-)
Full international (Bosnia)
• Strong but temperamental midfielder who joined Hamburg in a £1million transfer in summer 2000 after falling out of favour at Dortmund.
• International debut for Bosnia against Argentina in Cordoba in May 1998.

PLAYER
BARBOSA, Cedric
Midfielder, French, 179cm, 67kg
Born: 06.03.76, Aubenas, France
Clubs: Ales, Montpellier (1997-)
• Young midfielder who failed to establish himself in the Montpellier first team and was due to move on in summer 2000.

PLAYER
BARBU, Constantin
Forward, Romanian, 176cm, 70kg
Born: 16.05.71, Galati, Romania
Clubs: Arges (1994-97), Sumsung Blue (Kor) (1997), Arges (1998), Rapid Bucharest (1998-1999), Numancia (Spa) (1999-)

• Striker who made his name at Rapid Bucharest, scoring 74 goals in 124 games.
• A high-profile signing for Numancia following their fairytale promotion to the Spanish first division.
• A natural penalty-box player, but can also operate as a playmaker behind two main strikers.

PLAYER
BARDON, Cedric
Forward, French, 176cm, 76kg
Born: 15.10.76, Lyon, France
Clubs: Lyon (1992-98), Rennes (1998-)
• Bright and lively attacker who has not yet managed to tap all the potential he showed as a youngster at Lyon. Good touch and very unselfish, but does not convert enough chances.

COACH
BARIC, Otto
Born: 19.06.32
• Veteran coach who has worked across Europe over the past 30 years: Wacker Innsbruck (1970-72), LASK (1972-74), FC Zagreb (1974-76), Yugoslavia under-21 (1974-79), Dinamo Vincovci (1976-79), Dinamo Zagreb (1979-80), Sturm Graz (1980-82), Rapid Vienna (1982-85), Stuttgart (1985-86), Sturm Graz (1986-88), Dinamo Zagreb (1989-90), Vorwarts Steyr (1990-91), Salzburg (1991-95), Croatia assistant (1995-96), Croatia Zagreb (1996-97), Fenerbahce (1997-98), LASK (1998-99).
• National coach of Austria who succeeded Herbert Prohaska in April 1999 following a humiliating 9-0 defeat by Spain.
• A hugely successful coach in domestic Austrian football, winning a host of trophies and guiding Rapid Vienna and Salzburg to European finals and coaching the Yugoslavia under-21 side to the 1978 European title.

BARMBY, Nicky
Forward, English, 168cm, 72kg
Born: 11.02.74, Hull, England
Clubs: Tottenham (1991-95), Middlesbrough (1995-96), Everton (1996-2000), Liverpool (2000-)
Full international (England) 15 caps/3 goals
• Sharp, quick and technically blessed secondary forward who also operates on the left of midfield.
• Broke through at Spurs, but forced to move north, reportedly because of homesickness.
• Form at Everton in the 1999-2000 season prompted **Kevin Keegan** to include him in the England squad for Euro 2000, but did not play.
• Surprisingly joined Liverpool in July 2000 for £6million, making him the first player for 40 years to move from Everton to Anfield.
• Has already been transferred three times in his career, all for fees in excess of £5million.

BARNETT, Jonathan
• London-based agent and the representative of, among others, **Stephen McPhail** and **John Hartson**.
• **Contact:** Suite A, 8 New Cavendish St, London W1M 7IJ. Tel: 44 (0) 20 7935 1068.

BARON, Karsten
Forward, German, 196cm, 90kg
Born: 24.04.73, Berlin, Germany.
Clubs: Hertha Zehlendorf, Hamburg (1992-)
• Striker who returned to competitive action in 2000 after nearly two-and-a-half years out with a badly injured knee. A gangling, wafer-thin individual, he does not particularly look like a professional footballer, but appearances can be deceptive. He has great ball control, can dribble and turn defenders and knows how to tuck away chances.
• Surname pronouced Bay ron.

BARONIO, Roberto
Midfielder, Italian, 180cm, 74kg
Born: 11.12.77, Manerbio, Italy
Clubs: Brescia (1994-96), Lazio (1996-97), Vicenza (1997-98), Lazio (1998-99), Reggina (1999-)
• Highly promising young midfielder who played a key role in Italy's winning side at the 2000 European Under-21 championship.
• Spent the 1999-2000 season on loan at Reggina after failing to break into the Lazio first team.

BAROS, Milan
Forward, Czech, 184cm, 76kg
Born: 28.10.81, Czech Republic
Clubs: Banik Ostrava
• Striker who figured in the Czech Republic squad for the 2000 European Under-21 Championships, partly at the expense of injured team-mate Martin Lukes.

BARROSO
Full name: Jose Alberto da Mota Barroso
Midfielder, Portuguese, 180cm, 77kg
Born: 26.08.70, Braga, Portugal
Clubs: Sporting Braga (1990-92), Rio Ave (1992-93), Sporting Braga (1993-96), FC Porto (1996-98), Sporting Braga (1998-)
Full international (Portugal) 1 cap/0 goals
• A hugely influential player for his hometown club Sporting Braga, but failed to make the breakthrough during two seasons at FC Porto.

BARRY, Gareth
Defender, English, 183cm, 75kg
Born: 23.02.81, Hastings, England
Clubs: Aston Villa (1998-)
Full international (England) 2 caps/0 goals

• Promising teenager defender who Villa 'snatched' from Brighton, who had spotted him and eventually received compensation.

• Plays on the left side of a three-man central defence for Villa, but can also play at full-back or wing-back.

• A surprise call-up to England's Euro 2000 squad after impressing in two pre-tournament friendlies, but did not play in Holland and Belgium.

COACH
BARSEGHYAN, Suren
Armenian
Born: 06.04.50.

• National coach of Armenia since June 1998.

PLAYER
BARTEN, Mike
Defender, German, 181cm, 75kg
Born: 20.11.73, Lubeck, Germany
Clubs: Hansa Lubeck, Werder Bremen (1998-)

• Hard-working central defender who is not the most technical of players, but always gives a determined performance.

• Has been a useful squad player at Werder, but has not established himself in the first team.

PLAYER
BARTHEZ, Fabien
Goalkeeper, French, 183cm, 76kg
Born: 28.06.71, Lavelanet, France
Clubs: Toulouse (1991-92), Marseille (1992-95), Monaco (1995-2000), Manchester United (Eng) (2000-)
Full international (France) 38 caps/0 goals

• The most famous shaved pate in goalkeeping. A hero in his homeland thanks to his efforts in France's victorious World Cup 98 and Euro 2000 campaigns, and a recent £10million addition to the ranks of Manchester United.

• A strong character who exudes authority and charisma, he fills the role of keeper-sweeper to perfection, as well as excelling in the shot-stopping, positioning and courage departments. On the other hand, a couple of doubts persist.

• A variety of injuries meant him only starting one game in three for Monaco during the 1999-2000 season, while he has been known to flap at the odd cross and there will surely be plenty of those in the Premiership.

• The first goalkeeper to wear short-sleeved shirts.

• Champions Cup winner with Marseille in 1993, World Cup winner in 1998 and European Champion with France in 2000. Has also won three French League titles in 1993, 1997 and 2000.

• Surname pronounced Bar tez.

PLAYER
BARTON, Warren
Defender, English, 180cm, 76kg
Born: 19.03.69, London Stoke Newington, England
Clubs: Maidstone Utd (1989-90), Wimbledon (1990-95), Newcastle Utd (1995-)
Full international (England) 3 caps/0 goals

• Right-back who can also play in midfield. Hard-working player who came to professional football late after working as an insurance clerk.

• Had a brief spell as an England international during the Umbro Cup tournament in summer 1995, after which he moved to Newcastle for £5million.

PLAYER
BARTUAL, Jorge
Goalkeeper, Spanish, 182cm, 84kg
Born: 18.08.71, Valencia, Spain
Clubs: Valencia (1993-)

• Reserve keeper at Valencia since 1993, spending two seasons with Valencia B, before moving up to the first team for the 1995-96 season.

PLAYER
BASEGIO, Walter

Midfielder, Belgian, 180cm, 82kg
Born: 19.08.78, Belgium
Clubs: Anderlecht (1996-)
Full international (Belgium) 3 caps/0 goals
• Left-footed defensive midfielder who has great
vision and pace.
• Came through the youth system at Anderlecht,
winning Under-21 honours, and in March 1999, a
first senior cap against Bulgaria.

PLAYER
BASINAS, Angelos

Defender, Greek, 180cm, 76kg
Born: 04.01.76, Greece
Clubs: Panathinaikos (1996-)
Full international (Greece)
• Strong-tackling and adventurous right-back or
wing-back. A favourite of national coach **Vassilis
Daniil**.

PLAYER
BASLER, Mario

Midfielder, German, 186cm, 73kg
Born: 18.12.68, Neustadt, Germany
Clubs: Neustadt/Weinstr, Kaiserslautern, RW
Essen, Hertha Berlin, Werder Bremen, Bayern
Munich, Kaiserslautern
Full international (Germany) 30 caps/2 goals
• The wayward midfield genius is now with
Kaiserslautern after Bayern Munich kicked him
out in early 1999 for repeated nocturnal
escapades. But whatever his many detractors
might say, there is much more to 'Super Mario'
than late nights on a barstool and after-hours
scuffles. While he certainly is not the epitomy
of consistency, he is a proven match-winner,
a schemer of extraordinary invention and a
feared dead-ball specialist.

Fabien Barthez

Gabriel Batistuta

PLAYER
BASSEDAS, Christian
Midfielder, Argentinian
Born: 16.02.73, Buenos Aires, Argentina
Clubs: Velez Sarsfield (1990-2000), Newcastle (Eng) (2000-)
Full international (Argentina)
• Accomplished midfielder who joined Newcastle in a £3.5million transfer in May 2000, signing a five-year contract.
• A member of the Argentina squad at the 1997 Copa America and the 1996 Olympics.
• Winner of the Argentinian League, Libertadores Cup and World Club Cup during 10 seasons at Velez.

PLAYER
BASSILA, Christian
Defender, French, 194cm, 83kg
Born: 05.10.77, Paris, France
Clubs: Lyon (1996-99), Rennes (1999-)
• Tough but intelligent attacking midfielder who was a key figure in the Rennes side in 1999-2000.

PLAYER
BASZCZYNSKI, Marcin
Defender, Polish, 181cm, 71kg
Born: 7.06.77
Clubs: Ruch Chorzow
Full international (Poland) 1 caps/0 goals
• Promising young right-back who has quickly become a key man of Chorzow's defence.
• Started at amateur side Pogon Ruda Slaska and made his national team debut against Spain in January 2000.

ADMINISTRATOR
BATES, Ken
English
Born: 04.12.31
• Chairman and owner of Chelsea who has transformed the sporting and commercial fortunes of the under-achieving London club since taking control in 1982.

- Hands-on and highly-opinionated, he uses the club matchday programme to comment on the issues of the day.
- A key figure in the proposed redevelopment of Wembley stadium.
- Formerly a director at Oldham.

PLAYER
BATICLE, Gerald
Midfielder, French, 182cm, 78kg
Born: 10.09.69, Amiens, France
Clubs: Amiens (1990-91), Auxerre (1991-95), Strasbourg (1995-98), Auxerre (1998-99), Metz (2000-)
- Spent the first half of the 1999-2000 season wasting away on the bench and in the reserves after a dispute with his coach at Auxerre, **Guy Roux**. But during the winter break, this experienced striker moved on to Metz and his aerial power, mobility, selflessness and goals played a fundamental part in helping his new club stave off relegation.
- Nicknamed 'Baticlegol'.
- Surname pronounced Bah teek le.

PLAYER
BATISTUTA, Gabriel
Forward, Argentinian, 185cm, 73kg
Born: 01.02.69, Reconquista, Argentina
Clubs: Newell's Old Boys (1988-89), River Plate (1989-90), Boca Juniors (1990-91), Fiorentina (Ita) (1991-2000), Roma (Ita) (2000-)
Full international (Argentina) 73 caps/53 goals
- One of the greatest strikers in world football, a natural goalscorer who combines power, presence and precision in the penalty area.
- Made his name in his native Argentina with Boca Juniors, where he developed a prolific partnership with Diego Latorre, scoring 13 goals in 31 goals.
- Made his international debut against Brazil in June 1991 and has gone on to become his country's all-time top scorer.
- Stayed with Fiorentina for nine seasons,

earning himself hero status in Florence when he stayed with the club following relegation in 1993. In summer 1998, he turned down offers from Parma and Manchester United to stay at Fiorentina.
- In 1996 a statue of Batistuta was paid for and erected outside Fiorentina's ground by fans.
- Established a Serie A record in autumn 1994 when he scored in Fiorentina's first 11 matches.
- Won the Italian Cup in May 1996 when he scored twice as Fiorentina beat Atalanta 3-0 on aggregate in the Final.
- Provoked riots in Florence when he moved to Roma in June 2000 for £22million and a reported after-tax wage of £4.5million per year, making him the world's highest paid footballer.
- 'I always want to win – even when I'm playing cards with my wife.'

PLAYER
BATTLES, Laurent
Midfielder, French, 174cm, 68kg
Born: 23.09.75, Nantes, France
Clubs: Toulouse, Bordeaux
- His surname is appropriate. A rugged right-back or midfield grafter, he has very much been a second-stringer since arriving at Bordeaux at the start of the 1999-2000 season. But when called upon, he has not looked out of place, particularly impressing in the latter stages of the club's Champions League campaign.
- French Under-21 international.
- Surname pronounced Batt less.

PLAYER
BATTY, David
Midfielder, English, 172cm, 76kg
Born: 02.12.68, Leeds
Clubs: Leeds (1987-93), Blackburn (1993-96), Newcastle (1996-98), Leeds (1998-)
Full international (England) 42 caps/0 gls
- Tough-tackling midfielder who has won League titles with Leeds and Blackburn. An excellent short

David Beckham

passer in midfield, but often loses his discipline.
• Missed the vital penalty in England's 1998 World Cup shoot-out defeat by Argentina.
• Leeds fans displayed 'Batty is God' banners at Elland Road in protest at the player's sale to Blackburn.
• International debut 21.05.91, v USSR.)
• Missed Euro 2000 through injury.

PLAYER
BAUMANN, Frank
Defender, German, 187cm, 79kg
Born: 29.10.75, Wurzburg, Germany
Clubs: Nurnberg, Werder Bremen (1999-)
Full international (Germany) 2 caps/1 goals
• Cultured and calm sweeper who made his full debut for Germany last season against Norway, but just failed to make the final cut for Euro 2000.
• In excellent form during the 1999-2000 season for Bremen, it may well be that he eventually becomes the long-term successor to **Lothar Matthaus** as the national team libero.

PLAYER
BAUMGART, Steffen
Forward, German, 178cm, 77kg
Born: 05.01.72 Rostock, Germany
Clubs: Hansa Rostock (1994-98), Wolfsburg (1998-99), Hansa Rostock (2000-)
• In his second spell at Rostock, he is a no-nonsense striker of the straight-for-goal variety. A relatively small physical package, but one packed with determination and liveliness.

COACH
BAUP, Elie
French
Born: 17.03.55
• Head coach of Bordeaux since January 1998.
• A former goalkeeper with Third Division Mazamet and Muret who began his coaching career at Castelnaudary.
• Had long spells in charge of Toulouse (1983-91)

and Saint Etienne (1991-96) before joining the coaching staff of Bordeaux in July 1997.
• Was highly praised for the attacking football which took Bordeaux to the French League title in the 1998-99 season and is now rated one of France's foremost tacticians.
• Has a baseball cap permanently fixed to his head.
• An advocate of a well-organised, solid back-four guarded by a pair of defensive midfielders, it is not surprising that he admires the work of Carlos Alberto Parreira, Brazil's World Cup-winning boss in 1994. In attack, he favours slick short-passing triangles and a pair of midfield playmakers positioned on either flank.
• While goalkeeping coach at Toulouse, he nurtured the talent of a young **Fabien Barthez**.

COACH
BAXTER, Stuart
English
Born: 16.08.53
• One of the most successful English coaches of the 1990s, but virtually unknown in his own country.
• Won the Swedish championship with AIK in 1998 and 1999, having previously worked in Norway, Portugal, the United States and Japan.

PLAYER
BEATTIE, James
Forward, English, 185cm, 76kg
Born: 27.02.78, Lancaster, England
Clubs: Blackburn (1995-98), Southampton (1998-)
• Promising young striker who joined Southampton from Blackburn in July 1998 when £7.5million **Kevin Davies** went the other way.
• England Under-21 international.

AGENT
BECALI, Iaon
Romanian
• Romania's leading player agent, who has been

involved in the transfer to western Europe of virtually all of the country's leading players over the past decade.
• **Contact:** Calea Floreasca Nr. 91-97, Tronson 4, Bloc F1, Scare 1, Etaj 1, Bucharest, Romania. Tel: 40 1 210 0770.

PLAYER
BECK, Mikkel
Forward, Danish, 186cm, 77kg
Born: 12.05.73, Aarhus, Denmark
Clubs: B1909 (1992-93), Fortuna Koln (Ger) (1993-96), Middlesbrough (Eng) (1996-99), Derby (Eng) (1999-2000), QPR (2000, loan), AaB (2000, loan), Lille (Fra) (2000-)
Full international (Denmark) 19 caps/3 goals
• Striker who is willing, hard-working and promising, but never quite delivers the real thing.
• Helped B1909 win promotion to the Danish first division but was then sold to Fortuna Koln for £25,000 to solve a cashflow problem.
• Move to Middlesbrough in 1996 on a free 'Bosman' transfer was held up as Fortuna Koln tried to claim compensation.
• Struggled to score for Boro and suffered relegation in 1997.
• Father Carl played for Danish side AGF.

ADMINISTRATOR
BECKENBAUER, Franz
German
Born: 11.09.45
• The most powerful man in German football, a legendary figure who commands respect from all quarters of the German game.
• The only man to win the World Cup as a player, captain (1974) and coach (1990).
• Now combines his role as president of Bayern Munich with the position of vice-president of the German FA (DfB). Played an important role as the figurehead for Germany's successful bid to stage the World Cup in 2006.
• Nicknamed 'Der Kaiser' (The King).

PLAYER

BECKHAM, David

Midfielder, English, 182cm, 80kg

Born: 02.05.75, London Leytonstone, England
Clubs: Manchester United (1993-), Preston North End (1995, loan)
Full international (England) 34 caps/1 goal

• The most high-profile player in English football whose haircut, dress sense and social life receive as much press coverage as his football.
• Arguably the best right-sided midfielder in European football. Dead-ball specialist and a hugely influential player for club and country.
• Criticised for his indiscipline (red cards against Argentina at France 98 and Vasco da Gama in the 1999 World Club Championship), but has had to deal with unprecedented abuse from opposing fans over his marriage to Spice Girl Victoria Adams.
• Finished second to **Rivaldo** in the 1999 European Footballer of the Year poll.
• Won a football skills competition aged 10 at a Bobby Charlton Soccer School course; the prize was a trip to Barcelona to train with the then coach **Terry Venables**.
• George Best on Beckham: 'David Beckham isn't a great. He can't kick with his left foot, he can't tackle, he doesn't head the ball and he doesn't score many goals. Apart from that, he's all right.'
• 'I know I'm expected to pull myself to a new higher level every time I play. I accept that because that's what I want to do, to perform at the highest level.'
• 'If I get booked for saying something to the referee or kicking a player, then that's just me. I'm never going to change. The spotlight will always be on me, but it's something I'm learning to live with.'
• International debut: 01.09.96, v Moldova.

ADMINISTRATOR

BEEN, Harry

• General secretary of the KNVB (Dutch FA) and a member of the executive committee of UEFA.

Radek Bejbl

PLAYER
BEIERLE, Markus

Forward, German, 183cm, 78kg
Born: 02.06.72, Brachenheisen, Germany
Clubs: TSV Cleebronn, Union Bockingen, VfB Stuttgart, Ulm, Stuttgarter Kickers (1997-98), Duisburg (1998-)
• Considering that he had not played in the Bundesliga before the start of the 1998-99 season, he has done remarkably well in the top-flight over the last two years, proving himself to be a most able finisher thanks to his excellent right-foot and ability in the air.
• Surname pronounced Buy er ler.

PLAYER
BEINLICH, Stefan

German, Midfielder, 180cm, 75kg
Born: 13.01.72, Berlin, Germany.
Clubs: Dynamo Berlin, Bergmann-Borsig Berlin, Aston Villa (Eng) (1991-94), Hansa Rostock (1994-97), Bayer Leverkusen (1997-)
Full international (Germany) 4 caps/0 goals
• Classy playmaker who was somewhat unlucky not to be included in Germany's Euro 2000 squad. Arguably the owner of the best left foot in the Bundesliga, he is a refined creator and a huge threat from free-kicks, just as capable of scoring with a well-placed curler as a thunderous blast.
• Once played in England for Aston Villa.

PLAYER
BEJBL, Radek

Midfielder, Czech, 185cm, 78kg
Born: 29.08.72, Nymburg, Czech Republic
Clubs: Slavia Prague (1990-96), Atletico Madrid (Spa) (1996-2000), Lens (Fra) (2000-)
Full international (Czech Rep.) 50 caps/3 goals
• Influential central midfielder who has established himself as a crucial figure for the Czech Republic.
• A hard worker and tackler who covers a huge amount of ground for his team-mates, and also weighs in with some crucial passes.

• Made his name in the Slavia Prague side which reached the semi-finals of the 1996 UEFA Cup.
• Earned a transfer to Atletico Madrid in July 1996, having played a key role in the Czech Republic's surprise run to the Final of Euro 96.
• Indicated his intentions to move clubs in summer 2000, after suffering relegation from the Spanish Liga with Atletico, eventually joining French club Lens.
• International debut aged 20 against Egypt in January 1992.

PLAYER
BELIC, Milan

Forward, Yugoslav, 169cm, 64kg
Born: 29.8.77, Yugoslavia
Clubs: Vojvodina Novi Sad
• Diminutive striker with a fine touch. Fast, a strong dribbler and a good finisher. Was a candidate for Yugoslavia's Under-21 team, but remained uncapped at senior level after disciplinary problems (he stormed off the bench after a game's third substitution has been completed without him getting on the pitch).

PLAYER
BELKEVICH, Valentin

Defender, Belarus, 181cm, 70kg
Born: 27.01.73, Belarus
Clubs: Kyiv Dynamo
Full international (Belarus)
• A key figure in the success of Kyiv Dynamo in recent seasons, a right-footed defender who is versatile enough to be able to also play in midfield.
• Footballer of the Year in Belarus in 1995.

PLAYER
BELODEDICI, Miodrag

Defender, Romanian, 185cm, 75kg
Born: 20.05.64, Sokolovac, Romania
Clubs: Steaua (1982-89), Red Star Belgrade (Yug) (1990-92), Valencia (Spa) (1992-94), Valladolid (Spa) (1994-95), Villarreal (Spa) (1995-96), Atlante

(Mex) (1996-98), Steaua (1998-)
Full international (Romania) 52 caps/5 goals
• Veteran sweeper who was recalled by Romania for Euro 2000 at the age of 36.
• Won the European Cup with Steaua Bucharest in 1986 and became the first player to win the competition with two different clubs when he was a member of the Red Star Belgrade side which triumphed in 1991.
• Increasing civil unrest in Bucharest led him to take exile in Belgrade in 1988, spending three and a half seasons in international exile before feeling safe enough to resume his career with Romania.
• Moved to Spain in 1992 and had a short spell in Mexico before returning home to Steaua in 1998.

PLAYER
BELSUE, Alberto
Full name: Alberto Belsue Arias
Defender, Spanish, 171cm, 69kg
Born: 02.03.68, Zaragoza, Spain
Clubs: Zaragoza (1988-98), Alaves (1998-)
Full international (Spain) 17 caps/0 goals
• Right-back who was rated as the best in his position in Spain in the mid-1990s.
• A product of the Zaragoza youth scheme who played two games for Spain at Euro 96.
• Moved to Alaves in 1998 after 11 seasons at Zaragoza.
• International debut for Spain against Denmark in 1994.

PLAYER
BELSVIK, Petter
Forward, Norwegian, 188cm, 84kg
Born: 02.10.67, Lillehammer, Norway
Clubs: Molde (1989-91), Ham-Kam (1991-93), Start (1994-95), Stabaek (1996-)
• Striker who had scored 143 league goals prior to the 2000 season for four different clubs.
• Is closing in on the Norwegian all-time goal scoring record set by Odd Iversen, father of **Steffen Iversen**.

PLAYER
BEN SLIMANE, Mehdi
Forward, Tunisian, 170cm, 76kg
Born: 01.01.74, Kramm, Tunisia
Clubs: Marseille (Fra) (1996-97), Freiburg (Ger) (1997-)
Full international (Tunisia)
• Stocky (some would say podgy) winger with deft skill, well worth watching by opposing defenders.
• Moved to German club Freiburg after an injury-plagued season in Marseille.

PLAYER
BENADO, Arik
Defender, Israeli
Born: 5.12.73
Clubs: Maccabi Haifa
Full international (Israel) 43 caps/0 goals
• The mainstay in the Israel national team defence for the past four seasons. As a central defender has generally done a good job in keeping opposing attackers out of harm's way. Is good in the air, but lacks a few extra paces of speed. Is captain of Maccabi Haifa. Scores very few goals.

PLAYER
BENARBIA, Ali
Midfielder, French/Algerian, 171cm, 68kg
Born: 08.10.68, Oran, Algeria
Clubs: Narbonne, Martigues (1988-95), Monaco (1995-98), Bordeaux (1998-99), Paris Saint-Germain (1999-2000
• Cultured right-sided playmaker, who has served as vital attacking supply line at all his clubs. A wonderful creator, a midfielder never short of a defence-splitting through ball or accurate whipped cross.
• He is also renowned for being a charismatic team leader, a man to galvanise the troops. 'I'm only in football to win trophies. Second place is of no use at all to me. I expect every teammate of mine to be the same.'
• An instrumental figure in Bordeaux's 1999

French League title triumph before joining PSG.
• Recently indicated his readiness to play for Algeria after years of being ignored by France.

PLAYER
BENARRIVO, Antonio
Defender, Italian, 170cm, 69kg
Born: 21.08.68, Brindisi, Italy
Clubs: Brindisi (1986-89), Padova (1989-91), Parma (1991-)
Full international (Italy) 23 caps/0 goals
• Experienced full-back or wide midfielder whose willingness to get to the opponent's byline has made him an automatic choice at club level, and a useful international player in the past as well.
• Pace, experience and combative qualities make him a tough customer.

PLAYER
BENAYOUN, Yossi
Midfielder, Israeli, 180cm, 72kg
Born: 05.05.80, Israel
Clubs: Maccabi Haifa, Israel
Full international (Israel) 7 caps/4 goals
• One of the hottest talents in Israeli soccer, the young star is not without his faults. He has been sidelined by new national coach **Richard Moller Nielsen** and returned to the under-21s after disobeying an instruction by club coach Eli Cohen to be substituted in a League match in March 2000.
• Benayoun is fleet of foot and has an excellent instinct in front of goal. He has often broken down defences both for club and country.
• Had a short spell at the Ajax youth academy, but got homesick and returned to Israel.

PLAYER
BENITEZ, Miguel
Full name: Miguel Angel Benitez Pavon
Forward, Paraguayan, 169cm, 65kg
Born: 19.05.70, Santisima Trinidad, Paraguay
Clubs: Calpe (Spa) (1990-93), Atletico Madrid
(Spa) (1993-95), Merida (Spa) (1994-95), Espanyol (Spa) (1995-99)
Full international (Paraguay)
• Striker who played for Paraguay at the 1998 World Cup and has been a moderate success in Spain with Espanyol.
• Most effective in a deep-lying role, although he can play further forward, and did so when he finished as Paraguay's top scorer in the qualifying matches for the 1998 World Cup.

PLAYER
BENJAMIN
Full name: Benjamin Zarandona Esono
Midfielder, Spanish, 184cm, 76kg
Born: 02.03.76, Valladolid, Spain
Clubs: Real Valladolid (1994-98), Real Betis (1998-)
• Solid, hard-working midfield all-rounder who joined Betis from Valladolid in summer 1998 for £6.75million but struggled to justify the fee.
• Was likely to be sold by Betis following relegation in May 2000.

REFEREE
BENKO, Gunter
Austrian
Born: 12.07.55
• Works as a medical orderly.
• Awarded his FIFA Badge in 1993.

PLAYER
BEQAI, Arian
Goalkeeper, Albanian, 187cm, 80kg
Born: 20.08.76, Albania
Clubs: OFI Crete (Greece)
Full international (Albania) 6 caps/0 goals
• Capable keeper who has earned plaudits for his performances in the Greek League with OFI.
• Made his international debut for Alabania as a substitute against Turkey in January 1998.

PLAYER
BEREZOVSKI, Roman
Goalkeeper, Armenian, 190cm, 80kg
Born: 05.08.74, Armenia
Clubs: Zenit St Petersburg (Rus) (1994-)
Full international (Armenia)
• Armenian international keeper with good reactions. Has has been impressively consistent over the last few seasons for Zenit St Petersburg in the Russian League.

PLAYER
BERG, Arild
Midfielder, Norwegian, 173cm, 73kg
Born: 17.07.75, Norway
Clubs: Bodo Glimt (1998-)
• Youngest of three Berg brothers but struggles with allergic reactions and this has restricted his career.
• Has agreed to join Rosenborg at a time that suits him in the near future.

PLAYER
BERG, Henning
Defender, Norwegian, 184cm, 75kg
Born: 01.09.69 in Lorenskog, Norway
Clubs: Valerenga (1990-91), Lillestrom (1992), Blackburn (1993-97), Manchester United (1997-)
Full international (Norway) 72 caps/8 goals
• Soild, competent defender who has been a regular for Norway despite not playing every week for United, where he has a number of rivals for the spot alongside **Jaap Stam** in central defence.
• League winner with Blackburn, 1995. Member of Norwegian World Cup squads, 1994 and 1998.
• International debut: 13.05.92, v Faroe Islands.

PLAYER
BERG, Orjan
Midfielder, Norwegian, 172cm, 69kg
Born: 20.08.68, Norway
Clubs: Rosenborg (1988-90), Wettingen (Ger), Munich 1860 (Ger), Bodo/Glimt (1994-99), Rosenborg (1999-)

Full international (Norway) 19 caps/1 goal
• A skilled technician who decided against going back to Bodo/Glimt when his loan spell with Rosenborg was over.
• Oldest brother from a Bodo football family.

PLAYER
BERG, Runar
Midfielder, Norwegian, 179cm, 73kg
Born: 07.10.70, Tromso, Norway
Clubs: Rosenborg (1990), Tromso (1991), Bodo/Glimt (1992-96), Rosenborg (1997-99), Venezia (Ita) (1999-)
Full international (Norway) 3 caps/0 goals
• Midfielder who headed for Italy in 1999 to try his luck with Venezia after a successful career in the Norwegian League that included title victories with Rosenborg.

PLAYER
BERG HESTAD, Daniel
Midfielder, Norwegian, 183cm, 80kg
Born: 30.07.75, Norway
Clubs: Molde (1993-)
Full international (Norway) 5 caps/0 goals
• Young midfielder who has failed to fulfill the realise the expectations a couple of seasons ago that he would become a star player.
• Scores regularly with his head and loves to go forward.

PLAYER
BERGDOLMO, Andre
Defender, Norwegian, 187cm, 78kg
Born: 13.10.71, Oslo, Norway
Clubs: Lillestrom (1991-96), Rosenborg (1997-2000), Ajax Amsterdam (Hol) (2000-)
Full international (Norway) 27 caps/0 caps
• Stylish attacking full-back with a precise left foot. Gained great experience playing in the Champions League and for Norway.
• Played for Norway at Euro 2000 and joined Ajax after the tournament.

BERGER, Jorg
German
Born: 13.10.44

• Experienced coach who has taken charge of a number of German clubs in recent years.
• Played his entire career at Lokmotiv Leipzig in the old GDR before becoming youth coach in 1979.
• Then embarked on a coaching career which has taken in Carl Zeiss Jena, the East German national youth and B teams, Darmstadt, Ulm, Fortuna Dusseldorf, Hessen Kassel, Hannover 96, Freiburg, Eintracht Frankfurt, FC Koln, Schalke and Karlsruher. Also had a spell in Switzerland coaching FC Basel.
• Returned to Eintracht in spring 2000 and saved them from relegation. Dubbed 'The Fireman', he is a coach clubs turn to in times of trouble and thanks to his cool head in a crisis and his powers of motivation, Eintracht Frankfurt (twice) and Schalke have managed to dodge the relegation bullet.
• Defected from East Germany in 1979. 'Being in charge of a struggling club is nothing compared to standing at a frontier post and watching a border guard looking at your forged passport.'

PLAYER
BERGER, Patrik
Midfielder, Czech, 187cm, 80kg
10.11.73, Prague, Czech Rep
Clubs: Slavia Prague (1991-95), Borussia Dortmund (1995-96), Liverpool (1996-
Full international (Czech Rep) 40 caps/ 18 goals
• Left-sided midfielder who had his best season for Liverpool in 1999-2000.
• A Bundesliga winner with Dortmund in 1996 who scored a penalty in the Czechs' surprise appearance in the Final of Euro 96.
• International debut: 24.03.93, v Cyprus (1-1).
• Missed the Czech Republic's first two games at Euro 2000 through suspension after being sent off in the qualifers.

COACH
BERGEROO, Philippe
French
Born: 13.01.54

• Coach of Paris Saint-Germain since March 1999 when he succeeded the sacked Artur Jorge.
• As a player he was a goalkeeper with Bordeaux, Lille and Toulouse, winning three caps for France and was a member of the French squad which won the 1984 European Championship.
• Goalkeeping coach of the French national side from 1994 until the World Cup triumph in 1998, when he joined the back-room staff at PSG.
• Very much a coach in **Aime Jacquet**'s image, swearing by preparation and tactical discipline.

PLAYER
BERGKAMP, Dennis
Forward, Dutch, 185cm, 80kg
Born: 18.05.69, Amsterdam, Holland
Clubs: Ajax Amsterdam (1986-93), Internazionale (Ita) (1993-95), Arsenal (Eng) (1995-)
Full international (Holland) 79 caps/36 goals
• Gifted forward who began his career as a winger at Ajax before moving into a central attacking role, scoring 103 goals in 185 games.
• Appearances in European competition have been limited by his fear of flying, reportedly caused by a journalists' prank during the 1994 World Cup. When the Dutch team plane was preparing for take-off, the reporter joked his bag contained a bomb, grounding the plane and trigerring a nervous reaction in Bergkamp.
• Cost Arsenal £7.5m from Inter in July 1995 after failing to reproduce his Ajax goalscoring form in Serie A.
• International debut: 26.09.90, v Italy (lost 1-0)
• The Dutch national team's all-time top scorer, and announced his retirement after Euro 2000.
• Named after Manchester United player Denis Law, but the birth registrar insisted that Denis was a girl's name, so his parents were forced to name him Dennis.

Eyal Berkovic

PLAYER
BERGSSON, Gudni
Defender, Icelandic, 185cm, 81kg
Born: 21.07.65, Reykjevik, Iceland
Clubs: Tottenham (Eng), Bolton (Eng)
Full international (Iceland) 77 caps/1 goal
• Cultured full-back, ex-international skipper and qualified lawyer who made his name with Spurs. Although now approaching the end of his career, his defensive skills and eye for goal figured strongly in Bolton's promotion drive in the 1999-2000 season.

PLAYER
BERHALTER, Gregg
Defender, American, 180cm, 76kg
Born: 01.08.73, Englewood, United States
Clubs: University of North Carolina, FC Zwolle (Hol) (1994-96), Sparta Rotterdam (Hol) (1996-98), Cambuur (Hol) (1998-)
Full international (United States) 5 caps/0 goals
• American defender and a tight marker. Caused a stir when claiming **Ruud Van Nistelrooy** was simulating fouls, trying to get free-kicks.
• Not the most technical defender but has a great mentality. Before coming to Holland in 1994, his wife was an American international as well.

PLAYER
BERKOVIC, Eyal
Forward, Israeli, 170cm, 64kg
Born: 02.04.72, Haifa, Israel
Clubs: Maccabi Haifa (1992-96), West Ham (Eng) (1996-99), Celtic (Sco) (1999-)
Full international (Israel) 62 caps/8 goals
•One of Israel's biggest stars, Berkovic is the main playmaker and his world-class skills have often done the business for the national team. After Israel's 5-0 thrashing of Austria in Euro 2000 qualifying, Berkovic recieved perfect 10 marks for his performance.
• Has avoided serious injury throughout his career, although is not the toughest of competitors.

• Celtic paid out a club record transfer fee when bringing him to Parkhead from West Ham in the early stages of John Barnes' reign but his first season in Glasgow was tainted by mediocre performances and criticisms concerning his level of commitment. He is adamant, however, that he sees his future as a Celtic player.

BUSINESS
BERLUSCONI, Silvio
Born: 29.09.36
• Politician, club owner and media mogul who transformed the fortunes of Milan when he bought the club in 1986.
• A pioneer of pay-TV who once predicted a day when fans would be let into games for free to provide the atmosphere for those paying to watch at home. Also a long-term advocate of a European Superleague.
• An ambitious politician who has used the imagery and language of the football terraces to launch a political career which saw his 'Forza Italia' party briefly elected to power.

PLAYER
BERNINI, Andrea
Midfielder, Italian, 178cm, 72kg
Born: 10.06.73, Reggello, Italy
Clubs: Sangiovann. (1995-97), Montevarchi (1997-99), Reggina (1999-)
• Midfielder who impressed on the flank in his first season in Serie A with Reggina.

PLAYER
BERNTSEN, Tommy
Defender, Norwegian, 188cm, 87kg
Born: 18.12.73, Norway
Clubs: Lillestrom (1998-)
• Promising central defender who is strong in the air and very uncompromising.

PLAYER
BERRE, Morten
Forward, Norwegian, 181cm, 78kg
Born: 10.08.75, Oslo, Norway
Clubs: Skeid (1996-97), Haugesund (1998), Viking Stavanger (1999-)
• Pacy attacker who enjoys runs down the left flank.
• Joined Viking from Haugesund but started career with Skeid Oslo.

PLAYER
BERRETTA, Daniele
Midfielder, Italian, 177cm, 69kg
Born: 08.03.72, Rome, Italy
Clubs: Roma (1990-92), Vicenza (1992-93), Roma (1993-94), Cagliari (1994-95), Roma (1995-96), Cagliari (1996-)
• An important figure in midfield for Cagliari after failing to establish himself at Roma despite a bright start to his career in the Italian capital.

PLAYER
BERTHOLD, Thomas
Defender, German, 185cm, 81kg
Born: 12.11.64, Hanau, Germany
Clubs: Eintracht Frankfurt (1982-87), Hellas Verona (Ita) (1987-89), Roma (Ita) (1989-91), Bayern Munich (1991-93), Stuttgart (1993-)
Full international (Germany) 62 caps/1 goal
• Fiery, tough-tackling central defensive veteran whose competitive instincts have not at all been blunted by 18 seasons of demanding top-flight football.
• Began his career as a marauding right-back and appeared for Germany in three World Cup finals, including their victorious Italia 90 campaign.
• Missed the entire 1992-93 season through injury.
• Surname pronounced Bear tohld.

BERTI, Sergio

• Italian agent whose clients include **Slavisa Jokanovic**, **Gilles de Bilde** and **Vincenzo Montella**.
• **Contact:** Via F. Lli Rosselli, 11, I-51100, Pistoia, Italy.

PLAYER
BERTILSSON, Henrik
Forward, Swedish, 189cm, 87kg
Born: 16.10.69, Sweden
Clubs: Falkenbergs (1987-91), Halmstad (1991-94), Martigues (Fra) (1994-95), Orgryte (1995-98), Halmstad (1999-)
Full international (Sweden) 1 cap/0 goals
• A big striker who topped Sweden's scoring charts in the 1993 season, aged 18. A professional spell in France with Martigues followed, but he was virtually a forgotten man when he returned home, to Orgryte. However, Halmstad seem to have brought out best of this burly, but stylish player.

PLAYER
BERTIN, Teddy
Defender, French, 185cm, 80kg
Born: 06.08.69, Elixecourt, France
Clubs: Amiens, Le Havre (1991-97), Marseille (1997-98), Strasbourg (1998-)
• Highly-experienced, inspirational sweeper. Defensively very robust, with a good aerial game, his comfort on the ball makes him the ideal launchpad for his team's attacks. Also boasts a thunderous shot from free-kicks.
• While at Le Havre, he gave 50 tickets for a game with Paris Saint-Germain to kids from a poor part of town.
• Surname pronounced Ber tan.

PLAYER
BERTOTTO, Valerio
Defender, Italian, 179cm, 76kg
Born: 15.01.73, Turin, Italy
Clubs: Alessandria (1990-93), Udinese (1993-)

• No-nonsense centre-back who is a tough man-marker and has stayed loyal to Udinese since making his name at Alessandria.
• Can also play at right-back.

PLAYER
BESCHASTNYKH, Vladimir
Forward, Russian, 185cm, 83kg
Born: 01.04.74, Moscow, Russia
Clubs: Moscow Spartak (1992-94), Werder Bremen (Ger) (1994-96), Racing Santander (Spa) (1996-)
Full international (Russia) 46 caps/6 goals
• Strong-running striker who has performed well in Spain after an indifferent time in Germany with Werder Bremen.
• Fell out with Santander after calling for coach Gustavo Benitez to be sacked.
• Played for Russia at Euro 96 and won Russian League titles in 1993 and 1994.

PLAYER
BETO
Full name: Roberto Luis Gaspar Deus Severo
Defender, Portuguese, 185cm, 74kg
Born: 03.05.76, Lisbon, Portugal
Clubs: Campomaoirense (1995-96), Sporting Lisbon (1996-)
Full international (Portugal) 8 caps/0 goals
• Resourceful central defender who has been linked with a number of English clubs.
• Made his international debut for Portugal against Germany in 1997 and has been a regular member of the squad ever since, including Euro 2000.
• Member of the Portuguese team which won the 1994 European Under-18 championship.

PLAYER
BETTARINI, Stefano
Defender, Italian, 181cm, 79kg
Born: 06.02.72, Forli, Italy
Clubs: Internazionale (1990-91), Baracca (1991-

92), Lucchese (1992-94), Salernitana (1994-95), Lucchese (1995-96), Cagliari (1996-97), Fiorentina (1997-98), Bologna (1999), Venezia (1999-)
• Dashing left wing-back who has a reputation as a party-goer, but is strong and athletic and often scores spectacular goals.

ADMINISTRATOR
BETTEGA, Roberto
Born: 27.12.50
• Vice-president of Juventus and a hugely important figure at the club where he was such a successful player.
• Played 42 times for Italy as a centre-forward, scoring 19 goals.

PLAYER
BEYA, Zoubeir
Midfielder, Tunisian, 176cm, 69kg
Born: 15.05.71, Sahen, Tunisia
Clubs: Etoile du Sahel, Freiburg (1997-)
Full international (Tunisia)
• Classy Tunisian international midfielder at his best playing on the shoulder of the main strikers. A player of silky technique whom even in the most frantic game seems to have a lot of time on the ball.
• Surname also spelt Baya.

PLAYER
BEYE, Habib
Defender, Midfielder, 183cm, 78kg
Born: 19.10.77, Suresnes, France
Clubs: Paris Saint-Germain (1997-98), Strasbourg (1998-)
• Right-back who was playing as an amateur in the French fifth division when signed for PSG by **Claude Le Roy** in 1997. He followed Le Roy to Strasbourg, where he impressed everyone in the 1999-2000 season.

PLAYER
BEZHENAR, Serhiy
Defender, Ukrainian, 182cm, 81kg
Born: 09.08.70
Clubs: Dnipr, Kyiv Dynamo, Erzurumspor (Tur)
Full international (Ukraine) 23 caps/1 goal
• Former Soviet youth international who won the Ukrainian League title with Dynamo in 1995, 1996 and 1997 before a move to Turkey.

PLAYER
BEZRODNY, Artem
Midfielder, Russia, 180cm, 79kg
Born: 10.02.79, Russia
Clubs: Moscow Spartak
Full international (Russia) 1 cap/0 goals
• Up and coming young midfielder at Spartak. Fast, with good passing ability and ball control.
• Made his international debut for Russia against Andorra in September 1999.

PLAYER
BEZZAI, Houssin
Defender, Moroccan, 170cm, 72kg
Born: 04.11.78, Elaouyen, Morocco
Clubs: Sparta Rotterdam (Hol)
• Promising young defender who won the African Under-20 championship with Morocco in 1997.

PLAYER
BIA, Giovanni
Defender, Italian, 178cm, 73kg
Born: 24.10.68, Parma
Clubs: Parma (1984-86), Perugia (1986-90), Parma (1990), Trento (1990-91), Parma (1991-92), Cosenza (1992-93), Napoli (1993-94), Internazionale (1994-95), Udinese (1995-97), Brescia (1997-98), Bologna (1998-)
• Much-travelled central defender with an eye for goal.
• Established himself in the Italian top flight with Napoli, but since then has failed to hold down a regular first-team place.

PLAYER
BIAGINI, Leonardo

Forward, Argentinian/Spanish, 183cm, 75kg
Born: 13.04.77, Rosario, Argentina
Clubs: Newell's Old Boys (1993-95), Atletico Madrid (Spa) (1995-97), Merida (Spa) (1997-98), Mallorca (Spa) (1998-)

• Striker who has emerged at Mallorca as a player of real promise after struggling to establish himself at Atletico Madrid and Merida.

• Atletico Madrid president **Jesus Gil** took a real gamble on 18-year-old Biagini when he was signed for £1.3million from Newell's Old Boys in 1995.

• Scored only five goals in 49 League appearances for Atletico, and only one in 27 for Merida.

• Has excelled for Mallorca, both in the League and Europe, scoring crucial goals in the run to the 1999 Cup-winners Cup Final.

COACH
BICSKEI, Bertalan

Hungarian

• Coach of the Hungarian national side since 1998.

• A forward with Honved, he is in his second spell in charge of Hungary, having also coached Honved, Lucerne and in Egypt.

PLAYER
BIELI, Rainer

Striker, Swiss, 176cm, 73kg
Born: 22.02.79, Switzerland
Clubs: Kestenholz, Grasshopper (1995-98), Baden (1998-99), Neuchatel Xamax (1999-)

• Swiss Under-21 international striker. Up and coming youngster with 21 goals in the 1999-2000 season, second behind **Charles Amoah**.

• Tipped for a move back to Grasshopper for the 2000-2001 season.

Oliver Bierhoff

PLAYER
BIERHOFF, Oliver
Forward, German, 191cm, 90kg
Born: 01.05.68, Karlsruhe, Germany
Clubs: Bayer Uerdingen (1986-88), Hamburg (1988-90), Borussia Monchengladbach (1990), Salzburg (Aut) (1990-91), Ascoli (Ita) (1991-95), Udinese (Ita) (1995-98), Milan (Ita) (1998-)
Full international (Germany) 50 caps/30 goals
• Germany's captain and the scorer of the Golden Goal that gave them victory over the Czech Republic in the Final of Euro 96.
• A magnificent finisher, especially in the air, although he is not a player to build attacking moves around.
• Career did not take off until move to Italy, spending three years in Serie B with Ascoli and finishing as top scorer in Serie B with 20 goals.
• Moved to Milan in summer 1998 after finishing as top scorer in the Italian League with 27 goals while with Udinese. Won the *Scudetto* in his first season with Milan in 1999.
• Won 10 Under-21 caps for Germany, including a hat-trick on his debut against Switzerland.
• Made his senior debut in February 1996 against Portugal.
• 'I don't have **Ronaldo**'s speed, **Alessandro Del Piero**'s dribbling ability or **Gabriel Batistuta**'s power. I score simple goals.'

PLAYER
BIGNE, Yoann
Midfielder, French, 168cm, 65kg
Born: 23.08.77, Laval, France
Clubs: Rennes (1996-)
• French Under-21 international, a versatile all-rounder and a product of the Rennes youth system.

COACH
BIGON, Alberto
Italian
Born: 31.10.47
• Coach who was in charge at Napoli when they won the Italian League.
• A player with Milan and Perugia who made his name with Cesana, taking the small-town Italian club to ninth place in Serie A in 1988.
• At Napoli, he managed the side which contained Diego Maradona and Cereca and which won the Italian title in 1990.
• The following season, Napoli could only finish seventh, and Bigon moved on to second division Lecce and then Udinese.
• Since then he has only worked in fits and starts, winning the Swiss championship with Sion in 1997 and having disappointing spells at Perugia, where he was sacked eight games into the season, and Olympiakos, where he was involved in a series of disputes with **Zlatko Zahovic**.

PLAYER
BILIC, Slaven
Defender, Croatian, 190cm, 85kg
Born: 11.09.68, Split, Croatia
Clubs: Hajduk Split (1988-93), Karlsruhe (Ger) (1993-95), West Ham (Eng) (1995-97), Everton (Eng) (1997-99),
Full international (Croatia) 44 caps/3 goals
• Central defender who was a key player in the emergence of the Croatian national side in the mid-1990s, being appointed national team captain within two months of making his international debut, against Australia in 1992.
• Won the national championship and two Cups with Hajduk Split before a move to Germany, where he was voted into the Bundesliga team of the 1994-95 season by the media.
• Was accused of diving in the penalty area after clashing with **Laurent Blanc** in Croatia 1998 World Cup semi-final against France, resulting in a red card for the Frenchman, who missed the Final as a result.
• Suffered from injury problems after the 1998 World Cup and returned to Croatia while Everton pondered his future.
• Has a university degree in law.

PLAYER
BILICA
Full name: Fabio Alves da Silva
Defender, Brazilian, 187cm, 78kg
Born: 04.01.79, Brazil
Clubs: Vitoria Bahia (1998), Venezia (Ita) (1998-)
• Brazilian defender who has performed admirably in since a move to Italy's Serie A.

PLAYER
BINOTTO, Jonatan
Midfielder, Italian, 181cm, 75kg
Born: 22.01.75, Montebelluna, Italy.
Clubs: Juventus (1992-94), Ascoli (1994-95, Cesena (1995-96), Verona (1996-98), Bologna (1998-)
• Highly promising midfielder who failed to make the grade at Juventus, but has established himself in Serie A during spells at Verona and Bologna.

PLAYER
BIRINDELLI, Alessandro
Defender, Italian, 176cm, 73kg
Born: 12.11.74, Pisa, Italy.
Clubs: Empoli (1992-97), Juventus (1997-)
• Speedy right-back signed by Juventus from Empoli, where he was involved in successive promotion from the third division to Serie A.

PLAYER
BISGAARD, Morten
Midfielder, Danish, 178cm, 73kg
Born: 25.06.74, Randers, Denmark
Clubs: OB Odense (1993-98), Udinese (Ita) (1998-)
Full international (Denmark) 5 caps/0 goals
• Full-back or wide midfielder who was signed by Udinese in summer 1998 as a replacement for the Milan-bound **Thomas Helveg**.
• Has had trouble adapting to the discipline of Italian soccer, compared to the Danish League, where he was free to attack at will. His international career has suffered as a result.

PLAYER
BIZACKI, Krzysztof
Forward, Polish, 170cm, 71kg
Born: 07.04.73, Poland
Clubs: Ruch Chorzow
Full international (Poland) 2 caps/0 goals
• Small but skilful striker with a good nose for goal. With his scoring ability can trouble any defence. Played the best football of his career during the 1999-2000 season, helping his club qualify for the UEFA Cup.

PLAYER
BIZARRI, Albano Benjamin
Goalkeeper, Argentinian, 193cm, 89kg
Born: 09.11.77, Etruria, Argentina
Clubs: Racing Avellaneda (1996-99), Real Madrid (Spa) (1999-)
• Keeper bought by Real Madrid as an understudy for **Bodo Illgner**, but injuries, poor form and the emergence of **Iker Casillas** conspired to keep him on the sidelines.
• Argentinian Under-21 international and a member of the senior squad at the 1999 Copa America.

PLAYER
BJARMANN, Torgeir
Defender, Norwegian, 183cm, 82kg
Born: 24.06.68, Lorenskog, Norway
Clubs: Lillestrom (1988-)
• Reliable captain and central defender who has played more than 275 matches in 11 seasons for his club Lillestrom.
• Scores important goals from set-pieces.

PLAYER
BJERRE, Anders
Midfielder, Danish, 187cm, 85kg
Born: 27.05.69, Denmark
Clubs: KB (1990), B1903 (1991-92), FC Copenhagen (1992-93), Naestved (1993-94), Lyngby (1994-97), AGF (1997-)
• Midfielder who is now back with AGF Aarhus

fter a spell with Lyngby ended when the club xperienced financial difficulties.

PLAYER
BJORKAN, Asmund
Forward, Norwegian, 178cm, 78kg
Born: 03.07.73, Oslo, Norway
Clubs: Bodo/Glimt (1993-)
• One of the quickest players in the Norwegian league. Has been loyal to Bodo/Glimt where he as played more than 260 matches.

PLAYER
BJORKLUND, Joachim
Defender, Swedish, 184cm, 81kg
Born: 15.02.71, Vaxjo, Sweden
Clubs: Osters (1988-89), Brann Bergen (Nor) 1989-92), IFK Gothenburg (1992-95), Vicenza (Ita) 1995-96), Rangers (Sco) (1996-98), Valencia 1998-)
Full international (Sweden) 70 caps/0 goals
• Central defender who has been the mainstay of the Swedish national team defence since making is international debut against Australia in January 1992.
• Speedy defender with excellent timing and anticipation.
• Won Swedish League titles in successive years with Gothenburg in 1993, 1994 and 1995.
• The nephew of former Swedish national coach Tommy Svensson.

PLAYER
BJORNEBYE, Stig Inge
Defender, Norwegian, 181cm, 76kg
Born: 11.12.69, Elverum, Norway
Clubs: Strammen (1987-89), Kongsvinger (1989-91), Rosenborg (1992), Liverpool (Eng) (1992-2000), Blackburn (Eng) (2000-)
Full international (Norway) 73 caps/1 goal
• Reliable left wing-back who can also play in midfield.
• Joined Liverpool in 1993 after impressing in a

spell for Rosenborg. Struggled at first at Anfield, but gradually asserted himself.
• Unable to win a regular place in the Liverpool squad under **Gerard Houllier**, and rejoined former Liverpool coach **Graeme Souness** at Blackburn in summer 2000.

PLAYER
BJUR, Ole
Midfielder, Danish, 183cm, 78kg
Born: 13.09.68, Denmark
Clubs: Vanlose (1988-91), Brondby (1991-)
Full international (Denmark) 3 caps/1 goal
• Versatile campaigner who started his career as a striker but is now better known as a midfield grafter. Can also play at right-back.
• Looked to have a promising international career after scoring on his debut for Denmark against Sweden, but has since found opportunities limited.

PLAYER
BLAZEK, Jaromir
Goalkeeper, Czech, 185cm, 86kg
Born: 29.12.72, Czech Republic
Clubs: Ceske Budejovice, Bohemians, Slavia Prague, Sparta Prague (1999-)
• Young goalkeeper with a big physical presence who joined Sparta from Bohemians in the 1999-2000 season's winter break.
• Quickly established himself as the first-choice keeper at Sparta, turning in some impressive Champions League displays, and then edged out Slavia rival **Radek Cerny** for the third goalkeeping slot in the Euro 2000 squad.

PLAYER
BLEDZEWSKI, Andrzej
Goalkeeper, Polish, 184cm, 75kg
Born: 02.07.77, Poland
Clubs: Gornik Zabrze
• A talented keeper of a new generation with national team prospects. Played for second

division Baltyk Gdynia and Polonia Bytom before joining Gornik three years ago.
• Polish Under-21 international.

PLAYER

BLANC, Laurent

Defender, French, 190cm, 82kg
Born: 19.11.65, Ales, France.
Clubs: Montpellier (1983-91), Napoli (Ita) (1991-92), Nimes (1992-93), St Etienne (1993-95), Auxerre (1995-96), Barcelona (Spa) (1996-97), Marseille (1997-99), Internazionale (Ita) (1999-)
Full international (France) 95 caps/16 goals
• Highly accomplished sweeper who is strong in the air and a precise passer on the ground.
• Missed France's 1998 World Cup Final triumph after being unfairly sent off the semi-final against Croatia after Slaven Bilic over-reacted after being pushed in the box by Blanc.
• Made his name with Montpellier, being voted French Footballer of the Year in 1990, having already won the European Under-21 Championship with France in 1988.
• International debut against the Republic of Ireland in 1989.
• Spent less than a year at Napoli, but was deemed too adventurous for the Italians.
• Won the French League with Auxerre in 1996 and the European Cup-winners Cup with Barcelona in 1997.
• Surname pronounced Blon.

PLAYER

BLANC, Serge

Defender, French, 180cm, 77kg
Born: 22.09.72, Lyon, France
Clubs: Montpellier, Monaco, Lyon
• Can play stopper but he makes a far more meaningful contribution as an attacking left-back.
• Has won French Under 21 and Military honours.
• Too often in the bad books of referees.
• Name pronounced: Ser je Blon.

PLAYER

BLANCHARD, Jocelyn

Midfielder, French, 189cm, 78kg
Born: 28.05.72, Bethune, France
Clubs: Dunkerque, Metz, Juventus, Lens
• Right-sided or central midfielder now back in France after spending the 1998-99 season on the bench at Juventus.
• A schemer with an abundance of creativity and energy, as well as possessing a powerful right-footed shot. But has yet to rediscover the eye-catching form of his time in the Second Division with Dunkerque and then in the top flight with Metz.
• Name pronounced Jos lan Blon shar.

ADMINISTRATOR

BLATTER, Sepp

Born: 10.03.36
• President of FIFA since December 1998 when he succeeded Joao Havelange after defeating Lennart Johansson in a tightly-fought election.
• An economics graduate from Lausanne University in his native Switzerland, he worked in public relations and journalism before becoming Director of Technical Development Programmes at FIFA in 1975.
• Appointed general secretary of FIFA in 1981 and played a key role in introducing a number of FIFA initiatives, including the world under-17 and under-20 championships and the women's world cup.
• Has taken a more conciliatory approach to the FIFA presidency than the autocratic Havelange, but suffered a major defeat when the FIFA executive awarded the 2006 World Cup to Germany, rather than South Africa, whom Blatter had publicly backed.

COACH

BLAZEVIC, Miroslav

Croatian
Born: 10.02.35
• National coach of Croatia since March 1994

nd the man who has overseen his country's
dramatic arrival on the international scene in
the 1990s.
• Born in Travnik, Bosnia, but his two uncles
were killed in World War Two fighting for an
independent Croatia.
• Played right wing for Sarajevo, Rijaka and
Sion before a bad knee injury forced him into
premature retirement.
• A masterful tactician and clever motivator
who is an eternal optimist and favours attacking
football.
• Coached Sion, Lausanne and Grasshopper
before returning to Yugoslavia, where he became
a Croatian national hero by coaching Dinamo
Zagreb to the 1982 Yugoslav League title. He then
worked throughout Europe at Pristina, Dinamo
Zagreb, Nantes, PAOK and Dinamo again.
• Became national coach in 1994 on the personal
request of 'my friend' President Tudjman.
• Prone to exaggerated statements to the press.

COACH
BLOKHIN, Oleg
Ukrainian
Born: 05.11.52
• Coach of Ionikos Nikea, whom he helped
remain in First Division after taking over midway
through the 1999-2000 season. Went on to lead
Ionikos to the Cup Final, only to lose to AEK.
• One of the great players of the USSR in the
1970s and 1980s. His performances as a striker
for Kyiv Dynamo in winning the 1975 European
Cup-winners Cup earned him the accolade of
1975 European Footballer of the Year.
• Played in the 1982 and 1986 World Cup finals,
becoming the first Soviet player to win a century
of international caps.
• Only allowed to leave the Soviet Union to go to
Vorwarts Steyr of Austria when he was past his
best. Stayed in the West and has carved out a
useful career as a coach in Greece.

PLAYER
BLOMQVIST, Jesper
Midfielder, Swedish, 176cm, 71kg
Born: 05.03.74, Tavelsjo, Sweden
Clubs: Umea (1992-93), IFK Gothenburg (1993-
96), Milan (Ita) (1996-98), Parma (Ita) (1998),
Manchester United (Eng) (1998-)
Full international (Sweden) 29 caps/0 goals
• Left winger who sprung to prominence during
IFK's run to the 1995 Champions League
quarter-finals.
• Failed to make an impact at Milan, and,
because of injuires, has had to be content with
being Ryan Giggs's understudy at Old Trafford.
• Swedish player of the year in 1993 and a
member of the 1994 World Cup squad.
• Won a hat-trick of Swedish League titles in
1993, 1994 and 1996.

PLAYER
BLONDEAU, Patrick
Defender, French, 174cm, 73kg
Born: 27.01.68, Marseille, France
Clubs: Martigues (1988-89), Monaco (1990-97),
Sheffield Wed (Eng) (1997-98), Bordeaux (1998-
99), Marseille (1999-)
Full international (France) 2 caps/0 goals
• An enterprising and combative right-back. But
the Marseille captain did himself no favours
during the 1999-2000 season in his self-appointed
role of club rabble-rouser, going public with
criticism of a number of his teammates and
crudely attempting to intimidate opponents – he
slapped Monaco's Argentine star **Marcello
Gallardo** in the tunnel before a vital end of
season game.
• French League champion in 1997.
• Surname pronounce Blon doh.

PLAYER
BO, Lars Gaute
Goalkeeper, Norwegian, 185cm, 82kg
Born: 20.11.63, Norway
Clubs: Bryne, Varhaug, Viking (1996-)
Full international (Norway) 1 cap/0 goals
• Loyal veteran goalkeeper who returned to
Viking in 1996, having already retired. Has now
played more than 225 league matches for Viking.

PLAYER
BOA MORTE, Luis
Forward, Portuguese, 178cm, 72kg
Born: 04.08.77, Lisbon, Portugal
Clubs: Sporting Lisbon, Lourihanense (loan),
Arsenal (Eng) (1997-99), Southampton (Eng)
(1999-), Fulham (2000-, loan)
• Left-winger or striker who spent two years on
the fringes at Highbury before moving to
Southampton.
• Spent the 2000-2001 season on loan to Fulham.
• Former Portuguese Under-21 international.

PLAYER
BOATENG, George
Midfielder, Dutch, 182cm, 76kg
Born: 05.09.75, Accra, Ghana
Clubs: Excelsior (1994-95), Feyenoord (1995-97),
Coventry (Eng) (1997-99), Aston Villa (Eng) (1999-)
• All-rounder who cost Coventry £250,000 from
Feyenoord in December 1997 and quickly
established himself in the Premier League.
• Aston Villa were accused of an illegal approach
for Boateng, but finally got their man, at a price
tag of £6million in 1999.

PLAYER
BOBAN, Zvonimir
Midfielder, Croatian, 183cm, 79kg
Born: 08.10.68, Imotski, Croatia
Clubs: Dinamo Zagreb (1985-91), Bari (Ita) (1991-
92), Milan (Ita) (1992-)
Full international (Croatia) 51 caps/12 goals

• A national hero in Croatia after a 1990 Yugoslav
League match between Dinamo Zagreb and Red
Star Belgrade. During a fight between fans of
Dinamo and police, Boban intervened to defend a
young fan who was being attacked by a Serbian
policeman. He was banned for six months and
did not appear for Yugoslavia at the 1990 World
Cup.
• Joined Milan for a reported £8million in 1992.
• Member of the Milan side which won the
European Cup in 1994 and was many people's
player of the season when Milan pipped Lazio to
the 1999 Italian League title.
• Member of Yugoslavia's 1987 World Youth Cup-
winning side.
• Playmaker and captain of the Croatian side at
Euro 96 and France 98.

PLAYER
BOBIC, Fredi
Forward, German, 185cm, 77kg
Born: 30.10.71, Maribor, Slovenia
Clubs: Bad Cannstatt, Vfb Stuttgart, TSF
Ditzingen, Stuttgarter Kickers (1992-94), VfB
Stuttgart (1994-99), Borussia Dortmund (1999-)
Full international (Germany) 19 caps/2 goals
• Overall the wiry striker has a more than decent
scoring record in the Bundesliga – in six seasons
as a first-teamer he has managed 76 goals – and
while at VfB Stuttgart he was the country's top
marksman in the 1995-96 season with 17 goals.
• But over the last couple of years the domestic
League strike-rate of the Slovenian-born German
international has dipped considerably and he
looked particularly out of sorts during 1999-2000
for new club, Dortmund.
• His strengths are his aerial power and ability to
turn and shoot in one fluid movement, but even
his most ardent fans would have to admit, he has
been a little short of quality when playing for
Germany.
• Surname pronounced Bo beech.

BODE, Marco
Midfielder, German, 189cm, 85kg
Born: 23.07.69, Osterode, Germany
Clubs: VfB Osterode, Werder Bremen (1989-)
Full international (Germany) 22 caps/5 goals
• The German international all-rounder is never short on offers from other clubs, but has always remained loyal to Werder.
• He can play left-back, left wing, in the centre or the left-side midfield or as a striker, but his favourite position is on the left-side of midfield.
• Female listeners to a German radio station recently voted him the most erotic player in the country.
• Surname pronounced Bow der.

BOFFIN, Danny
Midfielder, Belgian, 172cm, 63kg
Born: 10.07.65, St Truiden, Belgium
Clubs: St Truiden (1986-87), FC Liege (1987-91), Anderlecht (1991-97), Metz (1997-)
Full international (Belgium) 42 caps/1 goal
• Perpetual motion and non-stop graft on the left-side of midfield. The Belgian international also boasts a fair turn of speed and is a good crosser of balls from the flank. Unfortunate not to be selected for Euro 2000.
• Surname pronounced Boff fan.

BOGARDE, Winston
Defender, Dutch, 190cm, 79kg
Born: 22.10.70, Rotterdam, Holland
Clubs: Sparta Rotterdam (1992-94), Ajax (1994-97), Milan (Ita) (1997-98), Barcelona (Spa) (1998-2000), Chelsea (Eng) (2000-)
Full international (Holland) 17 caps/ 0 goals
• Tough-tackling, physically strong left-side defender. Can play at centre-back or left-back but prefers the former.
• Made his league debut aged 17 and was used

as a left winger at Sparta, but was converted to a left-back by **Louis Van Gaal** at Ajax.
• Won a host of honours at Ajax: 1995 Champions League, two Dutch League titles, World Club Cup and European Supercup.
• Holland's best player at Euro 96, but lost his place in the national side after a series of injuries (he broke an ankle and missed France 98) and a quarrel with his then club Ajax.
• Sold by Ajax to Milan but joined Barcelona during the transfer window in the middle of the 1997-98 season, reuniting him with Van Gaal.
• International debut v Republic of Ireland, 1995.
• Surname pronounced Bo khard der

BOGDANOVIC, Goran
Forward, Yugoslav, 177cm, 70kg
Born: 27.4.67
Clubs: Sartid Smederevo
• Experienced and technically excellent striker who has come close to making the Yugoslav national side.

BOGDANOVIC, Rade
Forward, Yugoslav, 185cm, 85kg
Born: 21.05.70, Sarajevo, Yugoslavia
Clubs: Zeljeznikar Sarajevo (1991-93), Pohang Atoms (Kor) (1993-95), JEF United (Jap) (1997), Atletico Madrid (Spa) (1997-98), Werder Bremen (Ger) (1998-)
Full international (Yugoslavia) 3 caps/2 goals
• Striker who has formed a useful partnership at Werder Bremen with Peruvian **Claudio Pizarro**, winning the 1999 German Cup.

BOGHOSSIAN, Alain
Midfielder, French, 184cm, 82kg
Born: 27.10.70, Digne, France
Clubs: Marseille (1989-92), Istres (1992-93), Marseille (1993-94), Napoli (Ita) (1994-97),

Sampdoria (Ita) (1997-98), Parma (Ita) (1998-)
Full international (France) 22 caps/2 goals
• Combative and hard-working midfielder who made a surprise switch to Napoli in 1993 but has developed his game hugely in Italy.
• Joined Parma in summer 1998 in a £3.5million transfer from Sampdoria.
• World Cup winner with France in 1998, but missed Euro 2000 through injury.

PLAYER
BOHINEN, Lars
Midfielder, Norwegian, 185cm, 78kg
Born: 08.09.69, Vadso, Norway
Clubs: Valerenga (1988-90), Viking Stavanger (1990), Young Boys (Swi) (1990-1993), Nottingham Forest (Eng) (1993-1995), Blackburn (Eng) (1995-98), Derby (Eng) (1998-)
Full international (Norway) 49 caps/10 goals
• Experienced midfielder whose forthright opinions when dropped have caused problems with coaches.
• Lack of first-team action at Blackburn cost him his international career and he missed out on both the 1998 World Cup and Euro 2000.

PLAYER
BOKOV, Maxim
Defender, Russian, 180cm, 70kg
Born: 29.08.73, Russia
Clubs: Zenit St Petersburg (1990-96), CSKA Moscow (1997-)
Full international (Russia) 3 caps/0 goals
• Self-confident and strong centre-back with good positional sense.

PLAYER
BOKSIC, Alen
Forward, Croatian, 187cm, 81kg
Born: 21.07.70, Makarska, Croatia
Clubs: Hajduk Split (1987-91), Cannes (Fra) (1991-92), Marseille (Fra) (1992-93), Lazio (Ita) (1993-96), Juventus (Ita) (1996-97), Lazio (1997-

2000), Middlesbrough (Eng) (2000-)
Full international (Croatia) 32 caps/7 goals
• Talented, fast and powerful forward who creates more goals than he scores, but is still a hugely effective figure.
• Unlucky with injuries in recent years, missing the 1998 World Cup with a knee injury.
• Won one cap for Yugoslavia while at Hajduk.
• Signed by Marseille after scoring the winning goal in the 1991 Yugoslav Cup Final for Hajduk against Red Star. Was loaned out to Cannes but returned in 1992-93, winning a Champions Cup medal and finishing as top scorer in France.
• Moved to Lazio in November 1993 for £8million, spending a year at Lazio (1996-97).
• Son of a truck driver from Split. Travelled to Rome aged 13 to play for Hajduk in a youth tournament. The only souvenir he bought was a replica Lazio shirt.
• Linked with a move to Galatasaray in summer 2000, but eventually moved to Middlesbrough, becoming the Premiership's highest paid player on £63,000 a week.

PLAYER
BOLANO, Jorge
Midfielder, Colombian, 168cm, 63kg
Born: 28.04.77, Santa Maria, Colombia.
Clubs: Junior Barranquilla, (1993-99), Parma (Ita) (1999-), Perugia (Ita) (1999, loan)
Full international (Colombia)
• Pacy, diminutive midfield creator signed by Parma in 1999 after playing for Colombia in the Copa America. Loaned out to Perugia but returned to Parma in summer 2000 looking for first-team action.

PLAYER
BOLIC, Elvir
Forward, Bosnian, 185cm, 81kg
Born: 10.10.71, Zenica, Bosnia
Clubs: Red Star Belgrade, Fenerbahce (Tur), Rayo Vallecano (Spa) (2000-)

Full international (Bosnia)

• Striker who made a name for himself in Turkey before a move to Spain in summer 2000.

• Started out with Celik in his home town of Zenica, moving to Red Star Belgrade as a 20-year-old, winning the Yugoslav League in 1992.

• When the Yugoslav civil war broke out, he moved to Turkey's Galatasaray, but had trouble settling.

• 'War in Bosnia broke out and although I was not harassed for being a Muslim, my parents were in danger and I decided to leave.'

• Moved on to Gazientespor, where 'I felt better because my mother Fatima came with me.' After two years he joined Fenerbahce for £1.8million.

• Scored a memorable goal for against Manchester United in the Champions League in November 1996, United's first home defeat in Europe for many years.

• Made his international debut for Bosnia against Greece in September 1996.

PLAYER
BOLO
Full name: Juan Antonio Perez Bolo
Forward, Spanish, 185cm, 74kg
Born: 05.03.74, Bilbao, Spain
Clubs: Athletic Bilbao (1993-97), Osasuna (1997), Hercules (1997-98), Athletic Bilbao (1998), Rayo Vallecano (1999-)

• Hard-running, awkward-looking but committed striker whose goals helped Rayo Vallecano win promotion to the Spanish first division in 1999 and help become surprise League leaders in October 1999.

• Began his career at Bilbao, but was always on the fringes, spending time at Hercules and Osasuna before a move to Vallecano in January 1999.

PLAYER
BOMBARDA, Mariano
Forward, Argentinian/Italian, 188cm, 88kg
Born: 10.09.72, Cadiz, Spain
Clubs: Huracan, Groningen (Hol) (1994-96), Metz

(Fra) (1996), Groningen (Hol) (1996-98), Willem II (Hol) (1998-)

• Powerful centre-forward who looks very clumsy, but is surprisingly effective.

• Born in Spain and brought up in Argentina.

• Played briefly in France in 1996-97 (7 games, 1 goal).

AGENT
BONETTO Marcello

• Leading Turin-based agent who represents clients such as **Paolo Madini**, **Sebastiano Rossi**, **Diego Fuser**, **Ciro Ferrera**, **Michele Paramatti**, **Gianluca Zambrotta** and **Fabio Peruzzi**.

• **Contact:** Via San Quintino, 28, I-10121, Torino, Italy. Tel: 39 11 516 0411.

PLAYER
BONILLA, Victor
Full name: Victor Manuel Bonilla
Forward Colombian, 176cm, 76kg
Born: 23.01.71, Tumaco Narino, Colombia
Clubs: Deportivo Cali (1991-99), Real Sociedad (Spa) (1999-2000), Toulouse (Fra) (2000-)
Full international (Colombia)

• Colombian striker who has flopped since a 1999 move from America Cali, replacing **Darko Kovacevic**, and switched to France in summer 2000.

PLAYER
BONNISSEL, Jerome
Defender, French, 178cm, 68kg
Born: 16.04.73, Montpellier, France
Clubs: Montpellier (1993-96), Deportivo La Coruna (Spa) (1996-99), Bordeaux (1999-)

• Keanu Reeves lookalike and attack-conscious left-back who never needs any prompting to raid into opposition territory. Renowned for his neat link-up play and good final ball, he is the ex-captain of Montpellier and the French Olympic and Under-21 sides.

BONOMI, Mauro

Defender, Italian, 183cm, 74kg
Born: 23.08.72, Cremona, Italy
Clubs: Cremonese (1989-92), Lazio (1992-95), Cagliari (1995-96), Cesena (1996-97), Bologna (1997) Torino (1997-)
• Made his name as a youngster at Cremonese, impressing with his pace, technique and intelligence, and earning a move to Lazio. But a series of injuries have effectively destroyed what was a promising career.
• Failed to establish himself at Lazio because of the injuries and has moved on from club to club.

BOOTH, Scott

Forward, Scottish, 177cm, 77kg
Born: 16.12.71, Aberdeen, Scotland
Clubs: Aberdeen (1989-97), Borussia Dortmund (Ger) (1997-98), Utrecht (Hol) (1998, loan), Vitesse Arnhem (Hol) (1998, loan), Twente (Hol) (1999-)
Full international (Scotland) 17 caps/5 goals
• Striker who has been playing in Holland in recent seasons after a surprise move to Germany.
• Played for Scotland at Euro 96.

BORBOKIS, Vassilis

Defender, Greek, 182cm, 80kg
Born: 10.02.69, Serres, Greece
Clubs: Apollon (1992-93), AEK Athens (1993-97), Sheffield Utd (Eng) (1997-99), Derby (Eng) (1999-)
Full international (Greece) 2 caps/0 goals
• Right wing-back who can also play on the left of defence. Joined Derby after being refused permission by Sheffield Utd to return to Greece when injured.

BORDON

Full name: Marcelo Jose Bordon
Defender, Brazilian, 189cm, 85kg
Born: 07.01.76, Sao Paulo, Brazil
Clubs: Botafago (1993), Sao Paulo (1993-99), Stuttgart (Ger) (1999-)
Full international (Brazil)
• Centre-back who has quietly won over the critics since a move to Germany from Sao Paulo.

BORIMIROV, Daniel

Forward, Bulgarian, 184cm, 74kg
Born: 15.01.70, Vidin, Bulgaria
Clubs: Levski Sofia (1990-95), Munich 1860 (Ger) (1995-)
Full international (Bulgaria) 53 caps/5 goals
• Bulgarian international attacking midfielder or frontrunner with an abundance of speed, experience and versatility. Can line up as an orthodox striker, on the right or left of midfield and even in a deep midfield position, though he is not the most steely of customers.
• Won the Bulgarian League and Cup with Levski.

BORKELMANS, Vital

Defender, Belgian, 175cm, 72kg
Born: 10.06.63, Belgium
Clubs: Waregem (1986-89), Club Brugge (1989-2000), Gent (2000-)
Full international (Belgium) 22 caps/0 goals
• Veteran defensive midfielder who was recalled to the Belgian national side for the 1998 World Cup.
• Worked as a miner before becoming a full-time professional, and hence has a strong work ethic.
• Spent 12 seasons with Club Brugge.

BORNES, Joaquin

Full name: Joaquin Bornes Rincon
Defender, Defender, 187cm, 82kg
Born: 25.05.75, Los Palacios, Spain
Clubs: Recreativo (1994-99), Real Betis (1999-)
• Solid, dependable central defender who has shown signs that he could reach the very top.
• Strong in the air and reliable on the ground.

BOROVSKY, Sergei

- Former national coach of Belarus who returned to the post following the sacking of Mikhail Vergenko in October 1999.

BOSCHKER, Sander

Goalkeeper, Dutch, 184cm, 84kg
Born: 20.10.70, Lichtenvoorde, Holland
Clubs: FC Twente (1989-)

- Keeper who has been a loyal servant to Twente down the years. A consistent performer whose brothers are also goalkeepers.

BOSKOV, Vujadin

Yugoslav
Born: 16.05.31

- National coach of Yugoslavia from July 1999 to July 2000.
- Recalled from retirement to take charge of the Yugoslav national side at Euro 2000 following the sacking of Milan Zivadinovic.
- Played 57 times for Yugoslavia, including two World Cups. Played 512 League matches (20 goals) for FK Vojividina and had two seasons with Italy's Sampdoria.
- Has spent nearly 40 years as a coach, in his native Yugoslavia, Holland, Spain, Italy and Switzerland. Honours as a coach include the Yugoslav League in 1966 with FK Vojvodina, the Spanish title in 1980 with Real Madrid and the Italian Serie A crown with Sampdoria in 1991.

BOSKOVIC, Branko

Midfielder, Yugoslav, 184cm, 73kg
Born: 21.06.80, Backa Topola, Yugoslavia
Clubs: Red Star Belgrade

- One of Yugoslavia's brightest hopes. Left-footed with fine technique. A regular in the Under-21 side.

BOSMAN, Jean-Marc

- The man who sparked a revolution in the 1990s after he took his case to the European Court.
- Signed professional forms with Standard Liege as a 17-year-old in July 1982, the start of a modest career as a moderately good midfielder.
- Signed a two-year deal with RFC Liege in May 1988, with RFC Liege paying Standard a fee of £65,000. Two years later, RFC Liege offered Bosman a one-year extension, which he rejected and was placed on the transfer list, available for a fee of around £250,000.
- In July 1990, French club Dunkerque reached agreement with Bosman and a one-year loan deal (with a view to a permanent move) was agreed with RFC Liege. But Liege doubted Dunkerque's ability to pay and refused to sanction the transfer by refusing to submit the necessary paperwork to the Belgian FA. Liege suspended Bosman, and he instituted legal proceedings.
- In November 1990, a Belgian civil court freed Bosman to play for French third division Saint Quentin on loan.
- The case wound its way through the legal system in May 1991 after the Belgian Court of Appeal referred the case to the European Court. In the meantime, Bosman returned to Belgium and was unable to find a new club, but was not allowed to claim unemployment benefit.
- In May 1993, Bosman joined third division side Olympic Charleroi, moving on a year later to fourth division side Vise.
- In June 1995, the European Court of Justice heard Bosman's claim for £700,000 in damages and the advocate-general Carl Otto-Lenz advised the court to rule that western European football's transfer system was illegal.
- In December 1995, the European Court turned down an appeal by UEFA and ruled in his favour.
- Despite his legal success, Bosman was left penniless by the campaign and was forced to set up a fighting fund to raise money on his behalf.

Jean-Marc Bosman

PLAYER
BOSMAN, John
Forward, Dutch, 185cm, 82kg
Born: 01.02.65, Bovenkerk, Holland
Clubs: Ajax (1983-88), Mechelen (Bel) (1988-90), PSV (1990-91), Anderlecht (Bel) (1991-96), FC Twente (1996-99), AZ (1999-)
Full international (Holland) 30 caps/17 goals
• Veteran striker who is now winding down his career at AZ after 17 seasons in the top flight in Belgium and Holland in which his strike rate has remained one goal every two games.

PLAYER
BOSNICH, Mark
Goalkeeper, Australian, 187cm, 92kg
Born: 13.01.72, Fairfield, Australia
Clubs: Sydney Croatia, Manchester Utd (1989-91), Sydney Croatia, Aston Villa (1992-99), Manchester Utd (1999-)
Full international (Australia) 17 caps/1 goal
• Signed in June 1999 on a Bosman free transfer by Manchester Utd to replace **Peter Schmeichel**.
• Played three league games for United between 1990 and 1991, but returned to Australia having failed to obtain a work permit.
• Voted Oceania's Goalkeeper of the Century.
• Position at Old Trafford was placed in doubt by the arrival of **Fabien Barthez** in summer 2000. He was offered the chance to go on loan to Celtic but declined and was told he would be third choice behind Barthez and **Raimond Van der Gouw**.

PLAYER
BOSSCHAART, Pascal
Forward, Dutch, 176cm, 69kg
Born: 19.10.71, Amsterdam, Holland
Clubs: FC Zwolle (1996-99), Utrecht (1999-)
• Established left-back at Utrecht after making his League debut aged 17 for Zwolle.

PLAYER
BOSSIO, Carlos
Goalkeeper, Argentinian, 194cm, 96kg
Born: 01.12.73 Cordoba, Argentina
Clubs: Las Palmas, Cordoba (1988-90), Belgrano (1993-94), Estudiantes (1995-99), Benfica (Por) (1999-)
Full international (Argentina)
• Argentinian keeper who has had a difficult time at Benfica since a move there in the summer of 1999, being squeezed out by the impressive form of German keeper **Robert Enke**.

PLAYER
BOSVELT, Paul
Midfielder, Dutch, 183cm, 84kg
Born: 26.03.70, Doetinchem, Holland
Clubs: Go Ahead Eagles (1989-94), FC Twente (1994-97), Feyenoord (1997-)
Full international (Holland) 6 caps/0 goals
• Right-footed central midfielder and captain of Feyenoord with bags of stamina and commitment but also solid distribution skills.
• Performances for Feyenoord earned him a place in the Dutch squad for Euro 2000.

PLAYER
BOUCHIBA, Elbekay
Midfielder, Dutch, 175cm, 71kg
Born: 01.11.78, Weert, Holland
Clubs: AZ (1998-)
• Lively, skilful player who has spent much of his time at AZ on the bench.

PLAYER
BOUDARENE, Fabien
Midfielder, French, 178cm, 77kg
Born: 05.10.78, St Etienne, France
Clubs: St Etienne (1997-)
• French Under-21 international.

PLAYER
BOUKHARI, Nouradin
Forward, Moroccan
Born: 03.06.1980
Clubs: Sparta Rotterdam
• A tricky left winger who broke through in the 1999-2000 season. Regular scorer with an enormous potential. Learned his skills on the streets of Rotterdam.
• Has turned down an offer from the Dutch Under-21 team to play for Morocco.
• Could be one of the future stars of the Dutch League.

PLAYER
BOULD, Steve
Defender, English, 193cm, 90kg
Born: 16.11.62, Stoke, England
Clubs: Stoke (1980-88), Torquay (1992, loan), Arsenal (1988-99), Sunderland (1999-
Full international (England) 2 caps/0 goals
• Spent 11 seasons with Arsenal, winning two League titles, two FA Cups and the Cup-winners Cup as a key member of the famous back line.

PLAYER
BOUMA, Wilfred
Forward, Dutch, 180cm, 75kg
Born: 15.06.78, Helmond, Holland
Clubs: PSV Eindhoven (1994-96), MVV (1996-98), Fortuna Sittard (1998-99), PSV Eindhoven (1999-)
• Exciting young winger who is starting to establish himself at PSV after time spent away from the Philips Stadion with MVV and Fortuna Sittard.
• Highly effective down the left-wing and can also operate at left-back.
• Dutch Under-21 international.

PLAYER
BOUMSONG, Jean-Alain
Defender, French, 190cm, 84kg
Born: 14.12.79, Douala, Cameroon
Clubs: Le Havre (1998-2000), Auxerre (2000-)

• Under-21 central defender who is mature beyond his years and set for a brilliant career.
• A qualified mathematician.

PLAYER
BOUSSATTA, Dries
Forward, Dutch, 169cm, 64kg
Born: 23.12.72, Amsterdam, Holland
Clubs: Telstar (1991-92), Ajax (1992-94), Utrecht (1994-98), AZ (1998-)
Full international (Holland) 3 caps/0 goals
• First player from Holland's Moroccan community to an earn an international call-up.
• Right-sided midfielder who has found the move up to international level difficult.
• Given international debut by **Frank Rijkaard** against Germany in November 1998.

PLAYER
BOUTAL, Samuel
Forward, French, 180cm, 78kg
Born: 22.11.69, Bordeaux, France
Clubs: Pau, Red Star, Caen (1998-99), Troyes (1999-2000)
• Graceful Bordeaux-born forward or attacking midfielder, who enjoyed an impressive first season in the French top flight with Troyes. Speedy, lithe and a decent goalscorer.

PLAYER
BOWYER, Lee
Midfielder, English, 175cm, 61kg
Born: 03.01.77, London, England
Clubs: Charlton (1994-96), Leeds (1996-)
• Youngster who combines hard running and strong tackling with a good first touch and a sharp eye for goal.
• Long tipped for full international honours after regular appearances as an England Under-21 international and time spent training with the senior squad.

Paul Bosvelt

PLAYER
BOYD, Tom
Defender, Scottish, 180cm, 78kg
Born: 24.11.65, Glasgow, Scotland
Clubs: Motherwell (1983-91), Chelsea (Eng) (1991-92), Celtic (1991-2000)
Full international (Scotland) 65 caps/1 goal
• By far the longest serving player on the Celtic staff, club captain Boyd has seen and done it all since moving to Parkhead from Chelsea in 1992.
• With over 60 caps for Scotland, he has enjoyed a particularly successful career, the highlight of which occured when leading Celtic to the League title under Wim Jansen in 1998.

PLAYER
BOYE, Erik
Goalkeeper, Danish, 186cm, 77kg
Born: 07.02.64, Denmark
Clubs: Vejle, Kolding, Haderslev, Frederica, Vejle (1995-)
• Veteran keeper who has been on the verge of an international call-up for much of his career, but it has never arrived.

PLAYER
BOYE, Torben
Defender, Danish, 189cm, 80kg
Born: 02.05.66, Denmark
Clubs: AaB (1990-)
• Solid and dependable defender who has been with Danish club AaB all his career, from the Danish third division through to their League title successes in the mid-1990s.

PLAYER
BRABEC, Erich
Defender, Czech, 187cm, 81kg
Born: 24.02.77, Czech Republic
Clubs: Petra Drnovice
Full international (Czech Rep) 1 cap/0 goals
• Another of the village club Drnovice's crop of talented young players.

• Along with team-mate Zdenek Grygera, Brabec was a member of the Czech Under-21 squad that won silver at the European Championships in 2000.
• Made his first appearance for the full national team at the Carlsberg Cup friendly tournament over the 1999-2000 winter break.

PLAYER
BRAGSTAD, Bjorn Otto
Defender, Norwegian, 194cm, 84kg
Born: 05.01.71, Norway
Clubs: Rosenborg (1989-2000), Derby (Eng) (2000-)
Full international (Norway) 14 caps/0 goals
• Once a misfit in Rosenborg's central defence, this quiet stopper has established a reliable partnership with **Erik Hoftun** for club and country. Loyal player for over a decade before a summer move to England.

COACH
BRAKSTAD, Erik
Norwegian
Born: 19.04.51
• Has been in charge of Molde since taking over from Aage Hareide three years ago. Previous coaching career at Hodd. Prefers the 4-3-3 system with an emphasis on attacking football.

PLAYER
BRAMBILLA, Massimo
Midfielder, Italian, 178cm, 68kg
Born: 04.03.73, Vimercate, Italy
Clubs: Monza (1990-94), Reggiana (1994-95), Parma (1995-96), Bologna (1997), Torino (1998-)
• Hard-working central midfielder who failed to make the breakthrough into the big time during one and half seasons at Parma and has since moved on to Bologna and Torino.
• Italian Under-21 international.

AGENT
BRANCHINI, Giovanni

• Milan-based businessman who handles the European affairs of **Ronaldo**.
• Also represents **Rui Costa, Hidetoshi Nakata, Nicola Ventola, Flavio Conceicao, Guillermo Amor, Igor Kolivanov** and **Benito Carbone**.
• **Contact:** Corso Magenta 56, I-20123, Milano, Italy. Tel: 39 2 4818 700.

PLAYER
BRAND, Christian

Midfielder, German, 174cm, 67kg
Born: 23.05.73, Germany
Clubs: Werder Bremen (1996-99), Wolfsburg (1999-)
• Busy, agressive little attacking midfielder whose former stock-in-trade was taking on and beating defenders on the left flank. But towards the end of the 1999-2000 season he performed well in a central role, directing traffic with verve and vision and his long-term future looks to be there.
• Surname pronounced Brant.

PLAYER
BRANDAO

Full name: Ildebrando Dalsoto
Forward, Brazilian, 180cm, 76kg
Born: 14.05.70, Rio Grande, Brazil
Clubs: Coritiba (1997-98), Belenenses (Por) (1998-99), Vitoria Guimaraes (Por) (1999-)
• Striker who quickly established himself as a stalwart of Vitoria Guimaraes' attack in the 1999-2000 season.

PLAYER
BRANDO, Frederic

Midfielder, French, 76cm, 72kg
Born: 08.11.73, Cannes, France
Clubs: Toulon, Monaco, Le Havre, Marseille
• No half-measures with this defensive midfielder. Treats every game as though it was his last,

pressing and tackling with the same intensity in the first minute of a game as the last.
• Former Marseille coach **Rolland Courbis** once said he became tired just watching Brando's high-energy play.
• Surname pronounced Bron doh.

REFEREE
BRASCHI, Stefano

Italian
Born: 06.06.57
• Works as a commercial agent.
• Awarded his FIFA badge in 1995.

PLAYER
BRATIC, Vidak

Midfielder Yugoslav, 190cm
Born: 20.10.76, Yugoslavia
Club: Vojvodina Novi Sad
• Physically strong midfielder whose strength makes him valuable for the team. Can play also in central defence.

ADMINISTRATOR
BRAUN, Egidius

• President of the DFB (Deutscher Fussball-Bund, the German FA), since 1992 and a key figure within UEFA, where he is Treasurer.
• Played an instrumental role in Germany's successful bid to host the 2006 World Cup gaining the support of UEFA at the expense of England.
• Recently suffered health problems and was not present in Zurich for the vote on the 2006 World Cup.

PLAYER
BRAUNOVIC, Drasko

Defender, Yugoslav
Born: 20.12.66, Yugoslavia
Club: Valletta, Sliema, Birkirkara
• Talented defender who has won four consecutive Maltese League titles, the first three with Valletta.

BRAVO, Francisco

Full name: Francisco Javier Lopez Bravo
Defender, Spanish, 178cm, 77kg
Born: 06.04.74, Malaga, Spain
Clubs: Malaga (1994-)
• Solid, dependable centre-back who has worked his way up from Malaga's youth system to become club captain.
• Key member of Malaga's 1999 promotion-winning side.

BRDARIC, Thomas

Forward, German, 185cm, 78kg
Born: 23.01.75, Germany
Clubs: Neuffen, Nurtingen, Stuttgarter Kickers, Kirchheim, Stuttgart, Fortuns Dusseldorf, Fortuna Koln (1998-99), Bayer Leverkusen (1999-)
• Performed a valuable service during the 1999-2000 season as Leverkusen's back-up striker, weighing in with a half-dozen goals.
• Instinctive marksman who certainly did not look out of place in the Bundesliga in 1999-2000 following a move from Second Division Fortuna Koln.

BRECHET, Jeremie

Defender, French, 186cm, 77kg
Born: 14.08.79, Lyon, France
Clubs: Lyon (1998-)
• A product of the Lyon youth ranks and current French Under 21 international.
• In his short career, he has played at full-back, stopper and as a defensive midfielder, but most experts agree that his best position is left-back.
• Athletic, a good marker and very comfortable on the ball, he has been likened to **Paolo Maldini**.
• Surname pronounced Bray shay.

BREEN, Gary

Defender, Irish, 190cm, 75kg
Born: 12.12.73, London, England
Clubs: Maidstone (1991-92), Gilingham (1992-94), Peterborough (1994-96), Birmingham (1996-97), Coventry (1997-)
Full international (Rep Ireland) 31 caps/4 goals
• Right-footed central defender who has had a steady if unexceptional career, culminating in a move to Coventry in 1997.

BREITENREITER, Andre

Forward, German, 182cm, 71kg
Born: 02.10.73, Langenhagen, Germany
Clubs: Hannover 96 (1991-94), Hamburg (1994-97), Wolfsburg (1997-)
• Diminutive, highly-mobile frontrunner who can be used at the point of attack or in the 'hole' behind the strikers. Suffered a series of niggling injuries last term but looked sharp whenever he was in action, scoring seven times in 19 games.
• Former German Under-21 international.

BRENDESETHER, Geirmund

Defender, Norwegian, 176cm, 74kg
Born: 22.03.70, Norway
Clubs: Brann (1996), Arminia Bielefeld (Ger) (1996-97), Brann (1997-)
Full international (Norway) 6 caps/0 goals
• Attacking right full-back who returned to Brann after failing to impress in the German Bundesliga with Arminia Bielefeld. Has played more than 210 League matches.

PLAYER
BRESSAN, Mauro
Midfielder, Italian, 177cm, 76kg
Born: 05.01.71, Valdobbiadene, Italy.
Clubs: Montebelluna (1988-89), Milan (1989-91), Como (1991-94), Foggia (1994-95), Cagliari (1995-97), Bari (1997-99), Fiorentina (1999-)
• Hard-working player who performs a useful function in central midfield.
• On the books of Milan as a youngster, but did not play for the first team, instead making a name for himself at Bari, earning move to Fiorentina in summer 1999.

PLAYER
BREVI, Ezio
Midfielder, Italian, 180cm, 76kg
Born: 20.01.70, Rome, Italy
Clubs: Corsico (1990-93), Pre Sesto (1993-95), Firenzuola (1995-96), Triestina (1996-99), Reggina (1999-)
• A powerful midfielder who Reggina were looking to rely heavily upon following their promotion to Serie A.

PLAYER
BREWSTER, Craig
Forward, Scottish, 186cm, 80kg
Born: 13.12.66, Dundee, Scotland
Clubs: Forfar (1985-91), Raith Rovers (1991-93), Dundee United (1993-96), Ionikas (Gre) (1996-)
• Veteran Scottish striker who has completed his fourth year with Ionikos having played in 119 matches and scored 37 goals.

PLAYER
BRIDGES, Michael
Forward, English, 185cm, 70kg
Born: 05.08.78, North Shields, England
Clubs: Sunderland (1995-99), Leeds (1999-)
• Pacy striker who moved to Leeds in a £5million transfer in 1999 after finding limited opportunities at Sunderland.

Egidius Braun

• England Under-21 international.

PLAYER
BROCCHI, Cristian
Midfielder, Italian, 170cm, 67kg
Born: 30.01.76, Milan, Italy
Clubs: Milan (1994-95), Pro Sesto (1995-97), Lumezzane (1997-98), Verona (1998-)
• Talented attacking midfielder who has quickly established himelf as key man for Verona.

PLAYER
BROCKEN, David
Midfielder, Belgian, 178cm, 76kg
Born: 18.02.71, Belgium
Clubs: Lierse (1990-99), Anderlecht (1999), Standard Liege (2000-)
Full international (Belgium) 2 caps/0 goals
• Dependable right-back who has spent most of his career with Lierse before trying his luck in Brussels with Anderlecht. Moved on to Standard after just six months.

PLAYER
BROCKHAUSER, Istvan
Goalkeeper, Hungarian, 193cm, 88kg
Born: 03.05.64, Budapest, Hungary
Clubs: Vac (1987-88), Ujpest Dzoza (1988-92), Kispest Honved (1992-96), Gyori (1996), Genk (Bel) (1996-)
Full international (Hungary) 10 caps/0 goals
• Veteran Hungarian international keeper who has been a dependable presence in the Genk defence since his transfer from Gyori in 1996.
• 1998 Belgian Cup winner.

PLAYER
BROGGER, Lars
Forward, Danish, 182cm, 75kg
Born: 22.03.70, Denmark
Clubs: Ikast (1996-98), Silkeborg (1998-), Ikast (1999, loan)
• Striker who has struggled to live up to his billing as Silkeborg's most expensive signing. He returned to former club Ikast on loan, and gained in confidence enough to return to Silkeborg and start scoring goals.

PLAYER
BROGNO, Toni
Forward, Belgian, 170cm, 64kg
Born: 19.07.73, Italy
Clubs: RSC Charleroi (1994-97), Westerlo (1997-2000), Sedan (Fra) (2000-)
Full international (Belgium) 7 caps/0 goals
• Diminutive striker who finished as the joint top scorer in the Belgian League in the 1999-2000 season with 30 goals.
• A little dribbler who likes to create his own chances and always has his eye on the target.
• On the fringes of Belgium's Euro 2000 squad but missed the cut.
• International debut against Luxembourg in November 1998.
• Joined Sedan for £5million in August 2000.

COACH
BROOS, Hugo
Born: 10.04.52
• Former libero of Anderlecht and Club Brugge who was very successful as coach of Club Brugge and is currently in charge at Excelsior Mouscron, who qualified for the UEFA Cup under his guidance.
• Is tipped to be the next Belgian national team coach.

COACH
BROWN, Craig
Scottish
Born: 01.07.40
• Coach of Scotland since 1993, making him one of Europe's longest-serving national coaches.
• Following an unspectacular playing career with Dundee and Rangers which was cut short by injury, Brown became manager of Clyde before

taking up a coaching position with the Scottish FA.
• After operating as understudy to then national coach **Andy Roxburgh**, he was appointed national coach in 1993 and became the first ever coach to take Scotland to the European Championship finals in 1996. Two years later he led the Scots to the World Cup but failed narrowly to achieve qualification for Euro 2000.
• In terms of player quality, Brown has had less resources at his disposal than any other national coach in Scotland's history, making his achievments all the more remarkable.

PLAYER
BROWN, Wes
Defender, English, 186cm, 75kg
Born: 16.03.79, Manchester, England
Clubs: Manchester Utd (1996-)
Full international (England) 1 cap/0 goals
• Versatile youngster who missed most of the 1999-2000 season though injury, after breaking into the United first team (and the England national side) during the previous campaign.
• International debut: 28.04.99, v Hungary (1-1)

PLAYER
BRUGGINK, Arnold
Forward, Dutch, 185cm 77kg
Born: 24.07.77, Almelo, Holland
Clubs: FC Twente (1993-97), PSV Eindhoven (1997-)
• Former captain of Holland's Under-21 side, where he was a prolific scorer, just as he was alongside **John Bosman** at Twente, before a move to PSV.
• Time at PSV has proved very frustrating, with most of it spent on the bench, watching **Ruud Van Nistelrooy** and **Luc Nilis**. With Nilis gone to Villa, and Van Nistelrooy injured, the 2000-2001 season could prove more fruitful.

PLAYER
BRUNEL, Philippe
Forward, French, 176cm, 73kg
Born: 28.02.73, Boulogne-sur-Mer, France
Clubs: Boulogne, Lens (1993-), Gueugnon (1995-96)
• Local boy from the channel port of Boulogne, who apart from a season on loan to Gueugnon, has spent all his career at Lens.
• Hyperactive left-sided attacker, who has a good technique, runs strongly with the ball and is one of the best crossers in French football.

COACH
BUBENKO, Jozef
Slovakian
Born: 21.03.51
• Coach who steered Inter Bratislava to the Slovakian League and Cup double in 1999-2000.

PLAYER
BUCCI, Luca
Goalkeeper, Italian, 180cm, 80kg
Born: 13.03.69, Bologna, Italy
Clubs: Parma (1986-90), Casertana (1990-92), Reggiana (1992-93), Parma (1993-96), Perugia (1997), Torino (1998-)
Full international (Italy) 3 caps/0 goals
• Keeper who made his name in Parma's rise to the Italian First Division.
• Started out as a 16-year-old reserve in the Third Division Parma side coached by **Arrigo Sacchi**, making his professional debut with Parma in Serie B aged 17.
• Made his international debut as a second-half substitute for the injured **Gianluca Pagliuca** in a 3-1 win over Turkey in 1994, having been a surprise choice, uncapped, for Italy's 1994 World Cup squad.
• Italy's third-choice keeper at Euro 96.

PLAYER
BUCEK, Yurai
Goalkeeper, Slovakian, 204cm, 98kg
Born: 15.09.73, Slovakia
Clubs: Skoda Xanthi (Gre)
• Steady starter who only missed two matches during the 1999-2000 season. Consistent, unspectacular type.

PLAYER
BUCK, Andreas
Midfielder, Defender, 180cm, 78kg
Born: 29.12.67, Geislingen, Germany
Clubs: Vfl Kirchheim, Freiburg (1988-90), Stuttgart (1990-97), Kaiserslautern (1997-)
• Wide midfielder able to operate on either flank. Quick, tricky and a fine crosser of the ball, he was a Bundesliga winner with Stuttgart in 1991 and Kaiserlautern in 1997.
• Only two years ago, **Lothar Matthaus** was suggesting he should picked for Germany.
• Surname pronounced Boo kk.

PLAYER
BUDAN, Igor
Forward, Croatian, 185cm, 80kg
Born: 22.04.80, Rijeka, Croatia
Clubs: Rijeka (1997-99), Venezia (Ita) (1999-)
• Promising young forward who signed a four-year contract with Venezia in 1999.
• Played for Croatia at the 1999 World Under-20 championship in Nigeria.

PLAYER
BUFFON, Gianluigi
Goalkeeper, Italian, 190cm, 88kg
Born: 28.01.78, Carrara, Italy
Clubs: Parma (1994-95)
Full international (Italy) 14 caps/0 goals
• A hugely promising keeper who has been the cornerstone of Parma's success in recent seasons.
• Cool, gifted, with lightning reflexes and fast off his line. Only weakness is the classic Italian one

of vulnerability in the air.
• First choice keeper in the Italian national team under **Dino Zoff** but he missed Euro 2000 after a breaking a hand in a warm-up game against Norway.
• Has played five seasons in Serie A after making a spectacular debut as a 17-year-old in November 1995, in Parma's 0-0 home draw with Milan.
• International debut in the World Cup play-off against Russia in October 1997 when he appeared as a substitute in arctic conditions in Moscow following an injury to **Gianluca Pagliuca**.

PLAYER
BULAJIC, Spasoje
Defender, Slovenian, 186cm, 80kg
Born: 24.11.75, Slovenj Gradec, Slovenia
Clubs: Rudar Velenje, Publikum, Olimpia Ljubljana, Maribor, Koln (Ger)
Full international (Slovenia) 10 caps/1 goal
• Defender who was a member of Slovenia's squad at Euro 2000 but did not play,
• Won promotion to the Bundelisga with Koln in 2000.

PLAYER
BULATOV, Viktor
Midfielder, Russian, 180cm, 72kg
Born: 22.01.72, Russia
Clubs: Dinamo Stavropol (1994), Krylya (1995-97), Moscow Spartak (1997-)
Full international (Russia) 5 caps/0 goals
• Versatile player who is often used in central defence as well as in attack.

PLAYER
BULENT Korkmaz
Defender, Turkish, 181cm, 77kg
Born: 24.11.67, Istanbul, Turkey
Clubs: Galatasaray
Full international (Turkey) 55 caps/1 goal
• Central defender who has been with Galatasaray all of his career.

• An excellent man-marker but has not always been in favour at Galatasaray.
• Made his international debut for Turkey against the Republic of Ireland in 1990 and was a member of the Turkish squad at Euro 96.

PLAYER
BULYKIN, Dmitri
Forward, Russian, 193cm, 83kg
Born: 20.11.79, Russia
Clubs: Lokomotiv Moscow (1996-)
• Young striker with great potential. Very tall and strong with a good shot.

PLAYER
BUNJEVCEVIC, Goran
Defender, Yugoslav, 190cm, 77kg
Born: 17.02.73, Karlovac, Croatia
Clubs: Red Star Belgrade
Full international (Yugoslavia) 3 caps/0 goals
• One of the best players in the Yugoslav league. Left-footed, good technique, reads the game superbly. Plays in central defence, but can be used also in defensive midfield.
• Was brought up in Split (Croatia), came to Belgrade as a refugee and anonymous player.
• Studies journalism in his spare time.

PLAYER
BURGOS, German
Full name: German Adrian Ramon 'Mono' Burgos
Goalkeeper, Argentinian, 187cm, 93kg
Born: 16.04.69, Mar del Plata, Argentina
Clubs: Ferro Carril Oeste (1987-94), River Plate (1994-99), Mallorca (Spa) (1999)
Full international (Argentina) 24 caps/0 goals
• Long-haired rock music-loving goalkeeper who was signed by Mallorca to replace Carlos Roa, who had retired to join a religious sect.
• Is a talented keeper but has been criticised for not curbing his showman tendencies.
• Was banned for 12 matches last season for an off-the-ball attack on an Espanyol player.

• Plays in a rock band and has become a minor celebrity as a result.
• Member of Argentina's squad at the 1998 World Cup and the 1999 Copa America.

PLAYER
BURLEY, Craig
Midfielder, Scottish, 182cm, 82kg
Born: 24.09.71, Ayr, Scotland
Clubs: Chelsea (1990-97), Celtic (1997-99), Derby (1999-)
Full international (Scotland) 38 caps/3 goals
• Joined Chelsea straight from Ayrshire schools football and became a regular under **Glenn Hoddle**.
• Moved to Scotland after falling out of favour at Stamford Bridge and played a major role in winning the 1998 Scottish title.
• Nephew of Ipswich manager George Burley.

PLAYER
BURTON Deon
Forward, English/Jamaican, 173cm, 68kg
Born: 25.10.76, Ashford, England
Clubs: Portsmouth (1993-97), Cardiff (1996-97, loan), Derby (1997-), Barnsley (1998-99, loan)
Full international (Jamaica) 14 caps/6 goals.
• Striker who is more famous for the goals which took Jamaica to France 98 than any achievements in England. Began brightly at Portsmouth, but has struggled to make the starting line-up at Derby, going on loan to first division club Barnsley.
• Voted Jamaian Sports Personality of the Year in 1998 and nicknamed One Love because of the goals he scored in 1-0 wins which took Jamaica to France 98.
• Born in England to Jamaican parents, he agreed to play for Jamaica after impressing during a chance training session while on holiday in the Caribbean.

BUSHI, Alban
Forward, Albanian
Born: 24.08.73
Clubs: FK Tirana, Litex (Bul) Flamutari, Adanaspor (Tur) (1999-)
Full international (Albania) 24 caps/6 goals
• Experienced striker for the Albanian national side who is now earning a living in Turkkey, where he helped Adanaspor escape relegation in the 1999-2000 season, having previously helped Litex Lovech win the Bulgarian League title.

BUSHMANOV, Yevgeni
Defender, Russian, 180cm, 75kg
Born: 02.11.71, Russia
Clubs: Shinnik (1988-89), Moscow Spartak (1990-92), CSKA (1993-96), Torpedo Moscow (1996-98), Spartak (1998-)
Full international (Russia) 7 caps/0 goals
• Reliable central defender with good technique.

BUSUTTIL, Carmel
Midfielder, Maltese
Born: 26.06.1964, Malta
Clubs: Sliema Wanderers
Full international (Malta) 103 caps/23 goals
• Midfielder who is still the number one player in the Maltese League, despite his age.

BUT, Vladimir
Midfielder, Russian, 184cm, 80kg
Born: 24.09.77, Novorossick, Russia
Clubs: Chernomerets, Borussia Dortmund (1994-)
Full international (Russia) 1 cap/0 goals
• Young Russian midfielder who has mysteriously lost his way in recent times. A couple of years ago, the young Russian midfielder was being widely lauded for tirelesss box-to-box running, craft and powerful left-foot shooting. But recently, he has looked ill-at-ease when asked to deputise for the injured **Andy Moller** at Dortmund.

BUTA, Cornel
Defender, Romanian
Born: 01.11.77, Romania
Clubs: Dinamo Bucharest, Rapid Bucharest (2000-)
Full international (Romania)
• Highly promising young defender who made his international debut for Romania against Cyprus in February 2000.

BUTLER, Paul
Defender, Irish, 187cm, 83kg
Born: 02.11.73, Manchester, England
Clubs: Rochdale (1991-96), Bury (1996-98), Sunderland (1998-)
• Centre-back who played a solid role in Sunderland's promotion to the Premiership in 1999.
• Republic of Ireland B international.

BUTT, Hans-Jorg
Goalkeeper, German, 191cm, 92kg
Born: 28.05.74, Berlin, Germany
Clubs: TSV Grossenkneten, VfB Oldenburg, Hamburg
Full international (Germany) 1 cap/0 goals
• Unspectacular but highly-competent practitioner of the art of goalkeeping and fully deserves his elevation to the German squad. Takes a cool penalty and converted no less than nine in the course of the 1999-2000 season.
• Due to move to Bayer Leverkusen in 2001.

BUTT, Nicky
Midfielder, English, 178cm, 71kg
Born: 21.01.75, Manchester, England

Clubs: Manchester Utd (1992-)
Full international (England) 8 caps/0 goals.
• Tough midfielder who came through the youth ranks at United with **Paul Scholes**, **David Beckham** and Co, but has not achieved the same sort of international recognition.

PLAYER
BUZNIKIN, Maxim
Forward, Russian, 171cm, 73kg
Born: 01.03.77, Russia
Clubs: Moscow Spartak (1997-)
Full international (Russia) 2 caps/1 goal
• Has probably the best ball control of any player in the Russian League and makes use of his speed and low height to great effect.

COACH
BYSHOVETS, Anatoli
Russian
Born: 23.04.46
• Veteran Soviet and Russian coach who played as a striker for Dynamo Kiev from 1964 to 1973, winning the USSR League in 1966, 1967, 1968 and 1971. Won 40 caps and 15 goals from 1966 to 1972. Scored four goals in 1970 World Cup.
• Playing career was stopped by an injury at the age of 27.
• USSR Olympic manager in Seoul 1988, where they won the gold medals.
• Moscow Dynamo manager from 1988 to 1990. USSR-CIS team manager from 1990 to 1992. Worked with teams in Cyprus and South Korea until becoming Russian national team manager in August 1998.
• Currently without a team.

C

PLAYER
CABANAS, Ricardo
Midfielder, Spanish/Swiss
Born: 17.01.79
Clubs: Grasshopper
• Highly-promising Swiss Under-21 midfielder from Spanish stock. A talented pocket-sized schemer who has been with Grasshopper since the age of 13.

PLAYER
CABROL, Dario
Midfielder, Argentinian
Born: 31.01.72, Santa Fe, Argentina
Clubs: Union Santa Fe (1990-92), Racing Club (1992-93), Lanus (1993-95), Union Santa Fe (1994-2000), Toulouse (Fra) (2000-)
• Midfielder who moved to Europe in the summer of 2000 after more than a decade in the Argentinian League.

PLAYER
CACERES, Fernando
Defender, Argentinian, 180cm, 74kg
Born: 07.02.69, 180cm, 74kg
Clubs: Argentinos Juniors (1986-91), River Plate (1991-93), Zaragoza (Spa) (1993-96), Boca Juniors (1996), Valencia (Spa) (1997-98), Celta Vigo (Spa) (1998-)
Full international (Argentina) 24 caps/1 goals
• Experienced, dependable centre-back who started at Argentinos Juniors.
• Made his name at River Plate and played for Argentina at the 1993 Copa America and 1994 World Cup.
• At Zaragoza he won the European Cup-winners Cup in 1995 and was the only player to play in every minute of the campaign.
• Followed his Zaragoza coach **Victor Fernandez** to Celta Vigo for a reported £2.5million fee in

summer 1998, following brief spells back home with Boca Juniors and in Spain with Valencia.

PLAYER
CADAMARTERI, Danny
Forward, English, 172cm, 79kg
Born: 12.10.79, Bradford, England
Clubs: Everton (1996-)
• Pacy forward who broke through in the 1997-98 season. Also plays in midfield.
• England Under-21 international.

PLAYER
CADETE, Jorge
Full name: Jorge Paulo Cadete Santos Reis
Forward, Portuguese, 177cm, 65kg
Born: 27.08.68, Porto Amelia, Portugal
Clubs: Sporting Lisbon (1987-88), Vitoria Setubal (1988-89), Sporting Lisbon (1989-1994), Brescia (Ita) (1994-95) Celtic (1995-97), Celta Vigo (Spa) (1997-99), Benfica (1999), Bradford (Eng) (2000), Estrela Amadora (2000-)
Full international (Portugal) 33 caps/5goals
• Talented but unsettled striker who was captain of Sporting Lisbon under **Bobby Robson** in the early 1990s, when he was Portuguese League top scorer with 18 goals in 1992-93.
• Played in Italy in 1994-95, but could not prevent Brescia from relegation.
• Made Portugal's squad for Euro 96 after some excellent performances for Celtic in Scotland.
• Had a brief spell with Bradford in the final weeks of the 1999-2000 season, but returned to Portugal for the 2000-2001 campaign.

PLAYER
CAFU
Full name: Evangelista de Moraes Marcos
Defender, Brazilian, 176cm, 74kg
Born: 07.06.70, Sao Paulo, Brazil.
Clubs: Sao Paulo (1989-94), Real Zaragoza (Spa) (1994-95), Palmeiras (1995-97), Roma (Ita) (1997-)
Full international (Brazil) 91 caps/5 goals

• Flying right-back who is nicknamed 'Pendolino' after Italy's express trains because of his pacy overlapping runs.

• Captain of Brazil who played a key role at the 1998 World Cup finals.

• Started his career at Sao Paulo, where he won two Libertadores Cups in 1992 and 1993.

• Had a brief spell in Spain at Zaragoza, but returned to Brazil, to Palmeiras, a move which angered Sao Paulo, who claimed to have an agreement whereby they would have first choice of signing him if he returned from Europe.

• Included in the 1994 World Cup squad, appearing as a substitute in the Final following an injury to Jorginho.

PLAYER
CAIRES, Bruno
Full name: Bruno Ricardo Mendoca de Caires
Midfielder, Portuguese, 184cm, 80kg
Born: 02.04.76, Lisbon, Portugal
Clubs: Belenenses (1994-95), Benfica (1995-97)
Celta Vigo (1997-)
• Portuguese midfielder signed from Benfica in 1997, but has hardly been used by **Victor Fernandez**.

PLAYER
CAIRO, Ellery
Forward, Dutch, 175cm, 74kg
Born: 03.08.78, Rotterdam, Holland
Clubs: Feyenoord (1994-97), Excelsior (1997-99), Feyenoord (1999-)
• Lively right winger with great pace. Failed to make it to the starting line-up at Feyenoord despite starting in their youth ranks.

• Was set to move to FC Twente for the start of the 2000-2001 season.

• Dutch Under-21 international.

• Cousin Rodney plays at FC Utrecht.

COACH
CAJUDA, Manuel
Portuguese
• One of Portugal's top coaches of the moment, a man who, thanks to his organisational and motivational skills, has wrung the maximum out of a playing staff of theoretically modest potential at Sporting Braga.

• A man with a Cantona-like flair for the obtuse: 'Our players need to fight back against our current poor run of form and not run away like a patient when he sees the needle coming.'

PLAYER
CALADO
Full name: Jose Antonio Calada da Silva
Defender, Portuguese, 179cm, 78kg
Born: 01.03.76, Belenenses, Portugal
Clubs: Estrela Amadora (1993-95), Benfica (1995-)
Full international (Portugal) 4 caps/0 goals
• Useful utility player whose main weakness is his inconsistency.

• Performances for Benfica last season attracted interest from a number of English clubs.

AGENT
CALASSAN, Milan
• Yugoslav agent who is registered in France. Represents **Savo Milosevic**.

• **Contact:** 52, Avenue Gound, 77330 Ozoir, La Ferriere, France.

PLAYER
CALORI, Alessandro
Defender, Italian, 188cm, 87kg
Born: 29.08.66, Arezzo, Italy
Clubs: Arezzo (1984-85), Montevarchi (1985-89), Pisa (1989-91), Udinese (1991-99), Perugia (1999-)
• Central defender whose height makes him a threat at set-pieces.

COACH
CAMACHO, Jose Antonio
Spanish
Born: 08.06.55
- National coach of Spain since September 1998.
- A tough, uncompromising defender (centre-back or full-back) who spent 16 seasons at Real Madrid, where he was dubbed 'Macho' Camacho. Won the Spanish League nine times and the Cup four times. Won the UEFA Cup in 1985 and 1986.
- At one time, his total of 81 caps was a Spanish record, but has since been overtaken by Andoni Zubizarretta's total of 129.
- After retiring as a player he took up a coaching post in Real Madrid's youth system and rose to be number two to Alfredo Di Stefano with the seniors.
- Left Real to take charge of Espanyol (twice) and Sevilla, returning to Madrid in the summer of 1998. But he lasted only 22 days during the close season after falling out with then Real president **Lorenzo Sanz** over his choice of assistants.
- Took over as coach of Spain from **Javier Clemente** and succeeded in reviving the fortunes of the side, using players from many different clubs, not just Real Madrid and Barcelona, as favoured by Clemente.

PLAYER
CAMARA, Aboubacar 'Titi'
Forward, Guinean, 184cm, 80kg
Born: 17.11.72, Conakry, Guinea
Clubs: AS Kaloum Conakry, Saint-Etienne (Fra) (1990-95), Lens (Fra) (1995-97) Marseille (Fra) (1997-99), Liverpool (Eng) (1999-)
Full international (Guinea)
- Unpredictable but hard-working forward who joined Liverpool for £2.6million from Marseille.
- **Tony Vairelles** on Camara: 'He has an unusual way of dribbling and shooting, and he plays with his heart rather than his head. But that's why he surprises opponents. If you took away his style, you'd kill him.'
- Played at the 1994 and 1998 African Nations Cups.

Jose Antonio Camacho

PLAYER
CAMARA, Henri
Forward, Senegal
Born: 10.05.77
Clubs: Neuchatel Xamax, Strasbourg (Fra) (2000-)
Full international (Senegal)
• Impressive Senegal international striker who left Neuchatel Xamax for Strasbourg in summer 2000, only to find himself out in the cold when the Alsace club discovered they had more than their quota of non-EU players. The pacy and elusive African frontrunner was tipped to return to Xamax, though Bordeaux and Lens were also keen.

PLAYER
CAMARA, Kemoko
Goalkeeper, Guinea, 185cm, 77kg
Born: 05.04.75, Guinea
Clubs: Mouscron (Bel) (1996-97), Waregem (Bel) (1997-98), Mechelen (Bel) (1998-)
Full international (Guinea) 48 caps/0 goals
• Keeper who has established himself as number one at Mechelen over the past two seasons.

PLAYER
CAMARASA, Francisco
Full name: Francisco Jose Camarasa Castellar
Defender, Spanish, 183cm, 80kg
Born: 27.09.67, Valencia, Spain
Clubs: Valencia (1987-)
Full international (Spain) 14 caps/0 goals
• Veteran club captain at Valencia who played in the Spain defence in the 1994 World Cup. Suffered terrible injuries between 1996 and 1999. Was controversially banished to the Valencia reserves after criticising **Hector Cuper** in November 1999.

PLAYER
CAMERON, Colin
Midfielder, Scottish, 166cm, 60kg
Born: 23.10.72, Kirkcaldy, Scotland
Clubs: **Sligo** (1991-92), Raith Rovers (1992-96),
Hearts (1996-)
Full international (Scotland) 5 caps/1 goal
• Another Hearts player who has forced his way into the Scotland squad of late, Cameron's forceful midfield performances were a feature of Hearts play in the 1999-2000 season and the inspirational qualities of the former Raith Rovers player have led to his appointment as club captain at Hearts.

PLAYER
CAMINERO, Jose Luis
Midfielder, Spanish, 187cm, 90kg
Born: 08.11.67, Madrid, Spain
Clubs: Castilla (1987-89), Valladolid (1989-93), Atletico Madrid (1993-98), Valladolid (1998-)
Full international (Spain) 21 caps/8 goals
• Versatile, experienced but temperemental midfielder who has played as a winger, sweeper, central defender and all areas of midfield.
• Was rejected as a youngster by Real Madrid where his path was blocked by Michel. Joined Real Valladolid, where he was converted into a sweeper by Colombian coach Francisco Maturana.
• Signed by Atletico Madrid in 1993 for £900,000 and played a key role in the 1996 League and Cup double success.
• International debut against Chile in 1993.
• Spain's top scorer at the 1994 World Cup with three goals despite missing the second round through suspension. Also played at Euro 96.

PLAYER
CAMMARATA, Fabrizio
Forward, Italian, 178cm, 71kg
Born: 30.08.75, Caltanisetta, Italy
Clubs: Juventus (1992-94), Verona (1994-96), Torino (1996-97), Pescara (1997-98), Verona (1998-)
• Striker who showed great promise as a youngster, when he played alongside **Alessandro Del Piero** in Juventus's youth teams. But after being

released by Juventus, he struggled to find his feet, but looked to have established himself with Verona's promotion to Serie A in 1999.

PLAYER
CAMPBELL, Andy
Forward, English, 180cm, 73kg
Born: 18.04.79, Stockton, England
Clubs: Middlesbrough (1996-), Sheffield Utd (1998, 1999, loan)
• Exciting striking prospect who made his Premiership debut aged 16, but has yet to make the major breakthrough.

PLAYER
CAMPBELL, Kevin
Forward, English, 185cm, 85kg
Born: 04.02.70, London, England
Clubs: Arsenal (1988-95), Orient (1989, loan), Leicester (1989, loan), Nottingham Forest (1995-98), Trabzonspor (Tur) (1998-99), Everton (1999-)
• Strong-running striker who won a host of honours with Arsenal before being sold to Forest.
• Spell in Turkey ended in acrimonious circumstances when he accused Trabzonspor president Mehmet Ali Yilmaz of racism.
• Former England Under-21 international.

PLAYER
CAMPBELL, Sol
Defender, English, 188cm, 91kg
Born: 18.09.74, London Newham, England
Clubs: Tottenham (1992-)
Full international (England) 36 caps/0 goals
• Powerful centre-back whose reputation grows with every season. Plays on the left side of the defence, at centre-back or full-back, but can also play in midfield, and has been used by Spurs at centre-forward.
• Likened by **Glenn Hoddle** to **Marcel Desailly**.
• International debut: 18.05.96, v Hungary (won 3-0).

Sol Campbell

Fabio Cannavaro

ADMINISTRATOR
CAMPORA, Jean-Louis
• President of French club Monaco.

PLAYER
CAMUS, Daniel
Defender, Belgian, 177cm, 75kg
Born: 21.10.71, Belgium
Clubs: RWDM (1991-97), Genk (1997-99),
Mechelen (1999-)
• Midfield battler and a tough competitor in the
Belgian League.
• Joined Mechelen halfway through the 1999-
2000 season after failing to hold down a regular
first-team place at Genk.

PLAYER
CANABAL, Manuel
Full name: Manuel Canabal Fiestra
Forward, Spanish, 197cm, 93kg
Born: 10.11.74, Forcarel, Spain
Clubs: Pontevedra (1993-95), Merida (1995-97),
Real Madrid (1997), Valladolid (1998), Alaves
(1998-99), Rayo Vallecano (1999-)
• Tall striker who is surprisingly skilful given his
height and can also play in midfield.
• A massive flop at Real Madrid when signed
from Merida, but found success at Vallecano.

PLAYER
CANDELA, Vincent
Defender, French, 180cm, 76kg
Born: 24.10.73, Bedarieux, France
Clubs: Toulouse (1992-95), Guingamp (1995-96),
Roma (Ita) (1997-)
Full international (France) 23 caps/1 goal
• Left-back who is excellent going forward and
would have won more caps for the French
national side were it not for the excellence of
Bixente Lizarazu.
• Made his first division debut as a 20-year-old
with Toulouse, moving on to Guingamp and
joining Roma in January 1997.

• A member of France's World Cup-winning squad who played one game, against Denmark, in the 1998 finals.
• Was in exceptional form for Roma in the 1999-2000 season, leading to speculation that he would join Internazionale.
• International debut against Turkey, 09.10.96 (won 4-0).

PLAYER
CANIZARES, Jose
Full name: Jose Santiago Canizares Ruiz
Goalkeeper, Spanish, 181cm, 78kg
Born: 18.02.69, Madrid, Spain
Clubs: Real Madrid (1988-89), Castilla (1989-90), Elche (1990-91), Merida (1991-92), Celta Vigo (1992-94), Real Madrid (1994-98), Valencia (1998-)
Full international (Spain) 26 caps/0 goals
• Joined Real Madrid at 17 but was sent on loan to Elche and Merida, where former Real winger Juanito was the coach.
• Real sold him to Celta in 1992 for £300,000 but bought him back two years later for £2million after he was Spain's hero during the crucial 1994 World Cup qualifier against Denmark, making superb saves after appearing as a substitute following the 10th-minute sending-off of Andoni Zubizarretta.
• Seemed certain to keep goal in Spain's 1992 Olympic-winning team, but lost his place to Toni.
• Failed to win the number one slot at Real and was eventually sold to Celta Vigo. After two impressive seasons there, where he made his international debut, Madrid exercised the buy-back clause in the contract.
• Was then sold by Real for a second time in 1998, to Valencia.
• All along he has remained the national team's number two, behind Zubizarretta and then **Jose Molina**.
• Took over from Molina during Euro 2000, having not been used at Euro 96.

PLAYER
CANNAVARO, Fabio
Defender, Italian, 176cm, 75kg
Born: 13.09.73, Napoli, Italy
Clubs: Napoli (1991-95), Parma (1995-)
Full international (Italy) 40 caps/0 goals
• Experienced and tough centre-back blessed with excellent good timing. Strong in the air despite his lack of height.
• A ball boy at Napoli in the 1980s when Diego Maradona was the star turn.
• Made his international debut as a substitute against Northern Ireland in January 1997 and has stayed in the team virtually ever since.
• One of the few Italian players to come out of the 1998 World Cup campaign in France with his reputation enhanced and was exceptional as a linchpin of the defence which took Italy to the brink of success in Euro 2000.
• European champion with Italy at Under-21 level in 1994 and 1996.

PLAYER
CANTALUPPI, Mario
Defender, Swiss, 185cm, 86kg
Born: 11.04.74, Switzerland
Clubs: Grasshopper (1990-93), Basle (1994-96), Servette (1996-98), Grasshopper (1998), Basle (1998-)
Full international (Swizerland) 7 caps/3 goals
• Swiss international defender who has his eyes on a move to the Bundesliga and hopes for a move before his contract with Basle ends in 2003. Was happy to sign a four-year contract in 1999 after an 18-month injury-enforced break.
• Won the Swiss League with Basle in 2000.

PLAYER
CAPDEVILA, Joan
Full name: Joan Capdevelia Mendez
Defender, Spanish, 180cm, 78kg
Born: 02.03.78, Tarrega, Spain
Clubs: Tarrefa (1996-97), Espanyol (1997-99),

Atletico Madrid (1999-2000), Deportivo (2000-)
• Hard-working left-side midfielder or full-back.
• Came to attention at Espanyol, where his performances earned him a transfer to Atletico Madrid.
• Joined Deportivo in summer 2000 as part of a package of players from relegated Atletico, including **Jose Molina** and **Juan Valeron**.

COACH
CAPELLO, Fabio
Italian
Born: 18.06.46
• Coach of Roma since summer 1999 and the most successful Italian coach of the 1990s, following his triumphs with Milan and Real Madrid.
• An accomplished forward for Milan and Juventus who won 32 caps for Italy in the 1970s, scoring eight goals, including the winner against England at Wembley in 1993.
• Joined the backroom staff of Milan and became first-team coach in 1991 when **Arrigo Sacchi** resigned to become Italian national coach.
• Won three successive Italian League titles between 1992 and 1994, capped by a marvellous victory over Barcelona in the 1994 Champions Cup Final in Athens.
• Moved to Real Madrid in 1996 and won the Spanish League title in his first and only season.
• Returned to Milan for the 1997-98 season, but could only manage 10th place. Remained under contract to Milan, but was effectively resting for the final 18 months of his contract before the move to Roma.
• 'A coach is like a winemaker. He must produce the best wine from the grapes he has available.'

PLAYER
CAPONE
Full name: Carlos Alberto de Oliveira
Defender, Brazilian, 180cm, 79kg
Born: 23.05.72, Sao Paulo, Brazil
Clubs: Mogi Merim, Ponte Preta, Sao Paulo,

Kyoto Songo (Jap), Juventude, Galatsaray (Tur)
• Much-travelled Brazilian central defender, who has settled well in Turkey with Galatasaray.
• Played in the Champions League for Galatasaray, scoring against Milan, and then played a part in the triumphant 1999-2000 UEFA Cup campaign.
• Won the Brazilian Cup with Juventude.

PLAYER
CAPUCHO
Full name: Nuno Fernando Goncalves da Rosa
Midfielder, Portuguese, 180cm, 78kg
Born: 21.02.72, Barcelos, Portugal
Clubs: Gil Vicente (1999-92), Sporting Lisbon (1992-95), Vitoria Guimaraes (1995-97), FC Porto (1997-)
Full international (Portugal) 17 caps/2 goals
• Powerful midfielder whose tough-tackling is an asset to most midfield engine rooms.
• Also likes to attack, and his useful technique makes him a match for most defenders.
• World Youth Cup winner in 1991.
• International debut v Germany in February 1996.
• Played his way into Portugal's squad for Euro 2000, where he made two appearances.

PLAYER
CARBONARI, Horacio
Defender, Argentinian 188cm 85kg
Born: 02.05.74, Rosario, Argentina
Clubs: Rosario Central (1995-98), Derby (1998-)
• Derby's record signing in July 1998 – £2.7million from Rosario Central.
• Plays anywhere in defence, likes to get forward, with a powerful shot from set-pieces.

PLAYER
CARBONE, Benito
Forward, Italian, 168cm, 67kg
Born: 14.08.71, Bagnara Calabra, Italy
Clubs: Torino (1988-90), Reggina (1990-91), Casertana (1991-92), Ascoli (1992-93), Torino

(1993-94), Napoli (1994-95), Internazionale (1995-97), Sheffield Wed (Eng) (1997-99), Aston Villa (Eng) (1999-2000), Bradford (Eng) (2000-)
• Skilful, dimunitive playmaker who arrived in England after falling out of favour at Inter, and then fell out with Wednesday manager Danny Wilson, joining Villa on loan.
• A maker rather than a taker of goals.
• Former Italian Under-21 international.

PLAYER
CARBONI, Amedeo
Defender, Italian, 180cm, 73kg
Born: 06.04.65, Arezzo, Italy
Clubs: Arezzo (1984-85), Bari (1985-86), Arezzo (1986), Empoli (1986-87), Parma (1987-88), Sampdoria (1988-90), Roma (1990-97), Valencia (Spa) (1997-)
Full international (Italy) 18 caps/0 goals
• Left-back with pace, strength and experience of 12 seasons in Serie A.
• Brought to Spain's Valencia from Roma by Italian coach **Claudio Ranieri**.
• Sent off after just 30 minutes of his Valencia debut against Barcelona for a foul on Luis Figo.

PLAYER
CARDONI, Manuel
Midfielder, Luxembourg, 184cm, 82kg
Born: 22.09.72, Luxembourg
Clubs: Bayer Leverkusen (Ger) (1996-99), Jeunesse d'Esch (1998-)
Full international (Luxembourg) 37 caps/3 goals
• One of Luxembourg's leading players, who returned home to Jeunesse d'Esch after failing to make the grade in two seasons with Leverkusen.

PLAYER
CARDOSO, Rodolfo
Midfielder, Argentinian, 178cm, 76kg
Born: 17.10.68, Azul, Argentina
Clubs: AC Azul, Homburg (Ger) (1989-93), Freiburg (Ger) (1993-95), Werder Bremen (Ger)

John Carew

(1995-96), Hamburg (Ger) (1997-98), Boca Juniors (1998), Estudiantes De la Plata (1999), Hamburg (Ger) (1999-2000)
Full international (Argentina)

• Playmaker who made his name in the mid-1990s with Freiburg. Moves to Werder Bremen and Hamburg failed to work out and he returned to Argentina on loan, before a move back to Germany to play some of the best football of his career for Hamburg in 1999-2000.

• After five seasons of below-par performances and injury worries, the career of the Argentine playmaker was going nowhere a year ago and his employers at Hamburg only reluctantly allowed him to train with the first team when no buyers could be found. But Cardoso miraculously rediscovered his form on the training ground and soon found himself back in the first team, showing all the flair and vision which made him such an influential figure with Freiburg in the mid-1990s.

• International debut: December 1995, v Venezuela.

PLAYER
CAREW, John
Forward, Norwegian, 195cm, 89kg
Born: 05.09.79, Norway
Clubs: Valerenga (1998-99), Rosenborg (1999-2000), Valencia (Spa) (2000)
Full international (Norway) 16 caps/3 goals

• Tall, strong striker who joined Spanish club Valencia in July 2000. Has a good shot, shields the ball well and is strong in the air.

• Played for Valerenga while still a student, and opted to move to Rosenborg in 1999 despite strong interest from abroad.

• In Norway's squad for Euro 2000, but used only as a substitute.

• His father played in goal for Gambia.

PLAYER
CARLOS
Full name: Carlos Dominguez, Dominguez
Midfielder, Spanish, 168cm, 67kg

Born: 18.09.76, Seville, Spain
Clubs: Sevilla (1994-96), Mallorca (1997), Sevilla (1997-98), Mallorca (1998-99), Espanyol (1999-)

• Diminutive attacking midfielder who surprised many in the 1999-2000 season with his goals for Espanyol, having previously not shown any goalscoring tendencies.

• Spanish Under-21 international.

• Nicknamed 'Mighty Mouse'.

PLAYER
CARLOS GARCIA
Defender, Spanish, 183cm, 74kg
Born: 13.08.70, Durango, Spain
Clubs: Athletic Bilbao (1990-), Osasuna (1994-95)

• Powerful central defender who has spent his entire career, save for a season on loan to Osasuna in 1994-95, with Athletic Bilbao.

COACH
CARLOS MANUEL
Portuguese

• The Campomaiorense coach was constantly tipped for the axe last season, but he is nothing if not a fighter and saved his skin with a successful rearguard operation to keep the club in the First Division.

• During a coaching career with Braga, Sporting Lisbon, Salgueiros and now Campomaiorense, has proved himself excellent leader and motivator.

• A one-time midfield star for Portugal and Benfica. 'For Portugal I had the reputation of a player who scored vital goals at vital times. I want to experience the same exciting moments as a coach.'

PLAYER
CARNELL, Bradley
Midfielder, South African, 174cm, 70kg
Born: 22.01.77, South Africa
Clubs: WITS University, Kaiser Chiefs (1997-98), Stuttgart (Ger) (1998-)
Full international (South Africa)

• Highly promising young South African left-back or wing-back. Nippy, purposeful and an accurate provider of crosses. Has shown much character to recover from two knee ligament injuries.

PLAYER
CARNOT, Stephane
Midfielder, French, 170cm, 71kg
Born: 10.07.72, Quimper, France
Clubs: Guingamp (1995-97), Monaco (1997-98), Auxerre (1998-)
• Cultured, left-footed playmaker who looked ill-at-ease during an anti-climactic 1997-98 season in Monaco's star-studded ranks but whose career has revived over the last two years in the more homely surroundings of Auxerre.
• A lynchpin of the Guingamp side which earned promotion to the French top flight in 1985.

PLAYER
CARR, Stephen
Defender, Irish, 176cm, 78kg
Born: 29.08.76, Dublin, Ireland
Clubs: Tottenham (1993-)
Full international (Rep Ireland) 12 caps/0 goals
• Left wing-back whose performances for Spurs under **George Graham** earned him international recognition with the Republic of Ireland.

PLAYER
CARRAGHER, Jamie
Defender, English, 186cm, 83kg
Born: 28.01.78, Liverpool, England
Clubs: Liverpool (1996-)
Full international (England) 1 cap/0 goals
• Versatile product of Anfield youth system who has established himself in the Liverpool first team under **Gerard Houllier**.
• International debut: 28.04.99, v Hungary (1-1).

Iker Casillas

PLAYER
CARRICK, Michael
Midfielder, English, 182cm, 78kg
Born: 28.07.81, Wallsend, England
Clubs: West Ham (1999-), Swindon (loan),
Birmingham City (loan)
• Young midfielder who some are suggesting
could be as good as **Joe Cole**. Born and brought
up in the north east, but is coming through the
ranks in London at West Ham.

PLAYER
CARRIERE, Eric
Midfielder, French, 173cm, 61kg
Born: 24.05.73, Foix, France
Clubs: Auch, Muret, Nantes (1996-)
• Busy, neat central midfielder who can both
win the ball and use it intelligently. A French B
international, he was consistently impressive
during the 1999-2000 season for Nantes.

ADMINISTRATOR
CARRARO, Franco
Italian
Born: 06.12.39
• President of the Italian League since 1997 and
a key figure in the negotiation of pay-TV contracts.

PLAYER
CASANOVA, Laurent
Midfielder, French, 183cm, 81kg
Born: 28.04.71, Bastia, France
Clubs: Bastia (1991-95), Lyon (1995-96), Bastia
(1996-)
• A proud Corsican and Bastia's inspirational
skipper. Whether marking in central defence or in
a midfield holding role, he always gives full value
for money and was in outstanding form during
the 1999-2000 season.

PLAYER
CASCARINO, Tony
Forward, Irish, 190cm, 78kg

Born: 01.09.63, St Paul's Cray, England
Clubs: Gillingham (1981-87), Millwall (1987-90),
Aston Villa (1990-91), Celtic (1991-92), Chelsea
(1992-94), Marseille (1994-97), Nancy (1997-)
Full international (Rep Ireland) 90 caps/19 goals
• Many though his career was going downhill
when off-loaded by Chelsea in the summer of
1994. But he has enjoyed a marvellous Indian
summer in France, racking up the goals with
Marseille and then at Nancy.
• French defenders have rarely been able to
come to terms with the aerial power and
muscular style of the Republic of Ireland
international and in his adopted country he is
affectionately known as 'Grandad Goal'.

ADMINISTRATOR
CASEY, Des
• Irish member of the executive committee of UEFA.

PLAYER
CASILLAS, Iker
Goalkeeper, Spanish, 184cm, 80kg
Born: 20.05.81, San Sebastian, Spain
Clubs: Real Madrid (1998-)
Full international (Spain) 2 caps/0 goals
• Teenage keeper who made a remarkable debut
in the 1999-2000, beginning the campaign as the
number three at Real, and ending it on the
winning side in the European Cup Final and a
member of Spain's Euro 2000 squad.
• A member of Spain's team which won the 1999
Under-20 World Youth Cup in Nigeria.
• Called on by Real Madrid after injuries to **Bodo
Illgner** and poor form of **Albano Bizarri**.
• Madrid's goalkeeper coach Manuel Amiero:
'Casillas is a phenomenon. He's big, strong, but is
very quick and has great reflexes. Some people
criticise him because he comes a long way for the
ball sometimes but, if you watch, you'll see how
good his judgment is. When he comes out it's
because he knows he can get the ball – and
he does.'

CASSANO, Antonio

Midfielder, Italian, 175cm, 70kg
Born: 12.07.82, Bari, Italy
Clubs: Bari (1997-)
• Hugely promising young striker who has long been tipped for a move north to a bigger Italian club and away from his hometown club Bari.

CATANHA

Full name: Henrique Guedes da Silva
Forward, Brazilian, 177cm, 75kg
Born: 06.03.72, Sao Paulo, Brazil
Clubs: Salamanca (Spa) (1996-97), Leganes (Spa) (1997-98), Malaga (Spa) (1998-)
• Striker who has amazed Spain with his goalscoring feats over the past two seasons.
• Born in Brazil, but moved to Europe in 1995, joining Spanish side Salamanca, from where he moved on to Malaga, initially on loan.
• Scored 25 goals in 40 games for Malaga in the 1998-99 season as they won promotion to the Spanish first division. Then amazed everybody by finishing the 1999-2000 season with 24 goals, making him the second highest scorer in the League.
• Nickname Cataha means 'Red Crab'.
• Recently became a Spanish citizen and nearly made the Spain squad for Euro 2000.
• Linked with a summer 2000 move to Deportivo, but the transfer appeared to have collapsed after a failure to agree personal terms.

CAVALLERI, Tiberio

• Italian agent whose clients include **Christian Panucci**.
• **Contact:** Via Solferino N. 53, I-25121, Brescia, Italy. Tel: 39 30 45319/39 30 2400221.

CAVALLERO, Pablo Oscar

Goalkeeper, Argentinian, 184cm, 81kg
Born: 13.04.74, Buenos Aires, Argentina
Clubs: Velez Sarsfield (1996-98), Union Santa Fe (1998-99), Espanyol (Spa) (1999-2000), Celta Vigo (Spa) (2000-)
Full international (Argentina) 3 caps/0 goals
• Keeper who has established himself in Spain since moving from Union Santa Fe in 1999.
• Played for Argentina's silver medal-winning side at the 1996 Olympics.
• A non-playing member of Argentina's squad at the 1998 World Cup in France.

CAVASIN, Alberto

Italian
Born: 19.01.56
• Promising young coach who has been in charge of Lecce since summer 1999.
• Spent most of his coaching career doing the rounds of Serie C1 clubs, before impressing at Cesena during the 1998-99 campaign.

CAVEGLIA, Alain

Forward, French, 180cm, 83kg
Born: 28.03.68, Lyon, France
Clubs: Gueugnon (1989-90), Sochaux (1990-94), Le Havre (1994-96), Lyon (1996-1999), Nantes (2000), Le Havre (2000-)
• A regular scorer in the French League who returned to Le Havre in the summer of 2000 after failing to make an impact at Nantes after a mid-season move.

CAVENS, Jurgen

Forward, Belgian, 188cm, 82kg
Born: 19.08.78, Belgium
Clubs: Lierse (1995-)
Full international (Belgium) 3 caps/0 goals

• Promising young striker who was 1999 'Rookie of the Year' in Belgium after scoring twice in the 1999 Belgian Cup Final.

PLAYER
CEBALLOS, Jose Maria
Goalkeeper, Spanish, 182cm, 79kg
Born: 07.09.69, Cantabria, Spain
Clubs: Racing Santander (1989-)
• Solid rather than exceptional keeper who has spent his entire career at Santander.

ADMINISTRATOR
CECCHI GORI, Vittorio
Italian
Born: 27.12.42
• President of Fiorentina since 1993 when he inherited the 'family firm' from his father Mario.

PLAYER
CEH, Ales
Midfielder, Slovenian, 174cm, 77kg
Born: 07.04.68, Marburg, Austria
Clubs: Olimpia Ljubljana (1990-91), Grazer AK (1992-)
Full international (Slovenia) 56 caps/1 goal
• Hard-working holding midfielder who is good at maintaining possesion.
• Nicknamed 'Seedorf' at Grazer AK because he plays the same sort of holding role as **Clarence Seedorf**.
• Played for Slovenia at Euro 2000, and is the most capped Slovenian player, having played in the country's first international, against Estonia in June 1992.
• Won the League and Cup with Olimpia Ljubljana before a move to Austria.

PLAYER
CELIL Sagir
Midfielder, Turkish, 172cm, 66kg
Born: 15.04.74, Samsun, Turkey
Clubs: Samsunspor, Fenerbahce (2000-)

Full international (Turkey) 7 caps/0 goals
• Strong but skilful left-sided midfielder who was one of Samsunspor's best players until a £2million transfer to Fenerbahce in May 2000.

PLAYER
CENK Isler
Forward, Turkish, 180cm, 70kg
Born: 1974, Turkey
Clubs: Samsunspor, Adanaspor (1999-)
• Striker who made his name at Samsunspor before a big-money move to Adanaspor, where he was the club's record signing and highest-paid player. Has yet to repay the investment.

PLAYER
CERNY, Harald
Midfielder, Austrian, 177cm, 73kg
Born: 13.09.73, Vienna, Austria
Clubs: ASV Hinterbruhl, Bayern Munich (Ger) (1992-93), Admira Wacker (1994), FC Tirol (1994-96), Munich 1860 (Ger) (1995-)
Full international (Austria) 36 caps/3 goals
• Adventurous right wing-back with a good turn of pace and who usually delivers a decent final ball. However, he is rather small and lightweight and can easily be out-muscled when called to defend.
• On Bayern Munich's books early in his career but did not make the grade there.
• Surname pronounced Chair nee.

PLAYER
CERNY, Radek
Goalkeeper, Czech, 190cm, 85kg
Born: 18.02.74, Czech Republic
Club: Slavia Prague
Full international (Czech Republic) 1 cap/0 goals
• Replaced the now-retired Jan Stejskal in the Slavia goal after serving as his understudy for several seasons.
• A reliable keeper who was a key factor in Slavia having the best defensive record in the

1999-2000 season. After breaking into the national team, he was only excluded from the Euro 2000 squad as one of the four of the 26 Czech squad members not to travel to the Low Countries.

PLAYER
CESAR Martin
Full name: Cesar Martin Villar
Defender, Spanish, 185cm, 81kg
Born: 02.04.77 Oviedo, Spain
Clubs: Oviedo (1994-99), Deportivo La Coruna (1999-)
Full international (Spain) 3 caps/2 goals
• Solid, old-fashioned stopper who won the 2000 Spanish League title with Deportivo.
• Strong in the air and a big threat at set-pieces.
• Given his international debut by **Jose Camacho** against Poland on 18.08.99.
• Has been unlucky with injuries but is seen as a future first-choice for the national team.

PLAYER
CESAR Sanchez
Full name: Cesar Sanchez Domniguez
Goalkeeper, Spanish, 185cm, 82kg
Born: 02.09.71, Coria, Spain
Clubs: Valladolid (1991-)
• One of the best goalkeepers in Spain in recent seasons. An agile, brave keeper who is on the verge of winning international honours.
• Was signed by Real Madrid for the 1999-2000 season, but then sent back on loan to Valladolid.
• His future at Madrid became uncertain following the emergence of **Iker Casillas**, but he returned to the Bernabeu for the 2000-2001 season.

REFEREE
CESARI, Graziano
Italian
Born: 23.12.56
• Works as a commercial agent.
• Awarded FIFA badge in 1993.

COACH
CEULEMANS, Jan
Born: 28.02.57
• A former striker with Club Brugge and the Belgian national team during the glory days of the national team of the 1980s. His name is often chanted by the Brugge supporters when things aren't going well. However, he hasn't coached his favourite club yet. Was coach of Third Division team Ingelmunster before moving to Westerlo, whom he steered clear of relegation in the 1999-2000 season.

PLAYER
CHAINHO
Full name: Carlos Narciso Chainho
Born: 10.07.74, Luanda, Angola
Clubs: Estrela Amadora (1994-98), FC Porto (1998-)
• Forceful midfielder who battles for every ball, and is considered a key member of the Porto team.
• Four caps at Under-21 level for Portugal.

PLAYER
CHAMOT, Jose
Defender, Argentinian, 185cm, 78kg
Born: 17.05.69, Rosario, Argentina
Clubs: Rosario Central (1988-91), Pisa (Ita) (1990-93), Foggia (Ita) (1993-94), Lazio (Ita) (1994-98), Atletico Madrid (Spa) (1998-99), Milan (Ita) (1999-)
Full international (Argentina) 40 caps/2 goals
• Rugged and quick Argentinian defender who returned to Italy for the 1999-2000 season after a spell in Spain with Atletico.
• Can play anywhere across the back four, but prefers the left-back role.

PLAYER
CHERCHESOV, Stanislav
Goalkeeper, Russian, 183cm, 80kg
Born: 02.09.63, Moscow
Clubs: FC Tirol Innsbruck (Aut)
Full international (Russia) 39 caps/0 goals

• Veteran keeper who played for Russia at the 1994 World Cup and 1992 and 1996 European Championships.

PLAYER
CHIBA, Said
Midfielder, Moroccan, 183cm, 70kg
Born: 28.09.70, Casablanca, Morocco
Clubs: FIS Rabat (1992-94), Al-Hilal (Sau) (1994-96), Compostela (Spa) (1996-99), Nancy (Fra) (1999-)
Full international (Morocco)
• Although the right-sided Moroccan midfielder earned infamy at the last World Cup by attempting decapitate Ronaldo, there is fortunately more to his game, namely his neat and tidy constructive play and boundless energy.

PLAYER
CHIESA, Enrico
Forward, Italian, 176cm, 70kg
Born: 29.12.70, Genova, Italy.
Clubs: Pontedecimo (1986-87), Sampdoria (1987-90), Teramo (1990-91), Chieti (1991-92), Sampdoria (1992-93), Modena (1993-94), Cremonese (1994-95), Sampdoria (1995-96), Parma (1996-99), Fiorentina (1999-)
Full international (Italy) 15 caps/4 goals
• Pacy, skilful striker who can shoot with either foot and play on the flanks.
• Made his name at Sampdoria in the 1995-96 season, when he scored 22 goals in 27 games and earned a move to Parma.
• Scored on his international debut for Italy against Belgium in May 1996 and was tipped to be a dark horse of Euro 96, but his fortunes suffered with Italy's.
• Was in the shadow of the goalscroring exploits of **Hernan Crespo** at Parma, and was sold to Fiorentina in summer 1999.

PLAYER
CHIMENTI, Antonio
Goalkeeper, Italian, 184cm, 77kg
Born: 30.06.70, Bari
Clubs: Sambenedettese (1988-91), Tempio (1991-92), Monza (1992-93), Sambenedettese (1993), Salernitana (1993-97), Roma (1997-99), Lecce (1999-)
• Joined Roma in 1997 from Salernitana as a reserve, following 10 years in Serie B and C, and broke into the first team following an injury to Michael Konsel.
• Went a Roma club record 510 minutes without conceding a goal in Europe in the 1998-99 season.

PLAYER
CHIPPO, Youssef
Midfielder, Moroccan, 184cm, 77kg
Born: 10.05.73, Boujaad, Morocco
Clubs: Al Arabi (Qat) (1996), FC Porto (Por) (1997-99), Coventry (Eng) (1999-)
Full international (Morocco)
• Made a brief appearance at the Barcelona Olympics and since fullfilled much of his potential, first while earning petro-dollars in the Middle East, then in Portugal, and now as a pal for **Mustapha Hadji** at Coventry.

PLAYER
CHIVU, Cristian
Defender, Romanian, 183cm, 78kg
Born: 15.10.80, Resita, Romania
Clubs: Univ. Craiova (1998-99), Ajax (Hol) (2000-)
Full international (Romania) 8 caps/1 goal
• Highly promising left-sided defender who can also play at sweeper and in midfield.
• Joined Ajax for £3million during 1999-2000 season, playing 21 games in his first season.
• Has the talent to be the leader of the next generation of Romanian players, according to **Mircea Lucescu**.
• Made his international debut for Romania against Cyprus in August 1999 (2-2).

• Capped 20 times by Romania at Under-20 level.
• Member of Romania's squad at Euro 2000 and earned rave reviews for the way he dealt with **Luis Figo** and **David Beckham**.

COACH
CHOVANEC, Jozef
Czech
Born: 07.03.60
• Coach of Czech Republic who became the first man to lead a team to the European Championship finals without dropping a point in qualifying.
• More attack-minded than his predecessor Dusan Uhrin.
• A clever tactician who spent eight seasons as a player with Sparta Prague and then had a spell with PSV before returning home for four more years at Sparta.
• Won 52 caps (4 goals) for Czecohoslovakia as a sweeper, as well as eight Czech League titles with Sparta and one Dutch League crown with PSV.
• Player of the Year in Czechoslovakia in 1986.
• Within 12 months of his return to the Letna he had been appointed Sparta's coach. Won two straight Czech League titles and was made national team coach in January 1998.

PLAYER
CHRISTANVAL, Philippe
Defender, French, 185cm, 73kg
Born: 31.08.78, Paris, France
Clubs: Monaco (1997-)
• Supremely confident young sweeper who just missed the France Euro 2000 boat, but his time will come soon.
• A graduate of the Monaco youth system, he has been earmarked to be the long-term successor to **Laurent Blanc** in the national team.

PLAYER
CHRISTENSEN, Anders
Midfielder, Danish, 187cm, 73kg
Born: 26.07.77, Denmark

Clubs: Naestved (1997-99), Gent (Bel) (1999-)
• Pacy, strong midfielder who made the move to Belgium for the 1999-2000 season after impressing as a semi-professional in his native Denmark.

PLAYER
CHRISTENSEN, Bent
Forward, Danish, 180cm, 76kg
Born: 04.01.67, Copenhagen, Denmark
Clubs: Vejle (1986-87), Brondby (1987-91), Schalke (Ger) (1991-93), Olympiakos (Gre) (1993-94), Compostela (Spa) (1994-97), Genclerbirligi (Tur) (1997), Brondby (1997-)
Full international (Denmark) 26 caps/8 goals
• Striker who is now back in Denmark after mixed fortunes abroad.
• Top scorer in the Danish League three times in four seasons from 1988 to 1991 and played for Denmark in their historic campaign at Euro 92.
• Became the most expensive Danish player ever when he joined Schalke for £1.8million in 1991.
• His time in Germany did not work out, nor did a move to Olympiakos. But was a revelation at Spanish club Compostela and earned a recall to the Danish national side.
• Nicknamed 'Turbo' early in his career because of his speed.

PLAYER
CHRISTIAN
Full name: Christian Correa Dionisio
Forward, Brazilian, 186cm, 79kg
Born: 23.04.75, Porto Alegre, Brazil
Clubs: Internacional (1993), Maritimo (Por) (1993-94), Estrela Amadora (Por) (1994-95), Farense (Por) (1995-96), Internacional (1996-99), Paris Saint-Germain (Fra) (1999-)
Full international (Brazil)
• Striker who took three months to open his account for PSG following his £10 million move from Internacional of Porto Alegre. But when he did, the goals just did not stop flowing and he ended the 1999-2000 campaign with a total of

16, giving him fourth-place in the national scoring lists.
• Muscular, quick, an exceptional dribbler and a major threat in the air, he has an abundance of weapons in his arsenal.
• Failed to impress in a three-year spell in Portugal in the mid-1990s, and returned to Brazil.
• International debut: Brazil v Ecuador, September 1997.

PLAYER
CHRISTIE, Malcolm
Forward, English, 182cm, 70kg
Born: 11.04.79, Peterborough, England
Clubs: Derby (1998-)
• Promising young striker spotted playing in non-League football by Derby.

PLAYER
CHVALOVSKY, Ales
Goalkeeper, Czech, 183cm, 77kg
Born: 29.05.79, Czech Republic
Clubs: Chmel Blsany
• Keeper with the tiny village team Blsany, a heavy investor in young talent.
• Part of the Czech Under-21 team that won silver at 2000's European Championships.
• Is the son of Czech FA president **Frantisek Chvalovsky**, also a goalkeeper in his time.

ADMINISTRATOR
CHVALOVSKY, Frantisek
Czech
Born: 17.04.54.
• President of the Czech FA since 1995.

PLAYER
CIECHELSKI, Laurent
Defender, French, 180cm, 77kg
Born: 04.06.71, Gien, France
Clubs: Auxerre (1992-95), Gueugnon (1995-96), Auxerre (1996-)
• Versatile defender equally comfortable as a stopper or left-back. A product of the ever-prolific Auxerre youth system.
• Surname pronounced See chel ski.

PLAYER
CIOBOTARIU, Liviu
Defender, Romanian, 188cm, 84kg
Born: 07.01.71, Ghimpati, Romania
Clubs: Progresul (1992-94), National Bucharest (1994-98), Dinamo Bucharest (1998-99), Standard Liege (Bel) (1999-)
Full international (Romania) 24 caps/1 goal
• Central defensive stopper who has been a regular in the Romanian national team since the 1998 World Cup.
• Made his international debut for Romania agianst Macedonia in August 1997.
• Played four times for Romania at France 98, replacing the injured Daniel Prodan.
• Moved to Standard Liege in October 1999.
• Played for Romania at Euro 2000.

COACH
CIPRO, Frantisek
Czech
Born: 12.04.47
• Coach of Slavia Prague.

PLAYER
CIRIC, Dragan
Forward, Yugoslav, 180cm, 73kg
Born: 15.09.74, Jakovo, Yugoslavia
Clubs: Partizan Belgrade (1992-97), Barcelona (Spa) (1997-99), AEK Athens (Gre) (1999-)
Full international (Yugoslavia) 4 caps/0 goals
• The Yugoslav attacking midfielder or forward hardly featured at Barcelona following a move from Partizan Belgrade in the summer of 1997. But he has looked good since transferring to AEK Athens at the start of the 1999-2000 season, scoring 10 goals in his first campaign.
• Elegant, technical and well-balanced, he was Yugoslavia's Player of the Year in 1996.

PLAYER
CIRIC, Sasa
Forward, Macedonian
Born: 11.01.68, Bitula, Macedonia
Clubs: Metalurg Skopje, Pelister Bitola, Vardar Skopje, CSKA Sofia (Bul), Aarau (Swi), Nurnberg (Ger), Tennis Borussia Berlin (Ger) (1999-2000), FC Koln (Ger) (2000-)
Full international (Macedonia) 14 caps/5 goals
• Macedonia's leading striker, who won League and Cup honours with Vardar before a move abroad. A sharp striker with a keen eye for goal.

PLAYER
CIRILLO, Bruno
Defender, Italian, 187cm, 72kg
Born: 21.03.77, Trecase, Italy.
Clubs: Tricase (1996-98), Reggina (1998-)
• Promising young defender who is adaptable and has adjusted well to Italy's Serie A following promotion with Reggina.

PLAYER
CISSE, Aliou
Midfielder, French/Senegal, 180cm, 75kg
Born: 24.03.75, Ziguinchor, Senegal
Clubs: Lille, Sedan (1998-99), Paris Saint-Germain (1999-)
• Versatile campaigner and a valuable member of the PSG squad.
• No relation of **Edouard Cisse**.

PLAYER
CISSE, Edouard
Midfielder, French, 186cm, 75kg
Born: 30.03.78, Pau, France
Clubs: Pau, Paris Saint-Germain, Rennes (1998-99), Paris Saint-Germain (1999-)
• Former French Under-21 international whose athleticism, strength in the tackle and non-stop activity makes him a redoutable defensive midfielder.
• Surname pronounced See say.

PLAYER
CITKO, Marek
Forward, Polish, 178cm, 77kg
Born: 27.03.74, Poland
Clubs: Widzew Lodz, Legia Warsaw (2000-)
Full international (Poland) 10 caps/2 goals
• Livewire striker who voted 'Discovery of the Year' in 1996 and very quickly became the main man in the Polish national team. But an Achilles injury broke his career in 1997.
• Left Widzew for Legia in January 2000 and he is now trying to rebuild his career.

PLAYER
CIZEK, Martin
Midfielder, Czech, 187cm, 79kg
Born: 09.06.74, Czech Republic
Clubs: Banik Ostrava, Sparta Prague, Munich 1860 (Ger) (1999-)
Full international (Czech Republic) 18 caps/1 goals
• Midfielder who is comfortable on the ball but has yet to win a regular first-team place in Munich.

PLAYER
CLAUDIO LOPEZ
Full name: Claudio Javier Lopez
Forward, Argentinian, 178cm, 75kg
Born: 17.07.74, Rio Tercero, Argentina
Clubs: Racing Avellaneda (1992-96), Valencia (Spa) (1996-2000), Lazio (Ita) (2000-)
Full international (Argentina) 35 caps/5 goals
• Incredibly quick striker who is one of the most effective strikers in the world on the counter-attack. Powerful left foot.
• Moved to Valencia in summer 1996, but was forced to spend time on the sidelines after coach **Luis Aragones** resigned and his successor Jorge Valdano preferred to play **Ariel Ortega** in the role of second attacker.
• Played for Argentina's silver medal-winning side at the 1996 Olympics.

• Career at Valencia was revived by the arrival of Italian **Claudio Ranieri**, whose counter-attacking tactics suited Lopez perfectly.

• Played alongside **Gabriel Batistuta** in Argentina's attack at the 1998 World Cup.

• Success in the 1998-99 season, including two goals in Valencia's 1999 Spanish Cup victory, attracted attention of clubs around Europe.

• Continued to score regularly for Valencia in 1999-2000 season, as his club became the surprise team of the European campaign, reaching the Champions League Final against Real Madrid.

• Joined Lazio for a reported £16million in summer 2000.

• Nicknamed 'El Piojo' (The Louse) because of his scrawny stature as a boy.

CLAEYS, Geoffrey
Defender, Belgian, 186cm, 79kg
Born: 05.10.74, Bruges, Belgium
Clubs: Cercle Bruges (1992-96), Feyenoord (Hol) (1996-98), Anderlecht (1998-99), Eendrecht Aalst (1999-2000), Lierse (2000-)
Full international (Belgium) 3 caps/1 goal
• Defender who moved to Lierse in spring 2000 in a bid to get his career back on track after a disappointing time at Eendrecht Aalst.

• Made the breakthrough at Cercle Bruges, but played the best football of his career during two seasons in Holland with Feyenoord.

CLAESSENS, Gert
Midfielder, Belgian, 188cm, 78kg
Born: 21.02.72, Belgium
Clubs: Liege (1990-92), Genk (1992-94), Club Brugge (1994-99), Oviedo (Spa) (1999-)
Full international (Belgium) 4 caps/1 goal
• Tall Belgian midfielder who left Brugge in 1999, and has failed to win a regular place at Oviedo.

• Made his name while winning the Belgian League with Club Brugge.

CLAYTON
Forward, Brazilian, 175cm, 69kg
Born: 19.07.75, Sao Joao de Paraiso, Brazil
Clubs: Atletico Mineiro (1993-99), Santa Clara (Por) (1999-), FC Porto (Por) (2000-)
• Striker whose performances for Santa Clara led to a transfer to FC Porto.

CLEGG, Michael
Defender, English, 173cm, 72kg
Born: 03.07.77, Tameside, England
Clubs: Manchester United (1995-)
• Youngster who came through the youth system at Manchester United with great expectations. But he has found competition for first-team places very tough.

• Father owns a gym, younger brother Steve is a trainee at Old Trafford.

• Former England Under-21 international.

CLEMENT, Philippe
Midfielder, Belgian, 190cm, 86kg
Born: 22.03.74, Antwerp, Belgium
Clubs: Genk (1996-98), Coventry (Eng) (1998-99), Club Brugge (1999-)
Full international (Belgium) 11 caps/0 goals
• Ultility player who can operate in midfield or at full-back. A robust player whose physical presence is a useful asset for any side.

• Played twice for Belgium at the 1998 World Cup having made his name at Genk in the 1997-98 season as he helped them win the Belgian Cup and finish runners-up in the League.

• Moved to England after the 1998 World Cup, but his time at Premiership Coventry was plagued by ill luck as a hamstring strain and a broken cheekbone restricted his appearances and his ability to settle.

• Hopes of a regular place as a holding midfielder in the Belgian national side have been blocked by the good form of **Yves Vanderhaeghe**.

• Member of the Belgian squad at Euro 2000.

COACH
CLEMENTE, Javier
Spanish
Born: 12.03.50

• Basque by birth and nature, he was set for a promising playing career at Athletic Bilbao, but was forced to retire after suffering a serious knee injury aged 23. Moved on to the club's coaching staff, becoming youth coach and then first-team boss in 1980.

• Was forced out of Bilbao by player power in 1986 after his hard-working demands were not appreciated. Moved to Espanyol and steered them to the 1988 UEFA Cup Final.

• Appointed Spanish national coach in 1992, taking the team to two World Cups and the 1996 European Championships finals. Was either loved or hated by the fans and press for his often-criticised for his team selections.

• After an early exit from the 1998 World Cup, his fate was sealed when Spain lost to Cyprus in a Euro 2000 qualifer in September 1998.

• Failed to turn around the fortunes of Real Betis, moving on to Bilbao's great rivals Real Sociedad, who he saved from the drop.

PLAYER
CLESCENCO, Serghei
Forward, Moldovan, 171cm, 64kg
Born: 20.05.72, Moldova
Clubs: Zimbru Chisinau, Go Ahead Eagles (Hol), Zenit St Peterburg (Rus), Maccabi Haifa (Isr)
Full international (Moldova)

• Moldovan player of the year in 1999 and the country's most experienced international.

• Usually plays as a lone striker for the Moldovan national side.

Claudio Lopez

COCO, Francesco

Defender, Italian, 181cm, 78kg
Born: 08.01.77, Paterno, Italy
Clubs: Milan (1994-97), Vicenza (1997-98), Milan (1998-99), Torino (1999-)

• Left-back who made a name for himself in the 1994-95 season when he covered impressively for the injured **Paolo Maldini**. But since then, the presence of Maldini and his own injuries have inhibited his progress.

• A member of the Italian side which won the 2000 European Under-21 side, but was sent off in the Final.

COCU, Philip

Midfielder, Dutch, 182cm, 74kg
Born: 29.10.70, Eindhoven, Holland
Clubs: AZ (1988-90), Vitesse Arnhem (1990-95), PSV Eindhoven (1995-98), Barcelona (Spa) (1998-)
Full international (Holland) 46 caps/4 goals

• Hugely versatile all-rounder who can play at sweeper, centre-back central midfield, or on the left wing.

• Started out at the youth section of De Graafschap, but had to change when his family moved to Alkmaar.

• Made his League debut for AZ, playing two seasons in the Dutch second division before joining Vitesse.

• Broke a leg in his game for Vitesse but took over from the Ajax-bound John Van den Brom in 1993, impressing enough to earn a transfer to PSV in 1995.

• Joined Barcelona, despite strong interest from Internazionale, after the 1998 World Cup.

• International debut: v Germany, 24.04.96.

COELHO, Humberto

Portuguese
Born: 10.04.50
Full name: Humberto Manuel de Jesus Coelho

• National coach of Portugal from December 1997 to June 2000, when he resigned following his side's semi-final defeat by France at Euro 2000.

• A distinguished career as a player, an accomplished central defender with Benfica and Paris Saint-Germain.

• Won 64 caps over 15 years as an international for Portugal.

• Portugal's Player of the Year in 1981 and 1978 and a Portuguese league champion on eight occasions.

• Coached Salgueiros and Braga after retiring as a player, but then left to set up a soccer school and devote his time to working as a TV and radio pundit.

COHEN, Rafi

Goalkeeper, Israeli, 190cm, 84kg
Born: 28.11.70, Israel
Clubs: Hapoel Petah Tikva
Full international (Israel) 43 caps/0 goals

• The good-natured, quietly-spoken keeper has born the brunt of the Israel national team defence's mistakes, and his own. On more than one occasion he conceded early penalties against international opponents. Was sacked by former coach **Shlomo Scharf**, who blamed Cohen for Israel's 2-1 home loss to Spain in a Euro 2000 qualifier.

• After almost two years away from the team, Cohen was recalled by **Richard Moller Nielsen** as he began building his new squad.

PLAYER
COIS, Sandro

Midfielder, Italian, 178cm, 70kg
Born: 09.06.72, Fossano, Italy
Clubs: Saviglianese (1988-89), Torino (1989-94), Fiorentina (1994-)
Full international (Italy) 2 caps/0 goals
• Midfield ball winner, fetcher and carrier who won two full caps under **Cesare Maldini,** who had capped him 12 times at Under-21 level.
• Versatile enough to be played on either flank, in defence or, occasionally, in attack.

PLAYER
COLDING, Soren

Defender, Danish, 178cm, 75kg
Born: 02.09.72, Frem, Denmark
Clubs: Brondby (1991-)
Full international (Denmark) 29 caps/0 goals
• Long-time right-back for Brondby and one of the most reliable players in the Danish Superliga. Tough in the tackle, but distribution is not the best.
• A steady if unspectacular defender who was a regular in the Danish side at France 98 and Euro 2000 and has played a major role in Brondby's domestic success in recent years,
• International debut for Denmark against France in November 1996.

PLAYER
COLE, Andy

Forward, English, 180cm, 75kg
Born: 15.10.71, Nottingham, England
Clubs: Arsenal (1990-1992), Fulham (1991, loan), Bristol City (1992-93), Newcastle Utd (1993-95), Manchester United (1995-)
Full international (England) 7 caps/0 goals
• Prolific scorer at club level, but critics have suggested that he needs too many chances to be a reliable marksman at international level.
• Broke through under **Kevin Keegan**'s guidance at Newcastle.
• International debut: 29.03.95, v Uruguay.

Philip Cocu

PLAYER
COLE, Joe
Midfielder, English, 172cm, 70kg
Born: 08.11.81, London Islington, England
Clubs: West Ham (1998-)
• Supremely gifted teenager who has been hailed as the new saviour of English football.
• A broken leg in April 2000 ended any debate about whether he was too young to play at Euro 2000.

PLAYER
COLLAUTO, Mattia
Midfielder, Italian, 180cm, 70kg
Born: 10.11.73, Venice, Italy
Clubs: Como (1991-97), A. Catania (1994-95, loan), Cremonese (1997-99), Bari (1999-)
• Hard-working player who is effective down either flank. Signed by Bari in summer of 1999 to replace Fiorentina-bound **Mauro Bressan** and Juventus-bound **Gianluca Zambrotta**.

REFEREE
COLLINA, Pierluigi
Italian
Born: 13.02.60
• Works as a financial advisor.
• Awarded FIFA badge in 1995.
• The most recognisable official in European football, largely because of his distinctive bald head, but also because of a no-nonsense approach which has earned him the respect of players and coaches.
• In charge of 1996 Olympic Games Final between Nigeria and Argentina and 1999 Champions League Final between Manchester United and Bayern Munich.
• 'You usually know when a player has been really fouled or whether he is play-acting. It's to do with body language. There is something different about the way a player falls when it's involuntary. You don't necessarily see it if you are watching on TV. But down there on the pitch, you know.'

PLAYER
COLLINS, John
Midfielder, Scottish, 172cm, 68kg
Born: 31.01.68, Galsshiels, Scotland
Clubs: Hibernian (1985-90), Celtic (1990-96), Monaco (Fra) (1996-98), Everton (Eng) (1998-2000), Fulham (Eng) (2000-)
Full international (Scotland) 58 caps/12 goals
• Left-footed playmaker who has been the main creative force in Scotland's midfield in recent years.
• One of the first beneficiaries of the Bosman ruling when he joined Monaco on a free transfer from Celtic in July 1996.
• Left Everton in July 2000 to be reunited with **Jean Tigana**, his coach at Monaco.

PLAYER
COLLYMORE, Stan
Forward, English, 190cm, 89kg
Born: 22.01.71, Cannock, England
Clubs: Crystal Palace (1990-92), Southend (1992-93), Nottingham Forest (1993-95), Liverpool (1995-97), Aston Villa (1997-200), Fulham (1999, loan), Leicester (2000-)
Full international (England) 3 caps/0 goals
• Striker whose huge talent – running with pace at defenders – has been endangered by bust-ups, misunderstandings and disagreements with managers and coaches over the years.
• Failed to settle at Liverpool after refusing to move home from the Midlands following a £7million transfer in summer 1995. At Villa, manager **John Gregory** refused to speak to him, and eventually offloaded him to Leicester.
• 'I'm no angel, but I think I'm misunderstood more than anything else.'

COACH
COLOMBA, Franco
Italian
Born: 06.02.55
• Coach of Reggina since summer 1999.

• A useful midfielder with Bologna, he made his name as a coach with Salernitana, taking them to fifth place in the 1995-96 season and winning plaudits for the attractive football played.

• Was sacked by Salernitana the following season, but moved on to Reggina, where he steered them to seventh place in Serie B, earning a move to Vicenza. But he was sacked after 19 games of his first season as a Serie A coach. He returned to Reggina for the 1999-2000 season.

REFEREE
COLOMBO, Claude
French
Born: 01.10.60
• Professor of economic and social science.
• Earned his Fifa badge in 1995.

PLAYER
COLUCCI, Leonardo
Midfielder, Italian, 175cm, 70kg
Born: 29.12.72, Cerignola, Italy
Clubs: Cerignola (1989-93), Siracusa (1993-95), Lazio (1995-96), Reggiana (1996-97), Verona (1997-)
• Intelligent left-footed midfield organiser who was appointed as club captain during his fourth season with Verona.

PLAYER
COMISETTI, Alexandre
Forward, Swiss, 180cm, 74kg
Born: 21.07.73, Zurich, Switzerland
Clubs: Grasshopper, Yverdon (1992-93, Lausanne (1993-94), Yverdon (1994-95), Grasshopper (1995-99), Auxerre (Fra) (1999-)
Full international (Switzerland) 20 caps/3 goals
• A Swiss international left-winger or midfielder of no little pace and invention but who has not quite lived up to expectations following his move in 1999 from Grasshopper. Has been known to lead some of his Auxerre team-mates on mushroom picking expeditions.

Pierluigi Collina

CONGO, Edwin

Forward, Colombian, 183cm, 76kg
Born: 07.10.76, Bogota, Colombia
Clubs: Once Caldas, Real Madrid (Spa) (1999)
Real Valladolid (Spa) (1999-)
Full international (Colombia) 10 caps/2 goals
• Tall, strong striker with good technique who
joined Real Madrid after impressing for Colombia
at the 1999 Copa America, but was loaned out to
Valladolid as part of the deal that took keeper
Cesar to and from the Bernabeu stadium.

CONNOLLY, David

Forward, Irish, 172cm, 68kg
Born: 06.06.77, London Willesden, England
Clubs: Watford (1994-97), Feyenoord (Ho) (1997-
98), Wolverhampton (1998-99), Excelsior (Hol)
(1999-)
Full international (Rep. Ireland) 21 caps/1 goals
• Young striker who made a name for himself by
bucking the trend when favouring a move abroad
rather than to the English Premiership.

CONTE, Antonio

Midfielder, Italian, 178cm, 73kg
Born: 31.07.69, Lecce, Italy
Clubs: Lecce (1985-1991), Juventus (1991-)
Full international (Italy) 20 caps/2 goal
• Gutsy player who makes up for in attitude and
application what he lacks in natural talent.
• Returned from a serious knee injury to led Juve
to the 1998 Champions League Final against Real
Madrid, scoring a crucial late equaliser against
Olympiakos in the quarter-finals. 'There was only
four minutes left or we would have been out, and
in that hothouse it wasn't exactly easy to silence
85,000 passionate Greeks.'
• His career at Juventus was revived by the
arrival as coach of **Carlo Ancelotti**, who was a
similar type of player himself.

CONTICCHIO, Alessandro

Midfielder, Italian, 179cm, 71kg
Born: 19.01.74, Celleno, Italy
Clubs: Internazionale (1993-94), Gualdo (1994-
97), Lecce (1997-)
• Tough-tackling midfielder who graduated from
the youth ranks at Inter.

CONTINI, Giorgio

Forward, Swiss, 172cm, 66kg
Born: 04.01.74, Switzerland
Clubs: Winterthur (1992-94), Frauenfeld (1994-
95), Baden (1995-96), St Gallen (1996-)
• Strong-willed, wholehearted striker. Powerful
right-foot shot and says he models his play on
the Italian **Marco Simone**. Made great strides
during the 1999-2000 season.

CONTRA, Cosmin

Defender, Romanian, 180cm, 74kg
Born: 15.12.75, Timiisoara, Romania
Clubs: Dinamo Bucharest (1995-99), Alaves (Spa)
(1999-)
Full international (Romania) 15 caps/0 goals
• Promising right-back who been in and out of
the Romanian side over the past four years.
• Began his career with his hometown team
Politehnica Timisoara and then established
himself over three seasons at Dinamo Bucharest
before a move to newly-promoted Alaves in
summer 1999.
• Made his international debut for Romania
against Georgia in April 1996 but failed to dislodge
Dan Petrescu as first-choice right-back.
• Played a key role in Alaves' surprise top six
finish in the Spanish League in 1999-2000.
• Picked out by Romania coach **Emerich Jenei**
before Euro 2000 as a young player who
deserved a regular opportunity at international
level.

PLAYER
CONTRERAS, Pablo

Defender, Chilean, 180cm, 73kg
Born: 11.09.78, Santiago, Chile
Clubs: Colo Colo, Monaco (Fra)
Full international (Chile) 6 caps/0 goals
• Chilean international left-back with lots of snap in the tackle and solid distribution skills. Deserves more than a role as back-up at Monaco.

PLAYER
COOL, Fabian

Goalkeeper, French, 186cm, 80kg
Born: 29.09.74, L'Isle-Adam, France
Clubs: Auxerre (1994-).
• A worthy successor between the Auxerre posts to French international keepers, Joel Bats, Bruno Martini and **Lionel Charbonnier**.
• With the club since the age of 12, his first taste of the big-time was a Cup-winner Cup quarter-final against Arsenal in March 1995 which Auxerre lost 2-1 on aggregate.

ADMINISTRATOR
COOPER, Keith

• English head of FIFA's press relations since 1995. Always seen alongside FIFA president **Sepp Blatter** at press conferences.

PLAYER
CORDOBA, Ivan

Defender, Colombian
Born: 11.08.76, Medellin, Colombia
Clubs: Deportivo Rionegra (1993-94) Atletico Nacional (1994-97), San Lorenzo (Arg) (1998-2000), Internazionale (Ita) (2000-)
Full international (Colombia)
• Speedy centre-back who moved from San Lorenzo to Inter in January 2000 in a £10million transfer.
• Made his name with a weakened Colombia tean at the 1997 Copa America. His pace was a huge asset during the 1998 World Cup qualifiers.

Keith Cooper

• Dropped from Colombia's France 98 squad on the eve of the finals after losing form at club level.

• Re-established himself in the Colombia side for the 1999 Copa America after improved club form for San Lorenzo.

• 'He's not just the fastest defender in South America, he's the fastest in the world.' Oscar Ruggeri, San Lorenzo coach.

PLAYER
CORREA, Fernando Edgardo
Forward, Uruguayan, 179cm, 79kg
Born: 06.01.74, Montevideo, Uruguay
Clubs: River Plate Montevideo (1990-95), Atletico Madrid (Spa) (1995-96), Racing Santander (Spa) (1996-98), Atletico Madrid (Spa) (1998-)

• Skilful and fast striker who got a second chance at Atletico Madrid after failing to impress in his first spell in the Spanish capital following a £1million transfer from River Plate of Montevideo in 1995.

• Moved to Racing Santander in the summer of 1996 and scored 27 goals in two seasons, persuading Atletico to exercise the buy-back clause in the deal with Racing.

PLAYER
CORT, Carl
Forward, English, 194cm, 79kg
01.11.79, London, England
Clubs: Wimbledon (1996-2000), Lincoln (1997, loan), Newcastle (2000-)

• Product of the Wimbledon youth system, a young striker with good ball control despite his size.

• Suffered relegation with Wimbledon in May 2000, but was snapped up by Newcastle in a £7million transfer.

• England Under-21 international.

ADMINISTRATOR
CORTES GARCIA, Pedro
• President of Spanish club Valencia.

PLAYER
COSTACURTA, Alessandro
Defender, Italian, 182cm, 75kg
Born: 24.04.66, Orago, Italy
Clubs: Milan (1986-), Monza (1986-87, loan)
Full international (Italy) 59 caps/2 goals

• Versatile, experienced centre-back who has won 18 national and international titles in a 15-year career with Milan.

• Made his international debut for Italy against Norway in November 1991 in **Arrigo Sacchi**'s first game as national coach.

• Suspensions meant he missed out on Milan's 1994 European Cup victory over Barcelona and Italy's 1994 World Cup Final against Brazil.

• Nicknamed Billy because of his support as a kid for a Milan basketball team of the same name

PLAYER
COUPET, Gregory
Goalkeeper, French, 181cm, 80kg
Born: 31.12.72, Le Puy-en-Velay, France
Clubs: Saint-Etienne (1993-96), Lyon (1996-)

• Talented keeper whose strengths are coming for crosses and his ability to prevail in one-on-one situations. Kicking, however is another story

• Lyon fans do not generally appreciate players who arrive at their club from local rivals Saint-Etienne but Coupet is an exception.

COACH
COURBIS, Rolland
French
Born: 12.08.53

• Coach of Lens since summer 2000, when he replaced the sacked Francois Brisson.

• A colourful Mediterranean character who is a French media darling courtesy of his happy-go-lucky persona, quick-wit and undiplomatic language. But quips and barbs aside, his football credentials are impeccable.

• As a steely libero, he won the French League title three times, once with Marseille (1972) and

vice with Monaco (1978 and 1982).
Coached Toulon, Toulouse and Bordeaux (twice)
before taking charge at Marseille in summer 1997.
Took Marseille to second place in the French
league and a place in the UEFA Cup Final, which
they lost to Parma, but was sacked after a
disastrous 1999-2000 season.

'At first Marseille president **Yves Marchand**
told me he knew nothing about football and
would let me get on with the job. Then he gave
me a fitness guru who injured 24 of my players,
and lumbered me with a nutritionist, physio and a
doctor. Don't ever tell him, Marseille's defence is
not watertight. He'll employ a lifeguard.'

ADMINISTRATOR
RAGNOTTI, Sergio
Italian
Born: 09.01.40
Multi-millionaire owner of Lazio who has
poured millions into the club since becoming
president in 1992.

Has made his money from a business empire
which is centred on his merchant bank Cragnotti
and Partners Capital Investment. Key to his
wealth has been the success of a processed
foods company, Cirio, which sponsors Lazio. In
1999, Cirio employed 11,000 people and had a
turnover of £740million.

'Football is the most global business of the lot.
But in Italy, football is seen as the plaything of
the rich and not as part of the entertainment
industry. This is simply an old-fashioned
mentality which, fortunately for us, still prevails. I
say fortunately because otherwise we would not
have been able to overturn the established power
balance with the northern clubs.'

BRASSON, Bertrand
Defender, Belgian, 178cm, 79kg
Born: 05.10.71, Brussels, Belgium
Clubs: Anderlecht (1990-96), Napoli (Ita) (1996-
98), Anderlecht (1998-)

Full international (Belgium) 22 caps/1 goal
• Attacking full-back who has been back at
Anderlecht for the past two seasons after a two-
year spell in Italy where he suffered relegation
with Napoli.

PLAYER
CRESPO, Hernan
Forward, Argentinian, 184cm, 78kg
Born: 05.07.75, Florida, Argentina
Clubs: River Plate (1993-96), Parma (Ita) (1996-
2000) Lazio (Ita) (2000-)
Full international (Argentina) 21 caps/7 goals
• Argentinian who has been among the best
strikers in Serie A in recent seasons and hit the
headlines in summer 2000 with a world-record
transfer from Parma to Lazio.
• Made his name under then coach Daniel
Passarella at River Plate, winning the
Libertadores Cup and earning a move to Italy.
• Member of the Argentina team beaten by
Nigeria in the Final of the 1996 Olympics.
• Became the world's most expensive player for
two and a half weeks when he joined Lazio in
July 2000 in a transfer which valued him at just
under £37million. **Luis Figo**'s move to Real
Madrid eclipsed Crespo's record.

PLAYER
CRISTALLINI, Paolo
Midfielder, Italian, 179cm, 73kg
Born: 20.09.71, Milan, Italy
Clubs: Pisa (1989-94), Torino (1994-97), Bologna
(1997-98), Piacenza (1998-)
• Powerful midfielder who began his career as a
defender at Pisa.

PLAYER
CROSA, Diego
Defender, Argentinian, 180cm, 80kg
Born: 18.04.76, Rosario, Argentina
Clubs: Newell's Old Boys (1994-99), Real Betis
(Spa) (1999-)

- Argentinian defender who impressed in his first season in Spain with Betis following a £2million transfer from Newell's Old Boys.
- Was likely to leave Betis following relegation at the end of the 1999-2000 season, with a number of clubs tracking him.
- Holds joint Argentinian/Italian nationality.

COACH
CRUYFF, Johan
Dutch
Born: 25.04.47
- Legendary figure in the European game, forever associated with the 'total football' played by Ajax and Holland in the 1970s.
- Began at Ajax Amsterdam aged 12, after his mother, who worked as a cleaner at the club, persuaded the coaching staff to take her boy on.
- Made his international debut aged 19 and went on to inspire Ajax and Holland throughout the 1970s.
- Joined Barcelona for a world-record £922,000 after winning a hat-trick of European Cups with Ajax.
- Ended his playing career back in Holland at Feyenoord after a spell in the North American Soccer League.
- Voted European Footballer of the Year in 1971, 1972 and 1973.
- Coached Ajax to the 1987 European Cup-winners Cup. Took charge of Barcelona in 1989, winning four successive Spanish League titles and the 1992 European Cup in what is now seen as a golden era for the club.
- Ousted from Barcelona in 1996, he still lives in the city. But heart problems in recent years mean he is unlikely to take on another coaching position, preferring instead to stay in touch with the game through media work.

PLAYER
CRUYFF, Jordi
Forward, Dutch, 184cm, 68kg
Born: 09.02.74, Amsterdan

Clubs: Ajax, Barcelona (Spa) (1993-96), Manchester Utd (Eng) (1996-2000), Celta Vigo (Spa) (1999, loan), Alaves (Spa) (2000-)
Full international (Holland) 9 caps/1 goal
- Son of **Johan Cruyff**, born during his father's time in Barcelona and named after the patron saint of Catalunya.
- Played under his father at Barcelona, earning international recognition by Holland.
- Time at United hit by injuries and while he has inevitably suffered through comparisons with his father, the family name has also opened many doors during his career.

PLAYER
CRUZ, Julio Ricardo
Forward, Argentinian, 186cm, 80kg
Born: 10.10.74, Santiago del Estero, Argentina
Clubs: Banfield (1993-96), River Plate (1996-97), Feyenoord (1997-2000), Bologna (Ita) (2000-)
Full international (Argentina) 5 caps/0 goals
- Powerful striker with impressive physique, strong scoring instincts and good touch on the ball.
- Nicknamed El Jardinero (the Gardener).
- Scored 15 goals in his first season at Feyenoord, followed by 15 in 1998-99.

PLAYER
CUELLAR, Angel
Full name: Angel Manuel Cuellar Llanos
Forward, Spanish, 173cm, 73kg
Born: 13.09.72, Badajoz, Spain
Clubs: Real Betis (1990-95), Barcelona (1995-97), Real Betis (1997-)
Full international (Spain) 2 caps/0 goals
- Striker whose career has run into trouble since a move back to Betis from Barcelona, where he failed to hold down a regular place.
- Was expected to move on to a new club in summer 2000.

CUNNINGHAM, Kenny
Defender, Irish, 182cm, 74kg
Born: 28.06.74, Dublin, Ireland
Clubs: Millwall (1989-94), Wimbledon (1994-)
Full international (Rep Ireland) 31 caps/0 goals
• Attacking right-back who can also fill in at centre-half. Suffered relegation with Wimbledon in May 2000.

COACH
CUPER, Hector
Argentinian
Born: 16.11.55
• Has a magnificent record in Spain, establishing Mallorca as a power, first in the Spanish League and then in Europe, all achieved while working with limited resources.
• Took Mallorca to the 1998 Spanish Cup Final, where they lost on penalties to Barcelona, then reached the Cup-winners Cup Final the following season, which Mallorca lost to Lazio.
• Moved to Valencia in summer of 1999 and steered them to the 2000 Champions League Final.
• Played eight times for Argentina, but just missed out on a place in the 1978 World Cup squad.
• Made his name as a coach of modest Argentinian club Lanus, and was a virtual unknown when he arrived in Spain to take charge of Mallorca.
• Born in Argentina but has English roots: his great grandfather was called Cooper.

COACH
CURBISHLEY, Alan
English
Born: 08.11.57
• One of the most promising young managers in the English game who has twice won promotion to the Premier League with Charlton.

PLAYER
CURCIC, Sasa
Midfielder, Yugoslav, 176cm, 67kg
Born: 14.02.72, Belgrade
Clubs: Bolton (Eng), Aston Villa (Eng), Crystal Palace (Eng), New York/New Jersey MetroStars (US), Motherwell (Sco)
Full international (Yugoslavia) 14 caps/1 goal
• The Yugoslavian international has had an eventful career which has incorporated spells with Bolton, Aston Villa and Crystal Palace, as well as a stint in the US Major League with New York/New Jersey Metrostars. He arrived at Fir Park midway through last season but has yet to make any significant impact on the Scottish game.

PLAYER
CURTIAN, Alexandr
Midfielder, Moldovan, 174cm, 68kg
Born: 11.02.74, Moldova
Clubs: Zimbru Chisinau, Widzew (Pol), Hamburg (Ger), Zenit St Peterburg (Rus)
Full international (Moldova) 30 caps/2 goals
• Moldovan player of the year in 1993 and 1998, and captain and playmaker of the national side.

PLAYER
CUTAJAR, Michael
Midfielder, Maltese
Born: 14.02.71, Malta
Clubs: Birkirkara
Full international (Malta) 7 caps/1 goal
• Central midfielder who has been a key figure in Birkirkara's surge to the top of Maltese football.

PLAYER
CVITANOVIC, Mario
Defender, Croatian, 182cm, 78kg
Born: 06.05.75, Croatia
Clubs: Dinamo Zagreb
Full international (Croatia) 6 caps/0 goals
• Promising defender who has played for Croatia Zagreb in the Champions League and has been

linked with a move abroad.

CZERESZEWSKI, Sylwester
Midfielder, Polish, 183cm, 82kg
Born: 04.10.71, Poland
Clubs: Stomil Olsztyn, Legia Warsaw
Full international (Poland) 23 caps/4 goals
• A versatile player who can operate anywhere in midfield or attack. Previously with Stomil Olsztyn, where he was nicknamed Pele.

CZERWIEC, Ryszard
Midfielder, Polish, 174cm, 74kg
Born: 28.02.68, Poland
Clubs: Widzew, Guingamp (1997-98) Wisla Krakow (1998-)
Full international (Poland) 28 caps/0 goals
• After spending five years with Widzew moved to Guingamp in 1997. Returned to Poland after only a year. Playmaker with great distribution and vision who led his team to the 1998-99 championship. Despite 28 caps he has not yet performed for Poland as well as he has at club level.

D

DA COSTA, Francisco
Midfielder, Portuguese, 181cm, 74kg
Born: 01.12.74, Lisbon, Portugal
Clubs: Madeira, Monaco (Fra)
Full international (Portugal) 7 caps/1 goal
• Versatile Portuguese international who can play full-back or as a defensive midfielder. Combative and tactically-aware, the Lisbon-born player is not bereft of technical polish either.
• Nicknamed Costinha.
• Won the French League with Monaco in May 2000, but a transfer to Sporting Lisbon fell through in summer 2000.

PLAYER
DA ROCHA, Frederic
Forward, French, 176cm, 70kg
Born: 16.09.74, Cenon, France
Clubs: Nantes (1995-)
• A product of Nantes' prolific youth scheme, he has the versatility to play as an orthodox striker or slightly deeper on the right side. His one-touch play and movement is of a high standard, but he could certainly be more ruthless in front of goal.

PLAYER
DABANOVIC, Mladen
Goalkeeper, Slovenian, 196cm, 94kg
Born: 13.09.71, Slovenia
Clubs: Maribor (1992-96), Rudar (1995-99), Lokeren (Bel) (1999-)
Full international (Slovenia) 17 caps/0 goals
• Keeper who played in all three of Slovenia's matches at Euro 2000, having been a regular squad member since making his international debut against Iceland in February 1998.
• Says he would have studied to become a mechanical engineer if he had not been a footballer.

PLAYER
DABIZAS, Nicos
Defender, Greek, 184cm, 75kg
Born: 03.08.72, Amyndaeo, Greece
Clubs: Olympiakos (1994-97), Newcastle (Eng) (1997-)
Full international (Greece) 4 caps/2 goals
• Centre-back who can also play in midfield. Dangerous in the air at set-pieces.

PLAYER
DABO, Ousmane
Midfielder, French, 185cm, 83kg
Born: 08.02.77, Laval, France
Clubs: Rennes (1995-98), Internazionale (Ita) (1998-99), Vicenza (Ita) (1998, loan), Parma (Ita) (1999) Monaco (2000-)
• One of a number of young players plucked by Inter from Rennes in the summer of 1998, before being sent out on loan to Vicenza.
• Moved on to Parma in 1999, but could not break into a midfield dominated by **Dino Baggio** and **Alain Boghossian**, and moved back to France in summer 2000, as a makeweight that took **Sabri Lamouchi** to Italy.
• French Under-21 international.
• Surname prounounced Dah bo.

PLAYER
DABROWSKI, Christoph
Midfielder, German, 195cm, 80kg
Born: 01.07.78, Poland
Clubs: Hertha Berlin, Preussen Berlin, Schoneberg, Werder Bremen (1995-)
• Lanky German Under-21 midfielder whose forte is ball-winning and and striking accurate long diagonal balls. Born in Poland but now a naturalised German.
• Surname pronounced Dah brof ski.

Ali Daei

PLAYER
DACOURT, Olivier
Midfielder, French, 180cm, 78kg
Born: 25.09.74, Montreuil-sous-Bois
Clubs: Strasbourg (1992-98), Everton (Eng) (1998-99), Lens (1999-2000), Leeds (Eng) (2000-)
• Talented midfielder whose game took on an extra dimension during a season in the Premiership with Everton (1998-99). At Lens in the 1999-2000 season, he continued to make great strides, graduating from defensive midfielder to creator-in chief.
• Hits a mean free-kick and after years of goal-shyness, his finishing is finally coming together too – witness the marvellous chip with which he scored against Atletico Madrid in the UEFA Cup.
• Moved back to England in summer 2000 following a £7million transfer to Leeds.
• Surname pronounced Da kor.

PLAYER
DADASON, Rikhardur
Forward, Icelandic, 189cm, 84kg
Born: 26.04.72, Iceland
Clubs: Fram (1990-96), KR (1996), Kalamata (Gre) (1996-97), KR (1997), Viking Stavanger (Nor) (1998-2000), Stoke City (Eng) (2000-)
Full international (Iceland) 31 caps/9 goals
• Bustling international forward who won the hearts of Icelandic fans by scoring against world champions France in Reykjavik in 1998. Sporadically linked with a number of clubs around Europe.

PLAYER
DAEI, Ali
Forward, Iranian, 188cm, 82kg
Born: 21.03.69, Tehran, Iran.
Clubs: Estghal, Pirouzi, Al-Sadd Douha, Arminia Bielefeld (Ger), Bayern Munich (Ger), Hertha Berlin (Ger) (1999-)
Full international (Iran)

• The Iranian star striker lost his place in the Hertha starting line-up when **Alex** arrived. But as Daei proved in the Champions League in the 1999-2000 season, he is a frontrunner of high quality. A constant threat in the air and there is a touch of Cantona in him, the same upright stance and excellent close control.

• Dropped from the Iran squad during the qualifying campaign for France 98, but was reinstated when fans organised a petition the Internet.

• Voted Asian Footballer of the Year in 1999.

• Surname pronounced Die ee.

PLAYER
DAEMS, Filip
Midfielder, Belgian, 180cm, 74kg
Born: 31.10.78, Belgium
Clubs: Lierse (1998-)
• Left-side midfielder who got his chance at Lierse following the transfer of **Nico Van Kerckhoven** to Schalke.

PLAYER
DAEV, Vyacheslav
Defender, Russian, 185cm, 80kg
Born: 06.09.72, Russia
Clubs: Baltika Kaliningrad (1996-98), Torpedo Moscow (1999-)
• A key player at Torpedo, when he marshalls the Russian League's meanest defence. Strong central defender who is good at initiating the attack.

REFEREE
DALLAS, Hugh
Scottish
Born: 26.10.57
• Company director.
• Earned his FIFA badge in 1991.

PLAYER
DALMAT, Stephane
Midfielder, French, 180cm, 79kg
Born: 16.02.79, Tours, France

Clubs: Chateauroux (1997-98), Lens (1998-99), Marseille (1999-2000), Paris Saint-Germain (2000-)
• The complete midfield package of pace, skill and physical force and rightly considered one of France's brightest prospects. Can play in central, left or right midfield – the latter is his favourite slot – but whatever his position, his electrifying forward bursts are a constant theme.

• In three years, he has been the subject of three big-money transfers totalling £17.2 million (Chateauroux to Lens; Lens to Marseille; Marseille to Paris Saint-Germain).

• French Under-21 international.

• Surname pronounced Dal mah.

PLAYER
DAMJANAC, Nikola
Goalkeeper, Yugoslav, 190cm, 83kg
Born: 27.10.71, Mostar, Bosnia
Clubs: Partizan Belgrade
Full international (Yugoslavia)
• Once considered a great talent of Yugoslav football and was a member of the national team squad in 1999. But fatal errors in a UEFA Cup game against Leeds, as well as injuries, relegated him to the bench. Spent one season in the Dutch league with Roda.

PLAYER
DANI
Full name: Daniel da Cruz Carvalho
Forward, Portuguese, 182cm, 70kg
Born: 02.11.76, Lisbon, Portugal
Clubs: Sporting Lisbon (1994-96), West Ham (Eng) (1996, loan), Ajax (Hol) (1996-)
Full international (Portugal) 9 caps/0 goals
• Winger who attracts headlines (and female fans) because of his good looks, but also a useful footballer with skill, technique and pace.

• Was tipped to move on from Ajax in the summer of 2000 with the arrival of **Co Adriaanse**.

PLAYER
DANI Garcia Lora
Forward, Spanish, 183cm, 73kg
Born: 22.12.74, Barcelona, Spain
Clubs: Real Madrid (1992-98), Zaragoza (1995-97, loan), Mallorca (1998-99), Barcelona (1999-)
Full international (Spain) 4 caps/1 goal
• Striker who was rejected by Real Madrid and eventually sold by Mallorca to Barcelona for £10million.
• Earned a reputation as a prodigious goalscorer in the youth ranks at Real Madrid, but played only two first-team games at the Bernabeu before being loaned to Zaragoza, where he formed a useful partnership with **Fernando Morientes**.
• Returned to Real in the summer of 1997 as a partner for new signing Morientes, but he failed to make an impact and was sold for £1.6million to Mallorca in 1998.
• Enjoyed a spectacular season at Mallorca, scoring 12 League goals as Mallorca reached the European Cup-winners Cup Final against Lazio.
• International debut v Italy, November 1999.

PLAYER
DANI MALLO
Full name: Daniel Mallo Castro
Goalkeeper, Spanish, 185cm, 78kg
Born: 15.01.79, La Coruna, Spain
Clubs: Deportivo La Coruna (1999-)
• Highly promising young keeper who is tipped to take over as the first-choice at Deportivo in the near future.

COACH
DANIIL, Vasilis
Greek
Born: 03.08.38
• National coach of Greece since March 1999 and the departure of **Anghel Iordanescu**.
• Experienced Greek club coach who has had three spells in charge of Panathinaikos, twice winning the League and Cup.

PLAYER
DANJOU, Frederic
Defender, French, 186cm, 80kg
Born: 28.09.74 Clamart, France
Clubs: Auxerre (1994-99), Oviedo (Spa) (1999-)
• Strong accomplished central defender who became Real Oviedo's record signing when he joined from Auxerre for £2.5million.
• A French League and Cup winner with Auxerre in 1996.

PLAYER
DARASZ, Thomas
Forward, Austrian, 184cm, 77kg
Born: 05.11.77, Vienna, Austria
Clubs: Austria Vienna (1996-)
• Central midfielder who is now a well-established member of the first team at Austria Vienna.
• A competant all-rounder who is as adept at passing as tackling.

PLAYER
DARIO SILVA
Full name: Dobray Dario Silva Pareira
Forward, Uruguayan, 178cm, 71kg
Born: 02.11.72, Treinta y Tres, Uruguay
Clubs: Defensor (1992), Penarol (1993-95), Cagliari (Ita) (1995-98), Espanyol (Spa) (1999), Malaga (Spa) (1999-2000)
Full international (Uruguay)
• Uruguayan striker who spent the 1998-99 and 1999-2000 seasons on loan in Spain after coming unstuck with Cagliari in Italy.

PLAYER
DATORU, George
Forward, Nigeria, 176cm, 76kg
Born: 25.05.77, Port Harcourt, Nigeria
Clubs: Admira Wacker (Aut) (1997-98), Vorwarts Steyr (Aut) (1998-99), Austria Vienna (Aut) (1999-)
• Nigerian striker who has adapted well to life in Austria, despite relegation with Vorwarts Steyr. Has struck a useful partnership with **Christian**

Mayrleb since moving to Austria Vienna.

PLAYER
DAUGAARD, Kim

Midfielder, Danish, 179cm, 73kg
Born: 29.07.78, Denmark
Clubs: Herfolge, Brondby
Full international (Denmark) 2 caps/0 goals
• Playmaker who has established himself as a key man for Brondby in recent years, earning call-ups to the Danish squad, and winning his first cap in January 2000 against Sweden.

COACH
DAUM, Christoph

German
Born: 24.10.53
• Inspirational coach of Bayer Leverkusen and the man earmarked to become national coach of Germany in June 2001.
• Modest playing career with Eintracht Duisburg (1972-75) and FC Koln amateurs (1975-81) and began his coaching career with FC Koln's youth section, before progressing to assistant coach in 1985 and head coach for four seasons from 1986.
• Guided Stuttgart to the 1991-92 Bundesliga title before moving on to Turkey, where he spent two seasons in charge of Besiktas.
• Returned to Germany for the 1996-97 season and has overseen a transformation in the fortunes of Bayer Leverkusen, leading them to second, third, second and second place finishes in his four years in charge.
• A risk-taker who is never afraid to go for broke with an-out attacking strategy and always open to new ideas which might give his team the edge – in the 1999-2000 season he brought in a motivational guru who had the players walking over hot coals.
• He will forever be remembered for fielding too many foreigners when his Stuttgart side faced Leeds United in the Champions League in 1992-93.

Christoph Daum

Edgar
Davids

PLAYER
DAVIDS, Edgar
Midfielder, Dutch, 169cm, 68kg
Born: 13.03.73, Paramaribo, Surinam
Clubs: Ajax (1991-1996), Milan (Ita) (1996-1997), Juventus (Ita) (1997-)
Full international (Holland) 35 caps/4 goals
• Talent, technique and fighting spirit make Davids a key man for club and country.
• World-class midfielder who combines aggression with perceptive passing and visionary control.
• Grew up in Amsterdam, he came through the famed youth system at Ajax, where then coach **Louis Van Gaal** dubbed him 'The Pitbull'.
• By the age of 24 had won the Champions League, the European Supercup, the UEFA Cup, the World Club Cup, three Dutch leagues and the Dutch Cup.
• Stormed out of the Dutch training camp at Euro 96 after a row with coach **Guus Hiddink** over the influence of senior white players in the squad. At the time Davids was bitter that he and other young black players were on lowly-paid contracts at Ajax, despite having won the European Cup.
• Matured sufficiently for **Frank Rijkaard** to appoint him as Dutch vice-captain.
• Wears specially-made basketball-style goggles to protect his eyes after an operation to correct myopia. Cynics have suggested that the glasses are worn more for cosmetic than medical purposes.
• **Guus Hiddink** on Davids: 'He has more passion in his right toe than other internationals have in both legs.'
• **Johan Cruyff** on Davids: 'He provides emotion, fire. Holland absolutely need that fire to go further.'
• Joined Milan on a free transfer after Euro 2000, but broke a leg and failed to settle. Moved to Juventus for £3.4million in December 1997.
• Famously got out of his Porsche and beat up two would-be muggers who had stopped him at traffic lights in Milan shortly after his move there in 1996.
• 'Going to Milan was a big mistake. It was a bad time, the most bitter experience of my club career. But I have always tried to use it in a

positive way. It has allowed me to mature as a person. It taught me that being a world-class footballer is about being in control.'

COACH
DAVIES, Billy
Scottish
Born: 31.05.64
• Signed for Rangers as a schoolboy but, after failing to make any impact at Ibrox, turned out for St Mirren, Dunfermline and Motherwell in a 17-year playing career.
• Appointed manager of Motherwell at the age of 34, the youngest ever Scottish Premier League manager, but his lack of experience has been mitigated by his exceptional enthusiam and tactical awareness. Some inspired signings (Andy Goram, **John Spencer**, Ged Brannan and Ben Goodman) have helped push 'Well into the top half of the division, and the Fir Park side only narrowly missed out on UEFA Cup qualification in 1999-2000.

ADMINISTRATOR
DAVIES, DAVID
• Executive director of the English Football Association since 1999.
• A former TV reporter who became the FA's chief press officer before stepping up to a more general role in the aftermath of the resignations by secretary Graham Kelly and chairman Keith Wiseman.
• The author of **Glenn Hoddle**'s account of the 1998 World Cup, a book which ultimately cost Hoddle his job.

PLAYER
DAVIES, Kevin
Forward, English, 183cm, 85kg
Born: 26.03.77, Sheffield, England
Clubs: Chesterfield (1994-97), Southampton (1997-98), Blackburn (1998-99), Southampton (1999-)
• Strong young striker with good touch who starred in Chesterfield's 1997 run to the semi-finals of the FA Cup.

• Signed by Blackburn for in excess of £7million, but injuries and a relegation struggle conspired against him and he returned to Southampton for £1million.
• England Under-21 international.

PLAYER
DE ASCENTIS, Diego
Midfielder, Italian, 178cm, 77kg
Born: 31.07.74, Como, Italy
Clubs: Como (1995-96), Bari (1996-99), Milan (1999-)
• Former Italian Under-21 international who was signed by Milan in summer of 1999 to provide cover for **Demetrio Albertini**.
• A central midfield ballwinner who made his name at Bari after starting out at his hometown club Como.

PLAYER
DE BILDE, Gilles
Forward, Belgian, 180cm, 72kg
Born: 09.06.71, Zellik, Belgium
Clubs: Eendracht Aalst (1994-95), Anderlecht (1995-97), PSV (1997-99), Sheffield Wednesday (1999-)
Full international (Belgium) 24 caps/1 goal
• Player of the season in his first year at Eendracht Aalst, then moved to Anderlecht but couldn't live up to expectations and was banned after assaulting an Aalst player and fled to Holland, where he had an unsuccessful spell with PSV.
• A speedy but temperamental striker, most dangerous if given space.
• International debut: 16.11.94, Macedonia (1-1).
• Surname pronounced De Bill der.

PLAYER
DE BOER, Frank
Defender, Dutch, 179cm, 79kg
Born: 15.05.70, Grootebrock, Holland
Clubs: Ajax (1988-98), Barcelona (Spa) (1998-)
Full international (Holland) 81 caps/9 goals
• Accomplished left-sided centre-half who remains

Ed De Goey

one of the world's best defenders despite a difficult 1999-2000 season at Barcelona where he struggled to hold down a first-team place.

• A key member of the Ajax team throughout the 1990s, winning the UEFA Cup in 1992, the Champions League in 1995, five Dutch League titles (1990, 1994, 1994, 1996, 1997), the 1995 World Club Cup, and 1995 European Supercup.

• Missed Euro 96 through injury but was one of the best players at the 1998 World Cup, with some outstanding performances as Holland reached the semi-finals.

• Joined Barcelona in January 1999 after a protracted dispute ended in a £8million transfer finally being completed.

• Twin brother of **Ronald De Boer**.

• Father Cees is a former professional player.

• International debut v Italy, 26.09.90.

PLAYER
DE BOER, Ronald

Midfielder, Dutch, 179cm, 79kg
Born: 15.05.70, Grootebrock, Holland
Clubs: Ajax (1988-91), Twente (1991-93), Ajax (1993-98), Barcelona (Spa) (1998-2000), Rangers (Sco) (2000-)
Full international (Holland) 61 caps/13 goals

• Right-sided midfielder who has followed a similar career path to his identical twin brother **Frank de Boer** with the notable exception of 18 months spent at Twente.

• A key member of the Ajax team throughout the 1990s, winning the UEFA Cup in 1992, the Champions League in 1995, five Dutch League titles (1990, 1994, 1994, 1996, 1997), the 1995 World Club Cup, and 1995 European Supercup.

• Skilful and pacy, he can play anywhere on the right flank, but prefers right wing to right-back.

• Voted Dutch Footballer of the Year in 1994.

• Joined Barcelona in January 1999 after a protracted dispute ended in a £8million transfer finally being completed.

• International debut v San Marino, 24.03.93.

PLAYER
DE BOECK, Glen
Defender, Belgian, 189cm, 78kg
Born: 22.08.71, Belgium
Clubs: Mechelen (1992-95), Anderlecht (1995-)
Full international (Belgium) 23 caps/0 goals
• Was dropped to the bench by Anderlecht coach
Aime Antheunis halfway through the 1999-2000
season, but fought back, although he also lost his
place in the national team during that period.
• Strong in the air, has a good tackle. But loses
his concentration sometimes and gets too many
cards.

PLAYER
DE BRUL, Tjorven
Midfielder, Belgian, 188cm, 82kg
Born: 22.06.73, Belgium
Clubs: Lokeren (1991-94), Club Brugge (1994-)
Full international (Belgium) 10 caps/0 goals
• Accomplished full-back who has enjoyed
considerable success with Club Brugge in the
Belgian League, but has not been a favourite of
Belgian national coach **Robert Waseige**.

COACH
DE CANIO, Luigi
Italian
Born: 26.09.57
• Succeeded **Alberto Zaccheroni** at Udinese
and won many admirers for his approach after
making his name at Pescara in Serie B.
• An intellectual who demands hard work and
discipline from his players.

PLAYER
DE CLER, Tim
Defender, Dutch, 183cm, 70kg
Born: 08.11.78, Leiden, Holland
Clubs: Ajax (1998-)
• Dutch Under-21 international left-back who has
lost out at Ajax since the arrival of **Cristian
Chivu** during the 1999-2000 season.

PLAYER
DE FRANCHESHI, Ivone
Midfieler, Italian, 172cm, 68kg
Born: 01.01.74, Padova, Italy
Clubs: Padova (1993-98), Venezia (1998-99),
Sporting Lisbon (Por) (1999-)
• Italian whose arrival at Sporting Lisbon during
the 1999-2000 proved decisive in Sporting
winning their first League title for 18 years.

PLAYER
DE GIER, Jack
Forward, Dutch, 182cm, 81kg
Born: 06.08.68, Schijndel, Holland
Clubs: Den Bosch (1988-91), Cambuur (1991-94),
Go Ahead Eagles (1994-95), Willem II (1995-97),
Lierse (Bel) (1998), NEC (1998-)
• Striker in the Gerd Muller mould: deadly in the
penalty box, physical strong and a hard worker.
Obviously not as good as Muller, but has not
always got the credit he deserves.

PLAYER
DE GOEY, Ed
Goalkeeper, Dutch, 197cm, 83kg
Born: 02.12.66, Gouda, Holland
Clubs: Sparta Rotterdam (1985-90), Feyenoord
(1990-97), Chelsea (1997-)
Full international (Holland) 31 caps/0 goals
• Experienced keeper who has been a regular
selection at Chelsea despite **Gianluca Vialli**'s
rotation policy.
• First-choice for Holland at the 1994 World Cup,
but lost his place to **Edwin Van der Sar** during
the Euro 96 qualifiers.
• A member of the Dutch squad at Euro 96,
Euro 2000 and the 1998 World Cup.
• International debut: 16.12.92, v Turkey
(won 3-1).

DE HAAN, Foppe

Dutch

Born: 26.06.43

• The longest-serving coach in Holland, having been at at Heerenveen since 1985 and leading the team all the way from the Second Division to the Champions League.

• Despite losing his best players (**Jon Dahl Tomasson**, **Ruud Van Nistelrooy**) every season, he is still able to build an attractive and stable team.

• Comes from the region of Friesland, which is known for its sober and down-to-earth people.

DE JONG, John

Midfielder, Dutch, 179cm, 73kg

Born: 08.03.77, Den Haag, Holland

Clubs: Den Haag (1995-97), Utrecht (1998-)

• Hugely promising attacking midfielder, who has attracted interest from bigger clubs, but prospective buyers have shied away from paying Utrecht's asking price.

DE LA FUENTE, Jean-Paul

• French managing director of the sports media consultancy Media Content, which has advised a number of English Premier League clubs, including Manchester United, on the exploitation of TV rights.

DE LA PENA, Ivan

Midfielder, Spanish, 169cm, 69kg

Born: 06.05.76, Santander, Spain

Clubs: Barcelona (1994-98), Lazio (Ita) (1998-99), Marseille (Fra) (1999-2000), Barcelona (2000-)

• While 'The Little Buddha' did hint at a dazzling future as a playmaker during his early days at Barcelona, the harsh truth is that he has delivered little since moving to Lazio and then on loan to Marseille. Too often on the periphery of the action; too often in the treatment room.

DE LOS SANTOS, Gonzalo

Midfielder, Uruguayan, 190cm, 82kg

Born: 19.07.76, Montevideo, Uruguay

Clubs: Penarol (1995-97), Merida (Spa) (1997-98), Malaga (Spa) (1998-)

Full international (Uruguay)

• Uruguayan midfielder who has been a success in Spain despite playing for unsuccessful teams.

• Won the League title in Uruguay with Penarol, moving to Spain's Merida in 1997

• Reported to have a £40million buyout clause at Malaga.

DE LUCAS, Enrique

Full name: Enrique De Lucas Martinez

Midfielder, Spanish, 177cm, 75kg

Born: 17.08.78, Barcelona, Spain

Clubs: Espanyol (1996-)

• Promising young attacking midfielder who has come through the youth system at Espanyol, playing for the first team on a number of occasions, but has yet to win a regular place.

• Spanish Under-21 international.

DE MARCHI, Marco

Defender, Italian, 182cm, 74kg

Born: 08.09.66, Milan, Italy

Clubs: Como, Ospitaletto, Bologna (1987-90), Juventus (1991-92), Roma (1991-92), Juventus (1992-93), Bologna (1993-96), Vitesse Arnhem (Hol) (1997-)

• No-nonsense stopper who is the first Italian in the Dutch League, performing well at Vitesse.

DE NEEF, Thierry

Midfielder, French, 175cm, 68kg

Born: 27.10.66, Paris, France

Clubs: Sedan (1992-94), Nice (1994-97), Le Havre (1997-)

• Defensive midfielder who has been a key player at Le Havre since 1997.

PLAYER
DE NOOIJER, Dennis
Forward, Dutch, 183cm, 75kg
Born: 04.04.69, Oost-Souburg, Holland
Clubs: Sparta Rotterdam (1987-98), Heerenveen (1998-)
• Striker who was often mentioned as the next striker of Feyenoord but never made the trip across town.
• Numerous clubs like Anderlecht were interested in him but he insisted on a deal which includeed his twin brother **Gerard**.
• International career has been blocked by tendency to pick up injuries.

PLAYER
DE NOOIJER, Gerard
Midfielder, Dutch, 183cm, 76kg
Born: 04.04.69, Oost-Souburg, Holland
Clubs: Sparta Rotterdam (1988-98), Heerenveen (1998-)
• The other twin. Unlike his brother, he hasn't always been in the spotlight. Used to be a defender but is now an all-rounder. Prefers to play in midfield and was even striker when his brother was injured. Did remarkably well scoring several goals.

PLAYER
DE PATRE, Tiziano
Midfielder, Italian, 179cm, 74kg
Born: 18.12.68, Notaresco, Italy
Clubs: Giulianova (1984-87), Messina (1987-88), Atalanta (1988-89), Monza (1989-90), Atalanta (1990-91), Venezia (1991-92), Sambenedettese (1992-94), Pescara (1994-95), Lecce (1995-97), Ravenna (1997), Cagliari (1997-)
• Much-travelled midfield dynamo who has spent most of his career in the Italian Serie B.

PLAYER
DE PAULA, Oscar
Forward, Spanish, 180cm, 74kg
Born: 31.05.75, Duranga, Spain
Clubs: Badajoz (1992-95), Real Sociedad (1995-)
• Striker who is strong in the air and has a solid rather than spectacular scoring record for Sociedad.

PLAYER
DE PEDRO, Francisco Javier
Midfielder, Spanish, 180cm, 76kg
Born: 04.08.73, Logrono, Spain
Clubs: Real Sociedad (1992-)
Full international (Spain) 3 caps/1 goal
• Natural midfielder who can play in a number of positions, but is arguably most effective on the left.
• His form in the 1998-99 season earned him a call-up to the Spanish national squad from coach **Jose Antonio Camacho**, who believes that if you're in form, you're in.

PLAYER
DE ROSA, Gaetano
Defender, Italian, 177cm, 73kg
Born: 10.05.73, Dusseldorf, Germany
Clubs: Napoli (1991-93), Palermo (1993-94), Napoli (1994-95), Pistoiese (1995), Savoia (1995-97), Bari (1997-)
• Central defender who plays the old-fashioned way, as a sweeper. An elegant player with excellent distribution skills and a natural target for Italy's biggest clubs.

PLAYER
DE SANCTIS, Morgan
Goalkeeper, Italian, 190cm, 80kg
Born: 26.03.77, Guardiagrele, Italy
Clubs: Pescara (1994-97), Juventus (1997-99), Udinese (1999-)
• Highly promising young keeper who has played for Italy at Under-21 level.
• Progress at Juventus has been blocked by **Edwin Van der Sar** and **Angelo Peruzzi**, so he went on

loan to Udinese to gain first-team experience.

PLAYER
DE VISSER, Jan
Midfielder, Dutch, 180cm. 77kg
Born: 01.01.68, Hoorn, Holland
Clubs: AZ (1988-91), Heerenveen (1991-99), Feyenoord (1999-)
• Modest left half with great pace and workrate. Earned a transfer to Feyenoord in 1999 although he is approaching the autumn of his career.

PLAYER
DE VLIEGER, Gert
Goalkeeper, Belgian, 186cm, 74cm
Born: 10.16.71, Dendermonde, Belgium
Clubs: Beveren (1991-95), Anderlecht (1995-99), Harelbeke (1998-99, loan), Willem II (1999-)(Hol)
Full international (Belgium) 7 caps/0 goals
• Keeper who has been the main rival to **Filip De Wilde** for the number one spot in the Belgian national side.
• Made his international debut in February 1999, against Cyprus, following an injury to his then Anderlecht team-mate De Wilde.
• Established himself as first-choice for both clubs and country before De Wilde's form returned.
• Moved to Holland after losing his place to De Wilde at Anderlecht, and was number to two to De Wilde in Belgium's squad at Euro 2000.

PLAYER
DE WILDE, Filip
Goalkeeper, Belgian, 181cm, 78kg
Born: 05.07.64, Zele, Belgium
Clubs: Anderlecht (1987-96), Sporting Lisbon (Por) (1996-98), Anderlecht (1998)
Full international (Belgium) 33 caps/0 goals
• Solid rather than spectacular shot-stopper who returned to favour in the Belgian national team in time for Euro 2000.
• An experienced keeper who made his international debut in August 1989 but spent many years in the shadow of Michel Preud'homme, watching the 1990 and 1994 World Cups from the bench, before making the step up for France 98.
• Belgium's first-choice keeper at Euro 2000 after displacing **Geert De Vlieger** at both club and country level. Did not have a good tournament, making a number of bad errors that resulted in goals, and was sent off against Turkey.

PLAYER
DE WITTE, Chris
Forward, Belgian, 183cm, 70kg
Born: 13.01.78, Antwerp, Belgium
Clubs: Anderlecht (1995-97), FC Twente (Hol) (1997-)
• Striker who has settled well at Twente after arriving on loan from Anderlecht. Popular with Twente fans for his elaborate goal celebrations.

PLAYER
DEANE, Brian
Forward, English, 193cm, 87kg
Born: 07.02.68, Leeds, England
Clubs: Doncaster Rovers (1985-88), Sheffield Utd 1988-93), Leeds Utd (1993-97), Sheffield Utd (1997-98), Benfica (Por) (1998-99), Middlesbrough (1999-)
Full international (England) 3 caps/0 goals
• Strong target man who earned his reputation at long ball-playing Sheffield Utd. Returned to English football after an ill-fated spell under **Graeme Souness** at Benfica.

PLAYER
DEBEVE, Mickael
Midfielder, French, 182cm, 80kg
Born: 01.12.70, Abbeville, France
Clubs: Toulouse (1986-94), Lens (1994-), Le Havre (1999, loan)
• Loaned out by Lens to Le Havre during the 1999-2000 season, he is a whirlwind of grit and industry on the right side of midfield.

• A French champion with Lens in 1997-98 and the scorer of their winner when they defeated Arsenal in the Champions League the following season at Wembley.

PLAYER
DEBLOCK, Pierre
Midfielder, French, 178cm, 71kg
Born: 01.05.73, Auchel, France
Clubs: Amiens, Sedan (1998-)
• This right-sided attacking midfielder was in inspirational form for newly-promoted Sedan in the 1999-2000 season. An incisive passer, good finishing ability and full of drive.
• Surname pronounced Day block.

PLAYER
DECO
Full name: Anderson Luis de Souza
Midfielder, Brazilian, 174cm, 73kg
Born: 17.08.77, Sao Bernardo do Campo, Brazil
Clubs: Corinthians (1997), Alverca (Por) (1997-98) Salgueiros (Por) (1998), FC Porto (Por) (1999-)
• A 'heart and soul' midfielder who has proved to be an invaluable acquisition for Porto.

PLAYER
DEFLANDRE, Eric
Defender, Belgian, 178cm, 80kg
Born: 02.08.73, Liege, Belgium
Clubs: Standard Liege (1991-95), Ekeren (1995-96), Club Brugge (1996-2000), Lyon (Fra) (2000-)
Full international (Belgium) 24 caps/0 goals
• Hard-working attacking right-back who has been in and out of the Belgian national team in recent seasons.
• Made his name at Club Brugge after a move from Germinal Ekeren in 1996. Was a solid performer in the 1998 Belgian League title-winning side, missing just five games all season.
• Made his international debut against Holland in December 1996.
• Played in all of Belgium's games at France 98

after appearing as a substitute in the opening game. Fell out of favour following Belgium's workmanlike performances in France, but returned to the team in the months building up to Euro 2000.
• Performances for Belgium at Euro 2000 earned him a transfer to Lyon.

PLAYER
DEHU, Frederic
Defender, French, 187cm, 80kg
Born: 24.10.72, Villeparisis, France
Clubs: Lens (1991-99), Barcelona (Spa) (1999-2000)
Full international (France) 4 caps/0 goals
• Utility man signed as part of Louis Van Gaal's masterplan at Barcelona in the summer of 1999.
• An injury early in the League campaign put paid to any plans to be first-choice centre-back and he returned to France in the summer of 2000.
• A French League and Cup winner with Lens.

ADMINISTRATOR
DEIN, David
English
• Vice-chairman of Arsenal and a key shareholder who runs the club on a day-to-day basis.
• Member of UEFA's club competitions committee.

PLAYER
DEISLER, Sebastian
Midfielder, German, 182cm, 71kg
Born: 05.01.80, Lorrach, Germany
Clubs: FV Lorrach, Borussia Monchengladbach (1998-99), Hertha Berlin (1999-)
Full international (Germany) 6 caps/0 goals
• Precociously-talented attacking midfielder with the versatility to operate as a classic playmaker or wide on the right – hence the endless comparisons with David Beckham.
• There is absolutely no doubt about his delicate ball skills, vision and shooting from free-kicks. But what is worrying is the number of injuries he seems to pick up.

Alessandro Del Piero

COACH
DEL BOSQUE, Vicente
Spanish
Born: 23.12.50
• Has done an excellent job at Real Madrid after taking over from **John Toshack** in November 1999, steering Real to victory in the Champions League in May 2000 before agreeing to stay on for another season on a full-time contract.
• A former Real player who was previously in charge at the Bernabeu stadium on a caretaker basis, in 1994.

PLAYER
DEL GROSSO, Alessandro
Defender, Italian, 185cm, 75kg
Born: 27.08.72, Rome, Italy
Clubs: Celano (1989-91), Francavilla (1991-93), Avezzano (1993-96), Salernitana (1996-99), Bari (1999-)
• Left-back who likes to get forward and shoot from distance. Has stayed loyal to Bari, despite offers to move north.

PLAYER
DEL PIERO, Alessandro
Forward, Italian, 173cm, 73kg
Born: 09.11.74, Conegliano, Italy
Clubs: Padova (1991-92), Juventus (1992-)
Full international (Italy) 36 caps/11 goals
• The Golden Boy of Italian Soccer who was named in early 2000 as the world's richest footballer, after he negotiated a new contract with Juventus worth £3.6million a year, after tax.
• A brilliant free-kick taker with phenomenal technique and great vision.
• Joined Juventus in 1993 from Padova, showing enough of his ability for Juve to sell **Roberto Baggio** to Milan, safe in the knowledge that they had an ideal replacement.
• Troubled by injury in the 1998-99 season, and struggled to find the net in the 1999-2000 season, scoring just once from open play.

• Dubbed Pinturrichio by the Italian press after the 16th-century renaissaince maestro.
• Voted Italy's Young Player of the Year in 1995.
• Played for Italy at the 1996 European Championships in England and the 1998 World Cup in France, but was not at his best in either tournament after a long, demanding season in Serie A.

PLAYER
DELANEY, Mark
Defender, Welsh, 185cm, 73kg
Born: 13.05.76, Haverfordwest, Wales
Clubs: Cardiff (1998-99), Aston Villa (1999-)
Full international (Wales) 4 caps/0 goals
• Right wing-back who was picked up by Cardiff from the League of Wales aged 22.

PLAYER
DELAP, Rory
Defender, Irish, 183cm, 83kg
Born: 06.07.76, Sutton Coldfield, England
Clubs: Carlisle (1992-98), Derby (1998-)
Full international (Rep Ireland) 6 caps/0 goals
• Right wing-back noted for his long throw.

PLAYER
DELAY, Florant
Goalkeeper, Swiss, 179cm, 88kg
Born: 23.08.71, Switzerland
Clubs: Neuchatel Xamax (1991-95), Sion (1995), Neuchatel Xamax (1995-2000), Yugoslav (2000-)
• Keeper who recently joined the Yverdon club after a decade of service to Neuchatel Xamax.
• A calm and authoritative presence between the posts.

PLAYER
DELAYE, Philippe
Midfielder, French, 174cm, 66kg
Born: 26.06.75, Montbrison, France
Clubs: Montpellier (1992-)
• One of the rare satisfactions in a Montpellier

side which was relegated at the end of the 1999-2000 season. This busy, skilful central midfielder has an eye for a good through ball and weighs in with his share of goals.

PLAYER
DELLI CARRI, Daniele
Defender, Italian, 184cm, 75kg
Born: 18.09.71, Foggia, Italy
Clubs: Bisceglie (1988-90), Torino (1990-91), Lucchese (1991-93), Torino (1993-94), Genoa (1994-96), Piacenza (1996-)
• Centre-back whose battling qualities have been put to good use over the years in various relegation and promotion battles.

PLAYER
DELVECCHIO, Marco
Forward, Italian, 186cm, 80kg
Born: 07.04.73, Milan, Italy
Clubs: Internazionale (1990-92), Venezia (1992-93), Udinese (1993-94), Internazionale (1994-95), Roma (1995-)
Full international (Italy) 6 caps/1 goal
• Left-footed striker who has performed well at Roma over the past two seasons, finally fulfilling the promise he showed when coming through the Inter youth system.
• Strong in the air. Can look clumsy but what he lacks in subtlety he makes up in determination and hard work.
• Made his debut aged 19 for Inter against Fiorentina, but was then sent for spells at Venezia and Udinese, before returning to Inter.
• Joined Roma in November 1995 in exchange for Marco Branca.
• International debut for Italy against Norway in February 1999.

Denilson

PLAYER
DELY VALDES, Julio Cesar
Forward, Panamanian, 184cm, 80kg
Born: 12.03.67, Colon, Panama
Clubs: Atletico Colon (1985-87), Paraguayo (1988-89), Nacional (Uru) (1989-93), Cagliari (Ita) (1993-95), Paris Saint-Germain (Fra) (1995-97), Ovicdo (Spa) (1997-2000), Malaga (Spa) (2000-)
Full international (Panama)
• The most successful Panamanian footballer ever, having had successful spells in Uruguay, Italy, France and now Spain.
• Made his name at Cagliari in Italy, moving to Paris in 1995 and on to Oviedo after two years.
• A consistent goalscorer throughout his career.

PLAYER
DEMENKO, Maxim
Defender, Russian
Born: 21.03.76
Clubs: Zenit
Full international (Russia)
• Tall, powerful player who is the backbone of the club's midfield, although often is used as a libero or sweeper in the national team.

PLAYER
DEMETRADZE, Georgi
Forward, Georgian, 170cm, 72kg
Born: 26.09.76, Georgia
Clubs: Dinamo Tbilisi (1994-97), Feyenoord (Hol) (1997-98), Alaniya Vladikavkaz (Rus) (1998-2000), Kyiv Dynamo (Ukr) (2000-)
Full international (Georgia) 13 caps/0 goals
• Striker who was signed by Kyiv Dynamo as a replacement for the Milan-bound **Andrii Shevchenko**.
• Began his career with leading Georgian club Dinamo Tbilisi, scoring the winning goal in the 1995 Georgian Cup Final, before an unproductive spell in Holland at Feyenoord.

DENIAUD, Thomas

Forward, French, 184cm, 81kg
Born: 31.08.71, Nantes, France
Clubs: Auxerre (1991-99), Le Havre (1999-)

• A graduate of the much-celebrated Auxerre youth set-up, he looked assured of a bright future as a marksman when he celebrated one of his early first team outings for the club with a brace of fine headed goals in a 2-1 Champions League win away to Rangers in October 1996.

• But talented though he was, the presence in the Auxerre ranks of outstanding strikers such as **Lilian Laslandes** and **Stephane Guivarc'h** kept him on the outside looking in for several seasons and he moved on to Le Havre last summer.

• Surname pronounced Day nee oh.

DENILSON

Midfielder, Brazilian, 178cm, 72kg
Born: 24.08.77, Sao Paulo
Clubs: Sao Paulo (1995-98), Real Betis (Spa) (1998-)
Full international (Brazil)

• Left-winger famous for becoming the world's most expensive player in 1997 when Real Betis paid Sao Paulo a reported £22million.

• Practically unknown in Europe before Le Tournoi in France in June 1997, the four-nation tournament held to prepare for the 1998 World Cup, having made his international debut against Chile two months earlier in April 1997.

• Full of tricks and compared to Garrincha but struggled to justify the price tag at Betis.

• 'I'm as quick and skilful as they come. The transfer is definitely not over the top. I could have gone to the club of my choice in Italy or Spain, but I know I've made the right decision. In a couple of year's time Betis will be one of the biggest teams in Europe.'

• Suffered relegation in May 2000, and a return to Brazil, on loan to Flamengo, was funded by his boot sponsor Nike.

DENIZLI, Mustapha

Turkish
Born: 10.11.49

• National coach of Turkey since October 1996 until Euro 2000, after which he took over at Fenerbahce.

• A useful left-winger in a 18-year playing career, when he won 17 caps (3 goals).

• Top scorer in the Turkish League in 1980 with Altay and a Turkish Cup-winner in 1967.

• Gained great coaching experience when assisting Galatasaray's German manager Jupp Derwall in the mid-1990s, later becoming head coach and winning the Turkish League in 1988, 1989, 1993 and 1995 and the 1993 Turkish Cup.

DENNEBOOM, Romano

Forward, Dutch, 187cm, 79kg
Born: 29.01.81, Schiedam, Holland
Clubs: Heerenveen (1998-)

• Promising youngster, a Dutch Under-18 international, who broke into the Heerenveen first-team during the 1999-2000 season.

• Pacy striker with good technique, likened to **Patrick Kluivert**.

DENOUEIX, Raymond

French
Born: 14.05.48

• Coach of Nantes since 1997, when he suceeded Jean-Claude Suaudeau.

• Spent his entire playing career at Nantes, winning the French League in 1973 and 1977.

• In charge of the Nantes youth section between 1982 and 1997.

• Like all his predecessors on the Nantes bench, he swears by an attacking style based on one-touch play and considerable movement and is very hard to please, demanding maximum effort from his players.

Didier Deschamps

DERANJA, Zvonimir

Forward, Hajduk Split, 173cm, 75kg
Born: 22.09.79, Croatia
Clubs: Hajduk Split
• Exciting young forward who is nicknamed 'Popeye' because of his explosive pace.
• Has attracted interest from Serie A clubs, but has yet to command a first-team place at Hajduk because of the competition for places.

PLAYER
DESAILLY, Marcel

Defender, French, 185cm, 85kg
Born: 07.09.68, Accra, Ghana
Clubs: Nantes (1986-92), Marseille (1992-94), Milan (Ita) (1994-98), Chelsea (Eng) (1998-)
Full international (France) 72 caps/2 goals
• A tower of power at centre-back for club and country. Began his career at Nantes, continued as a stopper with Marseille, and served Milan with distinction for four-and-a-half seasons as a holding midfield player, before moving to Chelsea after the 1998 World Cup.
• Joined Milan after impressing in Marseille's 1993 European Cup Final win over Milan. A year later he became the first player to win the European Cup with different clubs in successive seasons when Milan beat Barcelona 4-0, with Desailly scoring the fourth goal.
• Played in all seven of France's matches when they won the World Cup in 1998, but was sent off against Brazil in the Final for a second bookable offence.
• Intern'l debut: 22.08.93, v Sweden (1-1).

PLAYER
DESCHAMPS, Didier

Midfielder, French, 174cm, 71kg
Born: 15.10.68, Bayonne, France
Clubs: Nantes (1985-90), Marseille (1990-94), Bordeaux (1991-92, loan), Juventus (Ita) (1994-99), Chelsea (Eng) (1999-2000), Valencia (Spa) (2000-)

Full international (France) 101 caps/4 goals.
• France's victorious captain at the 1998 World Cup who became the most capped French international of all time when he won his 83rd cap against Ukraine in March 1999.
• Started with his hometown club Bayonne and made his breakthrough in the French first division with Nantes and Marseille. Was furious when Marseille loaned him to Bordeaux during the 1999-91 season, but his superb form earned him a recall to Marseille.
• Went on to captain the Marseille team which won the European Cup amid controversy in 1993. Joined Juventus the following year and was midfield general in the 1996 European Cup win over Ajax.
• Derided by Eric Cantona as a 'water carrier' who lacks finesse or style, but Cantona's remarks failed to appreciate the crucial role played by Deschamps' hard work and accurate passing in central midfield.
• Did not enjoy playing in the English Premier League and moved to Spain in summer 2000 after a season at Chelsea.
• International debut: 29.04.89, v Yugoslavia (0-0).

PLAYER
DESIO, Hermes
Midfielder, Argentinian, 176cm, 73kg
Born: 20.01.70, Rosario, Argentina
Clubs: Independiente (1993-94), Celta Vigo (Spa) (1994-96), Salamanca (Spa) (1997), Alaves (Spa) (1997-)
• Midfield hatchet man who has been crucial to the rise of Alaves in recent seasons in Spain.
• Is highly effective in the midfield holding role, winning the ball for the more creative midfielders.
• Recently adopted Spanish citizenship.

PLAYER
DEVINEAU, Charles
Midfielder, French, 171cm, 65kg

Born: 02.08.79, Cholet, France
Clubs: Nantes (1998-)
• Promising French Under-21 international striker and another product of the Nantes youth system.

ADMINISTRATOR
D'HOOGHE, Michel
Belgian
Born: 08.12.45
• President of the Belgian FA and a member of the FIFA executive committee since 1988.
• A medical doctor and lecturer by profession.

PLAYER
DHEEDENE, Didier
Midfielder, Belgian, 183cm, 78kg
Born: 22.01.72, Rocourt, Belgium
Clubs: Germinal Ekeren (1990-97), Anderlecht (1997-)
• Midfielder transformed into a left-back and was underrated for a long time. His baldness gives you the impression he is over 30 but he is only 28 years old. Is not the most technical player but is reliable. Has a good work-rate, loves to go forward and has a great shot.

PLAYER
DHORASOO, Vikash
Midfielder, French, 168cm, 63kg
Born: 10.10.73, Honfleur, France
Clubs: Le Havre (1993-98), Lyon (1998-)
Full international (France) 2 caps/0 goals
• Diminutive playmaker whose fast breaks from deep, nimble footwork and energy had everyone predicting a glorious future for him a couple of years ago. But his game has lost some spark in recent times and his hopes of making France's Euro 2000 squad went west.
• The French-born son of parents from the South Sea island of Mauritius, he had to pass his A levels before his mother and father allowed him to turn pro.

Roberto Di Matteo

PLAYER
DI BIAGIO, Luigi
Midfielder, Italian, 175cm, 74kg
Born: 03.06.71, Rome, Italy.
Clubs: Lazio (1988-89), Monza (1989-92), Foggia (1992-95), Roma (1995-99), Internazionale (1999-)
Full international (Italy) 19 caps/2 goals
• Midfield anchor man, a solid performer with good vision and passing ability, but criticised for being part of a national team midfield which lacks creativity.
• Missed the penalty which cost Italy a place in the 1998 World Cup semi-finals after a 0-0 draw with France in Paris.
• Made his Serie A debut for Lazio in 1989, before playing at Foggia under **Zdenek Zeman** and then following Zeman to Roma.
• Signed a five-year contract with Inter in summer 1999.

PLAYER
DI CANIO, Paolo
Forward, Italian, 178cm, 72kg
Born: 09.08.68, Rome, Italy
Clubs: Lazio (1985-89), Ternana (1986-87, loan), Juventus (1990-93), Napoli (1993-94), Milan (1994-96), Celtic (Sco) (1996-97), Sheffield Wed (Eng) (1997-99), West Ham (Eng) (1999-)
• Talented individual with exceptional technique but suspect temperament.
• His career in England appeared to be over after he assaulted referee Paul Alcock after being shown a red card following a brawl between Arsenal and Sheffield Wednesday players in September 1998. He was subsequently banned for 12 matches and fined by the Football Association.
• Won the Italian League with Milan with 1996.

PLAYER
DI FRANCESCO, Eusebio
Midfielder, Italian, 177cm, 71kg
Born: 08.09.69, Pescara, Italy

Clubs: **Empoli** (1987-91), Lucchese (1991-95), Piacenza (1995-97), Roma (1997-)
Full international (Italy) 12 caps/0 goals
• Hard-working midfielder who is admired by coaches, including **Dino Zoff**, for his workrate and attitude but is not always appreciated by the fans.
• Joined Roma in 1997 after two impressive seasons with Piacenza. Made his Serie A debut with Empoli, but dropped down to Serie C in successive seasons and moved to Lucchese in Serie B.
• International debut against Wales in 1998.

PLAYER
DI LIVIO, Angelo
Midfielder, Italian, 173cm, 73kg
Born: 26.07.66, Rome, Italy
Clubs: Roma (1984-85), Reggiana (1985-86), Nocerina (1986-87), Perugia (1987-89), Padova (1989-93), Juventus (1993-99), Fiorentina (1999-)
Full international (Italy) 29 caps/0 goals
• Tenacious midfielder who is no longer an automatic choice at international level.
• Nicknamed the 'Little Soldier' for his never-say-die attitude and tireless running on the left or right flanks.

PLAYER
DI MATTEO, Roberto
Midfielder, Italian, 180cm, 73kg
Born: 29.05.70, Schaffhausen, Switzerland
Clubs: Schaffhausen (1988-91), Zurich (1991-92), Aarau (1992-93), Lazio (1993-96), Chelsea (Eng) (1996-)
Full international (Italy) 33 caps/1 goal
• Italo-Swiss who broke into the Italian national side during his time with Lazio. Quickly established himself as a battling all-round midfielder.
• Joined Chelsea in 1996 in a £4.9million transfer from Lazio. Had three good seasons, including scoring the fastest goal in a Wembley FA Cup Final, against Middlesbrough in May 1997, but lost out following the arrival of **Didier Deschamps**.
• International debut:16.11.94, Italy v Croatia.

PLAYER
DI NAPOLI, Arturo
Forward, Italian, 177cm, 75kg
Born: 18.04.74, Milan, Italy.
Clubs: Acireale (1993-94), Gualdo (1994-95), Napoli (1995-96), Internazionale (1996-97), Vicenza (1997-98), Empoli (1998-99), Piacenza (1999-)
• Striker who graduated from the youth ranks at Inter, but could not make the first team, and moved on to Vicenza and Empoli.
• Joined Piacenza as their most expensive signing in summer 1999, but could not prevent their relegation.

PLAYER
DI VAIO, Marco
Forward, Italian, 178cm, 76kg
Born: 15.07.76, Rome, Italy
Clubs: Lazio (1992-95), Verona (1995-96), Bari (1996-97), Salernitana (1997-99), Parma (1999-).
• Exciting young striker who made his name at Salernitana, earning a £10million transfer to Parma in summer 1999.
• Still has room for improvement through coaching, and may get more opportunities at Parma in the 2000-2001 season following the sale of **Hernan Crespo** to Lazio.

PLAYER
DIABATE, Lassina
Midfielder, Ivory Coast, 180cm, 75kg
Born: 16.09.74, Boique, Ivory Coast
Clubs: Bourges (1993-95), Perpignan (1995-97), Bordeaux (1997)
Full international (Ivory Coast)
• Ivory Coast international midfielder known principally for his work-rate and tactical know-how. But proved there is much more to his game by firing home a great winner against Lyon in the penultimate game of 1998-99, a victory which kept Bordeaux on course for the League title.
• Surname pronounced Dee ah bah tay.

PLAYER
DIALLO, Hamed
Forward, Cameroon, 173cm, 67kg
Born: 18.12.76, Zahia, Cameroon
Clubs: Le Havre (1997-98), Laval (1998-99), Le Havre (1999-2000)
• Exciting but inconsistent talent who was top scorer in the French second division in 1998-99.

PLAYER
DIATTA, Lamine
Defender, Senegal, 184cm, 76kg
Born: 02.07.75, Dakar, Senegal
Clubs: Red Star (Fra) (1998-99), Troyes (Fra) (1999-)
• Right-sided defender who has yet to make his mark in the French first division.

PLAYER
DIAWARA, Kaba
Forward, French, 183cm, 83kg
Born: 16.12.75, Toulon, France
Clubs: Toulon, Bordeaux (1995-98), Rennes (1998-99), Bordeaux (1999), Arsenal (Eng) (1999), Marseille (1999) Paris Saint-Germain (2000-)
• Powerful and quick left-footed striker, but at times his finishing is not as assured as it should be. Nor has it helped being on a transfer treadmill, shuttling between Bordeaux, Arsenal, Marseille and PSG in the last 18 months.
• Pronounced Dee ah wah rah.

REFEREE
DIAZ VEGA, Ramon
Spanish
Born: 01.09.54
• Bank public relations manager.
• Earned his FIFA badge in 1991.

PLAYER
DIDA
Goalkeeper, Brazilian, 195cm, 85kg
Born: 07.10.73, Irara, Brazil

Clubs: Corinthians, Milan (Ita) (2000-)
Full international (Brazil)
• Hugely talented keeper who is the natural successor to **Claudio Taffarel** as Brazilian number one.
• Won the World Club Championship with Corinthians before finally moving to Milan in summer 2000, a deal which had been agreed a year earlier.

PLAYER
DIEGO TRISTAN
Forward, Spanish, 186cm, 79kg
Born: 05.01.76, Seville, Spain
Clubs: Betis B (1995-98), Mallorca (1998-)
• Powerfully-built forward who failed to make the first team at Real Betis and was sold to Mallorca B, where he made a dramatic breakthrough, scoring freely for Mallorca in the 1999-2000 season, finishing the League campaign with 18 goals.
• Did not start playing football until the age of 17.

PLAYER
DIENG, Oumar
Defender, Senegalese/French
Born: 30.12.72, Dakar, France
Clubs: Lille (1989-94), Paris Saint-Germain (1994-96), Samporia (Ita) (1996-98), Auxerre (1998-99), Sedan (1999-)
• Central defender who has got his career back on track at Sedan after a miserable spell in Italy with Sampdoria.

PLAYER
DIMAS
Full name: Manuel Teiceira Dimas
Defender, Portuguese, 186cm, 78kg
Born: 16.02.69, Johannesburg, South Africa
Clubs: FC Porto, Amadora, Guimaraes, Benfica, Juventus (Ita), Fenerbahce (Tur), Standard Liege (Bel)
Full international (Portugal) 39 caps/0 goals
• Son of Portuguese emigrants to South Africa

who decided he would have a better life in his parents' homeland.
• Played for Portugal at Olympic and Under-21 level.
• Made an initial impression at Academica aged 17, catching the eye of FC Porto, who handed him a two-year contract but then let it expire.
• Had brief spells at Amadora and Vitoria Guimaraes before joining Benfica in 1994.
• Surprised Benfica fans with his versatility, playing in the centre of defence but also at left-back.
• In Portugal's squad for Euro 96 and Euro 2000.
• Bought by Juventus from Benfica to bolster an injury-hit defence in 1997.
• A competent defender, but a reluctance to attack from left-back meant he did not win a regular place at Juve, and was sold to Turkey, before moving on Belgium.

COACH
DIMITROV, Dimitar
Bulgarian
Born: 09.06.59
• National coach of Bulgaria since 1999.

PLAYER
DINOV, Serghey
Goalkeeper, English, 180 cm, 71kg
Born: 23.04.69, Chisinau, Moldova
Clubs: Tighina Bender, Bugeac Comrat, Nistru Otaci, Constructorul Chisinau
Full international (Moldova) 13 caps/0 goals
• Experienced campaigner who has been voted Moldova's best goalkeeper four years running between 1996 and 1999.

PLAYER
DIOMEDE, Bernard
Forward, French, 170cm, 70kg
Born: 23.01.74, Saint-Doulchard, France
Clubs: Auxerre, Liverpool (Eng) (2000-)
Full international (France)
• Outgoing Auxerre coach **Guy Roux** loves

wingers and the bright and lively Diomede has served him admirably on the left-flank since making his first-team debut in December 1992.
• Has won eight caps for France and appeared in three games in the triumphant World Cup 98 campaign but has never particularly convinced at the highest level. The next stage of his career should be a switch to a playmaking role.
• Surname pronounced Dee oh med.

PLAYER
DIOP, Pape Malik
Forward, Senegal, 185cm, 75kg
Born: 12.01.79 Sheriflo, Senegal
Clubs: Lens (1998-99), Strasbourg (1999-)
Full international (Senegal)
• Highly promising young defender who played for his country at the 2000 African Nations Cup.

PLAYER
DIOUF, El Hadji
Forward, Senegal, 182cm, 74kg
Born: 15.01.81, Dakar, Senegal
Clubs: Sochaux (1998-99), Rennes (1999-2000)
• Teenager from Senegal who has shown much promise both as an out-and-out striker or on the right side of attack. Has excellent pace and holds the ball up well.
• Surname pronounces Dee oof.

AGENT
DIOUF, Papa
• Marseille-based agent whose clients include **Joseph-Desire Job**, **Pascal Nouma**, **Marcel Desailly** and **William Gallas**.

PLAYER
DIRKX, Jurgen
Defender, Dutch, 182cm, 80kg
Born: 15.08.75, Reusel, Holland
Clubs: PSV Eindhoven (1994-95), Fortuna Sittard (1995-99), PSV Eindhoven (1999-)
• Young defender from the youth ranks of PSV.

Djalminha

Was on loan to Fortuna for several years and is now back at PSV. Not a regular in the starting line up as he tends to be inconsistent. Good marker, strong in the air, but lacks skills.

PLAYER
DIXON, Lee
Defender, English, 180cm, 72kg
Born: 17.03.64, Manchester, England
Clubs: Burnley (1982-84), Chester (1983-85), Bury (1985-86), Stoke (1986-88), Arsenal (1988-)
Full international (England) 22 caps/0 goals
• Right-back and stalwart of the seemingly ageless Arsenal backline for more than a decade.

PLAYER
DJALMINHA
Full name: Djalma Feitosa Dias
Midfielder, Brazilian, 178cm, 69kg
Born: 09.12.70, Sao Paulo, Brazil
Clubs: Flamengo (1990-93), Guarani (1993-94), Shimizu S-Pulse (Jap) (1994), Guarani (1995), Palmeiras (1996-97), Deportivo La Coruna (Spa) (1997-)
Full international (Brazil) 11 caps/4 goals
• Hugely skilful but highly temperamental midfielder who was the inspiration behind Deportivo's 2000 Spanish Liga triumph.
• Son of 1960s star Djalma Dias, who won 16 caps for Brazil.
• Unharried air and devastating left foot have invited comparisons with Brazil's 1970 midfield general Gerson.
• Failed to make the grade at Rio club Flamengo and was eventually kicked out in 1993 after coming to blows with team-mate Renato Portaluppi.
• Spent two years with Guarani but experienced further disciplinary problems and spent a year in Japan with Shimuzu S-Pulse.
• Brought back to Brazil by then Palmeiras coach Wanderley Luxermburgo. He formed a midfield partnership with **Rivaldo** in what was arguably the most attractive Brazilian clubs side of the

1990s, winning the Brazilian championship in 1996.

• When Rivaldo was sold by Deportivo to Barcelona in 1997, Djalminha replaced his former team-mate at Deportivo in a £6.6million transfer from Palmeiras.

• 'I'm an admirer of the old Brazilian style. I know that in modern football speed and power have become more important, but the emphasis in my game is on skill and technique.'

PLAYER
DJETOU, Martin
Defender, French, 180cm, 79kg
Born: 15.12.74, Brogohio, Ivory Coast
Clubs: Strasbourg, Monaco
Full international (France) 3 caps/0 goals
• Powerful and athletic individual with the Desailly-like quality of being able to operate in central defence or in a midfield holding role. Although born in the Ivory Coast, he has been a naturalised Frenchman for some time and currently finds himself in the senior national team waiting room. A talented cartoonist who loves to use his teammates and coaches as models.
• Surname pronounced Je too.

PLAYER
DJORDJEVIC, Predrag
Midfielder, Yugoslav
Born: 04.08.72, Yugoslavia
Clubs: Red Star Belgrade, Olympiakos (Gre)
Full international (Yugoslavia) 4 caps/0 goals
• Former Red Star Belgrade man who was voted the best midfielder in Greece for the 1999-2000 season by readers of *Ethnosport* magazine.
• Excellent distribution, a dead-ball specialist and does his share of chasing and harrying too. Won his first full cap for Yugoslavia against Switzerland in September 1998, but has subsequently faded from national team view.

PLAYER
DJORKAEFF, Youri
Midfielder, French, 179cm, 72kg
Born: 09.03.68 Lyon, France
Clubs: Grenoble (1984-89), Strasbourg (1990), Monaco (1990-95), Paris Saint-Germain (1995-96), Internazionale (Ita) (1996-99), Kaiserslautern (Ger) (1999-)
Full international (France) 67 caps/26 goals
• A richly talented French international schemer or out-and-out forward, he floats with menace in the attacking third, allying subtle creative powers with a potentially devastating right-foot shot. Might have joined Manchester United in the summer of 1999 but instead opted for a longer deal with Kaiserslautern and enjoyed a magnificent first season in the Bundesliga.
• 'I know I'm a good player. So it's hard not to become a little big-headed from time to time.'
• Managed by his father Jean, who played 48 times for France in the 1960s.
• Surname pronounced Jaw kie eff.

PLAYER
DJOROVIC, Goran
Defender, Yugoslav, 183cm, 79kg
Born: 11.11.71, Pristina, Yugoslavia
Clubs: Pristina (1992-93), Red Star Belgrade (1993-97), Celta Vigo (Spa) (1997-)
Full international (Yugoslavia) 43 caps/0 goals
• Strong, intelligent defender who is equally at home at left-back or centre-back.
• Began his career at Pristina, moving on to Red Star Belgrade.
• A popular figure at Spanish club Celta, where he plays in central defence. For the Yugoslav national team, he plays at left-back.
• Made his international debut in December 1994 against Brazil.
• Played in all of Yugoslavia's games at the 1998 World Cup and was a valuable member of the squad at Euro 2000.

DJUKIC, Miroslav

Defender, Yugoslav, 177cm, 75kg
Born: 19.02.66, Stitar Tabac, Yugoslavia
Clubs: Rad Belgrade (1988-91), Deportivo La Coruna (Spa) (1990-97), Valencia (Spa) (1997-)
Full international (Yugoslavia) 43 caps/0 goals
• Central defender who is an established member of the Yugoslav national side.
• Strong defender who is powerful in the air and comfortable bringing the ball out from the back.
• Famous in Spain as the player who missed the penalty which cost Deportivo La Coruna the 1993-94 Spanish League title.
• Moved to Valencia in summer 1997 and established a strong partnership with **Joachim Bjorklund** which was crucial to Valencia's progress to the 2000 Champions League Final.
• International debut against Turkey in 1991.

PLAYER
DJUKIC, Sladjan

Forward, Yugoslav, 183cm, 79kg
Born: 21.12.66, Ploca, Yugoslavia
Clubs: Brest, Lorient, Troyes
• The veteran Yugoslav attacker is playing slightly deeper these days, but has certainly lost none of his sharpness in front of goal. Great left foot.
• Surname pronounced Joo keech.

PLAYER
DMITRULIN, Yuri

Defender, Ukrainian, 175cm, 71kg
Born: 10.02.75, Ukraine
Clubs: Kyiv Dynamo
Full international (Ukraine) 23 caps/1 goal
• Another quality product of Kyiv Dynamo youth system. A left-sided defender who can play in any position in defence and likes to get forward and attack.

PLAYER
DODDS, Billy

Forward, Scottish, 173cm, 77kg
Born: 05.02.69, New Cumnock, Scotland
Clubs: Chelsea (Eng) (1986-88), Partick (1987-88), Chelsea (Eng) (1988-89), Dundee (1989-94), St Johnstone (1993-94), Aberdeen (1994-98), Dundee United (1998-)
Full International (Scotland) 18 caps/4 goals
• After treading the boards with Dundee, St Johnstone, Dundee United and Aberdeen, the 31-year-old striker moved to Ibrox mid season as cover for the injured Michael Mols. Dodds, a regular Scottish international for the past few years, has adapted well to life at Ibrox, scoring freely in his six months with Rangers.

COACH
DOLMATOV, Oleg

Russian
Born: 29.11.48
• Coach of CSKA Moscow who played as a midfielder for Kairat Alma-Ata (1967-1971) and Moscow Dynamo (1972-1979) and won 14 caps for the USSR 1971-1977.
• Joined CSKA Moscow in mid-season in 1998 and sensationally took the team from the bottom of the Russian League to second place.

COACH
DOMENECH, Raymond

French
• A keen student of the game, authoritative and open and jovial in his dealings with the press, France's Under-21 coach for the past six years could be a good bet to follow **Roger Lemerre** as the next manager of *Les Bleus*.
• During his playing days as a left-back with Lyon, Strasbourg, Bordeaux and Paris Saint-Germain, he was the hard man of French football, collecting a pile of red and yellow cards and generally frightening the life out of attackers. But when he retired he claimed the tough-guy routine

had been an act to gain a psychological edge, and that he was really an intellectual. He may be right; he has subsequently taken to the stage for a number of amateur dramatic productions.
• Cut his coaching teeth at Mulhouse and Lyon.

PLAYER
DOMI, Didier
Defender, French, 179cm, 71kg
Born: 02.05.78, Sarcelles, France
Clubs: Paris Saint-Germain (1996-99), Newcastle (1999-)
• Speedy, attack-minded left-back whose £3.25million transfer from PSG to Newcastle in January 1999 upset many people in France. His departure was seen as another example of the drain of young of French talent abroad.
• French Under-21 international.

PLAYER
DOMINGUEZ, Jose
Midfielder, Portuguese, 165cm, 62kg
Born: 16.02.74, Lisbon, Portugal
Clubs: Benfica, Birmingham (Eng) (1994-95), Sporting Lisbon (1995-97), Tottenham (Eng) (1997-)
Full international (Portugal) 3 caps/0 goals.
• Diminutive left-winger who had to move to the English first division (Benfica to Birmingham, £180,000, March 1994) to gain recognition.

PLAYER
DOMORAUD, Cyril
Defender, French, 180cm, 77kg
Born: 22.07.71, Lakota, France.
Clubs: Creteil (1992-94), Red Star (1994-96), Bordeaux (1996-97), Marseille (1997-99), Internazionale (Ita) (1999-)
Full international (Ivory Coast)
• Left-sided central defender who moved to Italy in 1999 and was given plenty of chances to prove himself, but he was reported to be looking for a move back to France in summer 2000.

PLAYER
DOLL, Oliver
Defender, Belgian, 181cm, 76kg
Born: 09.06.73, Belgium
Clubs: Seraing (1993-94), Anderlecht (1994-2000), Charleroi (2000-)
Full international (Belgium) 1 cap/0 goals
• Tough-tackling defender who struggled at Anderlecht in recent seasons, failing to claim a place in the starting line up. In his better days he came close to being selected for the national team. Joined **Enzo Scifo**'s Charleroi for the 2000-2001 season.

PLAYER
DOMINGOS
Full name: Domingos Jose Paciencia de Oliveira
Forward, Portuguese, 174cm, 63kg
Born: 02.01.69, Leca de Palmeira, Portugal
Clubs: FC Porto (1987-97), Tenerife (Spa) (1997-99), FC Porto (1999-)
Full international (Portugal) 34 caps/9 goals
• Veteran striker who is approaching the end of a long and fruitful career, spent mostly with FC Porto in Portugal.
• A national champion with Porto in 1988, 1990, 1992, 1993, 1995, 1996 and 1997.
• Played for Portugal at Euro 96 but failed to provide the cutting edge that Portugal's entertaining attacking play needed.
• International debut against United States in 1990.
• His qualities in the penalty box were once compared by former Porto coach **Bobby Robson** to **George Weah**.

PLAYER
DONATO
Full name: Donato Gama da Silva
Midfielder, Spanish, 174cm, 80kg
Born: 30.12.62, Rio de Janeiro, Brazil
Clubs: Vasco da Gama (1980-88), Atletico Madrid (1988-93), Deportivo La Coruna (1993-)
Full international (Spain) 12 caps/3 goals

• Veteran midfielder who has been a late starter in his native Brazil, where he only broke into professional football in Rio at the age of 19, and Spain, where he made his international debut for his adopted country at the age of 31.
• Trained as a locksmith before being signed by Rio club America.
• Voted Brazil's best defender in 1987.
• Maintains that God led him to Atletico Madrid and then inspired him to request Spanish nationality.
• Sold to Deportivo for £400,000 in 1993.
• Scored on his international debut against Denmark in 1992.
• Spanish League champion in 2000.

PLAYER
DONOVAN, Landon
Forward, American, 174cm, 66kg
Born: 04.03.82, United States
Clubs: Bayer Leverkusen (Ger) (1999-)
• American wonderkid who was acclaimed as player of the tournament at the 1999 World Under-17 championship.
• Signed by Leverkusen in February 1999 amid accusations of cradle-snatching.

COACH
DONCEVSKI, Andon
Macedonian
• The first national coach of independent Macedonia. A former striker who won the Yugoslavian Cup in 1961 with Vardar.

PLAYER
DORADO, Javier
Full name: Javier Dorado Bielsa
Defender, Spanish, 182cm, 77kg
Born: 17.02.77, Madrid, Spain
Clubs: Real Madrid (1997-)
• Blond attacking left-back, understudy of **Roberto Carlos** at Real Madrid. Was part of the Spain Under-21 squad in Slovakia in May 2000,

and was expected to be farmed out on loan for the 2000-2001 season.

PLAYER
DOS SANTOS, Manuel
Midfielder, French, 172cm, 65kg
Born: 28.03.75, Praia, Cape Verde Islands
Clubs: Monaco (1995-97), Montpellier (1997-99)
• Adventurous left-back, whose raids down the flank offer some interesting attacking options. Defensively, he is usually secure and he must rate among the top five in his position in France.

PLAYER
DOSEK, Lukas
Defender, Czech, 178cm, 75kg
Born: 12.09.78, Larlovy Vary, Czech Rep
Clubs: Viktoria Pilsen, Slavia Prague (1999-)
• Hard-tackling defender who can also push into midfield.
• A member of the Czech Under-21 team that were losing finalists in the 2000 European Championships.
• Twin brother of striker **Tomas Dosek**, with whom he joined Slavia from Viktoria Pilsen in 1999.

PLAYER
DOSEK, Tomas
Forward, Czech, 178cm, 75kg
Born: 12.09.78, Larlovy Vary, Czech Rep
Clubs: Viktoria Pilsen, Slavia Prague (1999-)
• Attacking midfielder who, when he moved with twin brother **Lukas Dosek** to Slavia from Viktoria Pilsen, switched to out-and-out attacker.
• A member of the Czech Under-21 team that finished as runners-up in the Euro 2000 team.

PLAYER
DOSPEL, Ernst
Midfielder, Austrian, 184cm, 70kg
Born: 08.10.76, Absdorf, Austria
Clubs: Austria Vienna (1995-)

Full international (Austria) 1 cap/0 goals
• Tough but flexible young defender who has been tipped for a long international career.

PLAYER
DOSTALEK, Richard
Midfielder, Czech, 186cm, 77kg
Born: 26.04.74, Czech Republic
Clubs: Slavia Prague
Full international (Czech Republic) 2 caps/0 goals
• No-nonsense red-headed midfielder who has ceased to figure in the Czech national team's plans since **Jozef Chovanec** took over from Dusan Uhrin.
• At his best he provides some substance to Slavia's surfeit of style; at worst, he can appear clumsy.

PLAYER
DOUGLAS, Robert
Goalkeeper, Scotland, 191cm, 94kg
Born: 24.04.72, Lanark, Scotland
Clubs: Livingstone (1995-97), Dundee (1997-)
• At a time when there is a dearth of good goalkeepers in Scotland, Douglas has risen quickly in status following some excellent performances in goal for Dundee.
• The former Livingstone keeper is now a regular in the Scotland squad.

PLAYER
DOWE, Jens
Midfielder, German,184cm, 79kg
Born: 01.06.68, Rostock, Germany
Clubs: Hansa Rostock (1989-94), Munich 1860 (1994-96), Hamburg (1996), Wolves (Eng), Sturm Graz (Aut) (1996-97), Hansa Rostock (1997-99), Rapid Vienna (Aut) (1999-)
• Experienced campaigner who has formed a useful partnership in Rapid Vienna's midfield with **Dejan Savicevic**.

PLAYER
DRAPER, Mark
Midfielder, English, 178cm, 78kg
Born: 11.11.70, Long Eaton, England
Clubs: Notts Co (1988-94), Leicester (1994-95), Aston Villa (1995-99), Rayo Vallecano (Spa) (1999-2000), Southampton (2000-)
• Clever midfielder who left Aston Villa in the autumn of 1999 to try his luck in Spain after falling out of favour with John Gregory.
• Former England Under-21 international.

PLAYER
DROBNY, Jaroslav
Goalkeeper, Czech, 193cm, 85kg
Born: 18.10.79, Czech Republic
Clubs: Ceske Budejovice
• Keeper who serves as a reliable deputy to **Ales Chvalovsky** at Under-21 level. Part of the squad that lost out to Italy in the final of the 2000 European Under-21 championships.

PLAYER
DROZDOV, Yuri
Defender, Russian, 192cm, 70kg
Born: 16.01.72, Russia
Clubs: Lokomotiv Moscow
Full international (Russia) 6 caps/0 goals
• Extremely effective man-marker and a solid team player.

PLAYER
DRULIC, Goran
Forward, Yugoslav, 182cm, 79kg
Born: 17.04.77, Yugoslavia
Clubs: Red Star Belgrade
• A prolific scorer and regular in the Yugoslav Under-21 team dubbed the 'Serbian **Christian Vieri**' by fans.
• Has a poor disciplinary record, collecting red cards in three important games for Red Star.
• Missed the 1999-2000 season with a serious knee injury.

Dion Dublin

PLAYER
DRULOVIC, Ljubinko
Midfielder, Yugoslav, 167cm, 68kg
Born: 11.09.68, Novaros, Yugoslavia
Clubs: Sloboda (1988-90), RAD (1990-92), Gil
Vicente (Por) (1992-94), FC Porto (Por) (1994-)
Full international (Yugoslavia) 29 caps/3 goals
• Fast and skilful left-footed wide midfielder who
has been one of the stars of FC Porto's success
in recent years.
• A great provider from the left and an
accomplished counter-attacker.
• Began his career in the lower reaches of the
Yugoslav league before a move to Belgrade club
Rad.
• Signed for Porto in 1994 after catching the eye
while playing for Portuguese club Gil Vicente.
• Made his international debut for Yugoslava,
aged 28, against Argentina in December 1996.
• Was a member of Yugoslavia's squad at the
1998 World Cup in France, but did not get off the
bench. **Vujadin Boskov** showed more faith in
him at Euro 2000, playing him from the start.
• FC Porto team-mate **Rui Barros**: 'Drulovic is a
real artist with the ball. He can open up a
defence with a perfect through ball in the blink of
an eye and even when running at full speed
down the wing he still has the technique to put in
a dangerous cross.'

PLAYER
DUBERRY, Michael
Defender, English, 185cm, 85kg
Born: 14.10.75, Enfield, England
Clubs: Chelsea (1993-99), Bournemouth (1995,
loan), Leeds (1999-)
• Strong, speedy centre-back who came through
the ranks at Chelsea, and was tipped for big
things. But left for Leeds in the summer of 1999
in a bid to gain regular first-team football after
being crowded out by the likes of **Marcel
Desailly** and **Frank Leboeuf** at Stamford Bridge.
• England Under-21 international.

PLAYER
DUBLIN, Dion
Forward, English, 187cm, 78kg
Born: 22.04.69, Leicester, England
Clubs: Norwich (1998), Cambridge U (1988-92), Manchester Utd (1992-94), Coventry (1994-98), Aston Villa (1998-)
Full international (England) 4 caps/0 goals
• Tall, powerful striker who is strong in the air, but with a sure touch. Can also operate as an emergency centre-back.
• Made his name as a prolific scorer with long ball-playing Cambridge United. Played only 12 League games for Manchester United after suffering a broken leg not long after a £1million move from Cambridge in August 1992.
• Revived his career at Coventry and provoked howls of protests from fans at Highfield Road when he was sold to Villa for £5.75 million in November 1998.

PLAYER
DUCROCQ, Pierre
Midfielder, French, 179cm, 75kg
Born: 18.12.76, Pontoise, France
Clubs: Paris Saint-Germain, Laval, Paris Saint-Germain
• PSG youth team graduate and excellent toiler in the midfield shadows. Reliable ball-winner and does a fine job serving as a screen in front of the defence.
• Surname pronouced Doo crow.

PLAYER
DUDEK, Jerzy
Goalkeeper, Polish, 187cm, 81kg
Born: 23.03.73, Rybaik, Poland
Clubs: Sokol Tychy (1995-96), Feyenoord (Hol) (1996-)
Full international (Poland) 5 caps/0 goals
• One of Europe's most promising keepers who has been linked with transfers to Manchester United and Real Madrid, among others.

• Played just 15 Polish first division games before being signed by Feyenoord as long-term successor to Ed De Goey.
• Combination of bravery, reflexes and unwavering concentration earned him an accolade as the best keeper in Dutch League in 1998-99 season.
• International debut as a substitute against Israel, in Tel Aviv, 25.02.98 (lost 2-0).

PLAYER
DUDIC, Ivan
Defender, Yugoslav, 180cm, 76kg
Born: 13.02.77, Belgrade, Yugoslavia
Clubs: Red Star Belgrade
Full international (Yugoslavia) 2 caps/0 goals
• Right full-back and regular in the Yugoslav Under-21 side before making a late entry into Yugoslavia's squad for Euro 2000.
• Made history on his international debut against China in Beijing in May 2000 when he was substituted at half-time, only to return to the action as a substitute 13 minutes into the second half.
• Strong in the tackle, he is also working hard to improve his attacking play.

PLAYER
DUGARRY, Christoph
Forward, French, 188cm, 78kg
Born: 24.03.72, Bordeaux, France
Clubs: Bordeaux, Milan (Ita), Barcelona (Spa), Marseille, Bordeaux
Full international (France) 43 caps/7 goals
• Versatile French international attacker who can play wide on either flank or through the middle, where his strength in the air is a potent weapon.
• An explosive mixture of the combative and the technical, he has a 1998 World Cup winners medal to his name, but in recent times his career has involved more lows than highs: largely inactive stints with Milan and Barcelona, a less than convincing time with Marseille, a six-match ban for brawling at the end of a Marseille-Bologna

UEFA Cup semi, a failed dope test – though he was later cleared by the French federation – and a return to first club Bordeaux last December after Marseille fans assaulted him.
• His best friend is French World Cup hero **Zinedine Zidane** and they co-own a chic brasserie in a smart part of Bordeaux.

PLAYER
DULJAJ, Igor
Midfielder, Yugoslav, 175cm, 73kg
Born: 29.10.79, Belgrade, Yugoslavia
Clubs: Partizan Belgrade
• Hard-working defensive central midfielder and another product of Partizan Belgrade's good youth work.
• Yugoslav Under-21 international.

PLAYER
DUMITRU, Florentin
Forward, Romanian,
Born: 25.05.77, Bolentin, Romania
Clubs: Sportul (1996-98), Astra (1998-)
Full international (Romania) 3 caps/0 goals
• Highy-rated young defender and one of the key figures in Romania's Under-21 side. Expected to become a regular in the senior side.

PLAYER
DUNDEE, Sean
Forward, South African/German, 187cm, 81kg
Born: 07.12.72, Durban, South Africa
Clubs: Karlsruhe, Liverpool (Eng), Stuttgart (1999-)
• South African-born striker who burst onto the Bundesliga scene with goal upon goal for Karlsruhe in the mid-1990s and, after he was granted German citizenship, he looked set for a bright future with the Nationalmannschaft.
• But injury and loss of form meant he never did play for Germany and his stock fell even further following a period stuck on the bench at Liverpool.
• Now showing signs of rediscovering his goal touch at Stuttgart.

PLAYER
DUNNE, Richard
Defender, Irish, 183cm, 83kg
Born: 21.09.79, Dublin, Ireland
Clubs: Everton (1996-)
Full international (Republic of Ireland) 3 caps/1 goal
• Big strong centre-half who was a member of the Republic of Ireland's victorious squad at the 1998 European Under-18 championships.

BUSINESS
DUPONT, Jean-Louis
• Brussels-based lawyer who represented **Jean-Marc Bosman** in his landmark case in the European Court. Has since become the leading lawyer for all sports-related legal matters; he was the man South Africa turned to for advice on challenging FIFA's decision on the hosting of the 2006 World Cup.

PLAYER
DURRANT, Ian
Midfielder, Scottish, 173cm, 65kg
Born: 29.10.66, Glasgow, Scotland
Clubs: Rangers (1984-98), Kilmarnock (1998-)
Full international (Scotland) 20 caps/0 gooals
• Like **Ally McCoist** and Andy Goram, Durrant was one of the Rangers stars of the **Walter Smith** era who found themselves surplus to requirements when **Dick Advocaat** took over at Ibrox. His move to Kilmarnock, however, helped revitalise his career and he remains a regular choice for the Scottish national side.

PLAYER
DURAND, Eric
Goalkeeper, French, 178cm, 80kg
Born: 13.05.65, Genelard, France
Clubs: Gueugnon, Martigues (1992-97), Bastia (1997-)
• Common French surname, uncommonly talented keeper. Did not make the grade at first

club Auxerre, but has subsequently bounced back in style at Gueugnon, Martiguues and Bastia and had a strong case when he bemoaned his omission from the French squad for the 1998 World Cup.
• Keeps in trim during the close season on his mountain bike.
• Surname pronounced Doo ron.

REFEREE
DURKIN, Paul
English
Born: 15.08.55
• Works as a fitter.
• Awarded his FIFA badge in 1994.

PLAYER
DUSCHER, Aldo
Midfielder, Argentinian, 184cm, 80kg
Born: 22.03.79, Esquel, Argentina
Clubs: Newell's Old Boys, Sporting Lisbon (Por) (1998-2000), Deportivo La Coruna (Spa) (2000)
• Made his name at Sporting Lisbon, starring in the 1999-2000 Portuguese League triumph.
• Started at Buenos Aires club Newell's Old Boys, making the £1.7million move to Sporting in summer 1998, along with Croat coach Mirko Jozic.
• Linked with a move to Italy in summer 2000, but eventually joined Spanish champions Deportivo.

PLAYER
DUTRUEL, Richard
Goalkeeper, French, 192cm, 86kg
Born: 24.12.71, Thonon-Les bains, France
Clubs: Paris Saint-Germain (1991-93), Caen (1993-95), Paris Saint-Germain (1995-96), Celta Vigo (Spa) (1996-2000), Barcelona (Spa) (2000-)
• French keeper who has made steady progress in Spain, joining Barcelona in summer 2000.
• Began at Paris Saint-Germain, where his progress was blocked by **Bernard Lama**.
• Went on loan to Caen, where his form earned a

Aldo Duscher

regular place in the French Under-21 side and, eventually, a £1.25million transfer to Celta Vigo in Spain.
• Established himself as a popular figure in Vigo and was one of the stars of Celta's 1998-99 UEFA Cup run, at one stage going a club record 520 minutes without conceding a goal.
• Barcelona followed his progress very closely and he joined the Catalan club on a free transfer in summer 2000.

PLAYER
DZODIC, Nenad
Defender, Yugoslav, 188cm, 75kg
Born: 04.01.77, Belgrade, Yugoslavia
Clubs: Zemun (1996-97), Montpellier (Fra) (1997-)
• Promising young defeder who left Yugoslavia at an early age, but has yet to establish himself at Montpellier.
• Yugoslav Under-21 international.

PLAYER
DZAMARAULI, Gocha
Midfielder, Georgian, 180cm, 73kg
Born: 23.07.71 Georgia
Clubs: Alania Vladikavkaz (Rus), Trabzonspor (Tur) (1998-99), Zurich (Swi) (1999-)
Full international (Georgia) 42 caps/5 goals
• Experienced international midfielder who has had spells with clubs in Russia, Turkey and now Switzerland.
• Surname also spelt Jamarauli.

PLAYER
DZHANASHIA, Zaza
Forward, Georgian, 176cm, 74kg
Born: 10.02.76, Georgia
Clubs: Samtredia (1994-96), Lokomotiv Mocow (Rus) (1996-)
• Georgian international striker with a fiery temper, but is skilful and quick, although he is often criticised for being overweight.
• Surname also spelt Janashia.

E

EADIE, Darren
Midfielder, England, 172cm, 73kg
Born: 10.06.75, Chippenham, England
Clubs: Norwich (1993-99), Leicester (1999-)
• Pacy left-sided midfielder who became Leicester's record signing in 1999 when he joined from Norwich for £3million in December 1999.
• England Under-21 international.

PLAYER
EARLE, Robbie
Midfielder, English/Jamaican, 176cm, 68kg
Born: 27.01.65, Newcastle under Lyme, England
Clubs: Port Vale (1982-1991), Wimbledon (1991-)
Full international (Jamaica) 10 caps/1 goal
• Combative all-rounder whose professionalism was cited by the then Jamaica coach Rene Simoes as a key factor in helping the Reggae Boyz qualify for the 1998 World Cup.
• Intelligent and eloquent off the pitch, he is keen to pursue a career in the media when he retires.
• 'The [English-raised] players have done a lot for the team, especially Robbie Earle as he is very bright, He's positive and his professional attitude has inspired out team.' Jamaican World Cup coach Rene Simoes.

ECHOUAFNI, Olivier
Midfielder, French, 184cm, 71kg
Born: 13.09.72, Marseille, France
Clubs: Marseille (1996-98), Strasbourg (1998-)
• Marseille-born midfielder who has been in the best form of his career. He has always been an industrious ball-winner and a player who keeps his passes shot and sweet. But in recent times, he has added a flair for goalscoring to his portfolio and in 1999-2000 he was Strasbourg's leading marksman with nine goals.

PLAYER
EDGAR
Full name: Edgar Patricio Carvalho Pacheco
Midfielder, Portuguese, 180cm, 82kg
Born: 07.08.77 Luanda, Angola
Clubs: Benfica (1995-98), Real Madrid (Spa) (1998-99), Malaga (Spa) (1999-2000)
Full international (Portugal) 1 cap/0 goals
• Promising young midfielder who was named by *World Soccer* as one the brightest young talents in European football and a potential star of the 2002 World Cup.
• Small, quick and powerfully built, he is most effective as a wide midfielder or winger.
• Born in Angola but moved to Lisbon at the age of 14 to join Benfica. Made his first-team debut under Artur Jorge but Benfica allowed his contract to run out in summer 1998.
• Signed by Real Madrid on a free transfer but sent on loan to Malaga, where he performed so well that he was signed permanently for £2million.

PLAYER
EDMILSON
Full name: Edmilson Goncalves Pimenta
Forward, Brazilian, 175cm, 72kg
Born: 17.09.71 Brazil
Clubs: Democrata (1993), Nacional (Por) (1993-94), Salgueiros (Por) (1994-95), FC Porto (Por) (1995-97), Paris Saint-Germain (Fra) (1997), Sporting Lisbon (Por) (1998-)
• Brazilian forward who has been a considerable asset in the Sporting Lisbon attack following a move from FC Porto.

PLAYER
EDU ALONSO
Full name: Eduardo Alonso Alvarez
Midfielder, Spanish, 177cm, 73kg
Born: 30.05.74, Bilbao, Spain
Clubs: Athletic Bilbao B (1992-96), Eibar (1996), Athletic Bilbao (1997), Salamanca (1997-99), Athletic Bilbao (1999-)

• Promising youngster who is confident and accomplished on the ball and has started to make an impact on the Bilbao first team following loan spells at Eibar and Salamanca.

COACH
EDVALDSSON, ATLI
Icelandic
Born: 1957
• Installed at the end of the 1998-99 season as the national coach of Iceland having led KR to a long-awaited double.
• A vastly experienced international who played his football in Germany and Turkey, he now carries the hopes of the nation on his back, following the standards set by **Gudjon Thordarson**.

ADMINISTRATOR
EDWARDS, Martin
Born: 24.07.45
• Chairman and chief executive of Manchester United from 1980, when he succeeded his father Louis, to July 2000, when he stood down in favour of **Peter Kenyon**.
• Almost sold the club for around £10million in the late 1980s, but held on and has seen the club's value multipy: Rupert Murdoch's BSkyB offered £632million in late 1998, but the deal was blocked by the Monopolies and Mergers Commission. Since then, he has gradually reduced his shareholding in the club.

PLAYER
EFFENBERG, Stefan
Midfielder, German, 186cm, 85kg
Born: 02.08.68, Hamburg, Germany
Clubs: Bramfelder, Victoria Hamburg, Borussia Monchengladbach (1987-90), Bayern Munich (1990-92), Fiorentina (Ita) (1992-94), Borussia Monchengladbach (1994-98), Bayern Munich (1998-)
Full international (Germany) 35 caps/5 goals
• Bayern coach **Ottmar Hitzfeld** likes to rotate his team to keep everybody fresh, but midfield

general Effenberg is the exception to the turnover rule and quite rightly so.
• The inspirational Bayern captain has been in the best form of his career over the past two seasons and represents Bayern's heart and soul.
• A driving force in the middle of the field, his technique and tactical brain are second to none and the once bad boy of German football has grown up to become a remarkable leader.
• What a shame that he has turned his back on international football.

PLAYER
EGGEN, Dan
Defender, Norwegian, 192cm, 82kg
Born: 13.01.70, Copenhagen, Denmark
Clubs: Frem (Den) (1990-93), Brondby (Den) (1993- 97), Celta Vigo (Spa) (1998-2000), Alaves (Spa) (2000-)
Full international (Norway) 21 caps/2 goals
• Curly-haired central defender who is hard to beat in the air and is a threat at set-pieces.
• Born in Denmark and has never played club football in his native Norway.
• Played for Norway at the 1998 World Cup and was surprisingly recalled for Euro 2000.

COACH
EGGEN, Nils Arne
Norwegian
Born: 17.09.41
• A player with Rosenborg, Valarenga and IF Oslo but far more successful as a coach with Rosenborg (1971-72), Norway Under-21 (1973), Norway (1974-77), Rosenborg (1978-85) Moss and Norway Olympic team (1986-87), Rosenborg (1988-present).
• Norway's most successful coach who has won seven League titles and four Cups with Rosenborg.
• Won 29 caps for Norway as a player.
• Great believer in teamwork: 'Success comes as a product of the work people around you have done. We do not fulful each other through ourselves but through others – that's teamwork.'

Stefan Effenberg

PLAYER
EHIOGU, Ugo

Defender, English, 189cm, 93kg
Born: 03.11.72, London Hackney, England
Clubs: West Brom (1989-1991), Aston Villa (1991-)
Full international (England) 1 cap/0 goals
• Tall, strong and intelligent centre-back who broke into the full England squad under **Terry Venables**, but whose subsequent career has been affected by injuries.
• Unsettled at Villa under coach **John Gregory** and was linked with a move to Manchester City in the summer of 2000.

PLAYER
EHRET, Fabrice

Midfielder, French, 183cm 71kg
Born: 28.09.79, Viganello, Switzerland
Clubs: Strasbourg (1998-)
• Left-sided French Under-21 midfielder or wing-back who is definitely one for the future. A youngster with lots of spirit, pace and a remarkable left-foot; he is already one of the foremost volleyers of a ball in France.
• Surname pronounced Err ray.

PLAYER
EIGENRAUCH, Yves

Defender, German, 179cm, 73kg
Born: 24.04.71, Minden, Germany
Clubs: SV Minden 05, Arminia Bielefeld, Schalke (1990-)
• Hard-nosed stopper or rampaging right-back whose total commitment has made him a long-time favourite with Schalke fans.
• A keen supporter of the Green Party.

PLAYER
EILTS, Dieter

Midfielder, German, 186cm, 74kg
Born: 13.12.64, Uppgant-Schott, Germany
Clubs: SV Hage, Werder Bremen (1984-)
Full international (Germany) 31 caps/0 goals

Giovane Elber

- One of the heroes of Germany's triumph at Euro 96, he remains an oustanding defensive midfielder even though his national team days have long gone.
- Incredibly competitive, a great ball-winner and full of tactical nous, he is very much a one-club man, the only member of Werder's 1987-88 title-winning side still operating in the top flight.
- Surname pronounced Ay elts.

PLAYER
EKAKUA ELONGIA, Elos
Forward, DR Congo, 184cm, 78kg
Born: 05.02.74, DR Congo
Clubs: Lokeren (1994-98), Club Brugge (1998-99), Anderlecht (1999-)
Full international (DR Congo)
- Skilful right winger from the DR Congo. Failed to make any impression at Lokeren and Club Brugge. Still **Aime Anthuenis**, who has a habit of giving confidence to African players, brought him to Anderlecht, and the gamble appears to have paid off.
- Scored several important goals in the 1999-2000 season, first as a substitute, later as a member of the starting line-up. Still has to add some consistency to his game.

PLAYER
EKSTROM, Par
Forward, Swedish, 194cm, 82kg
Born: 17.08.68, Sweden
Clubs: Mjallby (1996-87), Orebro (1998-)
- Tall, lanky striker who played for years in Sweden's lower divisions with Mjallby. Orebro signed him halfway through the 1998 season and after taking time to settle has proved a reliable goalscorer.

PLAYER
EKOKU, Efan
Forward, Nigerian, 185cm, 76kg
Born: 08.06.67, Manchester, England
Clubs: Bournemouth (1990-93), Norwich (1993-95), Wimbledon (1995-99), Grasshopper (Swi) (1999-)

Full international (Nigeria) 4 caps/0 goals
• Long-striding, athletic striker at his best when running at defences.
• Born in Manchester, but qualified to represent Nigeria because his father hails from the west African state.
• Nicknamed 'The Chief'.

PLAYER
EL FAKIRI, Hassan
Midfielder, Morocan, 181cm, 74kg
Born: 18.04.77, Nador, Morocco
Clubs: Lyn Oslo (Nor), Brann (Nor), Monaco (Fra) (2000-)
• Elegant and exciting young midfielder who arrived from Lyn Oslo prior to this season. Sparkled for Brann in the 1999 season and signed by Monaco. Played the spring 2000 season for Brann before leaving for French football.

PLAYER
EL HADRIOUI, Abdelkrim
Defender, Moroccan, 175cm, 73kg
Born: 06.03.72, Taza, Morocco
Clubs: FA Rabat, Benfica (Por) (1996-98), AZ (Hol) (1998-)
Full international (Morocco)
• Attacking full-back who has been a big hit in Holland since a move from Benfica.
• Played for Morocco at the last two World Cups and African Nations Cup and was a regular choice for his country even while out of favour at club level.

PLAYER
EL-KARKOURI, Talal
Defender, Moroccan, 186cm, 78kg
Born: 08.07.76, Casablanca, Morocco
Clubs: Raja Casablanca, Paris Saint-Germain (Fra) (1999-)
Full international (Morocco)
• PSG originally intended to send the young Moroccan centre-back on loan to Servette of

Geneva after signing him last January from Raja Casablanca. But thankfully for the Parisian powers that be, they had second thoughts about farming out the North African and now he's a first team regular.
• Reads the game well, strong in the air and has massive self-belief, at times too much.

PLAYER
EL KHATTABI, Ali
Midfielder, Dutch/Moroccan, 175cm, 74kg
Born: 17.01.77, Schiedam, Holland
Clubs: Sparta Rotterdam (1995-96), Heerenveen (1996-98), Sparta Rotterdam (1999-)
Full international (Morocco)
• Born in Holland but plays internationally for the country of his parents' birth.
• Made his international debut in November 1997 against Togo and was a member of Morocco's squad at the 1998 World Cup, when he desperately tried to learn French and Arabic to try to communicate with his new team-mates.
• Returned to Sparta halfway through the 1999 season after a short spell at Heerenveen.

PLAYER
EL SAKA, Abdelzaher
Defender, Egyptian, 183cm, 77kg
Born: 1974
Clubs: Denizlispor
• Egyptian international defender who played for his country at the 2000 African Nations Cup finals.
• Plays alongside his compatriot **Mohamed Youssef** at Denizlispor in Turkey.

PLAYER
ELBER, Giovane
Forward, Brazilian, 182cm, 79kg
Born: 23.07.72, Londrina, Brazil
Clubs: Londrina (1990-91), Grasshopper (Swi) (1991-94), Stuttgart (Ger) (1994-97, Bayern Munich (Ger) (1997-)
Full international (Brazil)

Emerson Ferreira

• Feline Brazilian striker with the instinct to be on hand for the tap-ins, and the technical craft and athleticism to pull spectacular goals out of his hat.

• In the past, a host of big-name overseas imports have flopped at Bayern. But Elber has lived up to all expectations since arriving from Stuttgart in 1997, scoring 14 goals in 1999-2000 to take his total to an impressive 79 in 162 Bundesliga games.

PLAYER
ELEFTHEROPOULOS, Dimitris
Goalkeeper, Greek, 190cm, 83kg
Born: 07.08.76, Greece
Clubs: Olympiakos (1996-)
Full international (Greece) 5 caps/0 goals
• Highly-regarded young keeper who has been prompting interest from several big-name overseas clubs thanks to his good work for Olympiakos in the Champions League – apart from a horrendous gaffe which gifted Juventus a goal in the quarter-final in 1998-99.

• Made his international debut the same season against Belgium and in 1999-2000 was voted the country's top keeper by readers of *Ethnosport* weekly magazine.

PLAYER
ELIAS, Joao
Forward, Angolan, 174cm, 68kg
Born: 12.12.73, Angola
Clubs: Beershot, Kortrijk, Mechelen (1996-)
• Angolan-born attacker who has excelled at Mechelen in a free role after struggling at Beerschot and Kotrijk, often clashing with coaches.

REFEREE
ELLERAY, David
English
Born: 03.09.54
• One of England's leading officials who combines his duties as a referee with his full-time job as a

housemaster at Harrow public school.
• Awarded FIFA badge in 1992.

PLAYER
ELLIOTT, Matt
Defender, Scottish, 191cm, 93kg
Born: 01.11.68, London Wandsworth, England
Clubs: Charlton (1988-89), Torquay (1989-92), Scunthorpe (1992-93), Oxford Utd (1993-97), Leicester (1997-)
Full international (Scotland) 9 caps/0 goals
• Tall, strong centre-back who has become a regular choice for his adopted country Scotland after 'discovering' Scottish grandparents.
• Often used as an emergency striker by Leicester because of his strength in the air.

ADMINISTRATOR
ELLIS, Doug
• Chairman of Aston Villa who is nicknamed 'Deadly Doug' because of his reputation for hiring and firing managers.

PLAYER
ELMANDER, Johan
Forward, Swedish, 188cm, 79kg
Born: 27.05.81, Gothenburg
Clubs: Orgryte (1999-2000), Feyenoord (Hol) (2000-)
• Skilful forward who was dubbed the new golden boy of Swedish soccer when he made a sensational debut for Sweden's Under-21 team, scoring one goal and creating another in front of a number of watching foreign scouts.
• Signed a contract with Feyenoord and was set to move to Holland in October 2000 despite interest from clubs in Italy and Spain.
• Swedish great Nils Liedholm: 'In Holland they are describing Elmander as a cross between **Dennis Bergkamp** and **Marco Van Basten**, and that's not good for someone who has not yet played for the senior national team.'

PLAYER
EMERSON Ferreira de Rosa
Midfielder, Brazilian, 179cm, 74kg
Born: 04.04.76, Pelotas, Brazil
Clubs: Botafogo (1992), Gremio (1992-97), Bayer Leverkusen (Ger) (1997-2000), Roma (Ita) (2000-)
Full international (Brazil)
• The Brazilian international midfielder was easily the most impressive player in the Bundesliga in the 1999-2000 season, being voted Player of the Year by his fellow professionals.
• He is a man of many parts – classic playmaker, elegant, elusive dribbler or tough-tacking ball-winner – and Leverkusen skipper **Jens Nowotny** is not too wide of the mark when he describes the Brazilian as 'the best midfield player in the world'.
• Leverkusen resisted as long as they could, but ultimately had to agree to let Emerson move to Roma in summer 2000.

PLAYER
EMERSON Luiz Firmino
Forward, Brazilian, 184cm, 78kg
Born: 28.07.73, Campinas, Brazil
Clubs: Sao Paulo (Ger), Hamburg (Ger) (1991-92), Atletico Juniors, Bellmare Hiratsuka (Jap) (`1995), St Pauli (Ger) (1996-97), MVV (Hol) (1997-)
• Much-travelled Brazilian not to be confused with his more illustrious namesakes.

PLAYER
EMERSON Moises Costa
Midfielder, Brazilian, 183cm, 77kg
Born: 12.04.72, Rio de Janeiro, Brazil
Clubs: Flamengo, Curitiba, Belenenses (Por) (1992-94), FC Porto (Por) (1994-96), Middlesbrough (Eng) (1996-97), Tenerife (Spa) (1997-2000), Deportivo La Coruna (Spa) (2000-)
• Midfielder who has excellent technique and a sharp eye for goal. Had a difficult time in England with Middlesbrough and then suffered relegation from the Spanish first division in 1998 with

Tenerife. But his form since then was good enough to secure a transfer to Deportivo in summer 2000.

PLAYER
EMERSON Thome
Defender, Brazilian, 186cm, 89kg
Born: 30.03.72, Porto Alegre
Clubs: Sheffield Wed (Eng) (1997-00), Chelsea (Eng) (2000), Sunderland (Eng) (2000-)
• Intelligent centre-back about whom little was known when he arrived in England in March 1998. Claims to have played for Benfica, but records do not show this.
• Moved to Chelsea in February 2000 after a string of good performances for Wednesday, and was then sold to Sunderland for £4million after Chelsea signed **Winston Bogarde**.

PLAYER
EMRE Asik
Defender, Turkish, 185cm, 72kg
Born: 24.10.73, Bursa, Turkey
Clubs: Fenerbahce, Instanbulspor
Full international (Turkey) 9 caps/1 goal
• Right-sided defender who made his name with a spectacular goal for Turkey against Sweden in a Euro 96 qualifying match in March 1995.
• First came to attention playing for the Turkish under-21 side, and Fenerbahce beat a host of clubs to his signature.
• Fell out with Fenerbahce coach Carlos Alberto Parreira in their Turkish League title-winning season in 1996, and switched to Instanbulspor.

PLAYER
EMRE Belozoglu
Midfielder, Turkish, 173cm, 68kg
Born: 07.09.80, Turkey
Clubs: Galatasaray
Full international (Turkey) 1 cap/0 goals
• Young midfielder who is seen by many as the next big star of Turkish football.
• An excellent passer of the ball, intelligent

reader of the game, with a powerful left foot shot.
• Came through the youth teams at Galatasaray, where he learned a great deal as understudy to **Gheorghe Hagi**.
• A big success in the Turkish Under-21 and Olympic sides, he made his full international debut for Turkey against Norway in February 2000.

ADMINISTRATOR
ENAULT, Gerard
• General secretary of the French FA.

PLAYER
ENERLY, Dagfinn
Forward, Norwegian, 180cm
Born: 09.12.72 Norway
Clubs: Skeid, Moss (1998-)
Full international (Norway) 1 cap/0 goals
• Quick striker who made his breakthrough with Skeid Oslo a couple of seasons ago. His goal scoring earned him a call for national duty but has played only one game for Norway.

COACH
ENGEL, Jerzy
Polish
Born: 06.10.52.
• Coach of Polish national team since replacing Janusz Wojcik in January 2000.
• Began his coaching career in 1975. After spending a few years with lower division clubs joined Legia Warsaw and finished second in 1986. Then moved to Cyprus to be runners-up with Apollon Limassol four years later before returning to Poland. In 1997 he took over as director and manager of Polonia Warsaw.

PLAYER
ENGELMAN, Petr
Goalkeeper, Finnish, 188cm, 78kg
Born: 10.03.77, Turku, Finland
Clubs: TPS Turku (1995-98), Aston Villa (Fin) (1998-)

Full international (Finland) 1 cap/0 goals
• Finnish keeper signed by Villa as reserve cover but has yet to make an impact.

PLAYER
ENGLEBERT, Gaetan
Midfielder, Belgian, 179cm, 68kg
Born: 11.06.76, Belgium
Clubs: Liege, RFC Liege, St Truiden (1997-98), Club Brugge (1998-)
• Former Belgian youth international who has quietly established himself in the Club Brugge midfield since a move from St Truiden two years ago.
• Efficient, uncomplicated passer and useful with free-kicks and corners.

PLAYER
ENGONGA, Vincente
Full name: Vincente Engonga Mate
Midfielder, Spanish, 181cm, 84kg
Born: 20.10.65, Torrelavega, Spain
Clubs: Valladolid (1991-92), Celta Vigo (1992-94), Valencia (1994-97), Mallorca (1997-)
Full international (Spain) 14 caps/1 goal
• Hard-working, tough-tackling, versatile midfielder who can perform the roles of both anchorman and playmaker.
• One of the relatively unsung heroes behind Mallorca's success in recent years.
• Son of Guinean immigrants.
• Made the late, late transition from journeyman to international honours when he made his debut for Spain against Russia in September 1998, aged 32.

PLAYER
ENKE, Robert
Goalkeeper, German, 185cm, 78kg
Born: 24.08.77, Jena, Germany
Clubs: Carl Zeiss Jena (1995-96), Borussia Monchengladbach (1996-99), Benfica (Por) (2000-)
• Hugely promising young keeper who

established himself at Benfica in the 1999-2000 season despite stiff competition.
• Made his name at Borussia Monchengladbach during their 1998-99 relegation season. Despite the setback, snapped by Benfica's German coach **Jupp Heynckes**.
• German Under-21 international.

PLAYER
ENYINNAYA, Ugochukwu 'Ugo'
Forward, Nigerian, 180cm, 80kg
Born: 08.05.81, Warri Nigeria
Clubs: RWDM (Bel) (1998-99), Bari (Ita) (1999-)
• Extremely quick striker who made an immediate impact in Serie A, scoring against Internazionale in only his second game for Bari.
• Used mostly as a substitute, when his pace causes maximum damage.

PLAYER
EPUREANU, Serghei
Midfielder, Moldovan, 174cm, 72 kg
Born: 12.09.76, Moldova
Clubs: Agro Chisinau, Zimbru Chisinau, Samsunspor (Tur)
Full international (Moldova) 25 caps/2 goals
• One of Moldova's leading players, with good technique and impressive passing range.
• 1999 Moldovan Footballer of the Year.

PLAYER
ERANIO, Stefano
Midfielder, Italian, 180cm, 74kg
Born: 29.12.66, Genoa
Clubs: Genoa (1984-92), Milan (1992-97), Derby (1997-)
Full international (Italy) 20 caps/3 goals
• Right-sided midfielder or wing-back who surprisingly left Milan in the summer of 1997 for a lucrative contract with Derby.
• A European Cup-winner with Milan in 1994.

PLAYER
ERCEG, Tomislav
Forward, Croatian, 183cm, 79kg
Born: 22.10.71, Croatia
Clubs: Hajduk Split, Lugano (Swi) (1995-96),
Grasshopper (Swi) (1996), Duisburg (Ger) (1996),
Hajduk Split (1997-98), Ancona (Ita) (1998),
Perugia (Ita) (1998), Hajduk Split (1998-)
Full international (Croatia) 4 caps/1 goal
• Prolific scorer for Hajduk Split who has failed
to find the net in his travels around Europe.

PLAYER
ERDELY, Miklos
Goalkeeper, Hungarian, 195cm, 85kg
Born: 30.03.81, Hungary
Clubs: Debrecen (1998-99), MTK (1999-)
• Promising young keeper who has been tipped
for a move west in the near future.

PLAYER
ERGUN Penbe
Midfielder, Turkish, 187cm, 80kg
Born: 17.05.72, Zonguldak, Turkey
Clubs: Genclerbirligi, Kilimlispor, Galatasaray
Full international (Turkey) 6 caps/0 goals
• Versatile campaigner who can play in defence
or midfield. Celebrated his 28th birthday by
winning the UEFA Cup with Galatasaray.
• Made his international debut for Turkey against
Russia in April 1994. Played only two more games
before a surprise call-up to the Turkish squad for
Euro 2000, when he made two appearances.

PLAYER
ERIBERTO
Full name: Eriberto da Conceicao Silva
Midfielder, Brazilian, 180cm, 80kg
Born: 21.01.79, Rio Bonito, Brazil
Clubs: Palmeiras (1997-98), Bologna (Ita) (1998-)
• Exciting attacking midfielder who creates a
buzz when he appears as a substitute.
• Brazilian Under-21 international.

Sven Goran Eriksson

PLAYER
ERIKSSON, Lars
Goalkeeper, Swedish, 186cm, 86kg
Born: 21.09.65, Stockholm, Sweden
Clubs: Hammarby (1986-88), IFK Norrkoping (1988-95), FC Porto (Por) (1995-98), Hammarby (1998-)
Full international (Sweden) 17 caps/0 goals
• One of the great personalities of Stockholm football who won the Swedish League with Norrkoping in 1989 and then had spells abroad in Belgium and Portugal.
• Spent years as number two to Thomas Ravelli in the Swedish goal. A good shot-stopper, but sometimes tends to stay on his line.

COACH
ERIKSSON, Sven Goran
Swedish
Born: 05.02.48
• Hugely respected coach who won the Italian League for the first time when Lazio pipped Juventus to the title on the final day of the 1999-2000 season.
• An amateur player who began his coaching career in his native Sweden in 1976 with Degerfors, moving on to IFK Gothenburg, where he won the Swedish League title in 1982 and two Swedish Cups (1979 and 1982).
• His success with IFK in the 1982 UEFA Cup brought him to the attention of clubs in south/western Europe, and he moved to Benfica for the 1982-83 season.
• Won the Portuguese League in both his seasons with Benfica, before heading for Italy and a contract with Roma. A second-place League finish behind Juventus in 1986 was the highlight of three seasons at Roma, and was followed by two disappointing years at Fiorentina.
• He returned to Portugal in 1989 for three further seasons at Benfica winning the League title again in 1991 and reaching the 1990 Champions Cup Final against Milan.

• Spent five relatively quiet seasons at Sampdoria, achieving a top-ten finish every year, but surprised many when he rejected a move to Blackburn Rovers, preferring instead a move to the hothouse atmosphere at Lazio.
• Reached the 1998 UEFA Cup Final, which Lazio lost to Internazionale, and then won the last ever European Cup-winners Cup Final in 1999.

COACH
ERLANDSEN, Arne
Norwegian
Born: 20.12.59
• In his third year with Lillestrom, where he has been successful despite the limited resources available. Career as a player with Lillestrom and Stromsgodset (223 league matches). Stresses the importance of collective hard-working football.

PLAYER
ERLINGMARK, Magnus
Midfielder, Swedish, 187cm, 82kg
Born: 08.07.68, Jonkoping, Sweden
Clubs: BK Forward (1985-88), Orebro (1989-92), IFK Gothenburg (1993-)
Full international (Sweden) 37 caps/1 goal
• An irrepressible performer for IFK in various positions in defence, midfield and attack. IFK signed him from Orebro where he was already a full international. Has won four consecutive Swedish League titles (1993-96). Aeriel power is a strong feature of his game.

PLAYER
ERTUGRUL Saglam
Forward, Turkish, 184cm, 80kg
Born: 19.11.69, Istanbul, Turkey
Clubs: Samsunspor, Besiktas
Full international (Turkey) 26 caps/11 goals
• Physically strong striker who burst onto the scene in Turkey in 1993-94 with 17 goals in 29 games for unfashionable Samsunspor and then had an even better debut season with Besiktas in

1995-96, scoring 23 times in 30 games as his new team clinched the Turkish League title.
• A non-playing member of the Turkish squad at Euro 96, he fell out of favour with national coach **Mustapha Denizli** and was only an outside consideration for Euro 2000.

ADMINISTRATOR
ERZIK Senes
Born: 18.09.42
• President of Turkish Football Federation and a member of the FIFA executive commitee since 1996. Also a vice-president of UEFA.
• An economist by profession.

PLAYER
ESCUDE, Julien
Defender, French, 184cm, 76kg
Born: 17.08.79, Chartres, France
Clubs: Cannes, Rennes
• French Under-21 left-back destined for a bright future. A tenacious tackler, reads the game well and links up intelligently with the midfield and attack.
• Surname pronounced Es koo day.

PLAYER
ESNAIDER, Juan Eduardo
Forward, Argentinian, 180cm, 77kg
Born: 05.03.73, Mar del Plata, Argentina
Clubs: Ferrocarril (1990-91), Real Madrid (Spa) (1991-93), Real Zaragoza (Spa) (1993-95), Real Madrid (Spa) (1995-96), Atletico Madrid (Spa) (1996-97), Espanyol (Spa) (1997-99), Juventus (Ita) (1999-)
Full international (Argentina)
• Fiery striker who was bought by Juventus to provide attacking cover in the 1998-99 season following a serious knee injury to **Alessandro Del Piero**.
• Made his name in Zaragoza 1995 Cup-winners Cup triumph, scoring in the Final.
• Surname pronounced Ess nye der.

PLAYER
ESPINA, Marcelo Fabian
Midfielder, Argentinian, 174cm, 73kg
Born: 28.04.67, Buenos Aires, Argentina
Clubs: Lanus (1992-93), Platense (1993-95), Colo Colo (Chi) (1995-99), Racing Santander (Spa) (1999-)
Full international (Argentina)
• Argentinian international midfielder who was signed by Santander from Santiago side Colo Colo in February 1999.
• Useful passer of the ball, with a powerful shot.

PLAYER
ESQUERDINHA
Full name: Jose Marcelo Januario Araujo
Midfielder, Portuguese, 175cm, 67kg
Born: 06.05.72, Caicara, Brazil
Clubs: Bahia (1995), Fluminense (1996), Vitoria Bahia (1996-98), FC Porto (Por) (1998-)
• Talented left-sided midfielder whose crosses were the main source of goals for Brazilian forward **Jardel** at Porto.

PLAYER
ESTEBAN Andres Suarez
Goalkeeper, Spanish, 177cm, 82kg
Born: 27.06.75, Aviles, Spain
Clubs: Aviles (1992-95), Oviedo (1995-)
• Solid keeper who could end up at a bigger club. Has been a regular since 1997.

PLAYER
ETO'O, Samuel
Midfielder, Cameroon, 180cm, 75kg
Born: 10.03.81, Nkon, Cameroon
Clubs: ECB, Real Madrid (Spa) (1997-), Leganes (Spa) (1997-98), Espanyol (Spa) (1998-99)
Full international (Cameroon)
• Attacking midfielder whose career in Spain has suffered in fits and starts, being signed by Real Madrid but sent on loan to Leganes and Espanyol. Played one game for

Espanyol...against Real Madrid.
• Appeared as a substitute for Cameroon at the 1998 World Cup.

PLAYER
EUSEBIO Sacristan Maria
Midfielder, Spanish, 170cm, 71kg
Born: 13.04.64, Valladolid, Spain
Clubs: Valladolid (1983-87), Atletico Madrid (1987-88), Barcelona (1988-95), Celta Vigo (1995-97), Valladolid (1997-)
Full international (Spain) 13 caps/0 goals
• Hugely gifted midfielder who is now winding down his career with at Valladolid after starring under **Johan Cruyff** at Barcelona.
• Won the European Cup and four Spanish League titles in seven seasons in Barcelona.

EX-PLAYER
EUSEBIO
Full name: Eusebio da Silva Ferreira
Born: 25.01.42
• One of the greatest players of all time and arguably the greatest African footballer ever – having been born and brought up in Mozambique, a Portuguese colony.
• Was brought to Europe for a trial at Sporting Lisbon in 1961, but Benfica virtually kidnapped him at the airport, waiting for the furore to die down before introducing him to the first team.
• In 13 seasons with Benfica, he won the Portuguese League seven times, the Portuguese Cup twice, was European Footballer of the Year in 1965, top scorer at the 1966 World Cup with nine goals, and Portuguese League top scorer seven times.
• A greatly gifted footballer, but also a wonderful sportsman, he has worked for many years as the public face of Benfica, and also fronted the successful Portuguese campaign to host the European Championships in 2004.

PLAYER
EVANILSON
Full name: Evanilson Aparecido Ferreira
Defender, Brazilian, 181cm, 67kg
Born: 12.09.75, Diamantina, Brazil
Clubs: Bayer Leverkusen (Ger)
Full international (Brazil)
• Brazilian international wing-back able to operate on either flank. A member of his country's Copa America-winning squad of 1999, he is still coming to terms with the more frenetic pace of the German game, but he does have many qualities.
• A solid defender, athletic, with a good sense of anticipation and raids with intelligence and flair on the wing.

COACH
EXBRAYAT, Rene
French
Born: 30.10.47
• Failed to stop the rot at Servette in the 1999-2000 season after spells at Esperance Tunis and Le Havre and Martigues.

PLAYER
EXTEBERRIA, Imanol
Full name: Imanol Exteberria Egana
Goalkeeper, Spanish, 187cm, 77kg
Born: 27.03.75, Bergara, Spain
Clubs: Athletic Bilbao (1995-)
• First-choice keeper between 1997 and 1999, when he lost his place to the younger Lafuente. Former Under-21 international.

PLAYER
EXTEBERRIA, Joseba
Full name: Joseba Exteberria Lizardi
Midfielder, Spanish, 177cm, 71kg
Born: 05.09.77, Elgoibar, Spain
Clubs: Real Sociedad (19994-95), Athletic Bilbao (1995-)
Full international (Spain) 30 caps/7 goals

- Versatile attacking midfielder or forward with chunky physique whose determination and enthusiasm make up for his relatively limited technical ability.
- Started at Sociedad but switched to rivals Athletic Bilbao in 1995.
- Happiest playing down the right-hand channels.
- First came to prominence at the world Under-20 championships in Qatar in 1995.
- Played for Spain at Euro 2000.

F

PLAYER
FABBRI, Nestor
Defender, Argentinian, 181cm, 80kg
Born: 29.04.68, Buenos Aires, Argentina
Clubs: Racing (1986-92), Lanus (1992-94), Boca Juniors (1994-98), Nantes (Fra) (1998-)
Full international (Argentina)
• Veteran sweeper who was a member of the Argentina squad which finished runners-up at Italia 90.
• Topped *France Football*'s Player of the Year rankings in 1998-99 and is the perfect organiser and calming influence in a Nantes side packed with youngsters.

PLAYER
FABER, Ernest
Defender, Dutch, 184cm, 73kg
Born: 27.08.71, Geldrop, Holland
Clubs: NEC (1990-91), Sparta Rotterdam (1991-92), PSV Eindhoven (1993-), Groningen (1993-94, loan)
Full international (Holland) 1 cap/0 goals
• Defensive hard man who has struggled to hold down a first-team place at PSV since joining from Sparta.
• Four Under-21 caps for Holland.

PLAYER
FABIO
Full name: Fabio Ramon Ramos Mereles
Forward, Paraguayan, 170cm, 63kg
Born: 14.06.80, Asuncion, Paraguay
Clubs: Rio Ave (Por) (1998-99)
• Young attacker or midfielder who impressed in the 1999-2000 season while still a teenager, but could not prevent Rio Ave from being relegated.

PLAYER
FABIO PINTO
Forward, Brazilian, 182cm, 75kg
Born: 09.10.80, Santa Catarina, Brazil
Clubs: Internacional (1997-98), Oviedo (Spa) (1998-)
• Signed as an 18 year-old wunderkid from Internacional of Porto Alegre in 1998.
• Has so far failed to adapt to the Spanish League but Oviedo remain patient and hopeful.

PLAYER
FABUS, Martin
Forward, Slovakian, 186cm, 82kg
Born: 11.11.76, Slovakia
Clubs: Ozeta Trencin (1996-99), Sigma Olomouc (Cze) (1999-)
Full international (Slovakia) 10 caps/2 goals
• Striker who finished as top scorer in the Slovakian League in 1999 with 19 goals, earning a move to Sigma Olomouc and establishing himself in the Slovakian national team.

PLAYER
FACIUS, Calle
Midfielder, Danish, 173cm, 76kg
Born: 01.01.76, Denmark
Clubs: AaB (1990-97), Ikast (1998), Vejle (1999-)
• Hard man of Danish football with a powerful tackle and fiercesome attitude. Made his name at Aab Aalborg.
• Former Danish Under-21 international.

PLAYER
FADIGA, Khalilou
Forward, Senegelese, 184cm, 75kg
Born: 30.12.74, Senegal
Clubs: Paris Saint-Germain (Fra), Standard Liege (Bel) (1994-95), Lommel (Bel) (1995-97), Club Brugge (Bel) (1997-)
Full international (Senegal)
• Striker who starred for Senegal at the 2000 African Nations Cup and is well established in Belgium after a spell early in his career at Paris Saint-Germain failed to work out.

PLAYER
FAGIANI, Daniel
Defender, Argentinian, 170cm, 71kg
Born: 22.01.74, Pujato, Argentina
Clubs: Newell's Old Boys (1994-99), Valencia (Spa) (1999-)
• Left-back signed from Newell's Old Boys in 1999, has failed to impress **Hector Cuper**. Was not used in the Champions League Final despite **Amedeo Carboni** being suspended.

PLAYER
FALCONE, Giulio
Defender, Italian, 184cm, 75kg
Born: 31.05.74, Atri, Italy
Clubs: Torino, (1992-96), Fiorentina (1996-99), Bologna (1999-)
• Talented defender who made an impressive Serie A debut with Torino in 1993 at the age of 19.
• Spent three seasons in Turin before Fiorentina beat Milan to his signature in 1996.
• Suffered weight problems early on in Florence, but recovered to win a place in the side.
• Yet to fulfill the promise shown in winning the 1996 European Under-21 championship.

PLAYER
FARINOS, Francisco
Full name: Francisco Javier Farinos Zapata
Midfielder, Spanish, 173cm, 69kg
Born: 29.03.78, Valencia, Spain
Clubs: Valencia (1996-2000), Internazionale (Ita) (2000-)
Full international (Spain) 1 cap/0 goals
• Young left-footed midfielder who came to the fore in Valencia's run to the 2000 Champions League Final.
• Combative and forceful, but with a useful touch. Can be a little wreckless at times.
• Inter beat city rivals Milan to sign him in a £10million transfer in May 2000.

PLAYER
FARNERUD, Pontus
Midfielder, Swedish, 180cm, 74kg
Born: 04.06.80, Helsingborg, Sweden
Clubs: Helsingborg (1998), Monaco (Fra) (1998-)
• Most of his time at Monaco has been spent on the bench, but his coaches in the principality firmly believe they have a star for tomorrow on their hands in the shape of the young Swede midfielder. A tireless, determined figure in central midfield and uses the ball well too, rarely giving away possession.

COACH
FASCETTI, Eugenio
Italian
Born: 23.10.38
• Coach of Bari since 1996 and a controversial figure in Italian football.
• Known for his 'organised confusion' tactical theory which has been responsible for a record six promotions to Serie A, with Varese, Lecce, Lazio, Torino, Verona and Bari.
• At Bari, he has introduced a number of promising youngsters, including **Gianluigi Zambrotta** and **Antonio Cassano**.

PLAYER
FATIH Aykel
Defender, Turkish, 180cm, 79kg
Born: 26.12.77, Istanbul, Turkey
Clubs: Galatasaray
Full international (Turkey) 18 caps/0 goals
• Product of Galatasaray's youth system and regarded as one of Turkey's brightest prospects.
• A right-sided defender who likes to get forward. Started off as a centre-back with his club but now plays right-back. Can also be used in midfield, which better suits his attacking instincts.
• International debut for Turkey against Wales in August 1997.
• Played in all of Turkey's games at Euro 2000.

FATIH Terim

Turkish
Born: 14.09.54
• The most successful Turkish coach of recent times, who guided Turkey to the finals of Euro 96 and won the 2000 UEFA Cup with Galatasaray.
• Played 51 times as a defender for Turkey, 31 as captain, and spent 13 years at Galatasaray.
• Made his name as a coach of the Turkish Under-21 side which won the 1993 Mediterranean Games.
• Returned to Galatasaray as coach in July 1996, winning the Turkish League and UEFA Cup.
• Moved to Italian side Fiorentina in summer 2000.

PLAYER
FAVALLI, Giuseppe

Defender, Italian, 181cm, 73kg
Born: 08.01.72, Orzinuovi, Italy
Clubs: Cremonese (1988-92), Lazio (1992-)
Full international (Italy) 2 caps/0 goals
• Left-back with strong attacking instincts who has spent eight seasons with Lazio.
• A solid performer in Serie A, but maybe lacking in international class.
• Signed from Cremonese after playing in Italy's 1992 Under-21 Euro championship-winning side.

PLAYER
FAZLI Ulusal

Forward, Turkish
Born: 1974
Clubs: Antalyaspor, Besiktas (2000-)
• Strong, technical striker with a good scoring record in the Turkish League. His goals for Antalyaspor earned him a transfer to Besiktas in the summer of 2000.

AGENT
FEDELE, Gaetano

• Italian agent who represents **Fabio Cannavaro**.
Contact: Via Scarlatti, 153, I-80127, Napoli, Italy.

PLAYER
FEHAR, Miklos

Forward, Hungarian, 184cm, 78kg
Born: 20.07.79, Tatabanya, Hungary
Clubs: Gyori ETO (1995-98), FC Porto (Por) (1998-2000), Salgueiros (2000-)
Full international (Hungary) 10 caps/1 goal
• Striker who moved on to Salgueiros during the 1999-2000 season after failing to make the breakthrough at Porto.
• Known as 'Miki'.

PLAYER
FEINDOUNO, Pascal

Forward, Guinean, 182cm, 77kg
Born: 27.02.81, Conakry, Guinea
Clubs: Bordeaux
Full international (Guinea)
• Teenage striker who has become a cult hero after scoring the last-minute goal against Paris Saint-Germain in the last game of the 1998-99 season which secured the French League title for Bordeaux.

PLAYER
FELDHOFER, Ferdinand

Defender, Austrian, 182cm, 70kg
Born: 23.10.79, Austria
Clubs: Sturm Graz (1997-)
• Highly promising young defender who is tipped for a long international career after starring for the Austrian Under-21 side.

PLAYER
FELIPE Gurendez Aldanondo

Defender, Spanish, 174cm, 71kg
Born: 18.11.75, Vitoria, Spain
Clubs: Athletic Bilbao (1994-97), Osasuna (1997-98), Athletic Bilbao (1998-)
• Utility player who can play in defence or midfield.
• Came through the youth ranks at Athletic Bilbao and capped by Spain at Under-21 level.

PLAYER
FERDINAND, Les
Forward, English, 181cm, 85kg
Born: 18.12.66, London Acton, England
Clubs: QPR (1987-95), Brentford (1988, loan),
Besiktas (1988-89, loan) Newcastle (1995-97),
Tottenham (1997-)
Full international (England) 17 caps/5 goals
• Tall, powerful striker who has been troubled by
injuries of late.
• A late developer who was spotted by QPR while
playing for non-League Hayes.
• Had his best season in 1995-96, scoring 25
league goals after a £6m transfer to Newcastle.
• Nicknamed Sir Les.
• Scored on his international debut for England
against San Marino in February 1993.

PLAYER
FERDINAND, Rio
Defender, English, 189cm, 82kg
Born: 07.11.78, London Peckham, England
Clubs: West Ham (1995-)
Full international (England) 9 caps/0 goals
• Young centre-back who has the talent and
temperament to become a great international libero.
• A second cousin of striker **Les Ferdinand**.

COACH
FERGUSON, Alex
Scottish
Born: 31.12.41
• The most successful British manager of the
1990s and arguably the greatest of all time.
• A useful player for St Johnstone, Dunfermline
and Rangers who took up coaching with Falkirk.
• Took charge of Scotland for the 1986 World Cup
following the sudden death of Jock Stein, having
overseen enormous success at Aberdeen.
• Took over at Manchester United in November
1986 and was fortunate to be given the time to
mould a side in his own image.
• Was on the verge of leaving Old Trafford in

1990, having won no trophies, but was saved by
victory over Crystal Palace in the 1990 FA Cup
Final replay.
• Has since gone to win the League six times,
the FA Cup a further three times, the 1991
European Cup-winners Cup, and the 1999
Champions League.
• **Martin Edwards:** 'Alex always had a hot tem-
per. He'd have caused a fight in an empty house.'

PLAYER
FERGUSON, Barry
Midfielder, Scottish, 180cm, 70kg
Born: 02.02.78, Glasgow, Scotland
Clubs: Rangers (Sco) (1996-2000)
Full International (Scotland) 7 caps/1 goal
• Although always highly regarded, Ferguson
struggled to make an impact under previous
Rangers manager **Walter Smith** but his talents
have been nurtured by **Dick Advocaat** and he is
now a regular in the Scottish national team.

PLAYER
FERGUSON, Duncan
Forward, Scottish, 190cm, 86kg
Born: 27.12.71, Stirling, Scotlan
Clubs: Dundee Utd (1990-93), Rangers (1993-95),
Everton (Eng) (1995-1998), Newcastle (Eng)
(1998-2000), Everton (Eng) (2000-)
Full international (Scotland) 7caps/1 goal
• Tall, quick, physical striker who is highly
effective in the air, but whose career has been
blighted by injury and indiscipline.
• Spent several weeks in prison in Glasgow after
being convicted of assualt on a fellow player.
• Nicknamed 'Duncan Disorderly'.
• Refuses to speak to the press and retired from
international football in 1998 although Scotland
coach **Craig Brown** insists the door is still open.
• His £7million transfer to Newcastle by cash-
strapped Everton in November 1998 provoked fan
protests and led to the resignation of Everton
chairman Peter Johnson.

Rio Ferdinand

PLAYER
FERNANDES, Fabrice
Forward, French, 176cm, 73kg
Born: 29.10.79, Aubervilliers, France
Clubs: Rennes
• Paris-born midfielder who is considered one of the best young playmakers in France. An outstanding dribbler and passer, he played with **Nicolas Anelka** at INF Clairefontaine, the French national soccer academy.

COACH
FERNANDEZ, Luis
French
Born: 02.10.59
• Born in Spain but a naturalised Frenchman, he coaches as he played. For France, Paris Saint-Germain, Racing Paris and Cannes he was a dynamic and combative, if provocative, defensive midfielder and such characteristics feature strongly in his management style.
• Throughout a game Fernandez is never still, prowling up and down the touchline and frantically signalling instructions to his players. Yet his success as a coach with Cannes, Paris Saint-Germain and Athletic Bilbao has not been achieved by semaphore and energy alone. He spends hours watching videos of games and working on tactics and is an inspirational dressing-room presence.
• Recently resigned after a three-year spell working in Bilbao, which started productively but ended in acrimony. In particular, he had much-publicized feuds with internationals **Julen Guerrero** and **Ismael Urzaiz**.
• Is a hot tip to eventually lead France.

PLAYER
FERNANDEZ, Heine
Forward, Danish, 180cm, 79kg
Born: 14.07.70, Denmark
Clubs: Silkeborg (1990-98), Viborg (1998-)
Full international (Denmark) 1 cap/0 goals

Alex Ferguson

• One of the most effective strikers in the Danish League who should have gained more recognition with the Danish national side.

• Won the Danish League title with Silkeborg in 1994 and was the Superliga's leading scorer in 1998-99 with 23 goals.

PLAYER
FERNANDO COUTO
Full name: Fernando Couto Silva Manuel
Defender, Portuguese, 184cm, 84kkg
Born: 02.08.69, Esphinho, Portugal
Clubs: FC Porto (1987-94), Parma (Ita) (1994-96), Barcelona (Spa) (1996-98), Lazio (Ita) (1998-)
Full international (Portugal) 68 caps/6 goals

• Shaggy-haired centre-back now back for his second spell in Italian football after two seasons at Barcelona.

• A strong man-to-man marker whose temperament can be a little suspect.

• Made his name at FC Porto after joining from regional league club Lourosa at the age of 17. Was sent out on loan to Famalicao and Academica.

• A member of the Portuguese team which won the World Youth title in Riyadh in 1989.

• Won the Portuguese League with FC Porto in 1992 and 1994 and the Portuguese Cup in 1991 and 1994.

• Surname pronounced Co to.

PLAYER
FERNANDO MEIRA
Full name: Fernando Jose Silva Freitas Meira
Midfielder, Portuguese, 188cm, 85kg
Born: 05.06.78, Guimaraes, Portugal
Clubs: Vitoria Guimaraes (1994-2000), Benfica (2000-)

• Highly versatile midfielder who was reported to have agreed contracts with Udinese and Vicenza in the summer of 2000, but eventually joined Benfica.

COACH
FERNANDO SANTOS
Portuguese
Full name: Fernando Manual da Costa Santos
Born: 10.10.54
• FC Porto boss who places much emphasis on a solid back four, patient approach play and attack on the flanks.
• Formerly head coach of Estrela Amadora and Estoril, he is very much an atypical figure in the game; he studied engineering at university and is a devout church-goer.
• Admits he is a hard coach to please. 'In my two seasons in charge of FC Porto, the team has won the Championship and finished second, but I'm anything but satisfied. I'm a perfectionist and I want more from the team. I demand more.'

PLAYER
FERRANTE, Marco
Forward, Italian, 176cm, 70kg
Born: 04.03.71, Velletri, Italy
Clubs: Napoli (1988-90), Reggiana (1990-91), Pisa (1991-92), Napoli (1992), Parma (1992-93), Piacenza (1993-94), Perugia (1994-95), Parma (1995), Salernitana (1995-96), Parma (1996), Torino (1996-)
• Much-travelled striker who showed talent as a youngster but has never fulfilled his potential.

PLAYER
FERRER, Albert
Defender, Spanish, 170cm, 73kg
Born: 06.06.70, Barcelona, Spain
Clubs: Tenerife (1989-90), Barcelona (1990-98), Chelsea (Eng) (1998-)
Full international (Spain) 36 caps/0 goals
• Accomplished right-back who won every Spanish domestic honour at Barcelona under **Johan Cruyff**, as well as the European Cup in 1992, and the 1997 European Cup-winners Cup.
• Was in and out of the Barcelona squad under **Bobby Robson**, left out in the cold by **Louis Van Gaal** and joined Chelsea after the 1998 World Cup.

• Played right midfield in Spain's gold-medal winning side at the 1992 Barcelona Olympics, but is most effective as a man-marking full-back.
• International debut: 04.09.91, v Uruguay (won 2-1).

COACH
FERRER, Lloren Serra
Spanish
Born: 05.05.53
• First-team coach at Barcelona, having been caretaker coach following the resignation of **Louis Van Gaal** in May 2000. Most recently in charge of Barcelona's youth section as 'co-ordinator of football' since 1997.
• Made his name with Mallorca, then took Betis from the second division into European competition.

PLAYER
FERRARA, Ciro
Defender, Italian, 180cm, 75kg
Born: 11.02.67, Naples, Italy
Clubs: Napoli (1984-94), Juventus (1994-)
Full international (Italy) 49 caps/0 goals
• Experienced 'footballer's footballer' who has won Italian League titles with Napoli and Juventus and the 1996 European Cup with Juve.
• Extremely versatile: can play as stopper, sweeper, marker, left-back or right-back.
• Began at Napoli, playing alongside Diego Maradona in the famous side which won two League titles and the UEFA Cup in the late 1980s.
• Missed France 98 World Cup after breaking a leg.

PLAYER
FERRARI, Matteo
Defender, Italian, 181cm, 77kg
Born: 05.12.79, Aflou, Algeria
Clubs: Spal (1995-96), Internazionale (1996-97), Genoa (1997-98), Lecce (1998-99), Bari (1999-)
• Promising youngster whom Inter are keen to develop, hence loan spells at Genoa, Lecce and Bari.
• A member of the victorious 2000 European Under-21 championship-winning squad.

PLAYER
FERREIRA, Francisco (Patxi)
Full name: Francisco (Patxi) Ferreira Colmenero
Defender, Spanish, 181cm, 77kg
Born: 22.05.67, Salamanca, Spain
Clubs: Athletic Bilbao (1984-89), Atletico Madrid (1989-93), Sevilla (1993-94), Atletico Madrid (1994-95), Valencia (1995-97), Athletic Bilbao (1997-)
Full international (Spain) 21 caps/0 goals
• Veteran central defender who has been playing top-flight football in Spain since 1984.
• Tough-tackling campaigner who is reliable and dependable rather than exceptional.
• Came through the youth ranks at Athletic, moving on to Atletico, where he won the Spanish Cup twice, and Sevilla.
• Returned to Bilbao in 1997 and played an important role as a squad player rather than first-choice centre-back.

COACH
FERREIRA, Jesualdo
Portuguese
• Former boss of the Portuguese Under-21 side who took over at the Alverca club during the 1999-2000 season. Studious, methodical and renowned as a fine strategist.

COACH
FERRERA, Emilio
Belgian
• Newcomer on the scene in Belgium. Of Spanish descent, he is a young coach who prevented Beveren from relegation in his first year in charge.
• His brother Manu, a former Anderlecht youth coach, is now in charge at Charleroi.

PLAYER
FERRON, Fabrizio
Goalkeeper, Italian, 182cm, 73kg
Born: 05.09.65, Bollate, Italy
Clubs: Milan (1985-86), Sambenedett (1986-88), Atalanta (1988-96), Sampdoria (1996-99),

Internazionale (1999-)
• Highly-rated keeper who has never quite realised his potential.
• After Sampdoria were relegated in 1999, he joined Inter as cover for **Angelo Peruzzi**.

PLAYER
FESTA, Gianluca
Defender, Italian, 183cm, 75kg
Born: 15.03.69, Cagliari, Italy
Clubs: Cagliari (1986-93), Fersulcis (1987-88), Inter (1993-1997), Roma (1993-94), Middlesbrough (1997-)
• No-nonsense centre-back who joined Boro from Inter in a £2.7m transfer in January 1997.

PLAYER
FEVZI Tuncay
Goalkeeper, Turkish, 194cm, 85kg
Born: 14.09.77, Mugla, Turkey
Clubs: Muglaspor, Besiktas
Full international (Turkey) 1 cap/0 goals
• Highly promising young keeper who is the understudy to **Rustu Recber** in the Turkish national team. Excellent reflexes, very athletic, with lots of experience despite his age.
• Made his international debut for Turkey against Norway in Feburary 2000 after a series of impressive displays for Besiktas.

PLAYER
FIGO, Luis
Full name: Luis Felipe Madeira Figo Caeiro
Forward, Portuguese, 180cm, 75kg
Born: 04.11.72, Lisbon, Portugal
Clubs: Sporting Lisbon (1989-95), Barcelona (Spa) (1995-2000), Real Madrid (Spa) (2000-)
Full international (Portugal) 65 caps/15 goals
• One of the greatest talents in the modern European game, a winger who loves to run at and beat defenders with his pace and wonderful skill.
• A member of the Portuguese side which won the world Under-20 title in Lisbon in 1991, and in

the squad which travelled to the 1994 European Under-21 finals.

• Began at Sporting Lisbon, winning the Cup in 1995. In the spring of 1995 both Parma and Juventus both claimed to have agreements to sign Figo for the following season. Both teams dropped their interest and Figo joined Barça for a bargain £1.5million.

• Considered to have been a huge success in Spain, playing a leading role in Barcelona's 1998 and 1999 Liga triumphs.

• The one Barcelona player to have stayed in favour under three different coaches: **Johan Cruyff**, **Bobby Robson** and **Louis Van Gaal**.

• Complained about Cruyff playing him out of position on the left wing, but it seems to have improved his game on both flanks.

• Voted Portuguese Footballer of the Year in 1999.

• International debut v Luxembourg 12.10.91.

• Became the world's most expensive footballer in July 2000 when he made the highly contentious £37million move from Barcelona to Real Madrid. His agent **Jose Veiga** signed an agreement with Real presidential hopeful **Florentino Perez**, but did not believe Perez had any chance of winning and wanted to use the contract to improve Figo's pay deal with Barça. But the whole thing backfired spectacularly when Perez surprisingly won the Real election.

PLAYER
FILEVSKI, Anton
Goalkeeper Macedonian, 192cm, 92kg
Born: 23.06.64, Skopje, Macedonia
Clubs: Zeleznik Belgrade (Yug)
Full international (Macedonia) 3 caps/0 goals
• Keeper whose excellent club form in 1999-2000 brought him a late debut with the national side.

PLAYER
FILIMONOV, Alexander
Goalkeeper, Russian, 193cm, 88kg
Born: 15.10.73, Russia

Clubs: Fakel (1992-93), Tekstilstedt (1994-95), Moscow Spartak (1996-)
Full international (Russia) 13 caps/0 goals
• Tall, physically imposing keeper, who was considered to be Russia's number one until the silly goal conceded from Ukraine's **Andrii Shevchenko** in the decisive, final-round Euro 2000 qualifier.

PLAYER
FILIPESCU, Iulian
Defender, Romanian, 187cm, 80kg
Born: 29.03.74, Slatina, Romania
Clubs: Steaua Bucharest (1992-96), Galatasaray (Tur) (1996-98), Real Betis (Spa) (1999-)
Full international (Romania) 38 caps/0 goals
• Reliable left-sided defender who can play at full-back, centre-back or in midfield, where he excels in a holding role, but can also shoot.

• A member of the Steaua side which won four Romanian League titles between 1993 and 1996.

• Introduced into the Romanian national team by Anghel Iordanescu, his original coach at Steaua, making his international debut against Yugoslavia in March 1996.

• Followed fellow countrymen **Gheorghe Hagi** and **Gica Popescu** to Turkey, where he twice sampled League title success with Galatasaray.

• Moved to Betis halfway through the 1998-99 season in a deal worth almost £5million.

• Played for Romania at Euro 2000.

PLAYER
FINIDI George
Midfielder, Nigerian, 185cm, 79kg
Born: 15.04.71, Puthovcourt, Nigeria
Clubs: Calabar Rovers, Ajax (Hol) (1993-96), Real Betis (Spa) (1996-2000), Mallorca (Hol) (2000-)
Full international (Nigeria)
• Exciting winger who was Dutch Footballer of the Year and a European Cup-winner during his time at Ajax.

• Famed for his elaborate goal celebration routines.

Luis Figo

• A regular for Nigeria who scored the goal against Algeria in 1993 which secured Nigeria's first qualification for the World Cup finals.

PLAYER
FINK, Thorsten
Midfielder, German, 181cm, 80kg
Born: 29.10.67, Dortmund, Germany
Clubs: Roland Marten, Borussia Dortmund, Wattenscheid (1989-94), Karlsruher (1994-97), Bayern Munich (1997-)
• Often unsung midfield workhorse but nonetheless terribly effective thanks to his non-stop fetching and carrying. Has not scored in the Bundesliga since March 1998, but was on target with a sweetly-struck shot from the edge of the box in Bayern's 4-2 win away to Real Madrid in the second phase of the 1999-2000 season's Champions League.
• German Under-21 international.

COACH
FINKE, Volker
German
Born: 24.03.48
• In charge of Freiburg since July 1991, he is the longest-serving of the current batch of Bundesliga coaches. No professional playing experience, but has worked wonders in transforming unfashionable Freiburg into a force in German football.
• Cerebral, innovative and always prepared to give youth its chance, his team plays some of the most attractive, attacking football in the country.

PLAYER
FIORE, Stefano
Midfielder, Italian, 177cm, 68kg
Born: 17.04.75, Cosenza
Clubs: Cosenza (1992-94), Parma (1994-95), Padova (1995-96), Chievo (1996-97), Parma (1997-99), Udinese (1999-)
Full international (Italy) 10 caps/1 goals
• Creative midfielder who sprang on to the

international scene a matter of weeks before Euro 2000, playing a key role in the Italian national side.
• Made his Serie A debut for Parma in December 1994, establishing himself as a stylish, swashbuckling orchestrator in central midfield.
• Was the £5.2million makeweight in the £22million deal which saw striker **Amoroso** move from Udinese to Parma in summer 1999.
• At Udinese, Fiore played more regularly and had the chance to establish his playmaking credentials, with **Dino Zoff** taking notice and giving him an international debut against Sweden in February.
• Zoff quickly established Fiore in the playmaking role for Italy, as much to head off those Italians who had been campaigning to see **Francesco Totti** in that position.
• Will join Lazio in summer 2001, according to the Roman club.

PLAYER
FIRICANO, Aldo
Defender, Italian, 184cm, 78kg
Born: 12.03.67, Trapani, Italy
Clubs: Cavese (1983-85), Udinese (1985-89), Nocerina (1986-87, loan), Cagliari (1989-96), Fiorentina (1996-)
• Vastly experienced sweeper who moved to Fiorentina in 1996 from Cagliari as part of the deal which also saw **Luis Oliveira** move to Florence, having played for the then Fiorentina coach **Claudio Ranieri** for three seasons at Cagliari.
• Has played under 18 different coaches in his career.

PLAYER
FJORTOFT, Jan-Aage
Forward, Norwegian, 192cm, 91kg
Born: 10.01.67, Alesund, Norway
Clubs: Gursken, Hodd, Hamarkameratene, Lillestrom (1988-89), Rapid Vienna (Aut) (1989-

93), Swindon Town (Eng) (1993-95), Middlesbrough (Eng) (1995-96), Sheffield United (Eng) (1996-97), Barnsley (Eng) (1997-98), Eintracht Frankfurt (Ger) (1998-)
Full international (Norway) 70 caps/20 caps
• Battle-hardened Norwegian centre-forward who fits the hustle and bustle of German football like a glove. He is good in the air, has a sharp eye for an opening and better close control than he is given credit for. His fighting spirit was a key ingredient in Eintracht's successful fights against relegation in the past two years.

PLAYER
FJORTOFT, Karl Oskar
Midfielder, Norwegian, 174cm, 62kg
Born: 26.07.75, Norway
Clubs: Hodd (1995), Rosenborg (1996-97), Molde (1997-)
• Midfield dynamo who left Rosenborg for Molde some seasons ago when he failed to establish himself in the side. Originally from Hodd's famous football academy.

PLAYER
FLAVIO CONCEICAO
Full name: Flavio da Conceicao
Midfielder, Brazilan, 178cm. 74kg
Born: 12.06.74, Santa Maria da Sierra, Brazil
Clubs: Rio Branco (1992-93), Palmeiras (1994-96), Deportivo La Coruna (Spa) (1997-2000), Real Madrid (Spa) (2000-)
Full international (Brazil)
• Midfield destroyer who also has impressive distribution skills, a powerful, accurate shot and a good goalscoring record.
• A regular international for Brazil under coach Wanderley Luxemburgo after making his name as midfield anchorman for the Brazil Olympic side.
• Signed by Deportivo from Palmeiras for £4million on a seven-year contact in 1996.
• Joined Real Madrid in summer 2000 as a replacement for Milan-bound **Fernando Redondo**.

PLAYER
FLEMING, Curtis
Defender, Irish, 178cm, 80kg
Born: 08.10.68, Manchester, England
Clubs: Middlesbrough (1991-)
Full international (Rep Ireland) 10 caps/0 goals
• Combative and versatile full-back who can play on either flank.

PLAYER
FLO, Jostein
Forward, Norwegian, 194cm, 95kg
Born: 03.10.64, Stryn, Norway
Clubs: Molde (1987-90), Lierse (Bel) (1990-91), Sogndal (1991-93), Sheffield Utd (Eng) (1993-96), Stromsgodset (1996-)
Full international (Norway) 23 caps/11 goals
• Veteran who played in the English Premier League and in Belgian football some seasons ago. Athletic striker who is strong in the air and has a good shot. He will be vital in his club's fight for promotion after relegation in 1999.
• Brother of **Tore Andre Flo**.

PLAYER
FLO, Tore Andre
Forward, Norwegian, 196cm, 85kg
Born: 15.06.73, Stryn, Norway
Clubs: Sogndal (1994), Tromdo (1995), Brann (1996-97), Chelsea (Eng) (1997-)
Full international (Norway) 51 caps/21 goals
• Tall striker with exceptional technique who has matured into a forward of international stature during three seasons at Chelsea.
• Has been a victim of **Gianluca Vialli**'s player rotation policy at Chelsea, leading him to be linked with a number of other clubs.
• Dubbed 'Flo-naldo' after scoring for Norway in a memorable friendly win over Brazil.
• International debut: 11.10.95, v England (0-0).

PLAYER
FLOWERS, Tim
Goalkeeper, English, 188cm, 91kg
Born: 03.02.67, Kenilworth, England
Clubs: Wolverhampton (1984-86), Southampton (1986-93), Swindon (1987, loan), Blackburn (1993-99), Leicester (1999-)
Full international (England) 11 caps/0 goals
• Excellent shot-stopper who made his name at Southampton, becoming England's most expensive goalkeeper when he joined Blackburn for £2.4million in November 1993.
• Fell from grace at Blackburn during the 1998-99 season because of a combination of injuries and loss of form. Has since revived his career at Leicester.
• International debut: 13.06.93, v Brazil (1-1).

PLAYER
FOE, Marc-Vivien
Midfielder, Cameroonian, 190cm, 85kg
Born: 01.05.75, Nkolo, Cameroon
Clubs: Canon Yaounde (1994), Lens (Fra) (1994-99), West Ham (Eng) (1999-2000), Lyon (Fra) (2000-)
Full international (Cameroon)
• Accomplished midfielder who was one of the stars of Cameroon's victory at the African Nations Cup.
• Won the French League title with Lens in 1998, but subsequent transfer to Manchester United was put on hold because of a broken leg.
• Surname pronounced Foe ay.

PLAYER
FOLETTI, Patrick
Goalkeeper, Swiss, 188cm, 93kg
Born: 27.05.74, Switzerland
Clubs: Grasshopper (1998-99), Lucerne (1999-)
• Keeper who is building a reputation for pulling off match-winning saves.

COACH
FOMENKO, Mikhail
Ukrainian
Born: 19.09.48
• Coach of Metallist Kharkiv and a former skipper of Kyiv Dynamo in the 1970s.
• A strict disciplinarian who made his name in Ukraine in 1990s when Kyiv Dynamo, under his guidance, defeated **Johan Cruyff**'s Barcelona 3-1 in Kyiv.

PLAYER
FONSECA, Daniel
Forward, Uruguayan, 182cm, 74kg
Born: 13.09.69, Montevideo, Uruguay
Clubs: Nacional Montevideo (1989-90), Cagliari (Ita) (1990-92), Napoli (Ita) (1992-94), Roma (Ita) (1994-97), Juventus (Ita) (1997-)
Full international (Uruguay)
• Serie A veteran who has scored consistently at Cagliari, Napoli, Roma and Juventus.
• Recent seasons at Juve have been dogged by injury and lack of first-team action.
• Played for Uruguay at the 1990 World Cup in Italy, where he first came to the attention of Serie A scouts, securing a transfer to Cagliari.

PLAYER
FONTOLAN, Davide
Midfielder, Italian, 182cm, 76kg
Born: 24.02.66, Garbagnate, Italy.
Clubs: Legnano (1982-86), Parma (1986-87), Udinese (1987-88), Genoa (1989-90), Internazionale (1990-96), Bologna (1996-)
• Attacking midfielder whose career has been a mild anti-climax, with injuries affecting his time at Inter.
• His fortunes have been revived at Bologna, but international honours have eluded him.

Tore Andre Flo

Marc-Vivien Foe

FORSSELL, Mikael

Forward, Finnish, 186cm, 79kg
Born: 15.03.81, Steinfurt, Germany
Clubs: HJK Helsinki, Chelsea (Eng) (1998-),
Crystal Palace (Eng) (2000-, loan)
Full international (Finland) 3 caps/0 goals
• Teenage goalscoring prodigy who signed a five-year contract with Chelsea in December 1998.
• Moved on loan at Crystal Palace after failing to make an impact on **Gianluca Vialli**'s rotation policy at Stamford Bridge.

PLAYER
FORTES, Carlos

Forward, Dutch, 170cm, 70kg
Born: 27.04.74, Rotterdam, Holland
Clubs: Sparta Rotterdam (1992-97), Vitesse
Arnhem (1997-)
• Lively left winger, who feared for the end of his career after suffering a double fractured leg in a European match against Braga.
• Returned to full fitness in the 1999-2000 season under the guidance of **Ronald Koeman**.

PLAYER
FORTUNE, Quinton

Midfielder, South African, 180cm, 76kg
Born: 21.05.77, South Africaa
Clubs: Tottenham (Eng), Mallorca (Spa) (1995-96), Atletico Madrid B (1996-99), Manchester United (Eng) (1999-)
Full international (South Africa)
• Youngest ever player to be capped by South Africa when he made his debut in 1996.
• Travelled to England aged 15 and was an apprentice at Spurs under **Terry Venables**, but moved on to Spain in 1995 after failing to obtain a work permit.
• Spent four seasons with Atletico Madrid B, playing only two first-team/A games.
• Played all three games for South Africa at 1998 World Cup.

FOURNET-FAYARD, Jean
• French member of the UEFA executive committee.

FOWLER, Robbie
Forward, English, 176cm, 73kg
Born: 09.04.75, Liverpool, England
Clubs: Liverpool (1992-)
Full international (England) 14 caps/3 goals
• Gifted striker whose goals have carried Liverpool in recent years, but who has been let down by injuries and his own indiscretions.
• During a local derby with Everton in 1999, he responded to crowd taunts about his alleged drug taking by pretending to snort the goal line in celebration of a goal.
• A prolific, instinctive scorer for Liverpool since his debut in 1993 but has yet to have a proper opportunity to transfer that form to the international arena.

FRAN
Full name: Francisco Javier Valeron Santana
Midfielder, Spanish, 179cm, 71kg
Born: 14.07.69, La Coruna, Spain
Clubs: Deportivo La Coruna (1988-)
Full international (Spain) 16 caps/2 goals
• A huge hero in La Coruna, where he is Deportivo's captain and longest-serving player, having started out in the club's youth ranks.
• Initially an inside-left, but now prefers to play wide on the left, where his skill and technique are put to excellent use.
• Largely ignored by former national coach **Javier Clemente** ('Fran has not captured my message') but has enjoyed a revival under **Jose Camacho** which coincided with Fran playing a key role in Deportivo's first Spanish League title success in 1999-2000.
• Recalled by Camacho to the Spanish national side, playing for Spain at Euro 2000.

FRANCISKOVIC, Ivica
Midfielder, Yugoslav, 178cm, 70kg
Born: 28.09.78, Subotica, Yugoslavia
Clubs: Partizan Belgrade, Spartak Subotica
• Skiful, left-footed playmaker who failed to make the grade with Partizan.
• Yugoslav Under-21 international.

FRANKOWSKI, Tomasz
Forward, Polish, 172cm, 62kg
Born: 16.08.74, Poland
Clubs: Strasbourg (Fra), Stade Poitiers (Fra) and FC Martigues (Fra), Nagoya Grampus Eight (Jap), Wisla Krakow
Full international (Poland) 3 caps/0 goals
• Striker who spent five years abroad before returning to help Wisla Krakow to win the Polish championship.
• Top scorer in the 1999-2000 Polish League with 21 goals. Voted discovery of 1998 in Poland.

FRANTZESKOS, Costas
Midfielder, Greek, 180cm, 72kg
Born: 04.01.69, Greece
Clubs: Panathinaikos (1990-94), OFI Crete (1994-96), PAOK Salonika (1996-2000), Kalamata (2000-)
Full international (Greece) 38 caps/8 goals
• Now in the twilight years of a long and successful career but still has much to offer in terms of accurate left-footed passing ability, imagination and prowess from set-pieces.

FREDERIKSEN, Soren
Forward, Danish, 178cm, 73kg
Born: 27.01.72, Denmark
Clubs: Viborg (1993-94), Silkeborg (1993-96), Viborg (1996), AaB (1996-)
Full international (Denmark) 6 caps/1 goal
• Bustling striker who shot AaB Aalborg to the

Robbie Fowler

Danish Superliga title in 1999.
• Keen on a move abroad, but trials at Leicester and Ipswich did not work out.
• Made his international debut for Denmark against England in March 1994 but has never been anything more than a fringe player at international level.

PLAYER
FREDGAARD, Carsten
Forward, Danish, 185cm 78kg
Born: 20.05.76, Denmark
Clubs: Lyngby (1995-99, Sunderland (Eng) (1999-)
Full international (Denmark) 4 cap/0 goals
• Highly sought-after attacking midfielder or striker while with Lyngby, but has failed to establish himself in the first team at Sunderland, going loan to West Brom.

PLAYER
FREI, Alexander
Forward, Swiss, 179cm, 69kg
Born: 15.07.79, Switzerland
Clubs: Basel (1997-98), Thun (1998-99), Lucerne (1999-)
• Promising young attacker currently catching the eye with his drive and eye for goal. Joined from Second Division Thun at the start of the 1998-99 season.

PLAYER
FRESI, Salvatore
Defender, Italian, 182cm, 72kg
Born: 16.01.73, La Maddalena, Italy
Clubs: Fiorentina (1990-91), Foggia (1991-93), Salernitana (1993-95), Internazionale (1995-), Salernitana (1998-99, loan)
• Touted as a future Italian national team libero after starring performances at Under-21 level.
• Won 20 Under-21 caps under **Cesare Maldini** while still with second division Salernitana and was expected to make the step up to the full national team, especially after a move to Inter in

summer 1995. But the arrival at Inter of **Roy Hodgson** scuppered his progress and he was played in midfield in a 4-4-2 formation.
• Reputation marred by a high tackle which broke Giovanni Stroppa's leg at Udinese.
• Spent most of the 1998-99 season back on loan at Salernitarna and has since failed to regain his place in the national squad.

PLAYER
FREUND, Steffen
Midfielder, German, 180cm, 68kg
Born: 19.01.70, Brandenburg, Germany
Clubs: Stahk Brandenburg (1988-91), Schalke (1991-93), Borussia Dortmund (1993-98), Tottenham (Eng) (1998-)
Full international (Germany) 21 caps/0 goals
• Gritty, hard-working midfielder who added bite to Spurs' midfield following his transfer from Dortmund in December 1998.
• Product of the East German youth system and a locksmith by trade.
• Won German League title in 1995 and 1996, European Championship in 1996 and European Champions Cup in 1997.

PLAYER
FREY, Sebastien
Goalkeeper, French, 189cm, 85kg
Born: 18.03.80, Thonon-les-Bains, France
Clubs: Cannes (1997-98), Internazionale (Ita) (1998-), Verona (Ita) (1999-2000, loan)
• Promising French Under-21 keeper who joined Inter as a teenager and spent a year on loan at Verona, returning to Milan in summer 2000.

PLAYER
FRICK, Mario
Midfielder, Liechtenstein, 183cm, 76kg
Born: 07.09.74, Liechtenstein
Clubs: St Gallen (Bel) (1994-96), Basel (Swi) (1996-1999), Zurich (Swi) (1999-)
Full international (Liechtenstein) 29 caps/3 goals

• Liechtenstein's only professional player, an attacking midfielder who has carved out a useful career in Belgium and Switzerland.

PLAYER
FRIEDEL, Brad
Goalkeeper, American, 193cm, 92kg
Born: 18.05.71, Lakewood, USA
Clubs: Brondby (Den) (1994-95), Galatasaray (Tur) (1995-96), Columbus Crew (1996-1997), Liverpool (Eng) (1997-)
Full international (United States) 65 caps/1 goal
• Tall, agile and very strong keeper who has won numerous caps for the US, but has struggled to command first-team club football in Europe.
• Edged out **David James** from the Liverpool goal but then lost out to **Sander Westerveld**. Lack of first-team action made it unlikely that his work permit would be renewed.

PLAYER
FRINGS, Torsten
Forward, German, 182cm, 80kg
Born: 22.11.76, Wursel, Germany
Clubs: Rhenania Alsdorf, Alemann Aachen, Werder Bremen (1996-)
• Promising young utility man tipped to play for Germany in the not-too-distant future. Can play as an attacking midfielder – on either left or right flank – right-back or up front and rarely has been found wanting.

REFEREE
FRISK, Anders
Swedish
Born: 18.02.63.
• Works as an insurance agent.
• Awarded FIFA badge in 1991.
• In charge of the Euro 2000 Final between France and Italy.

PLAYER
FROGGATT, Stephen
Midfielder, English, 177cm, 70kg
Born: 09.03.73, Lincoln, England
Clubs: Aston Villa (1991-94), Wolverhampton (1994-98), Coventry (1998-
• Left-winger whose form for Coventry following a £1.9million transfer from Wolves brought him into international contention.

PLAYER
FRYDEK, Martin
Midfielder, Czech, 169cm, 74kg
Born: 09.03.69, Hradec, Czech Republic
Clubs: Sparta Prague, Leverkusen (Ger), Teplice
Full international (RCS/Czech Rep) 43 caps/4 goals
• Pugnacious midfielder whose career has gone astray since a disastrous move from Sparta to Germany's Bayer Leverkusen.
• Rescued from Germany before the 1999-2000 season by Teplice, who fancied Frydek to boost their chances of getting through the Champions League's third qualifying round, but the player has continued to struggle with form back in the Czech League.

PLAYER
FUERTES, Esteban Oscar
Forward, Argentinian, 183cm, 85kg
Born: 26.12.72, Buenos Aires, Argentina
Clubs: Platense (1995-96), Racing (1996-97), Colon (1997-99), Derby County (Eng) (1999), Lens (Fra) (2000-)
• Striker who hit the headlines when his passport contained irregularities which prevented him from entering the UK to play for Derby.

PLAYER
FUKAL, Milan
Defender, Czech, 188cm, 84kg
Born: 16.05.75, Czech Republic
Clubs: Jablonec, Sparta Prague (1999-)
Full international (Czech Republic) 8 caps/1 goal

• Signed from Jablonec before the 1999-2000 season, Fukal proved to be the revelation of Sparta's Champions League campaign.
• The defender has developed a previously untapped talent for scoring vital goals – usually long-range strikes – and earned himself a place in the Euro 2000 squad after impressive European and domestic form.

COACH
FUNKEL, Friedhelm
German
Born: 10.12.53
• MSV Duisburg's disastrous form last season led to him being sacked after four years in charge of the Zebras. Yet he remains highly respected in Germany and was in the running to become the assistant to new Germany coach **Rudi Voller**.
• Provided leadership of the low-key, no-frills variety. A midfielder in the Bayer Uerdingen side which beat Bayern Munich in the Final of the 1985 German Cup.

PLAYER
FUSER, Diego
Midfielder, Italian, 183cm, 77kg
Born: 11.11.68, Venaria, Italy
Clubs: Torino (1986-89), Milan (1989-90), Fiorentina (1990-91), Milan (1991-92), Lazio (1992-98), Parma (1998-)
Full international (Italy) 24 caps/2 goals
• Right-sided midfield all-rounder and honest worker whose qualities are much admired by coaches.
• A Serie A veteran who made his debut for Torino aged 18 in the local derby against Juventus in April 1997.
• Played one season under Arrigo Sacchi at Milan, but left because of competition for midfield places.
• A member of Italy's squad at Euro 2000.
• Surprised many when Parma paid Lazio £4million for his services in summer 1998, but he has played some of his best football at Parma.

G

GAARDE, Allan
Midfielder, Danish, 195cm, 83kg
Born: 25.01.75, Denmark
Clubs: AaB (1997-)
• Attacking midfielder who won the Danish League title with AaB Aalborg in 1999. Height makes him a big threat in the air.

PLAYER
GABRI
Full name: Gabriel Garcia de la Torre
Midfielder, Spanish, 174cm, 73kg
Born: 10.02.79, Barcelona, Spain
Clubs: Barcelona (1998-)
• Hugely talented attacking midfielder with an abundance of vision and goalscoring nous.
• The star of Spain's world Under-20 triumph in Nigeria in 1999.
• One of the few local youngsters to break into the Barcelona first team under Dutch coach Louis Van Gaal despite intense competition.
• Demonstrated his huge potential by scoring crucial goals to help Barcelona continue their unbeaten progress into the quarter-finals of the Champions League.

PLAYER
GABRIEL, Petr
Midfielder, Czech, 190cm, 85kg
Born: 17.05.73, Czech Republic
Clubs: Sparta Prague, Kaiserslautern (Ger) (2000-)
Full international (Czech Republic) 10 caps/1 goal
• Often-ridiculed, physical defensive midfielder who had an impressive 1999-2000 season (despite breaking team-mate Vladimir Labant's leg in the Slavia-Sparta derby) and was drafted into the Euro 2000 team as a result.
• Joined Kaiserslautern in the summer of 2000.

PLAYER
GAILLOT, Philippe
Defender, French, 182cm, 80kg
Born: 28.02.65, Chateau-Salins, France
Clubs: Metz (1985-92), Valenciennes (1992-93), Metz (1993-)
• Apart from a season with Valenciennes, he has spent all his career with Metz, serving them admirably in the left-back berth for over 15 years. A relentless marker and very good in the air, he has clocked up more than 400 French League appearances.
• Pronounced Fee leep Guy oh.

PLAYER
GAJSER, Saso
Midfielder, Slovenian, 178cm, 76kg
Born: 11.02.74, Slovenia
Clubs: Maribor (1996-97), Rudar (1997-99), Gent (Bel) (1999-)
Full international (Slovenia) 6 caps/1 goals
• Midfielder from Slovenia and an anonymous but important part of Gent's success in the 1999-2000 season. Usually plays on the right flank.
• A member of his national squad at Euro 2000 but did not play.
• Has said he would be a policeman if he had not become a footballer.

PLAYER
GALANTE, Fabio
Defender, Italian, 185cm, 80kg
Born: 20.11.73, Montecatini Terme, Italy
Clubs: Empoli (1990-93), Genoa (1993-96), Internazionale (1996-99), Torino (1999-)
• Powerful centre-half with an eye for goal at set-pieces.
• Captain of the Italian Under-21 side which won the 1996 European Championship.

PLAYER
GALASEK, Tomas
Midfielder, Czech, 181cm, 75kg
Born: 15.01.73, Ostrava, Czech Rep
Clubs: Banik Ostrava (1991-96), Willem II (Hol) (1996-2000), Ajax (Hol) (2000-)
Full international (Czech Rep) 11 caps/0 goals
• Midfielder who followed coach Co Adriaanse from Willem II to Ajax in summer 2000.
• International debut against Finland, 08.03.95.

PLAYER
GALCA, Constantin
Midfielder, Romanian, 179cm, 73kg
Born: 08.03.72, Bucherest, Romania
Clubs: Arges Pitesti (1989-91), Steaua Bucharest (1991-96), Mallorca (Spa) (1996-97), Espanyol (Spa) (1997-)
Full international (Romania) 58 caps/4 goals
• Holding midfielder who provides a strong midfield presence for Espanyol and Romania. Good tackler with excellent distribution skills.
• A regular at Steaua Bucharest for five seasons, winning four Romanian League titles.
• Had an excellent first season in Spain with Mallorca, scoring 13 goals in 34 games, before moving to Espanyol.
• Played for Romania at the 1994 and 1998 World Cups, Euro 96 and Euro 2000.

PLAYER
GALIC, Marinko
Defender, Slovenian, 178cm, 80kg
Born: 22.04.70, Koper, Slovenia
Clubs: Koper, Maribor, Croatia Zagreb (Cro), Mura, Maribor
Full international (Slovenia) 55 caps/0 goals
• Central defender who started all three of Slovenia's games at Euro 2000.
• A stylish defender who plays sweeper for his club Maribor, and is the free man at the back for his country. But can be prone to making mistakes and occasional indiscipline.

• Says he would have trained to be a journalist is he had not become a footballer.

PLAYER
GALLARDO, Marcelo
Midfielder, Argentinian, 169cm, 70kg
Born: 18.01.76, Buenos Aires, Argentina
Clubs: River Plate (1992-99), Monaco (Fra) (1999-)
Full international (Argentina) 35 caps/1 goal
• Extremely gifted footballer with wonderful technique who is a product of the River Plate youth system.
• Joined Monaco in a £5million in summer 1999 and was voted France's Player of the Year in his first season. One of the principal reasons why Monaco romped to the 1999-2000 League title.
• The decision of 'Monegasque' coach Claude Puel to play the little Argentinian international on the left-side of midfield was a masterstroke, with Gallardo's dynamism and trickery proving the inspiration behind a large proportion of his team's goals. In the process, he has become a marked man in French football circles, singled out for some especially brutal treatment from opposing defenders.
• Sabri Lamouchi on Gallardo: 'He's the sort of player who is gven a sausage at the start of a move and turns it into caviar.'
• International debut: November 1994, v Chile.
• Surname pronounced Guy ah do.

PLAYER
GALLAS, William
Defender, French, 181cm, 72kg
Born: 17.08.77, Asnieres, France
Clubs: Caen (1996-97), Marseille (1997-)
• There is every chance that this outstanding young defender will soon break into the senior French side. Disciplined, athletic and quick, he can play at right-back but is even better as a centre-back. Very comfortable on the ball and scored a memorable winner when Marseille beat Manchester United in the Champions League.

ADMINISTRATOR
GALLIANI, Adriano

• Vice-president of Milan and the man designated
to run the club in the absence of president **Silvio
Berlusconi**. Responsible for all the club's
transfer dealings.

PLAYER
GALVEZ, Jose

Full name: Jose Galvez Estevez
Forward, Spanish, 180cm, 78kg
Born: 03.08.74, Mallorca, Spain
Clubs: Mallorca (1991-93), Valencia (1993-96),
Mallorca (1997-98), Real Betis (1998-)
• Promising forward who was edged out of the
picture at Betis by the arrival of **Denilson**.
• Plagued by inconsistency but an impressive
player when on top of his game.

PLAYER
GAMARRA, Carlos

Full name: Carlos Alberto Gamarra Pavon
Defender, Paraguayan, 179cm, 76kg
Born: 17.02.71, Ypacarai, Paraguay
Clubs: Cerro Porteno (1991-92), Independiente
(Arg) (1992-93), Cerro Porteno (1993-95),
Internacional (Bra) (1996-97), Benfica (Por)
(1997-98), Corinthians (Bra) (1998-99), Atletico
Madrid (Spa) (1999-2000), Flamengo (Bra, loan)
Full international (Paraguay)
• Accomplished central defender who is
comfortable on the ball and has excellent vision
and positional sense.
• Played for Paraguay at the 1998 World Cup
finals in France.
• Performances for Brazilian club Corinthians in
their 1998 national championship success earned
him rave reviews and the accolade of Brazilian
Player of the Year, an extraordinary award for a
foreign defender to win.
• Linked with a move to another club following
Atletico's relegation from the Spanish Liga in May
2000, and eventually returned to Brazil, to Flamengo.

Marcelo Gallardo

189

GANE, Ione
Forward, Romanian, 183cm, 77kg
Born: 12.10.71, Dranic, Romania
Clubs: Osasuna (Spa) (1996-98), St Gallen (Swi) (1998-)
Full international (Romania) 5 caps/0 goals
• A quick and opportunistic Romanian striker who won the Romanian Cup with Universitatea Craiova in 1991.

PLAYER
GANEA, Ioan
Forward, Romanian, 179cm, 79kg
Born: 19.08.73, Fagaras, Romania
Clubs: Brasov (1994-96), Univ. Craoiva (1996-98), Rapid Bucharest (1998-99), Stuttgart (Ger) (1999-)
Full international (Romania) 16 caps/9 goals
• The Romanian attacker has blown rather hot and cold since moving to the Bundesliga from Rapid Bucharest. But overall, seven goals in his first season in the West was not a bad return and provided he finds more consistency, he definitely has the touch, speed and composure in front of goal to make a big name for himself.
• The top scorer in the Romanian League in 1998-99 with 28 goals, he can also play deeper in a playmaking role.
• Surname prounouced Gan nay ah.

PLAYER
GANZ, Maurizio
Forward, Italian, 178cm, 70kg
Born: 13.10.68, Tolmezzo, Italy
Clubs: Sampdoria (1985-88), Monza (1988-89), Parma (1989-90), Brescia (1990-92), Atalanta (1992-95), Internazionale (1995-97), Milan (1997-)
• Much-travelled striker who was a surprise signing when he move across town from Inter to Milan in December 1997.

PLAYER
GARAY, Diego
Midfielder, Argentinian, 170cm, 69kg
Born: 01.02.75, Cordoba, Argentina
Clubs: Newell's Old Boys, Strasbourg
• When the Argentinian attacking midfielder arrived at Strasbourg a year ago, he was described by his new manager Claude Le Roy as 'one of the most gifted players I've ever seen'.
• Unfortunately, injuries and loss of form has left Garay giving fans in Alsace a quite different impression. The jury is out.

PLAYER
GARCIA CALVO, Jose Antonio
Defender, Spanish, 180cm, 78kg
Born: 01.04.75, Madrid, Spain
Clubs: Real Madrid B (1993-95), Real Madrid (1995-97), Valladolid (1997-)
• Central defender who failed to win a first-team place after coming through the youth ranks at Real Madrid, and despite impressing on his debut, a Champions League quarter-final against Juventus.
• Moved to Valladolid, where he quickly established himself as a regular.
• Spanish Under-21 international.

REFEREE
GARCIA-ARANDA Encinar
Spanish
Born: 03.03.56
• Professor of physical education.
• Awarded FIFA badge in 1993.

PLAYER
GARGO, Mohamed
Defender, Ghanaian, 181cm, 80kg
Born: 19.06.75, Tamale, Ghana
Clubs: Torino (Ita) (1991-93), Borussia Dortmund (Ger) (1993-94), Bayern Munich (Ger) (1994), Stoke City (Eng) (1995), Udinese (Ita) (1995-)
Full international (Ghana)

• One of the first Africans to be brought over to Italy as a teenager when Torino signed him as a 16-year-old. He has since matured into a highly versatile, highly-rated defender or defensive midfielder.
• Sent on loan by Torino to Germany and England, he was signed permanently by Udinese, who have reaped the benefits of having one of the best African players in Serie A on their books.

PLAYER
GARITANO, Ander
Midfielder, Spanish, 175cm, 70kg
Born: 26.02.69, Derio, Spain
Clubs: Athletic Bilbao (1985-96), Zaragoza (1996-)
• Attacking midfielder whose promise has never been fully realised during his time at Athletic Bilbao and Zaragoza.
• Came through the youth ranks at Athletic, his hometown club, but fell out with the club's golden boy **Julen Guerrero** and was snapped up by Zaragoza for a knockdown £500,000.

PLAYER
GARZJA, Luigi
Defender, Italian, 174cm, 73kg
Born: 07.07.69, San Cesario, Italy
Clubs: Lecce (1985-91), Reggina (1987-88, loan), Roma (1991-94), Cremonese (1994-96), Bari (1996-)
• Honest, hard-working professional and a useful man-marking defender. Popular captain at Bari.

PLAYER
GASPAR
Full name: Gaspar Galves Burgos
Defender, Spanish, 183cm, 88kg
Born: 07.07.79, Cordoba, Spain
Clubs: Atletico Madrid (1998-)
• Young reserve defender sparingly used by successive Atletico coaches **Claudio Ranieri** and **Radomir Antic**. Can play in any of the defensive positions.

ADMINISTRATOR
GASPERT, Joan
• Elected president of Barcelona in July 2000 after serving as vice-president to **Josep Lluis Nunez**.

PLAYER
GATTUSO, Gennaro
Midfielder, Italian, 176cm, 77kg
Born: 09.01.78, Corigliano Schiavonea, Italy
Clubs: Perugia (1995-97), Rangers (1997-98), Salernitana (1998-99), Milan (1999-)
Full international (Italy) 2 caps/0 goals
• Combative midfielder who won a Scottish League and Cup with Rangers in 1998 before returning to Italy via Salernitana in November 1998.
• Joined Milan in summer 1999 to provide cover for the Champions League campaign.
• Italy Under-21 international.

PLAYER
GAUCHO I
Full name: Eric Freire Gomes
Forward, Brazilian, 172cm, 64kg
Born: 22.09.72, Recife, Brazil
Clubs: Estrela Amadora (1996-), Ourana (1998-99)
• Striker who returned to form for Estrela Amadora in the 1999-2000 season after spending the 1998-99 season on loan at Ourana.

PLAYER
GAUTIERI, Carmine
Forward, Italian, 182cm, 76kg
Born: 20.07.70, Naples, Italy
Clubs: Turris (1989-91), Empoli (1991-92), Cesena (1992-93), Bari (1993-96), Perugia (1996-97), Roma (1997-99), Piacenza (1999-)
• Midfield workhorse who joined Empoli in 1991 but had to wait until 1994 to make his Italian first division debut with Bari.
• Spent two seasons with Roma, before heading to Piacenza in 1999.

Grigoris Georgatos

GAVA, Franck
Midfielder, French, 180cm, 75kg
Born: 03.02.70, Montargis, France
Clubs: Nancy (1986-92), Lyon (1992-96), Paris Saint-Germain (1996-98), Monaco (1998-99), Rennes (1999-)
Full international (France) 3 cap/0 goals
• The last three years have not been kind to the French international midfielder. Moves to PSG and Monaco did not work out as planned, he faded out of contention for a World Cup 98 berth and after signing for Rennes, he spent most of the 1999-2000 season in the treatment room. However, a fit Gava can still make a positive contribution as a left-sided or central creator.

GAVILAN, Diego
Forward, Paraguayan, 173cm, 68kg
Born: 01.03.80 Asuncion, Paraguay
Clubs: Cerra Porteno (19994-2000), Newcastle (Eng) (2000-)
Full international (Paraguay)
• Young attacking midfielder who attracted interest from European clubs following his performances for Paraguay at the 1999 Copa America, and signed for Newcastle in spring 2000.

GAYLE, Marcus
Forward, English/Jamaican, 188cm, 80kg
Born: 27.09.70, Hammersmith, England
Clubs: Brentford (1989-94), Wimbledon (1994-)
Full international (Jamaica) 9 caps/2 goals
• Tall, pacy striker who can also play as a left-winger. Strong in the air, particularly at set-pieces.
• A controversial inclusion in Jamaica's 1998 World Cup squad because he waited until the team had qualified before making himself available for selection.

COACH
GAZZAYEV, Valeri
Russian
Born: 07.08.54.
- Coach of Dynamo Moscow since 2000, his second spell in charge, after winning the Russian League title in 1995 during a second spell with Alaniya Vladikavkaz.
- A striker for a number of Soviet League teams, including Moscow Lokomotiv and Dynamo, from 1970 to 1986, playing eight times for the USSR national team between 1979 and 1983, scoring four goals.

PLAYER
GEBHARDT, Marco
Midfielder, German, 179cm, 73kg
Born: 07.10.72, Germany
Clubs: Askania Ballenstedt, Quedlinburger, SpVgg Thale, Hallescher, Anhalt Dessau, Lok Altmark Stendal, Verl, Eintracht Frankfurt (1997-)
- One of the revelations of the Bundesliga during the 1999-2000 season. The left-sided attacking midfielder consistently caught the eye with his wonderful crossing ability, tactical maturity and sense of self-sacrifice and was even touted as a possible eleventh-hour selection for Germany's European Championship squad. He has no time to waste if he does want an international career; he is already 27, having spent most of his footballing life playing with minor clubs in eastern Germany.

PLAYER
GENAUX, Regis
Defender, Belgian, 178cm, 78kg
Born: 31.08.73, Charleroi, Belgium
Clubs: Standard Liege (1990-96), Coventry (Eng) (1996), Udinese (Ita) (1997-)
Full international (Belgium) 22 caps/0 goals
- Strong attack-minded right-back who returned to the Belgian national side after establishing himself in Serie A, but missed Euro 2000 through injury.

PLAYER
GENTILE, Marco
Defender, Dutch, 184cm, 83kg
Born: 25.05.68, Den Haag, Holland
Clubs: Den Haag (1987-95), MVV (1995-97), Burnley (Eng) (1997-98), Volendam (1998-99), Willem II (1999-)
- Tough-tackling defender who has gained a reputation in Holland for collecting yellow and red cards. Played Champions League football in the autumn of his career but was often kept on the bench due for tactical reasons.

PLAYER
GEORGATOS, Grigoris
Defender, Greek, 174cm, 72kg
Born: 31.10.72, Piraeus, Greece.
Clubs: Panahaiki (1993-95), Olympiakos (1995-99), Inter (Ita) (1999-2000), Olympiakos (2000-)
Full international (Greece) 28 caps/3 goals
- Greek international midfielder who provides a dynamic presence on the left flank.
- Won three consecutive League titles with Olympiakos (1997-99).
- 'As a child I was always a supporter of Inter. I remember in 1983 travelling on a ship with Juventus fans who celebrated all night and did not allow me to sleep. From then on I was an enemy of their team and a supporter of their rivals.'
- *Corriere dello Sport*: 'He has a left foot that can make a lot of things happen. He runs, he dribbles, he marks and of course he crosses the ball. Something Inter have not seen since the days of **Roberto Carlos**.'
- Left Inter in July 2000 to return to Olympiakos. 'I missed Greece too much. No sum of money could make me feel differently.'

PLAYER
GERARD
Full name: Gerard Lopez Segu
Midfielder, Spanish, 180cm, 72kg
Born: 12.03.77, Barcelona, Spain

Geremi Ndjitap

Clubs: Barcelona B (1996-97), Valencia (1997-98), Alaves (1998-99), Valencia (1999-2000), Barcelona (2000-)

Full international (Spain) 3 caps/0 goals

• Young midfielder who burst onto the scene in the 1999-20000 season, scoring a hat-trick in Valancia's Champions League quarter-final defeat of Lazio.

• Started at hometown club Barcelona, where he made steady progress to the B team. He scored 10 goals in 32 matches, playing just in front of the defence, but was allowed by Barça to join Valencia.

• Was loaned out to newly-promoted Alaves for the 1998-99 season, and made a huge impression in Vitoria as a goalscoring midfield anchorman.

• Capped by Spain at Under-18 and Under-20 level.

• Called into Spain's senior national squad just before Euro 2000 and made his international debut against Luxembourg in June 2000.

• Kept his place in the squad for the finals in Belgium and Holland.

• 'It's so difficult to make the breakthrough at Barcelona. So many of the kids I played with wasted too many years waiting for a chance that they were never given.'

• Returned to Barcelona in summer 2000 in a £5million transfer.

COACH
GERARD, Eugene
Dutch

• After 15 years at OFI Crete, the Dutchman took heed of a heart condition and decided to retire at the end of the 1999-2000 season, though he will remain a technical adviser to the club.

• The coach who nurtured the talent of Greece and Ajax star striker **Nikos Machlas**.

PLAYER
GERBER, Heiko
Midfielder, German, 181cm, 73kg
Born: 11.07.72, Stillberg, Germany

Clubs: Stahl Lugau, Chemnitzer (1991-96), Arminia Bielefeld (1996-98), Nurnberg (1998-)
Full international (Germany) 2 caps/0 goals
• Dynamic and industrious left-sided midfielder who made his debut for Germany at the 1999 Confederations Cup in Mexico, but has since dropped right out of the national team reckoning. Always a solid and thrusting performer, but arguably a little short of genuine class at the highest level.
• Surname pronounced Gear ber.

GEREMI, Ndjitap
Midfielder, Cameroon, 180cm, 78kg
Born: 20.12.78, Bafoussam, Cameroon
Clubs: Racing Bafoussam (1995-96), Cerro Porteno (Par) (1996-97), Genclerbirligi (Tur) (1997-99), Real Madrid (Spa) (1999-)
Full international (Cameroon)
• Versatile midfielder spotted by **John Toshack** in Turkey and signed by Real Madrid.
• Member of Cameroon's victorous team at the 2000 African Nations Cup.
• Voted best foreign player in Turkey in 1999.
• Brings pace, strength and skill to the right-hand flank.

GERETS, Eric
Belgian
Born: 18.05.54
• Former Belgian international full-back, who played for Standard Liege, Milan, MVV Maastricht and PSV Eindhoven.
• Was a victim of an important bribery scandal in the 1980s which cost him his place in Milan. But he fought back and was skipper of the PSV team that won the European Champions Cup in 1988.
• Before joining PSV, he coached Lierse and Club Brugge. With all his clubs he has won the League championship.

GERRARD, Steven
Midfielder, English, 188cm, 78kg
Born: 30.05.80, Liverpool, England
Clubs: Liverpool (1998-)
Full international (England) 2 caps/0 goals
• Hugely promising young product of the Anfield youth system who broke into the full England team in time for Euro 2000.
• A mature, intelligent passer of the ball, combative and versatile (can play across midfielder and at right-back). Tipped for a long international career.

GERSHON, Shimon
Defender, Israeli, 186cm, 76kg
Born: 6.10.77
Clubs: Hapoel Tel Aviv.
Full international (Israel) 5 caps/0 goals.
• One of the bright prospects for the future in Israel's defence. He has a powerful shot and has scored several spectacular goals for his club. Is a certainty to take over as the leader in defence when **Amir Shelah** and **Alon Harazi** retire.

GIAN, Carlos
Full name: Dias Carlos Dantas
Midfielder, Brazilian
Clubs: Lucerne
• Skilful Brazilian midfielder with quick feet and above-average vision.

GIANNICHEDDA, Giuliano
Midfielder, Italian, 179cm, 75kg
Born: 21.09.74, Pontecorvo, Italy
Clubs: Sora (1992-95), Udinese (1995-)
Full international (Italy) 3 caps/0 goals
• Hard-working midfielder who has limited ability but is highly effective at winning the ball and distributing it.

David Ginola

• Will join Lazio at the end of the 2000-2001 season as part of a £24million deal which will also see **Stefano Fiori** move to Rome.

PLAYER
GIBSON, Neathan
Forward, South African, 189cm, 84kg
Born: 14.05.70, Malaysia
Clubs: Sarawak (Mly) (1997), Norrkoping (Swe) (1998), MyPa (Fin) (1999-)
• Towering South African target man. Has played in the USA, as well as in Sweden for Norrkopiing.
• Known for his physical style, and as one of the best headers of the ball in the Finnish League.

PLAYER
GIGGS, Ryan
Midfielder, Welsh, 177cm, 69kg
Born: 29.11.73, Cardiff, Wales
Clubs: Manchester United (1990-)
Full international (Wales) 26 caps/7 goals
• Pacy, penetrating left winger who has been the most successful player of Alex Ferguson's time as Manchester United manager, winning 15 major honours, including three League and FA Cup doubles.
• Captained England schoolboys but opted to play for Wales at senior level.
• On the books of Manchester City as a boy but joined United as a trainee in July 1990.
• Rarely, if ever, plays for Wales in friendly matches, which has led many in Wales to question his commitment.

PLAYER
GIGLIO, Stefan
Defender, Malta, 181cm, 74kg
Born: 26.02.79, Malta
Clubs: Valletta
Full international (Malta) 6 caps/0 goals
• The driving force in Valletta's midfield, but is let down his indiscipline.

ADMINISTRATOR
GILBERTO Parca Madail

Born: 14.12.44
• President of the Federacao Portuguesa de Futebol since March 1996 and a leading figure In Portugal's successful bid to host the European Championship finals in 2004.

PLAYER
GILEWICZ, Radoslav

Midfielder, Polish, 174cm, 64kg
Born: 08.05.71, Chelm, Poland
Clubs: GKS Tychy, Ruch Chorzow, St Gallen (Swi), Stuttgart (Ger) (1996-97), Karlsruhe (Ger) (1997-98), Tirol (Aut) (1998-)
Full international (Poland) 7 caps/0 goals
• Livewire striker who has been a big hit in Austria in the past two seasons.

PLAYER
GINOLA, David

Midfielder, French, 183cm, 74kg
Born: 25.01.67, Gassin, France
Clubs: Toulon (1985-88), Racing Paris (1988-90), Brest (1990-92), Paris Saint-Germain (1992-95), Newcastle (Eng) (1995-97), Tottenham (Eng) (1997-2000), Aston Villa (Eng) (2000-)
Full international (France) 17 caps/3 goals
• Gifted attacking midfielder who has delighted fans in England with his trickery on the pitch and charm off it. But he remains an enigma in France, where he has not enjoyed the same rapport with the public.
• Still remembered as the man whose mistake, late in a World Cup qualifying game against Bulgaria, cost France a place at USA 94.
• Voted 1999 Player of the Season by English players and media after winning the League Cup with Spurs.
• First came to prominence as a local lad playing for France in the Toulon Under-21 tournament.
• Joined Aston Villa in 2000 after falling out with **George Graham**.

PLAYER
GIOVANELLA, Everton

Midfielder, Brazilian, 175cm, 67kg
Born: 13.09.70, Caixas do Sul, Brazil
Clubs: Internacional Portre Alegre (1993), Estoril (Por) (1993-94), Trisense (Por) (1994-95), Belenenses (Por) (1995-96), Salamanca (Spa) (1996-99), Celta Vigo (Spa) (1999-)
• Midfielder who has made the transition from journeyman to wanted man after years of unexceptional progress in Portugal and Spain.
• Made the breakthrough at Salamanca aged 27, winning promotion to the Spanish first division.
• Developed at Salamanca into an exceptional holding midfielder, with excellent tackling skills and positional sense.
• Joined Celta for £1.75million in summer 1999.

PLAYER
GIOVANNI

Full name: Giovanni da Silva Oliveira
Midfielder, Brazilian, 190cm, 84kg
Born: 04.02.74, Belem, Brazil
Clubs: Sao Carlense (1994), Santos (1995), Barcelona (Spa) (1996-99), Olympiakos (Gre) (1999-)
Full international (Brazil)
• Attacking midfielder signed from Barcelona at the start of the 1999-2000 season. Despite injury problems, he generally settled well and was voted the best foreign player in the Greek League.
• Few players in world football have as much skill as Giovanni and he uses it in both creative and chance-taking mode. But he remains something of an enigma due to a tendency to be easily discouraged – witness the last World Cup finals. A good friend of Rivaldo.

COACH
GIRESSE, Alan

French
Born: 02.08.52
• Legendary player who has has twice coached Toulouse to promotion to the French first division.

- Says he still feels bitter about the way he was shown the door by Paris Saint-Germain after just three months in charge in the 1998-99 season.
- Some might argue he is too much of a nice guy to be a successful coach. Yet the experience amassed in a brilliant playing career as a midfield general for France and Bordeaux, along with the respect he commands from his players and his organisational skills, suggest otherwise.
- On hanging up his boots, he spent seven years as a general manager with Bordeaux and Toulouse before becoming the latter's head coach in November 1995. Prefers experienced players and still does not have an official coaching badge.

PLAYER
GIULY, Ludovic
Midfielder, French, 164cm, 62kg
Born: 10.07.76, Lyon, France
Clubs: Lyon (1994-97), Monaco (1997-)
Full international (France) 1 cap/0 goals
- Blew his chance of going to Euro 2000 with an insipid performance on his full debut for France against Scotland in early 2000. But the diminutive right-sided attacking midfielder can console himself with the thought that he consistently sparkled at club level in the 1999-2000 season and has too much flair to remain long in the international wilderness.
- Surname pronounced Julie.

PLAYER
GIUNTI, Federico
Midfielder, Italian, 176cm, 73kg
Born: 06.08.71, Perugia, Italy
Clubs: Citta di Castello (1987-91), Perugia (1991-97), Parma (1997-99), Milan (1999-)
Full international (Italy) 1 cap/0 goals
- Ball-winning central midfielder who has been used as cover for **Demetrio Albertini** and **Massimo Ambrosini** at Milan.
- Has won one cap for Italy, against Bosnia in November 1996.

PLAYER
GIVEN, Shay
Goalkeeper, Irish, 183cm, 74kg
Born: 20.04.76, Lifford, Ireland
Clubs: Blackburn (1994-97), Swindon (1995, loan), Sunderland (1996, loan), Newcastle (1997-)
Full international (Rep Ireland) 25 caps/0 goals
- Highly capable young keeper who was first-choice keeper for the Irish Republic while playing second fiddle to **Tim Flowers** at Blackburn. Moved on to be number one at Newcastle, but then lost out to **Steve Harper**.

PLAYER
GOGIC, Sinisa
Forward, Yugoslav/Cypriot, 185cm, 76kg
Born: 20.10.63, Yugoslavia
Clubs: Olympiakos (Gre) (1996-2000), APOEL (2000-)
Full international (Cyprus) 37 caps/8 goals
- Serbian-born striker who has carved out a useful career in Greece and Cyprus, taking Cypriot nationality and playing a leading role for the national side.

COACH
GOIKOETXEA, Andoni
Spanish
Born: 23.08.56
- Controversial Bilbao hardman of the 1980s. Was **Javier Clemente**'s assistant with the national team from 1992 to 1996 before they fell out.
- Did poorly at Salamanca, but in the 1999-2000 season managed to keep Numancia in the top flight. Spent summer of 2000 out of work after refusing a new deal in Soria.

PLAYER
GOJKOVIC, Jovan
Midfielder, Yugoslavia, 178cm, 71kg
Born: 07.01.75, Cacek, Yugoslavia
Clubs: Red Star Belgrade

Full international (Yugoslavia) 1 cap/0 goals
• Left-footed, technically strong midfielder who is seen by many in Yugoslavia as a possible successor to **Dejan Savicevic**. So far, though, he has yet to live up to his great potential.

PLAYER
GOKTAN, Berkant
Forward, Turkish/German, 176cm, 70kg
Born: 12.12.80, Germany
Clubs: Bayern Munich (1998-), Borussia Monchengladbach (1998-99, loan), Arminia Bielefeld (1999-2000, loan)
• Highly promising young striker of Turkish origin who came through the ranks at Bayern Munich only to find first-team opportunities limited. Has since spent time on loan at Monchengladbach and Arminia Bielefeld.

PLAYER
GOLDBAEK, Bjarne
Midfielder, Danish, 180cm, 77kg
Born: 06.10.68, Copenhagen, Denmark
Clubs: Naetved (1987), Schalke (Ger) (1987-89), Kaiserslautern (Ger) (1990-93), Tennis Borussia Berlin (Ger) (1994), FC Koln (Ger) (1994-96), FC Copenhagen (1996-98), Chelsea (Eng) (1998-2000), Fulham (Eng) (2000-)
Full international (Denmark) 24 caps/0 goals
• Right-sided midfielder who battles hard but is just below real international class. Moved between various Bundesliga sides before a return home to Copenhagen and then a surprise switch to Chelsea.
• Member of Danish squad at 1998 World Cup and Euro 2000.

PLAYER
GOLZ, Richard
Goalkeeper, German, 199cm, 95kg
Born: 05.06.68, Berlin, Germany
Clubs: Wacker 04 Berlin, Tegel, Hamburg (1987-98), Freiburg (1998-)

• Reliable keeper, who, at 199cm, is the tallest player in the Bundesliga. Naturally, he puts his height to good use when coming for crosses, but also excels in the positioning department and in one-on-ones.
• Undemonstrative, serious type.

PLAYER
GOMA, Alain
Defender, French, 183cm, 83kg
Born: 05.10.72, Sault, France
Clubs: Auxerre (1990-98), Paris Saint-Germain (1998-99), Newcastle (Eng) (1999-)
Full international (France) 1 cap/0 goals
• French central defender whose time at Newcastle has been affected by injury and the departure of the coach who signed him from PSG, **Ruud Gullit**.

PLAYER
GOMEZ, Juan
Midfielder, Argentinian, 180cm, 78kg
Born: 25.01.71, Curruzu Cuatia, Argentina
Clubs: Argentinos Juniors (1991-95), River Plate (1995-96), Real Sociedad (Spa) (1996-)
• Holding midfielder who is an extremely effective ball-winner.

COACH
GOMEZ, Mario
Argentinian
Born: 27.02.57
• Argentinian coach who took over from **Hector Cuper** first at Lanus then at Mallorca, in August 1999. Was removed just a month later on the pretext that had failed to get a work permit. He was going to be sacked anyway, after a disastrous start to the season.

PLAYER
GOMEZ, Ronald
Forward, Costa Rican, 188cm, 80kg
Born: 24.01.75, Guanacoste, Costa Roca

Clubs: Olympiakos (Gre) (1996-99), Iraklis (Gre) (1999-)
Full international (Costa Roca)

• Despite missing three months of the 1999-2000 season, there was still more than sufficient time for OFI Crete's Costa Rican striker to hit 19 goals. Pacy and opportunistic and much more in the way of co-ordination than his famous compatriot **Paulo Wanchope** of West Ham.

• Came second behind **Giovanni** in the ballot for best foreigner in the Greek League in 1999-2000.

PLAYER
GONIAS, Panayotis
Midfielder, Greek, 180cm, 80kg
Born: 06.10.71, Livadeia, Greece
Clubs: Levadeiakos (1988-92), Olympiakos (1992-96), Iraklis (1996-98), Sporting Gljon (Spa) (1998-99), Paniliakos Pirgos (1999-)

• Capable midfield schemer with ample skill and vision and a good shot from distance, which, unfortunately, he does not utilise as often as he could.

PLAYER
GOOR, Bart
Midfielder, Belgian, 183cm, 75kg
Born: 09.04.73, Neerpelt, Belgium
Clubs: Genk (1996-97), Anderlecht (1997-)
Full international (Belgium) 19 caps/3 goals

• Dynamic young attacking midfielder whose performances on the left side of midfield were seen to be crucial to the revival of the Belgian national side under **Robert Waseige**.

• Made his name at Anderlecht after one season at Genk, winning the Belgian League in 1999-2000.

• Made his international debut against Cyprus in February 1999.

• Has earned a reputation as a goalscoring midfielder for Belgium, scoring in friendly matches against Italy and Holland and against Sweden in the opening match of Euro 2000.

• Raymond Goethals: 'I don't see him as the

Bart Goor

revelation that most people are calling him. But I was impressed with him as a youngster and he's been making steady progress. The highest compliment I can pay him is that he looks totally in his element in international football.'

PLAYER
GORAINOV, Olexander

Goalkeeper, Ukrainian, 182cm, 78kg
Born: 29.06.75
Clubs: Metalist Kharkiv
• Promising keeper who after several good seasons with modest Metalist is a clear target for bigger clubs.

PLAYER
GORAM, Andy

Goalkeeper, Scottish, 181cm, 92kg
Born: 13.04.64, Bury, England
Clubs: Oldham (1981-87), Hibernian (1988-91), Rangers (1991-98), Nottts County (1998-99), Sheffield Utd (1998-99), Motherwell (1998-)
Full international (Scotland) 39 caps/0 goals
• It looked like the end of the road for Goram when he was freed by Rangers at the end of the 1997-98 season but, after turning out briefly for Sheffield United, Goram was signed for Motherwell by manager **Billy Davies** and, despite being haunted by various controversies, has managed to re-establish himself, at the age of 36, as one of Scotland's most reliable keepers.

PLAYER
GOTTARDI, Guerino

Defender, Italian, 175cm, 71kg
Born: 18.12.70, Berne, Switzerland.
Clubs: Young Boys Berne Swi) (1989-91), Neuchatel Xamax (Swi) (1991-95), Lazio (1995-)
• Utility player and useful wide man who can play in midfield or defence. His pace means he is often used as a late substitute.
• Born in Switzerland, married to a Swiss and hopes to play for the Swiss national team.

PLAYER
GOTTSKALKSSON, Olafur

Goalkeeper, Icelandic, 191cm, 88kg
Born: 12.03.68, Keflavik, Iceland
Clubs: Keflavik (1988-89), KR (1990-93), Keflavik (1993-97), Hibernian (Sco) (1997-)
Full international (Iceland) 9 caps/0 goals
• Experienced keeper who could have made a career in basketball. Currently out of the frame at Hibs, he will be looking for a move which could help recover his place in the Icelandic national side.

PLAYER
GOUGH, Richard

Defender, Scottish, 183cm, 76kg
Born: 05.04.62, Stockholm, Sweden
Clubs: Dundee Utd (1980-86), Tottenham (1986-87), Rangers (1987-98), San Jose Clash (USA), Nottingham Forest (1999), Everton (1999-)
Full international (Scotland) 61 caps/6 goals
• Veteran central defender who was reunited last year with his former Rangers boss **Walter Smith** at Everton, after a surprise return, aged 37, to English football from Major League Soccer.
• Captained Rangers to a host of honours in Scotland before leaving for the US.

PLAYER
GOULD, Jonathan

Goalkeeper, Scottish, 186cm, 86kg
Born: 18.07.68, London, England
Clubs: Halifax (1990-92), West Brom (1991-92), Coventry (1992-96), Bradford (1995-97), Gillingham (1996-97), Celtic (1997-)
Full international (Scotland) 1 cap/0 goals
• Son of former Wales coach Bobby Gould who was signed by Celtic three years ago while struggling to hold down a place with Bradford.
• Since then he has enjoyed international status with Scotland and has fought off the challenge of Russian keeper Dimitri Kharine to retain his place with Celtic. Despite some high-profile errors in

the 1998-99 season, he looks set to remain the club's number one choice.

PLAYER
GOUMAS, Yiannis
Midfielder, Greek, 184cm, 76kg
Born: 24.05.75, Greece
Clubs: Panathinaikos (1996-)
Full international (Greece) 9 caps/0 goals
• In fine form in 1999-2000 for Panathinaikos. A talented sweeper who is pushing hard for a regular spot in the Greek starting line-up after making his international debut in the 1998-99 season against Finland.

PLAYER
GOURVENNEC, Jocelyn
Midfielder, French, 183cm, 80kg
Born: 22.03.72, Brest, France
Clubs: Lorient (1990-91), Rennes (1991-95), Nantes (1995-98), Marseille (1998-99), Montpellier (1999-2000), Rennes (2000-)
• Injury troubles and ill-advised transfer to Marseille and Montpellier have held him back in recent years. But he remains an outstanding attacking midfielder, at his best playing just behind the strikers. A left-footer of subtle skills and proven goalscoring ability.
• Surname pronounced Goor ven eck.

PLAYER
GOVEDARICA, Dejan
Midfielder, Yugoslav, 193cm, 84kg
Born: 02.10.69, Zrenjanin, Yugoslavia
Clubs: Proleter (1989-92), Vojovidina Novi Sad (1992-95), Volendam (Hol) (1996-97), Lecce (Ita) (1998), RKC Waalwijk (Hol) (1998-)
Full international (Yugoslavia) 20 caps/2 goals
• Yugoslav midfielder and member of his national team at France 98. A key player for Yugoslavia but has never received the recognition he deserves. Returned to RKC in 1998 and is the heart and soul of the team. A regular scorer as well.

ADMINISTRATOR
GOVERNATO, Nello
• Sporting director of Lazio and the man responsible for the Roman club's transfer policy.

PLAYER
GRADY, James
Forward, Scottish, 170cm, 64kg
Born: 14.03.71, Paisley, Scotland
Clubs: Clydebank (1994-97), Dundee (1997-)
• In what was a turbulent 1999-2000 season for Dundee, Grady emerged as one of Scotland's most prolific strikers, the former Clydebank man scoring a succession of vital goals as the Dens Park side battled their way to Premier League survival.

COACH
GRAHAM, George
Scottish
Born: 30.11.44
• Returned to London in October 1998 to coach Tottenham, the great rivals of Arsenal, the club where he made his name in the 1990s, winning the League (twice), FA Cup and League Cups, culminating in the 1994 European Cup-winners Cup victory over Parma in Copenhagen.
• A flamboyant player, nicknamed 'Stroller' who won the League and FA Cup with Arsenal in 1971. Graham the player would probably not have been picked by Graham the manager, who prefers hard work and tactical discipline to flair and individuality.
• Started his coaching career at Millwall in December 1982, leading them to promotion to the old second division in 1985 and moving on to Arsenal a year later.
• Was sacked by Arsenal in February 1995 and subsequently banned from the game for 12 months after a financial scandal involving transfer 'bungs'. 'After eight and a half years, they sacked me in two minutes.'
• Took charge at Leeds in September 1996, but missed life in London and moved to Spurs where he has gradually won the fans over with solid

results rather than spectacular football.

• 'Winning isn't just about pretty football. It's about hunger and application.'

PLAYER
GRAMMOZIS, Dimitrios
Midfielder, Greek/German, 179cm, 76kg
Born: 08.07.78, Greece
Clubs: TuS Neviges, SSVg Velbert, Borussia Velbert, Wuppertaler, KFC Uerdingen, Hamburg (1998-)
• Dynamic and industrious midfielder able to line up on the left side or in a more central position. Uses his speed, quick feet and swashbuckling style to make explosive forward bursts.

COACH
GRANT, Avraham
Israeli
Born: 6.2.1955.
• Maccabi Tel Aviv's outgoing coach, who won the Israeli League with them twice and the State Cup once. Has been touted as a future national team coach.

PLAYER
GRAVELAINE, Xavier
Midfielder, France, 183cm, 77kg
Born: 05.10.68, Tours, France
Clubs: Laval, Caen, PSG, Strasbourg, Guingamp, Marseille, Montpellier, PSG, Watford (Eng), Le Havre
Full international (France) 4 caps/0 goals
• Athletic and highly-skilled frontrunner or attacking midfielder, but has also spent his entire career living up to his image of a rebel without a cause. Never in contention for the diplomatic corps, he says what he thinks and if coaches and club presidents do not appreciate it – too bad. Really should have won more than four full caps for France.
• 'In this business, players are thought of as meat, but even with meat, there are limits to what is acceptable.'
• Name pronounced Zav ee er Grav er len.

PLAYER
GRAVESEN, Thomas
Defender, Danish, 178cm, 74kg
Born: 11.03.76, Vejle, Denmark
Clubs: Vejle, Hamburg (Ger) (1997-2000), Everton (Eng) (2000-)
Full international (Denmark) 8 caps/0 goals
• Combative Dane whose infectious will-to-win makes him both a crowd favourite and highly effective team leader. Has the ability to play in any number of positions in defence or midfield. All he asks is to be in the thick of the action.

PLAYER
GRAY, Michael
Defender, English, 170cm, 68kg
Born: 03.08.74, Sunderland, England
Clubs: Sunderland (1992-)
Full international (England) 3 caps/0 goals
• Left-back who likes to attack, a legacy from his early days as a winger.
• Missed the crucial penalty in Sunderland's dramatic promotion play-off shoot-out against Charlton in May 1998. But less than a year later made his international debut against Hungary.

PLAYER
GREGOIRE, Stephane
Midfielder, French, 180cm, 78kg
Born: 02.02.68, Thouars, France
Clubs: Thouars, Rennes (1997-)
• Rennes skipper and a driving force on the right-side or in the centre of midfield. A late-developer, he spent most of his career in the French third division before top-flight Rennes recruited him in 1997 at the age of 29.
• Surname pronounced Gray gg wah.

COACH
GREGORY, John
English
Born: 11.05.54
• Coach of Aston Villa since February 1998, when

he was the surprise choice to succeed Brian Little, having been in charge at second division Wycombe Wanderers.

• A former Villa player who was capped by England six times, he led Villa on an impressive run away from the relegation zone.

• Refreshingly open in his dealings with the press, he has been critical of the influx of foreigners into English football, preferring mostly to 'buy British'.

PLAYER
GREILICH, Holger
Defender, German, 188cm, 82kg
Born: 12.07.71, Mainz, Germany
Clubs: Mainz 05, Munich 1860 (1997-)
• Highly-effective man marker, rugged, ruthless and rarely found wanting in a one-on-one duel. He has, however, had his share of injury problems of late, especially with his left knee.

PLAYER
GREINER, Frank
Midfielder, German, 173cm, 73kg
Born: 03.07.66, Furth, Germany
Clubs: Nurnberg (1987-88), Koln (1988-95), Kaiserslautern (1995-97), Wolfsburg (1997-)
• If Wolfsburg are backed by the Volkswagen car company, he is their convertible. He can take the guise of an implacable back-line marker, raiding right wing-back or play in central midfield.

PLAYER
GRENET, Francois
Midfielder, French, 180cm, 75kg
Born: 08.03.75, Bordeaux, France
Clubs: Bordeaux (1992-)
• With Bordeaux since the age of 14, he is the club's longest-serving player. A right-sided full-back or wing-back, he has represented France at Under 21 and B level.
• Surname pronounced Gray nay.

PLAYER
GRETARSSON, Arnar
Midfielder, Icelandic, 182cm, 73kg
Born: 20.02.72, Rejkkavik, Iceland
Clubs: Breidablik (1994-96), AEK Athens (Gre) (1997-)
Full international (Iceland) 44 caps/2 goals
• Experienced midfielder with nearly half a century of internationals to his credit. Should figure strongly in Iceland's World Cup qualifying.

COACH
GRIGA, Stanislav
Slovakian
• Coach of 1999 Slovakian champions Inter Bratislava.

PLAYER
GRIM, Fred
Goalkeeper, Dutch, 188cm, 87kg
Born: 17.08.65, Amsterdam, Holland
Clubs: Ajax Amsterdam (1986), Cambuur (1986-94), Ajax Amsterdam (1994-)
• Veteran keeper who has been reserve at Ajax since 1994, rarely playing until the departure of **Edwin Van der Sar** to Juventus in summer 1999.

PLAYER
GRIMANDI, Gilles
Defender, French, 180cm, 75kg
Born: 11.11.70, Gap, France
Clubs: Monaco (1991-97), Arsenal (Eng) (1997-)
• A French League title winner with Monaco in 1997 who joined Arsenal in June 1997 in a joint deal with **Emmanuel Petit** to be reunited with former coach **Arsene Wenger**.
• Dependable squad member who can play anywhere in defence or midfield.

PLAYER
GRISHIN, Sergei
Midfielder, Russian, 175cm, 70kg
Born: 18.11.73, Russia

Clubs: Torpedo Moscow (1991-92), Asmaral (1993-95), Moscow Dynamo (1996-)
Full international (Russia) 3 caps/1 goal
• Key man and a hard-worker for the Dynamo midfield, who also provides a mobile and physical presence on the wing.

PLAYER
GRONKJAER, Jesper
Forward, Danish, 187cm, 81kg
Born: 12.08.77, Thiburg, Denmark
Clubs: Aab Aalborg (1995-98), Ajax (Hol) (1998-)
Full international (Denmark) 12 caps/0 goals
• The rising talent of Danish football, a skilful and pacy left winger often compared to former Manchester United winger Jesper Olsen.
• Had a nightmare international debut, against Italy on 27.03.99, when his back pass gifted the Italians their opening goals in the Euro 2000 qualifier.

PLAYER
GRONLUND, Tommi
Midfielder, Finnish, 174cm, 71kg
Born: 09.12.69, Finland
Clubs: HJK Helsinki (1992-96), Ljungskile (Swe) (1997), Trelleborg (Swe) (1998-)
Full international (Finland) 25 caps/1 goal
• Finnish midfielder who has captained his country. A grafter rather than a stylist.

COACH
GROSS, Christian
Swiss
Born: 14.08.54
• Coach of Basle since 1999 who, since his departure from Tottenham, has remoulded he Swiss side into a strong, attack-minded team with one of the best defences in the Swiss League.
• A former international player with Grasshopper who became their coach and won two Swiss League titles with the Zurich club.

Jesper Gronkjaer

Josep Guardiola

GROTH, Martin

Midfielder, German, 181cm, 76kg
Born: 20.10.69, Hannover, Germany
Clubs: Langenhagen, Hannover 96 (1987-95), Hansa Rostock (1995-98), Hamburg (1998-)
• Very underrated right-sided midfielder and Hamburg skipper who missed much of the 1999-2000 season through injury. Secure defensively, rarely gives away possession and boasts a rocket-like right-foot shot.
• Surname pronounced Grurth.

GROZDIC, Nenad

Midfielder, Yugoslav, 169cm, 68kg
Born: 03.02.74, Kucevo, Yugoslavia
Clubs: Zvizd, Rudar, Obilic (1997-99), Vitesse Arnhem (Hol) (1999-)
Full international (Yugoslavia) 9 caps/0 goals
• Dynamic, skilful and reliable midfielder, but has yet to establish himself the Yugoslav national side despite impressing in his first season in Holland.

GRUJIC, Spira

Defender, Yugoslav, 188cm, 82kg
Born: 07.12.71, Pristina, Yugoslavia
Clubs: Radnicki Nis (1992-95), RWD Molenbeek (Bel) (1995-97), Anderlecht (Bel) (1997-98), FC Twente (Hol) (1998-)
• Tough centre-back signed from Anderlecht midway through the 1998-99 season to strengthen the Twente defence.

GRYGERA, Zdenek

Defender, Czech, 184cm, 74kg
Born: 14.05.80, Czech Republic
Clubs: Petre Drnovice
• Part of a rich vein of young talent at the village club of Drnovice.

• A member of the Czech Under-21 team that claimed silver at the European Championships in Slovakia in 2000.

PLAYER
GUARDIOLA, Josep
Full name: Josep Guardiola Sala
Midfielder, Spanish, 180cm, 70kg
Born: 18.01.71, Barcelona, Spain
Clubs: Barcelona (1990-)
Full international (Spain) 39 caps/5 goals
• Club captain and playmaker at Barcelona and a hugely popular player with the fans.
• Key member of Spain's gold medal-winning side at the 1992 Barcelona Olympics.
• Made his international debut for Spain in October 1992 against Northern Ireland after just 20 first-team appearances for Barcelona.
• Left out of Spain's 1996 European Championship squad after losing his club place to **Gheorghe Popescu.** Ruled out of France 98 with a knee injury, but was recalled for Euro 2000.
• Barça team-mate **Ruus Hesp** on Guardiola: 'Nobody has the ability to dictate the pace of the game like Pep. He sees things way before the rest of us. He's the world's best player in his position.'

PLAYER
GUDJOHNSEN, Eidur Smari
Forward, Icelandic
Born: 15.09.78, Iceland
Clubs: PSV Eindhoven (Hol), Bolton (Eng), Chelsea (Eng) (2000-)
Full international (Iceland) 4 caps/1 goal
• Free-scoring striker and one of the best players Iceland has ever produced. The subject of attention of several English Premiership sides during the summer of 2000, eventually joining Chelsea.
• Now almost back at his best after a double leg break three years ago which cost him his place at PSV Eindhoven and almost permanently ended his career.

PLAYER
GUDJONSSON, Bjarni
Midfielder, Icelandic, 174cm, 74kg
Born: 26.02.79, Akranes, Iceland
Clubs: IA (1995-97), Newcastle (Eng) (1997-98), Genk (Bel) (1998-99), Stoke City (Eng) (1999-)
Full international (Iceland) 7 caps/1 goal
• Skilful international midfielder familiar to Stoke fans for his opportunistic free-kick at the 1999-2000 Auto Windscreens Shield final. Joined his father **Gudjon Thordarson** at the Britannia Stadium from Newcastle in autumn 1999.

PLAYER
GUDJONSSON, Thordur
Forward, Icelandic, 176cm, 78kg
Born: 14.10.73, Akranes, Iceland
Clubs: IA, Bochum (Ger) (1996-97), Genk (Bel) (1997-2000), Las Palmas (Spa) (2000-)
Full international (Iceland) 36 caps/9 goals
• Fast, skilful attacking midfielder whose goals and assists made a major contribution to Genk's championship run in the 1998-99 season.
• Like his younger brother **Bjarni Gudjonsson** he began his career at IA, under the coaching direction of their father, **Gudjon Thordarson.**
• Other brother Johannes was also at Genk.
• 'Kicking a football was as natural for us as walking. That's what happens when your dad is obsessed with football. Dad was a defender but my game is all about going forward.'

COACH
GUDLAUGSSON, Pall
Icelandic
Born: 1958
• Widely experienced coach, despite a quiet career as a player. Spent two seasons coaching top-division side Leiftur, following a highly successful spell in the Faroe Islands, during which he coached the national side on its entry into the international arena.
• Took over at Keflavik at the end of the 1999-

2000 season, and will be looking to restore the fortunes of a club which by its own standards has disappointed in recent years.

PLAYER
GUDMUNDSSON, Tryggvi
Forward, Icelandic, 176cm, 75kg
Born: 30.07.74, Iceland
Clubs: IBV, Tromso (Nor)
Full international (Iceland) 15 caps/3 goals
• Free-scoring forward whose prolific goalscoring ways while with IBV won him a move to Norway, as well as a clutch of international caps.
• Partners **Rune Lange** up front at Tromso, where he has been a regular goalscorer.

PLAYER
GUEL, Tchiressoua
Midfielder, Ivory Coast, 166cm, 65kg
Born: 27.12.75, Sikensi, Ivory Coast
Clubs: ASEC Abidjan, Marseille (Fra) (1998-99), St Etienne (Fra) (1999-)
Full international (Ivory Coast)
• Pocket-sized midfield creator with a big talent. A star of the Ivory Coast national team, he can operate in a central playmaking role or in an advanced position on the right.
• Pronounced Cher ray soo ah Goo ell.

PLAYER
GUERRERO, Jose
Full name: Jose Felix Guerrero Lopez
Midfielder, Spanish, 177cm, 74kg
Born: 23.08.75, Portugalete, Spain
Clubs: Athletic Bilbao B (1994-96), Eibar (1996-97), Racing Santander (1997-98), Real Sociedad (1998-)
• Versatile utility player best known for being the younger brother of the much more talented **Julen Guerrero**.

PLAYER
GUERRERO, Julen
Full name: Julen Guerrero Lopez
Midfielder, Spanish, 179cm, 71kg
Born: 07.01.74, Portugalete, Spain
Clubs: Athletic Bilbao (1991-)
Full international (Spain) 38 caps/13 goals
• Undisputed Golden Boy of Spanish soccer before the arrival of **Raul** on the scene.
• A clever, cultured midfielder but injuries and a resulting loss of confidence have meant that his undoubted potential has never been fulfilled on the international stage.
• Guerrero means warrior in Spanish, but he is often accused of being too nice for his own good.
• Became Spain's second youngest international against Mexico in January 1993.
• Hugely popular with female fans, needing police protection during training camps to keep them at bay.
• A Basque icon after refusing to join Real Madrid in 1995. Under contract to Bilbao until 2007.
• Left out of Spain's squad for Euro 2000.

PLAYER
GUGA
Full name: Jose Augusto Santos
Forward, Brazilian, 180cm, 73kg
Born: 14.03.77, Brazil
Clubs: Gil Vicente (Por) (1998-)
• Striker whose goals helped Gil Vicente finish in fifth place in the Portuguese League in 1999-2000.

PLAYER
GUGLIELMINPIETRO, Andres
Midfielder, Argentinian, 185cm, 75kg
Born: 14.04.74, San Nicolas, Argentina
Clubs: Gymnasia Y Esgrima La Plata (1995-1998), Milan (1998-)
Full international (Argentina)
• Midfielder who is better known as GIULY as his full name will not fit on back of his shirt.

• Scored 22 goals in 105 for Gimnasia before joining Milan.

PLAYER
GUIE-MIEN, Rolf
Midfielder, Congo, 178cm, 70kg
Born: 28.10.77, Congo
Clubs: Inter Brazzaville, Karlsruher (Ger), Eintracht Frankfurt (Ger) (1999-)
Full international (Congo)
• Right-sided attacking midfielder from the Congo. A fine athlete, strong in the air and blessed with a fine range of ball skills. On the other hand, he still has much to learn tactically and sometimes lacks composure in his play. Used to turn up for training at Karlsruhe on a bike.
• Pronounced Gwee Meen.

PLAYER
GUIVARC'H, Stephane
Forward, French, 184cm, 78kg
Born: 06.09.70, Concarneau, France
Clubs: Brest, Guingamp (1991-95), Auxerre (1995-96), Rennes (1996-97), Auxerre (1997-98), Newcastle (Eng) (1998-99), Rangers (Sco) (1999), Auxerre (1999-2000)
Full international (France) 14 caps/1 goal
• Thanks to an indifferent France 98 and his failure to make the grade at Newcastle United and Rangers, he is regarded in some quarters as damaged goods. But for Guingamp, Rennes and in two spells at Auxerre, the Breton striker has invariably come up to scratch, proving himself a fine finisher with either head, right or left foot and was the French First Division's top scorer in both 1996-97 (Rennes) and 1997-98 (Auxerre).
• A nature lover, fisherman, connoiseur of fine wine and a throughly unassuming charcter, who has turned his back on a number of lucrative post-World Cup commercial contracts.
• 'I'm a footballer. I don't feel the need for self-publicity and advertisinng campaigns.'
• Surname pronounced Gee varsh.

COACH
GULLIT, Ruud
Dutch
Born: 01.09.62, Amsterdam, Holland
• Former European and World Footballer of the Year who captained Holland to victory in the European Championships in 1988.
• A highly intelligent footballer, from his time playing as sweeper for Haarlem, through his successful time at Milan in the late 1980s, to his first steps in coaching, with Chelsea.
• Became the world's most expensive footballer in 1987 when Milan paid PSV £6.5million. It proved to be money well spent, as he won the European Cup and two World Club Cups before knee injuries shortened his career.
• Twice quit international football with football, the second time on the eve of the 1994 World Cup.
• Moved to London in 1995 with Chelsea, becoming player-coach in 1996 after **Glenn Hoddle** moved to be England manager. Won the FA Cup but clashed with players and, crucially, **Ken Bates** and was sacked in spring 1998.
• Was a surprise choice to take charge of Newcastle in 1999, but failed to establish a rapport with the players, particularly Alan Shearer, and he headed back to Amsterdam in autumn 1999.

PLAYER
GUNES Ali
Midfielder, Turkish/German, 174cm, 67kg
Born: 23.11.78, Donaueschingen, Germany
Clubs: Braunlingen, Donaueschingen, Villingen, Freiburg (1996-)
• Wiry and lightweight he might appear, but this highly promising, hyperactive ball-winner certainly knows how to tackle. Not that he just confines himself to defensive duties. He is quick and comfortable on the ball and loves to get into forward positions.
• He was born in Germany, but has chosen to play for Turkey, the land of his parents.
• Pronounced Goo nes.

Ruud
Gullit

PLAYER
GUNNARSSON, Brynjar Bjorn
Midfielder, Icelandic, 184cm, 79kg
Born: 16.10.75, Iceland
Clubs: KR (1995-97), Moss (Nor) (1998), Orgryte (Swe) (1999), Stoke City (Eng) (2000-)
Full international (Iceland) 21 caps/3 goals
• Hard-tackling international midfielder whose pace, strength and passing ability has won him a growing number of admirers since his arrival at Stoke.

PLAYER
GUNNLAUGSSON, Arnar
Midfielder, Icelandic, 183cm, 74kg
Born: 06.03.73, Akranes, Iceland
Clubs: IA Akranes, Feyenoord (Hol) (1992-94), Nurnburg (Ger) (1994-95), IA (1995), Sochaux (Ger) (1995-96), IA (1997) Bolton (Eng) (1997-99), Leicester (Eng) (1999-), Stoke City (2000, loan)
Full international (Iceland) 30 caps/3 goals
• Attacking midfielder who has never quite fulfilled his early promise, despite a career which has taken him to Holland, France and England.
• Currently on loan at Stoke City.

PLAYER
GUNNLAUGSSON, Bjarki
Forward, Icelandic
Born: 06.03.73, Akranes, Iceland
Full international (Iceland) 25 caps/6 goals
• Attacking midfielder/striker who, like his twin, **Arnar**, has never fully fulfilled the promise of the days when the pair formed one of the most potent strike forces Icelandic domestic football has ever seen.

PLAYER
GUPPY, Steve
Midfielder, English, 180cm, 68kg
Born: 29.03.69, Winchester, England
Clubs: Wycombe (1993-94), Newcastle (1994), Port Vale (1994-97), Leicester (1997-)

Full international (England) 1 cap/0 goals
- Left-winger or wing-back who has established himself as one of the best crossers from the left in the English game.
- Signed by then Newcastle manager **Kevin Keegan** in August 1994 from Wycombe, but sold three months later. Called up by Keegen to the England squad in the months before Euro 2000.

PLAYER
GURENKO, Sergei
Defender, Belarus, 176cm, 72kg
Born: 30.09.72, Grodno, Belarus.
Clubs: Khimik (1989-91), Neman Grodno (1991-95), Lokomotiv Moscow (1995-99), Roma (Ita) (1999-)
Full international (Belarus) 40 caps/2 goals
- Powerful midfielder who can operate on either flank.
- Roma signed him after **Fabio Capello** was reported to have been impressed by his performance for Belarus againt Italy in a Euro 2000 qualifier.

PLAYER
GUSEV, Rolan
Midfielder, Russian, 175cm, 68kg
Born: 17.09.77, Russia
Clubs: Dinamo Moscow (1994-)
Full international (Russia) 2 caps/0 goals
- Talented all-rounder who is fast, a good passer and with a powerful shot.

PLAYER
GUSSEINOV, Timerlan
Forward, Ukrainian, 184cm, 81kg
Born: 24.01.68, Ukraine
Clubs: Chornomorets
Full international (Ukraine) 11 caps/8 goals
- Prolific striker signed by Chornomorets in 1993 from Zariya Lugansk. Has improved his game to be less of a solo player and more of a team player. But has great individual talent and is still capable of scoring wonderful goals.

PLAYER
GUSTAFSSON, Eddie
Goalkeeper, Swedish, 186cm, 75kg
Born: 31.01.77, Sweden
Clubs: IFK Norrkoping (1996-)
Full international (Sweden) 1 cap/0 goals
- Promising keeper who began with small club IFK Stockholm. Self-proclaimed buddhist.

PLAYER
GUSTAFSSON, Tomas
Defender, Swedish, 179cm, 77kg
Born: 07.05.73, Sweden
Clubs: Winnipeg Fury (Can (1990-91), IF Brommapojkama (1990-96), AIK (1996-99), Coventry (1999-)
Full international (Sweden) 5 caps/0 goals
- Pacy full-back who can operate on either flank.
- Spent a year in Canada as a teenager, playing for Winnipeg Fury.
- International debut: 18.08.99, v Austria (0-0)

PLAYER
GUSTAVSSON, Mikael
Defender, Swedish, 186cm, 78kg
Born: 15.08.74, Sweden
Clubs: Motala (1996), Halmstad (1997-)
Full international (Sweden) 2 caps/0 goals
- One of the best right-backs in the Swedish League and seen as a long-term successor to **Roland Nilsson** in the national team.

PLAYER
GUSTAVO
Full name: Gustavo De la Parra Navarro
Defender, Spanish, 182cm, 80kg
Born: 19.12.75, Madrid
Clubs: Atletico Madrid B (1996-99), Atletico Madrid (1999-)
- Versatile defender who was promoted to the Atletico full squad at the start of the 1999-2000 season.
- Can play in the centre or at right-back.

PLAYER
GUSTAVO LOPEZ

Full name: Gustavo Adrian Lopez
Midfielder, Argentinian, 174cm, 73kg
Born: 13.04.73, Valentin Alsina, Spain
Clubs: Independiente (1991-96), Real Zaragoza
(Spa) (1996-99), Celta Vigo (Spa) (1999-)
Full international (Argentina)
• Strong-running midfielder who can play at
right-back, right midfield or in a more central role.
• Spent four seasons at Independiente in Buenos
Aires before moving to Spain's Zaragoza.
• His time at Zaragoza was affected by a knee
injury. But when **Victor Fernandez** moved to
Celta Vigo as coach, he went back to Zaragoza to
sign Gustavo Lopez.

PLAYER
GUTI

Full name: Jose Maria Gutierrez Hernandez
Midfielder, Spanish, 181cm, 76kg
Born: 31.10.76, Madrid, Spain
Clubs: Real Madrid (1995-)
Full international (Spain) 1 cap/0 goals
• Stylish but extremely competitive midfielder
who has come through the ranks at Real Madrid.
• Tall, blond and good-looking, earning
comparisons with **Redondo** and making him one
of the pin-up boys of Spanish football.
• Member of Spain's Under-21 European
championship-winning side in 1998.
• Made his full international debut for Spain
against Croatia in Seville in May 1999.

PLAYER
GYAN, Christian

Defender, Ghanaian/Italian, 167cm, 75kg
Born: 02.11.78, Tema, Ghana
Clubs: Gapoha, Feyenoord (Hol) (1996-), Excelsior
(Hol)) (1997, loan)
Full international (Ghana)
• Strong, tough-tackling defender who benefitted
from a loan spell at second division Excelsior,

returning to Rotterdam to play an important role
for Feyenoord.

H

HAAGDOREN, Philip
Forward, Belgian, 175cm, 63kg
Born: 25.06.70, Belgium
Clubs: Lommel (1990-93), Anderlecht (1993-96), Beveren (1995-96), Lierse (1996-99), GBA (1999-)
Full international (Belgium) 1 cap/0 goals
• Once one of the biggest playing talents at Anderlecht, but he failed to claim a regular place as a midfielder, despite being a member of the Belgian national team squad.
• Moved to Lierse, where he established himself as the playmaker, and now at Germinal Beerschot Antwerp, where he has formed a great partnership with Marc Degryse. Now in his 30s, he is not as high-profile anymore, but is still a great distributor.

PLAYER
HAALAND, Alf-Inge
Midfielder, Norwegian, 186cm, 82kg
Born: 23.11.71, Stavanger, Norway
Clubs: Bryne (1993), Nottingham Forest (Eng) (1994-97), Leeds (Eng) (1997-2000), Manchester City (Eng) (2000-)
Full international (Norway) 33 caps/0 goals
• Hard-working, tenacious player who was one of the first Norwegians to break into the English game.

COACH
HAAN, Ari
Dutch
Born: 16.11.48
• Ex-Holland, Ajax and Anderlecht midfield star who went on to coach at Anderlecht, Standard Liege, Feyenoord and in Greece, where he has worked for PAOK Salonika and, since March 2000, at Paniliakos.
• Tactically above-average but not a coach who is in favour of dialogue with his players.

PLAYER
HAAS, Bernt
Defender, Swiss, 185cm, 80kg
Born: 08.04.78, Switzerland
Clubs: Grasshopper (1994-)
Full international (Switzerland) 9 caps/0 goals
• The teenage Haas was pitched into the Grasshopper first team some five years ago by then club coach **Christian Gross** and has since developed into a very polished performer at right-back, making his first appearance for Switzerland in the 1996-97 season.
• Linked recently to a move to France or Spain.

PLAYER
HAAS, Mario
Forward, Austrian, 182cm, 83kg
Born: 16.03.74, Graz, Austria
Clubs: Sturm Graz (1993-99), Strasbourg (Fra) (1999-)
Full international (Austria) 16 caps/2 goals
• The Austrian international striker was a prolific marksman at club level for Sturm Graz in his native land. But he found goalscoring an altogether more difficult prospect on moving to France at the start of the 1990-2000 season, managing only one in the entire campaign.
• Surname pronounced Ah ss.

PLAYER
HADJI, Mustapha
Midfielder, Moroccan, 184cm, 72kg
Born: 16.11.72, Ifrane, Morocco
Clubs: Nancy (1992-96), Sporting Lisbon (Por) (1996-97), Deportivo La Coruna (Spa) (1997-99), Coventry (Eng) (1999-)
Full international (Morocco)
• 1998 African Footballer of the Year and the pin-up boy of Moroccan soccer.
• First came to prominence at French Second Division side Nancy, where he turned down the chance to play for the French Under-21 side in 1994 because he wanted to play for the country of his birth, Morocco.

• Played for Morocco at the 1994 and 1998 World Cup finals after making his international debut in 1994 against Zambia.

PLAYER
HAGAN, Ebenezer
Midfielder, Ghanaian, 189cm, 70kg
Born: 01.10.75, Ghana
Clubs: Goldfields, Kalamata (Gre) (1995-98) Iraklis Thessaloniki (Gre) (1998-)
• Ghanaian attacking midfielder who was linked with a move away from Iraklis to a number of other Greek clubs in the summer of 2000.
• Skilful and dynamic, but does not score enough goals – only two in the 1999-2000 season. Works well with Iraklis's Cypriot attacker **Michalis Konstantinou**.

PLAYER
HAGI, Gheorghe
Midfielder, Romanian, 174cm, 73kg
Born: 02.05.65, Sacelen, Romania
Clubs: Farul Constanta (1982-83), Sportul Studentsec (1983-86), Steaua Bucharest (1987-90), Real Madrid (Spa) (1990-92), Brescia (Ita) (1992-94), Barcelona (Spa) (1994-96), Galatasaray (Tur) (1996-)
Full international (Romania) 125 caps/34 goals
• The greatest Romanian footballer of all time, dubbed the 'Maradona of the Carpathians' for his outstanding left-footed playmaking skills.
• Romania's most-capped player and voted Romanian Player of the Century in 1999.
• Started out at Farul Constanta, where the stadium has since been renamed in his honour.
• Made his international debut in August 1983 in a goalless draw with Norway, but was probably at the peak of his powers at the 1994 World Cup, leading Romania to the quarter-finals, where they lost on penalties. Struck a dramatic winner against Argentina in a thrilling second-round match.
• Won three League titles with Steaua, joining them in 1986, and played in the 1989 European

Cup Final against Milan, which Steaua lost 4-0.
• Never quite fulfilled his huge promise in spells at Real Madrid, Brescia and Barcelona, but maintained his fitness levels to carry on playing for Romania at the age of 35.
• Voted Romanian Player of the Year six times, playing in the 1990, 1994 and 1998 World Cups, at well as Euro 84, Euro 96 and Euro 2000.
• Retired from international football after the 1998 World Cup, only to be persuaded to return, initially for one match only, a crucial Euro 2000 qualifying match against Hungary, staying on for the remainder of the qualifying campaign and the finals.
• Lost much of his pace in the last few years of his career, but retained his superb technique and visionary skills.
• Won the Turkish League with Galatasaray and his first and only European trophy, the UEFA Cup, in May 2000, despite being sent off in the Final against Arsenal.

PLAYER
HAJRY, Redouane
Midfielder, Moroccan, 174cm, 75kg
Born: 05.03.63, Casablanca, Morocco
Clubs: Benfica (Por) (1987-88), Farense (Por) (1988-89), Uniao Madeira (Por) (1989-90), Farense (Por) (1990-)
Full international (Morocco)
• The heart and soul of Farense's midfield for more than 10 seasons, with more than 300 Portuguese League games to his credit.

PLAYER
HAJTO, Tomasz
Defender, Polish, 187cm, 81kg
Born: 16.10.72, Makow Podhalanski, Poland
Clubs: Halniak Makow Podhalanski, Goral Zywiec, Hutnik Krakow (1990-91), Gornik Zabrze (1993-97), Duisburg (Ger) (1997-)
Full international (Poland) 28 caps/4 goals
• Uncompromising Polish international centre-back, right-back or defensive midfielder who

fouls first and asks questions later. Was top of the German yellow card tables in 1998-99 and was again up to his old tricks in 1999-2000.
• Surname pronounced Hi toe.

PLAYER
HAKAN Sukur
Forward, Turkish, 185cm, 80kg
Born: 01.09.71, Sakarya, Turkey
Clubs: Sakaryspor (1988-90), Bursaspor (1988-92), Galatasaray (1992-95), Torino (Ita) (1995), Galatasaray (1996-2000), Internazionale (Ita) (2000-)
Full international (Turkey) 56 caps/28 goals
• Prolific goalscorer in the Turkish League who is trying his luck in Italy for a second time.
• Moved to Torino in 1995 but grew homesick and returned to Galatasaray after playing just five matches.
• Played for Turkey at Euro 96 and Euro 2000, scoring twice against Belgium in June 2000 to take the Turks into the quarter-finals.
• Nicknamed 'The Bull of the Bosphorus'.
• First wife died in the 1999 earthquakes.
• Joined Inter for the 2000-2001 season.

PLAYER
HAKAN Unsal
Midfielder, Turkish, 178cm, 80kg
Born: 14.05.73, Sinop, Turkey
Clubs: Karabukspor, Galatasaray
Full international (Turkey) 15 caps/0 goals
• Left-sided midfielder who returned from injury to play in Turkey's Euro 2000 qualifying play-offs against the Republic of Ireland.
• Made his international debut against Belgium in August 1996, but has rarely been a regular.

PLAYER
HAKANSSON, Jesper
Midfielder, Danish, 168cm, 64kg
Born: 14.08.80, Albertslund, Denmark
Clubs: BK Frem (1998-99), Heerenveen (Hol) (1999-)

Gheorghe Hagi

Dietmar Hamann

• Exciting young attacker midfielder who had trials with Manchester United but opted instead for first-team football at Heerenveen, scoring on his debut against Ajax in Amsterdam.
• The third youngest Dane to make his Under-21 debut (only **Thomas Sorensen** and **Michael Laudrup** were younger).

PLAYER
HALDAN, Catalin
Midfielder, Romanian, 175cm, 73kg
Born: 03.02.76, Bucharest, Romania
Clubs: Dinamo Bucharest (1994-)
Full international (Romania) 8 caps/1 goal
• Midfielder who played a crucial role in Dinamo's Romanian League title triumph in 2000.
• On the fringes of the Romanian national team, and travelled to Euro 2000 as part of the squad, but did not play.
• Capped 16 times at Under-21 level.
• Surname pronounced Hill dan.

PLAYER
HALFON, Alon
Defender, Israeli, 180cm, 72kg
Born: 02.07.73, Israel
Clubs: Hapoel Haifa
Full international (Israel) 4 caps/0 goals
• One of the less regular players among the Israeli national team defenders, Halfon is an adequate stand-in for any of the other more veteran members of the back line if and when they are unavailable.

COACH
HALIHODZIC, Vahid
Bosnian
Born: 15.10.52
• France has been a happy hunting ground for the Bosnian, who won 32 caps for Yugoslavia. While a striker with Nantes in the early 1980s, he was twice the First Division's top scorer (1982-83 and 1984-85) and after two near-misses, led Lille

to promotion to the top flight last season.

• A hard taskmaster, he insists on total commitment and concentration from his players and includes the word 'work' in virtually every sentence.

• Began his coaching career with his hometown club, Velez Mostar, but the outbreak of civil war in Yugoslavia, drew him back to France, where he took charge of Second Division Beauvais. Led Moroccan side Raja Casablanca to the African Champions League title in 1997.

PLAYER
HALLE, Gunnar
Defender, Norwegian, 183cm, 78kg
Born: 11.08.65, Larvik, Norway
Clubs: Lillestrom (1990), Oldham (Eng) (1991-1996), Leeds (Eng) (1996-1999), Bradford (Eng) (1999-)
Full international (Norway) 64 caps/5 goals
• Versatile model professional who can play anywhere in defence or midfield. Member of Norway's squad at the 1998 World Cup.

PLAYER
HALMAI, Gabor
Midfielder, Hungarian, 189cm, 74kg
Born: 07.01.72, Szekesfehervar, Hungary
Clubs: Videoton (1989-91), Kispest (1991-93), Ekeren (Bel) (1994-96), MTK (1996-)
Full international (Hungary) 50 caps/4 goals
• Experienced international midfielder who returned from a spell in Belgium to win the Hungarian League in 1998 and 1999.

PLAYER
HAMANN, Dietmar
Midfielder, German, 192cm, 82kg
Born: 27.08.73, Waldsassen, Germany
Clubs: Wacker Munich, Bayern Munich (1996-98), Newcastle (1998-99), Liverpool (1999-)
Full international (Germany) 27 caps/2 goals)
• Outstanding all-rounder who has suffered more

than his fair share of injuries, but combines tireless work in midfield with a deft touch.

• Spent nine seasons with Bayern Munich, before a £4.5million transfer to Newcastle after France 98.

• Signed by Liverpool for £7million in summer 1999.

• International debut: 15.11.97, v South Africa.

PLAYER
HAMEL, Sebastien
Goalkeeper, French, 182cm, 73kg
Born: 20.11.75, Arpajon, France
Clubs: Monaco, Le Havre (1997-)
• Competant young keeper who is now well established as first choice at Le Havre.

PLAYER
HAMI, Mandirali
Midfielder, Turkish, 179cm, 78kg
Born: 20.07.68, Arsin, Turkey
Clubs: Trabzonspor, Schalke (Ger), Trabzonspor
Full international (Turkey) 49 caps/8 goals
• Veteran attacker and free-kick specialist and an effective foil for star striker **Hakan Sukur** in the Turkish national side down the years.

• Tried his luck in Germany with Schalke, but was not a great success and returned to Trabzon, the club where he made his name and where he remains a local hero.

COACH
HEMMERG, Piet
Dutch
Born: 22.01.54
• Coach of Grasshopper following the departure of **Roy Hodgson** in May 2000, having previously been in charge of the youth team.

• A former player with Nijmegen, Utrecht and Ajax whose career was cut short by injury.

• Coached Groningen (1992-1995) before working as assistant to **Christian Gross** at Grasshopper. Had a spell in Saudi Arabia in charge of the national under-20 squad and then Al Ahli of Libya, before returning to Zurich.

PLAYER
HAMMING, Ronald

Forward, Dutch, 177cm, 70kg
Born: 09.01.73, Zeegse, Holland
Clubs: Groningen (1992-95), Fortuna Sittard (1995-)
• Key player in Fortuna's success in reaching the Dutch Cup Final. Has a good eye for goal, but struggled with injuries in the 1999-2000 season and often started on the bench.

PLAYER
HANUCH, Mauricio Fabio

Midfielder, Argentinian, 175cm, 75kg
Born: 16.11.76, Buenos Aires, Argentina
Clubs: Platense (1993-98), Independiente (1998-99), Sporting Lisbon (Por) (1999-)
• Argentinian midfielder who has yet to live up to expectations in Portugal following a move to Sporting, having nearly ended up at Benfica.

PLAYER
HANNAH, David

Midfielder, Scottish, 182cm, 73kg
Born: 04.08.73, Airdrie, Scotland
Clubs: Dundee Utd (1992-96), Celtic (1997-98), Dundee Utd (1999-)
• Now in his second spell at Tannadice, he retuned to the club after an unspectacular spell with Celtic, during which he appeared to lose much of the promise which he had displayed as a youngster with United and which had taken him to the verge of an international call-up.

PLAYER
HANSEN, Jonny

Midfielder, Norwegian, 178cm, 72kg
Born: 13.12.72, Knarvik, Norway
Clubs: Tromso (1994-97), Eendracht Aalst (Bel) (1997-99), Tromso (2000-)
Full international (Norway) 4 caps/0 goals
• Strong midfielder who returned to Tromso after two seasons as a squad player in Belgium.

COACH
HANSEN, Poul

Danish
Born: 04.12.53
• One of Denmark's most highly-rated coaches who took over from Benny Lennartsson at Lyngby during the 1998-99 season and has impressed many people with his forthright opinions.

PLAYER
HANSSON, Mikael

Midfielder, Swedish, 177cm, 70kg
Born: 15.03.68, Sweden
Clubs: Soderkopings (1988-89), Norrkoping (1990-1999), Helsingborg (2000-)
• Goalscoring left-sided midfielder who was signed by Helsingborg to replace the departed Norwegian winger Kenneth Storvik.

PLAYER
HAPAL, Pavel

Midfielder, Czech, 180cm, 78kg
Born: 27.07.69, Kromeric, Czech Republic
Clubs: Sigma Olomouc, Dukla Prague, Brest (Fra) (1991-92), Bayer Leverkusen (Ger) (1992-95), Tenerife (Spa) (95-98), Sigma Olomouc (1998-99), Tenerife (Spa) (1999), Sparta Prague (1999-)
Full international (Czech Republic)31 caps/1 goal
• Veteran attacking midfielder who missed out on Euro 96 because of one of a series of injuries that have marred his career.
• After a loan spell back home he made a permanent and relatively successful return to the Czech League with Sparta following several seasons with Spain's Tenerife.

PLAYER
HARAZI, Alon

Defender, Israeli, 178cm, 78kg
Born: 13.02.71, Israel
Clubs: Maccabi Haifa
Full international (Israel) 65 caps/1 goal

- Like **Arik Benado**, veteran defender Harazi has been one of the most reliable and consistent players in Israel's back line. He is not without fault, however, and has made one or two costly mistakes which have been expensive for the national team. Is the only player among the current defenders to have scored a goal.

PLAYER
HARAZI, Ronen
Forward, Israeli, 183cm, 77kg
Born: 30.03.70, Jerusalem, Israel
Clubs: Hapoel Tel Aviv
Full international (Israel) 53 caps/23 goals
- The most prolific scorer among Israel's active players, Harazi has been battling with injury for the past two seasons. Has an excellent touch in front of goal but his form has been erratic since picking up his injuries.

COACH
HAREIDE, Age
Norwegian
- One of Scandinavia's most succesful coaches, who has been in charge of Brondby since 1999, having previously been coach at Molde, where he made his name and helped to develop players such as **Ole Solskjaer** and **Oyvind Leonhardsen**, and Helsingborg, where he won the Swedish League and Cup.
- The first Norwegian to play in England, for Manchester City and Norwich, he likes his teams to play attacking football.

PLAYER
HARLEY, Jon
Midfielder, English, 175cm, 63kg
Born: 26.09.79, Maidstone, England
Clubs: Chelsea (1997-)
- Left-sided player and the most prominent young Englishman to break into Chelsea's first team during 1999-2000 despite the multinational competition.
- Under-21 international tipped for senior honours.

PLAYER
HARPER, Steve
Goalkeeper, English, 188cm, 83kg
Born: 14.03.75, Easington, England
Clubs: Newcastle (1993-), Bradford (1995, loan), Hartlepool (1997, loan), Huddersfield (1998, loan)
- Reserve at Newcastle for many years who displaced Shay Given at the end of the 1998-99 season, playing in the FA Cup Final in only his ninth appearance for the club.
- A qualified referee.

PLAYER
HARTE, Ian
Defender, Irish, 177cm, 78kg
Born: 31.08.77, Drogheda, Ireland
Clubs: Leeds (1995-)
Full international (Rep Ireland)
- Left-back with strong shot who broke into the Leeds first team in the 1997-98 season.
- Nephew of Leeds team-mate **Gary Kelly**.

PLAYER
HARTMANN, Michael
Midfielder, German, 173cm, 73kg
Born: 11.07.74, Henningsdorf, Germany
Clubs: Stahl Hennigsdorf, BSV Brandenburg, Hertha Berlin (1994-)
- Adaptable and consistent left-sided player who is just as effective as a left wing-back or left-sided defensive marker. Will run until he drops, tackles strongly and uses the ball well.

PLAYER
HARTSON, John
Forward, Welsh, 185cm, 92kg
Born: 05.04.75, Swansea, Wales
Clubs: Luton (1992-1995), Arsenal (1995-97), West Ham (1997-99), Wimbledon (1999-)
Full international (Wales) 18 caps/2 goals
- Tall, powerful forward who became the most expensive teenager in English football when Arsenal paid Luton £2.5million in January 1995.

Wimbledon broke their club record to sign him for £7million in January 1999.
• Twice failed a medical (injured knee) which prevented a transfer to Spurs and Rangers.

PLAYER
HASAN Ozer
Forward, Turkish, 182cm, 73kg
Born: 01.10.74, Turkey
Clubs: Trabzonspor, Altay
• Skilful attacker who made his name at Trabzonspor before switching to Altay.

PLAYER
HASAN Sas
Forward, Turkish, 176cm, 71kg
Born: 01.08.76, Turkey
Clubs: Galatasaray
Full international (Turkey) 2 caps/0 goals
• Controversial midfielder who on his day is the best midfield schemer in Turkish football.
• Banned for six months in 1999 after failing a dope test. Returned to star for Galatasaray in their successful UEFA Cup campaign.
• An excellent crosser of the ball and recognised as provider of the most assists in the Turkish League.

COACH
HASEK, Ivan
Czech
Born: 06.09.63
• Coach of Sparta Prague since July 1999, when he returned to Sparta after a spell working for the Czech FA. Helped Sparta retain their League title in 2000.
• A popular player during 10 seasons with Sparta (1981-90 and 1997-98), who was capped 56 times (5 goals).
• Also had spells in France (Strasbourg) and Japan (Sanfrecce and JEF United).

Jimmy Floyd Hasselbaink

HASEK, Martin

Midfielder, Czech, 180cm, 68kg
Born: 11.10.69, Czech Rep
Clubs: Sparta Prague
Full international (Czech Republic) 11 caps/0 goals
• Midfield ballwinner who missed out on Euro 2000 after losing his place in the Sparta team following injury.
• Younger brother of ice hockey superstar Dominik Hasek – a fact that is almost always referred to when Martin is mentioned in the Czech media.

HASI, Besnik

Midfielder, Croatian, 178cm, 72kg
Born: 29.12.71, Dakorica, Croatia
Clubs: Genk (Bel) (1996-97), Munich 1860 (Ger) (1997-98), Genk (Bel) (1998-2000), Anderlecht (Bel) (2000-)
• Talented midfielder who was a key player for Genk when they won the 1999 Belgian League title and the 2000 Belgian Cup Final, before switching to Anderlecht in the summer of 2000.

HASSELBAINK, Jarel 'Jimmy' Floyd

Forward, Dutch, 180cm, 85kg
Born: 27.03.75, Paramaribo, Surinam
Clubs: Campomaoirense (Por) (1995-96), Boavista (Por) (1996-97), Leeds (Eng) (1997-99), Atletico Madrid (Spa) (1999-2000), Chelsea (Eng) (2000-)
Full international (Holland) 8 caps/2 goals
• Striker with a high reputation as an expert finisher.
• Born in Surinam, raised in Holland, but made his name in Portugal, where his goals for Boavista brought him to the attention of English clubs, with Leeds, managed by **George Graham**, signing him in summer 1997.
• Finished as Leeds' top scorer two seasons in a row before a row over wages prompted his £12million move to Spain.

• Had an excellent season in Spain, finishing as League top scorer despite Atletico's relegation.
• Picked up the nickname Jimmy in Portugal after club officials did not want to announce the name of their new striker, saying instead that they had signed 'Jimmy'.
• Joined Chelsea in May 2000 in a £15million transfer.
• Unlucky to have missed out on Holland's squad for Euro 2000.

HASSLER, Thomas

Midfielder, German, 167cm, 67kg
Born: 30.05.66, Berlin, Germany
Clubs: Reinickendorfer Fuchse, Koln (1985-90), Juventus (Ita) (1990-91), Roma (Ita) (1991-94), Karlsruher (1994-98), Borussia Dortmund (1998-99), Munich 1860 (1999-)
Full international (Germany) 101 caps/11 goals
• The veteran playmaker's career seemed over when Borussia Dortmund declared him surplus to requirements towards the end of the 1998-99 campaign.
• But 'Icke' bounced back with avengeance in the 1999-2000 season at 1860, catching the eye with his exuberance and creative flair and earning a recall to the German squad for Euro 2000.
• Even at the age of 34, he stands head and shoulders above fellow Bundesliga midfielders in terms of technique, vision and the ability to realise the extraordinary.
• Won his 100th cap for Germany at Euro 2000.
• Surname pronounced Hess ler.

HATZ, Michael

Defender, Austrian, 184cm, 80kg
Born: 07.11.70, Vienna, Austria
Clubs: Rapid Vienna (1990-96), Reggiana (Ita) (1996-98), Lecce (Ita) (1997-98), Rapid Vienna (1998-)
Full international (Austria) 6 caps/0 goals
• Hard-working holding midfielder who was on

Magnus Hedman

the fringes of Austria's 1998 World Cup but missed out on the trip to France after suffering relegation to Italy's Serie B with Reggiana.

AGENT
HAUGE, Rune
Norwegian

• Controversial figure who was involved in the transfer of many Scandinavian players to England in the 1980s and 1990s, but was banned by FIFA following his involvement a bung scandal which also led to **George Graham**'s departure from Arsenal.

• Has since re-established himself and is registered in the Channel Islands. Clients include **Ronny Johnsen**, **Ole Gunnar Solskjaer**, **Peter Schmeichel** and **Lars Bohinen**.

PLAYER
HAXHI, Altin
Midfielder, Albanian, 170cm, 68kg
Born: 17.06.75, Albania
Clubs: Litex Lovech (Bul)
Full international (Albania) 20 caps/2 goals
• Albanian international midfielder who won the Bulgarian Leaague title with Litex in 1998.

PLAYER
HEDMAN, Magnus
Goalkeeper, Swedish, 193cm, 93kg
Born: 13.07.75, Stockholm, Sweden
Clubs: AIK Stockholm (1990-1997), Coventry (1997-)
Full international (Sweden) 26 caps/0 goals
• Swedish national team keeper who enjoys a high media profile in Sweden thanks to his popstar wife Magdalena.

• A solid, confident keeper who won the Swedish League in 1992 and Cup in 1996 and 1997 with AIK Stockholm.

• International debut: 09.02.97, V Romania (won 2-0).

PLAYER
HEGGEM, Vegard
Midfielder, Norwegian, 179cm, 76cm
Born: 13.07.75, Trondheim, Norway
Clubs: Orkdal, Rosenborg (1995-98), Liverpool
(Eng) (1998-)
Full international (Norway) 20 caps/1 goal
• Pacy right-back who likes to attack and can
move into midfield quite easily.
• Made the breakthrough at Rosenborg in 1997,
joining Liverpool in July 1998 for £3.5million.
• Scored on his international debut: 25.08.98, v
France (3-3).

PLAYER
HEINEN, Dirk
Goalkeeper, German, 187cm, 83kg
Born: 03.12.70, Kol-Zollstock
Clubs: Bayer Leverkusen (1992-)
• Very unfortunate to lose his first-team spot to
Adam Matysek after suffering a terrible head
injury in a pre-season friendly two years ago.
But courtesy of his outstanding shot-stopping
abilities, courage and cool temperament, his
career is again on the up.

PLAYER
HEINRICH, Jorg
Defender, German, 185cm, 75kg
Born: 06.12.69, Ramelow, Germany
Clubs: Kickers Emden (1992-94), Freiburg (1994-
96) Borussia Dortmund (1996-98), Fiorentina (Ita)
(1998-2000), Borussia Dortmund (2000-)
Full international (Germany) 30 caps/2 goals
• Pacy left wing-back who returned to Dortmund
from Italy in summer 2000.
• Ultra-competitive and dangerous at set-pieces.
• Trained as a salesman and started out in the
regional leagues of the former East Germany
where he came to the attention of scouts from
Freiburg, who gave him his Bundesliga debut in
1994-95.
• Joined Borussia Dortmund in January 1996

after Freiburg could not resist a £1.2 million offer.
Won the European and World Club Cups with
Dortmund.
• Started all five of Germany's games at France 98.
• 'His workrate is remarkable. But there is so
much more to his game. He is an excellent
crosser of the ball, shoots powerfully and
accurately and can head the ball pretty well too.'
Volker Finke.

PLAYER
HEINTZE, Jan
Defender, Danish, 171cm, 77kg
Born: 17.08.63, Tornby, Denmark
Clubs: PSV Eindhoven (Hol) (1982-94), Bayer/KFC
Uerdingen (Ger) (1994-96), Bayer Leverkusen
(Ger) (1996-99), PSV Eindhoven (Hol) (1999-)
Full international (Denmark) 65 caps/2 goals
• Powerful, tenacious attacking left-back who
has enjoyed an Indian Summer in his career.
• International debut against Finland, 29.04.87
(won 1-0), but spent several years in the
wilderness under the then national coach
Richard Moller Nielsen before returning to
favour under **Bo Johansson**.
• Won the European Cup with PSV in 1988.

PLAYER
HEINZE, Gabriel Ivan
Defender, Argentina, 178cm, 72kg
Born: 19.03.78, Crespo, Argentina
Clubs: Union de Crespo, Newell's Old Boys
(1997), Real Valladolid (Spa) (1998-), Sporting
Lisbon (Por) (1998-99, loan)
• Utility defender who can play across the back
four, but is happiest at left-back.
• Moved to Spain's Valladolid in 1998, but spent
the 1999-2000 season on loan at Sporting Lisbon.

PLAYER
HEJDUK, Frankie
Defender, American, 174cm, 66kg
Born: 05.08.74, California, USA

Clubs: Tampa Bay Mutiny (1996-98), Bayer Leverkusen (Ger) (1998-)
Full international (United States)
• American with flashy skills to go with his Californian surfer image and shoulder-length hair.
• A member of the United States squad at the 1998 World Cup but has struggled to establish himself in the Bundesliga.

PLAYER
HELDER
Full name: Helder Marino Rodrigues
Defender, Portuguese, 181cm, 83kg
Born: 21.03.71, Luanda, Angola
Clubs: Estoril (1991-92), Benfica (1992-96), Deportivo La Coruna (Spa) (1996-1999), Newcastle (Eng) (1999-)
Full international (Portugal) 33 caps/3 goals
• Versatile defender who won the Portuguese League in 1994 with Benfica and played for Portugal at Euro 96, before moving to Spain.

PLAYER
HELDT, Horst
Midfielder, German, 169cm, 68kg
Born: 09.12.69, Konigswinter, Germany
Clubs: Koln (1990-95), Munich 1860 (1995-99), Eintracht Frankfurt (1999-)
Full international (Germany) 2 caps/0 goals
• Started out as a pacy and tricky left-sided midfielder, but was not at all helped by being called the 'new Hassler'. Now he is a brilliant central playmaker of rare imagination and vision.
• Close to the full German squad.

PLAYER
HELGASON, Audun
Defender, Icelandic, 181cm, 74kg
Born: 18.06.74, Iceland
Club: FH (1992-95), Leiftur (1996-97), Viking Stavanger (Nor) (1998-)
Full international (Iceland) 16 caps/1 goal
• Right-sided full-back whose solid tackling and

well-timed passes have made him a regular in Iceland's international side.

PLAYER
HELGUSON, Heidar
Forward, Icelandic, 183cm, 77kg
Born: 22.08.77, Iceland
Clubs: Throttur (1997), Lillestrom (Nor) (1998-99), Watford (Eng) (1999-)
Full international (Iceland) 9 caps/0 goals
• Brought to Watford by **Graham Taylor** at the end of 1999. Scored in his first appearance, and has added a few goals since. Will be looking to consolidate his position in the national squad, albeit while playing in the English first division, having suffered relegation in May 2000.

COACH
HELISKOSKI, Jyrki
• One of Finland's senior coaches, who led HJK to three League championships in the late 1980s. Then spent a decade coaching various Finnish youth teams as well as the national Under-21 side.
• An advocate of a direct, long-ball game.

PLAYER
HELIN, Petri
Midfielder, Finnish, 179cm, 83kg
Born: 13.12.69, Finland
Clubs: HJK (1988-92), Ikast (Den) (1992-96), HJK (1996-97, PK-35 (1998), Jokerit (1999)
Full international (Finland) 15 caps/2 goals
• Hard-working midfielder who is often used in a wide role, where his direct style is most effective.
• Has won three Finnish League titles with HJK and also spent time in Denmark with Ikast.

PLAYER
HELLERS, Guy
Midfielder, Luxembourg, 186cm, 83kg
Born: 10.10.64, Luxembourg
Clubs: Bascharage, Hollerich, Metz (Fra), Standard Liege (Bel) (1989-)

Full international (Luxembourg) 55 caps/2 goals
• Luxembourg's most experienced player with more than half a century of caps and a decade's worth of experience of the Belgian League.

PLAYER
HELLSTROM, Mikael
Midfielder, Swedish, 176cm, 77kg
Born: 11.03.72, Sweden
Clubs: Hammerby (1990-)
Full international (Sweden) 1 cap/0 goals
• Pacy left-back or midfielder who has been at Hammerby for more than a decade. Has been unlucky to have been overlooked by Sweden's national coaches.

PLAYER
HELMER, Thomas
Defender, German, 185cm, 76kg
Born: 21.04.65, Herford, Germany
Clubs: Arminia Bielefeld (1994-86), Borussia Dortmund (1996-92), Lyon (Fra) (1992), Bayern Munich (1992-99), Sunderland (Eng) (1999), Hertha Berlin (1999-)
Full international (Germany) 68 caps/5 goals
• Veteran man-marker who can also play at sweeper or libero, a position he prefers.
• Played for Germany at the 1992 and 1996 European Championships and 1994 and 1998 World Cups.
• Joined Bayern amid controversial circumstances in 1992. Dortmund did not want to sell him to their rivals, so he joined French club Lyon, and moved to Bayern a month later. The £3.2million fee made him Bayern's most expensive player at the time.
• Joined Sunderland in summer 1999 on a free transfer but moved on to Hertha after a few weeks.

PLAYER
HELSTAD, Torstein
Forward, Norwegian, 186cm
Born: 28.04.77, Norway

Clubs: Brann (1998-)
• Very quick striker who loves to take on defenders in one-to-one situations. Enjoyed an excellent 2000 season in Norway and was linked with a move abroad.

PLAYER
HELVEG, Thomas
Defender, Danish, 179cm, 82kg
Born: 24.06.71, Odense, Denmark
Clubs: Odense (1989-93), Udinese (Ita) (1993-98), Milan (Ita) (1998-)
Full international (Denmark) 52 caps/2 goals
• An intelligent but tough player who can play in midfield or at right-back.
• Impressed for Denmark at the 1998 World Cup, where he played all five games for Denmark.
• Had an excellent 1997-98 season in Serie A with surprise team Udinese. Had a good World Cup, but subsequently found competition for places at Milan tough following a transfer in summer 1998.
• Danish Cup winner in 1991 and 1993 and Danish Player of the Year in 1994.
• Joined Udinese for £500,000 in 1993, and helped win promotion to Serie A in 1995.
• 'My role is basically the same whoever I play for. I must do my share of defensive duties, get forward as much as possible, and create chances. It's as simple as that.'
• **Alberto Zaccheroni** on Helveg: 'Thomas is quick, has incredible stamina and a good tactical brain. He used to get into promising attacking positions and then waste the opportunity with a poor cross. But he has worked hard on that aspect of his game, and his final ball is usually spot on.'

PLAYER
HEMMINGSEN, Michael
Defender, Danish, 190cm, 82kg
Born: 02.10.67, Denmark
Clubs: B1909 (1992), OB (1993-)
Full international (Denmark) 3 caps/0 goals

• Veteran campaigner who has been one of the most reliable defenders in the Danish League in recent seasons, but has rarely managed to earn an international call-up.

• Twin brother Carsten plays for FC Copenhagen.

PLAYER
HENCHOZ, Stefan
Defender, Swiss, 186cm, 78g
Born: 07.03.74, Billens, Switzerland
Clubs: Bulle, Neuchatel Xamax (1992-1995), Hamburg (Ger) (1995-97), Blackburn (Eng) (1997-99), Liverpool (Eng) (1999-
Full international (Switzerland) 41 caps/0 goals

• Uncompromising man-marker, strong in the air and supremely confident.

• Suffered relegation with Blackburn in 1999, but moved to Liverpool and formed a solid central defensive partnership with **Sami Hyypia**.

• A protege of **Roy Hodgson** at Neuchatel and played in of Switzerland's games at Euro 96.

PLAYER
HENDRIE, Lee
Midfielder, England, 175cm, 65kg
Born: 18.05.77, Birmingham, England
Clubs: Aston Villa (1994-)
Full international (England) 1 cap/0goals

• Promising talent who broke into the Aston Villa side under **John Gregory**, earning Under-21 and full England honours very rapidly.

• Father Paul played for Birmingham, cousin John for Bradford, Middlesbrough and Barnsley among others.

• International debut: 18.11.98, v Czech Rep.

COACH
HENDRIE , Tom
Scottish

• Manager of St Mirren who previously combined his part-time duties as manager of Alloa with a secure career as a teacher. He took a major personal gamble when he opted to take on the full-time position at St Mirren, but he is finally reaping the benefits of his decision, having guided the Paisley side to the first division championship during his first season in charge.

• Intelligent and articulate, Hendrie is seen as one of Scotland's brightest young coaches and is greatly respected by his managerial counterparts.

PLAYER
HENDRIKX, Marc
Forward, Belgian, 184cm, 80kg
Born: 02.07.74, Hamont, Belgium
Clubs: Lommel (1992-97), Genk (1997-)
Full international (Belgium) 10 caps/0 goals

• Two-footed full-back who has played much of his career as a right-winger, but who now operates as a left-back, where he uses his attacking instincts to great effect.

• Established as a first-team regular at Genk since 1998, when he featured in the Belgian Cup Final win over Club Brugge.

• Form in the 1998-99 season was recognised with an international call-up and a debut against Peru in the Kirin Cup in Japan in May 1995.

• Played for Belgium at Euro 2000.

PLAYER
HENRIKSEN, Rene
Defender, Danish, 183cm, 74kg
Born: 27.08.69, Denmark
Clubs: AB (1995-99), Panathinaikos (Gre) (1999-)
Full international (Denmark) 20 caps/0 goals

• Central defender who adapted well to his new sporting environment in Greece following a move in summer 1999 from AB Copenhagen to Panathinaikos.

• Powerful in the air and a decent reader of the game, he is a footballing late-developer, winning his first cap at the age of 29.

PLAYER
HENRY, Thierry
Forward, French, 188cm, 83kg

Born: 17.08.77, Les Ulis, France
Clubs: Monaco (1994-99), Juventus (Ita) (1999), Arsenal (Eng) (1999-)
Full international (France) 21 caps/8 goals

A teenage prodigy at Monaco, where he won the 1997 French League title and scored 20 goals in 105 League games, primarily as a winger.

• FIFA was called in during the summer 1997 after Henry signed contracts, through different agents, with both Monaco and Real Madrid. He stayed with Monaco.

• Scored three goals in six games for France's 1998 World Cup-winning side.

• Spent seven months at Juventus scoring only three times, before being reunited with **Arsene Wenger**, his first coach at Monaco, in August 1999.

• Converted by Wenger into a central striker and was one of the stars of France's Euro 2000 triumph.

• 'I never imagined that things could move so fast. I'm not living the life of a normal youngster any more. But I stay in touch with my old friends to avoid getting a big head. I was lucky to have a talent for playing football because I don't have a talent for studying!'

PLAYER
HERMANSEN, Chris

Forward, Danish, 179cm, 83kg
Born: 23.01.75, Denmark
Clubs: Esbjerg (1995-96), Herfolge (1996-97), AB (1998-)

• Striker who has been a regular scorer in the Danish League whichever club he has been with.

PLAYER
HERMANSSON, Andreas

Forward, Swedish, 179cm, 78kg
Born: 08.01.73, Sweden
Clubs: Umea (1991-94), Trelleborg (1995-97), IFK Gothenburg (1998-2000), Hammerby (2000-)

• A fast, tough centre-forward signed by Hammarby in 2000 after a lengthy on-off transfer from Gothenburg. Made his name at Trelleborg.

Thierry Henry

Andreas Herzog

PLAYER
HERPOEL, Frederic

Goalkeeper, Belgian, 183cm, 76kg
Born: 16.08.74, Belgium
Clubs: Anderlecht (1995-97), Gent (1997-)
Full international (Belgium) 1 cap/0 goals
• Keeper who earned notoriety when he made his international debut in the epic 5-5 friendly draw with Holland in September 1999.
• Belgium's number three keeper at Euro 2000, being called up to the final 22 following an injury to Ronny Gaspercic.

PLAYER
HERRERA, Martin

Goalkeeper, Argentinian, 185cm, 79kg
Born: 13.09.70, Rio Cuarto, Argentina
Clubs: Atlanta (1996-97), Toluca (Mex) (1997-98), Ferril Carril Oeste (1998-99), Alaves (Spa) (1999-)
• Strong, charismatic keeper whose performances for Alaves since arriving from Argentina helped Alaves to a top six finish in Spain in 1999-2000.
• Came through the Boca Juniors youth system in Argentina.

COACH
HERRERA, Francisco 'Paco'

Spanish
Born: 02.12.53
• A second division journeyman who took over from **Andoni Goikoetxea** at Numancia in 2000 and was expected to find the going tough in the top flight.

PLAYER
HERRLICH, Heiko

Forward, German, 186cm, 83kg
Born: 03.12.71, Freiburg, Germany
Clubs: Kollnau, Emmendingen, Freiburg, Bayer Leverkusen (1989-93), Monchengladbach (1993-95), Borussia Dortmund (1995-)
Full international (Germany) 5 caps/1 goal

Striker who was at the centre of a storm in the summer of 1995 when he threatened to quit the game if Borussia Monchengladbach did not allow him to move to Borussia Dortmund. The row was dragged through the courts before Herrlich got his transfer, but though an ever-willing competitor and strong in the air, a succession of injuries and inconsistency have dogged him during his time as a Dortmunder. The highlight of his career was finishing the 1994-95 season as the Bundesliga's top scorer with 20 goals.
• Surname pronounced Err lick.

BUSINESS
HERSOV, Rob
South African
• CEO of internet company Sportal, which runs official websites for Juventus, Paris Saint-Germain and Bayern Munich. Reported to have paid £7million to host UEFA's official Euro 2000 website.
• A member of one of South Africa's richest families.
• Previously worked for ENIC, owner of AEK Athens, Slavia Prague and Vicenza.

PLAYER
HERZOG, Andreas
Midfielder, Austrian, 183cm, 80kg
Born: 10.09.68, Vienna, Austria
Clubs: Admira Wacker (1987), First Vienna (1988), Rapid Vienna (1988-92), Werder Bremen (Ger) (1992-95), Bayern Munich (Ger) (1995-96), Werder Bremen (Ger) (1996-)
Full international (Austria) 79 caps/18 goals
• Elegant Austrian midfield creator with great passing ability and a rocket-like left-foot shot from free-kicks or open play.
• Known in his homeland early in his career as the 'White Gullit', he has played in Germany since 1992, appearing in 223 Bundesliga games for Werder and Bayern Munich and scoring 57 goals.
• Surname pronounced Hurts zog.

PLAYER
HERTZSCH, Ingo
Defender, German, 184cm, 80kg
Born: 22.07.77, Meerane, Germany
Clubs: Callenberger, Chemnitzer, Hamburg (1997-)
• Highly impressive young defender who is being tipped for international honours.
• German Under-21 international.

PLAYER
HESKEY, Emile
Forward, English, 188cm, 84kg
Born: 11.01.78, Leicester, England
Clubs: Leicester (1994-2000), Liverpool (2000-)
Full international (England) 9 caps/1 goal
• Big, bustling centre-forward who was given his chance at international level by Kevin Keegan.
• Joined Liverpool for £11million from Leicester in March 2000, renewing his England Under-21 partnership with Michael Owen.
• International debut: 28.04.99, v Hungary (1-1).

PLAYER
HESP, Ruud
Goalkeeper, Dutch, 194cm, 94kg
Born: 31.10.65, Bussum, Holland
Clubs: Fortuna Sittard (1987-94), Roda (1994-97), Barcelona (Spa) (1997-2000)
• One of the surprise stars of Barcelona's 1998 double-winning side.
• Played for modest clubs in Holland before becoming Louis Van Gaal's first official signing as Barcelona coach. Was expected to keep the substitutes' bench warm, but he took advantage of an injury to Vitor Baia and claim the first-choice spot.
• Goalkeeper of the Year in Holland in 1989.
• His performances for Barcelona earned him a call-up to the Dutch national squad for the 1998 World Cup.
• Agile keeper for such a big man, and useful with his feet, too – an asset valued by the Total Football-aspiring Dutch coaches at Barcelona.

Jupp Heynckes

PLAYER
HEURTEBIS, Tony
Goalkeeper, French, 180cm, 73kg
Born: 15.01.75, Saint-Nazaire, France
Clubs: Rennes (1995-99), Troyes (1999-)
• In the space of the 1999-2000 season he went from third choice at Rennes to being ranked as one of France's best keepers. His acrobatics and bravery were crucial to keeping Troyes' heads above water in the 1999-2000 campaign.
• Surname pronounced Err tay bees.

REFEREE
HEYNEMANN, Bernd
German
Born: 22.01.54
• Works as an engineer.
• Awarded his FIFA badge in 1989.

COACH
HEYLIGEN, Jos
Belgian
• The successor of **Aime Anthuenis** at 1999 Belgian champions Genk, but he couldn't cope with the pressure and was never able to motivate the players. Was sacked halfway through the 1999-2000 season.

COACH
HEYNCKES, Jupp
German
Born: 09.05.45
•Coach of Benfica since 1999 whose cv is headed by a Champions League victory with Real Madrid in 1998 and back-to-back Bundesliga crowns with Bayern Munich in the 1988-89 and 1989-90 campaigns.
• A master-builder of competitive sides, but man-management is not his strongest suit. Hence his problems with **Davor Suker** at Real, **Joao Pinto** at Benfica and the infamous Eintracht Frankfurt player rebellion of December 1994 when **Tony Yeboah**, **Jay-Jay Okocha** and Maurizio Gaudino

went on strike against his hard-line methods.
• Hardly endeared himself to Portuguese fans when he described the country's League as one of the least competitive in Europe.

PLAYER
HIBIC, Mirsad

Defender, Croatian/Bosnian, 185cm, 81kg
Born: 11.10.73, Zenica, Bosnia
Clubs: Hajduk Split (1991-96), Sevilla (Spa) (1996-)
Full international (Croatia) 3 caps/0 goals
Full international (Bosnia) 10 caps/3 goals
• Central defender who is comfortable on the ball and is most effective in the libero role.
• Arrived in Split as a refugee from Zenica in Bosnia and played three times for Croatia before reverting to his Bosnian nationality
• Joined Sevilla from Hajduk Split in 1997 for £750,000.

PLAYER
HIDEN, Martin

Defender, Austrian, 181cm, 75kg
Born: 11.03.73, Stainz, Austria
Clubs: Sturm Graz (1992-94), Salzburg (1994-96), Sturm Graz (1996-98), Leeds United (Eng) (1998-2000), Austria Vienna (2000-)
Full international (Austria) 7 caps/1 goal
• Central defender signed by **George Graham** for Leeds in summer 2000, but found opportunities at Elland Road limited and moved back to Austria for the start of the 2000-2001 season.

COACH
HIDDINK, Guus

Dutch
Born: 08.11.46
• Out of contract after being sacked by relegated Betis in the 1999-2000 season in Spain, when he failed to pull off a miracle.
• Best known as coach of Holland at the 1996 European Championships and 1998 World Cups.

• Played for a variety of Dutch clubs in the 1960s before moving to the North American Soccer League with Washington Diplomats and San Jose Earthquakes.
• Returned to Holland for a four-year spell as youth coach with De Graafschap. Then worked as assistant at PSV for three years before taking charge as coach, winning the 1987 European Cup.
• Took over from **Dick Advocaat** as Holland coach in autumn 1994 and took the Dutch to the semi-finals of France 98, although he failed to control internal discontent at Euro 96, falling out with **Edgar Davids** in particular.
• Did well in a previous spell in Spain, at Valencia, but never looked in control at Betis, or Real Madrid, whom he took charge of after the 1998 World Cup.

PLAYER
HIERRO, Fernando

Full name: Fernando Ruiz Hierro
Defender, Spanish, 187cm, 84kg
Born: 23.03.68, Malaga, Spain
Clubs: Real Valladolid (1987-89), Real Madrid (1989-)
Full international (Spain) 73 caps/23 goals
• Commanding centre-back who was used by former Spain coach **Javier Clemente** as a holding midfielder, but has now been restored to his natural position at the back, where he is a rock for club and country.
• Started out at Valladolid where his older brother Manolo was on the books, and joined Real for £1.4 million in 1989.
• Scored seven goals in 1989-90 as Real Madrid won the Spanish League scoring a record 107 goals.
• A non-playing member of Spain's squad at the 1990 World Cup, but played every game at USA 94 and again at Euro 96 and France 98.
• Name means 'iron' in Spanish.
• Former Real Madrid coach **Fabio Capello** callled Hierro 'the Spanish Baresi'.

PLAYER
HILARIO
Goalkeeper, Portuguese, 188cm, 85kg
Born: 21.10.75, Sao Pedro da Cova Portugal
Clubs: Naval (1994-95), Academica (1995-96), FC Porto (1996-98), Estrela Amadora (1998-99), FC Porto (1999-)
• Reserve keeper at FC Porto who came in when **Vitor Baia** was sidelined with a knee injury.

PLAYER
HILL, Delano
Defender, Dutch, 191cm, 79kg
Born: 29.04.75, Amsterdam, Holland
Clubs: Den Bosch (1995-96), RKC Waalwijk (1996-98), Willem II (1998-
• Tall left-back, who can also play in the centre. Strong tackler and good in the air.

PLAYER
HINCHCLIFFE, Andy
Defender, English, 179cm, 81kg
Born: 05.02.69, Manchester, England
Clubs: Manchester City (1986-90), Everton (1990-98), Sheffield Wed (1998-)
Full international (England) 7 caps/0 goals
• Left wing-back noted for his delivery at set-pieces.

PLAYER
HISLOP, Shaka
Goalkeeper, English/Trinidadian, 194cm, 91kg
Born: 22.0.69, London Hackney, England
Clubs: Howard Uni, Reading (1992-1995), Newcastle (1995-98), West Ham (1998-)
Full international (Trinidad & Tobago)
• Born in London and an England Under-21 international, but opted to play for country of his parents' birth.
• Made his name at Reading as the best keeper outside of the Premier League, earning a £1.5million move to Newcastle in summer 1995.

COACH
HITZFELD, Ottmar
German/Swiss
Born: 12.01.49
• Hugely successful Bundesliga coach, winning the German League title with Bayern Munich and Borussia Dortmund, the two most successful German teams of the 1990s.
• A mostly amateur career as a forward, but played 22 games (5 goals) in the German Bundesliga, as well as eight games for the Swiss national amateur side.
• Made his name as coach in Switzerland with FC Zug, Aarau and Grasshopper, winning the League title in successive seasons with Grasshopper in 1990 and 1991.
• Joined Borussia Dortmund in July 1991 and won back-to-back German League titles in 1995 and 1996 before crowning his achievements with a victory over Juventus in the 1997 UEFA Champions League Final.
• Suprisingly moved to an executive post at the club in summer 1997, before switching to Bayern Munich at the start of the 1998-99 season.
• Led Bayern to successive League titles in 1999 and 2000, but had to endure the heartache of losing to Manchester United in injury time in the 1999 Champions League Final.
• An excellent man-manager, sometimes a diplomat, other times a disciplinarian, he has had few problems exerting his authority over star-packed squads at Dortmund and Bayern. Tactically very astute, he produces teams which can switch effortlessly from one formation to another and is a master in the art of rotating his personnel.
• A former mathematics teacher.
• A target of the German FA to become national coach, but remains contracted to Bayern.

COACH
HODDLE, Glenn
English
Born: 27.10.57

• Since spring 2000 has been manager of Southampton, his first appointment since leaving the post of England manager in autumn 1999.

• A wonderfully gifted midfield player for Spurs, Monaco and England, winning 53 caps, although many argue it should have been many more. Won the FA Cup with Spurs and the French League at Monaco under **Arsene Wenger,** who pursuaded him to take up coaching.

• As a coach, took Swindon to the Premier League via the play-offs before leaving for Chelsea, whom he steered to an FA Cup semi-final.

• Did very well initially as England manager, qualifying automatically for the 1998 World Cup at the expense of Italy. But after defeat on penalties by Argentina, his position deteriorated.

• Comments about players in a book rushed out after the tournament, combined with comments to a journalist about his controversial belief in reincarnation, led to his departure as England coach.

• 'Managing England should be the best job in the world, but it has become a horrible job. To think of my children going into school and getting hammered because their dad is the England manager. Perhaps we should be looking for a guy who is divorced with no kids.'

COACH
HODGSON, Roy
English
Born: 09.08.47

• One of the most successful English coaches of the 1990s who took Switzerland to the 1994 World Cup finals and 1996 European Championship finals and has worked successfully around Europe for the past 20 years.

• Was on the books of Crystal Palace as a youngster, but failed to make the grade and moved to non-League Maidstone. Teamed up with Bobby

Houghton in the mid-1970s and began his coaching career at Halmstad in Sweden. Helped out Houghton at Bristol City before a return to Sweden with Orebro.

• Made his name in Switzerland, taking Neuchatel Xamax to the runners-up spot in the Swiss League in 1991 and 1992 before being appointed Swiss coach.

• Lured to Internazionale in 1996, guiding the Milan club to the 1997 UEFA Cup Final and then leaving to take charge at Blackburn.

• Took Blackburn to sixth place in the League, before events conspired against him and he left before Blackburn were relegated in May 1999.

• Returned to Switzerland, taking charge of Grasshopper, before moving on to a new challenge at FC Copenhagen in summer 2000.

• 'Coaching is about three things: knowledge, communication and leadership. The really good coach will score highly in all three areas.'

ADMINISTRATOR
HOENESS, Uli
Born: 05.01.52

• General manager of Bayern Munich, the club he won the European Cup with as a player. Responsible for much of Bayern's activities in the transfer market.

PLAYER
HOFFMANN, Daniel
Goalkeeper, German, 187cm, 89kg
Born: 27.10.71, Germany
Clubs: Hansa Roctock (1990-96), VfB Leipzig (1996-97), Munich 1860 (1997-)

• They like goalkeepers who go by the name of Hoffmann at 1860. In the 1998-99 campaign, it was Michael Hoffmann who stood between their posts and in the 1999-2000 season Daniel Hoffman did the honours, winning much praise for his cool and authoritative performances. Not bad considering he was playing in discomfort with a knee problem.

Erik Hoftun

PLAYER
HOFTUN, Erik
Defender, Norwegian, 186cm, 85kg
Born: 03.03.69, Kyrksaeterora, Norway
Clubs: Molde (1992-93), Rosenborg (1994-)
Full international (Norway) 22 caps/0 goals
• Solid, powerful centre-back who is difficult to get past and enjoys initiating attacks. Preferred to stay with Rosenborg instead of moving to Italian football a couple of years ago.

PLAYER
HOGH, Jes
Defender, Danish, 184cm, 74kg
Born: 07.05.66, Copenhagen, Denmark
Clubs: Aalborg, Brondby, Fenerbahce (Tur), Chelsea (Eng) (1999-)
Full international (Denmark) 57 caps/1 goals
• Experienced centre-back who combines skill and patience with strength and commitment.
• Turkish league winner in 1997, having been a Danish champion in 1995.
• International debut: 09.04.91, v Bulgaria (1-1).

PLAYER
HOGH, Lars
Goalkeeper, Danish, 180cm, 76kg
Born: 14.01.59, Denmark
Clubs: OB (1991-)
Full international (Denmark) 8 caps/0 goals
• Veteran goalkeeper who has played more than 800 games for OB Odense.
• Played for Denmark at the 1986 World Cup, but lost out to **Peter Schmeichel** during the 1990s.
• Owns and runs a shoe shop in his native Odense.

PLAYER
HOLLERBACH, Bernd
Midfielder, German, 177cm, 82kg
Born: 08.12.69, Wurzburg, Germany
Clubs: ASV Rimpar, Kickers Wurzburg, St Pauli, Kaiserslautern (1995), Hamburg (1996-)
• Left-sided midfielder with bags of vitality and

...assing ability. Not a first-choice but an ideal sub who immediately settles into the pace of a game.

PLAYER
HOLM, Thomas
Midfielder, Norwegian, 180cm, 73kg
Born: 19.02.81, Oslo, Norway
Clubs: Valarenga, Heerenveen (1998-)
• Teenager who moved to Holland to try his luck with Heerenveen, showing promise but raising speculation that he may have moved too soon.

AGENT
HOLMES, Jonathan
English
• One of England's leading agents who represents a number of players, including **Emile Heskey** and **Graeme Le Saux**.

PLAYER
HOLOVKO, Olexander
Defender, Ukrainian, 185cm, 76kg
Born: 01.06.72, Ukraine
Clubs: Kyiv Dynamo
Full international (Ukraine) (36 caps/0 goals
• Defender who has been a transfer target of Liverpool. Captain of both Kyiv Dynamo and Ukraine who plays all matches on equally high level. A battler with good technique who likes to attack from the back.

PLAYER
HOOGENDORP, Rick
Forward, Dutch, 180cm, 74kg
Born: 12.01.75, The Hague, Holland
Clubs: Den Haag (1994-95), MVV (1995-96), Dordrecht (1997-98), RKC (1999), Celta Vigo (Spa) (2000-)
• Tall, strong striker who was suprisingly signed by Celta Vigo in January 2000 after the club failed to sign Argentinian striker **Juan Esnaider**.
• Made his name in the Dutch second division, where he scored freely for RKC Walwijk.

PLAYER
HOOGMA, Nico-Jan
Defender, Holland, 185cm, 85kg
Born: 26.10.68, Heerenveen, Holland
Clubs: VV Drachten, Cambuur (1989-92), FC Twente (1992-98), Hamburg (Ger) (1998-)
• Experienced Dutch central defender whose solidity, good technique and know-how made him the keystone of an excellent three-man Hamburg rearguard in 1999-2000. No Bundesliga player shone more than him during the second half of the League campaign but there was no hint of call-up papers from Dutch national coach **Frank Rijkaard**.
• 'I'll never be a star.'

PLAYER
HOPKIN, David
Midfielder, Scottish, 175cm, 65kg
Born: 21.08.70, Greenock, Scotland
Clubs: Greenock Morton (1989-92), Chelsea (1992-95), Crystal Palace (1995-97), Leeds (1997-2000), Bradford (2000-)
Full international (Scotland) 7 caps/ 2 goals.
• Tenacious, hard-working midfield dynamo who likes to attack but has a short fuse.
• Fell out with **Glenn Hoddle** at Chelsea, but his goals – including a last-minute winner in the Wembley play-off final – earned Crystal Palace promotion in 1997.

PLAYER
HORNAK, Michal
Defender, Czech, 182cm, 72kg
Born: 28.04.70, Czech Republic
Clubs: Sparta Prague
Full international (Czech Republic) 37 caps/1 goal
• Ageing but still reliable Euro 96 veteran who can play a variety of roles in defence and midfield.
• Featured in the Euro 2000 qualifying campaign but a lack of regular first-team football ruled him out of contention for the Low Countries.

PLAYER
HORVATH, Pavel
Midfielder, Czech, 177cm, 78kg
Born: 22.04.75, Czech Republic
Clubs: Slavia Prague
Full international (Czech Republic) 10 caps/0
goals
• Talented all-rounder combining flair with steel
who was the heart and soul of the Slavia Prague
team for several seasons, taking responsibility for
nearly all dead-ball situations as well as fulfilling
a creative role in midfield.

COACH
HOULLIER, Gerard
French
Born: 03.09.47
• Coach of Liverpool since July 1998, when he
stepped down from his job as technical director
of the French FA to move to England, initially
working alongside existing manager Roy Evans,
and then take sole charge in November 1998.
• A dedicated Anglophile who fell in love with
Liverpool while a spending year in the city as a
student teacher in 1969. He watched from the
Kop terraces as Liverpool beat Dundalk 10-0 in
the Fairs Cup.
• Had no formal playing career, but begun his
coaching career aged 26 as coach of Le Touquet
before becoming youth coach at Arras and head
coach at Nouex Les Mines, leading them on two
successive promotions.
• Was in charge of Lens between 1982 and 1985,
leading them to promotion and UEFA Cup qualification before joining Paris Saint Germain and
steering them to the 1986 French League title.
• Joined the technical staff of the French
federation and was assistant to **Michel Platini**
before taking charge himself after Euro 92.
• Resigned in November 1993 after defeat by
Bulgaria in Paris in a final World Cup qualifying
match. Moved upstairs to become technical
director.

Pavel Horvath

COACH
HOUWAART, Henk
Dutch
• A Dutchman who has been working in Belgium for many years. Was successful at Club Brugge and Harelbeke, before moving Gent for the 2000-2001 season.

PLAYER
HOWEY, Steve
Defender, English, 187cm, 75kg
Born: 26.10.71, Sunderland, England
Clubs: Newcastle (1989-), Manchetser Cty (2000-)
Full international (England) 4 caps/0 goal
• Centre-back who has been hit by injuries but can be commanding in the air and on the ground.
• Started as a striker, before moving into midfield for the 1992-93 season.
• Made his international debut against Nigeria in November 1994, and was a non-playing squad member at Euro 96.
• Brother Lee played for Newcastle's rivals Sunderland.
• Joined newly-promoted Manchester City in a £3million transfer in the summer of 2000.

PLAYER
HREIDARSSON, Hermann
Defender, Icelandic, 185cm, 83kg
Born: 11.07.74, Iceland
Clubs: IBV, Crystal Palace (1997-98), Brentford (1999-99), Wimbledon (1999-)
Full international (Iceland) 29 caps/1 goal
• Big, hard-tackling international defender whose travels took him to Crystal Palace and Brentford, before Ron Noades sold him to Wimbledon last year for a club record fee.

PLAYER
HRISTOV, Georgi
Forward, Macedonian
Born: 30.01.76,
Clubs: Pelister Bitola (1993), Partizan Belgrade

(Yug) (1994-97), Barnsley (Eng) (1997-2000), NEC (Hol) (2000-)
Full international (Macedonia)
debut: 13.10 1993; 32 caps/9 goals
• Macedonia's leading striker despite a disappointing spell at Barnsley, where he added insult to his knee injury by criticising the local women as 'ugly'.
• Made his name at Partizan Belgrade, where he won three Yugoslav League titles before a £1.5million transfer to England.

PLAYER
HRISTOV, Marian
Midfielder, Bulgarian, 186cm, 80kg
Born: 29.07.73, Botevgrad, Bulgaria
Clubs: Balkan Botevgrad, Slavia Sofia (1994-95), Levski Sofia (1995-97), Kaiserslautern (1997-)
Full international (Bulgaria) 17 caps/3 goals
• Tall and robust Bulgarian attacking midfielder or striker. Good in the air with lots of physical presence and hard-working, but can appear clumsy.
• Surname pronounced Rish tof.

PLAYER
HUARD, Laurent
Midfielder, French, 173cm, 68kg
Born: 26.08.73, Fougeres, France
Clubs: Rennes (1990-99), Sedan (1999-)
• A bundle of energy and commitment in central midfield, but by no means is he just a workhorse. His technique is perfectly acceptable and he serves as a good springboard for counter-attacks. A Former French Under-21 international.
• Surname pronounced Hoo ah.

PLAYER
HUCKERBY, Darren
Forward, English, 177cm, 76kg
Born: 23.04.76, Nottingham, England
Clubs: Lincoln (1993-95), Newcastle United (1995-96), Millwall (1996, loan), Coventry City

Gerard
Houllier

(1996-99), Leeds United (1999-)

•Talented young striker who was signed by **Kevin Keegan** for Newcastle in November 1995, but suffered from the then lack of reserve team football at St James' Park. Keegan had not wanted the reserve team to 'carve up' the pitch at St James' Park.

• England Under-21 international.

PLAYER
HUGO COSTA
Full name: Hugo Alexandre Esteves Costa
Defender, Portuguese, 184cm, 74kg
Born: 04.11.73, Tramagal, Portugal
Clubs: Benfica (1991-92), Gil Vicente (1992-93), Beira-Mar (1993-95), Estrela Amadora (1995-96), Alverca (1996-)
• Hugely important player for Alverca, both in winning promotion to the Portuguese first division in 1998 and in staying there since then.

PLAYER
HUGO HENRIQUE
Full name: Hugo Henrique Castro da Silva
Forward, Brazilian, 184cm, 80kg
Born: 18.05.75, Pernambuco, Brazil
Clubs: Sergipe (1999), Rio Ave (Por) (1999-)
• Striker who can look awkward in front of goal, but is surprisingly effective as a goalscorer.

PLAYER/COACH
HUGHES, Mark
Forward, Welsh, 179cm, 83kg
Born: 01.11.63, Wrexham, Wales
Clubs: Manchester Utd (1980-1986), Barcelona (Spa) (1986-87), Bayern Munich (Ger) (1987-88), Manchester Utd (1988-95), Chelsea (1995-98), Southampton (1998-2000), Everton (2000-)
Full international (Wales)
• Veteran centre-forward who won a host of honours during two spells with Man United, including four FA Cup winners' medals and the Europe Cup-winners Cup (after scoring the

winning goal in 1991 Final against Barcelona.

• Remains adept at holding up the ball, despite declining pace.

• Appointed caretaker manager of Wales, alongside Neville Southall, eventually taking sole charge, after the resignation of Bobby Gould in June 1999.

PLAYER
HUGHES, Michael
Midfielder, Northern Irish, 169cm, 67kg
Born: 02.08.71, Larne, Northern Ireland
Clubs: Manchester City (1988-94), Strasbourg (1992-96), West Ham (1994-97), Wimbledon (1997-)
Full international (Northern Ireland) 54 caps/4 goals

• Winger who can play on either flank.

• Moved to France in summer 1992, but no truth in the rumour that Strasbourg wanted to sign M Hughes from Manchester (ie Manchester United **Mark Hughes**).

• Fell out with **Egil Olsen** and vowed to leave Wimbledon at the end of 1999-2000 season.

PLAYER
HUIBERTS, Max
Forward, Dutch, 181cm, 71kg
Born: 17.11.70, Zwolle, Holland
Clubs: Zwolle (1990-91), Roda JC (1991-95), Borussia Monchengladbach (Ger) (1995-97), AZ (1997-)

• Left winger, who had a promising career at Roda, but several injuries and a wrong decision to play in the Bundesliga at Borussia Monchengladbach put the blocks on an international career.

• Is now back in Holland trying to get his career back on track at AZ.

COACH
HULSHOFF, Barry
Dutch

• A member of the Ajax team that reigned supreme over Europe in the early 1970s, playing as a no-nonsense full-back.

• Did not have the correct qualification to coach in his home country, so he moved to Belgium where he was in charge with St Truiden and Beveren, before moving to Eendracht Aalst. Also works as a TV analyst.

PLAYER
HUSIN, Andrii
Midfielder, Ukrainian, 189cm, 78kg
Born: 11.12.72
Club: Kyiv Dynamo
Full international (Ukraine) 24 caps/0 goals

• Tough-tackling defensive midfielder whose battling qualities make him indispensable for both club and country. Particularly strong in the air.

• Surname also spelled Gusin.

PLAYER
HUTCHISON, Don
Midfielder, Scottish, 185cm, 75kg
Born: 09.05.71, Gateshead, England
Clubs: Hartlepool (1990), Liverpool (1990-94), West Ham (1994-96), Sheffield Utd (1996-98), Everton (1998-2000), Sunderland (2000-)
Full international (Scotland) 10 caps/5 goals).

• Talented, enigmatic central midfielder whose off-the-pitch disciplinary problems have restricted his career.

• Lacks pace, but is combative and creative, with an eye for goals.

• Born in England but opted to play for Scotland. Scored on his full debut, against Germany in Germany.

HUTTER, Adi
Midfielder, Austrian, 185cm, 77kg
Born: 11.02.70, Hohenems, Austria
Clubs: Grazer AK, Salzburg (1993-)
Full international (Austria) 14 caps/3 goals
• Hard-working midfielder who has been in and our of favour with the Austrian national team during his career, missing the cut for the 1998 World Cup squad.
• Adi is short for Adolf.

HUYSEGEMS, Stijn
Forward, Belgian, 186cm, 76kg
Born: 16.06.82, Belgium
Clubs: Lierse (1998-)
• Young striker of whom big things are expected in Belgium. Fast with a sharp eye for goal.

HYYPIA, Sami
Defender, Finnish, 192cm, 85kg
Born: 07.10.73, Porvvo, Finland
Clubs: MyPa (Hol) (1993-1995), Willem II (Hol) (1995-1999), Liverpool (1999-)
Full international (Finland) 32 caps/1 goal
• Towering centre-back who arrived in England in summer 1999 after winning many plaudits in Holland and was one of the players of the 1999-2000 season.
• Finnish Player of the Season in 1998.

I

PLAYER
IACHINI, Giuseppe
Midfielder, Italian, 168cm, 69kg
Born: 07.05.64, Ascoli Piceno, Italy
Clubs: Ascoli (1980-87), Verona (1987-89), Fiorentina (1989-94), Palermo (1994-96), Ravenna (1996-97), Venezia (1997-)
• Hardened veteran who is arguably the most experienced player in Serie A, having made his debut for Ascoli back in 1980.

PLAYER
IANNUZZI, Alessandro
Forward, Italian, 179cm, 70kg
Born: 09.10.75, Rome, Italy
Clubs: Lazio (1993-96), Vicenza (1996-97), Lecce (1997-98), Lazio (1998), Milan (1999), Reggina (1999-)
• Talented midfielder who moved to Reggina for the 1999-2000 season after failing to command a first-team place at Lazio and Milan.

PLAYER
IASCHWILI, Alexander
Forward, Georgian, 174cm, 71kg
Born: 23.10.77, Tiflis, Georgia
Clubs: Dynamo Tbilisi, VfB Lubeck, Dynamo Tbilisi, Freiburg (1997-)
Full international (Georgia) 8 caps/2 goals
• Georgian international striker who missed a large chunk of the past two seasons with knee ligament damage. But he remains an outstanding frontrunner, a player of clever movement, feints, tricks and goals.
• Surname pronounced Ee ash vili.

PLAYER
IBAGAZA, Ariel
Midfielder, Argentinian, 166cm, 67kg
Born: 27.10.76, Buenos Aires, Argentina
Clubs: Lanus (1994-98), Mallorca (Spa) (1998-)
• Diminutive left-footed playmaker who plays just behind the front two strikers.
• Another of the ex-Lanus players brought to Mallorca from Argentina by then coach Hector Cuper.

PLAYER
IDIAKEZ, Inigo
Full name: Inigo Idiakez Barkaiztegi
Born: 17.11.73, Bilbao, Spain
Clubs: Real Sociedad (1992-)
• Tall striker who remains a regular at Sociedad despite never having reached double figures in the scoring charts in a season.
• Spanish Under-21 international.

PLAYER
IKPEBA, Victor
Forward, Nigerian, 174cm, 69kg
Born: 12.06.73, Benin City, Nigeria
Clubs: ACB Lagos, Standard Liege (Bel) (1989-93), Monaco (Fra) (1993-99), Borussia Dortmund (Ger) (1999-)
Full international (Nigeria)
• The 1999-2000 season was a dreadful one for the Nigerian international attacker. He never adjusted to the German game following a move from Monaco and showed little of the pace, trickery and goalscoring of his six years in Monte Carlo. But much more seriously, 2000 was the year he lost his wife to cancer, a personal tragedy which far outweighs any event on a football pitch.
• African Footballer of the Year in 1997.
• Surname pronounced Ik pay bah.

COACH
ILIC, Josif
Yugoslav
Born: 1950
• National coach of Malta since July 1997. A strict disciplinarian who is still very much in favour after winning five of his 28 games in charge.

PLAYER
ILIC, Radisa
Goalkeeper, Yugoslav, 192cm, 85kg
Born: 20.09.77, Bajina Basa, Yugoslavia
Clubs: Partizan Belgrade
• One of the surprises of the 1999-2000 season in Yugoslavia. A member of the Under-21 squad.

PLAYER
ILIC, Sasa
Midfielder, Yugoslav, 177cm, 69kg
Born: 30.12.77
Clubs: Partizan Belgrade, Yugoslavia
• Another product of Partizan's successful youth scheme who is already team captain and one of the key players.
• A regular in Yugoslavia's Under-21 team before he fell out with former coach Milovan Djoric following a disastrous 6-2 home defeat by Croatia.

PLAYER
ILLES, Bela
Midfielder, Hungarian, 182cm, 76kg
Born: 27.04.68, Sarvar, Hungary
Clubs: Sarvar (1985-86), Haladas (1986-92), Kispest (1992-95), MTK (1995-)
Full international (Hungarian) 55 caps/12 goals
• Attacking midfielder who has played a crucial role in MTK's success in recent years. Finished as top scorer in the Hungarian League in 1998-99 with 22 goals.

PLAYER
ILLGNER, Bodo
Goalkeeper, German, 190cm, 85kg
Born: 07.04.67, Koblenz, Germany
Clubs: Koln (1985-96), Real Madrid (Spa) (1996-)
Full international (Germany) 54 caps/0 goals
• Tall, experienced international keeper who joined Real from Koln in 1996.
• A World Cup winner in 1990 and also played in the USA in 1994. Also played at Euro 88 and Euro 92.
• Played 322 Bundesliga games for Koln.

• Alternated with **Santiago Canizares** for the number one slot at Real, but was in goal for when Real beat Juventus to win the 1998 Champions League Final.
• Lost his place to teenager **Iker Casillas** following injury in the 1999-2000 season.
• Business affairs are managed by his wife Bianca.

PLAYER
ILIE, Adrian
Forward, Romanian, 180cm, 74kg
Born: 20.04.74, Craiova, Romania
Clubs: Elect. Craoiva (1991-93), Steaua Bucharest (1993-96), Galatasaray (Tur) (1996-97), Valencia (Spa) (1998-)
Full international (Romania) 37 caps/11 goals
• Explosive striker who was Romania's best player at the 1998 World Cup finals, scoring a brilliant individual goal against Colombia.
• Nicknamed 'The Cobra' because of his ability to strike from anywhere.
• Won three titles as a midfielder at Steaua before a move to Turkey which didn't work out, although he was converted to his now familiar position of striker. Transferred midway through 1997-98 season to Valencia and started to repay the large fee with 12 goals in his first 17 games.
• Romanian Player of the Year in 1998.
• International debut: 22.09.93, v Israel (won 1-0).

PLAYER
ILIE, Sabin
Forward, Romanian, 178cm, 75kg
Born: 11.05.75, Craiova, Romania
Clubs: Electroputere (1993-94), Brasov (1994-95), Steaua Bucharest (1995-97), Fenerbahce (Tur) (1997-98), Valencia (Spa) (1998-99), Lleida (Spa) (1998-99), Steaua Bucharest (1999), National Bucharest (2000-)
• Striker who has lived his career in the shadow of his older brother **Adrian Ilie**, but arguably is the more talented individual.
• Made his name in the 1996-97 season, when

he scored 31 goals for Steaua, earning a transfer to Turkey and subsequently to Spain, to Valencia, who sent him out on loan to Lleida in the Spanish second division. He struggled to make an impression abroad and returned to Steaua for the 1999-2000 season, but fell out of favour and moved across town to National.

PLAYER
ILIEV, Ivica
Forward, Yugoslav, 181cm, 77kg
Born: 27.10.79, Belgrade, Yugoslavia
Clubs: Partizan Belgrade
• Fast and skilful attacker Yugoslav Under-21 international.
• Impressed with his courage and coolness in his European club debut against Lazio in Rome in the 1998-99 Cup-winners Cup.

PLAYER
IMAZ, Andoni
Full name: Andoni Imaz Garmendia
Midfielder, Spanish, 177cm, 74kg
Born: 05.09.71, San Sebastian, Spain
Clubs: Real Sociedad (1991-99), Athletic Bilbao (1999-)
Full international (Spain) 1 cap/0 goals
• Hard-working midfielder who joined Athletic Bilbao in 1997 after seven seasons at Basque rivals Real Sociedad.

COACH
INACIO, Augusto
Portuguese
Born: 06.12.55
• Many thought the former Maritimo and Chaves coach did not have the requisite star quality to step into the breach at Sporting Lisbon after the Italian **Giuseppe Materazzi** was unceremoniously fired just six weeks into last season. But he confounded the critics by leading Sporting to their first Portuguese League title in 18 years.
• A former full-back for Portugal and FC Porto

Adrian Ilie

and prior to his appointment by Sporting, he was earning a living as football commentator for the Antenna 1 TV station.

• 'Expectations are permanently high at a big club like Sporting. I spend every day trying to dampen down euphoria, minimise problems and generally keep things in perspective.'

PLAYER
INCE, Paul
Midfielder, English, 178cm, 74kg
Born: 21.10.67, Ilford, England
Clubs: West Ham (1985-1989), Manchester United (1989-95), Internazionale (Ita) (1995-97), Liverpool (1997-99), Middlesbrough (1999-)
Full international (England) 53 caps/2 goals

• Combative midfielder, self-styled as the 'Guvnor', whose days as an all-action dynamo look numbered.

• Started as West Ham, but incurred the wrath of fans when he appeared for a photocall in a Man United shirt before a £1m transfer to Old Trafford had been agreed.

• Won the European Cup-winners Cup, two FA Cups and two League titles with United before a £8m move to Italy in July 1995.

• Earned rave reviews for his dynamic play in Serie A after an indifferent start.

• Played for England at Euro 96 and France 98, where he missed a penalty in the shoot-out against Argentina. Recalled by **Kevin Keegan** for Euro 2000, but appeared off the pace during defeats by Portugal and Romania.

PLAYER
INGESSON, Klas
Midfielder, Swedish, 190cm, 88kg
Born: 20.08.68, Odeshog, Sweden
Clubs: IFK Gothenburg (1986-90), Mechelen (Bel) (1990-93), PSV Eindhoven (Hol) (1993-94), Sheffield Wednesday (Eng) (1994-95), Bari (Ita) (1995-98), Bologna (Eng) (1999-2000), Marseille (Fra) (2000-)
Full international (Sweden) 58 caps/13 goals

Simone Inzaghi

- Midfielder who grew in stature during five seasons in Italy and is now one of the most accomplished midfield anchormen in Europe.
- Played for Sweden at the 1994 World Cup, but has declined to play for his country in recent years in protest at what he saw as criticism of him by the Swedish public.
- Joined Marseille in summer 2000.

PLAYER
INNOCENTI, Duccio
Defender, Italian, 186cm, 80kg
Born: 20.09.75, Prato, Italy
Clubs: Fiorentina (1994-95), Pontedera (1995-96), Lucchese (1996-98), Bari (1998-)
- Central defender who has established himself in Italy's Serie A with Bari after failing to make the breakthrough at Fiorentina.

PLAYER
INZAGHI, Filippo
Forward, Italian, 181cm, 74kg
Born: 09.08.73, Piacenza, Italy
Clubs: Piacenza (1991-92), Leffe (1992-93), Verona (1993-94), Piacenza (1994-95), Parma (1995-96), Atalanta (1996-97), Juventus (1997-)
Full international (Italy) 24 caps/7 goals
- Striker who specialises in six-yard 'poaching'.
- Slight of frame but a very sharp finisher.
- Nicknamed 'Pippo' and the elder brother of **Simone Inzaghi**.
- Joined Juventus for £9million in 1997 after finishing the 1996-97 season as Serie A top scorer with 24 goals for Atalanta.
- A prolific scorer at club level but has yet to transfer that form to the international stage.

PLAYER
INZAGHI, Simone
Forward, Italian, 183cm, 75kg
Born: 05.04.76, Piacenza
Clubs: Piacenza (1993-94), Carpi (1994-95), Novara (1995-96), Lumezzane (1996-97),
Piacenza (1997-99), Brescello (1997-98, loan), Lazio (1999-)
Full international (Italy) 1 cap/0 goals
- Younger brother of Juventus striker **Filippo Inzaghi**, but with more of a physical presence.
- Joined Lazio in a £10million transfer from Piacenza in summer 1999 after his 15 goals had saved Piacenza from relegation.
- Was expected to a bit-player but instead played a major role in Lazio's title-winning season, scoring four goals in the 5-1 Champions League defeat of Marseille.
- Called up by Italian coach **Dino Zoff** and made his international debut against Spain in March 2000, but missed the cut for Euro 2000.

PLAYER
IRWIN, Denis
Defender, Irish, 172cm, 67kg
Born: 31.10.65, Cork, Ireland
Clubs: Leeds (1983-86), Oldham (1986-90), Manchester United (1990-)
Full international (Rep Ireland) 56 caps/4 goals
- Softly-spoken left-back who has been one of the most loyal servants of **Alex Ferguson**'s time at Old Trafford.
- Set-piece specialist and regular penalty-taker who announced his retirement from international football in 2000.
- Only member of the 1999 United's Champions League winning side to have played in the victorious 1991 European Cup-winners Cup side.

PLAYER
ISMAEL, Valerien
Defender, French, 191cm, 81kg
Born: 28.09.75, Strasbourg, France
Clubs: Strasbourg (1993-97), Crystal Palace (Eng) (1998), Lens (1998-)
- Athletic, powerful central defender, who has lacked a little consistency in the last couple of years with Crystal Palace and Lens and who can be let down at times by wayward distribution.

Ivan Helguera

- But he remains an above-average marker, and as an organiser of the back-line and team leader, he is excellent.
- Surname pronounced Ish my ell.

PLAYER
ITO
Full name: Antonio Alvarez Perez
Midfielder, Spanish, 176cm, 69kg
Born: 21.01.75, Almendralejo, Spain
Clubs: Extremadura (1991-97), Celta Vigo (1997-98), Real Betis (1998-)
Full international (Spain) 1 cap/0 goals
- Talented midfield all-rounder, who combines technical ability with good vision.
- Famous for an 18-month rise from being the Spanish League's lowest paid player (while with Extremadura) to a spot in the national side.
- International debut against Russia in 1998.

PLAYER
IULIANO, Mark
Defender, Italian, 187cm, 80kg
Born: 12.08.73, Cosenza, Italy
Clubs: Salernitana (1990-92), Bologna (1992-93), Monza (1993-94), Salernitana (1994-96), Juventus (1996-)
Full international (Italy) 11 caps/1 goal
- Tall utility defender who can do a useful marking job when called upon.
- Prefers to wear 'Juliano' on the back of his shirt for superstitious reasons.
- Member of Italy's squad at Euro 2000, having made his international debut against Wales in September 1998. Played an impressive part in Italy's progress to the Final against France.

COACH
IRURETA, Javier
Spanish
Born: 01.04.48
- Journeyman Basque coach who has finally found success in La Coruna after unspectacular

spells in Bilbao, San Sebastian and Vigo.
• Was an elegant forward for Atletico Madrid in the 1970s. Is frequently criticized for being insufficiently adventurous, but his tactics paid in 1999-2000 as Deportivo won their first Spanish League title.

PLAYER
IVAN CAMPO
Defender, Spanish, 185cm, 81kg
Born: 21.02.74, San Sebastian, Spain
Clubs: Logrones (1992-93), Alaves (1993-95), Valladolid (1996), Valencia (1996-97), Mallorca (1997-98), Real Madrid (1998-)
Full international (Spain) 4 caps/0 goals
• Shaggy-haired central defender who has not always convinced at Real Madrid following a move from Mallorca in summer 1998.

PLAYER
IVAN HELGUERA
Full name: Ivan Helguera Bujia
Midfielder, Spanish, 184cm, 74kg
Born: 28.03.75, Santander, Spain
Clubs: Manchego (1995-96), Albacete (1997), Roma (Ita) (1997-98), Espanyol (1998-99), Real Madrid (1999-)
Full international (Spain) 10 caps/0 goals
• Talented and versatile midfielder who can also play in defence.
• Made plenty of headlines in summer 1997 when he signed for Roma after 14 games in the Spanish second division for Albacete.
• Espanyol coach **Jose Antonio Camacho** had tried to sign him in 1997, but after a disappointing year in Italy he returned home, to Espanyol.
• 'I knew that Italian football would be demanding, but **Zdenek Zemen** went over the top. Sometimes we used to train with 20kg weights on our backs. Zemen had pretty fixed ideas about the midfield, but I don't regret my original decision. Fortunately, Espanyol gave me a second chance to prove myself.'

• Was converted to a sweeper at Espanyol, where he won a place in the Spanish national side, now coached by Camacho, and in 1999 moved to Real Madrid for £4.8million.
• Made his international debut against Italy in November 1998, where he reverted to his role as midfield playmaker.
• Played for Spain at Euro 2000.

PLAYER
IVAN IGLESIAS
Full name: Ivan Iglesias Corteguera
Midfielder, Spanish, 178cm, 72kg
Born: 16.12.71, Gijon, Spain
Clubs: Sporting Gijon (1991-93), Barcelona (1993-95), Sporting Gijon (1995-96), Oviedo (1996-)
• Powerful midfielder who started out with Gijon, then tried his luck at Barcelona from 1993 to 1995. Has suffered from injuries recently.

PLAYER
IVAN, Marian
Forward, Romanian, 180cm, 75kg
Born: 01.06.69, Bucharest, Romania
Clubs: Brasov (1991-94), Dinamo Bucharest (1994-96), Brasov (1998-)
Full international (Romania) 3 caps/0 goals
• Strong-running striker who was a member of Romania's squad at the 1994 World Cup but has since fallen from favour.

PLAYER
IVAN PEREZ
Full name: Ivan Perez Munoz
Forward, Spanish, 173cm, 72kg
Born: 29.01.76, Madrid, Spain
Clubs: Real Madrid (1994-96), Extremadura (1996), Real Madrid (1997), Betis (1997-98), Bordeaux (Fra) (1999), Numancia (1999-)
• Striker who graduated from Real Madrid's youth ranks to play for Betis and signed by Bordeaux to replace the Arsenal-bound **Kaba Diawara**.
• Younger brother of **Alfonso**.

IVERSEN, Steffen

Forward, Norwegian, 185cm, 75kg
Born: 10.11.76, Oslo, Norway
Clubs: Nationalkam, Rosenborg (1996), Tottenham (Eng) (1996-)
Full international (Norway) 18 caps/6 goals
• Centre-forward whose time in England has been troubled by injuries but he remains one of Norway's biggest striking talents.
• Agile, strong in the air with a powerful shot.
• Father Odd remains the Norwegian League's all-time top scorer.
• International debut: 14.10.98, v Albania (2-2)

IVIC, Ilija

Forward, Yugoslav, 182cm, 78kg
Born: 17.02.71, Zrenian, Yugoslavia
Clubs: Proleter (1988-91), Red Star Belgrade (1991-94), Olympiakos (Gre) (1994-99), Torino (1999-)
Full international (Yugoslavia) 1 cap/0 goals
• Striker who was signed by Torino after scoring 26 goals for Olympiakos in the 1997-98 season, but failed to repeat his scoring success in Serie B.

IVIC, Tomislav

Croatian
Born: 30.06.33
• Veteran who has coached clubs across the Continent and further afield and took charge of Standard Liege midway through the 1999-2000 season, stepping down from his post of technical director to be coach.

IVIC, Vladimir

Midfielder, Yugoslav, 191cm, 85kg
Born: 07.05.77
Clubs: Partizan Belgrade
• Many in Yugoslavia insist that Vladimir has more natural talent than his older brother **Ilija Ivic**. However, in spite of his huge potential, his career seems to have been stagnating of late.

IWAN, Tomasz

Forward, Polish, 183cm, 78kg
Born: 12.06.71, Slupsk, Poland
Clubs: Roda JC (Hol) (1994-95), Feyenoord (Hol) (1995-97), PSV Eindhoven (Hol) (1997-)
Full international (Poland) 30 caps/4 goals
• Hard-working striker who has been a key man for Poland in recent seasons after a return to favour following a row with former coach Anton Piechniczek.
• Made his name at Roda JC before spending two seasons at Feyenoord. Used mostly as a sub by PSV in the Champions League.

IZZET, Muzzy

Midfielder, English/Turkish, 177cm, 69kg
Born: 31.10.74, London, England
Clubs: Chelsea (1993-96), Leicester (1996-)
Full international (Turkey) 1 cap/0 goals
• Dynamic central midfielder with a good eye for goal.
• Born in London to a Turkish Cypriot family and opted to play for Turkey in early 2000, after twice rejecting Turkish approaches in the hope of playing for England.
• Muzzy is short for Mustapha.

J

JACKSON, Darren

Forward, Scottish, 178cm, 70kg
Born: 25.07.66, Edinburgh, Scotland
Clubs: Meadowbank Thistle (1985-87), Newcastle (1987-89), Dundee Utd (1989-92), Hibernian (1992-97), Celtic (1997-98), Coventry (1998-99), Hearts (1999-)
Full international (Scotland) 28 caps/4 goals
• Having followed an eventful career path which has seen him play in the colours of Meadowbank, Newcastle, Dundee United, Hibs and Celtic, Jackson finally turned out for the team he supported as a boy when he signed for Hearts in March 1999.
• At the age of 34 his best days are no doubt behind him but his experience is being used by manager **Jim Jefferies** to nurture the talents of the promising youngsters at Tynecastle.

PLAYER
JACOBSSON, Andreas

Defender, Swedish, 189cm, 82cm
Born: 06.10.72, Sweden
Clubs: Landskrona (1990-94), Helsingborg (1994-)
Full international (Sweden) 10 caps/0 goals
• Arguably the best centre-back in the Swedish League. Made his debut in the top League with Landskrona in 1994, joining Helsingborg a year later. Has no apparent weaknesses and has been watched by a number of foreign clubs, led by Ipswich.

COACH
JACQUET, Aime

French
Born: 27.09.41
• Coach of France's 1998 World Cup-winning side.
• Played in midfield for Lyon and Saint Etienne and twice for France, though he was a steady League player rather than international-class.

• Learned the coaching trade as pupil to masters such as Albert Batteux and Jean Snella then developd his own reputation at Lyon, Bordeaux and Montepellier.
• He was appointed as France manager in January 1994 as successor to **Gerard Houllier**.
• Resigned after France's triumph at the 1998 World Cup, moving upstairs to the position of technical director.

PLAYER
JACQUET, Christophe

Defender, Swiss, 178cm, 74kg
Born: 02.04.76, Switzerland
Clubs: Yverdon (1998-2000), Servette (2000-)
Full international (Switzerland) 3 caps/0 goals
• Up-and-coming young right-back or central defender bought by Servette from Yverdon in the 2000 close season. Solid, consistent, tough-tackling.

PLAYER
JAIME

Full name: Jaime Sanchez Fernandez
Midfielder, Spanish, 175cm, 70kg
Born: 20.03.73, Madrid, Spain
Clubs: Real Madrid (1993-96), Racing Santander (1996-97), Deportivo La Coruna (1997-)
• Central midfielder who puts workrate and effort above skill.
• Came through the youth ranks at Real Madrid, but had to move to Racing Santander to get a regular game.
• Returned to Madrid and was a member of the squad which won the Champions League in 1998.
• Moved on to Deportivo, where he played an important role as Deportivo won their first Spanish League title in May 2000.

PLAYER
JAIRO, Luiz Filho

Midfielder, Brazilian, 178cm, 74kg
Born: 25.11.71, Brazil
Clubs: St Gallen (1998-)

• Diminutive right-sided Brazilian midfielder who came from nowhere – actually Second Division Wil – to play a big part in St Gallen's title win in the 1999-2000 season. He does not have the same skill levels as his hero, Zico, but all the same, has a delicate touch on the ball and is very dynamic.

Carsten Jancker

PLAYER
JAMES, David
Goalkeeper, English, 194cm, 95kg
Born: 01.08.70, Welwyn Garden City, England
Clubs: Watford (1988-1992), Liverpool (1992-99), Aston Villa (1999-)
Full international (England) 1 cap/0 goals
• Keeper whose time at Liverpool was characterised by brilliant performances interspersed with dreadful mistakes, earning the nickname 'Calamity'.
• Joined Villa in summer 1999 and restored his reputation with a series of strong performances on the way to the FA Cup Final.

PLAYER
JANCKER, Carsten
Forward, German, 193cm, 90kg
Born: 28.08.74, Wismar, Germany
Clubs: Wismar, Hansa Rostock, Koln (1993-95), Rapid Vienna (Aut) (1995-96), Bayern Munich (1996-)
Full international (Germany) 9 caps/3 goals
• Towering, powerful target man who constitutes a handful for even the most uncompromising of stoppers. But since moving to Bayern from Rapid Vienna four years ago, his touch and awareness have improved immeasurably. Great attitude, never stops battling until the final whistle.
• Surname pronounced Yank ker.

PLAYER
JANKAUSKAS, Edgaras
Forward, Lithuanian, 191cm, 84kg
Born: 12.03.75, Lithuania
Clubs: Zalgiris (1992-96), CSKA Moscow (Rus)

(1996), Torpedo Moscow (Rus) (1997), Club Brugge (Bel) (1997-99), Real Sociedad (Spa) (2000-)
Full international (Lithuania) 21 caps/4 goals
• Tall Lithuanian striker who has been a success in western Europe, with Club Brugge and Real Sociedad.
• Started out at leading Lithuanian club Zhalgiris Vilnius, who sold him to CSKA Moscow in 1996 for £200,000.
• Moved on to Bruges midway through the 1997-98 season in a £1.1million transfer and immediately hit it off, scoring eight goals in 17 games as Club Brugge won the Belgian title.
• Continued his goalscoring form following a move to Spain in early 2000.
• 'I've come to western Europe to learn, to improve my game, to rise to new challlenges, and so far I've not been disappointed.'

PLAYER
JANKULOVSKI, Dime
Goalkeeper, Swedish, 187cm, 89kg
Born: 18.06.77, Sweden
Clubs: Lundby (1997), Vastra Frolunda (1998-)
Full international (Sweden) 1 cap/0 goals
• Strong keeper who forced himself into Frolunda's first team midway through the 1998 season.
• Swedish Under-21 international.

PLAYER
JANKULOVSKI, Marek
Midfielder, Czech, 183cm, 82kg
Born: 09.05.77, Czech Republic
Clubs: Banik Ostrava, Napoli (Ita) (2000-)
Full international (Czech Republic) 3 caps/0 goals
• After playing a key role in the Under-21 European Championships silver-medal-winning Czech team, this young midfielder was a surprise selection for the Euro 2000 squad after national team boss **Jozef Chovanec** had initially ruled out using any youngsters.

PLAYER
JANSSEN, Anton
Midfielder, Dutch, 184cm, 76kg
Born: 10.08.63, Tiel, Holland
Clubs: NEC (1982-86), Fortuna Sittard (1986-87), PSV Eindhoven (1988-89), Kortrijk (Bel) (1989-91), Fortuna Sittard (1991-94), NEC (1994-)
• Veteran midfielder who will finish his career where it all started. Was a member of the PSV team that won the European Cup in 1988, taking one of the decisive spot-kicks in the shoot-out.
• Skilful player with a mean free-kick, but heart problems almost forced him to retire during the 1999-2000 season. A little underrated but has had an impressive career.

PLAYER
JANSSEN, Jochen
Forward, Belgian, 187cm, 84kg
Born: 22.01.76, Belgium
Clubs: Lommel (1995-97), Westerlo (1997-98), Club Brugge (1998-)
• Attacker who usually plays on the left. Has great pace and by the end of the 1999-2000 season he was getting on the scoresheet regularly. Had started the season on the bench but is definitely one for the future. Was a key player at Lommel and Westerlo.

AGENT
JANSSEN, Rob
Dutch
• Holland's leading player agent whose clients include **Marc Overmars**, **Dennis Bergkamp**, **Frank De Boer**, **Ronald De Boer**, **Edwin Van der Sar** and **Philip Cocu**.
• **Contact:** Oosthaven 39, NL-2801 PE Gouda, Holland. Tel: 00 31 (0) 182 550 888.

PLAYER
JANSSEN, Theo
Midfielder, Dutch, 180cm, 75kg
Born: 27.07.81, Arnhem, Holland

Clubs: Vitesse Arnhem (1998-)

• Danish Under-21 international who began his professional career in Holland, where he has impressed with some skilful play, but has raised questions about his temperament.

PLAYER
JARDEL, Mario

Full name: Mario Jardel Almeida Ribeiro
Forward, Brazilian, 188cm, 76kg
Born: 18.09.73, Fortaleza, Brazil
Clubs: Vasco da Gama (1993-94), Gremio (1995), FC Porto (Por) (1996-2000), Galatasaray (Tur) (2000-)
Full international (Brazil)

• One of the most effective goalscorers of recent years in Europe, winning the Golden Shoe two seasons in succession, in 1998 and 1999.

• Strong in the air and tidy on the ground, he was the main reason for Porto's success in recent seasons, scoring 129 League goals in four seasons.

• Criticised for scoring most of his goals against weak teams in the Portuguese League. But also scored regularly in the Champions League, his goals taking Porto into the quarter-finals of the 1999-2000 competition.

• Consistently overlooked by former Brazil coach Mario Zagallo, but has been picked on occasions by his successor Wanderley Luxemburgo.

• Made a surprise £11million switch to Turkey in summer 2000, replacing the Inter-bound **Hakan Sukur** at Galatasaray.

• 'In Portugal I had a lot of success, made my reputation and developed all my self-confidence. But four years is enough and the routine can affect your motivation. I needed a new environment and a new set of goals.'

PLAYER
JARNI, Robert

Midfielder, Croatian, 180cm, 77kg
Born: 26.10.68, Cakovec, Croatia
Clubs: Hajduk Split (1986-991), Bari (Ita) (1991-93), Torino (Ita) (1993-94), Juventus (Ita) (1994-

Mario Jardel

95), Real Betis (Spa) (1995-98), Real Madrid (Spa) (1998-99), Las Palmas (Spa) (1999-)
Full international (Croatia) 60 caps/1 goal
• Once one of the best left wing-backs in the world who has lost his way since a move from Betis to Real Madrid failed to work out.
• Once seen as one of the fastest footballers around who could run 100m in 11 seconds.
• Member of the Yugoslavia team which won the World Youth Cup in Chile in 1987. Appeared at the 1990 World Cup for Yugoslavia.
• Moved to Italy's Bari in 1992, but the transfer from Hajduk Split was complicated by a complicated legal dispute over £500,000 which he claimed he was due from the transfer.
• Won the Italian League with Juventus and the Croatian Cup twice with Hajduk.
• Once the proud owner of a collection of watches ...until a burglar broke into his home in Turin.
• Joined Real Madrid in 1998 after starring for Croatia at the World Cup, but not before turning down a move to Coventry at the last minute.
• Fell out of favour at Real and moved to second division Las Palmas winning promotion in 2000.

PLAYER
JAROSIK, Jiri
Midfielder, Czech, 194cm, 84kg
Born: 27.10.77, Czech Republic
Clubs: Sparta Prague
• Along with **Tomas Rosicky**, midfielder Jarosik is one of Sparta's emerging young stars, featuring in both the 1999-2000 Champions League campaign and in the 2000 European championship silver-medal-winning Czech Under-21 team.

PLAYER
JAUME, Diego
Full name: Diego Jaume Favaro
Defender, Uruguayan, 180cm, 78kg
Born: 09.10.73, Montevideo, Uruguay
Clubs: Huracan (1996-98), Bella Vista (1999),

Numancia (Spa) (2000-)
• Solid, dependable centre-back who played his part in the Numancia sucess story in the 1999-2000 season.

PLAYER
JAVI GONZALEZ
Full name: Javier Gonzalez Gomez
Forward, Spanish, 178cm, 70kg
Born: 22.03.74, Barakaldo, Spain
Clubs: Athletic B (1993-94), Alaves (1994-95), Sestao (1995-96), Celta Vigo (1996-97), Athletic Bilbao (1997-)
• Promising attacking midfielder who had to go on loan to Celta Vigo, Sestao and Alaves before getting regular games at Bilbao.

PLAYER
JAVI MORENO
Full name: Javier Moreno Varela
Born: 10.09.74, Valencia, Spain
Clubs: Barcelona C (1994-96), Barcelona B (1995-97), Cordoba (1996-97), Yeclano (1997-98), Alaves (1997-98), Numancia (1998-99), Alaves (1999-)
• Product of the youth ranks at Barcelona, who then did the rounds of the lower divisions, breaking through on loan at Numancia, where he scored 18 League goals in the 1998-99 season.
• One of the stars of Alaves' impressive form in the 1999-2000 season.

PLAYER
JAY, Frederic
Defender, French, 172cm, 70kg
Born: 20.9.76, Macon, France
Clubs: Auxerre (1996-)
• Another Auxerre youth team alumni whose versatility was a godsend to **Guy Roux**. Has played for the club at right-back, left-back and sweeper.

PLAYER
JEANNERRET, Sebastien
Defender, Swiss, 180cm, 70kg
Born: 12.12.73, Switzerland
Clubs: Neuchatel Xamax (1993-99), Servette (1999-)
Full international (Switzerland) 11 caps/0 goals
• Purposeful, reliable Swiss international full-back – right or left – who was thrown into the deep end when making only his second appearance for the national team against England at Euro 96.
• A watch repairer by trade.

COACH
JEFFERIES, Jim
Scottish
• Captained Hearts as a player and, despite achieving a degree of success and popularity in charge of Falkirk, could not resist the lure of returning to Tynecastle as manager in 1995.
• Since then, Jefferies has led the club to three major cup finals, with his greatest moment occuring in 1998 when he masterminded a 2-1 Scottish Cup Final defeat of Rangers to give Hearts their first major trophy for 25 years.

PLAYER
JEFFERS, Francis
Forward, English, 177cm, 68kg
Born: 25.01.81, Liverpool, England
Clubs: Everton (1998-)
• Young striker who was described as Everton's answer to **Michael Owen** after breaking through in the 1998-99 season amd earning a full international call-up.
• Demanded a transfer at the start of the 1999-2000 season – aged 18 – in a bid to get pay parity with Everton's senior players.
• England Under-21 international.

PLAYER
JEHLE, Peter
Goalkeeper, Liechtenstein

Born: 22.01.82
• Teenage goalkeeper who who played a vital role in Liechtenstein's first international victory, 2-1 over Azerbaijan in October 1998.
• Had trials with Crystal Palace, Liverpool and Leverkusen, but chose to complete his studies.

PLAYER
JELIC, Branko
Forward, Yugoslav, 184cm, 76kg
Born: 05.05.77, Cacak, Yugoslavia
Clubs: Borac Cacak, Red Star Belgrade (2000-)
• A mid-season signing by Red Star in the 1999-2000 season as a replacement for injured striker **Goran Drulic**. Demonstrated his talent and finishing qualities straight away, earning caps with Yugoslavia's Under-21 side.

COACH
JENEI, Emerich
Romanian
Born: 28.03.37
• National coach of Romania since January 2000, his second spell in charge.
• Has spent nearly 30 years in coaching, including several spells at Steaua, where he started out as youth team coach in 1971.
• A useful player for National Bucharest, Steaua and Kayserispor who won 12 caps for Romania.
• Coached the Steaua first team from 1975-76 and 1983-86, winning the 1986 European Cup on penalties against Barcelona.
• Took charge of the Romanian national team in 1986 and guided them to the 1990 World Cup finals.
• Had spells in charge of the Hungarian national team in the 1990s, as well as Panionios of Greece, and even spent time as Romania's secretary of state for sport.
• Was back as coach of Steaua when a row on TV between his **Victor Piturca** and **Gheorghe Hagi** led to Piturca quitting as Romania coach. Jenei was seen as a safe pair of hands to steady the ship for Euro 2000.

PLAYER
JENSEN, Claus
Midfielder, Danish
Born: 29.04.77, Denmark
Clubs: Lyngby, Bolton (Eng), Charlton (Eng) (2000-)
Full international (Denmark) 1 caps/0 goals
• Highly promising young midfielder who has already demonstrated his worth with his performances for the Danish Under-21 side and for Bolton.
• Became Charlton's most expensive signing when he joined the newly-promoted Premier League side for £4million in July 2000.

PLAYER
JENSEN, Daniel
Forward, Danish, 177cm, 72kg
Born: 25.06.79, Copenhagen, Denmark
Clubs: Heerenveen (1998-)
• Young striker who has impressed with confident performances in Holland since a move from his native Denmark in 1998.

PLAYER
JENSEN, Ioakim
Defender, Swedish, 187cm, 81kg
Born: 28.03.74, Sweden
Clubs: Ljungskile (1988), Inter Turku (Fin) (1999)
• Swedish centre-back who is rated as one of the best defenders in the Finnish League.
• Signed by Inter in 1999 from local side Panos Ljungskile.

COACH
JENSEN, John 'Faxe'
Danish
Born: 03.05.65
• Legendary midfielder who is held in fond affection by Danes after scoring the 1992 European Championship Final.
• Retired as a player in 1999 and took charge of village club Herfolge, and amazingly led them to the Danish League title in his first season.
• Moved to Arsenal after Euro 92 for £1.57 million, a transfer which led to the downfall of **George Graham** as Arsenal manager in a bung scandal involving Norwegian agent **Rune Hauge**.
• Won the European Cup-winners Cup with Arsenal in 1995, having become a cult figure at Highbury for going so long without a goal.
• Full international (Denmark) 69 caps/4 goals

PLAYER
JENSEN, Martin
Defender, Danish, 177cm, 68kg
Born: 25.07.78, Denmark
Clubs: Esbjerg
Full international (Denmark) 2 caps/0 goals
• Promising all-round defender who combines aggression with good technique.

PLAYER
JEPSEN, Allan
Midfielder, Danish, 175cm, 68kg
Born: 04.07.77, Copenhagen, Denmark
Clubs: Aarhus (1996-97), Hamburg (Ger) (1997-99), Heerenveen (Hol) (1999-)
• Versatile youngster who can play in midfield or in central defence.
• Danish Under-21 international.

PLAYER
JEREMIES, Jens
Midfielder, German, 176cm, 76kg
Born: 05.03.74, Gorlitz, Germany
Clubs: Motor Gorlitz, Dynamo Dresden (1994-95), Munich 1860 (1995-98), Bayern Munich (1998-)
Full international (Germany) 25 caps/1 goal
• Initially burst upon the German scene as an indifatigable midfield warrior who snapped at the heels of opposition playmakers. But with the passing years, he has added composure and a greater range of passing skills to his repertoire and such has been his development that he looks a likely lad to replace **Lothar Matthaus** at sweeper

John Jensen

for both club and country. But how he will be missed in midfield if he does make the switch.
• Pronounced Yens Yeah ray mees.

PLAYER
JERKAN, Nicola
Defender, Croatian, 188cm, 86kg
Born: 08.12.64, Sinj, Croatia
Clubs: Hajduk Split, Oviedo (Spa) (1990-96), Nottingham Forest (Eng) (1996-99), Rapid Vienna (Aut) (1997-98, loan), Charleroi (Bel) (1999-)
Full international (Croatia) 31 caps/2 goals
• Experienced centre-back and libero who is no longer a regular in the Croatian national side after a disappointing time at club level.
• Signed by Nottingham Forest after Euro 96 but played just 14 League games in three season.

PLAYER
JESS, Eoin
Forward, Scottish, 177cm, 73kg
Born: 13.12.70, Aberdeen, Scotland
Clubs: Aberdeen (1988-96), Coventry (Eng) (1996-97), Aberdeen (1997-)
Full international (Scotland) 8 caps/2 goals
• Other than a brief flirtation with English football, when he played for Coventry City, Jess has spent his entire playing career with Aberdeen, the club he joined as a teenager back in 1988. He tends to be regarded as being in the category of a player who failed to fulfill his early potential but he has shown in patches that he could still be a key player for the Dons.

ADMINISTRATOR
JESUS GIL
Spanish
Born: 12.03.33
• Hugely controversial and outspoken president of Atletico Madrid.
• Mayor of Marbella who made his fortune in property development, but spent time in prison in early 2000 after being found guilty of fraud.

- Has made more than 30 changes of coach since taking control of the club in June 1987.
- 'I don't kill managers for pleasure. They way people go on you'd think I was Dracula and liked drinking managers' blood. But if I need to change a coach another hundred times to get things right, I will. There are always hundreds more in the queue.'
- Pronounced Hay zus Hill.

PLAYER
JEUNECHAMP, Cyril
Midfielder, French, 175cm, 71kg
Born: 18.12.75, Nimes, France
Clubs: Nimes (1996-97), Auxerre (1997-)
- His steely tackling and boundless stamina makes him the ideal midfield enforcer, but his solid work is at times undermined by a hair-trigger temper. First made his name in 1996 when he helped Second Division Nimes reach the final of the French Cup, where they lost to Auxerre.
- Prononced See ril Jern shom.

PLAYER
JEVRIC, Dragoslav
Goalkeeper, Yugoslavia, 187cm, 74kg
Born: 08.07.74, Berane, Yugoslavia
Clubs: Obilic, Red Star Belgrade (1995-99), Vitesse Arnhem (Ho) (1999-)
- Talented but accident-prone keeper who made his name at Red Star Belgrade.

PLAYER
JO, Shoji
Forward, Japanese
Born: 17.06.75, Japan
Clubs: Yokohama Marinos, Valladolid (Spa) (1999-)
Full international (Japan)
- Striker who was signed by Valladolid in December 1999 by Spain's Valladolid following a hugely successful spell in Japan.
- Has good technical skills but has been

criticised for being a lightweight who disappears from games for long periods.
- Got off to a bright start in Spain, but injured his knee playing for Japan in a friendly in Spring 2000.
- Following an exploratory operation on his knee, surgeons discovered that he did was born without a cruciate ligament.
- Played for Japan at the 1998 World Cup.

PLAYER
JOACHIM, Julian
Forward, English, 169cm, 81kg
Born: 20.09.74, Peterborough, England
Clubs: Leicester (1992-96), Aston Villa (1996-)
- Small but extremely pacy striker who has had often to play second fiddle to other strikers at Villa (**Dwight Yorke**, **Dion Dublin**) but has consistently scored goals.
- Bid to play for St Vincent/St Kitts in the 2002 World Cup qualifier was blocked by FIFA because he had played for England Under-21s.
- England Under-21 international.

PLAYER
JOAO PINTO
Full name: Joao Manuel Vieira Pinto
Forward, Portuguese, 171cm, 62kg
Born: 19.08.71, Oporto, Portugal
Clubs: Boavista (1988-90), Atletico Madrileno (1990-91), Boavista (1991-92), Benfica (1992-2000), Sporting Lisbon (2000-)
Full international (Portugal) 62 caps/19 goals
- Forward whose career has never quite lived up to the promise shown when he became the first player to win the World Youth Cup twice in a row, in 1989 and 1991.
- Can play as a frontman or just behind the front two, his greatest asset being his ability to take on and beat defenders.
- Was sold by Boavista to Atletico Madrid of Spain in 1990, but was loaned out by Atletico's second division nursery club, Atletico Madrileno,

Joao Pinto

grew homesick and returned home.

• Portugal's Footballer of the Year in 1993 and winner of the Portuguese Cup in 1992 with Boavista and in 1993 with Benfica.

• Won the Portuguese League title with Benfica in 1994, when he scored a hat-trick away at Sporting to secure the title.

• Stayed at Benfica despite strong interest from Liverpool, but his influence declined and his contract was cancelled by the club in summer 2000. He then made a controversial move across town to Sporting.

• Called himself Joao Manuel Pinto to distinguish himself from the veteran Porto full-back and captain Joao Pinto.

PLAYER
JOAO TOMAS
Full name: Joao Henrique Pataco Tomas
Forward, Portuguese
Born: 27.05.75, Bairro, Portugal
Clubs: Academica, Benfica (2000-)
• Promising centre-forward acquired by Benfica from Academica.

PLAYER
JOB, Joseph-Desire
Forward, French/Cameroon, 185cm, 76kg
Born: 01.12.77, Venissieux, France
Clubs: Lyon (1997-99), Lens (1999-2000), Middlesbrough (Eng) (2000-)
Full international (Cameroon)
• Livewire young attacker still trying to shed the tag of eternal super-sub.

• Born in the suburbs of Lyon, he turned down a chance to play for the French Under-21s in favour of representative honours with Cameroon, the land of his parents, making his international debut against England at Wembley in November 1997.

PLAYER
JOCHEMSEN, Arco
Midfielder, Dutch, 187cm, 82kg
Born: 21.02.71, Barneveld, Holland
Clubs: Vitesse Arnhem (1994-)
• Player who can operate on several positions in defence or midfield. Strong and resilient. AZ and Anderlecht were both keen to hire his services in the summer of 2000.

COACH
JOHANSEN, Benny
• One of Denmark's most respected coaches who is back in Denmark, at Lyngby, after a spell in the Middle East.
• Made his name at FC Copenhagen, winning the League in 1993 and Cup in 1995.

PLAYER
JOHANSEN, Martin
Midfielder, Danish, 168cm, 65kg
Born: 22.07.72, Glostrup, Denmark
Clubs: KB (1990-91), 1903 (1991-92), FC Copenhagen (1992-97), Coventry City (Eng) (1997-98), Lyngby (1998-)
Full international (Denmark) 1 cap/0 goals
• Midfielder who is now back in Denmark, with Lyngby, after a difficult spell in England with Coventry.
• Dribbling skills have led him to be likened to **Michael Laudrup**.
• Brother of **Michael Johansen**.

PLAYER
JOHANSEN, Michael
Midfielder, Danish, 186cm, 74kg
Born: 30.03.80, Denmark
Clubs: Aab Aalborg
• Midfielder who returned to Denmark in January 2000 after a stint in England with Bolton Wanderers.
• Brother of **Martin Johansen**.

ADMINISTRATOR
JOHANSSON, Lennart
Born: 05.11.29
• Swedish president of UEFA, who has been in office since 1990 having been a member of the executive committee since 1988.
• Was unsuccessful in his bid to win the presidency of FIFA in 1998, losing out to **Sepp Blatter** in the race to succeed Joao Havelange, despite being the favourite.
• Chairman of Stockholm side AIK Stockholm from 1967 to 1980, becoming chairman of the Swedish FA in 1984.

COACH
JOHANSSON, Bo
Swedish
Born: 28.11.42
• Swede who spent four years as national coach of Denmark, standing down after Euro 2000.
• Previously coached provincial Danish side Silkeborg to their first League title.
• Started at Swedish second division side Kalmar in 1973 as player-coach, having played 390 games (135 goals) in tototal.
• Has also worked in Greece, at Panionios, Norway, with FK Jerv, and Finland, at HJK Helksinki.
• In charge of the Icelandic national team 1990-91.
• Laid-back approach is appreciated by the players, if not the press.

PLAYER
JOHNSEN, Espen
Goalkeeper
Born: 20.12.79
Clubs: Start
• Goalkeeping talent who contributed strongly to his club's promotion in the 1999 season. Agile and acrobatic keeper who is wanted by top English clubs.
• Norwegian Under-21 international.

Lennart Johansson

PLAYER
JOHNSEN, Ronny
Defender, Norwegian, 190cm, 85kg
Born: 10.06.69, Tonsberg, Norway
Clubs: Lyn (1992-93), Lillestrom (1994-95),
Besiktas (1995-96), Manchester Utd (1996-)
Full international (Norway) 41 caps/2 goals
• Pacy centre-back who can also play as a
defensive midfielder.
• Missed the 1999-00 season through injury.
• Started his career as a striker.

PLAYER
JOHNSEN, Seth
Midfielder, English, 177cm, 70kg
Born: 12.03.79, Birmingham, England
Clubs: Crewe Alexandra (1996-99), Derby (1999-)
• Promising young midfielder who can also play
at full-back.
• A product of Crewe's successful youth system
who delayed a move to Premier League Derby in
1999 to stay and help Crewe's relegation fight.
• England Under-21 international.

COACH
JOHNSON, Gary
English
• National coach of Latvia and a former manager
of Cambridge United.

PLAYER
JOHNSON, Samuel
Midfielder, Ghanaian, 182cm, 84kg
Born: 25.07.73, Accra, Ghana
Clubs: Hearts of Oak, Anderlecht (Bel),
Gazientepspor (Tur), Fenerbahce (Tur) (1999-)
Full international (Ghana)
• Tough-tackling midfielder who has revived his
international career after breaking a leg at the
1994 African Nations Cup finals in Tunisia.
• Began at Accra club Hearts of Oak, before
spending two seasons at Anderlecht, where he
earned notoriety for scoring for both sides in the

Belgian Cup Final.
• Turned down Italian club Perugia in favour of a move to Turkey.

PLAYER
JOHNSTON, Allan
Midfielder, Scottish, 175cm, 69kg
Born: 14.12.73, Glasgow, Scotland
Clubs: Hearts (1990-97), Sunderland (1997-2000), Rangers (2000-)
Full international (Scotland) 9 caps/2 goals
• Winger who can operate on both flanks.
• Starred in Sunderland's 1998-99 promotion to the Premier League, but fell out of favour and switched to Rangers in the summer of 2000.

PLAYER
JOKANOVIC, Predrag
Midfielder, Yugoslav, 186cm, 85kg
Born: 26.10.68, Belgrade, Yugoslavia
Clubs: Zemun (1990-91), OFK Belgrade (1992-93), Uniao Madeira (Por) (1993-95), Maritimo (Por) (1995-)
• Yugoslav midfielder who has played an important role in Maritimo's survival in the Portuguese first division.

PLAYER
JOKANOVIC, Slavisa
Midfielder, Yugoslav, 191cm, 89kg
Born: 16.08.68, Novi Sad, Yugoslavia
Clubs: Cantera Novis Sad (1985-88), Vojvodina (1988-90), Partizan Belgrade (1990-93), Real Oviedo (Spa) (1993-95), Tenerife (Spa) (1995-99), Deportivo La Coruna (Spa) (1999-)
Full international (Yugoslavia) 53 caps/8 goals
• Experienced holding midfielder who provides a useful link between defence and attack.

PLAYER
JOKOVIC, Nocko
Midfielder, Danish/Yugoslav, 178cm, 79kg
Born: 03.07.73, Yugoslavia

Clubs: AGF (1992-96), Silkeborg (1996-)
• Powerful striker who has put problems off the pitch behind him to re-establish himself in the Danish League.
• Born in Serbia but has played for Denmark at Under-21 level after making a name for himself at AGF.
• Left AGF after a disagreement with coaching staff and was taken on by Silkeborg. He continued to score goals, but was involved in a fight in a nightclub and was jailed for 30 days and was sacked by Silkeborg. However, he has since returned to AGF.

REFEREE
JOL, Dick
Dutch
Born: 29.03.56
• Company director.
• Awarded FIFA badge in 1993.

COACH
JOL, Martin
Dutch
Born: 16.01.56
• A former player with Den Haag, Bayern Munich and West Bromwich Albion and now a coach with a great future.
• Won the Dutch cup with Roda JC in 1997 before joining RKC Waalwijk for the 1999-2000 season, RKC having only escaped relegation by winning a play-off three years running. He then steered RKC into a stable mid-table position.

PLAYER
JONES, Matthew
Midfielder, Welsh, 180cm, 72kg
Born: 01.09.80, Llanelli, Wales
Clubs: Leeds (1997-)
• Leading member of Leeds' 1997 FA Youth Cup-winning side who was tipped for big things after breaking into the first team in 1999-2000.
• Welsh Under-21 international.

PLAYER
JONES, Paul
Goalkeeper, Welsh, 190cm, 89kg
Born: 18.04.67, Chirk, England
Clubs: Wolverhampton (1991-96), Stockport (1996-97), Southampton (1997-)
Full international (Wales) 14 caps/0 goals
• Keeper who followed manager Dave Jones from Stockport to Southampton in July 1997 and earned international recognition in 1997.

PLAYER
JONK, Wim
Midfielder, Dutch, 184cm, 76kg
Born: 12.12.66, Volendam, Holland
Clubs: FC Volendam, Ajax (1988-93), Internazionale (Ita) (1993-95), PSV (1995-98), Sheffield Wed (Eng) (1998-)
Full international (Holland) 49 caps/1 goal
• Talented playmaker who took over from Jan Wouters at Ajax, winning the Cup-winners Cup in 1993, and then left for Internazionale.
• Couldn't impress in Serie A, although he had a better time than fellow Dutchman **Dennis Bergkamp** and scored the only goal of the second leg of the 1994 UEFA Cup Final, won by Inter.
• One of the Dutch stars of USA 94, but missed Euro 96 because of problems at Inter. Returned to play at France 98 after re-establising his reputation back in Holland at PSV.

PLAYER
JORGE ANDRADE
Full name: Jorge Manuel Almeida Gomes Andrade
Midfielder, Portuguese, 184cm, 73kg
Born: 09.04.78, Lisbon
Clubs: Estrela Amadora (1997-)
• Midfielder who has starred for Estrela in recent seasons, particularly in games against Benfica and FC Porto and become a target for the top two as a result.

PLAYER
JORGE COSTA
Full name: Jorge Paulo Costa Almeida
Defender, Portuguese, 188cm, 86kg
Born: 14.10.71, Oporto, Portugal
Clubs: Funchal (1990-91), Maritimo (1992-92), FC Porto (1993-)
Full international (Portugal) 31 caps/0 goals
• Tough, powerful central defender and captain of FC Porto who makes up for in aggression what he lacks in technique and sublety.
• Starred for Portugal in their 1991 World Youth Cup success.
• Winner of six Portuguese League titles and three Cups with FC Porto.
• Nicknamed 'The Tank' for his uncompromising attitude.
• Made his international debut for Portugal against Bulgaria in November 1992, but lost out to **Fernando Couto**, **Paulo Madeira** and **Helder** as first-choice central defender. Established himself in the side in the run-up to Euro 2000.

PLAYER
JORGE COUTO
Full name: Jorge Antonio Pinto do Couto
Midfielder, Portuguese, 170cm, 71kg
Born: 01.07.70, Santa Maria da Feira, Portugal
Clubs: Gil Vicente (1988-89), FC Porto (1989-96), Boavista (1996-)
Full international (Portugal) 6 caps/0 goals
• Experienced midfielder and a key figure in Boavista's success of recent seasons. Relied upon by coach **Jaime Pacheco** to unlock opposition defences.

COACH
JORGE JESUS
Portuguese
Born: 27.07.54
• A 4-4-2 man who took Felgueiras to promotion to the top flight in 1994-95. Despite serving Estrela Amadora well over the past two years –

they finished eighth in both campaigns – his contract was surprisingly not renewed in summer 2000.
• A firm believer in sportsmanship and made it clear last season that he felt Sporting Lisbon's Argentinian striker **Alberto Acosta** was too prone to dive for penalties.

PLAYER
JORGE SILVA
Full name: Jorge Soares da Silva
Goalkeeper, Portuguese, 183cm, 77kg
Born: 13.01.72, Lamengo, Portugal
Clubs: FC Porto (1990-91), Rio Ave (1991-92), FC Porto (1992-93), Rio Ave (1993-95), Salgueiros (1995), FC Porto (1995-96), Salgueiros (1996-)
• Useful keeper who has established himself at Salgueiros after spells at Rio Ave and FC Porto.

PLAYER
JORGE SOARES
Full name: Jorge Manuel Guerreiro Silva
Defender, Portuguese, 187cm, 83kg
Born: 22.10.71, Messejana, Portugal
Clubs: Farense (1990-96), Benfica (1996-98), Maritimo (1998-)
• Former Benfica defender who has adapted well to his new surroundings at Maritimo.

PLAYER
JORGENSEN, Martin
Midfielder, Danish, 177cm, 78kg
Born: 06.10.75, Oersted, Denmark
Clubs: AGF Aarhus (1993-97), Udinese (Ita) (1997-)
Full international (Denmark) 24 caps/3 goals
• Midfielder who has become the key creative player in the Danish national side since the retirement of **Brian** and **Michael Laudrup**.
• Most effective on the left flank, where his pace and trickery can leave opponents bemused. However, he can struggle against tight marking.
• Joined the local IF Midtjurs club at the age of

four, learning skills and technique before playing in organised, competitive matches. As a teenager, he helped AGF Aarhus win the 1996 Danish Cup, and went on to earn a record 31 caps for the Danish Under-21 side.
• Signed for Udinese in 1997 while still uncapped at senior level, and grew in stature during three years at Udine. Was tipped for a £10million move to a big Italian or Spanish club in summer 2000.
• In Denmark's Euro 2000 squad, but struggled with injuries throughout.

PLAYER
JOSE MARI
Full name: Jose Mari Romero Payon
Forward, Spanish, 184cm, 78kg
Born: 10.12.78, Seville, Spain
Clubs: Sevilla (1995-97), Atletico Madrid (1997-99), Milan (Hol) (1999-)
• Spanish Under-21 international who made a surprise £10million move to Milan midway through the 1999-2000 season.
• Showed great potential at Atletico, but struggled to establish himself in Serie A, and was linked with a return to Spain in summer 2000.

COACH
JOSE ROMAO
Portuguese
Born: 13.04.52
• Much-travelled coach who has worked at Famalicao, Belenenses, Tirsense, Academica Coimbra, Chaves and Alverca.
• Not unsurprisingly for a coach whose destiny seems to be a life of struggle with cash-strapped clubs in the lower reaches of the top flight, his gameplans are generally high on damage limitation and low on adventure.

Jorge Costa

PLAYER
JOVANOVSKI, Zoran
Defender, Macedonian, 188cm, 94kg
Born: 21.08.72
Clubs: Teteks Tetovo (1990-93), Vardar Skopje (1993-97), Helsingborg (Swe) (1997-99)
Full international (Macedonia) 5 caps/1 goal
• Macedonian defender who is strong in the air and was rated as one of the best defenders in the Swedish championship while with Helsinborg.

PLAYER
JUAN CARLOS
Full name: Juan Carlos Gomez Diaz
Forward, Spanish, 174cm, 70kg
Born: 05.04.73, Cordoba, Spain
Clubs: Atletico Madrid (1993-94), Marbella (1994-95), Atletico Madrid (1995-97), Valladolid (1997-98), Sevilla (1998-)
• Striker who started out at Atletico Madrid, winning the League and Cup double in 1996.
• Moved on to Valladolid, joining Sevilla for £1million in 1998.

PLAYER
JUANELE
Full name: Juan Castano Quiros
Forward, Spanish, 175cm, 170kg
Born: 10.04.71, Gijon, Spain
Clubs: Sporting Gijon (1991-94), Tenerife (1994-99), Zaragoza (1999-)
Full international (Spain) 5 caps/2 goals
• Striker who is yet another product of the famed youth system at Sporting Gijon, where he played alongside **Luis Enrique** and **Abelardo**.
• Had a short-lived spell at Barcelona after winning five caps for Spain.
• Was a member of Spain's squad at the 1994 World Cup, but was the only outfield player not to feature.

PLAYER
JUANFRAN
Full name: Juan Francisco Garcia Garcia
Defender, 180cm, 78kg
Born: 15.07.76, Rafelbunol, Spain
Clubs: Levante (1994-97), Valencia (1997-99),
Celta Vigo (1999-)
Full international (Spain) 1 cap/0 goals
• Left-back who began as a forward in the
Valencia youth system.
• Converted to a full-back at Levante, where he
made his League debut and did enough to earn a
return to Valencia.
• Moved to Celta in 1999 following interest from
Barcelona and Real Madrid.

PLAYER
JUGOVIC, Vladimir
Midfielder, Yugoslav, 179cm, 75kg
Born: 30.08.69, Trstenik, Yugoslavia
Clubs: Red Star Belgrade (1989-92), Sampdoria
(Ita) (1992-95), Juventus (Ita) (1995-97), Lazio (Ita)
(1997-98), Atletico Madrid (Spa) (1998-99),
Internazionale (Ita) (1999-)
Full international (Yugoslavia) 37 caps/3 goals
• All-rounder who combines hard work and ball-
winning with visionary passing and playmaking.
Has been one of the most transferred players in
recent Serie A history.
• Has won the European Cup with two different
clubs (Red Star, 1991 and Juventus, 1996).
• Joined Lazio from Juventus in summer 1997,
reportedly against the wishes of then Juve coach
Marcello Lippi.
• Troubled by injuries over the past year, which
led him to miss most of the Euro 2000 qualifying
campaign.

PLAYER
JULIO CESAR
Full name: Julio Cesar Santos Correa
Defender, Brazilian, 186cm, 77kg
Born: 17.08.78, San Luis De Maranhao, Brazil

Clubs: America, Valladolid (Spa) (1996-99), Real
Madrid (Spa) (1999-)
• Fast, strong entre-back who moved to Spain
from Brazil in 1996, joining Valladolid.
• Potential was spotted by **John Toshack**, who
brought him to the Bernabeu in summer 1999.
• Seen as a long-term replacement for **Fernando
Hierro**.

PLAYER
JULIO SALINAS
Full name: Julio Salinas Fernandez
Forward, Spanish, 188cm, 82kg
Clubs: Athletic Bilbao (1982-86), Atletico Madrid
(1986-88), Barcelona (1988-94), Deportivo La
Coruna (1994-95), Sporting Gijon (1995-97),
Yokohama Marinos (Jap) (1997-99), Alaves (1999-)
Full international (Spain) 56 caps/22 goals
• Veteran striker and a living legend in Spanish
football who returned to Spain after a spell in
Japan and was expected to hang up his boots
but carried on playing for Alaves.
• Played for Spain at the 1986, 1990 and 1994
World Cups and at Euro 96.
• Owns a chain of hair-care shops.

PLAYER
JUNINHO
Full name: Osvaldo Giraldo Junior
Midfielder, Brazilian, 167cm, 59kg
Born: 22.02.73, Sao Paulo
Clubs: Ituano (1992) San Paulo (1993-1995),
Middlesbrough (Eng) (1995-1997), Atletico Madrid
(Spa) (1997-), Middlesbrough (Eng) (2000, loan),
Vasco da Gama (2000-, loan)
Full international (Brazil)
• Tiny midfielder whose performances for Brazil
at the 1995 Umbro Cup in England brought him to
the attention of Middlesbrough.
• As a teenager, he underwent an intense course
of nutritional and medical care to build his body
strength and height.
• Moved to Spain in 1997 after suffering

relegation with Boro, but broke a leg in April 1998 and missed out on France 98.

• Returned to England in 2000 on loan after falling out of favour at Atletico, whose relegation in May 2000 placed his future in Madrid in doubt. Middlesbrough refused to pay Atletico's asking price to complete a permanent transfer, and he returned to Brazil, on loan to Vasco da Gama for the 2000-2001 season.

PLAYER
JURIETTI, Franck
Defender, French, 180cm, 78kg
Born: 30.03.75, Valence, France
Clubs: Lyon, Gueugnon, Bastia, Monaco (2000-)
• Just too good for a club of Bastia's modest resources to hang on to. For some time now, a band of some of the biggest clubs in France and the continent have been drooling over this former Under-21 international.
• Tireless and tactically aware, he is Monsieur Universal, switching effortlessly from right to left-back and from central to right midfield.

PLAYER
JUSKOWIAK, Andrzej
Forward, Polish, 185cm, 82kg
Born: 03.11.70, Gostin, Poland
Clubs: Lech Poznan (1987-92), Sporting Lisbon (Por) (1992-95), Olympiakos (Gre) (1995-96), Borussia Monchengladbach (Ger) (1996-98), Wolfsburg (Ger) (1998-)
Full international (Poland) 34 caps/13goals
• Polish international striker who has been a sure supplier of goals at Wolfsburg since arriving two years ago from Borussia Monchengladbach – 13 in 1998-99; 11 in 1999-2000.
• Very strong in the air, an excellent runner off the ball and does not really have a weaker foot.
• Was the top scorer with seven goals at the 1992 Olympics, helping Poland to the silver medal.
• Surname pronounced Yus koh vee ack.

Vladimir Jugovic

K

KACHLOUL, Hasan
Midfielder, Moroccan, 185cm, 75kg
Born: 19.02.73, Agadir, Morocco
Clubs: Nimes (Fra) (1992-95), Dunkerque (Fra)
(1995-96), Metz (Fra) (1996-97), St Etienne (Fra)
(1997-98), Southampton (Eng) (1998-)
Full international (Morocco)
• Playmaker signed by Southampton after a short
trial. Has adapted well to the English game,
sparking interest from bigger clubs.
• Member of the Moroccan squad at the 1994
World Cup and the 2000 African Nations Cup.

PLAYER
KACHURO, Petr
Forward, Belarus
Born: 02.08.72
Clubs: Dynamo Minsk, Shefield United (Eng)
Full international (Belarus) 25 caps/4 goals
• A skilful inside forward who is a regular for the
Belarussian national team and one of the country
most successful exports in recent years, albeit to
the confines of the English first division with
Sheffield United.

PLAYER
KACZOROWSKI, Pawel
Midfielder, Polish, 180cm, 70kg
Born: 22.03.74, Poland
Clubs: Pogon Zdunska Wola, KSZO Ostrowiec,
Lech Poznan (1999-)
Full international (Poland) 2 caps/0 goals
• Had spells with Pogon Zdunska Wola and KSZO
Ostrowiec before a move to Lech last year. Made
an imediate impression at Poznan that resulted in
his national team debut in January 2000.

PLAYER
KADLEC, Miroslav
Defender, Czech, 187cm, 82kg
Born: 22.06.64, Uherske Hradiste, Czech Republic
Clubs: Kaiserslautern (Ger), Petra Drnovice
Full international (Czech Rep.) 64 caps/2 goals
• Veteran sweeper whose penalty against France
put the Czechs into the final at Euro 96.
• After a long, successful spell in Germany, Kadlec
moved back to the Czech Republic so his children
could be educated in his home country.
• Despite retiring from international football,
unfounded rumours persistently linked him with a
Euro 2000 slot following injury to Jan Suchoparek.

PLAYER
KAHN, Oliver
Goalkeeper, German, 188cm, 87kg
Born: 15.06.69, Karlsruhe, Germany
Clubs: Karlsruhe (1987-94), Bayern Munich (1994-)
Full international (Germany) 27 caps/ 0 goals
• Whatever his rival for the German national
team goalkeeping shirt, Jens Lemann, might
say, the Bayern man is undisputably the country's
number one and, moreover, is one of the most
accomplished in the world.
• A brilliant shot-stopper and excellent in one-
against-one situations, he also exudes authority
and is an outstanding organiser of a defence.
• Not everyone loves him, though. A Freiburg fan
hit him on the head with a golf ball during a
Bundesliga match in the 1999-2000 season. 'It's
only sport. What happened to me is madness.'
• 'In the last few seasons I have won the UEFA
Cup, the German championship and the German
Cup twice. But I am never satisfied. Once you
have won one trophy you only want to win
another. I am a perfectionist.'

PLAYER
KALAC, Zeljko
Goalkeeper, Australian, 202cm, 91kg
Born: 16.12.72, Sydney, Australia

Clubs: Sydney Utd (1995-96), Leicester City (Eng) (1995), Sydney Utd (1996-98), Roda JC (Hol) (1998-)
Full international (Australia)
• Giant keeper, one of the tallest players in the European game, who established himself in the Dutch League with Roda after experiencing work permit problems in England at Leicester.

PLAYER
KALADZE, Kaha
Defender, Georgian, 186cm, 76kg
Born: 27.02.78, Tbilisi, Georgia
Clubs: Din. Tbilisi (1993-97), Kyiv Dynamo (Ukr) (1997-)
Full international (Georgia) 23 caps/0 goals
• Central defender who has played an important role in the success of Kyiv Dynamo in recent years.

PLAYER
KALISZAN, Arkadiusz
Midfielder, Polish, 195cm, 89kg
Born: 13.11.72, Poland
Clubs: Warta Poznan, Roda JC (Hol), Warta Poznan, Hutnik Krakow, Polonia Warsaw (1998-)
Full international (Poland) 1 cap/0 goals
• Tall and physical hard man with great determination. His short-fuse temper is a major drawback. Started at second division Warta Poznan. After short spell with Dutch club Roda JC he rejoined Warta. Then played for Hutnik Krakow before a move to Polonia two years ago.

PLAYER
KALLON, Mohamed
Forward, Sierra Leone, 187cm, 71kg
Born: 06.10.79, Sierra Leone.
Clubs: Lugano (Swi) (1995-97), Bologna (Ita) (1997), Genoa (1997-98), Cagliari (1998-99), Reggina (1999-)
Full international (Sierra Leone)
• Former teenage prodigy who was once believed to be the world's youngest international. Apart from a short spell with Genoa in the Italian second division, has so far failed to live up to his billing.

Oliver Kahn

PLAYER
KALOU, Bonaventure
Forward, Ivory Coast, 182cm, 77kg
Born: 12.01.78, Oume, Ivory Coast
Clubs: Oume, ASEC Abidjan, Feyenoord (1997-)
Full international (Ivory Coast)
• Youngster whose pace and skills have made him a cult figure during three seasons at Feyenoord.
• Made his debut for Ivory Coast, aged 20, against Cameroon in February 1998
• 'I want to become one of the best African footballers ever. **George Weah** is my motivation. He went to France for trials as an unknown and look where he is today.'

PLAYER
KALUZNY, Radoslaw
Defender, Polish, 192cm, 83kg
Born: 02.02.74, Poland
Clubs: Zaglebie Lubin, Wisla Krakow
Full international (Poland) 15 caps/3 goals
• Came through the youth ranks at Zaglebie Lubin, moving to Wisla in 1998. A free-kick specialist who is strong in the air.

PLAYER
KAMARK, Pontus
Defender, Swedish, 177cm, 78kg
Born: 05.04.69, Vasteras, Sweden
Clubs: Skiljebo, Vasteras, IFK Gothenburg (1989-95), Leicester City (Eng) (1995-99), AIK Stockholm (1999-)
Full international (Sweden) 53 caps/0 goals
• Versatile defender, a former captain of IFK Gothenburg, who played in England for Leicester before moving back to Sweden in 1999. A reliable all-rounder and man-marker, he suffered a career-threatening knee injury playing for Sweden against Denmark in April 2000 and was ruled out of Euro 2000.
• Played four games for Sweden when they finished third at the 1994 World Cup.
• Surname pronoucned Kaw mark.

COACH
KAMPMAN, Harri
Finnish
• Best remembered for his spell with FC Mypa, where he finished as a League runner-up four times on the trot.
• Coached Motherwell for a short spell before returning to Finland and eventually taking over at Tampere United, a newly-merged club.
• An important influence over the career of **Jari Litmanen**, and while at HyPa he helped to launch the careers of **Sami Hyypia** and **Joonas Kolkka**.

COACH
KANATLAROVSKI, Dragan
Macedonian
Born: 08.11.60
• National coach of Macedonia since summer 1999. A former player with Pelister, Vardar, Red Star Belgrade, Deportivo La Coruna, Karsiyakaspor. A coach with Pelister, Pobeda and Vardar.

PLAYER
KANCHELSKIS, Andrei
Forward, Russian, 181cm, 79kg
Born: 23.01.69, Kirovograd, Ukraine
Clubs: Kyiv Dynamo (USSR), (1988-89), Shaktyor Donesk (USSR) (1990-91), Manchester United (1990-95), Everton (Eng) (1995-97), Fiorentina (Ita) (1996-8), Rangers (Sco) (1998-)
Full international (Russia) 36 caps/0 goals
• Fast, direct winger who played his best football at Manchester United before a £7million transfer to Fiorentina.
• Took time to settle when arriving at Ibrox from Fiorentina and appeared to have difficulty in adapting to the Scottish game, but played particularly well towards the end of of the 1999-2000 season with some strong running performances on the right wing.
• Born in Ukraine to a Lithuanian father and Ukrainian mother, but one of a number of high-profile former Soviet internationals who opted to

Nwankwo Kanu

play for Russia after the break-up of the USSR.
• Played at the 1992 European championships for the CIS and for Russia at Euro 96 but missed the 1994 World Cup after a dispute with coach Pavel Sadyrin.

PLAYER
KANDAUROV, Serghii
Midfielder, Ukrainian, 175cm, 72kg
Born: 02.12.72, Ukraine
Clubs: Metallist Kharkov (1990-93), Maccabi Haifa (Isr) (1993-98), Benfica (Por) (1998-)
Full international (Ukraine) 6 caps/0 goals
• Playmaker at Benfica, where his considerable talent has been recognised, although he lacks consistency. Started his career with Metallist before a move to Israel. He seldom scores goals but is often the creator.

PLAYER
KANU, Nwankwo
Forward, Nigerian, 194cm, 83kg
Born: 01.08.76, Owerri, Nigieria.
Clubs: Federation Works (1991-2, 30/9), Iwanyanwu (1992-93), Ajax (Hol) (1993-96) Internazionale (Ita) (1996-99), Arsenal (Eng) (1999-)
Full international (Nigeria)
• Tall, deceptively skilful forward who was voted African Footballer of the Year in 1996 and 1999.
• Made his debut for Ajax aged 16 and had already won the European Cup, World Club Cup, three Dutch League titles and the world Under-17 youth championship, when aged 19, he inspired Nigeria's triumph at the 1996 Olympic Games.
• Said in 1993 that his ambition was 'to be the best player in the world'.
• Signed by Inter for £5million in 1996 but diagnosed by a serious heart condition before he could play and underwent surgery to replace an aortic valve.
• Made a full recovery but, following arrival of **Ronaldo** at Inter, found himself surplus to striking requirements.

KAPETANOVIC, Sead

Midfielder, Bosnian, 181cm, 73kg
Born: 21.01.72, Hamburg
Clubs: Wolfsburg, Borussia Dortmund (1999-)
Full international (Bosnia)
• Versatile player who has had little chance to demonstrate his abilities at Dortmund since a move from Wolfsburg in 1999.

PLAYER
KAPSIS, Michalis

Defender, Greek, 182cm, 78kg
Born: 18.10.73 Greece
Clubs: Panathinaikos, AEK Athens (1998-)
Full international (Greece)
• Very dependable and proficient AEK Athens left-back. A former star of the Greek Under-21s who was drafted into the senior set-up in the immediate post-USA 94 period.

PLAYER
KARANKA, Aitor

Full name: Aitor Karanka De la Hoz
Defender, Spanish, 181cm, 79kg
Born: 18.09.73, Vitoria, Spain
Clubs: Athletic Bilbao (992-97), Real Madrid (1997-)
Full international (Spain) 1 cap/0 goal
• Central defender who missed much of the 1997-98 season with a heart condition.
• Caused dismay in Bilbao when he bought out his contract with Athletic to join Real in August 1997.
• Finally broke up the central partnership of **Fernando Hierro** and **Manuel Sanchis**.
• 14 caps at Under-21 level for Spain.
• Outstanding in the 2000 Champions League Final against Valencia.
• Won his one and so far only full cap against Armenia, 26.04.95.

PLAYER
KARDASH, Vassyl

Midfielder, Ukrainian, 184cm, 73kg
Born: 14.01.73, Ukraine
Clubs: Karpaty, Maccabi Haifa (Isr), Chornomorets, Kyiv Dynamo (1996)
Full international (Ukraine) 10 caps/0 goals
• Experienced utility midfielder who, despite clear talent, has not been a regular for either his club or national team, often because of injuries.

PLAYER
KAREMBEU, Christian

Midfielder, French, 180cm, 75kg
Born: 03.12.70, New Caledonia
Clubs: Nantes (1990-95), Sampdoria (Ita) (1995-97), Real Madrid (Spa) (1997-2000), Middlesbrough (Eng) (2000-)
Full international (France) 44 caps/1 goal
• Versatile performer who can play in defence or midfield, but is happiest in central midfield, where his hard work and impressive stamina are put to best use.
• Fell out with Sampdoria during the 1997-98 season, demanding a transfer to Madrid. Samp would have preferred to sell him to Barcelona, but they eventually relented and sold him to Real.
• Won the Champions League in May 1998 and the World Cup six weeks later.
• Won the 1995 French League title with Nantes,
• Gained notoriety in Spain for his relationship with wonderbra model Adriana Skleranikova.
• Born on the Pacific island of Lifou, New Caledonia, he staged a very public protest at an Italian League match against French nuclear tests in the Pacific.
• Joined Middlesbrough for £2.1million after playing at Euro 2000 for France.

PLAYER
KARHAN, Miroslav

Defender, Slovakian, 188cm, 81kg
Born: 21.06.76, Trnava, Slovakia

Clubs: Spartak Trnava (1994-99), Real Betis (Spa) (1999-2000), Besiktas (Tur) (2000-)
Full international (Slovakia) 36 caps/1 goal
• Promising central defender who emerged as a key man at the back for Betis in 1999-2000, moving on to Turkey after Betis were relegated.
• A libero with good all-round defensive qualities who likes to get forward and shoot from distance.
• Signed by Betis from Spartak Trnava in summer 1998 for £1.6million.

PLAYER
KARIC, Amir
Midfielder, Slovenian, 180cm, 81kg
Born: 31.12.73, Orahovica Donja, Slovenia
Clubs: Rudar Velenje, Maribor, Gamba Osaka (Jap), Maribor
Full international (Slovenia) 24 caps/1 goal
• Versatile defender or midfielder who started all three games for Slovenia at Euro 2000.
• Mostly used on the left side, either as left-back, left-sided centre-back or holding midfielder. Rarely gets forward to join the attack.
• Returned to Maribor in 1999 after a 12-month spell in Japan with Gamba Osaka.

PLAYER
KARLSSON, Anders
Goalkeeper, 184cm, 85kg
Born: 27.04.63, Sweden
Clubs: Orebro (1983-)
• Relatively short for a keeper, but makes up for it with his experience and agility. A wonderful servant to Orebro who seems to get better with age.

PLAYER
KARNEBEEK, Andre
Defender, Dutch, 179cm, 76kg
Born: 01.03.71, Goor, Holland
Clubs: FC Twente (1989-)
• Left-back and former youth international. A reliable campaigner.

Valery Karpin

KARPIN, Valery

Midfielder, Russian, 185cm, 76kg
Born: 02.02.69, Tallinn, Estonia
Clubs: CSKA Moscow (1987-88), Fakel Voronezh (1989), Spartak Moscow (1990-94), Real Sociedad (Spa) (1994-96), Valencia (Spa) (1996-97), Celta Vigo (Spa) (1997-)
Full international (Russia) 52 caps/16 goals
• Highly effective right-sided midfielder who has been one of the most successful Russians to play in the Spanish League.
• Hard-working player who has a strong shot and a good eye for goal.
• Born in Estonia, and represented Estonia at youth level in basketball and ice hockey, before concentrating on football.
• A youth team player at CSKA Moscow, but made his name at Spartak Moscow.
• Played for the USSR at Under-21 level, but opted to play for Russia after being overlooked by Estonia.
• Transferred to Spain's Real Sociedad for £500,000 in 1994, moving to Celta Vigo for £2.5million after a spell at Valencia.

KARWAN, Bartosz

Midfielder, Polish, 180cm, 75kg
Born: 13.01.76, Poland
Clubs: GKS Katowice, Anderlecht (Bel), Legia Warsaw (1997-)
Full international (Poland) 4 caps/0 goals
• Speedy right-midfielder or forward. Made his name with GKS Katowice. Had a half-year adventure in Belgium with Anderlecht but played only for the amateur team.

KASHTAN, Dror

Israeli
Born: 01.10.44
• Israel's most successful coach of recent years, Kashtan won his sixth League title with Hapoel Tel Aviv in the 1999-2000 season, having previously won championships with Maccabi Tel Aviv and Betar Jerusalem.
• Was a leading contender to succeed **Shlomo Scharf** as national team coach before the IFA opted for **Richard Moller Nielsen**.

KASTENDEUCH, Sylvain

Defender, French, 180cm, 72kg
Born: 31.08.63, Hayange, France
Clubs: Metz (1982-84), Red Star (1984-85), Metz (1985-90), Saint-Etienne (1990-93), Toulouse (1994), Metz (1994-)
Full international (France) 9 caps/0 goals
• Veteran sweeper and Metz skipper who is still delivering the goods at the age of 37. No other active French player can match his total of 555 domestic League games and he was within reach of **Alain Giresse**'s all-time record of 586 at the start of the 2000-2001 season.
• He was on the receiving end of Eric Cantona's ire in the latter's last game in French football before his departure for the Premiership.
• Surname pronounced Kast ten doy ch.

KATANEC, Srecko

Slovenian
Born: 17.07.63
• National coach of Slovenia since July 1998.
• As a player, Katanec had spells at Olimpia Ljubjiana, Dinamo Zagreb, Partizan Belgrade, Stuttgart and Sampdoria, winning the Cup-winners Cup in 1990 and the Italian League in 1991.
• Won 29 caps (four goals) for Yugoslavia.
• Began his first coaching job in 1997 at HIT Gorica, while also in charge of the Slovenian Under-21 side.
• A tough, hard-working player, he has introduced the same qualities into his sides as a coach.

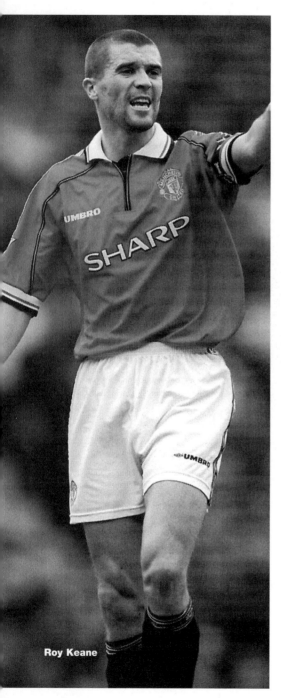

Roy Keane

COACH
KATALINIC, Ivan
Croatian
Born: 1951
• Coach of Hajduk Split.

PLAYER
KAUFMAN, Jiri
Forward, Czech, 180cm, 75kg
Born: 28.11.79, Czech Republic
Clubs: Petra Drnovice
• Striker with Drnovice, a village team that relies on developing young talent for its survival at the highest level. Scored twice for the Czech Under-21s in the spring of 2000 in a friendly against Israel designed to help Under-21 boss Karel Bruckner assess his future selection options.

PLAYER
KAVIEDES, Jaime Ivan
Forward, Ecuador, 182cm, 71kg
Born: 24.10.77, Santo Domingo, Ecuador
Clubs: Emelec (1998), Perugia (Ita) (1998-99), Celta Vigo (Spa) (1999-)
Full international (Ecuador)
• Ecuadorian striker signed from Perugia in 1999, but a big flop in Vigo. Enfuriated coach **Victor Fernandez** by returning late from holiday in January 2000.
• Made his name in Ecuador when he scored a record 43 goals in 40 games during the 1998 season for Emelec, a goal tally which made him the world's most prolific striker.

PLAYER
KEANE, Robbie
Forward, Irish, 175cm, 84kg
Born: 08.07.80, Dublin, Ireland
Clubs: Wolverhampton (1997-99), Coventry (1999-2000), Internazionale (Ita) (2000-)
Full international (Rep Ireland) 18 caps//6 goals
• Hugely promising striker and the most exciting talent to come out of Ireland in recent years.

• His performances for Wolves in the English first division attracted attention from a host of English Premier League clubs, with Coventry winning the battle for his signature in 1999 for £6million, out-bidding Aston Villa's offer of £5.5million.
• **Alex Ferguson** on Keane: 'I would pay no more than £500,000 for that lad, and leave him in the reserves.'
• Joined Inter in July 2000 for £11million after the Italian club failed to sign **Marcelo Salas**.
• International debut: March 1998, v Czech Rep.
• The star of Ireland's 1998 European Under-18 championship triumph.
• 'How unpredicable things are! This time last year I was getting ready to play for Wolves in the first division. Now I've got to get ready to play alongside people like **Ronaldo**, **Vieri**, **Blanc** and **Seedorf**.'

PLAYER
KEANE, Roy
Midfielder, Irish, 179cm, 81kg
Born: 10.08.71, Cork, Ireland
Clubs: Nottingham Forest (1990-93), Manchester Utd (1993-)
Full International (Rep Ireland) 46 caps/5 goals
• Dynamic, domineering central midfielder who has played a crucial part in Manchester United's success in the 1990s.
• Joined United in July 1993 from Forest for a then UK record £3.75million.
• Missed the 1999 Champions League Final through suspension.
• Signed a new contract in January 2000 which made him the Premier League's highest paid player on £50,000 a week.
• Succeeded Eric Cantona as United captain in summer 1997.
• Nicknamed 'Damien' after the character in the film *The Omen*.
• **Alex Ferguson**: 'He's the most victimised player in the game. He only needs to make one tackle and he's booked.'

PLAYER
KECHINOV, Valeri
Forward, Russian, 179cm, 72kg
Born: 05.08.74, Russia
Clubs: Pakhtakor Tashkent (1991-93), Moscow Spartak (1994-)
Full international (Russia) 6 caps/2 goals
• Accomplished all-round attacker who has a good shot and excellent ball control, but often misses games through injury.
• Member of Russia's squad at Euro 96.

COACH
KEEGAN, Kevin
English
Born: 14.02.51
• National coach of England who succeeded **Glenn Hoddle** in 1999, initially on a four-match basis while he was still in charge of First Division Fulham.
• An outstanding player who won 63 caps (21 goals) for England and was named European Footballer of the Year two years running in 1978 and 1979 while with Hamburg.
• Retired as a player in 1986 and pursued business interests in Spain.
• Was tempted back into football in February 1992 to manage Newcastle, who were on the brink of relegation to the old Third Division.
• Steered Newcastle to the top of the Premier League title, before quitting abruptly in January 1997.
• Made a surprise return with Fulham in May 1998 and steered them into the First Division before answering the call to manage England.
• An eternal optimist whose infectious enthusiasm rubs off on his players.
• 'I always thought managers were more involved but when it comes down to it, I just sit there and watch like everyone else.'

Harry Kewell

PLAYER
KEHRLI, Raphael
Midfielder, Swiss, 184cm, 77kg
Born: 14.09.77, Switzerland
Clubs: Young Boys (1998-99), Basle (1999-2000),
Lucerne (2000-)
• Right-sided midfielder of the all-action variety
who hits a good cross.

PLAYER
KEISI, Adoram
Defender, Israeli, 185cm, 74kg
Born: 17.06.72, Israel
Clubs: Maccabi Haifa
Full international (Israel) 9 caps/0 goals
• A tall and strong defender, he is fast enough to
become a danger man to the opposition's
defence. Has scored on several occasions for
Maccabi Haifa, but has yet to live up to his full
potential at international level.

PLAYER
KELLER, Marc
Midfielder, French, 181cm, 78kg
Born: 14.01.68, Colmar, France
Clubs: Mulhouse (1987-91), Strasbourg (Ger)
(1991-96), Karlsruhe (Ger) (1996-98), West Ham
(Eng) (1998-)
Full international (France) 6 caps/1 goal
• Left wing-back with strong shot who made his
name at Strasbourg and moved to England after
suffering relegation with Karlsruhe in 1998.

PLAYER
KELLER, Kasey
Goalkeeper, American, 187cm, 86kg
Born: 27.11.69, Washington, USA
Clubs: Portland University, Millwall (Eng) (1991-
96), Leicester City (Eng) (1996-99), Rayo
Vallecano (Spa) (1999-)
Full international (United States) 44 caps/0
goals
• American goalkeeper and the most successful

American playing in Europe.
• Played gridiron football and baseball as a boy, and did not take up soccer until the age of 14.
• Moved to England to play for Millwall while also studying at university.
• Joined Leicester for £900,000 in 1996, winning the League Cup and playing a major part in their establishment as a regular force in the English Premiership.
• Played for the United States in the 1998 World Cup finals in France, having made his international debut against Colombia in 1990.
• Voted American Player of the Year in 1999.
• Joined Rayo Vallecano on a Bosman-style free transfer in summer 1999.
• Was one of the stars of newly-promoted Vallecano's amazing early-season run in the 1999-2000 Spanish campaign.

PLAYER
KELLY, Gary
Defender, Irish, 174cm, 68kg
Born: 09.07.74, Drogheda, Ireland
Clubs: Leeds (1991-)
Full International (Rep Ireland) 31 caps/1 goal
• Right-back and uncle of Leeds team-mate **Ian Harte**.
• Missed the 1998-99 season through injury, but returned to play an important role in the Leeds revival under **David O'Leary**.
• Product of the Dublin youth club Home Farm.

PLAYER
KENNEDY, Peter
Midfielder, Northern Irish, 175cm , 75kg
Born: 10.09.73, Lurgan, Northern Ireland
Clubs: Notts Co (1996-97), Watford (199-)
Full International (Northern Ireland) 6 caps/0 goals
• Left-sided player who played a key role in Watford's 1999 promotion to the Premier League.

PLAYER
KEOWN, Martin
Defender, English, 185cm, 78kg
Born: 24.07.66, Oxford.
Clubs: Arsenal (1984-86), Brighton (1985, loan), Aston Villa (1986-89), Everton (1989-93), Arsenal (1993-)
Full international (England) 33 caps/2 goals
• Solid and thoroughly dependable centre-back who has been one of the cornerstones of Arsenal's near legendary defence in recent years, forming a hugely successful partnership with **Tony Adams** for both club and country.
• Played 22 League games for Arsenal after coming through the club's youth system, but moved to Villa to get regular football. Re-signed by Arsenal from Everton for £2million in February 1992.
• International debut: 19.02.92, v France (won 2-0).

PLAYER
KERE, Mahamadou
Defender, Burkino Faso, 182cm, 76kg
Born: 02.01.82, Burkina Faso
Clubs: Santos (Bra) (1997) Charleroi (Bel) (1998-)
Full international (Burkino Faso)
• Defensive midfielder from Burkina Faso who can also play in defence. A quiet player, not the stereotypical African player who likes to show off.
• Despite his age and only recent graduation from the youth ranks, he is very mature.
• Known in Belgium for scoring one of the most curious own goals ever seen. In the 1999-2000 season, Charleroi goalkeeper Mrmic handled the ball outside his penalty area; everybody was waiting for the referee to give a free-kick and a red card. Kere hammered the ball into his own goal out of frustation. But instead of whistling for a free-kick, the referee decided to allow the goal.

PLAYER
KERKAR, Karim
Midfielder, French, 174cm, 67kg
Born: 03.01.77, Givors, France

Clubs: Gueugnon, Le Havre
• Creative midfielder who impressed in 1999-2000 following a move to Le Havre from Gueugnon.

PLAYER
KETSBAIA, Temuri
Forward, Georgian, 174cm, 68kg
Born: 18.03.68, Gale, Georgia
Clubs: Dinamo Tbilisi (1987-90), Anorthosis (Cyp) (1991-1994), AEK Athens (Gre) (1994-97), Newcastle (Eng) (1997-)
Full international (Georgia) 40 caps/13 goals
• Shaven-headed attacker who has been popular with the fans during his time in Newcastle, but often let down on the pitch by his unpredictability and inconsistency.

PLAYER
KEWELL, Harry
Forward, Australian, 181cm, 74kg
Born: 22.09.78, Sydney, Australia
Clubs: Leeds (1995-)
Full international (Australia) 9 caps/3 goals
• The brightest talent to come out of Australia for many years, having joined Leeds in December 1995 from the Australian Academy of Sport.
• Voted PFA Young Player of the Season in April 2000 after a season in which he became a key player for Leeds and one of the most exciting forwards on display in the Premier League.

PLAYER
KEZMAN, Mateja
Forward, Yugoslav, 178cm, 71kg
Born: 12.04.79, Vrsac, Yugoslavia
Clubs: Zemun, Radnicki Nis, Loznica, Sartid, Partizan Belgrade, PSV Eindhoven (Hol) (2000-)
Full international (Yugoslavia) 3 caps/1 goal
• One of the biggest hopes of Yugoslav soccer. Shoots equally well with both feet. A regular with the Yugoslav Under-21 team and a late inclusion in Yugoslavia's squad for Euro 2000.

• Earned notoriety at Euro 2000 after being sent off after less than two minutes after appearing as a substitute against Norway in Bruges.
• Joined PSV for £7million in July 2000.

PLAYER
KHLESTOV, Dmitri
Defender, Russian, 177cm, 70kg
Born: 21.01.71, Russia
Clubs: Moscow Spartak (1989-)
Full international (Russia) 43 caps/0 goals
• Reliable, resilient defender who graduated from the Spartak youth ranks and has remained with the club throughout his career.
• Nicknamed 'Baresi' because of the physical resemblence to the former Milan and Italy defender, but also because of his tough defending style.
• **Oleg Romantsev**: 'He marks the opponent like nobody else in Europe.'

PLAYER
KHOKLOV, Dmitro
Midfielder, Russian, 189cm, 82kg
Born: 22.12.75, Moscow
Clubs: CSKA Moscow (1993-96), Torpedo Moscow (1997), PSV Eindhoven (Hol) (1997-1999), Real Sociedad (Spa) (2000-)
Full international (Russia) 22 caps/0 goals
• Attacking Russian midfielder bought from PSV Eindhoven in January 2000 to help Sociedad's fight against relegation.

PLAYER
KHOMUKHA, Dmitri
Midfielder, Tajikistan, 174cm, 69kg
Born: 23.08.69
Clubs: Kopetdag (1985-87), CSKA 2 (1988), SKA Karpety (1989), Metallist (Ukr) (1989-94), Erzu Grozny (1994), Zenit (1995-96), CSKA Moscow (1997-)
Full international (Tajikistan)
• Experienced midfield campaigner who is

probably the best free-kick taker in the Russian League.

PLAYER
KIELBOWICZ, Tomasz
Midfielder, Polish, 178cm, 67kg
Born: 21.02.76, Poland
Clubs: Rakow Czestochowa, Widzew Lodz (1999), Polonia Warsaw (1999-)
Full international (Poland) 2 caps/0 goals
• Dynamic left-midfielder who loves to attack and always causes danger for opponents. Joined Widzew Lodz from second division Rakow Czestochowa. Then moved to Polonia.
• Won his first international cap against France in February 2000.

PLAYER
KIHLSTEDT, Magnus
Goalkeeper, Swedish, 190cm, 86kg
Born: 29.02.72, Sweden
Clubs: Oddevold (1991-96), Lillestrom (Nor) (1997-98), Brann (Nor) (1999-)
Full international (Sweden) 6 caps/0 goals
• Tall Swedish keeper who joined Brann after an excellent spell with Lillestrom.
• Was Sweden's third-choice keeper at Euro 2000, having been pushed down the pecking order by the rise of **Mattias Asper**.

PLAYER
KIKO
Full name: Francisco Narvaez Machon, Kiko
Forward, Spanish, 189cm, 86kg
Born: 26.04.72, Cadiz, Spain
Clubs: Cadiz (1990-93), Atletico Madrid (1993-)
Full international (Spain) 26 caps/5 goals
• Supremely gifted striker who is more of a creator than scorer of goals. Expert at holding the ball, but also a clever improviser on the pitch.
• A cult hero in Spain after scoring five goals (including the last-minute winner in the Final) for Spain's victorious 1992 Olympic side.

• Joined Cadiz aged 13 and spent six years living in a boarding house. Sold to Atletico for £500,000 when Cadiz were relegated in 1993.
• Collected 10 yellow cards and two expulsions in the 1994-95 season.
• A League and Cup winner with Atletico in 1996 and a past 'Andalusian of the Year'.
• Future in Madrid was placed in doubt following Atletico's relegation at the end of the 1999-2000 season, but he signed a new contract in summer 2000.

PLAYER
KILI GONZALEZ
Full name: Cristian Alberto 'Kily' Gonzalez
Midfielder, Argentinian, 175cm, 71kg
Born: 04.08.74, Rosario, Argentina
Clubs: Rosario Central (1993-95), Boca Juniors (1995-96), Zaragoza (Spa) (1996-99), Valencia (Spa) (1999-)
Full international (Argentina)
• Left-sided midfielder who established himself in Spain with Zaragoza, scoring 15 goals in 92 games over three seasons.
• Excellent, battling performances for Valencia in his first season meant there was no debate about his place in the starting line-up for the Champions League Final against Real Madrid.

PLAYER
KIMONI, Daniel
Defender, Belgian, 178cm, 75kg
Born: 18.01.71, Belgium
Clubs: Standard Liege (1993-96), Genk (1996-)
Full international (Belgium) 3 caps/0 goals
• Central defender who is an accomplished man-marker and occasional international for Belgium.

PLAYER
KINCL, Marek
Forward, Czech, 188cm, 91kg
Born: 03.04.73, Czech Republic
Clubs: Slovan Liberec, Viktoria Zizkov (2000-),

Georgi Kinkladze

Sparta Prague (2000-)
Full international (Czech Republic) 1 cap/0 goals
• Moved to the capital from Slovan Liberec during the 1999-2000 season on the back of a impressive scoring record and continued to find the net with Zizkov, leading to a summer 2000 move across town to champions Sparta.

PLAYER
KINDER, Vladmir
Defender, Slovakian
Born: 04.03.69, Slovakia
Clubs: Middlesbrough (Eng), Drnovice (2000), Hannover (Ger) (2000-)
Full international (Slovakia) 34 caps/1 goall
• Slovak international left-back who landed at Drnovice for the second half of the 1999-2000 season following a miserable period in England with Middlesbrough.
• After putting his career back on track, Kinder lined up a move to Hannover in summer 2000.

PLAYER
KINGSTON, Richard
Goalkeeper, Ghanaian, 185cm, 85kg
Born: 13.06.78, Ghana
Clubs: Galatasaray (Tur), Sakaryaspor (Tur), Goztepe (Tur) (1999-)
Full international (Ghana)
• First-choice keeper for the Ghana national team who made a name for himself at Sakaryaspor after failing to make the breakthrough at Galatasaray.
• Injured 43 minutes into his international debut against Brazil.
• A non-playing member of Ghana's squad at the 1996 and 1998 African Nations Cup finals, but was the number one at the 2000 finals.

PLAYER
KINKLADZE, Georgi
Midfielder, Georgian, 173cm, 74kg
Born: 06.07.73, Tbilisi, Georgia

Clubs: Dinamo Tbilisi (1992-94), Saarbrucken (Ger) (1994), Dinamo Tbilisi (1994-95), Manchester City (Eng) (1995-98), Ajax Amsterdam (Hol) (1998-2000), Derby (Eng) (2000-)
Full international (Georgia) 37 caps/7 goals
• Mercurial midfielder who returned to England, to Derby, during the 1999-2000 season after a difficult time in Holland with Ajax.
• Georgian Player of the Year in 1993 who joined Manchester City in 1995 for £2million after City beat Real Madrid to his signature.
• Stayed with City when they were relegated in 1998, but not when they dropped down a further division a year later.

PLAYER
KINSELLA, Mark
Midfielder, Irish, 172cm, 75kg
Born: 12.08.72, Dublin
Clubs: Charlton Athletic
Full international (Rep Ireland) 16 caps/1 goal
• Captain of Charlton and and arguably the best player in the English first division when Charlton won promotion to the Premier League in 2000.

PLAYER
KIPARISSIS, Thomas
Forward, Greek, 184cm, 82kg
Born: 26.03.70, Greece
Clubs: Skoda Xanthi (1996-)
Full international (Greece) 12 caps/2 goals
• Determined, skilful frontrunner and well-regarded by Greek national coach **Vassilis Daniil**. More of an attacking foil than goalscorer, he only managed seven goals in the 1999-2000 season.
• Took his time to break into the Greek national team: he was 29 when he won his first cap in 1999 against Switzerland.

COACH
KIPIANI, David
Georgian
Born: 18.11.51
• National coach of Georgia, appointed for a second spell in charge following the resignation of **Johan Boskamp**.
• Also coach of club side Torpedo Kutaisi.

PLAYER
KIRALY, Gabor
Goalkeeper, Hungarian, 190cm, 85kg
Born: 01.04.76, Szombathely, Hungary
Clubs: Halades Szombathely (1993-97), Hertha Berlin (Ger) (1997-)
Full international (Hungary) 19 caps/0 goals
• Agile Hungarian goalkeeper who always plays in grey tracksuit bottoms for superstitious reasons. A keeper cum sweeper with good footballing skills and outstanding shot-stopping ability, he makes spectacular dashes off his line to confront onrushing forwards and will come a long way to punch. However, he can be erratic, alternating between the good and the downright ugly.
• International debut for Hungary against Austria in March 1998.
• Surname pronounced Kee rah lee.

COACH
KIRASTAS, Yiannis
Greek
• Ex-Paniliakos coach recruited by Panathinaikos in the summer of 1999 to replace the Argentinian Juan Ramon Rocha. Guided 'Pana' to runners-up spot in the Greek championsip in the 1999-2000 season and was voted the best coach in the country by First Division managers, players and club presidents.

BUSINESS
KIRCH, Leo
German

• Media mogul known as the German Rupert Murdoch. Through the Leo Kirch Group, he is hugely influential in the field of global TV rights, having purchased the rights to the 2002 World Cup from FIFA.

PLAYER
KIRCHLER, Roland
Midfielder, Austrian, 186cm, 77kg
Born: 29.09.70, Innsbruck, Austria
Clubs: Tirol (1990-)
Full international (Austria) 8 caps/ 0 goals
• Midfielder who turned down a move to Sturm Graz at the 11th hour in summer 1999, to stay loyal to FC Tirol and was rewarded with an international debut.

PLAYER
KIRILOV, Rosen
Defender, Bulgaria, 184cm, 95kg
Born: 04.01.73 Bulgaria
Clubs: Vidin, CSKA Sofia, Liteks, Adanaspor (Tur)
Full international (Bulgaria) 12 caps/0 goals
• Solid defender who won the Bulgarian League title with Liteks before joining the growing band of Bulgars earning a living in Turkey.

PLAYER
KIRSTEN, Ulf
Forward, German, 175cm, 81kg
Born: 04.12.65, Riesa, Germany
Clubs: Chemie Riesa, Stahl Riesa, Dynamo Dresden (1983-90), Bayer Leverkusen (1990-)
Full international (East Germany/Germany) 49 caps/14 goals, 51 caps/21 goals
• Chunky striker and cast-iron guarantee of goals – 10 seasons in the Bundesliga have brought him 159 goals and he has been the country's top scorer three times (1993, 1997, 1998). An abrasive, single-minded individual who is never afraid to

Ulf Kirsten

go in where it hurts and is a dead-eye finisher.
• A former star of top East German side Dynamo Dresden and the DDR national team, he is said to be eyeing a move to a club in the United States.
• Pronounced Oolf Care sten.

BUSINESS
KIRTON, Glen
• Made his name as the tournament director of Euro 96 in England before heading to Switzerland to work for ISL, the marketing company used by FIFA.

PLAYER
KISHISHEV, Radostan
Defender, Bulgarian, 167cm, 72kg
Born: 04.09.75, Bulgaria
Clubs: Neftochimik Bourgas, Liteks Lovech, Bursaspor (Tur), Neftochimik Bourgas, Charlton Athletic (Eng) (2000-)
Full international (Bulgaria) 33 caps/0 goals
• Versatile right-sided defender who can the right-back or right wing-back role or play on the right side of a three-man central defence.
• Played in all three games for Bulgaria at the 1996 European Championship.
• Won the Bulgarian League with Liteks in 1998 and then spent a season in Turkey before returning to his first club Neftochimik.

PLAYER
KITZBICKLER, Richard
Midfielder, Austrian, 175cm, 70kg
Born: 12.01.74, Worgl, Austria
Clubs: Tirol (1992-97), Salzburg (1997-)
Full international (Austria) 2 caps/0 goals
• One of the stars of the 1998-99 season in Austria and seen as one of the key men in the rebuilding of the national team under Otto Baric.

PLAYER
KJAER, Peter
Goalkeeper, Danish, 187cm, 88kg
Born: 05.11.65, Denmark
Clubs: Vejle (1990-92), Silkeborg (1992-)
Full international (Denmark) 2 caps/0 goals
• Experienced keeper who was third-choice for Denmark at Euro 2000, and likes to follow the example fo Peter Schmeichel and charge upfield for corners.
• Voted Goalkeeper of the Year in Denmark in 1999.

PLAYER
KJOLO, Mike
Defender, Norwegian, 180cm, 80kg
Born: 27.10.71, Oslo, Norway
Clubs: Strommen, Skeid (1996-97), AIK Stockholm (Swe) (1998-99), Stabaek (2000-)
Full international (Norway) 1 cap/0 goals
• Solid full-back who returned from AIK in Sweden in 2000, having made his international debut for Norway against Sweden in February 2000.

PLAYER
KLOMPE, Tieme
Defender, Dutch, 180cm, 70kg
Born: 08.04.76, Roden, Holland
Clubs: Heerenveen (1996-)
• Young defender who has impressed since making his Dutch League debut for Heerenveen as a teenager in the 1996-97 season. Has been ever-present in their backline ever since.

PLAYER
KLOS, Stefan
Goalkeeper, German, 182cm, 85kg
Born: 16.08.71, Dortmund, Germany
Clubs: Borussia Dortmund (1991-98), Rangers (Sco) (1998-)
• Signed by Dick Advocaat from Borussia Dortmund midway through the 1998-99 season, the German has displaced Lionel Charbonnier as first choice at Ibrox.

Patrick Kluivert

• Former Olympic and Under-21 international.
• Surname pronounced Close.

PLAYER
KLOS, Tomasz
Defender, Polish, 186cm, 78kg
Born: 07.03.73, Zgierz, Poland
Clubs: LKS Lodz (1995-98), Auxerre (1998-)
Full international (Poland) 19 caps/1 goal
• Polish international who can line up as a rugged, no-holds barred stopper, but makes far more of a contribution as a raiding right-back. Scored nine goals from full-back when LKS Lodz clinched the Polish League in 1997-98.
• Surname pronounced Close.

PLAYER
KLUIVERT, Patrick
Forward, Dutch, 188cm, 81kg
Born: 01.07.76, Amsterdam, Holland
Clubs: Ajax (1994-1997), Milan (Ita) (1997-98), Barcelona (Spa) (1998-)
Full international (Holland) 45 caps/28 goals
• Prodigiously talented young striker who burst onto the European scene as a teenage substitute in the 1995 European Cup Final, scoring the only goal of the game as Ajax beat Milan.
• Revived his career under **Louis Van Gaal** at Barcelona after a torrid time in Italy with Milan.
• Joined Milan on a free transfer from Ajax after refusing to sign a new contract in Amsterdam.
• Time in Milan was affected by the aftermath of two court cases, the first when he was involved in the death a prominent Amsterdam theatre director in a hit and run car accident, the second when he was cleared of rape.
• His disciplinary record has been disappointing, as has his goalscoring tally, although the team-mates who benefits from his effortless running and clever lay-offs would disagree.
• Was Holland's outstanding player at Euro 2000, scoring a hat-trick against Yugoslavia and finishing as the tournament joint top scorer.

PLAYER
KLYUYEV, Denis
Midfielder, Russian, 175cm, 70kg
Born: 07.09.73, Russia
Clubs: Dynamo Moscow (1994-95), Feyenoord (Hol) (1994-99), Dynamo Moscow (1999-)
• Experienced playmaker who recently rejoined Dynamo after a long spell abroad with Feyenoord, where he never established himself as a regular.

PLAYER
KMETSCH, Sven
Midfielder, German, 178cm, 77kg
Born: 13.08.70, Bautzen, Germany
Clubs: Motor Bautzen, Dynamo Dresden (1988-95), Hamburg (1995-98), Schalke (1998-)
Full international (Germany) 2 caps/0 goals
• An intensely hard-working and tactically-aware defensive midfielder or right-back, he was on the verge of the German national team when he left Hamburg for Schalke two years ago.
• But injury and a dip in form seems to have put paid to his international aspirations. Besides his energy and application, he has a potent right-foot shot.

BUSINESS
KNAPP, Barclay
• Chief executive of NTL, the digital and cable TV company which has bought live rights to the English Premier League and has stakes in Aston Villa, Newcastle, Middlesbrough and Leicester.

PLAYER
KNAVS, Aleksander
Defender, Slovenian, 190cm, 86kg
Born: 05.12.75, Maribor, Slovenia
Clubs: Olimpia Ljubljana (1993-97), Tirol (1997-)
Full international (Slovenia) 24 caps/1 goal
• English-type stopper, a tough competitor and good header of the ball.
• Member of the Slovenian squad at Euro 2000,

playing in two games.
• International debut 05.02.98 v Iceland.

PLAYER
KNOPPER, Richard
Midfielder, Dutch, 181cm, 70kg
Born: 29.08.77, Rijswijk, Holland
Clubs: Ajax (1997-)
• Came through Ajax's youth teams after switching from Feyenoord aged 16.
• Filled the attacking midfield role vacated at Ajax by **Jari Litmanen**'s 1999 move to Barcelona.
• 'I've tried to copy Litmanen's style. I've studied his moves, and we've talked a lot. Jari gave me valuable advice. The big thing is you mustn't be afraid to fail. Mentally you must be strong. That's where a lot of players go wrong.'
• Holland Under-21 international.

PLAYER
KNUDSEN, Jens Martin
Goalkeeper, Faroe Islands
Born: 11.06.67, Faroe Islands
Clubs: Leiftur Olafsfjordur (Ice)
Full international (Faroe Is) 56 caps/0 goals
• Keeper who is best known for the bobble hat worn while keeping goal for the Faroe Islands, though he has not worn the hat for some seasons in an attempt to be taken more seriously.

PLAYER
KOBIASCHVILI, Levan
Midfielder, Georgia,183cm, 79kg
Born: 10.07.77, Georgia
Clubs: Metalurg Rustawi, Dynamo Tbilisi (1996-97), Alania Vladikavkaz ((Rus) (1997), Freiburg (Ger) (1998-)
Full international (Georgia) 26 caps/0 goals
• One of the foremost left-wing-backs in the Bundesliga. Works incredibly hard on his flank, is an excellent crosser of the ball and is a free-kick specialist.
• Surname pronounced Co bee ash vili.

PLAYER
KOCH, Georg
Goalkeeper, German, 194cm, 95kg
Born: 03.02.72, Bergisch Gladbach, Germany
Clubs: Bayer Leverkusen, Fortuna Dusseldorf (1991-97), PSV Eindhoven (Hol) (1997-98), Arminia Bielefelf (1998-)
• Intensely competitive keeper with lots of courage and athleticism. But he can go overboard with the hard-man act; while playing for Bielefeld last season he brought down Hertha Berlin's **Michael Preetz** and while the latter lay writhing in agony with a broken arm, all Koch could do was stand over Preetz and berate him for diving.

PLAYER
KOCH, Harry
Defender, German, 184cm, 75kg
Born: 15.11.69, Bamberg, Germany
Clubs: Hallstadt, TSV Vestenbergsgreuth, Kaiserslautern (1995-)
• With his 70s-style curly perm and full-blooded commitment, this uncompromising right-sided defensive marker is a cult hero at Kaiserslautern.
• First made a name for himself back in 1994 when his amateur side Vestenbergsreuth knocked Bayern Munich out of the German Cup.

PLAYER
KOCH, Patrick
Midfielder, Swiss, 181cm, 73kg
Born: 15.12.75, Switzerland
Clubs: Lucerne (1998-99), Neuchatel Xamax (1999-)
• Cultured attacking midfielder with good touch and vision.

PLAYER
KOCIC, Aleksander
Goalkeeper, Yugoslav
Born: 18.03.69
Clubs: Vojvodina Novi Sad, Perugia (Ita), Empoli (Ita), Red Star Belgrade
Full international (Yugoslavia) 16 caps/0 goals

• Yugoslavia's first-choice keeper during the qualifying campaign for France 98, but a bad knee injury kept him out of the finals. Returned to the squad for Euro 2000, but a toe injury again kept him out of the finals.
• Moved to Italy in 1996, but struggled to win a regular place at Perugia and Empoli.

PLAYER
KODRO, Meho
Forward, Bosnian, 188cm, 81kg
Born: 12.01.67, Mostar, Bosnia
Clubs: Velez Mostar (1985-92), Real Sociedad (Spa) (1991-95), Barcelona (Spa) (1995-96), Tenerife (Spa) (1996-99), Alaves (Spa) (1999-)
Full international (Bosnia) 10 caps/3 goals
• Striker who was the talk of Spain when he finished as League top scorer four years ago, but has not recovered from a disastrous two-year spell at Barcelona.
• Made his name at Real Sociedad, where he finished as the Spanish League's top scorer in 1995, scoring 25 goals in 35 games.
• Failed to spark at Barcelona, where he suffered in the shadow of **Ronaldo** and other big names.
• Sold to Tenerife, but suffered relegation in 1999 and went on loan to Alaves, where he recovered some form and confidence.

COACH
KOEMAN, Ronald
Dutch
Born: 21.03.63
• Former Dutch international with an outstanding playing career. Won European cups with PSV and Barcelona and won the European Championships with Holland in 1988.
• One of the few players to have played for all of Holland's big three clubs – Ajax, Feyenoord and PSV – and is now expected to have a great coaching career, and probably be more successful that his former team-mates **Ruud Gullit** and **Frank Rijkaard**.

- Has already been linked with Barcelona as a future coaching job.
- A fan of fresh, attacking football, he has been coach of Vitesse Arnhem since 2000.

COACH
KOEVERMANS, Wim
Dutch
Born: 28.06.60
- Former defender with Groningen and Fortuna Sittard and a member of the Dutch national team that won the European title in 1988, although as cover for **Frank Rijkaard** he didn't play.
- Now coach at MVV Maastricht, who were relegated at the end of the 1999-2000 season.

PLAYER
KOGLER, Walter
Defender, Austrian, 185cm, 78kg
Born: 12.12.67, Wolfsberg, Austria
Clubs: Sturm Graz (1990-92), Austria Vienna (1992-96), Salzburg (1996-98), LASK (1998-99), Tirol (1999-)
Full international (Austria) 25 caps/1 goal
- Centre-back who was a member of Austria's squad at the 1998 World Cup, but did not play.
- Dependable and reliable rather than outstanding.

PLAYER
KOHLER, Jurgen
Defender, German, 186cm, 84kg
Born: 06.10.65, Lambsheim, Germany
Clubs: Jahn Lambsheim, Waldhof Mannheim, Koln (1987-89), Bayern Munich (1989-91), Juventus (Ita) (1991-95), Borussia Dortmund (1995-)
Full international (Germany) 105 caps/2 goals
- Mean and magnificent stopper still going strong after no less than 17 years, straining every sinew to stop strikers in their tracks. A superb tackler, quick, strong in the air and bristling with competitiveness, he has won absolutely everything: the World Cup, the Champions League, the UEFA Cup and Bundesliga and Serie A titles.
- He was for a time, the world's most expensive defender, moving from Bayern Munich to Juventus in 1991 for £4million. His £1million move to Bayern in 1989 had already made him the most expensive German defender.
- Dubbed 'Iron Foot', a most appropriate nickname for this fearless man-marker.
- Surname Pronounced Curl ler.

PLAYER
KOLIVANOV, Igor
Forward, Russian, 178cm, 70kg
Born: 04.07.65, Moscow, Russia
Clubs: Dinamo Moscow (1986-91), Foggia (Ita) (1991-96), Bologna (Ita) (1996-)
Full international (Russia) 35 caps/12 goals
- Atttacking midfielder or striker who has been one of the most successful Russians in Italy in recent years.
- Soviet Footballer of the Year in 1991 after scoring 18 goals in one season for Dynamo Moscow, including five in one game. A European Under-21 champion with the USSR in 1990.
- Made his international debut for the USSR in August 1989, against Poland, making 24 appearances for the Soviets and the Confederation of Independent States (CIS).
- Voted the best left-sided midfielder in Italy in the 1993-94 season.
- Missed half of the 1994-95 season after an injury picked up while playing for Russia against San Marino. His absence was blamed for Foggia's relegation.
- Played for Russia at Euro 96, having been their top scorer in the qualifiers with five goals.
- **Yuri Nikiforov** on Kolivanov: 'Igor is a brilliant forward. he can score goals and he can make them. He has a fantastic left foot, is lively and brave and is a real handful to mark. He's class and it's proved by the fact that he has been playing in Italy for many years. Italian clubs don't keep bad players.'

Jan Koller

PLAYER
KOLKKA, Joonas
Midfielder, Finnish, 175cm, 71kg
Born: 28.09.74, Lahti, Finland
Clubs: MyPa 47 (1994-95), Willem II (Hol) (1995-98), PSV Eindhoven (Hol) (1998-)
Full international (Finland) 27 caps/6 goals
• Winger who has been hyped as the 'new **Jari Litmanen**' ever since he had a trial with Ajax in winter 1995. Joined Willem II instead, playing 68 games, scoring 16 goals and earning a move to PSV.
• Scored on his international debut for Finland against Estonia in October 1994, aged 20.

PLAYER
KOLLE, Axel
Midfielder, Norwegian, 184cm, 76kg
Born: 23.01.73, Oslo, Norway
Clubs: Frederikstad, Lyn (1991-93), Stabaek (1994), Lyn (1995), Stabaek (1996-)
• Gifted midfielder with a variety of technical skills but lacks a little in physical presence.

PLAYER
KOLLER, Jan
Forward, Czech, 202cm, 103kg
Born: 30.03.73, Lhota, Czech Rep
Clubs: Sparta Prague (1994-96), Lokeren (Bel) (1996-99), Anderlecht (Bel) (1999-)
Full international (Czech Rep) 17 caps/13 goals
• Giant, towering centre-forward who has been a prolific goalscorer for the Czech Republic over the past two seasons.
• Won the 1995 Czech League title and the 1996 Czech Cup with Sparta.
• Made his name in Belgium at Lokeren where he finished as top scorer in the Belgian League in 1999 with 24 goals, six ahead of his nearest rival.
• Moved to Anderlecht in summer of 1999 and won the Belgian League title in his first season.
• Scored on his international debut, ironically against Belgium in February 1999.

• Led the Czech Republic's attack at Euro 2000 after scoring in all of the last five qualifying matches.

COACH
KOLLER, Marcel
Swiss
Born: 11.11.60
• Coach of St Gallen who led the club to only their second Swiss League championship since 1904.
• A former international defender with Grasshopper until beginning his coaching career in the mid-1990s.

ADMINISTRATOR
KOLOSKOV, Viacheslav
• President of the Russian Football Association and a member of the executive committee of UEFA. Won election to the FIFA executive committee in July 2000 at the expense of **Joseph Mifsud**.

PLAYER
KOLVIDSSON, Helgi
Midfielder, Icelandic, 180cm, 82kg
Born: 13.09.71, Iceland
Clubs: IK Kopavogur, Pfullendorf (Ger), Lustenau (Aut), Mainz 05 (Ger) (1998-2000), Ulm (Ger) (2000-)
Full international (Iceland) 6 caps/0 goals
• International midfielder whose speed, strength and uncompromising style have made him a firm favourite with fans of the Iceland national side.

PLAYER
KOMBAYASI, Paulinho
Forward, Brazilian, 171cm, 70kg
Born: 09.01.70. Osaso, Brazil
Clubs: Ionikos Nikea (Gre)
• Brazilian attcker who can line up in midfield, in the 'hole' just behind the strikers or as a conventional frontman. A lithe and elusive runner with the ball and usually finishes well. But can be selfish at times.

PLAYER
KOMLJENOVIC, Slobodan
Defender, Yugoslav, 187cm, 72kg
Born: 02.01.71, Yugoslavia
Clubs: SG Hoechst, Eintracht Frankfurt (1992-97) (Ger), Duisburg (1997-99) (Ger), Kaiserslautern (Ger) (1999-)
Full international (Yugoslavia) 21 caps/3 goals
• Classy Yugoslav international utility man. Totally at ease whether playing sweeper, stopper, wing-back or in a midfield holding role. Born in Yugoslavia but brought up in Germany.
• International debut against Brazil in December 1994, but has not always been first-choice.
• Surname pronounced Komel yay no veetch.

PLAYER
KOMPALA, Adam
Midfielder, Polish, 178cm, 71kg
Born: 16.08.73, Poland
Clubs: Gornik Zabrze, Ruch Radzionkow, Gornik Zabrze
• Started his career with Gornik. Then moved to Ruch Radzionkow. Returned to Zabrze in order to further his career. Named Polish 'Discovery of Year' for 1999-2000.

PLAYER
KONDE, Oumar
Defender, Swiss, 187cm, 85kg
Born: 19.08.79, France
Clubs: Basle, Freiburg (Ger)
• Swiss Under-21 defender who has done well in Germany with Freiburg after starting out at Basle.

PLAYER
KONDRASHOV ,Andrei
Defender, Russian, 190cm, 83kg
Born: 07.08.72, Russia
Clubs: Zenit St Petersburg (1996-)
Full international (Russia) 1 cap/0 goals
• Strong, powerful centre-back who is an imposing presence in the Zenit back-line.

PLAYER
KONE, Soufiane
Forward, French, 183cm, 80kg
Born: 08.06.80, Toulouse, France
Clubs: Nancy
- It speaks volumes for the talent of this young striker that Italian clubs Juventus and Parma have been tailing him. But the Serie A recruitors will have to be patient.
- The powerfully-built goalscorer – nicknamed Brutor' by his teammates at Nancy – ironically spent much of the 1999-2000 season on the sidelines with a series of muscular problems.
- Born in France to parents from the African state of Mali.
- Pronounced Soo fee anne Ko nay.

PLAYER
KONIG, Miroslav
Goalkeeper, Slovakian, 188cm, 80kg
Born: 01.06.72, Slovakia
Clubs: Slovan Bratislava (1995-)
Full international (Slovakia) 17 caps/0 goals
- Keeper who has made a huge contribution to the success of Slovan Bratislava in the Slovakian League in recent seasons, earning international recognition as a result.
- Set a Slovakian League record in 1999 when he kept 12 successive clean sheets, going 1,129 minutes without conceding a goal.

PLAYER
KONJIC, Muhamed
Defender, Bosnian, 193cm, 86kg
Born: 14.05.70, Bosnia-Herzegovina
Clubs: Slobada Tuzla (1990-92), Croatia Belisce (Cro) (1992-93), Croatia Zagreb (Cro) (1993-96), Zurich (Swi) (1996-98), Monaco (Fra) (1997-99), Coventry (Eng) (1999-)
Full international (Bosnia) 22 caps/0 goals
- Centre-back who has captained Bosnia and won the French League with Monaco in 1997.
- Joined Coventry in February 1998, but

struggled to hold down a regular place.

COACH
KONKOV, Anatoliy
Ukrainian
Born: 13.09.49
- A leading defender with Shakhtar and Kyiv Dynamo during his playing days. Appointed as national coach of Ukraine in 1995 but failed to qualify for the finals of Euro 96. Seen as one of the leading disciples of **Valeri Lobanovsky**.

PLAYER
KONSEL, Michael
Goalkeeper, Austrian, 186cm, 77kg
Born: 06.03.62, Vienna, Austria
Clubs: Rapid Vienna (1985-97), Roma (Ita) (1997-99), Venezia (Ita) (1997-99)
Full international (Austria) 43 caps/0 goals
- Austrian international number one who is agile but not the tallest of keepers.
- Made a surprise move to Serie A at the age of 35 after 13 successful seasons with Rapid Vienna, but lost his place at Roma after injury and moved on to Venezia.
- Played in all three of Austria's games at the 1998 World Cup.

PLAYER
KONSTANTINIDIS, Kostas
Midfielder, Greek, 188cm, 82kg
Born: 31.08.72, Greece
Clubs: Panathinaikos (1998-99), Hertha Berlin (Ger) (1999-)
Full international (Greece) 26 caps/1 goal
- Extremely versatile Greek international who is nominally a midfielder but can play in any number of postions: sweeper – where his reading of the game is excellent – full-back, even in attack.
- Capped 35 times at Under-21 level by Greece.
- Surname pronounced Kon stant tee nee dees.

KONSTANTINOU, Michalis
Forward, Cypriot, 187cm, 82kg
Born: 19.02.78, Cyprus
Clubs: Iraklis Thessaloniki
Full international (Cyprus) 15 caps/4 goals
• Cypriot striker who scored 22 League goals for Iraklis in the 1999-2000 season, double his tally for the previous campaign. Still some rough edges to his game – his first touch is not great – but he certainly knows how to get on the end of chances and put them away.

KONTERMAN, Bert
Defender, Dutch, 188cm, 84kg
Born: 14.01.71, Rouveen, Holland
Clubs: PEC Zwolle (1989-90), FC Zwolle (1990-93), Cambuur (1993-96), Willem II (1996-98), Feyenoord (1998-2000), Rangers (Sco) (2000-)
Full international (Holland) 11 caps/0 goals
• Defender who has earned comparisons with **Jaap Stam** after following the same career path (playing with Stam at Zwolle, Cambuur and Willem II, where he switched from midfield to defence).
• Powerful centre-back quick and strong in the air.
• International debut in March 1999 against Argentina, impressing with his marking of **Gabriel Batistuta**.
• Grew up in Holland's bible belt, and nearly gave up football because he had reservations about playing on Sundays.
• Linked with a move abroad throughout the 1999-2000 season, eventually joining Rangers.

KORAC, Milorad
Goalkeeper, Yugoslav, 186cm, 82kg
Born: 10.03.69, Posega, Yugoslavia
Clubs: Obilic Belgrade
• Proved with consistent performances that he belongs among the best keepers in Yugoslavia, making him a candidate for the national team.

KORNAUKHOV, Oleg
Goalkeeper, Russian, 179cm, 68kg
Born: 14.01.75, Russia
Clubs: Torpedo Moscow (1991-97), Shinnik (1997), CSKA Moscow (1998-)
Full international (Russia) 1 cap/0 goals
• Experienced keeper who is very good on his goal line, although he can be insconsistent.
• Number three goalie in the Russian national team.

KORNEEV, Igor
Forward, Russian, 172cm, 77kg
Born: 04.09.67, Moscow, Russia
Clubs: CSKA Moscow (1986-91), Espanol (1991-94), Barcelona (1994-95), Heerenveen (1995-97), Feyenoord (1997-)
Full international (Russia) 14 caps/3 goals
• Former Russian international playmaker who has not been an automatic choice at Feyenoord, but is capable of great things on his day.
• Played only 12 times for Barcelona before moving to Holland.

KORNYUKHIN, Yevgeni
Goalkeeper, Russian, 193cm, 80kg
Born: 07.03.67, Russia
Clubs: Vympel Rybinsk (1992-94), Rostelmash (1994), Zenit St Petersburg (1995), Energiya (1996), Shinnik (1997), Torpedo Moscow (1998-)
• Strong physical defender, a good tackler who likes to attack down the flanks. Spent most of his career in the lower Russian leagues before a move to Shinnik in 1997.

KORNFEIN, Itzik
Goalkeeper, Israeli
Born: 24.09.71, Israel
Clubs: Betar Jerusalem

Full international (Israel) 5 caps/0 goals
• Solid keeper who has saved his club on many occasions with some spectacular heroics, but has always been eclipsed by other goalkeepers. Was recently recalled to international duty with Israel.

PLAYER
KORSOS, Gyorgy
Midfielder, Hungarian, 180cm, 72kg
Born: 22.08.76, Gyor, Hungary
Clubs: Raba ETO (1992-93), Gyori (1993-99), Sturm Graz (Aut) (1999-)
Full international (Hungary) 17 caps/1 goal
• Promising young midfielder who made his debut for Hungary against Lithuania in May 1998, aged 21.
• Distinguished by his shoulder length blond hair.

PLAYER
KOSSOVSKYI, Vittaliy
Midfielder, Polish/Ukrainian, 172cm, 66kg
Born: 11.08.73, Ukraine
Clubs: Kyiv Dynamo
Full international (Ukraine) 24 caps/2 goals
• Fast, mobile midfielder who has made a big contribution to Kyiv Dynamo's Champions League campaign in recent seasons.

COACH
KOSTNER, Gunter-Lorenz
German
Born: 30.01.52
• Could not prevent Koln's relegation in 1997-98, but redeemed himself in 1999-2000 by helping newly-promoted little Munich club, Unterhaching to an excellent tenth place in the Bundesliga. His insistence that his team play hard but fair and do not show dissent has worked – no other Bundesliga side collected fewer bookings than Haching in 1999-2000.
• Made 91 Bundesliga appearances in a playing career for Borussia Monchengladbach, Bayer Uerdingen and Arminia Bielefeld.

Darko Kovacevic

• Coached Stuttgart, Stuttgarter Kickers Koln before returning to Unterhaching for a second spell in charge in 1998, having coached them from 1994 to October 1997.

PLAYER
KOUBA, Petr
Goalkeeper, Czech, 186cm, 82kg
Born: 28.09.69, Prague, Czech Republic
Clubs: Bohemians (1988-90), Sparta Prague (1991-96), Deportivo La Coruna (Spa) (1996-97), Kaiserslautern (Ger) (1997-98, loan), Viktoria Zizkov (1998-99, loan), Deportivo La Coruna (Spa) (1999-)
Full international (Czech Republic) 40 caps/0 goals
• One of the Czech Republic's heroes at the 1996 European Championships.
• Moved to Deportivo in Spain after the 1996 finals, but struggled to win a regular place, with **Jacques Songo'o** preferred by coach **John Toshack**.
• His Czech passport proved a major obstacle to progress at Deportivo, where Songo'o has dual French/Cameroon nationality, allowing him EC status.
• Spent 1997-98 season on loan to Kaiserslautern, but did not play. Returned home for the 1998-99 season, playing 11 games on loan for Viktoria Zizkov.
• Father Pavel was a keeper for Dukla Prague and won three caps for Czechoslovakia in the 1960s.
• International debut v Australia 30.01.91.

PLAYER
KOUMANTARAKIS, George
Forward, South African/Greek, 192cm, 82kg
Born: 27.03.74, Greece
Clubs: Manning Rangers (1997-98), Lucerne (Swi) (1998-99), Basle (Swi) (1999-)
Full international (South Africa) 2 caps/0 goals
• Quick-witted striker who born in Greece, brought up in South Africa and is now scoring goals in Swizerland with Basle. Two full caps for South Africa, where he used to star for Supersport United. Lots of star quality.

PLAYER
KOVAC, Nico
Midfielder, Croatian/German, 176cm, 72kg
Born: 15.10.71, Berlin, Germany
Clubs: Rapid Wedding, Hertha Zehlendorf, Hertha Berlin (1991-96), Bayer Leverkusen (1996-99), Hamburg (1999-)
Full international (Croatia) 9 caps/1 goal
• A Croat international of immense versatility: he can play at the back, right-or left-side of midfield and in attack. His best position, however, is as a raiding left wing-back and he has been compared to the Germany and Bayern Munich great Paul Breitner. Used to play alongside his brother **Robert Kovac** at Leverkusen.
• Surname pronounced Ko vatch.

PLAYER
KOVAC, Robert
Defender, Croatian/German, 182cm, 78kg
Born: 06.04.74, Berlin, German
Clubs: Rapid Wedding, Hertha Zehlendorf, Nurnberg (1995-96), Bayer Leverkusen (1996-)
Full international (Croatia) 9 caps/1 goal
• Tenacious defensive man-marker rated among the best in his position in German football.
• He does, however, have one failing, a tendency for foul play; in the 1999-2000 season he collected no less than 13 yellow cards.
• Surname pronounced Ko vatch.

PLAYER
KOVACEVIC, Darko
Forward, Yugoslav, 187cm, 79kg
Born: 18.11.73, Kovin, Yugoslavia
Clubs: Radnicki (1991-92), Proleter (1992-94), Red Star Belgrade (1994-96), Sheffield Wednesday (Eng) (1996), Real Sociedad (Spa) (1996-99), Juventus (Ita) (1999-)
Full international (Yugoslavia) 36 caps/5 goals
• Striker who was Juventus's record signing in 1999 when he joined from Real Sociedad for £14million.

• Has scored goals wherever he has played – apart from a year in Sheffield, where he had work permit problems and failed to settle.
• An excellent predatory striker who is strong in the air. Described by former Yugoslavia coach **Vujadin Boskov** as the best striker in Europe.
• Ex-Red Star Belgrade coach Ljubomir Petrovic: 'Darko is the sort of natural opportunist who will score goals anywhere. He's an impeccable finisher with either head or feet and crucially he has a steely determination in his character.'

PLAYER
KOVACEVIC, Sasa
Forward, Yugoslav, 169cm, 68kg
Born: 29.03.73, Zemun, Yugoslavia
Clubs: Obilic, CSKA Sofia (Bul), Obilic
Full international (Yugoslavia) 1 cap/0 goals
• Captain and key player in 1997-98, when Obilic took the Yugoslav championship title. Returned to the club after a short spell with CSKA Sofia.

PLAYER
KOVALEV, Sergiy
Midfielder, Ukrainian, 176cm, 70kg
Born: 21.11.71, Ukraine
Clubs: Shakhtar Donetsk
Full international (Ukraine) 10 caps/1 goal
• Another product of the Shakhtar youth school. Widely considered one of the best midfielders in Ukraine. A skilful organiser of fast counter-attacks.

PLAYER
KOVTUN, Andriy
Goalkeeper, Ukrainian, 182cm, 74kg
Born: 28.02.68, Ukraine
Clubs: Kyiv Dynamo, Vorskla Poltava
Full international (Ukraine) 2 caps/0 goals
• Former Kyiv Dynamo goalkeeper who found his home club in Poltava, where he is club captain and a big favourite with the fans.

PLAYER
KOVTUN, Yuri
Defender, Russian, 189cm, 77kg
Born: 05.01.70, Russia
Clubs: SKA Rostov (1989-90), Rostelmash (1991-93), Dinamo Moscow (1993-99), Moscow Spartak (1999-)
Full international (Russia) 31 caps/1 goal
• The toughest player in the Russian League, an unyielding player who has collected a record number of red and yellow cards.
• A member of Russia's squad at Euro 96.

PLAYER
KOZLOV, Alexei
Defender, Russian, 185cm, 77kg
Born: 18.08.75 Russia
Clubs: Dinamo Moscow (1994-98), Urulan (1999), Dinamo Moscow (2000-)
• Defender who rejoined Dinamo after a season with Uralan and is now a candiate to fill the right-back position in the Russian national team.

PLAYER
KOZNIKU, Ardian
Forward, Croatian, 178cm, 78kg
Born: 23.10.67, Dakovica, Croatia
Clubs: Pristina, Hajduk Split, Cannes (Fra), Le Havre (Fra), APOEL Nicosia (Cyp), Bastia (Fra), Dinamo Zagreb (formerly Croatia Zagreb)
Full international (Croatia) 7 caps/2 goals
• Striker who scored the first goal in the newly-formed Croatian League, for Hajduk against Istra Pula in 1992.
• Made his international debut against Slovakia in April 1994 and was a non-playing member of the Croatia squad at the 1998 World Cup.

PLAYER
KRALJ, Ivica
Goalkeeper, Yugoslav, 197cm, 93kg
Born: 26.03.73, Kotor, Yugoslavia
Clubs: Partizan Belgrade (1995-98), FC Porto

(Por) (1998-99), PSV Eindhoven (Hol) (1999-)
Full international (Yugoslavia) 36 caps/0 goals
• Seen as the future Yugoslav national keeper after three impressive seasons with Partizan. But poor form with Porto and PSV have reduced his stock, although he was first choice for the Yugoslavs at Euro 2000.
• Cites Bruce Grobbelaar as his idol.
• International debut: v Argentina, 28.12.96, in Mar del Plata (won 3-2).

PLAYER
KRAMER, Morten
Defender, Norwegian, 184cm, 78kg
Born: 10.07.67, Tromso, Norway
Clubs: Tromso (1986-)
• Veteran defender who has played more than 250 matches for his club. Strong in the air.

COACH
KRAUSS, Bernd
Austrian
Born: 08.05.57
• The ex-Austrian international full-back made his name as the highly-rated young coach of Borussia Monchengladbach, opting for an avant-garde defensive concept – by German tactical standards – of four men in a line and no sweeper. He continued to prosper while guiding Real Sociedad to third place in the Spanish Liga in 1997-98, but failed to build on that and was sacked in October 1999.
• Lasted only 67 days at Borussia Dortmund during the 1999-2000 season.

PLAYER
KRCMAREVIC, Slobodan
Forward, Yugoslav, 178cm, 74kg
Born: 12.06.67, Yugoslavia
Clubs: Panionios Nea Smyrni
• The Yugoslav striker could not stop scoring in the Cypriot League for Apollon Limasol and Anorthosis Famagusta – 31 goals in 1997-98 and

1998-99. But since arriving in Greece at Panionos in summer 1999, he has found a goalscorer's lot to be much tougher, scoring just seven times.

PLAYER
KREEK, Michel
Midfielder, Dutch, 184cm, 74kg
Born: 16.01.71, Amsterdam, Holland
Clubs: Ajax (1989-94), Padova (1994-96), Perugia (1996-97), Vitesse Arnhem (1997-)
Full international (Holland) 1 cap/0 goals
• Experienced midfielder whose career revived following a move back to Holland in 1997.
• Captain of Vitesse in their best-ever season (1998-99), earning a recall to the Dutch national side, almost four years after making his debut, against France in 1995.
• One of the first players to have his own Internet site.

PLAYER
KREMENLIEV, Emil
Defender, Bulgarian, 178cm, 74kg
Born: 13.08.69, Sofia, Bulgaria
Clubs: Slavia Sofia, Levski Sofia, Olympiakos (Gre), CSKA Sofia
Full international (Bulgaria) 27 caps/0 goals
• Right-sided defender who was a member of Bulgaria's squad at the 1994 World Cup and 1996 European Championship.
• Spent four seasons with his hometown club Slavia, before moving across town to Levski and then on to the Greek League. Now back home with CSKA Sofia.

PLAYER
KREUZER, Oliver
Defender, German, 182cm, 73kg
Born: 13.11.65, Mannheim, Germany
Clubs: Karlsruher (1985-91), Bayern Munich (1991-97), Basle (Swi) (1998-)
• One of the leading defenders in the Swiss League, where he is idolised by fans at Basle,

Runar Kristinsson

who have the best defence in the League.
• Hopes to continue playing till 2001 and then join the management at Basle.

PLAYER
KRISTAL, Marko
Midfielder, Estonian, 178cm, 79kg
Born: 02.06.73, Estonia
Clubs: Flora Talinn, Lahti (Fin) (1999-)
Full international (Estonia)
• A skilful midfielder or forward who, at 27, is only a few caps short of playing his 100th international match for Estonia.
• Moved to Lahti in Finland with his Flora team-mate Indrek Zelinski.
• A target for a number of foreign clubs in the past.

PLAYER
KRISTINSSON, Runar
Midfielder, Icelandic, 177cm, 72kg
Born: 05.09.69, Iceland
Clubs: KR (1987-94), Orgryte (Swe) (1994-97), Lillestrom (Nor) (1997-2000)
Full international (Iceland) 82 caps/3 goals
• Stylish Icelandic international and a regular goal scorer from his midfield position who looked set to go to a foreign club during the summer of 2000.
• Iceland's most capped player of all time who will be the key man in his country's 2002 World Cup qualifying campaign.

PLAYER
KRIVOKAPIC, Radovan
Midfielder, Yugoslavia
Born: 14.08.78, Yugoslavia
Clubs: Vojvodina Novi Sad
• Promising all-rounder who plays an attacking role in central midfield.
• Yugoslav Under-21 international.

PLAYER
KROGH, Mogens

Goalkeeper, Danish, 190cm, 84kg
Born: 31.10.63, Hjorring, Denmark
Clubs: Ikast (1990-91) Brondby (1991-)
Full international (Denmark) 10 caps/0 goals
• A faithful understudy to **Peter Schmeichel** down the years, first at Brondby and then with the Danish national team.
• A reliable keeper who has never realised his dream of playing in the English Premier League.
• A vociferous spokesman for the Danish players' union.

PLAYER
KRSTAJIC, Mladen

Defender, Yugoslavia, 191cm, 83kg
Born: 04.03.73, Zenica, Bosnia
Clubs: Partizan Belgrade, Werder Bremen (Ger) (2000-)
Full international (Yugoslavia) 4 caps/0 goals
• Tall, strong left-back who is excellent in the air and dangerous at set-pieces. Moved during the summer of 2000 to Germany's Werder Bremen.
• Candidate for Yugoslavia's Euro 2000 squad, but just missed the cut.

REFEREE
KRUG, Hellmut

German
Born: 19.05.56
• Works as a Sports educationalist.
• Awarded FIFA badge in 1991.

PLAYER
KRYSZALOWICZ, Pawel

Forward, Polish, 182cm, 77kg
Born: 23.06.74
Clubs: Gryf Slupsk, Zawisza Bydgoszcz, Amica Wronki (1994-)
Full international (Poland) 5 caps/0 goals
• A speedy and powerful striker who played in Poland's lower divisions before a move to Amica

five years ago. Won his first international cap as a substitute against Sweden in October 1999.

PLAYER
KUFFOUR, Samuel Osei

Defender, Ghanaian, 175cm, 75kg
Born: 03.09.76, Kumasi, Ghana
Clubs: Fantomas Kumasi, King Feisals Babies Club Kumasi, Torino (Ita), Bayern Munich (Ger) (1994-95), Nurnburg (Ger) (1995-96), Bayern Munich (Ger) (1996-)
Full international (Ghana)
• Everyone remembers the images of the devastated young Ghanaian stopper beating the ground with frustration after Bayern were undone in the 1999 Champions League by a pair of late, late Manchester United goals. A year on, Kuffour is just as intensely competitive and is earning even more praise for his man-marking abilities and boundless enthusiasm.
• Named the Bundesliga's best defender in the 1998-99 season.
• Played for Ghana at the 1991 Under-17 world championship and 1993 Under-20 World Youth Cup.
• His former Bayer coach **Giovanni Trapattoni** is a big fan. 'Kuffour is shaping up to be an out-standing centre-back. In terms of athleticism and commitment, he is is first rate. He sticks so close to his striker that you expect to follow his man to the opposition changing room at half-time.'
• 'When I was 13, I told my mum I didn't want to go to school. I wanted to play football. Then I was invited to the national camp. I had no boots and there was no help from anywhere. But we had a small black and white television. My mum sold it to buy my boots.'
• Surname pronounced Koo four.

PLAYER
KUHBAUER, Dietmar

Midfielder, Austrian, 175cm, 72kkg
Born: 04.04.71, Heiligenkreutz, Austria
Clubs: Admira Wacker (1990-92), Rapid Vienna

Sammuel Kuffour

(1992-97), Real Sociedad (Spa) (1997-2000-), Wolfsburg (Ger) (2000-)
Full international (Austria) 38 caps/4 goals
• Attacking midfielder who provides a useful link between midfield and attack.
• Twice voted Austrian Footballer of the Year.
• Moved to Spain in 1997 after the tragic death of his pregnant wife Michaela following a car crash. She had been driving to meet him from the airport when the accident happened and was on a life support machine for a considerable time afterwards.
• Moved to Germany in summer 2000.

PLAYER
KUHN, Allan
Midfielder, Danish, 184cm, 77kg
Born: 02.03.68, Denmark
Clubs: Lyngby (1990-97), Orgryte (Swe) (1997-)
• Former Danish Under-21 international. A left-sided midfielder with a good tactical grasp.

PLAYER
KUIVASTO, Toni
Defender, Finnish, 187cm, 82kg
Born: 31.12.75, Finland
Clubs: Ilves (1992-96), MyPa (1997-98), HJK Helsinki (1999-)
Full international (Finland) 15 caps/0 goals
• A strapping stopper, now in his second season with HJK Helsinki.

PLAYER
KUKA, Pavel
Forward, Czech, 183cm, 78kg
Born: 19.07.68, Prague, Czech Republic
Clubs: Slavia Prague 1989-93), Kaiserslautern (Ger) (1993-98), Nurnberg (Ger) (1998-99) Stuttgart (Ger) (1999-)
Full international (Czech Rep) 81 caps/26 goals
• Yes, the Czech international striker suffered his share of injuries in the 1999-2000 season and has always been a great maker of chances too.

But only one goal from 20 Bundesliga starts for Stuttgart was not good enough. On his day, his pace, sleight of foot and directness can trouble any defence.
• Surname pronounced Koo kah.

PLAYER
KULAWIK, Tomasz
Midfielder, Polish, 174cm, 69kg
Born: 04.05.69, Poland
Clubs: Boleslaw Bukowo, Gornik Wojkowice, Zaglebie Sosnowiec, Wislaw Krakow (1990-)
Full international (Poland) 2 caps/0 goals
• Creative attacking midfielder who has spent the last 10 years with Wisla.

PLAYER
KULIK, Vladimir
Forward, Russian, 180cm, 70kg
Born: 18.02.72, Russia
Clubs: Zenit St Petersburg (1991-96), CSKA (1997-)
• Striker who has been a regular scorer in the Russian League. A good finisher who is especially dangerous in the penalty box.

PLAYER
KULOVITS, Enrico
Midfielder, Austrian, 178cm, 72kg
Born: 29.12.74, Gussing, Austria
Clubs: Oberwart (1993-96), Grazer AK (1996-)
• Goalscoring midfielder who was born in Austria to Croatian parents, but is now a naturalised Austrian.
• Versatile all-rounder who can also play in defence.

PLAYER
KUQI, Shefki
Forward, Albanian/Finnish, 189cm, 88kg
Born: 10.11.79, Yugoslavia
Clubs: Lahti (1998-)
Full international (Finland) 9 caps/1 goal

• A bullish centre-forward who moved to Finland at the age of 12 from Kosovo.
• Now has a Finnish passport and has already made his international debut.
• Started out at MP Mikkeliu, then tried his luck at HJK Helsinki before loan spells in Scotland and Norway.

PLAYER
KURZ, Marco
Defender, German, 185cm, 76kg
Born: 16.05.69, Stuttgart, Germany
Clubs: Sindelfingen, Stuttgart (1989-90), Nurnberg (1990-94), Borussia Dortmund (1994-95), Schalke (1995-98), Munich 1860 (1998-)
• Tough-tackling, highly-competitive and mobile centre-back. A member of the Bundesliga-winning Dortmund squad of 1994-95 and played for Schalke when they beat Internazionale in the Final of the 1997 UEFA Cup.
• Surname pronounced Korts.

AGENT
KUTNER, Steve
• London-based agent whose clients include **Frank Lampard.**
• Contact: 6 Lansdowne Mews, London W11 3BH, England. Tel: 44 (0) 707 122 13 33.

PLAYER
KUZBA, Marcin
Forward, Polish, 183cm, 75kg
Born: 15.04.77, Torro Mazowieckia, Poland
Clubs: Gornik Zabrze, Auxerre (Fra) (1998-99), Lausanne (Swi) (1999-)
Full international (Poland) 2 caps/0 goals
• Polish striker now rebuilding his career at Lausanne after failing to make an impression at Auxerre. First made a name for himself at Gornik Zabrze.

PLAYER
KUZMANOVSKI, Stevica

Defender, Yugoslav, 178cm, 71kg
Born: 16.11.62, Tetovo, Macedonia
Clubs: Rad Belgrade, OFK Belgrade
• One of the best sweepers in the Yugoslavia
League. Now with OFK after playing for many
years with Rad.

PLAYER
KVARME, Bjorn Tore

Defender, Norwegian, 186cm, 81kg
Born: 17.06.72, Trondheim, Norway
Clubs: Rosenborg (1991-96), Liverpool (Eng)
(1996-99), St Etienne (Fra) (1999-)
Full international (Norway)
• Tough-tackling Norwegian who is a guarantee
of total commitment and unleashed energy
whether playing central defender, left or
right-back.
• Honesty is his policy; when his wife was ill last
season and he could not play, he refused to
accept his salary.

PLAYER
KVISVIK, Raymond

Midfielder, Norwegian, 179cm, 79kg
Born: 08.11.74, Norway
Clubs: Moss (1998), Brann (1998-)
Full international (Norway) 1 cap/0 goals
• Midfielder who scores spectacular goals with
his lethal left foot. Arrived from Moss a couple of
seasons ago and has won one cap for Norway.

L

LAAKSONEN, Pasi
Goalkeeper, Finnish, 191cm, 88kg
Born: 15.08.72, Finland
Clubs: PK-35 (1997-98), Jokerit (1999-)
Full international (Finland) 4 caps/0 goals
• A late starter in the Finnish top division who has attracted interest from clubs in England.
• Made his international debut for Finland in the 4-3 win over Belgium in August 1999.
• A tall and agile keeper who is arguably the best number one in the Finnish League.

PLAYER
LABANT, Vladimir
Midfielder, Slovak, 183cm, 72kg
Born: 08.06.74, Slovakia
Clubs: Ziliina, Dukla Banska Bystrica, Slavia Prague (Cze) (1997-99), Sparta Prague (Cze) (1999-)
Full international (Slovakia) 8 caps/2 goals
• Slovak defender who controversially moved to Sparta from fierce rivals Slavia Prague in the summer of 1999 but ironically broke his leg in his first game against his former team.

PLAYER
LABBADIA, Bruno
Forward, German, 178cm, 76kg
Born: 08.02.66, Darmstadt, Germany
Clubs: Schneppenhausen, Weiterstadt, Darmstadt (1994-87), Hamburg (1987-89), Kaiserslautern (1989-91), Bayern Munich (1991-94), Koln (1994-96), Werder Bremen (1996-97), Arminia Bielefeld (1998-)
Full international (Germany) 2 caps/0 goals
• Much-travelled veteran striker who has piled up the goals wherever he has played. The identikit penalty area predator, always on the lookout for a half-chance and blessed with very quick reactions and excellent heading abilty for a small man.
• In the 1999-2000 season, he reached the milestone of a century of Bundesliga goals.
• Surname pronounced La ba dee ah.

PLAYER
LACHUER, Yann
Defender, French, 176cm, 70kg
Born: 05.08.72, Champigny-sur-Marne, France
Clubs: Creteil, Auxerre, Chateauroux, Auxerre (1997-98), Paris Saint-Germain (1998-), Bastia (1999-2000, loan)
• After a disappointing 1998-99 season at Paris Saint-Germain, he spent 1999-2000 on loan to Bastia and saw his stock rise considerably with a string of top-quality performances for the Corsicans.
• A creative midfielder of substantial finesse and vision, he helped Chateauroux to the the Second Division title in 1997.
• Surname pronounced Lash were.

COACH
LACOMBE, Bernard
French
Born: 15.08.52
• Coach of Lyon for four seasons until the summer of 2000, when he stepped up aside to be replaced by **Jacques Santini**.
• Won 38 caps for France, scoring 12 goals and was a member of the 1984 European Championship-winning squad. Also played for Lyon, Saint Etienne and Bordeaux, winning the French League title in 1984, 1985 and 1987 with Bordeaux.
• When he retired as a player, he said he had no intention of going into coaching and spent seven years as Lyon's general manager. But he was finally persuaded by Lyon president Jean-Michel Aulas to take over the first-team reins in October 1996 and proved to be a good choice, qualifying the club for Europe in each of his four seasons at

Paul Lambert

the helm. But after much criticism in the 1999-2000 season – Lyon lost in the preliminary round of the Champions League and he was accused of orchestrating his players' violent play in a League game against Monaco – he decided to resign and is now an adviser to Aulas.

COACH
LACOMBE, Guy
French
Born: 12.06.55
• Highly-rated young coach who took Guingamp back up to the top flight in the 1999-2000 season and did so in some style, abandoning the Breton team's traditional defensive tactics and insisting on a decidedly more adventurous approach based on a short-passing game and lots on penetration on the flanks.
• A former youth team coach at Cannes (1990-95), he brought on such gems as future French internationals **Zinedine Zidane**, **Johan Micoud** and **Patrick Vieira**.
• A right-winger and then a midfielder for Nantes, Lens, Tours, Toulouse, Rennes, Lille, Cannes and a member of the French side which struck gold at the 1984 Olympics.

PLAYER
LACRUZ, Jesus Maria
Full name: Jesus Maria Lacruz Gomez
Defender, Spanish, 175cm, 72kg
Born: 25.04.78, Pamplona, Spain
• Promising youngster who is seen as having a great future at Bilbao, but has yet to find his best position, or establish himself as first choice.

PLAYER
LADIC, Drazen
Goalkeeper, Croatian, 184cm, 87kg
Born: 01.01.63, Croatia
Clubs: Varteks, Iskra Bugojno (Bos), Croatia (now Dinamo) Zagreb (1986-)
Full international (Croatia) 59 caps

• Veteran goalkeeper who has made almost 800 appearances for Dinamo Zagreb since 1986.
• Excellent shot-stopper, especially penalties, but does have a tendency to drop occasional clangers.
• First-choice keeper and record cap-holder for the Croatian national team. Played all of Croatia's seven games at the 1998 World Cup and all three at Euro 96.

COACH
LAGERBACK, Lars
Swedish
Born: 16.07.48
• Joint national coach of Sweden at Euro 200 and a key member of the Swedish national coaching set-up through the 1990s.
• After a modest career as a player and career in Sweden's lower divisions, he was taken on by the Swedish FA in 1990 and held a series of positions (youth, B team) before being appointed as assistant to **Tommy Soderberg** in 1998.
• Soderberg made him his full partner in late 1999.
• Has a degree in economics.

PLAYER
LAGONIKAKIS, Andreas
Midfielder, Greek, 176cm, 75kg
Born: 04.06.72, Greece
Clubs: Panathinaikos (1998-99), Rapid Vienna (Aut) (1999-)
• Midfield all-rounder who has strengthened Rapid since his summer 1999 move from Greece.

PLAYER
LALATOVIC, Nenad
Defender, Yugoslav, 188cm, 85kg
Born: 22.12.77, Belgrade, Yugoslavia
Clubs: Red Star Belgrade
• Talented left-back who can play also in central defence. Member of Yugoslavia's Under-21 team.

PLAYER
LAMA, Bernard
Goalkeeper, French, 183cm, 75kg
Born: 07.04.63, Saint-Symphorien, France
Clubs: Besancon (1983-84), Lille (1984-89), Metz (1989-90), Brest (1990-91), Lens (1991-92), Paris Saint-Germain (1992-97, West Ham (Eng) (1997-98), Paris Saint-Germain (1998-2000), Rennes (2000-)
Full international (France) 43 caps/0 goals
• Early in 2000, PSG informed their veteran keeper that the 1999-2000 campaign would be his last between the Parisian posts. But how they must regret that decision now. Lama was in sensational form in the second half of 1999-2000 and was the most accomplished custodian in the top flight.
• A keeper of great authority, sharp reflexes and a sure appreciation of angles.
• 'I certainly don't feel ready to be put out to grass. I think I can still be of service to a club with some ambition.'
• Pronounced Ber nar La mah.

PLAYER
LAMBERT, Paul
Midfielder, Scottish, 179cm, 69kg
Born: 07.08.69, Glasgow, Scotland
Clubs: St Mirren (1985-94), Motherwell (1993-96), Borrusia Dortmund (Ger) (1996-98), Celtic (1997-)
Full International (Scotland) 24 caps/1 goal
• Having collected a European Cup winners medal with Dortmund in 1997, Lambert has all the credentials to become a Scottish footballing legend, but he has found difficulty in translating such form into the differing environment of the game in his homeland, although injuries have played a part of late in his inconsistency.

PLAYER
LAMBOURDE, Bernard
Midfielder, French, 184cm, 85kg
Born: 11.05.71, Guadaloupe
Clubs: Cannes (1991-96), Angers (1994-95, loan), Bordeaux (1996-97), Chelsea (Eng) (1997-)

- Utility man who can fill a number of positions.
- Signed from Bordeaux for £1.6m in July 1997.

LAMOUCHI, Sabri
Midfielder, French, 175cm, 73kg
Born: 09.11.71, Lyon, France
Clubs: Ales (1991-94), Auxerre (1994-98), Monaco (1998-2000), Parma (Ita) (2000-)
Full international (France) 11 caps/1 goal
- In a previous sporting life at Auxerre, he was a refined attacking midfielder. But after moving to Monaco, the French international assumed ball-winning duties in the middle of the park and took to his new role with aplomb.
- 'I just want to play. Remember, I was one of the six unlucky players cut from the French squad on the eve of the last World Cup and it still hurts.'
- Surname pronounced La moo she.

LAMPARD, Frank
Midfielder, English, 183cm, 76kg
Born: 21.06.78, Romford, England
Clubs: West Ham (1995-), Swansea (1996, loan)
Full international (England) 1 cap/0 goals
- Promising young central midfielder with football in his blood: uncle is West Ham manager **Harry Redknapp**; father Frank (senior) played more than 600 games for West Ham.
- England Under-21 international.

LANDREAU, Mickael
Goalkeeper, French, 176cm, 77kg
Born: 14.05.79, Machecoul, France
Clubs: Nantes (1996-)
- A good bet to eventually succeed **Fabien Barthez** in the French national team goal. He has definitely been on the fast-track to stardom, making his first team debut for Nantes at the age of 17 and becoming the club's captain while still a teenager. The current French Under-21 keeper

is a prodigious talent, but he can nonetheless be prone to the odd boob.
- Pronounced Mee ky ell Lon dro.

LANG, Didier
Midfielder, French, 179cm, 77kg
Born: 15.12.70, Metz, France
Clubs: Metz, Sporting Lisbon (Por), Sochaux, Troyes (1999-)
- A left-sided midfielder with a defensive brief. But that does not prevent the Troyes skipper playing a full part when his side are in constructive mode. Delivers good free-kicks and corners and is strong in the air too.
- Surname pronounced Long.

LANGE, Rune
Forward, Norwegian, 190cm, 85kg
Born: 24.06.77, Norway
Clubs: Tromso (1997-)
- Much wanted striker who prior to the 2000 season had scored 47 goals in 61 Norwegian League matches.
- Has agreed personal terms with Rosenborg and is expected to move in the spring of 2001.

LANGE, Timo
Midfielder, German, 180cm, 79kg
Born: 19.01.68, Grevesmuhlen, Germany
Clubs: Stahl Brandenburg (1986-91), Hallescher (1991-92), Hansa Rostock (1992-)
- Always dependable right wing-back. Solid in the tackle, very disciplined and scurries forward to good effect. Lives and breathes Rostock's cause.
- Surname pronounced Lang ger.

LAPINSKI, Tomasz
Defender, Polish, 183cm, 79kg
Born: 01.08.69, Poland

Clubs: Widzew Lodz (1987-99), Legia (2000-)
Full international (Poland) 36 caps/0 goals
• Cultured central defender with a great vision. 'Favourite son' of Legia coach **Franciszek Smuda**. After spending 12 and a half years with Widzew (winning two championships in 1996 and 1997) he followed Smuda and joined Warsaw's side in January.
• Won a silver medal with the 1992 Olympic squad.

PLAYER
LAQUAIT, Bertrand
Goalkeeper, French, 184cm, 79kg
Born: 13.04.77, Vichy, France
Clubs: Nancy (1997-)
• Up-and-coming keeper with a growing band of admirers both within and outside the French borders. A French Under-21 cap, his brother Stephane was once a midfielder with Troyes.
• Surname pronounced Lak kay.

PLAYER
LARDIN, Jordi
Full name: Jordi Lardin Cruz
Midfielder, Spanish, 171cm, 64kg
Born: 04.0673, Barcelona, Spain
Clubs: Espanyol (1992-97), Atletico Madrid (1997-)
Full international (Spain) 3 caps/0 goals
• Exciting attacking midfielder blessed with skill and pace.
• Product of the Espanyol youth system who spent five seasons in Barcelona before Atletico won the battle to sign him.
• Former Under-21 international who got his break at senior level under **Jose Antonio Camacho**, his coach at Espanyol.

AGENT
LARIOS, Jean-Francois
• Paris-based agent who represents **Sylvain Wiltord**, **Salilou Lassisi** and **Herve Alicarte**.
• **Contact:** 43, rue Copernic, F-75116 Paris, France. Tel: 00 33 1 4500 5494.

PLAYER
LAROS, Louis
Midfielder, Dutch, 170cm, 69kg
Born: 12.03.73, Dordrecht, Holland
Clubs: Willem II (1990-92), MVV (1992-94), Willem II (1994-95), Vitesse Arnhem (1995-)
• A speedy winger who kept **Marc Overmars** out of the starting line-up at Willem II. Usually plays on the left. Is promising but not as consistent as Overmars.

PLAYER
LARRAINZAR, Domingo
Full name: Domingo Larrainzar Santamaria
Defender, Spanish, 181cm, 75kg
Born: 08.09.69, Pamplona, Spain
Clubs: Osasuna (1988-96), Malaga (1996-)
• Older brother of Bilbao defender **Inigo Larrainzar**, signed from Osasuna in 1996. Helped Malaga move from the third to first division in Spain.

PLAYER
LARRAINZAR, Inigo
Full name: Inigo Larrainzar Santamaria
Defender, Spanish, 173cm, 70kg
Born: 05.06.71, Pamplona, Spain
Clubs: Osasuna (1989-93), Athletic Bilbao (1993-)
Full international (Spain) 1 cap/0 goals
• Dependable right-back signed from Osasuna in 1993. Capped for Spain under **Javier Clemente**.

PLAYER
LARRAZABAL, Aitor
Full name: Aitor Larrazabal Bilbao
Defender, Spanish, 172cm, 68kg
Born: 21.06.71, Bilbao, Spain
Clubs: Athletic Bilbao (1989-)
• Left-sided defender who joined Athletic Bilbao as a schoolboy and has stayed for 11 seasons.
• A solid, dependable defender with a useful free-kick.
• Spanish Under-21 international.

Henrik Larsson

PLAYER
LARSSON, Henrik
Forward, Swedish, 178cm, 72kg
Born: 02.09.71, Helsingborg, Sweden
Clubs: Hogaborgs (1989-91), Helsingborg (1992-93), Feyenoord (Hol) (1993-97), Celtic (Sco) (1997-)
Full International (Sweden) 50 caps/11 goals
• Few would argue that Larsson is the finest player to have worn the Celtic shirt in recent years but his progress was halted by a horrific double leg break sustained during a UEFA Cup tie against Lyon. The dreadlocked Swede missed much of the 1999-2000 season because of the injury but made a strong recovery and even played for Sweden at Euro 2000.

PLAYER
LASLANDES, Lilian
Forward, French, 186cm, 82kg
Born: 04.09.71, Pauillac, France
Clubs: Saint-Seurin (1991-92), Auxerre (1992-97), Bordeaux (1997-)
Full international (France) 7 caps/3 goals
• Purists like to criticise Laslandes, sneering that he stands for the triumph of efficiency over style. But the fact remains that, first at Auxerre and then with Bordeaux, this hulking striker has led the line with honours and fully deserves his international caps. His touch and finishing ability have improved with each passing year and he is the most selfless of team-mates.
• 'I don't let the critics affect my morale. For several years now, a Laslandes has been worth between 10 and 15 goals and 6 to 10 assists.'
• Pronounced Lil lee on Las lond.

PLAYER
LASSEN, Peter
Forward, Danish, 193cm, 88kg
Born: 04.10.66, Denmark
Clubs: Frem (1991-93), Hvidore (1993-95), AB (1995-96), Eendracht Aalst (Bel) (1997-98), Silkeborg (1998-)
Full international (Denmark) 3 caps/1 goal

• A natural finisher whose goals for Silkeborg since returning home from Belgium have taken him to the brink of an international career aged 33.

PLAYER
LASSISI Saliou
Defender, Ivory Coast, 185cm, 80kg
Born: 15.08.78, Abidjan, Ivory Coast
Clubs: Rennes (Fra) (1995-98), Parma (Ita) (1998-), Sampdoria (Ita) (1998-99, loan)
Full international (Ivory Coast)
• Promising young defender who has yet to show his best form in Italy.

PLAYER
LATAL, Radoslav
Midfielder, Czech, 179cm, 72kg
Born: 06.01.70, Prague, Czech Republic
Clubs: Sigma Olomouc (1987-89), Dukla Prague (1989-91), Sigma Olomouc (1991-94), Schalke (1994-)
Full international (Czech Rep) 55 caps/3 goals
• Relatively unsung Czech international of no little adaptability who does a most efficient job whether at right-back or the right-side of midfield. Not a player for flights of fancy, just hard graft, drive and lots of intelligent support play.
• Pronounced Lah tal.

PLAYER
LATAPY, Russell
Midfielder, Trinidad & Tobago, 168cm, 64kg
Born: 02.08.68, Trinidad & Tobago
Clubs: Academica (Por) (1993-94), FC Porto (Por) (1994-96) Boavista (Por) (1996-98), Hibernian (Sco) (1998-)
Full international (Trinidad & Tobago)
• Midway through the 1999-2000 season, Hibs boss **Alex McLeish** was reported as unsatisfied with Latapy's work rate. The midfielder responded immediately with a series of breathtaking performances which have established him as one of the most exciting and entertaining players in the Scottish game at present.

PLAYER
LATUHERU, Bart
Forward, Dutch, 176cm, 69kg
Born: 08.11.65, Capelle aan den Ijssel, Holland
Clubs: Excelsior (1985-89), Vitesse Arnhem (1989-95), AZ (1996-98), NEC (1998-)
Full international (Holland) 1 cap/0 goals
• Veteran forward who is reaching the end of his career and has been a regular scorer in the Dutch first division.

PLAYER
LAUDRUP, Brian
Midfielder, Danish, 186cm, 82kg
Born: 22.02.69, Vienna, Austria
Clubs: Brondby (1986-89), Bayer Uerdingen (Ger) (1989-90), Bayern Munich (Ger) (1990-92), Fiorentina (Ita) (1992-93), Bayern Munich (Ger) (1993-94), Rangers (Sco) (1994-98), Chelsea (Eng) (1998), FC Copenhagen (1998-99), Ajax Amsterdam (Hol) (1999-2000)
Full international (Denmark) 82 caps/21 goals
• Hugely talented Danish international winger who announced his retirement in the summer of 2000.

COACH
LAUDRUP, Michael
Danish
Born: 15.06.64
• One of Denmark's greatest players who announced his retirement after the 1998 World Cup and was appointed as assistant to new national coach **Morten Olsen** in July 2000.

PLAYER
LAUREN
Full name: Lauren Bisan Etame-Mayer
Midfielder, Cameroonian, 180cm, 72kg
Born: 19.01.77, Lohdji Kribi, Cameroon
Clubs: Utrera (Spa) (1995-96), Sevilla B (Spa) (1996-97), Levante (Spa) (1997-98), Mallorca (Spa) (1998-2000), Arsenal (Eng) (2000-)
Full international (Cameroon)

- Hard-working midfielder who provides an attacking option on the right.
- One of the stars of Cameroon's 2000 African Nations Cup victory, despite speaking only Spanish and so unable to communicate in French with his team-mates.
- Born in Cameroon, but parents emigrated to Spain when he was young.
- Played in the last ever European Cup-winners Cup Final for Mallorca against Lazio.
- Linked with a host of big clubs in the summer of 2000, and eventually joined Arsenal for £5 million.

PLAYER
LAURENT, Pierre
Forward, French, 173cm, 65kg
Born: 13.12.70, Tulle, France
Clubs: Brive (1993-94), Bastia (1994-97), Leeds (1997), Bastia (1997-)
- Hails from the rugby-playing region of south-west France, but Laurent turned out to be a footballing winger, equally at ease on the right or left-flank.
- Now in his second spell at Bastia after an ill-fated transfer to Leeds United in 1997, but injury and the excellent form up front of Andre and **Frederic Nee** have restricted his opportunities.
- Surname pronounced Lor ron.

PLAYER
LAURSEN, Jacob
Defender, Danish, 183cm, 80kg
Born: 06.10.71, Vejle, Denmark
Clubs: Vejle (1990-1992), Silkeborg (1992-96), Derby (Eng) (1996-)
Full international (Denmark) 25 caps/0 goals
- Versatile player who can operate as a right wing-back or as a tough-tackling man-marker.
- Started career in midfield, but switched to defence by Silkeborg (and future Denmark) coach **Bo Johansson**.
- Retired from international football in spring 2000 to spend more time with his family.
- International debut: 08.01.95, v Saudi Arabia.

Garba Lawal

PLAYER
LAURSEN, Martin

Defender, Danish, 188cm, 79kg
Born: 26.02.77, Farvoug, Denmark
Clubs: Silkeborg (1995-98), Verona (Ita) (1998-2000), Parma (Ita) (2000-)
Full international (Denmark) 3 caps/0 goals
• Strrong, powerful central defender who has excelled in Italy, earning a move to Parma in summer 2000.

PLAYER
AUX, Phillipe

Goalkeeper, German, 182cm, 82kg
Born: 25.01.73, Germany
Clubs: Borussia Dortmund, Ulm (1994-)
• In his first season in the Bundesliga, 1999-2000, he proved beyond all doubt what a fine keeper he is and Ulm's eventual relegation was no reflection on him.
• Excels as a shot-stopper and in one-against-one situations.
• Surname pronounced Low kks.

PLAYER
LAVILLE, Florent

Defender, French, 185cm, 83kg
Born: 07.08.73, Valence, France
Clubs: Lyon (1993-)
• Resourceful, rugged centre-back who came up through the Lyon youth ranks and has represented France at Under-21 level. Does, however, have a tendency to lose self-control and make rash challenges. On intimate terms with the members of the country's disciplinary committee.
• Surname pronounced La veel.

PLAYER
LAWAL, Garba

Midfielder, Nigerian, 182cm, 73kg
Born: 22.05.74, Kaduna, Nigeria
Clubs: Roda JC (Hol) (1996-)
Full international (Nigeria)

• Solid performer who works hard in the Nigerian midfield, supporting the likes of **Finidi George** and **Austin Okocha**.
• Former accountancy student who gave up his academic ambitions to concentrate on football.
• Won an Olympic gold medal in 1996 and was a regular for Nigeria at France 98.

PLAYER
LAWAREE, Axel

Forward, Belgian, 176cm, 72kg
Born: 09.10.73, Belgium
Clubs: Seraing (1993-96), Standard Liege (1996-98), Sevilla (Spa) (1997-98), Mouscron (1998-)
• Striker who has had spells with Sevilla and several clubs in Belgium. A hard-working player but not very skilful. However, he still can be dangerous and formed a good pairing with **Marcin Zewlakow** at Mouscron after succeeding **Frederic Pierre**.

PLAYER
LAZETIC, Nikola

Midfielder, Yugoslav, 174cm, 69kg
Born: 09.02.78, Kosovska Mitrovica, Yugoslavia
Clubs: Red Star, Vojvodina, Obilic Belgrade, Fenerbahce (Tur) (2000-)
Full international (Yugoslavia) 1 cap/0 goals
• Attacking midfielder with great speed and good technique. Played at right wing-back with Red Star and Vojvodina, but is at his best when he plays behind the strikers.
• A possible transfer to Germany or Spain was on the cards for summer 2000, but he eventually joined Fenerbahce of Turkey.

PLAYER
LAZZARO LIUNI, Leandro

Forward, Argentinian, 186cm, 75kg
Born: 08.03.74, Argentina
Clubs: Slovan Liberec (Cze)
• Lazzaro Liuni's achievement of winning the Czech League's 'foreign player of the year' award

Frank
Leboeuf

for 1999-2000 has been likened to being the one-eyed man in the kingdom of the blind, but the powerful Argentinian striker has done as much as anyone to dispel the idea that imports can't adapt to life in the Czech League.

COACH
LE GUEN, Paul
French
Born: 01.03.64

• Former French national team skipper who, on ending an outstanding playing career as a defensive midfielder with Brest, Nantes and Paris Saint-Germain, was offered the job of coaching First Division Rennes and he immediately proved himself a more than safe pair of hands, leading the club to fifth place in the League in 1998-99.

• Won 17 caps for France.

• A taciturn Breton with a eye for fine tactical detail and, because he was playing up until recently, is something of a big brother to his players.

PLAYER
LE SAUX, Graeme
Defender, English, 178cm, 74kg
Born: 17.10.68, Jersey, Channel Islands
Clubs: Chelsea (1987-93), Blackburn (1993-97), Chelsea (1997-)
Full international (England) 35 caps/1 goal

• Left-back who began his career as a winger and is stronger going forward than defending.

• Rejoined Chelsea for £5million in August 1997 after four years with Blackburn, where he won the 1995 League title.

• Has faced criticism from fellow players who dislike his broadsheet-reading, antique-hunting lifestyle, but is as competitive on the pitch as the next player.

COACH
LE ROY, Claude
French
Born: 05.11.51
• A globetrotter who has coached French clubs
Amiens, Grenoble and Strasbourg, the Al-Shabab
club in the United Arab Emirates and the national
teams of Malaysia, Senegal and Cameroon – he
led the latter to the African Nations Cup in 1988
and again took charge of the Indomitable Lions at
France 98 – as well as occupying key management
roles at Paris Saint-Germain and Strasbourg.
• Joined Strasbourg in June 1998 as general
manager, but poor results led to him taking over
from sacked coach **Pierre Mankowski** early in
the 1999-2000 season.
• Scholarly and very media-friendly, his many
articles in the French press reveal a true
romantic of the game.
• Played for Rouen, Ajaccio, Avignon, and Laval.

PLAYER
LE TISSIER, Matthew
Midfielder, English, 186cm, 89kg
Born: 14.10.68, Guernsey, England
Clubs: Southampton (1986-)
Full international (England) 8 caps/0 goals
• One of the great unfulfilled talents of English
football whose loyalty to Southampton has
probably counted against his international career.
• Born in the Channel Islands and could have
played for France.

PLAYER
LEBEOUF, Frank
Defender, French, 184cm, 76kg
Born: 22.01.68, Marseille, France
Clubs: Hyeres (1986), Meaux (1986-88), Laval
(1988-91), Strasbourg (1991-96), Chelsea (1996-)
Full international (France) 30 caps/3 goals
• Cultured, accomplished centre-back who is
visionary in his ability to turn defence into attack.
A regular scorer from set-pieces.

• Made his debut for France while with
Strasbourg, but his international career took off
only following his £2.5million transfer to Chelsea.
• Played in France's 1998 World Cup Final victory
over Brazil following suspension to **Laurent Blanc**.
• International debut: 22.07.95, v Norway (0-0).

COACH
LECLERQ, Daniel
French
Born: 04.09.49
• Enjoyed a wonderful baptism as a first-team
coach, guiding Lens to the French title in 1997-
98. But resigned after Lens made a disastrous
start to the 1999-2000 season. However, he is now
keen for a comeback and unsucessfully proposed
his services to Marseille in summer 2000.
• Does not take himself too seriously and is a
coach with a distinct attacking philosophy, one
happy to include four forwards in his line-up.
• 'For me, football is only effective when it's
being enjoyed and that means going forward
whenever possible. I've always been convinced
you can build a competitive side by making
attacking football your number one priority.'
• Caught the eye in the 1970s with his long blond
mane and cultured ability as a playmaker or
libero for Lens and Marseille. Won the French
League in 1971 and 1972 with Marseille and the
French Cup in 1975 with Lens.

PLAYER
LEE, Robert
Midfielder, English, 179cm, 76kg
Born: 01.02.66, London West Ham, England
Clubs: Charlton (1983-92), Newcastle (1992-)
Full international (England) 21 caps/3 goals
• All-rounder who began as a winger at Charlton,
but was converted into a box-to-box central mid-
fielder by **Kevin Keegan** at Newcastle.
• Fell out with **Ruud Gullit**, but restored to the
Newcastle first-team by **Bobby Robson**.
• International debut: October 1994, v Romania.

COACH
LEEKENS, Georges
Belgian
Born: 18.05.49
- Best known for his time in charge of the Belgian national team, but now working as coach of Lokeren.
- A defender with Club Brugge who has coached a host clubs in Belgium and further afield. Was in charge at Kortrijk, Anderlecht, Cercle Bruges, Club Brugge, Mechelen, Trabzonspor and Charleroi, before leading Mouscron from the Belgian second division to the top of the first division.
- Appointed national coach in 1997 following the sacking of Wilfried Van Meir.

ADMINISTRATOR
LEFKARITIS, Marios
- President of the Cyprus Football Association and a leading member of the executive committee of UEFA.

PLAYER
LEGWINSKI, Sylvain
Midfielder, French, 185cm, 72kg
Born: 06.10.73, Clermont-Ferrand, France
Clubs: Clairefontaine, Monaco (1992-99), Bordeaux (2000-)
- Rather surprisingly off-loaded by Monaco midway through the 1999-2000 season. But has settled well at Bordeaux and certainly has much to offer, either in a holding role just in front of the back-line, or on the right-side of midfield. A man of simple tastes. While all his ex-Monaco teammates would turn up for training in the mandatory Porsches and Mercedes, he would arrive in an old banger.
- Surname pronounced Leg vin ski.

PLAYER
LEHKOSUO, Mika
Midfielder, Finnish
Born: 08.01.70
Clubs: HJK Helsinki, Perugia (Ita), HJK Helsinki

Roger Lemerre

Full international (Finland) 17 caps/1 goal.
• Hard-shooting midfielder, who spent some time with Italy's Perugia after starring for HJK in the Champions League, but is now back in Finland.
• A little slow but a steady performer nonetheless.

PLAYER
LEHMANN, Jens
Goalkeeper, German, 187cm, 80kg
Born: 10.11.69, Essen, Germany
Clubs: DJK Heisingen, SW Essen, Schalke (1991-98), Milan (Ita) (1998), Borussia Dortmund (1998-)
Full international (Germany) 12 caps/0 goals
• Probably wishes he had not gone too far in the self-promotion stakes, constantly proclaiming that he rather than **Oliver Kahn** should keep goal for Germany. The 1999-2000 season was a disappointing one for him, marked by a number of inexplicable blackouts: uncertainty when coming for crosses, mis-controlled back-passes and handling errors.
• His strong points are undoubtedly his reflexes, his good work on his line. In December 1997, he equalised with a last-minute header for Schalke against Dortmund.
• Moved to Italy in summer 1998, having won the UEFA Cup a year earlier, but had a miserable time.
• Surname pronounced Lay man.

PLAYER
LEIGHTON, Jim
Goalkeeper, Scottish, 185cm, 85kg
Born: 24.07.58, Johnstone, Scotland
Clubs: Aberdeen (1978-88), Manchester Utd (1988-92), Reading (1991-92), Dundee (1992-93), Sheffield Utd (1992-93), Hibernian (1993-97), Aberdeen (1997-)
Full international (Scotland) 91 caps/0 goals
• It looked like his long, and apparently unending career had finally come to a halt when new Dons boss **Ebbe Skovdahl** signed David Preece from Darlington in 1999 but an injury to Preece early in the season gave Leighton, 42, his chance, and he has held his place as first-choice keeper.

PLAYER
LEITNER, Jurgen
Midfielder, Austrian, 181cm, 76kg
Born: 18.10.75, Vienna, Austria
Clubs: Austria Vienna (1993-)
• Versatile all-rounder who can play in defensive midfield or, if needed, in the backline. On the fringes of the Austrian national squad under **Otto Baric**.

PLAYER
LEKO, Ivan
Midfielder, Croatian, 178cm, 75kg
Born: 07.02.78, Croatia
Clubs: Hajduk Split
Full international (Croatia) 3 caps/0 goals
• Highly promising young midfielder who has been linked with a move to Italy, but decided to stay in Croatia for a while longer. A strong all-rounder with a powerful free-kick.
• Captain of the Croatian Under-21 side.

PLAYER
LEMBI, Nzelo
Midfielder, DR Congo, 179cm, 75kg
Born: 25.08.75, DR Congo
Clubs: Lokeren (Bel) (1992-95), Club Brugge (1995-)
Full international (DR Congo)
• Powerful central defender with good technique although he can lack for pace at times.
• Considered one of the best defenders in the Belgian League, his future at Brugge was uncertain with his contract due to expire in summer 2000.

COACH
LEMERRE, Roger
French
Born: 18.06.41
• National coach of France who succeeded **Aime Jacquet** after the 1998 World Cup triumph.
• A prominent member of France's backroom staff during the World Cup, acting as number two to Jacquet.
• Prior to and even during Euro 2000, many in

the French media were questioning his ability to lead *Les Bleus*, suggesting he lacked authority, tactical nous and communication skills. But following his team's triumph at Euro 2000, where his astute team selections and assured handling of his squad came up trumps, only the final complaint remains.

• A former right-back or central defender for France, Sedan, Nantes, Nancy and Lens, he coached Red Star of Paris, Lens, Paris FC, Strasbourg and Esperance of Tunis and then spent a dozen years in charge of the French Military side – whom he guided to the world title in 1995 – before joining the backroom staff of then France coach **Aime Jacquet** early in 1998.

PLAYER
LENDVAI, Miklos
Midfielder, Hungarian, 178cm, 74kg
Born: 07.04.75, Zalaegerszeg, Hungary
Clubs: Zalaegerszegi (1991-96), Bordeaux (Fra) (1996-97), Lugano (Swi) (1997-98), Ferancvaros (1998-99), Geel (Bel) (1999-)
Full international (Hungary) 9 caps/0 goals
• Hungarian midfielder who returned to the national team thanks to his performances in Belgium. Despite that, his newly promoted side Verbroedering Geel were relegated after only one season. Could go to another Belgian first division club for the 2000-2001 season.
• A former striker with Ferencvaros.

PLAYER
LENGYEL, Roman
Midfielder, Czech, 191cm, 86kg
Born: 03.11.78, Czech Republic
Clubs: Ceske Budejovice, Sparta Prague (2000-)
• Young midfielder who kept his place in the Czech squad that won silver at the 2000's European Under-21 Championships despite appearing infrequently for Sparta since his move from Ceske Budejovice in the 1999-2000 Czech season's winter break.

PLAYER
LENNON, Neil
Midfielder, Northern Irish, 177cm, 78kg
Born: 25.06.71, Lurgan, Northern Ireland
Clubs: Manchester City (1989-90), Crewe Alexandra (1990-96), Leicester (1996-)
Full international (N. Ireland) 33 caps/2 goals
• Feisty central midfielder who has played a 5crucial playmaking role in Leicester's success in recent seasons.
• Signed an improved contract with Leicester in August 2000, turning down an offer from former manager **Martin O'Neill** at Celtic.

AGENT
LENS, Siegfried
• Dutch agent whose main client is **Patrick Kluivert**.
• **Contact:** Pro Athlete Sports Management, Planetenweg 27, NL-2132 HN Hoofddorp, Netherlands. Tel: 00 31 (0) 23 555 45 990.

PLAYER
LENTINI, Gianluigi
Forward, Italian, 181cm, 79kg
Born: 27.03.69, Carmagnola, Italy
Clubs: Torino (1985-88), Ancona (1988-89), Torino (1989-92), Milan (1992-96), Atalanta (1996-97), Torino (1997-)
Full international (Italy) 13 caps/0 goals
• Winger who became the world's most expensive player in summer 1992 when he joined Milan for £13million, a figure that some have alleged should not have counted as a world record because it also covered Lentini's wages, not just the transfer fee.
• Was set for a glorious career at the top of Serie A, but never recovered from a crash in 1994, when he wrote off his sports car in a high-speed smash and spent the following months in a coma.
• Recovered some form on loan to Atalanta and rejoined Torino at the end of the 1996-97 season. Hinted at retirement during the summer of 2000.

PLAYER
LEO FRANCO
Full name: Leonardo Neoren Franco
Goalkeeper, Argentinian, 189cm, 79kg
Born: 20.05.77, San Nicolas, Argentina
Clubs: Independiente (1995-97), Merida (Spa) (1997-98), Mallorca (Spa) (1999-)
• Young keeper who played regularly for Mallorca in the 1999-2000 season following a lengthy ban on first-choice keeper **German Burgos**.
• Member of Argentina's winning squad at the 1997 world Under-20 championships in Malaysia.

PLAYER
LEONARD, Philippe
Defender, Belgian, 185cm, 77kg
Born: 14.02.74, Liege, Belgium
Clubs: Standard Liege, Monaco (Fra)
Full international (Belgium) 18 caps/0 goals
• Unassuming character who was consistency personified in the Monaco left-back spot last season and deservedly forced his way back into the Belgian national team reckoning.
• Once was rather happy-go-lucky in his approach to the game, but has become more applied and disciplined in recent years, working particularly hard on improving his right foot. Boasts a fearsome shot from distance.
• Surname pronounced Lay oh nard.

PLAYER
LEONARDO
Midfielder, Brazilian, 177cm, 71kg
Born: 05.09.69, Niteroi, Brazil
Clubs: Flamengo (1987-1989), Sao Paulo (1990-1991), Valencia (1991-1993), Sao Paulo (1993), Kashima Antlers (1994-96), Paris Saint-Germain (1996-97), Milan (1997-)
Full international (Brazil)
• Left-sided player who played left-back for Brazil at the 1994 World Cup but was his country's main playmaker four years later in France.
• Notorious for being sent off at USA 94 for a

totally uncharacteristic elbowing of Tab Ramos.
• An intelligent, eloquent (speaks five languages fluently) and often opinionated player off the pitch. Gave journalists at the 1997 Copa America a 10-minute lecture on the role of the sports media.
• Revived his career at PSG after two seasons out of the spotlight in Japan.
• Has won League titles on three continents, in Brazil, Japan and Italy.

PLAYER
LEONHARDSEN, Oyvind
Midfielder, Norwegian, 177cm, 73kg
Born: 25.06.70, Kristiansund, Norway
Clubs: Molde (1989-91), Rosenborg (1992-94), Wimbledon (Eng) (1994-97), Liverpool (Eng) (1997-99), Tottenham (Eng) (1999-)
Full international (Norway) 66 caps/16 goals)
• Combative, hard-working midfielder who made his Norway debut aged 19 in **Egil Olsen**'s first game in charge of Norway.
• Has found a new lease of life at Tottenham after a move from Wimbledon to Liverpool failed to work out.
• Missed Euro 2000 through injury.
• International debut: 31.10.90, v Cameroon.

AGENT
LERBY, Soren
• Former Danish international.
• **Contact:** Proactive Sports Management, Pieter Braaijweg 53, NL-1099 DK Amsterdam, Netherland. Tel: 00 31 206 263 335.

PLAYER
LERINC, Leo
Midfielder, Yugoslav, 189cm, 79kg
Born: 30.12.75, Novi Sad, Yugoslavia
Clubs: Vojvodina Novi Sad, Red Star Belgrade
• Tall, skilful attacking midfielder, who put in some great performances in the summer of 1998, when Vojvodina reached the InterToto Cup semi-finals.

PLAYER
LEROY, Jerome
Midfielder, French, 183cm, 71kg
Born: 04.11.74, Bethune, France
Clubs: Paris Saint-Germain, Laval, PSG (1996-99), Marseille (2000-)
• Performed well on the right-side of the Marseille midfield following a transfer from Paris Saint-Germain mid-way through last season. Allies good ball skills and elusive running to an intense competitive spirit, though he must cut out the bad boy act – he was sent off three times in 1999-2000.
• Surname pronounced Ler wah.

PLAYER
LEROY, Laurent
Forward, French, 178cm, 64kg
Born: 16.04.76, Saint-Saulve, France
Clubs: Valenciennes, Cannes, Servette (Swi) (1998-99), Paris Saint-Germain (1999-)
• Nimble, gutsy attacker who was one of the revelations of the 1999-2000 French championship, forming an extremely complimentary front-line partnership with the Brazilian, **Christian** and developing nicely as a goalscorer. His speciality is the overhead kick.
• A Swiss champion with Servette in 1998-99.
• Surname pronounced Ler wah.

BUSINESS
LESCURE, Pierre
• President of French broadcaster Canal Plus, the owners of Paris Saint-Germain.

PLAYER
LESIAK, Andrzej
Defender, Polish, 191cm, 87kg
Born: 21.05.66, Zary, Poland
Clubs: Katowice (1991-92), Tirol Innsbruck (Aut) (1992-94), Dynamo Dresden (Ger) (1994-95), SV Ried (Aut) (1995-96), Rapid Vienna (Aut) (1996-97), Salzburg (1997-98), SV Ried (Aut) (1999-)

Full international (Poland) 18 caps/1 goal
• Much-travelled Polish international defender, who is now is his second spell at SV Ried in Austria.

PLAYER
LETIZI, Lionel
Goalkeeper, French, 187cm, 80kg
Born: 28.05.73, Nice
Clubs: Nice (1991-96), Metz (1996-)
Full international (France) 2 caps/0 goals
• French international keeper with sharp reflexes, cross-catching ability and a good command of his box. But the flip side is a tendency to make crass mistakes. Comes from a goalkeeping family; his father and grandfather were keepers with top clubs on the Cote d'Azur.
• Pronounced Lee oh nel Le tee zee.

REFEREE
LEVNIKOV, Nikolai
Russian
Born: 15.05.56
• Awarded his FIFA badge in 1992.

PLAYER
LIBEROPOULOS, Nikos
Forward, Greek, 186cm, 79kg
Born: 04.08.75, Greece
Clubs: Panathinaikos (1996-)
Full international (Greece) 23 caps/6 goals
• One of the great hopes of Greek football, the Panathinaikos attacker is at his most dangerous when given licence to roam just behind the main strikers. Has quick feet, lots of creativity and is a cool converter of chances.
• Rumoured to be on the verge of a move abroad in the summer of 2000, but instead accepted an improved contract with 'Pana'.

COACH
LIENEN, Ewald
German
Born: 28.11.53
• Highly-rated coach of Koln since May 1999 who oversaw their promotion to the German Bundesliga after they finished runaway leaders of the second division.
• In the 1970s, he was a long-haired Marxist-anarchist with Borussia Monchengladbach but he now preaches discipline to his players.
• Teamwork and discipline are his watchwords. No shop floor democracy; he's the boss.
• Played 333 Bundesliga matches for Monchengladbach, Arminia Bielefeld and Duisburg.
• Took charge of Duisburg amateurs in 1989 and the senior side in 1993, before moving to Tenerife in 1995 and Hansa Rostock in 1997.

PLAYER
LIMA, Francesco
Midfielder, Brazilian, 180cm, 82kg
Born: 17.04.71, Manhaus, Brazil
Clubs: Uniao Sao Joao (1995), Sao Paulo (1995), Gazientepsor (Tur) (1996-98), FC Zurich (Swi) (1998-99), Lecce (Ita) (1999-2000), Bologna (Ita) (2000-)
• Midfield all-rounder, who can create goals as well as break down opposition attacks. He impressed for Lecce in the 1999-2000 season and secured a move to Bologna in the summer of 2000.

PLAYER
LINARES, David
Midfielder, French, 181cm, 71kg
Born: 05.11.77, Venissieux, France
Clubs: Lyon
• Right-sided midfielder and former French youth international who has established himself in the Lyon ranks over the past few seasons.

PLAYER
LINCAR, Eric
Midfielder, Romanian, 180cm, 68kg
Born: 16.10.78, Oradea
Clubs: Bihor Oradea, Viitorul Oradea, Steaua Bucharest, Bordeaux (Fra), Steaua Bucharest (1997-)
Full international (Romania) 3 caps/0 goals
• Much-travelled midfielder who is now back in Romania after a brief spell in France with Bordeaux.
• Made his international debut for Romania against Belgium in April 1999.
• A member of the Romania's squad at Euro 2000.

PLAYER
LINDBERG, Janne
Midfielder, Finnish, 171cm, 72kg
Born: 24.05.66 Finland
Clubs: Kumu (1990), Haka (1991), MyPa (1992-94), Greenock Morton (Sco) (1994-98), MyPa (1998-)
Full international (Finland) 34 caps/1 goal
• Former Finnish international who is still going strong despite a recent long-term lay-off with an ankle injury.
• Hard-working, and also quite tough.
• Back in Finland with MyPa after spells in Scotland with Morton and in Germany with Mannheim.

PLAYER
LINDELOF, Samuli
Forward, Finnish, 178cm, 80kg
Born: 18.01.76, Finland
Clubs: Inter Turku (1995-)
• Potentially one of Finland's best attackers, whose career has been hindered by injuries.
• A strong, skilful player, who has stayed loyal to Inter even when they were relegated in 1997.

PLAYER
LINDEROTH, Tobias
Midfielder, Swedish, 174cm, 69kg
Born: 21.04.79, Sweden
Clubs: Hassleholms (1995), Elfsborg (1996-97),

Jari Litmamen

Stabaek (1999-)
• Young midfielder who left Swedish football to play under his father, coach **Anders Linderoth**. Loves to go forward and score goals.

PLAYER
LINKE, Thomas
Defender, German, 182cm, 77kg
Born: 26.12.69, Sommerda, Germany
Clubs: Rotweiss Erfurt (1988-92), Schalke (1992-98), Bayern Munich (1998-)
Full international (Germany) 17 caps/0 goals
• Ever-improving centre-back who has been carving out a niche for himself in the German national team in the last year or two. He may not be particularly tall and does not appear to pump iron, but still gets the job done. An extremely determined character whose timing in the tackle and in the air is usually exemplary.
• Surname pronounced Link ker.

COACH
LIPPI, Marcelo
Italian
Born: 12.04.48
• Dapper Paul Newman lookalike with a penchant for slim cigars and Serie A success.
• As a player, Lippi spent almost his entire career at Sampdoria, finishing with one season at Lucchese. He scored seven goals in 239 Serie A appearances and appeared in two B internationals for Italy.
• Began his coaching career on the staff at Sampdoria (1984-85), moving on to Pontedera (1985-86) Siena (1986-87), Pistoiese (1987-88), Carrarese (1988-89), Cesena (1989-91), Lucchese (1991-92), Atalanta (1992-93) and Napoli (1993-94).
• At all his clubs, he earned a reputation for teams that worked hard off the ball and were tactically flexible.
• His reputation was sealed when he led two teams with limited resources, Atalanta and Napoli, to seventh and sixth place respectively in 1993 and 1994, earning a call to Juventus.

• Won the double in his first season in Turin, and went on to win the Champions League in 1996, beating Ajax on penalties, the 1996 European Supercup and the 1996 World Club Cup.
• Quit Juventus in spring 1999 rather than see out his contract to the end of the season. Made a controversial switch to Internazionale for the 1999-2000 season.

PLAYER
LISZTES, Kristijan
Midfielder, Hungarian, 179cm, 72kg
Born: 02.07.76, Budapest, Hungary
Clubs: Ferencvaros (1993-96), Stuttgart (Ger) (1997-)
Full international (Hungary) 14 caps/0 goals
• Immensely-gifted Hungarian playmaker blessed with bewitching ball-skills and marvellous distribution. But he does tend to drift out of games and physically he is not the strongest.
• Surname pronounced Lish tes.

PLAYER
LITMANEN, Jari
Midfielder, Finnish, 181cm, 82kg
Born: 20.02.71, Lahti, Finland
Clubs: Reipas (1987-90), HJK (1991), MyPa (1992), Ajax (Hol) (1992-99), Barcelona (Spa) (1999-)
Full international (Finland) 62 caps/15 goals
• Attacking midfielder who was the creative heart of Ajax's triumphs on the European stage in the mid-1990s.
• A useful ice hockey player as a teenager but followed in his father's footsteps by opting for a footballing career, starting at Reipas Lahti aged 15.
• Joined Ajax for £200,000 in 1992 and went on to score 91 goals in 159 matches.
• Finland's most celebrated footballer and the country's all time top-scorer at international level.
• Joined Barcelona on a free transfer in 1999, but encountered opposition because he was seen to be a favourite of coach **Louis Van Gaal**.
• Injuries restricted his role in Barcelona's 1999-2000 to a minimal one.

• Shies away from publicity and refuses to lead a celebrity lifestyle. 'I understand my responsibility as a media personality. But there are things that I believe belong only to myself. That is where I try to draw the line.'
• Nicknamed 'Litti'.

PLAYER
LITOS
Full name: Carlos Manuel de Oliveira Magalhaes
Defender, Portuguese, 185cm, 81kg
Born: 25.02.74, Paranhos, Portugal
Clubs: Campomaiorense (1992-93), Boavista (1993), Estoril (1993-94), Rio Ave (1994-95), Boavista (1995-)
Full international (Portugal) 2 caps/0 goals
• Central defender who has been a key figure for Boavista under coach **Jaime Pacheco**.

PLAYER
LIZARAZU, Bixente
Defender, French, 169cm, 72kg
Born: 09.12.69, Saint-Jean-de-Luc, France
Clubs: Bordeaux (1988-96), Athletic Bilbao (Spa) (1996-97), Bayern Munich (Ger) (1997-)
Full international (France) 58 caps/2 goals
• Pacy and enterprising left-back or wing-back who never misses an opportunity to go forward in support of the attack, working his way forward with neat one-twos and either delivering an inviting low pull-back or cutting inside for a shot at goal. His defensive work is up to the mark too; he is a crisp tackler and solid cover man.
• From the French Basque country, his second love is surfing.
• Pronounced Bee sent tee Lee zah rah zoo.

AGENT
LJUNG, Roger
Swedish
• Former player turned agent.
• **Contact:** Fagelsangsvagen 10, S-237 34 Bjarred, Sweden, Tel: 00 46 46 291 921.

Attilio Lombardo

PLAYER
LJUNGBERG, Fredrik
Midfielder, Swedish, 176cm, 75kg
Born: 16.04.77, Sweden
Clubs: Halmstad (1994-98), Arsenal (Eng) (1998-)
Full international (Sweden) 17 caps/2 goals
• Livewire attacking midfielder who combines pace and technique on the left flank, though he can also play on the right.
• Won the Swedish League with Halmstad.
• Scored four mins, 42 seconds into his Arsenal debut, against Man United on 20.09.98.
• International debut: 24.01.98, v US (lost 1-0).

PLAYER
LLORENS, Carlos
Full name: Carlos Llorens Mestre
Defender, Spanish, 178cm, 73kg
Born: 01.09.69, Alicante, Spain
Clubs: Valencia B (1990-91), Tomelloso (1991-92), Cartagena (1992-93), Elche (1993-94), Levante (1994-95), Lleida (1995-97), Leganes (1997-98), Rayo Vallecano (1998-)
• Much-travelled all-rounder who can play in defence of midfield and was a key member of the Rayo Vallecano team which won promotion to the Spanish first division in 1999.

COACH
LOBANOVSKY, Valeri
Ukrainian
Born: 06.01.39
• The most successful coach in the history of Soviet football, winning more titles than any other.
• Guided Kyiv Dynamo to two European Cup-winners Cups in 1975 and 1986, the best European record of any Eastern European side.
• Coach of the Soviet team which lost to Holland in the Final of the 1988 European Championship.
• Returned from a lucrative spell of coaching national teams in the Middle East (UAE and Kuwait) to transform an average Kyiv team into one of the best in Europe.

- 'Lobanovsky creates a psychology of winners.' **Grigoriy Surkis**, Kyiv Dynamo president.
- Suffered from ill-health in recent years (a heart condition attributed to his alleged fondness for alcohol) but still made himself available to coach the Ukraine national team for the 2002 World Cup qualifiers after the resignation of **Josef Szabo**.

PLAYER
LOBONT, Bogdan
Goalkeeper, Romania, 183cm, 75kg
Born: 18.01.78, Hunedoara, Romania
Clubs: Corvinul Hunedoara, Rapid Bucharest (1999-99), Ajax Amsterdam (Hol) (2000-)
Full international (Romania) 11 caps/0 goals
- Highly promising young keeper who came to the fore in the 1998-99 season, winning the Romanian League with Rapid and earning a transfer to Amsterdam.
- Started with hometown club Corvinul, switching to Dinamo in August 1997 and winning the Romanian Cup in the 1997-98 season.
- Capped by Romania at Under-18 and Under-21 level. International debut: 02.09.98, v Liechtenstein (won 7-0).
- A member of Romania's squad at Euro 2000, where he was number two to **Bogdan Stelea**

PLAYER
LOCATELLI, Tomas
Forward, Italian, 175cm, 72kg
Born: 09.06.76, Bergamo, Italy
Clubs: Atalanta (1992-95), Milan (1995-96), Udinese (1997-)
Full international (Italy) 2 caps/0 goals
- Highly promising young midfielder who has not yet lived to the great promise he showed while graduating from the Atalanta youth system.
- Moved to Milan in 1995, but he could not establish himself in a troubled side and went on loan to Udinese, who eventually bought his contract outright.
- A left-footed playmaker with great ability.

PLAYER
LOKO, Patrice
Forward, French, 177cm, 72kg
Born: 06.02.70, Sully-sur-Loire, France
Clubs: Nantes (1988-95), Paris Saint-Germain (1995-99), Lorient (1999), Montpellier (1999-)
Full international (France) 26 caps/7 goals
- The best days of this veteran French international striker are clearly behind him. But he still has much to offer in terms of intelligent movement, will-to-win and finishing nous.
- Was the French First Division's top scorer with 22 goals for Nantes in their championship-winning season of 1994-95. Subsequently suffered from personal and emotional problems while in Paris, but has got his life and career back on track at Montpellier.

PLAYER
LOKVENC, Vratislav
Forward, Czech, 196cm, 89kg
Born: 27.09.73, Czech Republic
Clubs: Sparta Prague, Kaiserslautern (Ger) (2000-)
Full international (Czech Republic) 31 cap/3 goals
- Tall, clumsy-looking striker who is more skilful than his appearance would suggest.
- Lokvenc has continued to develop his game in the 1999-2000 season and under Czech coach **Jozef Chovanec** has become a regular member of the national team squad.

PLAYER
LOMAS, Steve
Midfielder, Northern Irish, 182cm, 74kg
Born: 18.01.74, Hanover, Germany
Clubs: Manchester City (1991-97), West Ham (1997-)
Full international (Northern Ireland) 35 caps/2 goals
- Strong, committed central midfielder whose leadership skills have been put to good effect as captain of both club and country.

PLAYER
LOMBARDO, Attilio
Midfielder, Italian, 175cm, 72kg
Born: 06.01.66, Santa Maria La Fossa, Italy.
Clubs: Pergocrema (1983-85), Cremonese (1985-89), Samdoria (1989-95, Juventus (1995-97), Crystal Palace (1997-98), Lazio (1999-)
Full international (Italy) 18 caps/3 goals
• One of the most famous bald heads in European football.
• Made his name as a flying winger with Sampdoria, winning the Italian League in 1991, and joining Juve in 1995 in time to win the Champions League (1996) and another title (1997).
• Moved to London in summer 1997 and played a spirited role in Crystal Palace's relegation battle, even stepping in as caretaker manager for the final matches.
• Stayed with Palace following relegation but returned to Italy in January 1991, appearing as a substitute for Lazio the last-ever Cup-winners Cup Final.
• Nicknamed 'Popeye' because of his bald head.

PLAYER
LONDONO, Oscar
Midfielder, French/Colombian, 173cm, 65kg
Born: 07.02.71, France
Clubs: Lausanne (Swi) (1991-94), Grenchen (Swi) (1994-95), Kriens (Swi) (1995-96), Lausanne (Swi) (1996-2000), Servette (Swi) (2000-)
• Skilful, lively Franco-Colombian schemer who joined Servette from Lausanne in summer 2000.
• A fast-improving left-sided performer, he can play full-back if required. Used to live in France and commute to Lausanne training sessions every day on a steamer across Lake Geneva.
• About to acquire Swiss citizenship.

PLAYER
LONFAT, Johan
Midfielder, Swiss, 178cm, 69kg
Born: 11.09.73, Switzerland

Clubs: Sion (1992-98), Servette (1998-)
Full international (Switzerland) 6 caps/0 goals
• Intelligent defensive midfielder whose great work in Servette's title-winning campaign of 1998-99 catapulted him into the Swiss squad.
• An excellent passer of the ball.

PLAYER
LONSTRUP, Christian
Defender, Danish, 186cm, 82kg
Born: 04.04.71, Copenhagen, Denmark
Clubs: Boldklub (1990), B1903 (1991-92), FC Copenhagen (1993-96), Cagliari (Ita) (1996-98), FC Copenhagen (1998-)
• Elegant former midfield playmaker who has been converted into a sweeper during his second spell at FC Copenhagen.
• A late developer who played for Denmark against Thailand in the King's Cup in 1996 following the withdrawal of **Michael Laudrup**.
• Returned to Copenhagen after a spell in Italy with Cagliari, having played for both Boldklub and B1903, the two clubs which merged to form FC Copenhagen.

COACH
LOOSE, Ralf
• National coach of Liechtenstein.

PLAYER
LOPEZ, Juan Manuel
Full name: Juan Manuel Lopez Martinez
Defender, Spanish, 183cm, 78kg
Born: 03.09.69, Madrid, Spain
Clubs:: Atletico Madrileno (1990-91), Atletico Madrid (1991-)
Full international (Spain) 11 caps/0 goals
• Versatile defender who can play at right-back or central defence.
• Olympic champion in 1992 and a Spanish League and Cup winner with Atletico in 1996.
• Called up to the Spanish squad for Euro 96 as a late replacement for the injured **Albert Ferrer**.

A one-club man who was promoted from
nursery side Atletico Madrileno to Atletico's
senior squad in 1991.
  Most effective as a central man-marker,
although his disciplinary record is poor. Attempts
to use him as a midfield ball-winner have failed.

REFEREE
LOPEZ NIETO, Antonio Jesus
Spanish
Born: 25.01.58
  Lists his occupation as a manufacturer.
  Awarded his FIFA badge in 1993.

PLAYER
LOPEZ REKARTE
Full name: Aitor Lopez Rekarte
Defender, Spanish, 173cm, 71kg
Born: 18.08.75, San Sebastian, Spain
Clubs: Real Sociedad (1994-)
  Mistake-prone defender who has become
unpopular due to a series of absurd sendings-off.
• Spanish Under-21 international.

COACH
LORANT, Werner
German
Born: 21.11.48
• The boss of 1860 Munich since July 1992, the
former Eintracht Frankfurt midfielder is the
second longest-serving coach in the Bundesliga
today and has built a side in his own image:
aggressive and direct.
• A character with a hair-trigger temper and just
as likely to clash with match officials, his players
or members of his own coaching staff. Once
performed a bungee jump off the Broadcast
Tower in Hamburg.
• Played more than 300 Bundesliga for a variety
of clubs, including Borussia Dortmund, Rot-Weiss
Essen, Saarbrucken, Eintracht Frankfurt and Schalke.
• Began his coaching career with Schweinfurt in
1986, moving on Viktoria Aschaffenburg in 1990.

PLAYER
LOREN
Full name: Lorenzo Juarro Garcia
Defender, Spanish, 182cm, 80kg
Born: 07.10.66, Membrillos, Spain
Clubs: Real Sociedad (1984-89), Athletic Bilbao
(1989-91), Burgos (1991-93), Real Sociedad (1993-)
• Started out as a striker, but was converted to a
defender at Sociedad. Had an unsuccessful spell
at Bilbao, then spent two years helping Burgos to
stay in the top flight, before returning to Sociedad.

COACH
LORENS, Edward
Polish
Born: 28.12.53
• Coach of Ruch Chorzow.
• Played seven seasons with Ruch before moving
to lower division clubs in Austria and in Australia.
As a coach had a spell at Ruch and Gornik
Zabrze. Then was in charge of the Poland Under-
21 side and had a year as national team assistant
before rejoining Ruch in 1999.

PLAYER
LOSADA, Roberto
Full name: Roberto Losada Rodriguez
Forward, Spanish, 180cm, 71kg
Born: 25.10.76, Vigo, Spain
Clubs: Oviedo (1994-98), Toledo (1998-99), Oviedo
(1999-)
• Promising young striker who has started to make
an impact at Oviedo after a spell on loan at Toledo.
• A product of Oviedo's youth system.

PLAYER
LOSKOV, Dmitri
Midfielder, Russian, 178cm, 68kg
Born: 12.02.74, Russia
Clubs: Rostelmash (1991-96), Lok. Moscow (1997-)
Full international (Russia) 2 caps/0 goals
• Midfielder with good work-rate and an
excellent free-kick taker.

PLAYER
LOVENKRANDS, Peter
Forward, Danish, 181cm, 68kg
Born: 29.01.80, Denmark
Clubs: AB (1998-2000), Rangers (Sco) (2000-)
• One of Danish football's brightest prospects. Extremely fast, with good technique, but has already been troubled by injuries.

PLAYER
LOZANO, Harold
Midfielder, Colombian, 190cm, 76kg
Born: 30.03.73, Cali, Colombia
Clubs: America Cali (1991-95), Palmeiras (Bra) (1995), America (1995-96), Valladolid (Spa) (1996-)
Full international (Colombia)
• Colombian who is used in a defensive holding role but can also play in a more creative role.
• Played for Colombia at the 1998 World Cup.

PLAYER
LUCCIN, Peter
Midfielder, French,178cm, 67kg
Born: 09.04.79, Marseille, France
Clubs: Cannes (1996-97), Bordeaux (1997-98), Marseille (1998-99), Paris Saint-Germain (2000-)
• Under-21 international who is one of France's most exciting youngsters. Began his career as a midfield all-rounder, a dedicated ball-winner with a great deal of skill and vision to boot. But it increasingly looks as though his long-term future is as a sweeper. His idol is **Frank Rijkaard**.
• Made the controversia movel from Marseille to rivals PSG alongside **Stephane Dalmat** in summer 2000.
• Surname pronounced Loo san.

COACH
LUCESCU, Mircea
Romanian
Born: 21.07.45
• One of the most successful Romanian coaches of recent times.

• As a player, he starred for Dinamo Bucharest and the Romanian national side.
• As a coach, he established his reputation after four seasons with Corvinul, which led to a four-year stint in charge of the Romanian national side.
• Moved on to Dinamo Bucharest, where he won the Romanian League title in 1990 after three successive second-place finishes.
• Moved to Italy in 1990, spending one season with Pisa before a six-year stretch at Brescia and a short spell at Reggiana.
• Returned to Romania to take up a post with Rapid Bucharest but was called back to Italy in April 1999 to take temporary of Internazionale following the resignation of **Luigi Simoni**.
• Won the Romanian League title with Rapid in 1999-2000 before being appointed by Galatasaray to replace Fiorentina-bound **Fatih Terim**.

PLAYER
LUCHKEVICH, Igor
Midfielder, Ukrainian, 176cm, 63kg
Born: 19.11.73, Ukraine
Clubs: Metalurg Zaporizha, Metalurg Donetsk, Karpaty
Full international (Ukraine) 2 caps/0 goals
• One of the most gifted players in the Ukrainian League. Has good technique and is an elegant mover on the pitch.

PLAYER
LUCIC, Teddy
Defender, Swedish, 187cm, 75kg
Born: 15.04.73, Gothenburg, Sweden
Clubs: Lundby (1989-92), Vastra Frolunda (1993-95), IFK Gothenburg (1996-98), Bologna (Ita) (1998-99), AIK Stockholm (1999-)
Full international (Sweden) 31 caps/0 goals
• Left-back or stopper who made his name with the Gothenburg clubs, Frolunda and IFK. A

Luis Enrique

controversial move to Italy's Bologna did not come off, and he returned to Sweden.
• A steady performer whose father is Croatian and mother Finnish.

PLAYER
LUDVIGSEN, Per Ove
Defender, Norwegian, 194cm, 91kg
Born: 20.05.66, Brann, Norway
Clubs: Fyllingen (1990-93), Brann (1994-)
• Veteran who used to be a striker but now has a job in central defence. Local hero who joined from neighbouring Fyllingen in 1994.

COACH
LUIS ARAGONES
Spanish
Born: 28.07.38
• The grandfather of Spanish coaches, with a record number of first division matches. Signed for Mallorca in summer of 2000 after a poor season at Oviedo. Turned down the Spain job in 1998. Has previously been in charge at Atletico Madrid (four times), Betis (twice), Barcelona, Sevilla and Valencia.

PLAYER
LUIS CEMBRANOS
Full name: Luis Cembranos Martinez
Midfielder, Spanish, 172cm, 71kg
Born: 06.06.72, Lucerne, Switzerland
Clubs: Barcelona C (1991-92), Figueres (1992-93), Barcelona B (1993-94), Barcelona (1994-95), Espanyol (1994-98), Rayo Vallecano (1998-)
Full international (Spain) 1 caps/0 goals
• Dimunitive attacking midfielder who plays just behind the forwards.
• Made his name at Espanyol after being rejected by Barcelona.

PLAYER
LUIS ENRIQUE

Full name: Luis Enrique Martinez Garcia
Midfielder, Spanish, 180cm, 73kg
Born: 08.05.70, Gijon, Spain
Clubs: Sporting Gijon (1989-91), Real Madrid (1991-96), Barcelona (1996-)
Full international (Spain) 51 caps/12 goals

• Dynamic all-rounder who is key man for both Barcelona and Spain.

• Famous for being the first and so far only player to cross Spanish football's great divide, leaving Real Madrid to join Barcelona in summer 1996.

• A product of Sporting Gijon's famous football school at Mareo, where he played alongside **Abelardo** and **Javier Manjarin**.

• Rejected by Barcelona after a five-day trial and refused to undergo a similar trial with Atletico Madrid. Spent two seasons as a striker at Sporting.

• Joined Real Madrid in 1991 for £1.25million, and began the transition from striker to goal-challanged all-rounder, playing in all positions except goalkeeper.

• A key member of Spain's 1992 Olympic gold medal-winning side and made his full international debut as a substitute against Romania in April 1991.

• Ended the 1994 World Cup with a broken nose after a clash with the elbow of Mauro Tassotti in Spain's quarter-final defeat by Italy.

• Moved to Barça after Euro 96, scoring twice on his debut, against Oviedo on September 1 1996.

• 'Moving to Catalonia was the best thing I ever did. I met my wife here, my baby was born here and I'm back by the sea again.'

• Became a born-again striker at Camp Nou, scoring 17 goals in 1996-97 and being voted Most Valuable Player by 70 per cent of fans, despite the presence of Ronaldo in the side.

• **Javier Clemente** on Luis Enrique: 'If Luis Enrique was a girl, I'd marry him.'

Teddy Lucic

PLAYER
LUIS FERNANDEZ
Defender, Spanish, 173cm, 67kg
Born: 27.06.72, Cantabria, Spain
Clubs: Racing Santander (1993-96), Real Betis (1996-)
• Fast left-sided defender signed by Betis in 1996 to provide cover for **Robert Jarni**.
• Began with Gimnastica Torrelavega in his native Canatbria before moving to Racing Santander for first division football in 1993.
• Established himself in 1998-99 season following the departure of Jarni to Real Madrid, but then lost out to **David Rivas**.

PLAYER
LUIS HELGUERA
Full name: Luis Helguera Bujia
Born: 09.06.76, Santander, Spain
Clubs: Manchego (1995-97), Zaragoza (1997-2000), Udinese (Ita) (2000-)
• Promising youngster who came through the ranks at Zaragoza, where they hoped he would fill the midfield holding role.
• Younger brother of Real Madrid's **Ivan Helguera**.
• Switched to Italian club Udinese in July 2000.

PLAYER
LUNDEKVAM, Claus
Defender, Norwegian, 191cm, 83kg
Born: 22.02.73, Norway
Clubs: Brann (1993-96), Southampton (Eng) (1996-)
Full international (Norway) 8 caps/0 goals
• Centre-back who is elegant but strong on the ball and likes to play himself out of danger.
• Cost Southampton £400,000 from Brann in September 1996.

PLAYER
LUNG, Tiberiu
Goalkeeper, Romanian
Born: 24.12.78, Craiova, Romania

Clubs: Univ. Craoiva (1997-)
Full international (Romania) 1 cap/0 goals
• Highly promising young keeper who established himself in the first team at Univ. Craiova at the age of 21 and broke into the Romanian national team.
• Was unlucky to have just missed the cut for Romania's Euro 2000 squad.

PLAYER
LUPESCU, Ioan
Midfielder, Romanian, 183cm, 75kg
Born: 09.12.68, Bucharest, Romania
Clubs: Dinamo Bucharest (1986-90), Bayer Leverkusen (Ger) (1990-96), Borussia Monchengladbach (Ger) (1996-98), Dinamo Bucharest (1998-)
Full international (Romanla) 72 caps/6 goals
• Veteran defender who played his way back into Romania's squad for Euro 2000 with a series of consistent displays for Dinamo Bucharest in the Romanian League.
• Played most of his career in midfield but now used as a left-sided defender.
• Won the Romanian League and Cup double in 1990 with Dinamo and the 1993 German Cup with Leverkusen.
• Member of Romania's squad at the 1990 and 1994 World Cups and 1996 European Championships.

PLAYER
LUPPI, Gianluca
Defender, Italian, 181cm, 74kg
Born: 23.08.66, Crevalcore, Italy
Clubs: Bologna (1984-90), Juventus (1990-92), Fiorentina (1992-95), Atalanta (1995-96), Ravenna (1996-97) Venezia (1997-)
• Vastly experienced central defender whose career looked to have peaked following a move to second division Ravenna, but some accomplished displays in Serie B earned him a move to Venezia.

PLAYER
LUQUE, Alberto
Full name: Juan Antonio Luque Ramirez
Forward, Spanish, 183cm, 80kg
Born: 11.03.78, Barcelona, Spain
Clubs: Mallorca (1997-99), Malaga (1999-2000)
• Promising young forward with good technique.
• Gained valuable first-team experience during the 1999-2000 season on loan at Malaga from Mallorca.
• Spanish Under-21 international.

PLAYER
LURLING, Anthony
Midfielder, Dutch, 173cm, 70kg
Born: 22.04.77, Den Bosch, Holland
Clubs: Den Bosch (1994-99), Heerenveen (1999-)
• Young attacking midfielder who has established himself at Heerenveen despite injuries at the start.
• Dutch Under-21 international.

PLAYER
LUYINDULA, Pegguy
Forward, French, 178cm, 72kg
Born: 25.05.79, Kinshasa, Congo
Clubs: Niort, Strasbourg (1998-99)
• Promising young forward who was born in Kinshasa in the former Zaire, but has since become a naturalised Frenchman and has starred for the Under-21s.
• Combative, quick and skilful, though he must improve his goals per chances ratio.

PLAYER
LUZHNYI, Oleh
Defender, Ukrainian, 182cm, 77kg
Born: 05.08.68, Ukraine
Clubs: Dynamo Kyiv (1990-99), Arsenal (Eng) (1999-)
Full international (USSR/Ukraine) 8/35 caps/0 goals
• Right-sided defender who can play at full-back

or, if needed, in central defence.
• Spent more than a decade at Dynamo Kyiv, winning seven consecutive Ukrainian League titles from 1993 to 1999.
• Nicknamed 'The Horse' because of his tendency to gallop forward.

PLAYER
LYKKE, Henrik
Defender, Danish, 186cm, 77kg
Born: 03.04.70, Denmark
Clubs: Lyngby (1991-93), FC Copenhagen (1993-94) Lille (Fra) (1994-95), Herfolge (1995-96), FC Copenhagen (1997), Herfolge (1998-)
Full international (Denmark) 3 caps/0 goals
• Much-travelled defender who is now back at Herfolge after spells in France and Copenhagen.
• Won the Danish League title with Lyngby and played a key role in Herfolge's remarkable triumph in the 1999-2000 season.

M

1988 French Cup Final.

PLAYER
MACHERIDIS, Triantafilos
Midfielder, Greek, 188cm, 83kg
Born: 10.11.73, Greece
Clubs: AEK Athens (1997-98), PAOK (1998-2000), Benfica (Por) (2000)
• Greek midfielder for whom Benfica have high hopes in the 2000-2001 season.
• Surname also spelt Maheridis.

PLAYER
MACHLAS, Nikos
Forward, Greek, 183cm, 75kg
Born: 16.06.73, Iraklion, Greece
Clubs: OFI Crete (1990-1996), Vitesse Arnhem (Hol) (1996-99), Ajax Amsterdam (Hol) (1999-)
Full international (Greece) 50 caps/16 goals
• One of Europe's in-demand strikers of recent seasons who moved to Ajax in summer 1999 for £5million after winning the Golden Shoe for scoring 42 goals in 63 League games for Vitesse.
• Time at Ajax has been affected by injuries, but he remains a fine prospect.

PLAYER
MADAR, Mickael
Forward, French, 183cm, 86kg
Born: 08.05.68, Paris, France
Clubs: Sochaux (1986-89), Laval (1989-90), Sochaux (1990-92), Cannes (1992-94), Monaco (1994-96), Deportivo La Coruna (Spa) (1996-98), Everton (Eng) (1997-98), Paris Saint-Germain (1999-)
Full international (France) 3 caps/1 goal
• Not the most elegant striker ever to walk on to a pitch. But thanks to his muscular approach, spirit and more skill than he is given credit for, he is always an awkward customer for defenders to supress.
• Unfortunate to miss a penalty when his Sochaux team lost a shoot-out to Metz in the

PLAYER
MADSEN, Michael
Defender, Danish, 191cm, 82kg
Born: 24.01.74, Fredriksberg, Denmark
Clubs: AB Copenhagen (1996-98), Bari (1998-)
Full international (Denmark)
• Strong, pacy central defender who has not featured a great deal at Bari since a move there in 1998, and was set to move to a new club in the summer of 2000.

PLAYER
MADSEN, Jens
Midfielder, Danish, 183cm, 80kg
Born: 01.02.70, Denmark
Clubs: OB, AaB (1994-95), Vejle (1995-99), Herfolge (2000-)
Full international (Denmark) 3 caps/0 goals
• Hugely experienced midfield campaigner who made a valuable contribution to Herfolge's amazing Danish title victory in 1999-2000.
• Played in Europe for Brondby and AaB.

PLAYER
MADSEN, Peter
Defender, Danish, 183cm, 76kg
Born: 26.04.78, Denmark
Clubs: Brondby (1996-)
• One of the brightest talents in Danish football, a striker or attacking midfielder with exceptional pace and vision.
• Voted the discovery of the 1998-99 season after establishing himself as a regular in the Danish Under-21 side. A promising career with the senior side beckons.

COACH
MAGATH, Felix
German
Born: 26.01.53
• Another whose character seems to have

changed completely since crossing the line from player to coach. For Hamburg and Germany, he was the cultured playmaker who elegantly pulled the strings in midfield and was not exactly renowned for his work-rate. As a coach, though, he is the hardest of hard taskmasters, infamous for his gruelling training regimes.

PLAYER
MAGLEBY, Christian
Midfielder, Danish, 178cm, 74kg
Born: 08.06.77, Denmark
Clubs: Lyngby (1996-)
Full international (Denmark) 3 caps/0 goals
• Pacy, skilful left-sided midfielder who likes to run at defences. Career has been affected by a series of injuries.

PLAYER
MAHDAVIKIA, Mehdi
Midfielder, Iranian, 172cm, 72kg
Born: 24.07.77, Iran
Clubs: Pirouzi, Bochum (Ger) (1998-99), Hamburg (Ger) (1999-)
Full international (Iran)
• High-class Iranian attacker of nimble footwork, pace and altruism whom Hamburg like wide on the left. Never seems to have a bad game and also has the versatility to play in central midfield or as a wing-back.
• Surname pronounced Mah dah veek ee ah.

PLAYER
MAHOUVE, Marcel
Midfielder, Cameroonian, 179cm, 74kg
Born: 16.01.73, Douala Cameroon
Clubs: Montpellier (1997-)
Full international (Cameroon)
• Central defender who has established himself at Montpellier over the past three seasons.
• Played once for Cameroon at the 1998 World Cup.

PLAYER
MAIER, Bernd
Midfielder, German, 172cm, 68kg
Born: 30.11.74, Germany
Clubs: Ulm, SV Grosskucken, Ulm (1996-)
• Versatile youngster able to play on either flank in defence or virtually anywhere in midfield. On his debut as a professional in a Second Division game in 1998 against Stuttgarter Kickers, he scored for Ulm and then put through his own goal.
• Surname pronounced My er.

PLAYER
MAIER, Ladislav
Goalkeeper, Czech, 185cm, 89kg
Born: 04.01.66, Boskovice, Czech Rep
Clubs: Boby Brno, Drnovice, Slovan Liberec (1993-98), Rapid Vienna (Aut) (1999-)
Full international (Czech Rep) 6 caps/0 goals
• Reliable keeper who has found his best form in the twilight of his career following a move to Austria.
• Ony started playing at the top level in 1993, aged 26.
• Made his international debut in 1995 against Kuwait and made the Czech squad for Euro 2000.
• Voted Czech goalkeeper of the year in 1998 and 1999.

COACH
MAIFREDI, Luigi
Italian
Born: 20.04.47
• Much-travelled coach who was in charge of Juventus for the 1991-92 season.
• Made his name by taking second division Bologna into Serie A in 1988, keeping them there for the next two seasons.
• Since his time in Turin, he has worked in brief spells at Genoa, Venezia, Brescia, Pescara, Esperance of Tunisia, and Albacete of Spain.

MAIN, Alan
Goalkeeper, Scottish, 182cm, 82cm
Born: 05.12.67, Elgin, Scotland
Clubs: Dundee Utd (1986-95), Cowdenbeath
(1988-89, loan), St Johnstone (1995-)
• Main has now spent the last five years at
McDiarmid Park since joining St Johnstone from
his first club, Dundee United. During that time he
has displayed a supreme level of consistency and
an exemplary big match temperament, which has
resulted in him becoming a regular fixture in
Craig Brown's international squads.

PLAYER
MAINI, Giampiero
Midfielder, Italian, 186cm, 81kg
Born: 29.09.71, Rome, Italy
Clubs: Roma (1989-91), Lecce (1991-93), Ascoli
(1993-94), Roma (1994-95), Vicenza (1995-97),
Milan (1997-98), Bologna (1998-99), Parma
(1999-)
Full international (Italy) 1 cap/0 goals
• Much-travelled midfielder who played a big
part in Vicenza's 1997 Italian Cup triumph.
• Made his international debut for Italy against
England at Le Tournoi in June 1997, but has not
played since.

PLAYER
MAJAK, Slawomir
Midfielder, Polish, 185cm, 76kg
Born: 12.01.69, Radomsko, Poland
Clubs: Zagelbie Lubin, Hannover 96 (Ger),
Widzew Lodz, Hansa Rostock (Ger) (1997-)
Full international (Poland) 22 caps/0 goals
• Polish international who has established
himself on the left side of the Hansa Rostock
midfield, and has weighed in with some crucial
goals.
• Polish Footballer of the Year in 1997.
• Made his international debut against Azerbaijan
in November 1995.

PLAYER
MAJDAN, Radoslaw
Goalkeeper, Polish, 185cm, 79kg
Born: 10.05.72, Poland
Clubs: Pogon Szczecin
Full international (Poland) 1 cap/0 goals
• Dynamic keeper who has good reflexes. Has
remained loyal to Pogon, where he started his
career. Thanks to his solid league performances
made his national team debut against Spain in
January 2000.

COACH
MAJEWSKI, Stefan
Polish
Born: 31.01.56
• Coach of Polish side Amica Wronki.
• A former national team player who was in the
Poland team which finished third in the World
Cup in 1982. Made his name with Legia before
joining Kaiserslautern and then Arminia Bielefeld.
• Began his coaching career with youth and
amateur teams in Germany. After short spells
with Polonia Warsaw in 1994 and 1996, he took
over Amica in the 1998-99 season and led them
to victory in the Polish Cup.

PLAYER
MAKAAY, Roy
Forward, Dutch, 188cm, 75kg
Born: 03.03.75, Wijchen, Holland
Clubs: Vitesse Arnhem (1993-97), Tenerife (Spa)
(1997-99), Deportivo La Coruna (Spa) (1999-)
Full international (Holland) 8 caps/0 goals
• Striker whose goals helped Deportivo La
Coruna win their first Spanish League title in May
2000.
• A quick forward who is a strong runner on the
ground and can be highly effective in the air.
• Made his name at Vitesse Arnhem, where his
all-round forward play led to him being touted as
the new **Marco Van Basten**.
• Moved to Tenerife, where he performed well

Paolo Maldini

but could not prevent his team's relegation.
• Was linked with Barcelona, whose then coach **Louis Van Gaal** wanted to added another Dutchman to the Orange legion at Camp Nou. Instead, he chose Deportivo, a decision which proved correct when Deportivo won the League.
• Was a member of the Dutch squad at Euro 2000.

PLAYER
MAKELELE, Claude
Midfielder, French, 174cm, 70kg
Born: 18.02.73, Kinshasa, Democratic Republic of Congo
Clubs: Nantes (1992-97), Marseille (1997-98), Celta Vigo (Spa) (1998-2000), Real Madrid (Spa) (2000-)
Full international (France) 3 caps/0 goals
• Strong-running player who plays mostly on the right side of midfield, where his pace and trickery are highly effective.
• Made his name at Nantes, winning the French League title, earning a transfer to Marseille and winning two caps for France.
• Helped Marseille to second place in the French League in 1998, before joining Celta Vigo in summer 1998 for £1.5million.
• Father played for Zaire (now the Democratic Republic of Congo).

PLAYER
MALADENIS, Christos
Midfielder, Greek, 180cm, 79kg
Born: 23.05.74, Pigadia Xanthias, Greece
Clubs: Xanthi, AEK Athens (1996-)
• An attacking midfielder who does not always start for AEK, but often comes up trumps as a super-sub, immediately settling into the rhythm of a game and scoring a goal; he did just that in AEK's Cup Final victory over Ionikos in the 1999-2000 season.
• Makes good late runs into the box and is a composed finisher.

MALBRANQUE, Steed
Midfielder, French, 172cm, 73kg
Born: 06.01.80, Mouscron, Belgium
Clubs: Lyon (1997-)
• One of the most promising young talents in France, an attacking midfielder blessed with uncommon touch, vision and poise. He is confident too and recently claimed that Lyon were not playing him enough. Interested parties such as Arsenal, Bologna and Lens are keenly watching this space.
• Surname pronounced Mal bron ke.

MALDARASANU, Marius
Midfielder, Romanian,
Born: 19.04.75, Ploiesti, Romania
Clubs: Petrolul (1996-98), Rapid Bucharest (1998-)
Full international (Romania) 5 caps/0 goals
• Midfielder who was on the fringes of Romania's squad in the run-up to Euro 2000, but missed the cut.

MALDINI, Cesare
Italian
Born: 05.02.32
• Coach of the Italian national team at the 1998 World Cup in France.
• Coaching philosophy stands for the traditional Italian values of pragmatism, Mediterranean flair and a solid defence, complete with sweeper.
• As a player, he was captain of Milan, winning the European Champions Cup at Wembley in 1963 and playing 14 times for Italy.
• As a coach, he was number two to Enzo Bearzot in Italy's triumphant World Cup campaign in 1982 and guided Italy's Under-21 side to three European titles in 1992, 1994 and 1996.

MALDINI, Paolo
Defender, Italian, 186cm, 83kg
Born: 26.06.68, Milan, Italy
Clubs: Milan (1984-)
Full international (Italy) 110 caps/7 goals
• The darling of Italian soccer who is approaching elder statesman status and is a hugely influential figure for Milan and Italy.
• Has been one of the world's best defenders for more than a decade after making his Serie A debut aged 16 and his international debut at 19. A complete defender who supplements attack with his forays down the left flank.
• Winner of six League and six European titles with Milan.
• Son of coach **Cesare Maldini**.
• One of only two Italians (the other is **Dino Zoff**) to win more than 100 caps.
• Made his League debut aged 16 in a 1-1 draw with Udinese in January 1995. Has now played more than 400 times in Serie A.
• Voted World Player of the Year in 1994 by readers of *World Soccer*.

MALESANI, Alberto
Italian
Born: 05.06.54
• Coach of Parma since 1998 who oversaw victory in the 1999 UEFA Cup Final over Marseille.
• Began his coaching career with Chievo, winning promotion to Serie B in 1994, and moving on to Fiorentina for one season in 1997-98.
• Succeeded **Carlo Ancelotti** in summer 1998 and guided Parma to the double of UEFA Cup and Italian Cup in 1999.
• Takes a flexible approach to tactics, switching from the 4-4-2 system employed by Ancelotti, to a 4-3-1-2 with a midfield playmaker.

COACH
MALINEN, Juha
Finnish
Born: 16.07.58
• One of Finland's most charismatic coaches, who worked for many years at TPS Turku.
• Now in his third season with MyPa, where in the 1998 season he did well to guide the club to third place after a very difficult start.

PLAYER
MAMIC, Zoran
Defender, Croatian, 190cm, 83kg
Born: 30.09.71, Zagreb, Croatia
Clubs: Bochum (Ger), Bayer Leverkusen (Ger) (1999-)
Full international (Croatia) 6 caps/0 goals
• Experienced central defender who joined Leverkusen from relegated Bochum in 1999, but has found opportunities limited, Jens Nowotny the first choice sweeper.
• Strong in the air and highly mobile, he missed out on Croatia's final 22 for the 1998 World Cup.

PLAYER
MANCINI, Francesco
Goalkeeper, Italian, 180cm, 79kg
Born: 12.10.68, Matera, Italy
Clubs: Matera (1984-87), Bisceglie (1987), Foggia (1987-95), Lazio (1995-96), Foggia (1996-97), Bari (1997-)
• Accomplished keeper who played under **Zdenek Zeman** at Foggia and Lazio and has settled well at Bari.
• No relation of **Roberto Mancini**.

PLAYER/COACH
MANCINI, Roberto
Forward, Italian, 179cm, 78kg
Born: 27.11.64, Jesi, Italy
Clubs: Bologna (1981-82), Sampdoria (1982-97), Lazio (1997-2000).
Full international (Italy) 36 caps/4 goals

• Veteran playmaker who ended his career at Lazio after 15 seasons at Sampdoria.
• One of the most talented players of his generation who would have won more honours if he had moved on from Sampdoria earlier.
• A goalmaker rather than goalscorer, he formed the 'Terrible Twins' partnership with **Gianluca Vialli** at Sampdoria in the early 1990s.
• Joined Lazio's coaching staff in summer 2000.

COACH
MANE
Full name: Jose Manuel Esnal
Spanish
Born: 23.03.50
• Straightforward and plain-talking coach who has worked wonders to take Alaves from the Spanish second division into the UEFA Cup. Originally came to fame by defeating Real Madrid in the 1998 Spanish Cup.

PLAYER
MANEL
Full name: Jose Manuel Menendez Herminia
Midfielder, Spanish, 170cm, 64kg
Born: 07.01.77, Aviles, Spain
Clubs: Aviles (1989-92), Real Oviedo (1992-99), Deportivo La Coruna (1999-)
• Reserve midfielder signed from Oviedo in 1999. Has so far failed to impress Deportivo coach **Javier Irureta**.

PLAYER
MANGONE, Amedeo
Defender, Italian, 185cm, 74kg
Born: 12.07.68, Milan, Italy
Clubs: Pergicrema (1987-89), Solbiatese (1989-93), Bari (1993-96), Bologna (1996-99), Roma (1999-)
• Solid centre-back who quickly established himself alongside **Antonio Carlos** in the Roma defence following a summer 1999 move from Bologna.

PLAYER
MANICHE
Full name: Nuno Ricardo Oliveira Ribeiro
Midfielder, Portuguese, 173cm, 69kg
Born: 11.11.77, Lisbon, Portugal
Clubs: Benfica (1995-96), Alverca (1996-98), Benfica (1998-)
• Promising youngster who broke through into the Benfica side in 1999-2000, but still has a lot of work to do to establish himself as a major player.
• Portuguese Under-21 international.

PLAYER
MANIERO, Filippo
Forward, Italian, 185cm, 82kg
Born: 11.09.72, Padova, Italy
Clubs: Padova (1989-90), Atalanta (1990-91), Padova (1991), Ascoli (1991-92), Padova (1992-95), Sampdoria (1995-96), Verona (1996-97), Parma (1997-98), Milan (1998), Venezia (1998-)
• Much-travelled striker who has established a useful partnership with **Mauricio Ganz** at Venezia. Their goals were the main factor in keeper Venezia in Serie A.

PLAYER
MANIGHETTI, Gian Paulo
Defender, Italian, 178cm, 74kg
Born: 24.01.69, Filago, Italy
Clubs: Piacenza (1986-91), Bari (1991), Piacenza (1991-92), Monza (1992-94), Bari (1994-98), Piacenza (1998-)
• Experienced defender who was tipped to move on to another club following Piacenza's relegation from Serie A in May 2000.

PLAYER
MANJARIN, Javier
Full name Javier Manjarin Peres
Midfielder, Spanish, 173cm, 73kg
Born: 31.12.69, Gijon, Spain
Clubs: Sporting Gijon (1989-93), Deportivo La Coruna (1993-)
Full international (Spain) 13 caps/2 goals
• Attacking midfielder and another product of the famed Sporting Gijon football school at Mareo.
• Member of Spain's 1992 Olympic squad, but did not play in the gold medal-winning side.
• Transferred to Deportivo in 1993 for a reported £1.4million fee.
• Made his international debut as a substitute in Spain's 6-0 defeat of Cyprus in 1995.

COACH
MANKOWSKI, Pierre
French
Born: 05.11.51
• Coach of Strasbourg since 1998 until 2000.
• Most of his best work as a coach has been achieved in the lower divisions, notably taking Caen from the Third Division to the First between 1985 and 1988 and winning promotion to the elite with Le Havre in 1991.
• Studious, methodical and a trained physiotherapist, he formed a double-act with **Claude Le Roy** for Cameroon and at Paris Saint-Germain and Strasbourg. However, the pair split acrimoniously when 'Manko' was fired by Strasbourg and Le Roy took his place.
• Former Lens and Amiens player.

PLAYER
MANNINGER, Alex
Goalkeeper, Austria, 187cm, 83kg
Born: 04.06.77, Salzburg
Clubs: Vorwaerts Steyr (1995), Salzburg (1995-96), Sturm Graz (1996-97), Arsenal (Eng) (1997-)
Full international (Austria) 4 caps/0 goals
• Hugely promising keeper who signed for Arsenal in June 1997 for £500,000 after a two-day trial.
• Filled in ably for the injured David Seaman when Arsenal won the 1998 Double, but unable to displace Seaman as number one.
• Austrian Under-21 international.
• A qualified mechanic.

COACH
MANOJLOVIC, Tomislav
Yugoslav
Born: 15.6.39
• An inspiring and authoritative trainer who has worked with Rad Belgrade, Proleter Zrenjanin, Kikinda and Vojvodina Novi Sad. Had success with Vojvodina, reaching the InterToto Cup semi-finals in 1998 and a UEFA Cup place in 1998-99. Currently not active as a coach.

PLAYER
MANSOURI, Yazid
Midfielder, French, 175cm, 69kg
Born: 25.02.78, Revin, France
Clubs: Le Havre (1997-)
• One of the revelations of the 1999-2000 season in France. Dynamic defensive midfielder who has been the epitomy of consistency and dogged spirit for Le Havre.

COACH
MANUEL JOSE
Portuguese
Born: 09.04.46
• The former Boavista and Benfica coach did an excellent job at Uniao Leira during the 1999-2000 season, steering the team away from the relegation zone.
• A highly-respected figure in the Portuguese game, he recently spoke about the future of domestic football at the national Parliament.

PLAYER
MANUEL PABLO
Full name: Manuel Pablo Garcia Diaz
Defender, Spanish, 170cm, 70kg
Born: 25.01.76, Gran Canaria, Spain
Clubs: Las Palmas (1996-98), Deportivo La Coruna (1998-)
• Full-back who is starting to show the form at Deportivo which saw him touted as a future Spanish international.

Alex Manninger

- A former Under-21 international, he struggled to settle in at Deportivo, failing to win a place in the starting line-up following a move from Las Palmas.
- But he gradually won coach **Javier Iureta** and the Depor fans over, and made a useful contribution to the team's successful League campaign in 1999-2000.

PLAYER
MAOULIDA, Toifilou
Forward, French, 185cm, 75kg
Born: 08.06.79, Mayotte, Madagascar
Clubs: Montpellier (1997-)
- Promising French Under-21 right-sided attacker who, despite finding himself in a sinking ship in 1999-2000, continually impressed with his hard-running, neat approach work and flair for stealing into goalscoring positions.
- Pronounced Twa fee loo Mao lee dah.

PLAYER
MAPEZA, Norman
Midfielder, Zimbabwean, 177cm, 75kg
Born: 12.04.72, Harare, Zimbabwe
Clubs: Galatasaray (Tur), Altay (Tur)
Full international (Zimbabwe)
- Skilful midfielder who was loaned to Altay after a change of coaching staff at Galatasaray, who had signed him from his native Zimbabwe.

PLAYER
MARCELINO
Full name Marcelino Elena Sierra
Defender, Spanish, 188cm, 84kg
Born: 26.09.71, Gijon, Spain
Clubs: Sporting Gijon (1993-96), Mallorca (1996-99), Newcastle (1999-)
Full international (Spain) 5 caps/0 goals
- Centre-back who joined Newcastle for £6million in 1999 after starring in Mallorca's run to the 1999 European Cup-winners Cup Final.

ADMINISTRATOR
MARCHAND, Yves
- President of Marseille since June 1999.

PLAYER
MARCHEGIANI, Luca
Goalkeeper, Italian, 188cm, 77kg
Born: 22.02.66, Ancona, Italy.
Clubs: Jesi (1984-87), Brescia (1987-88), Torino (1988-93), Lazio (1993-)
Full international (Italy) 9 caps/0 goals
- Former international who is still among the best keepers in Serie A.
- Perhaps his only weakness is his poor footwork, which cost him his international future after a disastrous performance in against Switzerland in 1992.
- European Cup-winners Cup winner In 1999, and League champion 2000.
- Known as 'The Duke' for his elegant playing style.

PLAYER
MARCO
Full name: Marco Antonio Pogioli
Forward, Brazilian, 178cm, 74kg
Born: 09.06.75, Brazil
Clubs: FC Jazz (Fin) (1997-99), FC Haka (Fin) (2000-)
- Brazilian striker who has carved out a career for himself in Finnish football, first at FC Jazz, and now at FC Haka.
- Only of medium height, but surprisingly in the air.

PLAYER
MARCOLINI, Michele
Midfielder, Italian, 177cm, 71kg
Born: 02.10.75, Savona, Italy
Clubs: Torino (1993-94), Sora (1994-97), Bari (1997-)
- Left-footed attacking midfielder who has established himself as the main creator at Bari since arriving in the Italian south in 1997.

MARCOS, Alberto
Full name: Alberto Marcos Rey
Born: 15.02.74 Camarma de Esteruelas, Spain
Clubs: Real Madrid (1993-95), Real Valladolid (1995-)
• Industrious left-back who came through the youth ranks at Real Madrid, but failed to establish himself in the first team.
• Joined Valladolid in 1995, winning a regular place almost immediately.

MARCOS ASSUNCAO
Full name: Marcos dos Santos Assuncao
Midfielder, Brazilian, 178cm, 74kg
Born: 25.07.76, Caieiras, Brazil
Clubs: Rio Branco (1994-95), Santos (1995-97), Flamengo (1998), Santos (1999), Roma (Ita) (1999-)
Full international (Brazil)
• Occasional Brazilian international who added some muscle and flair to Roma's midfield after joining from Flamengo for £5million in summer 1999.

MARCOS VALES
Full name: Marcos Vales Illanes
Midfielder, Spanish, 181cm, 75kg
Born: 05.04.75, La Coruna, Spain
Clubs: Deportivo La Coruna (1992-94), Sporting Gijon (1994-97), Real Zaragoza (1997-)
Full international (Spain) 1 cap/0 goals
• Attacking midfielder who has been troubled by inconsistency during his career, failing to hold down a regular place at Deportivo and Zaragoza.
• Capped at youth level by Spain and on the fringes of the senior national team squad during **Javier Clemente**'s time in charge.

MARESCA, Enzo
Midfielder, Italian, 180cm, 77kg
Born: 10.02.80, Italy
Clubs: Cagliari, West Bromwich (Eng), Juventus (1999-)
• One of the brightest talents in Italian soccer who has followed unorthodox career path from the Milan youth system to Juventus via Sardinia, the English first division and a £5million transfer back to Italy. And all while still a teenager.
• Captain of the Italian Under-20 side and a strong, intelligent right-footed central midfield playmaker.

MARGAS, Javier
Defender, Chilean, 185cm, 69kg
Born: 10.05.69, La Cisterna, Chile
Clubs: Colo Colo (1995), America (Mex) (1996-97), Univ. Catolica (1997-98), West Ham (Eng) (1998-)
Full international (Chile)
• Accomplished, experienced centre-back who has been Chile's best defender for some years.
• Was Chile's representative in the FIFA All-Star game before the draw for the 1998 World Cup.
• Joined West Ham in August 1998 for £2million from Universidad Catolica, but his time in London has been affected by injuries.

MARGIOTTA, Massimo
Forward, Italian, 188cm, 85kg
Born: 27.07.77, Maracaibo, Venezuela
Clubs: Pescara (1993-97), Cosenza (1997-98), Lecce (1998), Reggiana (1999), Udinese (1999-)
• Big, strong target man, who got the chance to prove himself in Serie A during 1999-2000 after spending his career up until then in Serie B.
• Uses his height and weight to great effect in the penalty area, and consequently is not the most elegant of strikers.

PLAYER
MARINESCU, Lucian
Midfielder, Romanian, 185cm, 78kg
Born: 24.06.72, Bucharest
Clubs: Rapid Bucharest (1996-98), Salamanca
(Spa) (1998-1999), Farense (Por) (2000-)
Full international (Romania) 8 caps/0 goals
• Accomplished midfielder who adapted well to
the Portuguese League and helped Farense avoid
relegation in the 1999-2000 seasoon.

PLAYER
MARIO
Full name: Mario Alberto Rosas Montero
Midfielder, Spanish, 166cm, 62kg
Born: 22.05.80, Malaga, Spain
Clubs: Barcelona (1997-99), Alaves (2000, loan-)
• Young attacking midfielder used sparingly by
Louis Van Gaal. Has now been loaned out to
Alaves.

PLAYER
MARIO LOJA
Full name: Mario Jorge Amaro Loja
Defender, Portuguese, 180cm, 71kg
Born: 27.12.77, Setubal, Portugal
Clubs: Vitoria Setubal (1996-)
• Defender who was the main organiser at the
back for Vitoria Setubal, but failed to inspire his
team-mates and they were relegated at the end
of the 1999-2000 season.

PLAYER
MARIO SILVA
Full name: Mario Fernando Magalhaes da Silva
Defender, Portuguese, 175cm, 73kg
Born: 24.04.77, Oporto, Portugal
Clubs: Boavista (1995-)
• Product of the Boavista youth system who
made his Portuguese League debut in the
1995-96 season.
• Capped once by Portugal at Under-20 level.

COACH
MARKEVITCH, Miron
Ukrainian
Born: 01.02.51
• Coach of Ukrainian club Metalurg Zaporizha.
• Has never played at the highest level, and he
coached a number of small clubs following the
break-up of the Soviet Union. Made his name five
years ago when he was appointed head coach of
Karpaty Lviv and turned them into one of the
strongest clubs in Ukraine.

PLAYER
MARKIC, Diego
Midfielder, Argentinian, 180cm, 73kg
Born: 09.01.77, Nunez, Argentina
Clubs: Argentinos Juniors (1996-99), Bari (Ita) (1999-)
• Argentinian Under-21 international who showed
glimpses of real talent in his first season in Italy.

PLAYER
MARKOVIC, Sasa
Forward, Yugoslav, 180cm, 70kg
Born: 17.09.71, Yugoslavia
Clubs: Cukaricki (1995-97), Radnicki (1997),
Zeleznik (1997-98), Red Star Belgrade (1998),
Stuttgart (Ger) (1998-2000), Obilic (2000-)
• The Yugoslav League's top scorer with Zeleznik
Belgrade and Red Star in 1997-98, but a complete
flop with VfB Stuttgart, where he spent one and a
half seasons, returning home in spring 2000.

PLAYER
MARLET, Steve
Forward, French, 180cm, 72kg
Born: 10.01.74, Pithiviers, France
Clubs: Red Star 93, Reyes, Auxerre (1996-)
• With former club Red Star of Paris, he
invariably played as a central striker, but
following a move to Auxerre, he has excelled on
the right wing. Not just a supplier of good
crosses; he is a good finisher, too.
• Surname pronounced Mar lay.

PLAYER
MAROCCHI, Giancarlo
Midfielder, Italian, 179cm, 76kg
Born: 04.07.65, Imola, Italy
Clubs: Bologna (1982-89), Juventus (1989-96), Bologna (1996-)
Full international (Italy) 11 caps/0 goals
• Highly experienced midfield campaigner who returned to Bologna in 1996 after a successful seven seasons at Juventus.

PLAYER
MARQUEZ, Rafael
Defender, Mexican, 182cm, 76kg
Born: 13.02.79, Zamora, Mexico
Clubs: Atlas, Monaco (Fra) (1999-)
• In his first season in European club football, the classy young Mexican central defender was nothing less than a revelation. Strong in the air and in the tackle and oozing determination, he is the sort of stopper who considers it a personal affront if a striker gets the better of him; fortunately for his self-esteem, few in the French top flight did in 1999-2000.
• Surname pronounced Mah kes.

PLAYER
MARSCHALL, Olaf
Forward, German, 186cm, 80kg
Born: 19.03.66, Torgau, Germany
Clubs: BSG Chemie Torgau, Lokomotiv Leipzig (1983-90), Admira Wacker (Aut) (1993-94), Dynamo Dresden (1993-94), Kaiserslautern (1994-)
Full international (East Germany) 4 caps/0 goals (Germany) 13 caps/3 goals
• Veteran front-man whose strike-rate tailed off in the 1999-2000 season – he only managed four goals. But that's not the whole story, with Marschall making a decent contribution with his good link-up play, unselfishness and pressing of defenders in possession.

PLAYER
MARTEINSSON, Peur
Forward, Icelandic, 186cm, 83kg
Born: 14.07.73, Iceland
Clubs: Fram (1994-95), Hammarby (1996-99), Stabaek (Nor) (1999-)
Full international (Iceland) 15 caps/0 goals
• Quick-thinking attacker who made several appearances as a substitute for the Icelandic national side in the qualifying stages of Euro 2000.

PLAYER
MARTEL, Didier
Forward, French, 181cm, 78kg
Born: 26.10.71, Saint Raphael, France
Clubs: Auxerre, Nimes, Chateauroux, Valencia (Spa), Paris Saint-Germain (1997-98), Utrecht (1998-)
• Dangerous French striker with enormous skill and a strong free-kick.

PLAYER
MARTENS, Jan-Pieter
Forward, Belgian, 176cm, 70kg
Born: 23.09.74, Biezen, Belgium
Clubs: Mechelen (1993-96), Roda (Hol) (1996-97), Sturm Graz (1998-)
• A regular for Sturm Graz following a January 1998 move from Holland. Good eye for goal.

AGENT
MARTINA, Silvano
• Italian-based agent whose clients include **Gianluigi Buffon, Alessandro Pistone, Luigi Turdo**.
• **Contact:** Residenza Sagittario, 23, I-20080 Basiglio, Italy. Fax: 00 39 2 9075 60 47.

AGENT
MARTINEZ, Javier Gonzalez
• Spanish agent whose clients include **Pedro Munitis**.
• **Contact:** Avda. Murrieta 22, 48980 Santurce (Vizcaya), Spain.

MARTINS, Corentin

Midfielder, French, 170cm, 67kg
Born: 11.07.69, Brest, France
Clubs: Brest (1989-91), Auxerre (1992-96), Deportivo La Coruna (Spa) (1996-98), Strasbourg (1998-99), Bordeaux (1999-)
Full international (France) 14 caps/1 goal
• Supremely gifted playmaker who climaxed a brilliant five-year spell at Auxerre by helping them achieve a League and Cup double in 1995-96. However that was the high watermark of his career. He mysteriously stayed on the bench throughout Euro 96 and in subsequent spells with Deportivo La Coruna in Spain, Strasbourg and on loan to Bordeaux, he has sparkled only sporadically.
• The son of Portuguese immigrants to Brittany – hence the typical Breton christian name Corentin.
• Pronounced Kor ran tan Mar teenz.

MARTYN, Nigel

Goalkeeper, English, 187cm, 91kg
Born: 11.08.66, St Austell, England
Clubs: Bristol Rovers (1987-89), Crystal Palace (1989-96), Leeds United (1996-).
Full international (England) 14 caps/0 goals
• Arguably the most consistent keeper in the Premier League. An excellent shot-stopper who has been unlucky to have played number two to David Seaman at England level.
• Britain's first million-pound keeper when he joined Crystal Palace.

MASCARDI, Carlos Gustavo

• Argentinian agent who specialises in the transfer of South Americans to Italy. Clients include **Juan Veron**, **Faustino Asprilla**, **Hernan Crespo** and **Nelson Vivas**.
Contact: Sarmiento 385, 1041 Buenos Aires, Argentina. Tel: 00 54 1 785 3234.

MASINGA, Philomen 'Phil'

Forward, South African, 187cm, 77kg
Born: 21.06.69, Stillfontein, South Africa
Clubs: Jomo Cosmos (1990), Mamelodi Sundowns (1991-93), Leeds United (Eng) (1994-96), St Gallen (Swi) (1996), Salernitana (Ita) (1996-97), Bari (Ita) (1997)
Full international (South Africa)
• Striker whose languid style and lanky legs have earned him a reputation as a goalscorer in Europe, although he has not always been appreciated at home in South Africa.
• Began his professional career at Jomo Cosmos, moving on to Mamelodi Sundowns, where success in local competitions earned him a move to England. He slotted in well at Leeds, but a dreadful miss against Manchester United cost him a regular place and he moved on to Switzerland after two seasons.
• After six months with St Gallen, he joined Salernitana in Italy's Serie B and then went on loan to Bari in Serie A. He was Bari's top scorer two seasons running and is now well established as one of the leading Africans playing in Europe.
• Was a member of the South African national side which played against Cameroon in July 1992, the first match since the lifting of international sporting sanctions. Masinga has gone on to become South Africa's leading goalscorer of all time, but vowed in 1999 to only play for the national side in away games after being jeered and booed by local fans.

MATARRESE, Antonio

• Italian member of the FIFA executive committee and a former president of the FIGC (Federazione Italiana Gioco Calcio) the Italian FA.
• Until June 2000, was a vice-president and executive commitee member of UEFA but was voted off at the UEFA Congress during Euro 2000.

Olaf Marschall

MATERAZZI, Giuseppe
Italian
Born: 05.01.46
• Much-travelled coach who is back in Italy after a disappointing spell in Italy with Sporting Lisbon. Was coach of Lazio for two seasons (1989-91) and Bari for four seasons (1992-96), and has also been in charge of Pisa, Messina, Casertana, Padova, Brescia and Piacenza.
• Father of **Marco Materazzi**.

PLAYER
MATERAZZI, Marco
Defender, Italian, 193cm, 92kg
Born: 19.08.73, Lecce, Italy
Clubs: Marsala (1993-94), Trapani (1994-95), Perugia (1995-96), Carpi (1996), Perugia (1997-98), Everton (Eng) (1998-99), Perugia (1999-)
• Central defender who returned to Perugia in 1999 after a disappointing year in England with Everton.

ADMINISTRATOR
MATHIEZ, Marcel
• President of the Swiss FA.

PLAYER
MATTHAUS Lothar
Defender, German, 174cm, 72kg
Born: 21.03.61, Erlangen, Germany
Clubs: Borussia Monchengladbach (1979-84), Bayern Munich (1984-88), Internazionale (Ita) (1988-92), Bayern Munich (1992-2000), New York/New Jersey MetroStars (USA) (2000-)
Full international (Germany) 150 caps/22 goals
• Officially the world's most capped footballer and arguably the greatest player of the 1990s. The only outfield player to have appeared in five World Cup finals and holds the record for the most World Cup finals appearances: 25.
• Began his professional career with Monchengladbach in 1979, making his

international debut in 1980 against Holland. Joinied Bayern in 1984, winning the German League title in 1985, 1986 and 1987 before a move to Italy where he won the 1989 League title and the 1991 UEFA Cup.

• Captained Germany to victory in the 1990 World Cup Final and was named German, European and World Footballer of the Year.

• Returned to Germany in 1992 and won further honours with Bayern Munich, but missed Germany's triumph at the 1996 European Championships in England after a public row with Jurgen Klinsmann and coach **Berti Vogts** ('My biggest mistake').

• Switched to sweeper in the latter years of his career, winning the Geman Footballer of the Year award in 1999 and winning a world record 144th cap for Germany against Holland in February 2000.

• Moved to New York in spring 2000 to join MetroStars, but made little contribution to their cause and was widely tipped for a swift return to Europe.

• 'I certainly wasn't a Maradona. I was a very fast player who saw a space and used it. If I dribbled past someone they didn't catch up with me. What Maradona saw in the small space, I could see over long distances.'

PLAYER
MATTEO, Dominic
Defender, English, 186cm, 74kg
Born: 24.04.74, Dumfries, Scotland
Clubs: Liverpool (1992-2000), Sunderland (1995, loan), Leeds (2000-)
• Tall, versatile defender who played in a three-man central defence under Roy Evans at Liverpool, and at full-back in **Gerard Houllier**'s back four.
• Rejected overtures from Scotland in hope of adding senior England honours to his Under-21 caps, but changed his mind in summer 2000.
• Joined Leeds in August 2000 after failing to command a first team place at Anfield.

PLAYER
MATTIASSON, Christer
Forward, Swedish, 175cm, 75kg
Born: 29.07.71
Clubs: Elfsborg (1996-98), AIK Stockholm (1998-)
Full international (Sweden) 2 caps/0 goals
• Striker who made a dramatic first season in the Swedish Allsvenskan for Elfsborg in 1997, scoring 14 League goals and earning a move to AIK a year later.
• A penalty-box opportunist, nicknamed 'Opportunist'.

PLAYER
MATYSEK, Adam
Goalkeeper, Poland, 191cm, 90kg
Born: 19.07.68, Poland
Clubs: Gornik Zabrze, Slask Breslau, Fortuna Koln (Ger) (1995-98), Gutersloh (Ger), Bayer Leverkusen (Ger) (1998-)
Full international (Poland) 29 caps/0 goals
• Polish international keeper who was given his chance in the Leverkusen goal when first-choice **Dirk Heinen** was sidelined with a serious head injury on the eve of the 1998-99 season and performed so ably that Heinen was eventually forced into the role of understudy.
• Steady rather spectacular. Good positioning, reflexes and distribution.

COACH
MATZOURAKIS, Yiannis
Greek
• Appointed Olympiakos coach in the final weeks of the 1999-2000 season, the ex-Xanthi boss was the Piraeus club's third coach of the campaign, following in the footsteps of Dusan Bayevic and Alberto Bigon.
• Matzourakis kept a firm hand on the tiller as Olympiakos collected their fourth national title. It was the second title of his career; the first was when leading APOEL Nicosia to the Cypriot championship 10 years ago.

PLAYER
MAUL, Ronald
Midfielder, German, 173cm, 72kg
Born: 13.02.73, Jena, Germany
Clubs: Geisstal, Carl Jeiss Jena, Osnabruck, Arminia Bielefeld (1996-)
Full international (Germany) 2 caps/0 goals
• Left wing-back, who earned his first cap for Germany in the Confederations Cup in Mexico in 1999, but has since faded from the international scene. Sturdy, dynamic and tactically disciplined.
• Surname pronounced Mowl.

PLAYER
MAURICE, Florian
Forward, French, 175cm, 73kg
Born: 20.01.74, Sainte-Foy-les-Lyon
Clubs: Lyon (1992-97), Paris Saint-Germain (1997-98), Marseille (1998-)
Full international (France) 6 caps/1 goal
• Talented striker who might well have gone to Euro 2000 with France if he had not been sidelined with a knee injury. A natural goalpoacher with a shoot-on-sight policy, but also has a strong steak of unselfishness in his make-up and has the mobility and awareness to create chances too.
• Surname pronounced Mor reece.

PLAYER
MAURO SILVA
Full name: Mauro da Silva Gomes
Midfielder, Brazilian, 180cm, 80kg
Born: 12.01.68, San Bernarrdo do Campo, Brazil
Clubs: Bragantino, Deportivo La Coruna (Spa) (1992-2000)
Full international (Brazil) 57 caps/0 goals
• Skilful, strong and industrious central midfielder who is a living legend in Galicia after eight seasons at Deportivo.
• A World Cup winner with Brazil in 1994, when he played in all seven games in the USA.
• Spanish Liga winner with Deportivo in 2000,

Phil Masinga

but left the club in July 2000 after his contract was mysteriously terminated.

• **John Toshack** on Mauro Silva: 'He's the best in the world in his position. When he's on form, he works like a horse.'

PLAYER
MAVROGENIDIS, Dimitris
Defender, Greek, 180cm, 70kg
Born: 23.12.76, Greece
Clubs: Aris Salonika (1996-97), Olympiakos (1997-)
Full international (Greece) 16 caps/1 goal
• Top-rated right-back or right-sided midfielder with Olympiakos. Previously with Aris Salonika and recently linked with Italian side Torino.

PLAYER
MAY, David
Defender, English, 184cm, 79kg
Born: 24.06.70, Oldham, England
Clubs: Blackburn (1988-94), Manchester Utd (1994-)
• Solid centre-back who joined United in July 1994 for £1.4m, but missed much of following three seasons through injury and was then pushed down the pecking order by the arrival of **Jaap Stam** at Old Trafford.

PLAYER
MAYRLEB, Christian
Forward, Austrian, 177cm, 76kg
Born: 08.06.72, Wels, Austria
Clubs: SV Ried (1993-94), Admira Wacker (1994-96), Tirol (1996-98) Austria Vienna (1998-)
Full international (Austria) 14 caps/3 caps
• Midfielder who was one of the players of the 1998-99 season in Austria, scoring 17 times in the League for Austria Vienna and attracting the attention of many foreign scouts.
• Good close control and powerful in the air.

PLAYER
MAX, Martin
Forward, German, 182cm, 79kg
Born: 07.08.68, Tarnowitz, Poland
Clubs: Borussia Monchengladbach (1989-95), Schalke (1995-99), Munich 1860 (1999-)
• The Bundesliga's top marksman in the 1999-2000 season with 19 goals, a total all the more impressive because it it contained only one penalty.
• A pacy and brave forward who can finish with aplomb with either right foot, left foot or head.

PLAYER
MAXIMOV, Yurii
Midfielder, Ukrainian, 187cm, 85kg
Born: 08.12.68, Herson, Ukraine
Clubs: Dnepr Dnjepropetrowsk (1992-94), Dynamo Kyiv (1994-97), Werder Bremen (Ger) (1997-)
Full international (Ukraine) 23 caps/5 goals
• In his two-and-a-half years with Werder the Ukrainian right-sided or central midfielder has spent a fair proportion of his time in the treatment room. But when fit, he can be a very useful performer indeed, a dynamic, hard-working figure in the engine room and one with the knack of stealing late into the box to score goals.
• A fey figure in the Kyiv Dynamo midfield in the mid-1990s who transferred to Werder £1.5 million.
• After some personal problems with **Josef Szabo** again, he returned to the Ukraine national side under **Valeri Lobanovsky**.
• Surname pronounced Max ee mof.

PLAYER
MAZINHO
Full name: Iomar do Nascimento
Midfielder, Brazilian, 176cm, 74kg
Born: 08.04.66, Santa Rita, Brazil
Clubs: Santa Cruz (1983-85), Vasco da Gama (1985-90), Lecce (Ita) (1990-91), Fiorentina (Ita) (1991-92), Palmeiras (1992-94), Valencia (Spa) (1994-96), Celta Vigo (Spa) (1996-2000)

Full international (Brazil)
- Highly effective holding midfielder who is approaching the end of his career.
- A member of Brazil's winning squad at the 1994 World Cup.
- Moved to Celta after being prematurely discarded by Valencia, but released by Celta in summer of 2000.

PLAYER
MAZZANTINI, Andrea
Goalkeeper, Italian, 182cm, 76kg
Born: 11.07.68, La Spezia, Italy
Clubs: Pro Patia (1987-88), Sarzanese (1988-90), Livorno (1990-91), Spezia (1991-93), Venezia (1993-96), Internazionale (1996-98), Perugia (1999-)
- A late developer who has finally won a regular first-team place in a Serie A at Perugia after years of doing the rounds of the lower Italian divisions and of sitting on the bench at Inter.

PLAYER
MAZZARELLI, Giuseppe
Defender, Swiss, 180cm, 79kg
Born: 14.08.79
Clubs: FC Zurich (1990-95), Manchester City (Eng) (1995-96), FC Zurich (1996-97), Grasshopper (1997-99), St Gallen (1999-)
Full international (Switzerland) 3 caps/0 goals
- A highly competitive central defender or midfielder who was outstanding for the 1999-2000 season's surprise champions in Switzerland, St Gallen.
- Won his first cap for Switzerland against the United Arab Emirates in September 1994.

PLAYER
MAZZOLA, Alessandro
Midfielder, Italian, 182cm, 74kg
Born: 15.06.69, Varese, Italy
Clubs: Varese (1987-92), Catanzaro (1992-95), Reggiana (1995-97), Piacenza (1997-)
- Hard-working midfielder who plays a crucial if

unglamorous role for Piacenza.

COACH
MAZZONE, Carlo
Italian
Born: 19.03.37
- Veteran campaigner with great experience and tactical nous.
- After a solid playing career as a full-back with Ascoli and Roma, he made his narme as a coach with Ascoli from 1968 to 1975, winning promotions from Serie C1 to Serie A.
- After three seasons at Fiorentina he returned to Ascoli and then moved on to a succession of clubs, none of which has ever been able to provide him with a platform for wider success.
- His most impressive success in recent years came with Bologna, whom he took to a UEFA Cup semi-final in 1999. But a disagreement with club directors forced him to move on to Perugia.

PLAYER
MAZZONI, Javier
Forward, Argentinian, 181cm, 78kg
Born: 04.08.72 Quilmes, Argentina
Clubs: Nantes (Fra) (1996-98), Lausanne (Swi) (1998-)
- Pony-tailed Argentine striker who flopped during two seasons in France with Nantes, but is having more luck in Switzerland at Lausanne.
- An old-style bustling front-man, his nickname is appropriately 'El Tank'.
- Scored in Lausanne's 2-0 win over Grasshopper in the 1999 Cup final.

PLAYER
MBOMA, Patrick
Forward, Cameroon, 185cm, 85kg
Born: 15.11.70, Douala, Cameroon
Clubs: Paris Saint-Germain (Fra) (1990-92), Chateauroux (Fra) (1992-93), Paris Saint-Germain (Fra) (1993), Chateauroux (Fra) (1993-94), Paris Saint-Germain (Fra) (1994-95), Metz (Fra) (1995-

96), Paris Saint-Germain (Fra) (1996), Gamba Osaka (Jap) (1997-98), Cagliari (Ita) (1998-2000), Parma (Ita) (2000-)
Full international (Cameroon)
• Much travelled Cameroon international striker who was born in Cameroon but raised in France.
• A bit-player at Metz and Paris Saint-Germain before a move to Japan in 1997, when his career took off, scoring 29 goals in 34 J.League games for Gamba Osaka and earning a move to Italy.
• Made his international debut in 1996 for Cameroon in a friendly against Liberia, but did not impress and was left out of the squad for the 1996 African Nations Cup. Was recalled for the start of the 1998 World Cup qualifers and has scored regularly ever since.
• Joined Parma in summer 2000 after Cagliari's relegation from Serie A.

PLAYER
McALLISTER, Gary
Midfielder, Scotland, 185cm, 72kg
Born: 25.12.64, Motherwell, Scotland
Clubs: Motherwell (1981-85), Leicester (1985-90), Leeds (1990-96), Coventry (1996-2000), Liverpool (2000-)
Full international (Scotland) 57 caps/5 goals
• Accomplished midfield playmaker who won the 1992 English League title with Leeds.
• Scotland's captain at Euro 96, but missed 1998 World Cup with a serious knee injury and announced his retirement from international football in the 1999-2000 season.
• Made a surprise switch to Liverpool in June 2000.

PLAYER
McATEER, Jason
Midfielder, Irish, 185cm, 82kg
Born: 18.06.71, Liverpool
Clubs: Bolton, Liverpool, Blackburn
Full international (Rep. Ireland)
• Industrious and versatile player who began as a central midfielder but moved to right wing-back at Liverpool.
• Moved to Blackburn after falling from favour at Liverpool, amid allegations that he was a leading member of a gang of Liverpool players who had been dubbed the Spice Boys by the press because of their love of clothes and nightclubs.

PLAYER
McCALL, Stuart
Midfielder, Scottish, 173cm, 75kg
Born: 100.06.64, Leeds, England
Clubs: Bradford (1982-88), Everton (1988-91), Rangers (1992-98), Bradford (1998-)
Full international (Scotland) 40 caps/1 goal
• Veteran midfield ball-winner who returned to Bradford in 1998 after enjoying great success in Scotland with Rangers and played a major role in Bradford's promotion to the Premier League.
• Born in Leeds to Scottish parents.

PLAYER
McCANN, Gavin
Midfielder, English, 181cm, 70kg
Born: 10.01.78, Blackpool, England
Clubs: Everton (1995-98), Sunderland (1998-)
• Hard-working midfielder sold by Everton to Sunderland for £500,000 in November 1998.

PLAYER
McCARTHY, Benedict
Forward, South African, 182cm, 76kg
Born: 12.11.77, Kaapstad, South Africa
Clubs: Seven Stars (1997), Ajax Amsterdam (Hol) (1997-99), Celta Vigo (Spa) (1999-)
Full international (South Africa)
• Talented young striker who was the star of the 1998 African Nations Cup in Burkina Faso.
• Made his name initially in Holland at Ajax, where his goals helped the club win the 1998 Dutch League title.
• Signed by Celta Vigo for a club record £3.75million as a replacement for Bulgarian

striker **Luboslav Penev** in July 1999.
• 'Retired' from international football with South Africa to concentrate on his club career in Spain.

COACH
McCARTHY, Mick
Irish
Born: 07.02.59
• National coach of the Republic of Ireland since 1996, when he suceeded Jack Charlton.
• A central defender for Barnsley, Manchester City, Celtic and Millwall, he won 57 caps for the Republic of Ireland, scoring two goals and appearing in the 1990 World Cup finals.
• A proud Yorkshireman who made his name as a coach at Millwall, he has had the unenviable task of following Charlton as the Republic's manager.

COACH
McCLAREN, Steve
English
• Assistant to **Alex Ferguson** at Old Trafford since Brian Kidd's departure to manage Blackburn in 1999. Previously assistant manager at Derby, where he gained a reputation for thorough preparation and always being open to new ideas and coaching methods.

PLAYER
McCOIST, Ally
Forward, Scottish, 178cm, 76kg
Born: 24.09.62, Bellshil, Scotland
Clubs: St Johnstone (1978-81), Sunderland (1981-83), Rangers (1983-98), Kilmarnock (1998-)
Full international (Scotland) 60 caps/19 goals
• Now 36 years old, McCoist is playing out the final stages of a distinguished career with Kilmarnock and, while his appearances in the first team have been necessarily sporadic, his positive influence at the club is apparent and his appetite for scoring goals remains undiminished.

BUSINESS
McCORMACK, Mark
American
• Pioneering of sports marketing and once famously dubbed 'most powerful man in sport' by *Sports Illustrated* magazine.
• Through his company IMG, he is involved in all aspects of the business of football, from representing players to the sale of TV rights.

COACH
McILROY, Sammy
Northern Irish
Born: 02.08.54
• Coach of Northern Ireland since early 2000 after making a name for himself as a coach by taking non-League Macclesfield into the English Football League.
• A member of the Northern Ireland side at the 1982 World Cup, he won 88 caps (5 goals) during a distinguished playing career at Manchester United, Stoke and Manchester City.

COACH
McLEISH, Alex
Scottish
• Coach of Scottish side Hibernian.
• After winning 77 Scotland caps and countless medals during a highly successful playing career with Aberdeen, McLeish entered the world of club management with Motherwell in 1994 and subsequently moved to Hibernian, transforming the fortunes of the Edinburgh side who were struggling in the First Division at the time.
• After achieving promotion to the Premier League, McLeish revitalised the team by signing players of international quality such as **Franck Sauzee** and **Russell Latapy**, helping Hibs to consolidate their position in the top division in the 1999-2000 season.

McMANAMAN, Steve
Midfielder, English, 184cm, 68kg
Born: 11.02.72, Liverpool, England
Clubs: Liverpool (1990-99), Real Madrid (Spa) (1999-)
Full international (England) 29 caps/3 goals
• Mercurial midfielder who has started to fulfill his great potential, scoring for Real Madrid in the 2000 Champions League Final against Valencia.
• A product of the youth system at Liverpool, his home town, although he supported Everton as a boy. Joined Real in 1999 at the end of his contract at Liverpool.
• An FA Cup winner with Liverpool in 1992 and added a League Cup triumph in 1995.
• Nicknamed 'Shaggy' at Liverpool because of his long hair.
• International debut v Uruguay in 1995, but has consistently failed to reproduce his club form for England. He was the subject of intense speculation before and during Euro 2000 as to whether **Kevin Keegan** would play him on the left, or take a gamble, using him in a free role.
• Was considered to have been a success in his first season in Spain with Real Madrid, but he was told in no uncertain terms by coach **Vincente del Bosque** that he was unlikely to feature in the first team in 2000-2001 following the arrival of **Luis Figo**.

PLAYER
McNAMARA, Jackie
Defender, Scottish, 173cm, 60kg
Born: 24.10.73, Glasgow, Scotland
Clubs: Dunfermline (1992-96), Celtic (1996-)
Full international (Scotland) 10 caps/0 goals
• Son of the Celtic midfielder of the same name, Jackie jnr has developed into an exceptionally talented defender since arriving at the club from Dunfermline four years ago. His defensive qualities are complemented by his ability to push forward and he has become a regular for Scotland.

PLAYER
McPHAIL, Stephen
Midfielder, Irish, 177cm, 76kg
Born: 09.12.79, London, England
Clubs: Leeds (1996-)
Full international (Rep. Ireland) 3 caps/1 goal
• Left-footed midfielder with great passing ability who broke into the Leeds first team in the 1998-99 season after impressing in the club's youth system.
• Republic of Ireland Under-21 international.

PLAYER
McSWEGAN, Gary
Forward, Scottish, 172cm, 68kg
Born: 24.09.70, Glasgow, Scotland
Clubs: Rangers (1986-93), Notts County (1993-95), Dundee United (1995-98), Hearts (1998-)
Full international (Scotland) 2 caps/1 goal
• After spending his formative years at Ibrox, McSwegan played for both Notts County and Dundee United before finally ending up at Hearts. Managed only seven goals in his first season at Tynecastle but his form in the 1999-2000 season led to a call up to the Scottish national side.

AGENT
MEDINA MARTIN, Jesus
• Barcelona-based agent whose clients incluse **Jordi Lardin**.
• **Contact:** Paseo de Gracia, 98, E-08008 Barcelona, Spain. Tel: 00 343 448 00 30.

COACH
MEEUWS, Walter
Belgian
Born: 11.07.51
• Former libero of Standard Liege, Ajax and the Belgian national team. Was Belgian national coach in the early 1990s but was never able to deal with the pressure of succeeding the highly popular Guy Thijs. Unlike Thijs he opted for a more and (by Belgian standards) unusual

Patrick Mboma

attacking style, which he learned from **Johan Cruyff** during his Ajax days. When the results weren't good he was forced to leave very quickly.
• Later led Antwerp to the Cup-winners Cup Final against Parma at Wembley. Previously at Lommel, now at Lierse, where he is working with a very talented squad that lacks consistency.

PLAYER
MEHLEM, Michael
Defender, Austrian, 184cm, 81kg
Born: 01.05.77, Austria
Clubs: LASK (1997-)
• Versatile youngster, who can play at centre-back or in central midfield if required.
• Another of the growing crop of young players to have coe through at LASK, where financial restraints force them to develop young talent.

PLAYER
MEIJER, Erik
Forward, Dutch, 189cm, 87kg
Born: 0.2.08.69, Meerssem, Holland
Clubs: Fortuna Sittard (1990-91), MVV (1991-93), PSV (1993-95), Uerdingen (Ger) (1995-96), Bayer Leverkusen (Ger) (1996-99), Liverpool (Eng) (1999-2000)
Full international (Holland) 1 cap/0 goals
• Much-travelled striker whose biggest strength is his heading ability. Has not seen much first-team action at Liverpool, despite injuries to **Robbie Fowler** and **Michael Owen** and looked set for a return to mainland Europe in the summer of 2000.

REFEREE
MEIER, Urs
Swiss
Born: 22.01.59
• Works as a grocer.
• Awarded his FIFA badge in 1994.

PLAYER
MELCHIOT, Mario

Defender, Dutch, 187cm, 76kg
Born: 04.11.76, Amsterdam, Holland
Clubs: Ajax Amsterdam (1996-99), Chelsea (1999-)
• Tall, long-legged utility player who won a Dutch League and Cup double with Ajax in 1998.
• Joined Chelsea in summer 1999, but injured in pre-season. Recovered in time to play a highly effective role in Chelsea's 2000 FA Cup Final victory over Aston Villa.
• Dutch Under-21 international.

PLAYER
MELIS, Martino

Midfielder, Italian, 180cm, 70kg
Born: 24.11.73, Cagliari, Italy
Clubs: Empoli (1989-95), Chievo (1995-98), Verona (1998-)
• Skilful left-sided midfielder who has been criticised for his poor workrate, but is a clever, creative player.

PLAYER
MELLBERG, Olof

Defender, Swedish, 186cm, 81kg
Born: 03.09.77, Stockholm, Sweden
Clubs: Degerfors (1996-97), AIK Stockholm (1998), Racing Santander (Spa) (1999-)
Full international (Sweden) 7 caps/0 goals
• Versatile defender who can play in a number of postions.
• Member of Sweden's squad at Euro 2000.
• A useful tennis player as a teenager who nearly chose racquets ahead of football.
• Former Swedish Under-21 international

PLAYER
MELLI, Alessandro

Forward, Italian, 179cm, 75kg
Born: 11.12.69, Agrigento, Italy
Clubs: Parma (1985-94), Modena (1988-89, loan),

Sampdoria (1994), Milan (1994-95), Parma (1995-97), Perugia (1998-)
Full international (Italy) 2 caps/0 goals
• Veteran striker who has never fufilled the great promise he showed as a youngster after making his professional debut aged 16 and helping his former club Parma climb through the divisions.

REFEREE
MELO PERREIRA, Vitor Manuel

Portuguese
Born: 21.04.57
• Works as a 'telecommunications expert'.
• Awarded his FIFA badge in 1992.

PLAYER
MENA, Oscar

Full name: Oscar Alcides Mena
Midfielder, Spanish/Argentinian, 182cm, 80kg
Born: 30.11.70, Lujan, Argentina
Clubs: Lujan (1991-92), Cambaceres (1992-94), Platense (1994-96), Lanus (1996-97), Mallorca (Spa) (1997-98), Atletico Madrid (Spa) (1998-)
• Right-footed central midfielder who made the breakthrough under **Hector Cuper** at Mallorca in the 1997-98 season, scoring seven goals in 35 games.
• Signed by Atletico Madrid in 1999, but his performances have been affected by injury.

PLAYER
MENDEZ, Gustavo

Defender, Uruguayan, 176cm, 73kg
Born: 03.02.71, Montevideo, Uruguay
Clubs: Nacional (1991-95), Vicenza (1995-99), Torino (1999-)
Full international (Uruguay)
• Hugely versatile player who can fill a number of positions in defence and midield, making him an invaluable squad player.
• Joined Torino after Vicenza's relegation from Serie A in 1999.

Benni McCarthy

PLAYER
MENDIETA, Gaizka
Full name: Gaizka Mendieta Zabala
Midfielder, Spanish, 173cm, 69kg
Born: 17.03.74, Bilbao, Spain
Clubs: Castellon (1991-92), Valencia (1992-)
Full international (Spain) 17 caps/4 goals
• Outstanding playmaker whose skill and vision should have earned him many more caps for Spain, but he fell out with former coach **Javier Clemente**.
• Starred for Valencia in the 1999 Spanish Cup triumph and their run to the 2000 Champions League Final.
• Joined Valencia aged 19 from second division Castellon, but did not seem likely to develop into anything more than a journeyman full-back.
• The transformation came under Italian coach **Claudio Ranieri** who encouraged Mendieta to lead the team's pressing tactics from central midfield. He ended the 1997-98 season as captain.
• Valencia tripled his salary in summer 1999 to stave off bids from Real Madrid and Athletic Bilbao.
• International debut against Austria in March 1999.
• Father was a goalkeeper with Castellon.

PLAYER
MENDOZA, Andres
Forward, Peruvian, 182cm, 773kg
Born: 02.05.78, Lima, Peru
Clubs: Sporting Cristal (1995-2000), Club Brugge (Bel) (2000-)
Full international (Peru)
• Peruvian striker who was bought by Club Brugge in January 2000 to replace Real Sociedad-bound **Edgaras Jankauskas**. Has had problems adapting so far, but is strong in the air and dangerous in the penalty area.

PLAYER
MENDY, Frederic
Midfielder, French, 182cm, 75kg
Born: 29.11.73, Marseille, France
Clubs: Martigues (1993-97), Bastia (1997-)
• A pillar of the Bastia side, he can play as a
defensive midfielder or as a stopper. A key
member of the French Military side which won
the world title in 1995.

PLAYER
MENIRI, Medhi
Defender, French, 188cm, 85kg
Born: 29.06.77, Troyes, France
Clubs: Nancy, Metz (2000-)
• French Under-21 international defender who
joined Metz in the summer of 2000 after being
relegated with Nancy in 1999-2000.

PLAYER
MERINO, Juan
Full name: Juan Merino Ruiz
Midfielder, Spanish, 176cm, 74kg
Born: 24.08.70, Cadiz, Spain
Clubs: Real Betis (1990-)
• Solid, dependable utility defender who is no
longer first choice at Betis. Can play anywhere in
defence or midfield, especially in a ball-winning
role.

REFEREE
MERK, Markus
German
Born: 21.04.57
• Works full-time as a dentist.
• Awarded his FIFA badge in 1992.

PLAYER
MERSON, Paul
Forward, English, 182cm, 83kg
Born: 20.03.68, London, England
Clubs: Arsenal (1985-97), Brentford (1987, loan),
Middlesbrough (1997-98), Aston Villa (1998-)

Full international (England) 21 caps/3 goals
• Talented forward whose career has been plagued
by much-publicised off-the-pitch problems.
• Won League, FA Cup and European Cup-winners Cup honours with Arsenal, but a move north
to Middlesbrough turned sour and he failed to
settle following tearful revelations of drinking,
gambling and drug addictions.
• Resurrected his career with a move south to
Villa, but announced his international retirement
in April 2000 after being ignored by **Kevin
Keegan**.
• 'I've had some bad days. If you go into the
hairdressers five times by the end of the week
you're going to have a haircut. So I just avoid
pubs. Every now and then I'll go in and have a
coke. But it's a day-to-day thing. Tomorrow, who
knows, it could be completely different.'

PLAYER
MERT Korkmaz
Midfielder, Turkish, 180cm, 76kg
Born: 16.08.71, Turkey
Clubs: Kocaelispor, Gazientepsor
Full international (Turkey) 5 caps/0 goals
• Strong-tackling midfield ball-winner who was
very close to being included in Turkey's squad for
Euro 2000, but just missed out.
• Made his international debut for Turkey against
Russia in April 1998. Went on to start in the first
two qualifying matches for Euro 2000, but then
was dropped.

PLAYER
METTOMO, Lucien
Defender, French/Cameroon, 183cm, 80kg
Born: 19.04.77, Douala, Cameroon
Clubs: Ocean Kribi, St Etienne (1996-)
Full international (Cameroon)
• Powerful young stopper in the Basile Boli
mould, who is on the verge of great things. A
member of the Cameroon squad which won the
2000 African Nations Cup.

MEYRIEU, Frederic
Midfielder, French, 172cm, 75kg
Born: 09.02.68, La Seyne, France
Clubs: Marseille (1985-87), Le Havre (1987-88), Marseille (1988-89), Bordeaux (1989-90), Toulon (1990-93), Lens (1993-97), Metz (1997-)
• A combustible character he might be. But there can be no question about Meyrieu's class as a playmaker. He has a magnificent left foot, bags of invention and is one of the country's most deadly free-kick exponents.
• Surname pronounced May ree ur.

COACH
MEZY, Michal
French
Born: 01.08.48
• Charismatic figure from the Camargue region of south-west France, who seems to have been permanently in transit between the posts of general manager and first-team coach at Montpellier.
• In 1990, he made history as French football's first president-coach, combining both roles at Nimes, but he did not last long.
• Though a fine motivator and a great believer in youth and attacking football, he could not prevent Montpellier being relegated last season.
• In the 1970s, he was one of France's most skilled midfielders, starring for Nimes, Lille and Montpellier and playing 17 times for France.

PLAYER
MICHAELSEN, Jan
Midfielder, Danish, 182cm, 79kg
Born: 28.11.70, Denmark
Clubs: AB (1996-)
Full international (Denmark) 2 caps/0 goals
• Aggressive hard-working right-sided midfielder whose performances for AB in recent seasons have taken him to the fringes of the Danish national side.

PLAYER
MICHALKE, Kai
Forward, German, 172cm, 65kg
Born: 05.04.76, Bochum, Germany
Clubs: SG Werne, Bochum (1994-99), Hertha Berlin (1999-)
• A former German Under-21 star, this attacking midfielder or frontrunner was tipped for greatness two or three years ago. But has found the competition for places slightly too hot to handle at Hertha. A pity; he has a great left-foot, is a nippy dribbler and never holds anything back on the pitch.
• Surname pronounces Mee shal ker.

PLAYER
MICHEL I
Full name: Miguel Angel Sanchez
Midfielder, Spanish, 174cm, 67kg
Born: 30.10.75, Madrid, Spain
Clubs: Rayo Vallecano B (1992-94), Rayo Vallecano (1994-), Almeria (1996-97, loan)
• Tireless worker in midfield for Rayo Vallecano, having coming through the ranks of Rayo B.
• Named after former Real Madrid star Michel Gonzalez.

PLAYER
MICHEL II
Full name: Miguel Angel Carrilero
Forward, Spanish, 188cm, 85kg
Born: 18.07.77, Madrid, Spain
Clubs: Conquese (1996-97), Rayo Vallecano B (1997-98), Penafiel (1998-99), Rayo Vallecano (1999-)
• Strong and hard-working midfielder who played a key role in Rayo Vallecano's promotion to the Spanish first division in 1999.
• Named Michel II to distinguish him from his namesake at Vallecano.

MICHEL, Lubos

Slovak
Born: 16.05.68
Works as a school teacher.
Awarded his FIFA badge in 1994.

PLAYER
MICHEL SALGADO

Full name: Michel Salgado Fernandez
Defender, Spanish, 173cm, 73kg
Born: 22.10.75, Pontevedra, Spain
Clubs: Celta (1993-99), Salamanca (1996-97), Real Madrid (1999-)
Full international (Spain) 17 caps/0 goals
Swashbuckling right-back who made his name at Celta Vigo with his raiding moves down the right during their 1998-99 UEFA Cup campaign.

Early career at Celta reached a crossroads in 1996 when he was farmed out to second division Salamanca on loan. But his performances in their promotion-winning campaign persuaded Celta to take him back.

Moved to Real Madrid in the summer of 1999. Was unlucky with injuries but recovered sufficiently to play in the winning Champions League Final side against Valencia in May 2000.
• Made his international debut against Cyprus on 05.09.99, which was **Javier Clemente**'s last game in charge (Spain lost 3-2).
• Established his national team credentials with a man-of-the-match performance against Italy in November 1998.

PLAYER
MICHOPOULOS, Nikos

Goalkeeper, Greek, 190cm, 86kg
Born: 20.02.70, Greece
Clubs: PAOK Thessaloniki (1996-)
Full international (Greece) 11 caps/0 goals
• Capable keeper who particularly impressed during the 1999-2000 season for PAOK.

PLAYER
MICIC, Dragan

Forward, Yugoslav, 173cm, 62kg
Born: 22.09.69, Bijeljina, Yugoslavia
Clubs: Red Star Belgrade
• A prolific scorer in the Yugoslav League but still only the eternal super-sub.

PLAYER
MICOUD, Johan

Midfielder, French, 188cm, 82kg
Born: 24.07.73, Cannes, France
Clubs: Cannes (1992-96), Bordeaux (1996-2000), Parma (Ita) (2000-)
Full international (France) 7 caps/0 goals
• At times in the 1999-2000 season, he allowed his high standards to slip and it was ironic that it was the campaign when he made a sure-footed entry onto the French national team stage. But when Micoud gets it right, he is the total midfield package: wonderful passing ability, caressing ball-control, physical presence, goals and excellent set-pieces.
• The comparisons with one Eric Cantona are anything but unfounded; the same upright stance, elegance and arrogance.
• Path at international level has been blocked by **Zinedine Zidane**, but his career progressed in the summer oof 2000 with a transfer to Parma.
• Surname pronounced Mee koo.

PLAYER
MIECIEL, Marcin

Forward, Polish, 186cm, 76kg
Born: 22.12.75, Poland
Clubs: Legia Warsaw
Full international (Poland) 11 caps/1 goal
• Quick, promising striker who has excellent technique on the ball. Can be used in midfield as well. Has not made the most of his potential yet, although he scored on his international debut for Poland.

Gaizka Mendieta

ADMINISTRATOR
MIFSUD, Joseph
Born: 13.01.50
• President of the Maltese Football Association and a member of the FIFA executive committee since 1998 until 2000, when he lost his place after a vote at the UEFA congress during Euro 2000.
• A lawyer by profession.

PLAYER
MIFSUD, Michael
Forward, Maltese, 176cm, 70kg
Born: 17.04.81, Malta
Clubs: Sliema Wanderers
Full international (Malta) 2 caps/0 goals
• Promising young striker who is seen as the successor to **Carmel Busuttil** in the Maltese national team.

AGENT
MIGLIACIO, Alain
• French-based representative of **Zinedine Zidane.**
• **Contact:** Residence Alexandra, 2, Chemin Vert, F-69160 Tassin La Demi-Lune, France. Tel: 00 33 4 72 38 05 01.

PLAYER
MIHAJLOVIC, Sinisa
Defender, Yugoslav, 185cm, 78kg
Born: 20.02.69, Vukovar, Croatia.
Clubs: Vojvodina (1988-90), Red Star Belgrade (1990-92), Roma (Ita) (1992-94), Sampdoria (Ita) (1994-98), Lazio (Ita) (1998-).
Full international (Yugoslavia) 47 caps/5 goals
• Former midfielder who was converted into a world-class sweeper by **Sven Goran Eriksson** at Sampdoria in 1996.
• Cut his teeth at Borovo and Vojvodina clubs, transferring to Red Star Belgrade halfway through the 1990-91 season and playing a key role in the 1991 European Cup triumph.

• A free-kick expert whose left-foot shots can travel at up to 150km/hour. An excellent reader of the game who can start counter-attacks with his long passes out of defence.

• Followed Eriksson to Lazio in 1998 and was one of the stars of Lazio's 1999-2000 successful Italian League title challenge.

• Born into a mixed family in the former Yugoslavia, with a Serb father and Croat mother.

• When he returned to his native city of Vukovar in Croatia, he was shocked by what he discovered. 'The city was wiped out like some sort of Hiroshima, our house reduced to rubble. I stopped the car close to my old school. I wanted to retrace the path I used to take as a child every morning, but the school wasn't there any more. I found a poster of the Yugoslav national team with me in it. There was a bullet mark over my heart.'

• Was a highly vocal critic of the NATO bombing of Serbia and he caused controversy before Euro 2000 when it emerged he had signed up to Slobodan Milosevic's Socialist Party, which he denies.

PLAYER
MIHALCEA, Adrian
Forward, Romanian, 180cm, 74kg
Born: 24.05.76, Slobozia, Romania
Clubs: Dinamo Bucharest 1996-
Full international (Romania) 10 caps/0 goals
• Promising forward whose goals for Dinamo have attracted interest from clubs in Italy and Spain.

PLAYER
MIJATOVIC, Predrag
Forward, Yugoslav, 177cm, 73kg
Born: 19.01.69, Podgorica, Yugoslavia.
Clubs: Buducnost (1988-89), Partizan Belgrade (1989-93), Valencia (Spa) (1993-96), Real Madrid (Spa) (1996-99), Fiorentina (Ita) (1999-)
Full international (Yugoslavia) 51 caps/22 goals
• One of Yugoslavia's leading strikers and an attacker of pace, hair-trigger reactions and exceptional technique.

• The hero of Real Madrid's 1998 European Cup triumph after scoring the only goal of the Final against Juventus.

• Born in Montenegro and made his mark in the Yugoslav League with Budocnost Titograd and Partizan Belgrade, notching 44 goals in 90 matches.

• Signed by Valencia in 1993 after the Spanish club lost out to Barcelona in the race to sign Brazilian Romario.

• At Valencia, he was the undisputed star of the 1995-96 season, scoring 28 goals as his team finished as runners-up in the Spanish League, and being voted Footballer of the Year.

• Has been criticised for his tendency to lose his footing easily in and around the penalty area. **Jesus Gil** once accused him of being 'epileptic', to which Mijatovic responded: 'It's only jealosy. Anyway, it takes real skill to be a good actor.'

• Joined Real Madrid for a reported £4.8million in summer 1997.

• Was the top scorer in the European section of the qualifiers for France 98, scoring 14 goals, including seven in the play-off mauling of Hungary.

• Moved to Fiorentina in 1999, but struggled with fitness, needing an operation on a heel.

• Made his international debut aged 20 for Yugoslavia against Finland, 23.08.89.

PLAYER
MIKHALEVICH, Pavel
Midfielder, Belarus, 172cm, 66kg
Born: 22.01.74, Minsk, Belarus
Clubs: NEC (1993-)
• Belarussian midfielder who went to Nijmegen, Holland, as part of a student exchange but stayed to play for the local club NEC. Had a bad season in 1999-2000 after suffering from an Achilles tendon that ruled him out for months.

• Has never been a member of his country's senior or Olympic squads because the Belarussian federation can not cover the travelling expenses.

Michel Salgado

PLAYER
MIKIC, Mihael
Forward, Croatian, 176cm, 71kg
Born: 06.01.80, Zagreb Croatia
Clubs: Dinamo Zagreb
• Promising young striker who has been dubbed the 'Croatian **Michael Owen**' because of similarities in looks and playing style.
• Starred for Croatia at the 1998 European Under-18 championships in Cyprus, winning a place in UEFA's all-star team.

PLAYER
MIKULENAS, Grazodas
Forward, Lithuanian, 185cm, 83kg
Born: 16.12.73, Lithuania
Clubs: Zalgiris Vilnius, Polonia Warsaw (Pol) (1996-98), Croatia Zagreb (Cro) (1998-)
Full international (Lithuania) 11 caps/1 goal
• Striker who moved to Zagreb with his Polish wife in January 1999 after a successful spell in Poland where he was voted Player of the Season by Polish soccer writers.
• Made his international debut for Lithuania against Poland in September 1997.

PLAYER
MILANESE, Mauro
Defender, Italian, 186cm, 83kg
Born: 17.09. 71, Trieste, Italy
Clubs: Massese (1991-92), Triestina (1992-94), Cremonese (1994-95), Torino (1995-96), Napoli (1996-97), Parma (1997), Internazionale (1998-99), Perugia (1999-)
• Journeyman full-back who fought his way up from the lower reaches of the Italian League to play in Serie A.
• Joined Inter in January 1998 after his place at Parma. Has since moved on to Perugia.

PLAYER
MILANIC, Darko

Defender, Slovenian, 184cm, 82kg
Born: 18.12.67, Koper, Slovenia
Clubs: Partizan Belgrade (1990-93), Sturm Graz (Aut) (1993-)
Full international (Slovenia) 44 caps/0 caps
• Veteran stopper and useful man-marker who can be relied upon to display great authority at the back.
• Won honours with the former Yugoslavia and played for Slovenia in Euro 2000.
• International debut for Slovenia: v Cyprus, 18.11.92 (1-1).

PLAYER
MILD, Hakan

Midfielder, Swedish, 182cm, 75kg
Born: 14.06.71, Trolhattan, Sweden
Clubs: IFK Gothenburg (1989-93), Servette (Swi) (1993-95), IFK Gothenburg (1995-96), Real Sociedad (Spa) (1996-1998), IFK Gothenburg (1998-)
Full international (Sweden) 58 caps/6 goals
• A mainstay for both IFK and Sweden who has had spells abroad in Switzerland and Spain.
• Returned home from Real Sociedad in 1999 for family reasons. A model player for coaches because of his work-rate and discipline.

AGENT
MILEWSKI, Jurgen

• Former player who is now a successful agent in Germay. Clients include **Alexander Zickler**, **Olaf Marschall**, **Dariusz Wosz**, **Jiri Nemec** and **Slobodan Komljenovic**.
• **Contact:** BTN Sport, Hudtwalckerstrasse 11, D-22299 Hamburg, Germany. Tel: 00 49 40 4607 6633.

PLAYER
MILINOVIC, Zeljko

Defender, Slovenian, 189cm, 86kg
Born: 12.01.76, Ljubljana, Slovenia
Clubs: Olimpia Ljubljana (1993-94), Zeleznicar

(1994-95), Maribor (1995-98), LASK (Aut) (1998-)
Full international (Slovenia) 21 caps/1 goal caps
• Reliable centre-back who is often used in a man-marking role.
• A member of the Slovenia squad at Euro 2000.
• International debut: Slovania v Austria, 18.03.97, v Austria (won 2-0).

PLAYER
MILLER, Kenny

Forward, Scottish, 175cm, 68kg
Born: 23.12.79, Edinburgh, Scotland
Clubs: Hibernian (1997-2000), Rangers (2000-)
• At the age of 19, Miller is regarded as one of the most promising prospects in Scotland and settled in easily to the Hibs first team, showing remarkable temperament and composure together with an insatiable goalscoring appetite.
• He joined Rangers in the summer of 2000 and, given his level of progress, it is only a matter of time before he aspires to full international recognition.
• Scottish Under-21 international.

PLAYER
MILOSEVIC, Savo

Forward, Yugoslav, 186cm, 85kg
Born: 02.09.73, Bijelina, Yugoslavia
Clubs: Partizan Belgrade (1992-95), Aston Villa (Eng) (19995-98), Zaragoza (Spa) (1998-2000), Parma (Ita) (2000-)
Full international (Yugoslavia) 49 caps/25 goals
• Tall, powerful forward who made his name at Partizan Belgrade before being signed on the basis of a video tape by Aston Villa for £3million in summer 1995.
• Won the League Cup with Villa, scoring in the Final, but left in disgrace after allegedly spitting at fans.
• Rediscovered his scoring touch in Spain and his goals helped Zaragoza challenge for a Champions League spot in 1999-2000 season.
• International debut: 23.12.94, v Brazil (lost 2-0).

Sinisa Mihajlovic

• Played for Yugoslavia at Euro 2000, where he surprised many with his goalcoring feats as he finished as the tournament's joint top scorer on six goals.

• Linked with a move to Italy in summer 2000 and eventually joined Parma in a £16million move.

• 'After six months at Aston Villa I wanted to move. I felt uncomfortable playing as a second striker. It was not Villa that I wanted to escape from, but English football, which did not suit me.'

PLAYER
MILOSEVSKI, Petar
Goalkeeper, Macedonian, 188cm, 82kg
Born: 06.12.73
Clubs: Pelister Bitola (1990-94), Vardar Skopje (1994-98), Trabzonspor (Tur) (1998-)
Full international (Macedonia) 16 caps/0 goals

• One of the most successful Macedonians abroad, with Trabzonspor in Turkey since 1998.

• A Macedonian title-winner in 1994 and 1995 and Cup-winner in 1995.

PLAYER
MILLA, Luis
Full name: Luis Milla Aspas
Midfielder, Spanish, 173cm, 69kg
Born: 12.03.66, Terual, Spain
Clubs: Barcelona (1986-90), Real Madrid (1990-97), Valencia (1997-)
Full international (Spain) 3 caps/0 goals

• Veteran midfield playmaker who is more often to be found on the bench these days.

• Came through at Barcelona under **Johan Cruyff**, but became one of the few players to join arch-rivals Real Madrid after falling out with Cruyff.

• Won two further Spanish League titles in Madrid before moving to Valencia in summer 1997. Lost his place in the starting line-up during the 1999-2000 season following injury and the rise of young midfielders **Gerard** and **Farinos**.

PLAYER
MILLS, Danny
Defender, English, 177cm, 75kg
Born: 18.05.77, Norwich, England
Clubs: Norwich (1994-98), Charlton (1998-99), Leeds (1999-2000)
• Quick right-back or wing-back who joined Leeds in summer 1999 for £3million after relegation with Charlton, but found life at Elland Road tough-going.
• England Under-21 international.

REFEREE
MILTON NIELSEN, Kim
Danish
Born: 03.08.60
• Awarded his FIFA badge in 1988.
• Sent **David Beckham** off during England's game against Argentina at the 1998 World Cup.

PLAYER
MINAVAND, Minavaud
Midfielder, Iranian, 183cm, 76kg
Born: 30.11.75, Tehran, Iran
Clubs: Pirouzi (1998), Sturm Graz (1998-)
Full international (Iran)
• Left-side midfielder who played all three games for Iran at the 1998 World Cup.

AGENT
MINGUELLA, Jose
• Barcelona-based businessman whose most famous client is **Rivaldo**. Also represents **Albert Ferrer**, **Sergi** and **Josep Guardiola**.
• **Contact:** C/Miret Sans I, 60, E-08034, Barcelona, Spain, Tel: 00 343 280 29 77.

PLAYER
MINKO, Valeri
Midfielder, Russian, 182cm, 80kg
Born: 08.08.71, Russia
Clubs: CSKA Moscow (1989-)
Full international (Russia) 4 caps/0 goals

• Tall, slim winger who is a legend at CSKA Moscow because of his loyalty to the club and his refusal to quit football following a kidney operation.

PLAYER
MIONNET, Cedric
Forward, French, 170cm, 65kg
Born: 08.07.74, Montreuil-sur-Mer, France
Clubs: Lens (1996-97), Sedan (1997-)
• At the start of the 1999-2000 season, many thought this adroit striker could be in line for a French national team call-up, but although it has not yet happened, his chance has far from gone.
• Speedy, able to glide past defenders and a cool finisher, he was rejected as a youngster by first division Lens, who claimed he was too small to make the grade.
• He used to work at a centre for handicapped people.
• Pronounced Say dreek Mee oh nay.

PLAYER
MIRKOVIC, Zoran
Defender, Yugoslav, 183cm, 75kg
Born: 21.09.71, Belgrade, Yugoslavia.
Clubs: Rad Belgrade (1989-93), Partizan Belgrade (1993-96), Atalanta (Ita) (1996-98), Juventus (Ita) (1998-)
Full international (Yugoslavia) 39 caps/0 goals
• Versatile defender who plays as an adventurous right-back for his country, but has often played at centre-back at club level.
• Was left out of Yugoslavia's squad for Euro 2000, after receiving a three-match ban following a red card in the final qualifying match.

PLAYER
MITRITA, Dumitru
Defender, Romanian, 168cm, 69kg
Born: 23.06.71, Craoiva, Romania
Clubs: Univ. Craoiva (1990-91), Electrop. Craoiva (1991-94), Univ. Craoiva (1994-97), Heerenveen

(Hol) (1997-)
Full international (Romania) 1 cap/0 goals
• Left-back who has settled well at Dutch club Heerenveen following a move from Romania in 1997.

PLAYER
MISSE-MISSE, Jean Jacques
Forward, Cameroonian, 180cm, 76kg
Born: 07.08.68, Yaounde, Cameroon
Clubs: Charleroi (Bel) (1993-96), Sporting Lisbon (Por) (1996-97), Trabzonspor (Tur) (1997-98), Dundee United (Sco) (1997-98), Chesterfield (Eng) (1997-98), Ethnikos Asteras (Gre) (1998-)
• Powerful yet adroit Cameroon international forward with the Ethnikos club. Enjoyed the best spell of his career when his 15 goals helped Belgian side Charleroi qualify for the UEFA Cup in 1993-94.

PLAYER
MIZRAHI, Alon
Forward, Israeli
Born: 22.11.71, Israel
Clubs: Maccabi Haifa, Nice (Fra), Hapoel Haifa, Betar Jerusalem
Full international (Israel) 29 caps/13 goals
• Since leaving for French second division side Nice in the 1998-99 season, Mizrahi, who has a good instinct in front of goal has been out of form. He has failed to find it since returning to Israel in the 1999-2000, when he joined Hapoel Haifa before moving on to Betar.

PLAYER
MJALLBY, Johan
Midfielder, Swedish, 186cm, 85kg
Born: 09.02.71, Sweden
Clubs: AIK Stockholm (1989-98), Celtic (Sco) (1998-)
Full international (Sweden) 22 caps/3 goals
• Brought to Celtic by Dr **Josef Venglos** from AIK Stockholm, Mjallby has delivered some solid

performances in the heart of the Parkhead back four and has covered well in recent itmes during the injury-enforced absences of **Alan Stubbs**.
• Played in all three of Sweden's games at Euro 2000.

PLAYER
MJELDE, Mons Ivar
Forward, Norwegian, 185cm, 85kg
Born: 17.11.67, Norway
Clubs: Brann (1989-90), Lillestrom (1992-94), Austria Vienna (Aut) (1994-96), Brann (1996-)
Full international (Norway) 3 caps/2 goals
• Veteran striker who enjoyed success with Austria Vienna before he returned home to Brann. Very strong in the air and has played more than 160 League matches in Norway.

PLAYER
MOENS, Oscar
Goalkeeper, Dutch, 190cm, 89kg
Born: 01.04.73, 's Gravenzande, Holland
Clubs: Excelsior (1992-96), Go Ahead Eagles (1996), AZ (1996-)
Full international (Holland) 1 cap/0 goals
• Eccentric keeper who loves to bring a certain showiness to his saves.
• International debut: v Ghana, October 1998, selected ahead of **Ed De Goey** and **Ruud Hesp** to give him some experience.

AGENT
MOGGI, Alessandro
• One of Italy's leading agents. Players represented include **Fabrizio Ravanelli**, **Francesco Tottii**, **Marco Di Vaioi**, **Salvatore Fresi** and **Fabio Galante**.
• Contact: Via Petrarca, 181, I-80122, Napoli, Italy.

ADMINISTRATOR
MOGGI, Luciano
• Director of Juventus who is responsible for most of the Italian club's transfer activities.

PLAYER
MOHAMED, Datti Aliyu
Forward, Nigerian, 178cm, 70kg
Born: 14.03.82, Makada, Nigeria
Clubs: Padova (Ita) (1997), Ravenna (Ita) (1998), Milan (Ita) (1998-)
• Raw but very exciting talent who was brought over from his native Nigeria as a 14-year-old and has been closely protected and nurtured by Milan, who gave him his Serie A debut as a 16-year-old against Bologna in January 1998.

PLAYER
MOLDOVAN, Viorel
Forward, Romanian, 178cm, 74kg
Born: 08.08.72, Bucharest, Romania
Clubs: Dinamo Bucharest (1993-95), Neuchatel Xamax (Swi), Grasshopper (Swi) (1997-98), Coventry City (Eng) (1998), Fenerbahce (Tur) (1998-2000), Nantes (Fra) (2000-)
Full international (Romania) 52 caps/21 goals
• Striker who is first choice with the Romanian national team, but has had a chequered club career in western Europe since leaving Steaua.
• Made his name in Europe at Swiss club Grasshopper, earning a transfer to Coventry City, but he failed to settle.
• Played for Romania in the 1998 World Cup, where he scored against England, and Euro 2000, where he won the penalty which put England out of the tournament.
• Linked with a move from Turkey to Spain in the summer of 2000, but moved to Nantes.

PLAYER
MOLINA, Jose Francisco
Full name: Jose Francisco Molina Jimenez
Goalkeeper, Spanish, 183cm, 80kg
Born: 08.08.70, Valencia, Spain
Clubs: Valencia B (1992-93), Villarreal (1994), Valencia (1994), Alabacete (1994-95), Atletico Madrid (1995-2000), Deportivo La Coruna (2000-)
Full international (Spain) 9 caps/0 goals

• Keeper who for years was notorious for having played only for Spain in an outfield role, having been kept out of the national side by Zubizarretta and making his debut as a substitute winger for 14 minutes of a game against Norway after Spain had run out of outfield players.
• Inspirational member of the Atletico Madrid side which won the League and Cup double in 1996.
• Was Spain's first-choice keeper at Euro 2000, but lost his place after a mistake gifted Norway the winning goal in Spain's opening game.

PLAYER
MOLLER, Andreas
Midfielder, German, 180cm, 76kg
Born: 02.09.67, Frankfurt, Germany
Clubs: 1919 Frankfurt, BSC Schwarz-Weiss, Eintracht Frankfurt (1985-87), Borussia Dortmund (1987-90), Eintracht Frankfurt (1990-92), Juventus (Ita) (1992-94), Borussia Dortmund (1994-2000), Schalke (2000-)
Full international (Germany) 85 caps/30 goals
• **Franz Beckenbauer** once said of the veteran left-sided playmaker: 'Moller was the biggest talent of his generation. But he has never made the best of all the ability he has. We will be waiting until he is 40 and still be feeling dissatisfied with him.'
• Such a judgment is a little unfair. He has won his share of honours – the World Cup and the European Championship with Germany and Bundesliga titles and the Champions League with Dortmund – and in a 15-year career has more often than not thrilled with his blistering pace, delicate skills and shooting power.
• A figure you either love or hate, he caused a sensation in the summer of 2000 by quitting Dortmund for arch Ruhr rivals, Schalke.
• Surname pronounced Mer ler.

PLAYER
MOLLER, Peter
Forward, Danish, 190cm, 83kg
Born: 23.03.72, Gistrup, Denmark

Clubs: AaB (1990-93), FC Copenhagen (1992-94), FC Zurich (Swi) (1994-95), FC Copenhagen (1995), Brondby (1995-97), PSV Eindhoven (Hol) (1997-98), Oviedo (Spa) (1998-), Brondby (2000) **Full international** (Denmark) 20 caps/4 goals
• Powerful striker who returned to Brondby on loan in April 2000 in an attempt to kickstart a promising career which has gone wrong in Holland and Spain.
• Made his name in Brondby's 1996 Danish League title-winning side, scoring 32 goals in 69 games.
• Moved to PSV in 1997 but failed to win a regular place, despite some useful performances.
• Played for Denmark in the 1998 World Cup, scoring against Nigeria as the Danes swept into the quarter-finals.
• Sold to Oviedo after the World Cup, but failed to establish himself as a regular and moved back to Denmark in a bid to win a place in Denmark's squad at Euro 2000.

COACH
MOLLER NIELSEN, Richard
Danish
Born: 19.08.37
• National coach of Israel who famously guided Denmark to the 1992 European Championship title after they had been called up as last-minute-entrants in place of Yugoslavia.
• A solid defender (nicknamed Lionheart) who won two caps for Denmark, but whose career was cut short by injury.
• Won the League title with Odense in 1977 and 1982, and coached the Danish Olympic and Under-21 sides. Was right-hand man to **Sepp Piontek** during the Danish Dynamite days of the 1980s, becoming Denmark coach in 1990.
• A DIY fan who was ripping out his kitchen and preparing to install a new one when he got the call to take the Danes to Euro 92. 'After the semi-final victory over Holland, I have to admit that my first thought was that I had another week's delay before starting work on that kitchen.'

• Took charge of Finland after Euro 96, moving on to Israel after the Israalis has sacked **Shlomo Scharf** after losing the Euro 2000 play-offs to Denmark.

PLAYER
MOLNAR, Miklos
Forward, Danish, 182cm, 80kg
Born: 10.04.70, Copenhagen, Denmark
Clubs: B1908, Standard Liege (Bel), Fremad, Hvidore, Frem, Servette (Swi), Saint Etienne (Fra), Lyngby, Sevilla (Spa), Standard Liege (Bel), Kansas City Wizards (USA)
Full international (Denmark) 18 caps/2 goals
• Much travelled forward who gives the Danish national side a physical presence in attack.
• Made his international debut in 1990 against Sweden but has never managed to establish himself as a regular for Denmark.
• Made it into Denmark's squad for Euro 2000 after some impressive performances in pre-tournament friendlies, but played only 26 minutes as a substitute.

PLAYER
MOLS, Michael
Forward, Dutch, 177cm, 71kg
Born: 17.12.70. Amsterdam, Holland
Clubs: Cambuur (Hol) (1991-93), Twente (1993-97), Utrecht (1997-99), Rangers (Sco) (1999-)
Full international (Holland) 6 caps/0 goals
• A regular goalscorer during his first few months with Rangers after signing from Utrecht, the Dutchman's progress was halted following a knee injury sustained in the Champions League tie against Bayern Munich. But he remains an exciting prospect.

COACH
MOMMENS, Raymond
Belgian
• Holds the Belgian record for League appearances. A former player with Charleroi

before being appointed as coach during the 1999-2000 season, only to be sacked after five months in charge.

COACH
MONDONICO, Emiliano
Italian
Born: 09.03.47
- Coach of Torino since 1998.
- A tough disciplinarian who has gained a reputation for getting the best from small teams with modest resources.
- Made his name at Cremonese where he discovered **Gianluca Vialli** and won promotion to Serie A in 1983.
- Moved on to Atalanta, via Como, winning promotion to Serie A and leading the unfashionable club to sixth place in the League in 1989.
- During his first spell at Torino (1990-1994), he took the Turin club to third place in the League, the UEFA Cup Final (lost to Ajax) and the 1993 Italian Cup.
- Won promotion to Serie A in 1995 during a second spell with Atalanta, but suffered relegation three years later and moved back to Torino.
- Pulled off another promotion in 1999, returning Torino to the top flight.

PLAYER
MONDRAGON, Farid
Goalkeeper, Colombian 191cm, 93kg
Born: 21.06.71, Cali, Colombia
Clubs: Argentinos Juniors (Arg) (1993-94), Independiente (Arg) (1994-99), Zaragoza (Spa) (1999), Independiente (Arg) (1999-2000), Metz (Fra) (2000-)
Full international (Colombia)
- Tall, athletic and reliable keeper who was Colombia's first-choice at the 1998 World Cup, having been a squad member in 1994.
- Moved to France in the summer of 2000.

PLAYER
MONTANO, Johnnier
Midfielder, Colombian, 173cm, 76kg
Born: 14.01.83, Cali, Colombia
Clubs: America Cali (1997-98), Atletico Quilmes (1998-99), Parma (Ita) (1999-)
Full international (Colombia)
- Touted as one the great new stars of Colombian football after starring at the 1999 Copa America at the age of just 16.
- Began in the youth set-up of Deportivo Cali, but was whisked away by Argentinian second division club Quilmes before he had played professional football in his own country.
- Spotted by European scouts when playing for Colombia at the annual Under-20 Toulon tournament. Parma beat competition from Manchester United, Paris Saint-Germain and Ajax to offer Quilmes £1.1million.
- Played for Colombia at the 1999 South American youth championships and received a full international debut before the Copa America in June 1999. Replaced the injured Faustino Asprilla in the Colombia squad for the tournament in Paraguay and a made a number of dramatic appearances as a substitute.

PLAYER
MONTELLA, Vincenzo
Forward, Italian, 172cm, 68kg
Born: 18.06.74, Pomigliano d'Arco, Italy.
Clubs: Empoli (1990-95), Genoa (1995-96), Sampdoria (1996-99), Roma (1999-)
Full international (Italy) 6 caps/0 goals
- Striker who makes up for his lack of height with pace and a goalscorer's sixth sense.
- Made his name at Sampdoria, scoring 12 goals in 18 matches in his first Serie A season in 1996-97.
- Was controversially transferred to Sampdoria from cross-town rivals Genoa in 1996. Having scored 21 Serie B goals for Genoa in 1995-96, a number of big clubs targeted him, but his contract was jointly owned by Genoa and his previous

club Empoli. Genoa tried to buy out Empoli's half, but Samp got there first.
• Joined Roma for £15million in summer 1999 after Sampdoria's relegation to Serie B.
• A member of Italy's squad at Euro 2000. Played in the Final against France as a substitute.
• The youngest of five brothers, he almost had to give up football in 1993 because of a heart infection.
• Known for his trademark 'aeroplane' goal celebrations.

PLAYER
MONTENEGRO, Daniel
Midfielder, Argentinean, 172cm, 68kg
Born: 28.03.79, Buenos Aires, Argentina
Clubs: Huracan (1997-99), Marseille (Fra) (1999-)
• Right-footed midfielder signed by Marseille after playing for Argentina ar the 1999 World Under-20 Youth Cup.

PLAYER
MONTERO, Jean-Louis
Defender, French, 177cm, 72kg
Born: 28.04.71, Bar-sur-Seine, France
Clubs: Troyes, Lorient, Sedan
• Gutsy Basque right-back who goes by the name of Jean-Louis in French football circles, but whose christian name according to his passport is Juan-Luis. More a stay-at-home full-back than a raiding one, but an impressive performer all the same.
• Surname pronounced Mon tay roh.

PLAYER
MONTERO, Paolo
Defender, Uruguayan, 179cm, 74kg
Born: 03.09.71, Montevideo, Uruguay
Clubs: Penarol (1990-91), Atalanta (1992-96), Juventus (1996-).
Full international (Uruguay)
• Tough-tackling centre-back signed by Juventus from Atalanta in 1996. Given his Serie A debut by **Marcello Lippi** at Atalanta in 1992.

PLAYER
MONTERRUBIO, Olivier
Forward, French, 171cm, 67kg
Born: 08.08.76, Gaillac, France
Clubs: Nantes (1996-)
• Missed much of last season with a complicated thigh problem. But when he is fit, he is one of the most potent forwards in the country, a compelling mixture of pace, mesmerising footwork and vision. He scored the winner from the penalty spot when Nantes beat Sedan in the 1999 French Cup Final.
• Surname pronounced Mon tay roo bee oh.

PLAYER
MOORE, Joe-Max
Midfielder, American
Born: 23.2.71, USA
Clubs: New England Revolution (1996-99), Everton (Eng) (2000-)
Full international (United States) 79 caps/20 goals
• Experienced international who played in two of the USA's three matches at France 98.
• Free-kick specialist whose time back in the USA after a two-year spell in Germany was blighted by injury.

AGENT
MORABITO, Vincenzo
• Italian agent who specialises in the Scandinavian market. Players representated by him include **Henrik Larsson, Peter Moller, Stefan Schwarz, Klas Ingesson, Fredrik Ljungberg, Kennet Andersson** and **Jon Dahl Tomasson.**
• **Contact:** Villa La Rocca Buterone 46, I-06060 Ponticelli Citta' della Pieve, Italy. Tel: 00 39 578 22 30 54.

COACH
MORACE, Carolina
• The first female professional coach in Italy, who took charge of Italian C1 side Viterbese in 1999.
• A legend in Italian women's soccer having won 12 League titles and 150 international caps.

ADMINISTRATOR
MORATTI, Massimo
Born: 11.05.45
- President of Internazionale since February 1995.
- Son of Angelo, club owner during the 1960s when Inter the European Cup under legendary coach Helenio Herrera.
- Moratti's family wealth is derived from the oil industry.

PLAYER
MORAVCIK, Lubomir
Midfielder, Slovakian, 173cm, 72kg
Born: 22.06.65. Nitra Slovakia
Clubs: Plastika Nitra (1989-90), St Etienne (Fra) (1990-96), Bastia (Fra) (1996-8), Duisburg (Ger) (1998-9), Celtic (Sco) (1998-)
Full International (Slovakia) 34 caps/6 goals
- Eyebrows were raised when Dr **Jozef Venglos** signed Moravcic, a fellow Slovakian, from Duisburg during the 1998-99 season, especially as the player, then aged 33, appeared to be past his best.
- 'Lubo', however, has answered his critics in the best possible way and he is, without doubt, one of Scottish football's most visionary players at present.

COACH
MORCH, Ole
Danish
Born: 28.05.48
- Coach of Danish side AB since November 1998, though he has not has it easy, falling out with key players and not bringing the long-awaited success back to AB.

PLAYER
MOREIRA, Daniel
Midfielder, French, 178cm, 74kg
Born: 08.08.77, Maubeuge, France
Clubs: Valenciennes, Guingamp (1996-98), Lens (1998-)

- Although he scored the winning goal in Lens' French League Cup final victory over Metz in 1999, he has struggled over the last two years to live up to his billing as one of France's most promising young playmakers. From the northern town of Maubeuge, he has always been a Lens supporter, but was rejected by the club as a teenager and headed off to learn his trade with Guingamp in Brittany.
- Surname pronounced Maur ree ay rah.

PLAYER
MORFEO, Domenico
Midfielder, Italian, 170cm, 67kg
Born: 16.01.76, Pescina, Italy
Clubs: Atalanta (1992-97), Fiorentina (1997-99), Milan (1998-99, loan), Cagliari (1999, loan), Verona (1999-)
- Talented midfielder whose career has failed to take off, as many had expected, with disappointing spells at Milan and Fiorentina.
- Was reunited for the 1999-2000 season with his former coach and mentor **Claudio Prandelli.**

PLAYER
MORIENTES, Fernando
Full name: Fernando Morientes Sanchez
Forward, Spanish, 184cm, 78kg
Born: 05.04.76, Toledo, Spain
Clubs: Albacete (1993-95), Zaragoza (1995-97), Real Madrid (1997-)
Full international (Spain) 12 caps/9 goals
- Outstanding young centre-forward whose rapid rise forced **Davor Suker** out of the Real Madrid side in the 1997-98 season.
- Had a fairytale international debut, scoring two goals in the first five minutes against Sweden on 25.03.98.
- A member of Spain's squad at the France 98 World Cup, but was a surprise omission from the final 22-man Spanish party for Euro 2000, despite scoring for Real Madrid in the 2000 Champions League Final and providing an

Peter Moller

outstanding foil to the predatory instincts to **Raul**.
• Played alongside **Raul** at the 1995 Under-20 world championship in Qatar and the 1996 Olympics.
• Holds the remarkable record of having scored on his debuts for Albacete, Zaragoza, Real Madrid, Spain Under-18s and Under 20s, and the senior national side.
• **Christian Panucci** on Morientes: 'He has the same air about him as **Marco Van Basten**.'
• Surprisingly left out of Spain's Euro 2000 squad.

PLAYER
MORIERO, Francesco
Midfielder, Italian, 173cm, 67kg
Born: 31.03.69, Lecce, Italy.
Clubs: Lecce (1986-92), Cagliari (1992-94), Roma (1994-97), Internazionale (1997-).
Full international (Italy) 8 caps/2 goals
• Old-fashioned right winger who was one of the revelations of the 1997-98 season for Inter, earning a place in Italy's 1998 World Cup team, starting four of the five matches in France.
• Was all set to move to Milan in summer 1997 from Roma, but was traded to Inter instead in place of Brazilian sweeper **Andre Cruz**.

PLAYER
MORNAR, Ivica
Forward, Croatian, 188cm, 83kg
Born: 12.01.74, Split, Croatia
Clubs: Hajduk Split (1991-96), Eintracht Frankfurt (Ger) (1996), Sevilla (Spa) (1996-97), Ourense (Spa) (1997-98), Standard Liege (Bel) (1998-)
Full international (Croatia) 6 caps/0 goals
• Striker who has not quite lived up to his billing of a few years ago, when he was considered the most promising young Croatian forward in Europe.
• Very quick with good technique.
• Was brought to Standard Liege by **Tomislav Ivic** and has played some of the best football of his career in Belgium following frustrating spells in Germany and Spain.

PLAYER
MOROZ, Hennadiy
Midfielder, Ukrainian, 182cm, 74kg
Born: 27.03.75
Clubs: CSKA Kyiv, Kryvbas
Full international (Ukraine) 4 caps/0 goals
• Powerful, dynamic Ukraine international attacker with an eye for spectacular goals. The main inspiration behind Kryvbas's rise to the second place in the Ukrainian League.

PLAYER
MORRIS, Jody
Midfielder, English, 165cm, 64kg
Born: 22.12.78, London, England
Clubs: Chelsea (1996-)
• Diminutive but highly effective midfielder and one of the few young English players to break into Chelsea's multinational team under **Gianluca Vialli**.
• England Under-21 international.

PLAYER
MOSTOVOI, Alexander
Midfielder, Russian, 181cm, 77kg
Born: 22.08/68, Saint Petersburg, Russia
Clubs: Spartak Moscow (1987-91), Benfica (Por) (1992-93), Caen (Fra) (1993-94), Strasbourg (Fra) (1994-96), Celta Vigo (Spa) (1996-)
Full international (Russia) 29 caps/8 goals
• Talented creative midfielder whose career has been let down by disputes off the pitch.
• Started out at Spartak Moscow before a move to Portugal's Benfica in 1992.
• Obtained Portuguese citizenship after arranging to marry a local woman, but the marriage did not last.
• Was one of the stars of Celta's 1998-99 UEFA Cup run.
• Has been dropped by Russia on a number of occasions following public rows with the coach and the authorities.

PLAYER
MPENZA, Emile
Forward, Belgian, 177cm, 75kg
Born: 04.07.78, Brussels, Belgium
Clubs: Kortrijk, Mouscron (1996-97), Standard Liege (1997-99), Schalke (Ger) (2000-)
Full international (Belgium) 27 caps/8 goals
• A speedster of a forward, the young Belgian international made an instant impact in German football following his move during the 1999-2000 season from Standard Liege to Schalke, scoring six goals in his first seven games for his new club and generally terrorising Bundesliga markers with his pace and tricks.
• One of Belgium's best players at Euro 2000, he was rumoured to be using his enhanced reputation to secure a lucrative transfer during the summer of 2000.
• Known in Germany as 'Magic', he is dating a former Miss Belgium.
• Younger brother of **Mbo Mpenza**, with whom he began his career at Kortrijk, before moving on to Mouscron and Standard Liege.
• Made his international debut against Northern Ireland in February 1997.

PLAYER
MPENZA, Mbo
Forward, Belgian, 175cm, 76kg
Born: 12.04.76, Kinshasa, DR Congo
Clubs: Kortrijk, Mouscron (1996-97), Standard Liege (1997-99), Sporting Lisbon (Por) (2000-)
Full international (Belgium) 19 caps/0 goals
• Strong, fast striker or right winger and older of two footballing brothers.
• Has suffered from comparisons with his younger brother **Emile Mpenza**, who is considered to be the more talented footballer.
• Made his international debut against Wales in March 1997 and was a member of the Belgian squad at the 1998 World Cup and at Euro 2000.
• Born in the Democratic Republic of Congo, the homeland of his parents, who moved to Belgium

when he was two months old.

• Came through at Mouscron under the guidance of former national team coach **Georges Leekens**.

• He and his brother once had to be smuggled over the Austrian border for a youth tournament when they did not have enough time to get passports.

PLAYER
MRMIC, Marijan
Goalkeeper, Croatian, 186cm, 80kg
Born: 06.05.65, Varazdin, Croatia
Clubs: Cibalia Vinkovci (1992-93), Varteks (1993-96), Besiktas (Tur) (1996-98), Varteks (1998-99), Charleroi (Bel) (1999-)
Full international (Croatia) 14 caps/0 goals

• Keeper who is in the autumn of his career. Was the understudy of **Drazen Ladic** for a long time in the Croatian national side. Played in Austria and Turkey before joining Charleroi, where he helped saved his team from relegation.

PLAYER
MUHR, Berhard
Defender, Austrian, 179cm, 76kg
Born: 17.03.77, Austria
Clubs: LASK (1998-)

• Accomplished sweeper who mature beyond his years.

• Austrian Under-21 international.

PLAYER
MUJCIN, Edin
Midfielder, Bosnian, 174cm, 72kg
Born: 14.01.70
Clubs: Marsonia (1992-96), Croatia Zagreb (1996-)
Full international (Bosnia) 12 caps/1 goal

• Bosnian midfielder who has been a regular with Croatia Zagreb in the Champions League, having fled to Croatia to escape the trouble in Bosnia.

COACH
MULLER, Joel
French
Born: 02.01.52

• The longest-serving current French First Division coach, he has been in charge of the Metz first team since 1989 and guided the club to second place in the French League in 1998, their best ever finish.

• Previously spent five years as the director of the club's youth system. Not surprising then that his Metz side has always featured a hardcore of young talent, but he does like an experienced back four.

• Once a defender with Lyon, Nice, Dunkerque and Metz, he was linked to the post of general manager at Strasbourg over the summer of 2000.

PLAYER
MULLER, Patrick
Midfielder, Swiss, 182cm, 69kg
Born: 17.12.76, Switzerland
Clubs: Servette (1995-98), Grasshopper (1999-2000), Lyon (Fra) (2000-)
Full international (Switzerland) 15 caps/1 goal

• A Swiss international starlet of amazing versatility, he started out as a left-sided schemer or forward of considerable pace and flair, but latterly has shown up well in a libero role.

• He first came to prominence at Servette and once looked set to play for Juventus, only for the Italians to wriggle out of the deal.

• Left Grasshopper for Lyon in France.

BUSINESS
MULLER, Roberto
• President and chief executive of the Muller Sports Group, which acts an agent for the football investment of Texas company Hicks, Muse, Tate and Furst.

• Was previously a successful sportswear manufacturer as president of Reebok international.

PLAYER
MULLER, Sasha
Midfielder, Swiss, 175cm, 67kg
Born: 28.02.70, Switzerland
Clubs: St Gallen (1994-95), Lucerne (1995-97), St Gallen (1997-)
Full international (Switzerland) 4 caps/0 goals
• Switzerland and St Gallen international midfielder whose strength is his passing ability. Few goals, but much good approach work. A revelation for St Gallen during the 1999-2000 season.

PLAYER
MUNITIS, Pedro
Full name: Pedro Munitis Alvarez
Born: 19.06.75, Santander, Spain
Clubs: Racing Santander (1993-2000), Real Madrid (2000-)
Full international (Spain) 12 caps/2 goals
• Fast and skilful winger who had an exceptional season in 1999-2000, earning a call-up by Spain and a place in the Euro 2000 squad.
• Born and brought up in Santander, where he came through the youth ranks at Racing.
• Spent the 1997-98 season on loan at Badajoz, before returning to Santander and establisihing himself as a major talent.
• Was one of Spain's best performers at Euro 2000 and joined Real Madrid in summer of 2000.

PLAYER
MUNTEANU, Catalin
Midfielder, Romanian
Born: 26.10.79, Bucharest, Romania
Clubs: Steaua Bucharest, Salamanca (Spa) (1997-)
Full international (Romania)
• Midfield talent whose star has waned since a move to Salamanca and relegation to the Spanish second division.
• Made his international debut against Spain in November 1997 but missed the 1998 World Cup trip.
• Scored 17 goals as Steaua won the 1998 Romanian League title.

PLAYER
MUNTEANU, Dorinel
Midfielder, Romanian, 170cm, 70kg
Born: 25.06.68, Gradinari, Bucharest
Clubs: Inter Sibiu (1989-91), Dinamo Bucharest (1991-93), Cercle Bruges (Bel) (1993-95), Koln (Ger) (1995-99), Wolfsburg (Ger) (1999-)
Full international (Romania) 90 caps/11 goals
• Acccomplished performer who started his footballing life at left-back, then switched to the left side of midfield and these days occupies a central midfield berth. Street-wise, nimble on the ball and hits a mean free-kick.
• Surname pronounced Moon tee ah nu.
• Named as Romania captain in August 2000.
• No relation to **Catalin Munteanu**.

PLAYER
MURATI, Edwin
Midfielder, French/Albanian, 171cm, 68kg
Born: 12.11.75, Tirana, Albania
Clubs: Tirana, Paris Saint-Germain, Chateauroux, Paris Saint-Germain, Fortuna Dusseldorf, Paris Saint-Germain
Full international (Albania) 7 caps/0 goals
• Albanian international who invariably gives value for money on the left side of midfield. Industrious, dynamic and loves to get forward.
• Surname pronounced Moo rah tee.

PLAYER
MURAWSKI, Maciej
Defender, Polish, 184cm, 80kg
Born: 20.02.74, Poland
Clubs: Zryw Zielona Gora, Sleza Wroclaw, Polonia Bytom, Lech Poznan, Legia Warsaw (1998-)
Full international (Poland) 2 caps/0 goals
• Solid defender who can also operate as a defensive midfielder. Started his career at amateur club Zryw Zielona Gora before moving to second division Sleza Wroclaw and Polonia Bytom. Then chose to develop his talent at first division Lech Poznan.

PLAYER
MURPHY, Danny
Midfielder, English, 175cm, 67kg
Born: 18.03.75, Chester, England
Clubs: Crewe (1994-97), Liverpool (1997-), Crewe (1999, loan)
• Hard-working midfielder who has never quite established himself as a first-team regular at Anfield after coming through the ranks at Crewe.
• England Under-21 international.

COACH
MUSLIN, Slavoljub
Yugoslav
Born: 15.6.53
• Coach of Red Star Belgrade since September 1999 who guided his team to the Yugoslav League and Cup double in 1999-2000.
• As a midfielder with Red Star he won the Yugoslav League three times and was a UEFA Cup finalist in 1978-79. He continued his playing career in France at Brest, where he also began coaching career moving on to Pau, Bordeaux, Lens, Le Mans Raja Casablanca.
• His biggest success came when he reached the UEFA Cup Final with Bordeaux in 1996, having qualified through the InterToto Cup, but he was surprisingly sacked before the Final.

PLAYER
MUSTAPHA Dogan
Defender, German, 180cm, 75kg
Born: 01.01.76, Isparta, Turkey
Clubs: Bayer Uerdingen, Fenerbahce (Tur) (1997-)
Full international (Germany) 2 caps/0 goals
• The first Turkish-born player to play for Germany.
• Born in the southern Turkish town of Yalvaz, but was only two when his family moved to Germany's Ruhr region. Came through the youth ranks at Bayer (now KFC) Uerdingen and joined Fenerbahce in a £1million transfer in 1997.
• Can play as a central defensive marker,

Alexander Mostovoi

sweeper or holding midfielder.
• Capped by Germany at Under-21 level and dubbed 'The new **Jurgen Kohler**' by Under-21 coach Hannes Lohr.
• International debut: Germany v USA, July 1999.
• Joachim Low on Dogan: 'During his time in Turkey he has really blossomed. His defensive game has become much sharper through competing with all the tricky, technical forwards. He's a very determined character who gives absolutely everything.'
• 'It wasn't difficult for me to choose Germany rather than Turkey. I was brought up and went to school in Germany and I'm proud to play for Germany. It's my country.'

PLAYER
MUTU, Adrian
Forward, Romanian, 178cm, 72kg
Born: 08.01.79, Bucharest, Romania.
Clubs: Arges Pitesti, Dinamo Bucharest (1998-99), Internazionale (Ita) (1999-)
Full international (Romania) 7 caps/1 goal
• Golden Boy of Romanian football who turned down offers from Parma and PSV Eindhoven to join Inter in early 2000 after scoring 18 goals in half a season for Dinamo Bucharest.
• Regular Under-21 international and a member of Romania's squad for Euro 2000.

COACH
MUURINEN, Antti
Finnish
Born: 05.04.54
• National coach of Finland, succeeding **Richard Moller Nielsen** in 2000, having previously coached HJK.

PLAYER
MUZZI, Roberto
Forward, Italian, 180cm, 72kg
Born: 21.09.71, Rome, Italy
Clubs: Roma (1989-93), Pisa (1993-94), Roma

(1994), Cagliari (1994-99), Udinese (1999-)
• Striker who was given the unenviable task of replacing the Parma-bound **Marcio Amoruso** at Udinese for the 1999-2000 season, but fully justified his £8million transfer fee by scoring 12 goals.
• Came through the Roma youth system, but established his reputation as a goalscorer at Cagliari, scoring 58 goals in five seasons in Sardinia.

PLAYER
MYHRE, Thomas
Goalkeeper, Norway, 192cm, 90kg
Born: 03.11.73, Sarpsborg, Norway
Clubs: Moss, Viking Stavanger (1993-97), Everton (Eng) (1997-), Birmingham (Eng) (2000, loan)
Full international (Norway) 13 caps/0 goals
• Tall and commanding keeper who joined Everton from Viking Stavanger for £700,000 in November 1997 after an impressive trial period.
• Went on loan to Birmingham in March 2000 to gain first-team football in a bid to win back his international place with Norway after breaking a leg. Did so successfully, and played in all three of Norway's games at Euro 2000.
• International debut: 22.04.98, Denmark (won 2-0).

PLAYER
MYKLAND, Erik
Midfielder, Norwegian, 172cm, 63kg
Born: 21.07.71, Risoer, Norway
Clubs: Start, Utrecht (Hol), Linz (Aut), Panathinaikos (Gre) (1997-2000), Munich 1860 (Ger) (2000-)
Full international (Norway) 75 caps/2 goals
• Midfield dynamo who was Norway's most impressive player at Euro 2000. He had announced his retirement from internartional football after France 98, but then changed his mind.
• A move to Munich 1860 had already been

arranged before Euro 2000, but his displays in the Low Countries encouraged a number of big clubs to make enquiries about his availability.

PLAYER
MYZIN , Sergiy
Midfielder, Ukrainian, 183cm, 75kg
Born: 25.09.72, Ukraine
Clubs: Kyiv Dynamo, Chornomorets, Karpaty, Kryvbas
Full international (Ukraine) 6 caps/0 goals
• Recently signed by Kryvbas from financially troubled Karpaty. A speedy player who likes to run at defenders.

N

NADAL, Miguel Angel
Full name: Miguel Angel Nadal Homar
Defender, Spanish, 187cm, 82kg
Born: 28.07.66, Mallorca, Spain
Clubs: Mallorca (1986-91), Barcelona (1991-99), Mallorca (1999-)
Full international (Spain) 47 caps/2 goals
• Tough, imposing centre-back who won a host of honours with Barcelona in the early 1990s after arriving from Mallorca in 1991.
• He was suspended for two games at the 1994 World Cup after being sent off after 29 minutes of Spain's opening match against South Korea. He then missed the first two games of Euro 96 following a red card in the qualifiers.
• Fell out with former Barcelona coach **Louis Van Gaal** and returned to Mallorca in the summer of 1999.
• Dubbed the 'Beast of Barcelona' by the British tabloid press.
• A junior tennis champion.

PLAYER
NADJ, Albert
Midfielder, Yugoslav, 173cm, 68kg
Born: 29.10.74, Zemun, Yugoslavia
Clubs: Partizan Belgrade (1992-96), Betis (Spa) (1996-98), Oviedo (Spa) (1998-)
Full international (Yugoslavia) 29 caps/3 goals
• Tireless worker in the midfield anchor position, a non-stop battler who is no technical slouch either.
• A solid consistent performer who signed for Betis in 1996 after eight seasons at Partizan Belgrade. Moved to Oviedo in 1999.
• Three times League and Cup winner in Yugoslavia with Partizan.

PLAYER
NAGOLI, Kennedy
Midfielder, Zimbabwean, 179cm, 68kg
Born: 24.04.73, Zimbabwe
Clubs: Zisco, Welcome Eagles (SAf), Jomo Cosmos (SAf), Aris Thessaloniki (1997-)
• Zimbabwean midfielder who has been a consistent performer in the Greek League for Aris since a move from South Africa in 1997.

PLAYER
NAKATA, Hidetoshi
Midfielder, Japanese, 175cm, 72kg
Born: 22.01.77, Yamanashi, Japan
Clubs: Bellmare Hiratsuka (1995-98), Perugia (Ita) (1998-99), Roma (Ita) (2000-)
Full international (Japan)
• A marketing phenomenon and the most talented and charismatic player ever to come out of Japan.
• Moved to Roma from Perugia in January 2000 in a deal that was estimated to have cost Roma £50million.
• A massive pin-up in Japan, with lucrative sponsorship deals with Fila sportswear, Subaru cars, Aau Plus drinks, Armani, Prada, Mastercard and a Japanese supermarket.
• No mean footballer either, a skilful midfielder who plays with poise and confidence and is not afraid to try something out of the ordinary.
• Japanese international striker Kazuyoshi Miura on Nakata: 'You have to have good control to play with Nakata. The ball comes so fast.'
• Perugia sold more than 70,000 'Nakata 7' shirts in Japan during his 18-month spell at the club.
• Nakata claims his internet site receives 200,000 hits a day. He uses the website to communicate with the press, because he refuses to speak in person to all but a handful of journalists.
• Has played for Japan at all leveld, including the 1998 World Cup in France and the Under-20 World Youth Cup.
• Won an Asian Cup-winners Cup medal with Bellmare Hiratsuka in 1995.

Hiroshi Nanami

NALETILIC, Marko

- Croatia's leading player agent whose clients include **Mark Viduka**, **Robert Prosinecki** and **Dario Simic**. Also represents a number of Belgians, including **Branko Strupar**, **Nico Van Kerckhoven** and **Gert Verheyen**.
- **Contact:** Kuslanova 26, Zagreb 10000, Croatia.

PLAYER
NALIS, Lilian

Midfielder, French, 185cm, 78kg
Born: 29.09.71, Nogent sur Marne, France
Clubs: Auxerre, Laval, Caen, Guingamp, Le Havre, Bastia (2000-)
- Much travelled attacking midfielder who joined Bastia after Le Havre were relegated in May 2000.

PLAYER
NANAMI, Hiroshi

Midfielder, Japanese, 177cm, 68kg
Born: 28.11.72, Shizuoka, Japan
Clubs: Jubilo Iwata (1995-99), Venezia (Ita) (1999-)
Full international (Japan)
- Left-sided midfielder and the third Japanese to play in Italy after **Hidetoshi Nakata** and Kazuyoshi Miura.
- Excellent at covering, running and well-judged through balls and can play further forward if needed.
- Played for Japan at the 1998 World Cup.

PLAYER
NANDO

Full name: Fernando Martinez Perales Nando
Defender, Spanish, 172cm, 72kg
Born: 31.05.67, Valencia, Spain
Clubs: Valencia (1987-92), Deportivo La Coruna (1992-97), Sevilla (1998-)
Full international (Spain) 2 caps/0 goals
- Veteran left wing-back whose pace and trickery still cause problems for defenders.
- Joined Sevilla midway through the 1997-98 season on a free transfer from Deportivo.

NANO

Full name: Fernando Macedo da Silva
Forward, Spanish, 187cm, 80kg
Born: 20.04.82
Clubs: Barcelona, Spain (1999-)
• Prodigious young talent who, at 17 years and four months, became Barcelona's youngest ever debutant when he played against Zaragoza on 22.08.99.
• Member of Spain's victorious 1999 team at European under-16 level.
• Arsenal attempted to sign him in the summer of 1999, but were rebuffed.
• Tall, powerful 18-year old left-winger used by **Louis Van Gaal** in the 1999 Supercup clashes against Valencia. Since then, he has continued to shine for Barcelona B.
• A magnificent prospect.

NANU, Stefan

Defender, Romanian, 182cm, 78kg
Born: 08.09.68, Filias, Romania
Clubs: Electrop. Craoiva (1991-95), Farul Constanza (1995-97), Rapid Bucharest (1997-99), Vitesse Arnhem (Hol) (1999-)
Full international (Romania) 7 caps/0 goals
• Powerful defender who has struggled to establish himself in Holland following a move from Rapid Bucharest in 1999.

NASCIMENTO, David

Defender, Portuguese, 184cm, 84kg
Born: 16.03.66, San Vicente, Cape Verde Islands
Clubs: Barrelnse, Vitoria Setubal, Benfica Branco, Vitoria Guimaraes, RKC Waalwijk (Hol) (1991-92), Roda JC (Hol) (1992-94), Utrecht (Hol) (1994-98), RKC Waalwijk (Hol) (1999-)
• Veteran Portuguese defender who is in command of the RKC defence. A reliable stopper.

NASTASE, Valentin

Midfielder, Romanian, 183cm, 80kg
Born: 04.10.74, Calinesti, Romania
Clubs: Gloria Bistrita (1993-94), Arges Ploesti (1994-99), Dinamo Bucharest (1999-)
Full international (Romania) 3 cap/0 goals
• Midfielder who can also play in defence. Won the Romanian League with Dinamo Bucharest in May 2000.

NAVAS, Mauro

Midfielder, Argentinian, 177cm, 76kg
Born: 20.10.74, Buenos Aires, Argentina
Clubs: Banfield (1993-95), Racing Avellaneda (1995-97), Udinese (Ita) (1998-99), Espanyol (Spa) (1999-)
• Highly promising right-back of whom big things are expected at Espanyol.
• Former Argentina youth international who moved to Italy in 1997, playing 30 games for Udinese.

NAWALKA, Adam

Polish
Born: 23.10.57
• Coach of Polish side Wisla Krakow.
• Spent 10 years as player with Wisla, winning the League championship in 1978. In the same year he went to Argentina with Poland for the World Cup.
• Relatively inexperienced as a coach. Replaced Wojciech Lazarek in March 2000 to become the fourth coach at Wisla that season.

NAYBET, Noureddine

Defender, Moroccan, 182cm, 73kg
Born: 18.07.70, Casablanca, Morocco
Clubs: Nantes (Fra) (1993-94), Sporting Lisbon (Por) (1994-96), Deportivo La Coruna (Spa) (1996-)
Full international (Morocco)

Pavel Nedved

• Dominant, no holds-barred central defender signed by then Depor coach **John Toshack** from his former club Sporting Lisbon in summer 1996.
• One of the best Africans playing in Europe, and the sweeper and captain at Deportivo.
• Won an African Champions Cup medal with Wydad before moving to Europe, to Nantes.
• Played 62 games over two seasons for Sporting before the move to Spain.
• A veteran of two World Cups (1994 and 1998).
• Linked with a host of big clubs after his dominating performances at the heart of Deportivo's defence during their 2000 Liga triumph.

PLAYER
N'DIEFI, Pius
Forward, Cameroon, 174cm, 74kg
Born: 05.07.75, Douala, Cameroon
Clubs: Lens (1993-95), Valence (1995-96), Sedan (1996-)
• Sedan love their African players and Cameroon international attacker N'Diefi is another example. Not a regular goalscorer, but an invaluable team player thanks to his speed off the mark, mazy dribbling and unselfish play.
• Helped Cameroon win the African title in 2000, although he missed the Final through injury.
• Pronounced Pee oos Enn Dee fee.

PLAYER
NDO, Joseph
Midfielder, Cameroon, 180cm, 80kg
Born: 28.07.76, Yaounde, Cameroon
Clubs: Neuchatel Xamax (Swi) (1998-99), Strasbourg (Fra) (1999-2000)
Full international (Cameroon)
• Right-sided wing-back who first made a name for himself in Cameroon's France 98 campaign. Good technique means he is very efffective going forward. But defensively, he can seem slightly under-strength.
• He is the son of Cameroon's top comic actor.
• Surname pronounced Enn doh.

NEDVED, Pavel

Midfielder, Czech, 177cm, 70kg
Born: 30.08.72, Cheb, Czech Republic.
Clubs: Dukla Prague (1991-92), Sparta Prague (1992-96), Lazio (Ita) (1996-).
Full international (Czech Rep) 46 goals/9 goals
• Probably the best Czech player in the world for the past three years, winning the Cup-winners Cup and Italian League title with Lazio and playing a leading role in the Czech Republic qualifying for Euro 2000.
• A great shot from long-range and an all-action left-sided midfielder.
• Won three Czech League titles with Sparta Prague.
• Performances for the Czech Rep at Euro 96 earned him a transfer to Rome in July 1996.
• Offered a contract extension to 2003 by Lazio president **Sergio Cragnotti**, who described Nedved as 'not for sale at any price'.
• Czech Player of the Year in 1997-98.
• Nicknamed 'Rocket' because of his powerful shot.

NEE, Frederic

Forward, French, 181cm, 72kg
Born: 18.04.75, Bayeaux, France
Clubs: Caen (19966-98), Bastia (1998-))
• This rangy striker from Normandy was in marvellous goalscoring form for the Corsicans in the 1999-2000 season. Difficult to stop when he gathers speed on his goalbound gallops and his finishing has improved immeasurably over the last year or two.
• Pronounced Fray day reek Nay.

NEESKENS, Johan

Dutch
Born: 15.09.51
• Former international star, who was an essential part of Ajax's supremacy in the early 1970s.

• Also played at Barcelona and New York Cosmos before problems (divorce, alcohol) took over his life. Managed to bounce back and after coaching some lesser known clubs in Germany and Switzerland, he was appointed **Guus Hiddink**'s assistant during the 1998 World Cup.
• Refused to succeed Hiddink when he found out he was only fourth or fifth choice. Was also **Frank Rijkaard**'s assistant at Euro 2000.
• Says he missed the daily routine and was set to coach NEC Nijmegen for the 2000-2001 season.

NEGRO, Paolo

Defender, Italian, 182cm, 73kg
Born: 16.04.72, Arzignano, Italy.
Clubs: Brescia (1989-90), Bologna (1990-92), Brescia (1992-93), Lazio (1993-)
Full international (Italy) 7 caps/0 goals
• Experienced, solid defender who has notched up seven seasons in Serie A and been on the fringes of the Italian national side since making his debut against Croatia in November 1994.
• Strength is his versatility: he can play at full-back or in central defence, where he excelled for Lazio in the 1998-99 season alongside **Alessandro Nesta**.
• Winner of two European Under-21 titles.
• Signed as a central defender from Brescia in 1993 and converted into an attacking right-back by then Lazio coach **Zdenek Zeman**.

NEHODA, Zdenek

• Former player turned agent whose clients include **Patrik Berger** and **Tomas Repka**.
• **Contact:** Bubenecska 19, CZ-19000 Praha 6, Czech Republic.

NELISSE, Robin

Forward, Dutch, 188cm, 78kg
Born: 25.01.78, Rotterdam, Holland

Oliver Neuville

Clubs: Feyenoord (1997-99), Cambuur (1999-)
• Youngster who looks to have a good future at Cambuur after establishing himself as a useful substitute in the 1998-99 season.

COACH
NELO VINGAGDA
Portuguese
Born: 10.10.54
• Rumoured in the summer of 2000 to be taking over at Belenenses, but instead chose to remain at Maritimo, whom he took to a creditable sixth place in the 1999-2000 campaign.
• An advocate of neat, attacking football and one for whom giving away possession is a cardinal sin. He used to be an assistant coach at Benfica and led the Portuguese Olympic side to the semi-finals of the 1996 Games in Atlanta.
• Known for his honesty; if his team plays poorly and still wins, he lets everyone know they were lucky.

PLAYER
NEMEC, Dejan
Goalkeeper, Slovenian, 184cm, 79kg
Born: 01.03.77, Murska Sobota, Slovenia
Clubs: Mura Murska Sobota
• Slovenia's third-choice keeper at Euro 2000, having been a key figure in the Slovenian Under-21 side.
• Was linked with a transfer to Club Brugge during the summer of 2000.

PLAYER
NEMEC, Jiri
Midfielder, Czech, 176cm, 74kg
Born: 15.05.66, Prague, Czech Republic
Clubs: Ceske Budejovice, Dukla Prague, Sparta Prague, Schalke (Ger) (1993-)
Full international (Czech Rep) 82 caps/1 goal
• Experienced old Czech midfield warhorse renowned for his battling qualities, relentless activity and foraging runs.

- The Czech Player of the Year in 1997, he helped Schalke win the UEFA Cup the same year and toiled for his country in their successful Euro 96 campaign.
- Surname pronounced Nem etch.

PLAYER
NEQROUZ, Rachid
Defender, Moroccan, 188cm, 84kg
Born: 10.04.72, Kasr Souk, Morocco.
Clubs: MC Oujda (1990-94), Young Boys Berne (Swi) (1994-97), Bari (Ita) (1997-)
Full international (Morocco)
- Versatile defender who has adapted well to Serie A following an unexpected move from Switzerland.

PLAYER
NERLINGER, Christian
Midfielder, German, 182cm, 80kg
Born: 21.03.73, Dortmund, Germany
Clubs: TSV Forstenried, Bayern Munich (1993-98), Borussia Dortmund (1998-)
Full international (Germany) 6 caps/1 goal
- Muscular left-sided midfielder who has many qualities: a powerful shot, aerial ability and great stamina. But subtlety and a flair for the producing the unexpected are not among them. On the fringes of the German national team until injury scuppered his Euro 2000 hopes.
- His father Helmut was a Bundesliga professional too, playing for Bayern Munich and Dortmund – the two professional staging posts of Christian's career.

PLAYER
NERVO, Carlo
Forward, Italian, 182cm, 71kg
Born: 29.10.71, Bassano del Grappa, Italy
Clubs: Bassano (1988-89), Monza (1989-90), Bassano (1990-91), Cittadella (1991-92), Mantova (1992-94), Bologna (1994-)
- Forward who has been with Bologna for the past six seasons, winning promotion from Italy's

Serie C to Serie A in successive seasons. Has not always been a regular, but a useful squad member.

PLAYER
NESMACHNY, Andriy
Defender, Ukrainian, 178cm, 71kg
Born: 28.02.79, Ukraine
Clubs: Kyiv Dynamo
Full international (Ukraine) 1 cap/0 goals
- Revelation of the 1999-2000 Ukrainian season. A highly promising right-sided defender who played regularly for Dynamo in the Ukraine League and the Champions League. Dynamo seemed to have found the ideal replacement for Oleh Luznhyi.

PLAYER
NESTA, Alessandro
Defender, Italian, 187cm, 79kg
Born: 19.03.76, Rome, Italy
Clubs: Lazio (1992-)
Full international (Italy) 30 caps/0 goals
- One of the most accomplished defenders in Serie A and a lynchpin of the Italian national team. A stylish but tough central defender who can play at sweeper, marker or stopper.
- Scorer of the decisive penalty in the Final shoot-out that won Italy the 1996 European Under-21 championship.
- Called up to Italy's squad for Euro 96, but did not play, making his debut three months later against Moldova.
- Spotted aged 10 by Roma scouts, who offered his local team Cinecitta Calcio £4,000 as a holding fee. But Nesta senior, Giuseppe, a lifelong Lazio fan, thought otherwise and took him along to Lazio for a trial.
- Injured while playing for Italy against Austria in the first round of France 98, prompting Lazio president Sergio Cragnotti to send a £4.5million bil to the Italian federation for compensation.
- Outstanding for Italy as the *Azzurri* surprised many by reaching the Final of Euro 2000.

PLAYER
NEUENDORF, Andreas
Midfielder, German, 178cm, 72kg
Born: 09.02.75, Berlin, Germany
Clubs: BFC Preussen, Fuchse, Renickend, Bayer Leverkusen (1994-97), Hertha Berlin (1997-)
• Agressive flame-haired midfield grafter who has also shown up well in the sweeper position. Was on the fringes of the German national team a year ago, but injuries forced him to miss almost half of the 1999-2000 campaign and he had drifted out of the international reckoning.
• Surname pronounced Noy en doorf.

PLAYER
NEUVILLE, Oliver
Forward, German, 171cm, 64kg
Born: 01.05.73, Locarno, Switzerland.
Clubs: Gambarogno, Locarno, Servette (1992-96), Tenerife (Spa) (1996-97), Hansa Rostock (1997-99), Bayer Leverkusen (1999-2000)
Full international (Germany) 17 caps/1 goal
• Diminutive, livewire attacker who despite playing in the majority of Germany's Euro 2000 qualifiers, was sensationally omitted from the squad for the European finals. Paid the ultimate price for a patchy second-half of the 1999-2000 season, but should bounce back.
• Whether playing through the middle or out on the right, he is a forward of pace, intelligent movement and delicate touch, both a purveyor and taker of chances.
• Of Italo-Swiss stock, he owes his German passport to the fact that his father was born in the Rhineland border town of Aachen.
• Surname pronounced Noy vil.

PLAYER
NEVILLE, Gary
Defender, English, 178cm, 72kg
Born: 18.02.75, Bury, England
Clubs: Manchester United (1992-)
Full international (England) 39 caps/0 goals

• Captain of United's victorious 1992 FA Youth Cup team and already hugely experienced, having made his debut for United in September 1992, against Moscow Torpedo in the UEFA Cup.
• Right-back who links well with **David Beckham** on United's right flank, but is less sure of himself when he switches to centre-back, where his lack of height has proved a problem.
• Was best man at Beckham's wedding.
• **Alex Ferguson**: 'If he was an inch taller he'd be the best centre-half in Britain.'
• Played in four of England's five matches at Euro 96, and three out of four at France 98.
• International debut: 03.06.95, v Japan (won 2-1).

PLAYER
NEVILLE, Philip
Defender, English, 178cm, 75kg
Born: 21.01.77, Bury, England
Clubs: Manchester United (1994-)
Full international (England) 29 caps/0 goals
• Younger brother of **Gary Neville**; twin sister Tracy is a British netball international. Father Neville is commerical manager at Bury FC.
• Signed, with his brother, a seven-and-a-half year contract with United in 1997.
• Non-playing member of England's Euro 96 squad, but left out of final 22 for France 98. Played all three games for England at Euro 2000, but was criticised for giving away the penalty which gave Romania victory in the final group match.
• International debut: 23.05.96, v China (won 3-0).

PLAYER/ADMINISTRATOR
NEVIN, Pat
Forward, Scottish, 169cm, 65kg
Born: 06.09.63, Glasgow, Soctland
Clubs: Clyde (1981-83), Chelsea (1983-88), Everton (1988-92), Tranmere (1992-97), Kilmarnock (1997-99), Motherwell (1999-)
Full international (Scotland) 28 caps/5 goals
• At 36, Nevin is one of the elder statesmen of

Scottish football and, unusually, combines his playing career with his role as chief executive of Motherwell. Still supremely fit, he continues to contribute on the field in the manner which has been evident during his time with Clyde, Chelsea and Tranmere.

PLAYER
NGOTTY, Bruno
Defender, French, 185cm, 86kg
Born: 10.06.71, Lyon, France
Clubs: Lyon (1988-95), Paris Saint-Germain (1995-98), Milan (Ita) (1998-2000), Marseille (2000-)
Full international (France) 6caps/0 goals
• Tough centre-back who scored seven goals in 80 games for PSG before a move to Milan in 1998.
• Strong in the air with a powerful shot – he scored the winning goal from a free-kick for PSG in the 1996 Cup-winners Cup Final against Rapid Vienna.
• Moved back to France, to Marseille, in summer 2000.

PLAYER
NICOLAE, Marius
Forward, Romanian, 184cm, 79kg
Born: 16.05.81, Bucharest, Romania
Clubs: Dinamo Bucharest (1996-)
Full international (Romania) 3 caps/1 goal
• Teenage striker who came through the Dinamo Bucharest ranks in the 1999-2000 season, atttracting considerable interest from western European clubs.
• Scored on his international debut, Romania v Latvia, February 2000.

PLAYER
NIELSEN, Allan
Midfielder, Danish, 180cm, 71kg
Born: 13.03.71, Esbjerg, Denmark
Clubs: Esbjerg (1988), Bayern Munich (Ger) (1988-1991), Sion (Swi) (1991), OB Odense (1991-93), FC Copenhagen (1993-95), Brondby (1994-96), Tottenham (Eng) (1996-2000), Wolves (Eng)

(2000, loan), Watford (Eng) (2000-)
Full international (Denmark), 35 caps, 7 goals
• Attacking midfielder whose teenage promise earned him a move to Bayern Munich, aged 17, but he only played once.
• Famously scored within 60 seconds of his international career, as a substitute against Armenia, but his career since then has had more downs than ups.
• Went on loan to Wolves in April 2000 to gain first-team action in a bid to hold onto his international place for Euro 2000.

PLAYER
NIELSEN, Anders
Midfielder, Danish, 182cm, 75kg
Born: 23.11.72, Kalundborg, Denmark
Clubs: Lyngby (1993-96), PSV Eindhoven (Hol) (1996-97), RKC Waalwijk (Hol) (1997-98) Sparta Rotterdam (Hol) (1998-)
• Midfielder who has carved out a career for himself in Holland, with RKC and now Sparta, after failing to make the grade at PSV.

PLAYER
NIELSEN, David
Defender, Danish, 183cm, 75kg
Born: 01.12.76, Denmark
Clubs: FC Copenhagen (1996-)
• Flamboyant striker who has been plagued by inconsistency but remains a favourite with fans at FC Copenhagen.
• Famous for his colourful haircuts.

PLAYER
NIELSEN, Jimmy
Goalkeeper, Danish, 191cm, 88kg
Born: 06.08.77, Denmark
Clubs: Millwall (Eng) (1994-95), AaB (1995-)
Full international (Denmark) 1 cap/0 goals
• The best young keeper in the Danish League who is now established back in Denmark at AaB after a move to English club Millwall did not work out.

• Capped by Denmark at Under-21, B and senior levels.

• Voted Danish Goalkeeper of the Year in 1998 and linked with a return to England, to Aston Villa or Newcastle.

PLAYER
NIELSEN, Michael
Midfielder, Danish, 183cm, 81kg
Born: 11.02.65, Denmark
Clubs: Frem (1992-93), FC Copenhagen (1993-)
Full international (Denmark) 1 caps/0 goals

• Veteran who plays a hugely influential role at FC Copenhagen, as captain and key midfielder, prompting and protecting the younger players in the squad.

• Nicknamed Mio.

PLAYER
NIEMI, Antti
Goalkeeper, Finnish, 186cm, 83kg
Born: 06.07.72, Oulu, Finland
Clubs: HJK (1991-95), FC Copenhagen (1995-97), Rangers (Sco) (1997-99), Hearts (Sco) (1999-)
Full international (Finland) 39 caps/0 goals

• Originally brought to Scotland from FC Copenhagen by ex-Rangers boss **Walter Smith**, the Finnish goalkeeper was surprisingly off-loaded by **Dick Advocaat** early in the 1999-2000 season. He was immediately signed by Hearts manager **Jim Jefferies**, whose faith in the player has been rewarded by a series of solid performances which helped the Tynecastle side to a place in the 2000-2001 UEFA Cup.

PLAYER
NIEUWENBURG, John
Defender, Dutch, 176cm, 71kg
Born: 24.12.78, Den Haag, Holland
Clubs: Sparta Rotterdam (1996-1999), Ajax (1999-)

• Signed by Ajax in a £2.5million deal from Sparta in 1999. Took time to bed in at Amsterdam, but has the talent to succeed.

PLAYER
NIGMATULLIN, Ruslan
Goalkeeper, Russian, 187cm, 71kg
Born: 07.10.74, Russia
Clubs: KamAZ (1993-94), Moscow Spartak (1995-97), Lokomotiv Moscow (1998-)
Full international (Russia) 2 caps/0 goals

• Tall, keeper, famous in Russia as a Renat Dasayev lookalike. Took **Alexander Filimonov**'s place in the Russian national squad after Filimonov was injured.

PLAYER
NIHAT Kahveci
Forward, Turkish, 175cm, 71kg
Born: 23.11.79, Turkey
Clubs: Besiktas

• Young, up-and-coming striker who has graduated from the youth ranks at Besiktas and is expected to win a regular first-team place soon.

• Used mostly as a substitute.

PLAYER
NIKIFOROV, Yuri
Defender, Russia, 188cm, 88kg
Born: 16.09.70, Odessa, Ukraine
Clubs: SKA Odessa (1987), Chernomorets (1988-93), Spartak Moscow (1993-96), Sporting Gijon (Spa) (1996-98), PSV Eindhoven (Hol) (1998-)
Full international (Russia) 40 caps/6 goals

• International sweeper who began his career as a forward, being dubbed one of the world's most promising strikers by Pele after his performances for Russia's European under-16 title-winning side.

• Once voted Russia's sexiest footballer by a poll of female fans.

• Played in two of Russia's games at Euro 96.

• Joined PSV after relegation in 1998 with Gijon, quickly being appointed captain.

• Won the Dutch League title with PSV in 1999-2000.

PLAYER
NIKOLAIDIS, Demis
Forward, Greek, 174cm, 72kg
Born: 17.09.73, Germany
Clubs: Ethinkos, Apollon, AEK Athens (1996-)
Full international (Greece) 30 caps/11 goals
• Despite summer 2000 speculation that
Liverpool and two or three Serie A sides were
interested, the Greek international frontrunner
remains the main man of the AEK Athens attack.
Quick, technically accomplished, a menace when
running at defences from deep and an assured
finisher. Inconsistency, however, is his weak
point.

PLAYER
NIKOLOV, Oka
Goalkeeper, Macedonian, 187cm, 86kg
Born: 25.05.74, Macedonia
Clubs: Eintracht Frankfurt (Ger) (1991-)
Full international (Macedonia)
• Keeper who has lost out to **Dirk Heinen** at
Eintracht and has been tipped to move on.

PLAYER
NIKOLOVSKI, Igor
Defender, Macedonian, 186cm, 80kg
Born: 16.07.73, Paris, France
Clubs Rabotnicki (1990), Metalurg (1991-93),
Vardar (1993-96), Antwerp (Bel) (1996-98),
Sakaryaspor (Tur) (1998-99), Trabzonspor (Tur)
(1999-)
Full international (Macedonia) 31 caps/1 goal
• Clever defender who has played in Turkey for
the past two seasons, earning a £1million
transfer to Trabzonspor in summer 1999.

PLAYER
NIKOPOLIDIS, Antonis
Goalkeeper, Greek, 188cm, 87kg
Born: 14.10.71, Greece
Clubs: Panathinaikos (1996-)
Full international (Greece) 7 caps/0 goals

• His good form between the posts for
Panathinaikos last season propelled him into the
national set-up and he was especially impressive
in a friendly victory over Romania in March 2000.
A late-developer, he has had to wait until his late
20s to blossom into an international-class keeper.

PLAYER
NILIS, Luc
Forward, Belgian, 183cm, 76kg
Born: 25.05.67, Hasselt, Belgium
Clubs: Winterslag (1984-86), Anderlecht (1986-
94), PSV Eindhoven (Hol) (1994-2000), Aston Villa
(Eng) (2000-)
Full international (Belgium) 56 caps/10 goals
• Gifted striker who has never reproduced his
prolific club form on the international stage for
Belgium.
• Winner of Dutch League in 1997 and 2000.
• Has a great touch on the ball, and is an
unselfish player who works well with a prolific
partner, such as **Ruud Van Nistelrooy**.
• International career surprisingly took a long time
to take off – he scored more than 100 goals in
six seasons for Anderlecht, while his first goal for
Belgium, against Zambia, took four years coming.
• Fell out with Belgian coach **Georges Leekens**
after Belgium's poor 1998 World Cup campaign,
but returned to the fold under new coach **Robert
Waseige** in time for Euro 2000.

REFEREE
NILSSON, Karl-Erik
Swedish
Born: 06.05.57
• Awarded his FIFA badge in 1994.

PLAYER
NILSSON, Mikael
Defender, Swedish, 186cm, 83kg
Born: 28.09.68, Falkoping, Sweden
Clubs: Falkoping (1985-87), IFK Gothenburg (1987-)
Full international (Sweden) 22 caps/0 goals

• A loyal one-club man in the Swedish Allsvenskan who joined IFK in 1987 and figured in all their triumphs in the 1990s. At home in defence or midfield, and packs a fiercesome shot.

PLAYER
NILSSON, Roland
Defender, Swedish, 179cm, 76kg
Born: 27.11.63, Helsingborg
Clubs: Helsingborg (1981-82), IFK Gothenburg (1983-89), Sheffield Wednesday (Eng) (1989-94), Helsingborg (1994-97), Coventry City (Eng) (1997-99), Helsingborg (1999-)
Full international (Sweden) 112 caps/2 goals
• The elder statesman of Swedish football who returned to his hometown club Helsingborg in 1999 from Coventry and then led them to their first title after 58 years.
• Won the UEFA Cup with IFK in 1987.
• A cultured right-back, the third Swede to collect more than 100 caps.

PLAYER
NIMNI, Avi
Midfielder Israeli, 186cm, 75kg
Born: 26.04.72, Tel Aviv, Israel
Clubs: Maccabi Tel Aviv, Atletico Madrid (Spa), Derby (Eng), Maccabi Tel Aviv
Full international (Israel) 47 caps/9 goals
• One of the most talented players in Israeli soccer, Nimni's dribbling abilities are spectacular. But he is not the most dedicated of workers and has a tendency to get injured.
• A badly-worked transfer deal saw Nimni go to Atletico Madrid in a multi-million dollar deal, but he was soon sidelined and his Spanish agent was holding back on a transfer for fear of not recouping his investment. Nimni spent a few months at Derby County before opting to return to his home club, Maccabi Tel Aviv.

PLAYER
NINIADIS, Andreas
Midfielder, Greek, 169cm, 63kg
Born: 18.02.71, Greece
Clubs: Olympiakos (1996-)
Full international (Greece) 15 caps/2 goals
• Underrated Olympiakos man who prefers a deep berth on the left side of midfield, but has the adaptability to take on other roles in the engine room.
• Greek international and an outstanding passer of the ball, but can be injury-prone.

PLAYER
NIOPLIAS, Nikos
Midfielder, Greek, 172cm, 70kg
Born: 17.01.65, Kozani, Greece
Clubs: Panathinaaikos, OFI Crete (1996-)
Full international (Greece) 44 caps/1 goal
• Veteran OFI Crete midfield general who should reach the milestone of 450 Greek League appearances in the 2000-2001 season.
• Although in his mid-30s, he remains one of the most creative players in the country, supplementing his flair with hard work and competitiveness.
• A former Greek international, he has spent the bulk of his career with OFI Crete, but also has worn the colours of Panathinaikos.

ADMINISTRATOR
NIZZOLA, Luciano
• President of the Italian FA since December 1996.

PLAYER
NJANKA, Pierre
Defender, Cameroon, 181cm, 83kg
Born: 15.03.75, Douala, Cameroon
Clubs: Neuchatel Xamax, Strasbourg
Full international (Cameroon)
• The versatile Cameroon international has the ability to play at left-back or as a central defensive marker. Speedy and athletic, he scored a magnificent individual goal for Cameroon

against Austria at the last World Cup.
• Surname pronounced Enn jan ka.

PLAYER
NJEGUS, Zoran
Midfielder, Yugoslav, 183cm, 75kg
Born: 25.06.73, Uzice, Yugoslavia
Clubs: Slobisa Uzice (1988-95), Red Star
Belgrade (1995-98), Atletico Madrid (Spa) (1998-)
Full international (Yugoslavia) 4 caps/0 goals
• Hard-working, versatile all-rounder who can
play in defence or midfield but is most effective
on the right side of midfield, where he works
tirelessly up and down the flank.
• Signed by **Arrigo Sacchi** for Atletico Madrid
after three seasons at Red Star Belgrade, but did
not win a regular first-team place and was
demoted to Atletico B.
• His fortunes revived under **Claudio Ranieri** and
then **Radomir Antic**, but his future at Atletico
was uncertain following relegation in May 2000.

PLAYER
NOEL-WILLIAMS, Gifton
Forward, English, 186cm, 91kg
Born: 21.01.80, London Islington, England
Clubs: Watford (1997-)
• Big, bustling centre-forward who made his
League debut aged 16 and remains a player of
huge promise, despite relegation from the English
Premier League in May 2000.

PLAYER
NOLAN, Ian
Defender, Northern Irish, 180cm, 76kg
Born: 09.07.70, Liverpool, England
Clubs: Tranmere (1991-94), Sheffield Wed (1994-
2000), Bradford (2000-)
Full international (Northern Ireland) 12 caps/0
goals
• Full-back and one-time captain of Sheffield
Wednesday, who missed the 1998-99 season
through injury.

PLAYER
NONDA, Shabani
Forward, Burundi, 182cm, 77kg
Born: 06.03.77, Bujumbura, Burundi
Clubs: Young Africans, Vaal Professionals (SAf),
Zurich (Swi) (1995-98), Rennes (Fra) (1998-2000),
Monaco (Fra) (2000-)
Full international (DR Congo)
• Many are calling the striker from Burundi the
'new **George Weah**' and it is anything but a half-
baked comparison. After all, Nonda has the same
power, delicate touch and goalscoring flair.
• Known as 'Chris' after his favourite Saint-
Christopher medaillon.
• Joined Monaco in July 2000 for £13.5million,
briefly a French record before the transfer of
Nicolas Anelka back to PSG. Signed by Monaco
to replace Juventus-bound **David Trezeguet**.
• Has opted to play for DR Congo, the country of
his parents' birth.

COACH
NORDIN, Olle
Swedish
Born: 23.11.49
• Coach of OFK Norrkoping and one Sweden's
most respected coaches.

PLAYER
NORNES, Jan-Frode
Defender, Norwegian, 187cm
Born: 08.01.73, Norway
Clubs: Eik, Odd Greenland (1999-)
Full international (Norway) 1 cap/0 goals
• Selected for national duty in 1999, this full-
back epitomises the attacking eagerness and
commitment his club, the part-timers of Odd, are
relying on to survive.

PLAYER
NOUMA, Pascal
Forward, French, 188cm, 82kg
Born: 06.01.72, Epinay-sur-Seine, France

Clubs: Paris Saint-Germain (1989-92), Lille
(1992-93), Caen (1993-94), Paris Saint-Germain
(1994-96), Strasbourg (1996-98), Lens (1998-)
• A frontrunning enigma, the sort of striker who
will score difficult goals, but has a tendency to
spurn straightforward chances. Given his
muscular frame, strength in the air and dribbling
ability, he really ought to average more than
seven or eight League goals per season. But
consistency is not his forte. Has appeared for
France at every level but the seniors.

COACH
NOUZARET, Robert
French
Born: 29.09.43
• Coach of Saint Etienne since 1998 who guided
the famous French club back into the First Division.
• Despite hailing from the rival Loire city of Lyon,
the veteran coach has certainly done a good job
at Saint Etienne, overseeing promotion to the top
flight in his first season in charge and then
surpassing expectations by leading *Les Verts* to a
great sixth-place finish in 1999-2000.
• A 4-4-2 man, who doesn't like sweeper systems
and prefers his two central defenders to
alternately cover and mark. He places much
emphasis on neat, quick attacking play.
• Spent the bulk of his career (13 years) as
coach and general manager of Montpellier –
winning them promotion in 1981 – but has also
been in charge of Orleans, Saint-Die, Bourges,
Lyon, Caen and the Ivory Coast.
• An ex-midfielder with Lyon, Bordeaux,
Montpellier and Gueugnon.

PLAYER
NOVAK, Djoni
Midfielder, Slovenian, 172cm, 73kg
Born: 04.09.69, Ljubljana, Slovenia
Clubs: Olimpia Ljubljana, Partizan Belgrade,
Fenerbahce (Tur), Le Havre (Fra), Sedan (Fra) (1999-)
Full international (Slovenia) 53 caps/2 goals

Pascal Nouma

• Experienced, hard-working right-sided defender or midfielder who has been a key member of the Slovenian national side for some years and played in all three of Slovenia's games at Euro 2000.
• A placy player who likes to get forward, but is also an adept defender.

PLAYER
NOVAKOVIC, Nebojsa
Forward, Swedish, 177cm, 68kg
Born: 29.10.64, Yugoslavia
Clubs: Dinamo Vinkovci (1988-91), Vasalunds (1991-92), Djurgarden (1993-96), AIK Stockholm (1997-)
• Bosnian Serb who now has a Swedish passport. An attacking midfielder of poise and refined shooting: his lobbed goal against Barcelona in the 1999-2000 Champions League will not be forgotten in a hurry.
• One of the biggest stars of the Swedish Allsvenskan, AIK are his third Stockholm club.
• Nicknamed 'Nescho'.

PLAYER
NOWOTNY, Jens
Defender, German, 187cm, 87kg
Born: 11.01.74, Spielberg, Germany
Clubs: Spielberg, Germania Friedrichstal, Karlsruher (1991-96), Bayer Leverkusen (1996-)
Full international (Germany) 22 caps/0 goals
• Leverkusen skipper and cool, collected sweeper. Physical, pacy and enterprising, he is especially impressive when running with the ball deep into enemy territory. Can also operate as a defensive marker or on the left-side of midfield.
• While at Karlsruhe, he used to spend his spare time helping at a centre for the disabled.
• Pronounced Yens No vot nee.

PLAYER
NOVOTNY, Jiri
Defender, Czech, 179cm, 75kg
Born: 07.04.70, Czech Republic
Clubs: Sparta Prague
Full international (Czechoslovakia) 12 caps/1 goal (Czech Republic) 24 caps/2 goals
• Solid rather than sensational Sparta captain and sweeper.
• The veteran Novotny was one of national team coach **Jozef Chovanec's** options when attempting to replace the injured **Jan Suchoparek** at Euro 2000 but otherwise isn't an automatic national team choice.

PLAYER
NUMAN, Arthur
Defender Dutch 180cm 70kg
Born: 14.12.69. Heemskerk Holland
Clubs: Haarlem (1987-91), Twente (1990-92), PSV Eindhoven (1992-98), Rangers (Sco) (1998-)
Full international (Holland) 40 caps/0 goals
• Numan's initial period at Ibrox was plagued by injury but the Dutchman has enjoyed an excellent 1999-2000 season, operating at full back but continually pushing forward and scoring a number of goals and forcing his way back into **Frank Rijkaard's** plans for Euro 2000.
• Played for Holland at the 1998 World Cup and at Euro 2000.

ADMINISTRATOR
NUNEZ, Josep Lluis
Spanish
Born: 07.09.31
Full Name: Josep Lluis Nunez Clemente
• President of Barcelona until summer 2000, when he stepped down amid mounting criticism of him and then coach **Louis Van Gaal.**

NUNO GOMES

Full name: Miguel Soares Pereira Ribeiro
Forward, Portuguese, 180cm, 76kg
Born: 05.07.76, Amarante, Portugal
Clubs: Boavista (1994-97), Benfica (1997-2000), Fiorentina (Ita) (2000-)
Full international (Portugal) 17 caps/4 goals
• The most promising striker to emerge from Portugal in recent years, who has attracted the interest of many foreign clubs.
• Made his name at Boavista, going on to score regularly for Benfica.
• A prolific scorer at youth and Under-21 level, but failed to scored in his first 15 outings for the senior national side after making his international debut as a substitute against France, a 3-2 defeat.
• One of the surprise stars of Euro 2000, his goals helped Portugal to reach the semi-finals and he secured a lucrative transfer to Fiorentina in July 2000.

NURMELA, Mika

Midfielder, Finnish
Born: 26.12.71, Oulu, Finland
Clubs: Oulun Luistinseura (1988-89), Rauman Pallo (1990), FC Haka (1991-92), Malmo (Swe) (1993-95), Emmen (Hol) (1995-99), Heerenveen (Hol) (1999-)
Full international (Finland) 15 caps/0 goals
• Finnish international right winger who joined Heerenven from second divisio Emmen. Has great pace and is one of the the best crossers in the Dutch League. Can also score himself.

NWOKO, Chucks

Forward, Maltese, 173cm, 72kg
Born: 21.11.78, Nigeria
Clubs: Birkirkara
Full international (Malta) 18 caps/0 goals
• Big bustling Nigerian-born striker whose unselfish style is his number one asset. Now holds a Maltese passport and will be a key figure in **Josif Ilic**'s plans for the Maltese national team.

NYARKO, Alex

Midfielder, Ghanaian, 183cm, 79kg
Born: 15.10.73, Accra, Ghana
Clubs: Sportul (Rom) (1994-95), Basle (Swi) (1995-97), Karlsruhe (Ger) (1997-98), Lens (1998-2000), Everton (Eng) (2000-)
Full international (Ghana)
• Ghanaian international midfielder who is at his best in a screening role in front of the defence. Works incessantly and usually emerges the winner in any physical duel.
• Pronounced Nee ah ko.

O

PLAYER
O'BRIEN, John
Midfielder, American, 178cm, 75kg
Born: 29.08.77, Los Angeles, United States
Clubs: Ajax Amsterdam (Hol), Utrecht (Hol) (1998-99), Ajax Amsterdam (Hol) (1999-)
Full international (United States) 4 caps/0 goals
• American who learned his football in the youth ranks of Ajax, but couldn't make the step up to the first team straightaway.
• Was sent on loan to FC Utrecht but the club's assistant coach Jan Wouters took O'Brien back to Ajax when he became head coach.
• A combative midfielder with great pace, but a victim like so many others of the crisis Ajax went through in the 1999-2000 season. Was a regular on the bench and was often used as a right back or on the right flank in midfield. In truth, he has had difficulties adapting to the highest level.

COACH
O'LEARY, David
Irish
Born: 02.05.58
• Manager of Leeds United since October 1958 when he succeeded **George Graham**.
• Took Leeds into the Champions League by finishing third in the English Premiership in 1999-2000. He ditched Graham's defensive-minded tactics and introduced some bold attacking football and had no hesitation in promoting youth.
• A softly-spoken former centre-back for Arsenal and the Republic of Ireland (68 caps/1 goal), O'Leary has adapted to coaching quickly and intelligently.

PLAYER
O'NEIL, Brian
Defender, Scottish, 185cm, 84kg
Born: 06.09.74, Paisley, Scotland
Clubs: Celtic (1991-97), Aberdeen (1997-98), Wolfsburg (Ger) (1998-)
Full international (Scotland) 4 caps/0 goals
• Centre-back or defensive midfielder whose career has taken off after making a surprise switch to the Bundesliga in 1998.
• Made his international debut for Scotland against Australia in March 1996

PLAYER
O'NEIL, John
Midfielder, Scottish, 173cm, 73kg
Born: 06.07.71, Belfast, Northern Ireland
Clubs: Dundee United (1988-94), St Johnstone (1994-)
• Another capture from Tayside rivals Dundee United, O'Neil joined St Johnstone in 1994 and is one of the club's longest-serving players. A highly skilful midfielder, O'Neil carries out his duties with minimum fuss and maximum efficiency and, while he is not the most flamboyant of players, his reliability means that he is virtually an automatic choice in the team's starting line-up.

PLAYER
O'NEILL, Fabian
Midfielder, Uruguayan
Born: 14.10.73, Paso de los Torros, Uruguay.
Clubs: Nacional (1992-95), Cagliari (Ita) (1995-2000), Juventus (Ita) (2000-)
Full international (Uruguay)
• The mainstay of the Cagliari midfield for five seasons until they were relegated in May 2000, when he was signed by Juventus.

O'NEILL, Martin

Northern Irish
Born: 01.03.52
• Charismatic manager of Celtic since July 2000, when he left Leicester City for Glasgow.
• A European Cup winner with Nottingham Forest in 1980 who played 64 times (8 goals) for Northern Ireland.
• Made his name as a young manager at Wycombe Wanderers, taking them into the Football League before taking charge at first division Leicester and overseeing their promotion to the Premier League.
• Twice won the League Cup with Leicester before accepting the offer to manage Celtic. Had previously rejected an offer to manage Leeds, but boardroom changes at Leicester are thought to have influenced his decision to leave in summer 2000.

OAKLEY, Matthew

Midfielder, English, 178cm, 76kg
Born: 17.08.77, Peterborough, England
Clubs: Southampton (1995-)
• Hard-working midfield link man who has excelled in Southampton's relegation struggles of recent years.
• England Under-21 international.

OBAJDIN, Josef

Forward, Czech, 178cm, 72kg
Born: 07.11.70, Podebrady, Czech Republic
Clubs: Sparta Prague
Full international (Czech Republic) 1 cap/0 goals
• Versatile veteran who performs a variety of roles for Sparta, frequently appearing as a substitute, often to good effect.
• Has broken into the national team just once but remains a key member of the Sparta squad.

OBERLEITNER Markus

Midfielder, German, 178cm, 75kg
Born: 16.08.73, Germany
Clubs: Unterhaching, Bayern Munich, Fortuna Dusseldorf (1996-97), Unterhaching (1997-)
• A neat and inventive midfield general who hardly put a foot wrong during the 1999-2000 season. Scored with an accurate header when Unterhaching beat Leverkusen on the final day of last season – thus helping Unterhaching's Munich neighbours Bayern snatch the League title.
• Surname pronounced Oh bear light ner.

OBRADOVIC, Milan

Defender, Yugoslav, 182cm, 73kg
Born: 03.08.77
Clubs: Obilic Belgrade
• Promising centre-back who is a regular in Yugoslavia's Under-21 side.

OFORI-QUAYE, Peter

Forward, Ghanaian, 182cm, 72kg
Born: 21.03.80, Ghana
Clubs: Kalamata (Gre) (1995-97), Olympiakos (Gre) (1997-)
• Highly promising young striker who has made a name for himself in Greece over the past five seasons.
• Scored on his debut for provincial club Kalamata aged 16 and joined Olympiakos for £2.5million in 1997.
• A member of the Ghana side which finished fourth at the 1997 Under-20 world championships.

OGNJANOVIC, Konstantin

Forward, Yugoslav, 184cm, 78kg
Born: 05.05.73, Podgorica, Yugoslavia
Clubs: Red Star Belgrade, OFK Belgrade
• Striker who could not break through at Red

Star because of the strong competition, but has been a prolific scorer at OFK.
• Son of a former Yugoslav national bank president.

PLAYER
OGNJENOVIC, Perica
Midfielder, Yugoslav, 170cm, 63kg
Born: 14.02.77, Smederevska Palanka, Yugoslavia
Clubs: Red Star Belgrade (1994-98), Real Madrid (Spa) (1999-), Valladolid (Spa) (2000, loan)
Full international (Yugoslavia) 12 caps/2 goals
• Pacy and highly promising young forward whose career has stalled at Real Madrid after a rapid rise at Red Star.
• Broke into the Red Star first team as a teenager in 1994-95, impressing everyone with his cunning, pace and technique.
• Yugoslav president Milan Milanjic on Ognjenovic: 'He is probably the most gifted of the new generation. The future belongs to him. He's so very quick. He's a player of incredible natural attacking intincts. He's a natural, an orginal. He can create, he can score, he poses a lot of problems for defenders.'
• Made three substitute apppearances for Yugoslavia at the 1998 World Cup.
•Joined Real Madrid in the transfer window in the 1998-99 season, but failed to win a regular first-team place. Went on loan to Valladolid for the 2000-2001 season.

PLAYER
OGUN Temizkanoglu
Defender, Turkish, 181cm, 76kg
Born: 06.10.69, Germany
Clubs: Trabzonspor, Fenerbahce
Full international (Turkey) 64 caps/5 goals
• Experienced, versatile defender who is usually used as a libero with the Turkish national team, though he can switch to stopper if required. Can also play in midfield, where he plays a holding role for his club Fenerbahce.
• Born in Germany and discovered playing in

amateur football by Trabzonspor, who took him to Turkey.
• Made his international debut for Turkey against the Republic of Ireland in May 1990.

PLAYER
OGUZ Cetin
Midfielder, Turkish, 180cm, 74kg
Born: 15.02.63, Germany
Clubs: Fenerbahce, Adanaspor
Full international (Turkey) 70 caps/3 goals
• One of the greatest midfield talents to have come out of Turkey, who is now winding down his career at Adanaspor.
• Midfield playmaker and Turkey's most capped player after beating the previous record set by **Fatih Terim**.
• Born in Germany but forever associated with Fenerbahce, where he won many honours.
• Nicknamed 'The Emperor'.

PLAYER
OHENE, Kennedy
Forward, Ghanaian, 186cm, 74kg
Born: 28.03.73, Ghana
Clubs: Ankaragucu
Full international (Ghana)
• Striker who has found success as one of the growing band of Ghanaians in Turkey, having moved there from Al Nasr of Saudi Arabia.
• Captain of the Ghana side which won the bronze medal at the 1992 Olympics in Barcelona and now a regular for the senior Ghana side.

PLAYER
OHREL, Christophe
Defender, Swiss, 176cm, 73kg
Born: 07.04.68, St-Die, France
Clubs: Lausanne (1987-92), Servette (1992-94), Rennes (Fra) (1994-95), St Etienne (Fra) (1995-96), Lausanne (1996-)
Full international (Switzerland) 56 caps/6 goals
• The Lausanne defensive midfielder used to be

Jay-Jay Okocha

a favourite of ex-Swiss national team manager **Roy Hodgson**. Never spectacular but highly-effective thanks to his tidy link-up play and industry on the right side of midfield.

PLAYER
OJEDA, Pedro Rafael
Full name: Pedro Rafael Ojeda Bustos
Forward, Argentinian
Born: 14.11.72, San Luis, Argentina
Clubs: Racing Avellanada (1998-), Numancia (Spa) (1999-)
• Very tall forward who is, as to be expected, very strong in the air.
• A big hit in his first season in Spain.

PLAYER
OKAN Buruk
Midfielder, Turkish, 169cm, 69kg
Born: 19.10.73, Istanbul, Turkey
Clubs: Galatasaray
Full international (Turkey) 14 caps/1 goal
• Former boy wonder of Turkish football who is starting to show some of the talent he displayed as a teenager.
• A prominent member of the Turkish side which won the European Under-18 title in 1992.
• Made his international debut while still a teenager, against San Marino in October 1992, prompting national coach **Sepp Piontek** to declare: 'The boy is a natural. It's incredible that someone so young has taken football here by storm.'
• But in February 1993, he broke a leg playing for Galatasaray in a Turkish Cup semi-final. When he returned a year later, his form and confidence had ebbed away.
• He was a bit-player at Galatasaray for three seasons, before returning to form in the 1997-98 season, when **Fatih Terim** took over as coach and switched him to the right side of midfield.
• Recalled to the national team in April 1998 for a friendly against Russia.

PLAYER
OKOCHA, Augustine 'Jay-Jay'
Midfielder, French, 173cm, 70kg
Born: 14.08.73, Enugu, Nigeria
Clubs: Enugu Rangers, Neunkirchen (Ger),
Eintracht Frankfurt (Ger) (1992-96), Fenerbahce
(Tur) (1996-98), Paris Saint-Germain (Fra) (1998-)
Full international (Nigeria)
• Playmaker whose qualities are not in doubt. He
has wonderful vision, explosive shooting and can
perform tricks with the ball which mere mortals
can only dream about. However, he can overdo
the showmanship and be frustratingly inconsistent.
• Arguably his most effective period at club level
was in Turkey with Fenerbahce, where
'Okochamania' broke out and he played under
the pseudonym of Mohamed Yavuz.

PLAYER
OKON, Paul
Defender, Australian, 180cm, 75kg
Born: 05.04.72, Sydney, Australia
Clubs: Marconi (1989-91), Club Brugge (Bel)
(1991-96), Lazio (Ita) (1996-2000), Middlesbrough
(Eng) (2000-)
Full international (Australia) 14 caps/0 goals
• Talented and versatile player – if fit. Career has
been thwarted by knee problems.
• Captain of Australian national team and the first
Australian national to play in Serie A.

PLAYER
OKPARA, Godwin
Defender, Nigerian, 176cm, 71kg
Born: 20.09.72, Wan Ogbaku, Nigeria
Clubs: Obanta Utd, Eendracht Aalst (Bel) (1991-
96), Strasbourg (Fra) (1996-)
Full international (Nigeria)
• Versatile and accomplished Nigerian international
whose best work is as a sweeper or central
defensive marker, though he can also play in
midfield. Never gets ruffled and performs his
duties with a minimum of fuss.

PLAYER
OKTAY, Derelioglu
Forward, Turkish, 181cm, 68kg
Born: 7.12.75, Istanbul, Turkey
Clubs: Besiktas, Gazientepspor
Full international (Turkey) 14 caps/8 goals
• Striker whose strong running and work-rate
have made him the perfect foil for Hakan Sukur
in the Turkish national side.
• Enjoyed a wonderful start to his international
career, scoring four goals in his second game,
against San Marino in September 1995, having
made his debut against Sweden in November
1995.
• Made one substitute appearance for Turkey at
Euro 2000, against Portugal in the quarter-final.
He would have played more, but he fell out of
favour at Besiktas during the 1999-2000 season,
and went on loan to Gazientepspor.

COACH
OKUKA, Dragan
Yugoslav
Born: 02.04.54
• Coach of Buducnost Podgorica, who had a fine
player career as a right winger with Velez Mostar.
Won the Yugoslav title with Obilic Belgrade in
1997-98.

PLAYER
OKUNOWO, Gbenga Samuel
Defender, Nigerian, 182cm, 79kg
Born: 01.03.79, Ibadan, Nigeria
Clubs: Liberty, Shooting Stars, Barcelona (Spa)
(1997-99), Benfica (Por) (1999-2000)
• Right-back who broke into the Barcelona first
team in the autumn of 1998, surprising many
with his confidence and maturity.
• Spotted by Barcelona scouts at the 1996 World
Youth championships in Portugal.
• Spent the 1999-2000 season on loan at
Benfica.

Sunday Oliseh

PLAYER
OLAIZOLA, Javier
Defender, Spanish, 176cm, 75kg
Born: 28.11.69, San Sebastian, Spain
Clubs: Eibar (1991-92), Burgos (1992-94), Eibar (1994-95), Mallorca (1995-)
• Solid, tough-tackling man-marker who has been the mainstay of Mallorca's defence in recent years.
• A runner-up in the 1999 European Cup-winners Cup Final, when Mallorca lost to Lazio.

PLAYER
OLEMBE, Salomon
Midfielder, French/Cameroon, 170cm, 65kg
Born: 08.12.80, Yaounde, Cameroon
Clubs: Nantes (1997-)
Full international (Cameroon)
• Became the youngest-ever international to appear at Wembley, when he played for Cameroon against England in 1998 aged just 17. Nantes prefer to use him at left-back, but a time will surely come when he brings his brilliant ball skills and quick wits to the playmaker role.
• Surname pronounced Oh lem bay.

PLAYER
OLESEN, Allan
Defender, Danish, 178cm, 70kg
Born: 25.01.74, Denmark
Clubs: Bronshoj (1995-96), AB (1996-2000), Saint Etienne (Fra) (2000-)
Full international (Denmark) 2 caps/0 goals
• Defender whose pace, determination and ball control took him to the verge of Denmark's squad for Euro 2000 and earned a transfer to Saint Etienne.
• Joined AB in 1996 but came into his own in the 1999-2000 season following the departure of **Rene Henriksen** to Greece. His League performances were recognised by a call-up to the Danish squad for a training camp in Spain during the winter break.
• Six caps at Under-16 level for Denmark.

PLAYER
OLI
Full name: Oliveira Jesus Alvarez Gonzalez
Forward, Spanish, 175cm, 73kg
Born: 02.04.72, Oviedo, Spain
Clubs: Real Oviedo (1992-97), Real Betis (1997-)
Full international (Spain) 2 caps/0 goals
• Striker who made his name at Oviedo, scoring 20 League goals in the 1998-97 season.
• A dependable goalscorer who made his international debut for Spain under **Javier Clemente**, but has yet to impress **Jose Antonio Camacho**.
• Joined Betis in 1997 for £4million.

PLAYER
OLISEH, Azubuike
Midfielder, Nigeria, 182cm, 72kg
Born: 18.11.78, Lagos, Nigeria
Clubs: Julius Berger, Anderlecht (Bel) (1995-99), Utrecht (Hol) (1999-)
• Younger brother of Nigerian international **Sunday Oliseh** who came through the youth ranks at Anderlecht before moving to Holland in attempt to gain first-team experience.

PLAYER
OLISEH, Sunday
Midfielder, Nigerian, 183cm, 74kg
Born: 14.09.74, Abavo, Nigeria
Clubs: Julius Berger (1988-90), FC Liege (Bel) (1990-94), Reggiana (Ita) (1994-95), Koln (Ger) (1995-97), Ajax (Hol) (1997-99), Juventus (Ita) (1999-2000), Borussia Dortmund (Ger) (2000-)
Full international (Nigeria
• Defensive midfield player who has been one of the most successful Nigerians in Europe.
• Played for Nigeria at the 1994 and 1998 World Cups. Was blamed by many in Nigeria for the defeat by Italy in the second round of USA 94. A sloppy throw-in by Oliseh allowed **Roberto Baggio** to race away and score.
• A member of the Nigerian squad which won the 1994 African Nations Cup, he also played in the 2000 Nations Cup finals.
• Made his international debut aged 18 for Nigeria against Ethiopia in April 1993, a 6-0 victory in an African Nations Cup qualifier.
• Left Nigeria aged 16, determined to make a name for himself in European football.
• Had an unhappy spell in Belgian football at FC Liege, where he was spotted by the then Nigeria coach, Dutchman Clemens Westerhof.
• Returned to Germany in summer 2000, having not won a first-team place at Juventus.
• 'In Europe we learn tactical discipline, but African players have a better intelligence and are learning to play with better conditioning and order. We are so much better than we ever were.'

PLAYER
OLISADEBE, Emmanuel
Forward, Nigerian/Polish, 177cm, 73kg
Born: 22.12.73, Nigeria
Clubs: Jasper United, Polonia Warsaw (1997-)
• Has settled extremely well in Warsaw since arriving from Nigerian club Jasper United in 1997. Was 'discovered' by Poland coach **Jerzy Engel** who wanted the Nigerian to play for Poland after he was granted Polish citizenship.

PLAYER
OLIVARES, Percy
Full name: Percy Celso Olivares Polanco
Defender, Peruvian, 182cm, 77kg
Born: 05.06.68, Lima, Peru
Clubs: Nurnburg (Ger) (1992-93), Tenerife (Spa) (1993-96), Fluminense (Bra) (1996), PAOK (Gre) (1996-98), Panathinaikos (Gre) (1998-)
• Quick and resourceful Peruvian left-back who joined Panathinaikos from PAOK Salonika at the start of the 1998-99 season.
• Announced his international retirement in 2000. 'I want to dedicate myself to Panathinaikos.'

PLAYER
OLIVE, Renato

Midfielder, Italian, 176cm, 77kg
Born: 06.04.71, Putignano, Italy
Clubs: Pesaro (1989-92), Lecce (1992-96), Fidelis
Andria (1996-97), Perugia (1998-)
• Experienced midfielder with great energy,
commitment and leadership skills.

PLAYER
OLIVEIRA, Luis

Full name: Airton Luis Oliveria Barroso
Forward, Belgian, 175cm, 71kg
Born: 24.03.69, Sao Luis, Brazil
Clubs: Anderlecht (1988-92), Cagliari (1992-96),
Fiorentina (Ita) (1996-99), Cagliari (Ita) (1999-
2000), Bologna (Ita) (2000-)
Full international (Belgium) 31 caps/9 goals
• Brazilian-born striker who has been one of the
best strikers in Serie A in recent years.
• Liked Belgium so much after signing for
Anderlecht from a Brazilian junior club aged 16
that he changed his nationality.
• Scored on his debut for Belgium against Tunisia
in 1992 and then moved to Italy, to Cagliari.
• Joined Fiorentina for £5.5million in summer
1996, moving back to Cagliari in 1999 and then
on to Bologna after Cagliari were relegated in
May 2000.

COACH
OLSEN, Egil

Norwegian
Born: 22.04.42
• Norway's most famous coach, an eccentric
whose direct, long-ball tactics worked for
Norway, taking them to the second round of the
1994 and 1998 World Cup finals, but failed at
Wimbledon, who were relegated in 1999-2000,
shortly after Olsen had quit.
• As a player, Olsen was an individualist who
played 16 times for his country. As a coach, he
believes in collective effort and organisation.

Victor Onopko

398

- Became a lecturer in physical education while coaching part-time. He took Lyn Olso from the third division back to the first and then took charge of the Norwegian Under-21s.
- Was appointed coach of the senior national side in October 1990 and transformed their fortunes.
- His radical political ideas (Marxist-Leninist), poker-playing activities and wellington boots (because of an old back injury) have made him a controversial figure.
- Joined Wimbledon in 1999, but the players could not adapt to his tactics.
- Nicknamed Drillo.
- 'The penetrative, direct style is the most effective. We'll stick with it even though other countries are going in the opposite direction. It's an easy philosophy.'

PLAYER
OLSEN, Frode
Goalkeeper, Norwegian, 188cm, 86kg
Born: 12.10.67, Norway
Clubs: Rosenborg (1990), Stromsgodset (1991), Start (1992-96), Stabaek (1997-99), Sevilla (Spa) (1999-2000)
Full international (Norway) 14 caps/0 goals
- Acrobatic keeper with good shot-stopping skills and excellent reflexes. Enjoys playing the clown and can be at fault on high crosses.
- Joined Sevilla on loan from Stabaek during the 1999-2000 season.
- International debut v Estonia, 06.02.95.

COACH
OLSEN, Morten
Danish
Born: 14.08.49
- Former international and leading member of the Danish Dynamite side of the 1980s, coached by **Sepp Piontek**, winning 102 caps (4 goals).
- Has had mixed success in a coaching career which has taken him to Germany and Holland.
- Sacked by Ajax despite winning the 1998

League title, amid accusations that he had tried to alter the Amsterdam's club famous playing style.

PLAYER
OLSEN, Odd Inge
Midfielder, Norwegian, 183cm, 79kg
Born: 28.12.69, Norway
Clubs: Molde (1996-)
Full international (Norway) 2 caps/0 goals
- Arguably the one Norwegian midfield player who covers most kilometres during a season than any other. Scores a high number of goals each season and was unlucky to miss out on Norway's Euro 2000 squad.

ADMINISTRATOR
OMDAL, Per Ravn
Born: 20.08.47
- President of the Norwegian Football Federation and a member of the FIFA excecutive committee since 1994. Also a vice-president of UEFA.
- An industrialist by profession.

PLAYER
OMER Catkic
Goalkeeper, Turkish, 182cm, 82kg
Born: 15.10.74, Eskisehir, Turkey
Clubs: Eskisehirspor, Gazientepspor
- Keeper who was a late call-up to Turkey's Euro 2000 squad after an injury to Engin Ipekoglu. Earned his call after helping Gazientepspor to third place in the Turkish League.

PLAYER
ONOPKO, Victor
Defender, Russian, 188cm 79kg
Born: 11.10.69
Clubs: Shakhtar Donesk (1989-91), Moscow Spartak (1992-94), Oviedo (Spa) (1995-)
Full international (Russia) 76 caps/6 goals
- Hugely experienced defender who can also play in midfield. Most effective as a libero, where his ball-playing skills come to the fore.

Ariel Ortega

• Russia's Player of the Year in 1992 and 1993, Oviedo signed him in 1995, beating off competition from Atletico Madrid.
• Captain of Russia at Euro 96.

PLAYER
OOIJER, Andre
Defender, Dutch, 185cm, 76kg
Born: 11.07.74, Amsterdam, Holland
Clubs: Volendam (1994-95), Roda JC (1995-98), PSV Eindhoven (1998-)
Full international (Holland) 4 caps/0 goals
• Versatile campaigner who was signed by PSV in summer 1998 after losing Philip Cocu to Barcelona.

PLAYER
OPDAM, Barry
Defender, Dutch, 186cm, 77kg
Born: 27.02.76, Leiden, Holland
Clubs: AZ (1996-)
• Central defender who blossomed during the 1999-2000 season. Also a regular scorer.

PLAYER
ORBU, Gennadiy
Midfielder, Ukrainian, 170cm, 68kg
Born: 23.07.70, Ukraine
Clubs: Rotor Volgograd (Rus), Shakhtar Donetsk
Full international (Ukraine) 17 caps/0 goals
• Product of Shakhtar youth system, a hard-working wide midfielder who covers large areas of the pitch during a game. A precise and powerful shot.

PLAYER
ORETAN, Chris
Forward, Nigerian, 173cm, 73kg
Born: 08.09.80, Nigeria
Clubs: Naxxar Lions (Mlt)
• Nigerian striker who has made a big impact in Maltese football and is now looking for a bigger challenge, preferably in England or Spain.

PLAYER
ORLANDINI, Pierluigi
Midfielder, Italian, 181cm, 77kg
Born: 09.10.72, San Giovanni Bianco, Italy
Clubs: Atalanta (1990-92), Lecce (1992-93), Atalanta (1993-94), Internazionale (1994-96), Verona (1996-97), Parma (1997-99), Milan (1999-)
• Former Under-21 international who has been a fringe player at a number of Serie A clubs, without making the proper breakthrough.

PLAYER
ORTEGA, Ariel
Midfielder, Argentinian, 170cm, 64kg
Born: 04.03.74, Ledesma, Argentina
Clubs: River Plate (1991-96), Valencia (Spa) (1996-98), Sampdoria (Ita) (1998-99), Parma (Ita) (1999-) River Plate (2000- loan)
Full international (Argentina) 68 caps/16 goals
• Hugely gifted attacker midfielder who is the closest Argentina have come to finding a successor to Diego Maradona.
• The 'new Maradona' tag has weighed heavily on him during his career, but he shown more than enough to justify the hype. Has outstanding ball control, playmaking skills and a sharp eye for goal.
• Joined Valencia from River Plate for £8million in 1997, but fell out with coach **Claudio Ranieri**.
• Starred for Argentina in the 1998 World Cup qualifiers, finishing as their top scorer and missing only one match. Scored two wonderful goals for Argentina against Jamaica at France 98, but was sent off against Holland in the quarter-final against Holland.
• Spent a season in Italy with Sampdoria before switching to Parma in 1999 as a replacement for Lazio-bound **Juan Veron**.
• 'My greatest attribute is dribbling at speed. But I'm missing many things. If I didn't make mistakes I'd be Maradona. And there's only one Maradona!'
• Returned to Argentina on loan for the 2000-2001 season.

PLAYER
OSHADOGAN, Joseph
Defender, Ghanaian, 182cm, 75kg
Born: 27.06.76, Genoa
Clubs: Pisa (Ita) (1993-94), Foggia (Ita) (1994-99), Reggina (Ita) (1999-)
• Defender who established himself under **Zdenek Zeman** at Foggia, but found a move to Reggina a little more problematic.

PLAYER
OSMANOVIC, Dejan
Forward, Yugoslav, 176cm
Born: 29.01.73, Vranje, Yugoslavia
Clubs: Hajduk Kula
• Fast and technically strong attacker. The only ethnic Gypsy to have made the grade in Yugoslavia's top flight.

PLAYER
OSMANOVSKI, Yksel
Forward, Swedish, 173cm, 68kg
Born: 24.02.77, Skravlinge, Sweden
Clubs: Malmo (1995-98), Bari (Ita) (1998-).
Full international (Sweden) 8 caps/2 goals
• Livewire forward or midfielder who is a clever operator on the ball.
• Former Swedish Under-21 international who made his senior international debut against the USA in January 1998.
• Joined Bari as part of the £2.5million deal which took him and **Daniel Andersson** to Italy in 1998.
• Had an impressive first season in Serie A, scoring six goals.

PLAYER
OSCAR
Full name: Oscar Garcia Junyent
Midfielder, Spanish, 179cm, 77kg
Born: 26.04.73, Barcelona, Spain
Clubs: Barcelona (1991-94), Albacete (1994-95), Barcelona (1995-99), Valencia (1999-2000), Espanyol (2000-)

• Young midfielder who was one of the highest profile casualties of **Louis Van Gaal**'s regime at Barcelona.

• Joined Valencia in 1999 after failing to get a regular game in Barcelona alongside the Dutch imports. Returned to the city of Barcelona, to Espanyol, in summer 2000.

• Seen as one of the brightest prospects to come through Barcelona's youth system in recent years, along with his brother, **Roger**.

PLAYER
OSCAR VALES
Midfielder, Spanish, 175cm, 79kg
Born: 13.09.74, Bilbao, Spain
Clubs: Athletic Bilbao (1993-97), Celta Vigo (1997-99), Athletic Bilbao (1999-)

• Ultility player who has came thorugh the youth ranks at Athletic Bilbao but has not yet managed to establish himself as a regular in the first team.

• Has spent time in the Athletic Bilbao B squad and on loan to Celta Vigo.

COACH
OSIM, Ivica
Yugoslav
Born: 06.05.41

• Former coach of Yugoslavia, Partizan Belgrade and Panathinaikos who has been in charge of Sturm Graz, winning the Austrian League in 1999.

PLAYER
OSMAN Ozkoglu
Defender, Turkish, 188cm, 81kg
Born: 26.08.71, Aydin, Turkey
Clubs: Ayssinspor, Trabzonspor
Full international (Turkey) 6 caps/0 goals

• Powerful central defender who uses his height to great effect at set-pieces, but can also bring the ball out of defence effectively.

• Made his international debut for Turkey against Canada in June 1995.

• A member of Turkey's squad at Euro 2000.

PLAYER
OSTERC, Milan
Forward, Slovenian, 185cm, 83kg
Born: 04.07.75, Murska Sobota
Clubs: Beltinci, Gorica, Hercules (Spa) (1998), Olimpia Ljubljana
Full international (Slovenia) 25 caps/5 goals

• Striker who played in all three of Slovenia's games at Euro 2000 as a substitute.

• Strong in the air, with enough flair to get past defenders on the ground.

• Had an unsuccessful spell in Spain with second division Hercules in 1998, but was tipped for a return to Spain in the summer of 2000.

PLAYER
OTERO, Jorge
Full name: Jorge Otero Bouzos
Defender, Spanish, 175cm, 70kg
Born: 28.01.69, Nigran, Spain
Clubs: Celta Vigo (1987-94), Valencia (1994-97), Real Betis (1997-)
Full international (Spain) 9 caps/0 goals

• Versatile defender who started out at Celta and played in the 1994 World Cup. Sold to Valencia in 1994, then followed **Luis Aragones** to Betis three years later. Hard and uncompromising.

• Member of Spain's squad at the 1994 World Cup and Euro 96.

PLAYER
OTERO, Marcelo
Forward, Uruguayan, 177cm, 70kg
Born: 14.04.71, Montevideo, Uruguay
Clubs: Rampla (1991-92), Penarol (1993-95), Vicenza (Ita) (1995-99), Sevilla (Spa) (1999-)
Full international (Uruguay

• Uruguayan international striker who made his name at Italian club Vicenza, scoring freely as they won the Italian Cup and then reached the semi-finals of the European Cup-winners Cup.

• Joined Sevilla in 1999 as the club's biggest signing on their return to the Spanish first division.

OTTO, Oliver

Midfielder, German, 183cm, 75kg
Born: 21.11.72, Germany
Clubs: TSV Wernau, Stuttgart (1993-94), Ulm (1994-)
Defensive midfielder who is consistent, industrious and a fine reader of the game. Discarded by Stuttgart six years ago after only making six first team appearances for them.

OUDE KAMPHUIS, Niels

Midfielder Dutch, 179cm, 75kg
Born: 14.11.77, Hengelo, Hollnd
Clubs: Twente (1994-99), Schalke (Ger) (1999-)
Dutch Under-21 international winger who showed great promise while at Twente, and has settled well at Schalke despite injury worries.

OUDEC, Nicolas

Forward, French,
Born: 28.10.71, Lorrent, France
Clubs: Nantes, Deportivo La Coruna (Spa), Paris Saint-Germain, Montpellier
Full international (France) 7 caps/1 goal
• Striker who made his name in the early 1990s at Nantes, winning the French league title in 1995. But he lost his way following a move to Spain, ending up at relegated Montpellier.

OUEDRAOGO, Rahim

Defender, Burkina Faso
Born: 08.10.80, Bobo Dioulasso, Burkina Faso
Clubs: ASSB, FC Twente (1998-)
Full international (Burkina Faso)
• Midfielder from Burkina Faso, sometimes used as right-back. Has found it difficult to adapt to his new environment and has spent a lot of time on the bench.

OULARE, Souleymane

Forward, Guinea, 180cm, 82kg
Born: 16.10.72, Conakry, Gui
Clubs: St Niklaas (Bel) (1991-92), Beveren (Bel) (1992-94), Waregem (Bel) (1994-96), Genk (Bel) (1996-99), Fenerbahce (Tur) (1999-)
Full international (Guinea)
• Strong-running striker who made a name for himself when Genk won the 1999 Belgian League title. He was sold to Turkish side Fenerbahce, where he was injured early on struggled to establish himself.

OVCHINNIKOV, Sergei

Goalkeeper, Russian, 190cm, 92kg
Born: 11.10.70, Moscow, Russia
Clubs: Lokomotiv Moscow (1991-97), Benfica (Rus) (1997-2000)
Full international (Russia) 18 caps/0 goals
• Experienced keeper who has been edged out of Benfica by **Robert Enke**.
• Nicknamed 'The Boss' while in Russia, where he was one of the heaviest players in the League.
• Russian goalkeeper of the year in 1994 and 1995 and Russia's third-choice keeper at Euro 96.

OVERMARS, Marc

Forward, Dutch, 174cm, 72kg
Born: 29.03.73, Ernst, Holland
Clubs: Go Ahead Eagles (1990-91), Willem II (1991-92) Ajax Amsterdam (1992-97), Arsenal (Eng), (1997-2000), Barcelona (Spa) (2000-)
Full international (Holland) 60 caps/13 goals
• Deep-lying left-winger who always causes problems for opponents with electric pace and dribbling skills.
• Started at Go Ahead Eagles, but made his name in Amsterdam, as one of the stars of Ajax's class of 1995.
• Played in all 11 of Ajax's matches when they

won the 1995 Champions Cup.

• Joined Arsenal in a £7million transfer in July 1997, winning the League and Cup double in his first season.

• Missed Euro 96 through injury, but appeared in five of Holland's six matches at France 98.

• Joined Barcelona in summer 2000 as part of a £32 million deal which also saw **Emmanuel Petit** leave Arsenal for Spain. Overmars was valued at £25million.

• International debut: 24.02.93, v Turkey (won 3-1).

PLAYER
OWEN, Michael

Forward, English, 172cm, 67kg
Born: 14.12.79, Chester, England
Clubs: Liverpool (1996-)
Full international (England) 22 caps/6 goals)

• Striker whose goal against Argentina at France 98 catapulted him to superstardom overnight.

• A prolific goalscorer at youth and schoolboy level, who scored 12 goals in seven games for England schoolboys.

• John Owens, England schoolboys coach: 'He scored adult goals in schoolboy football. The sort of goals that would not have looked out of place in the Premiership, and that is a sign of a rare talent.'

• Mental and physical strain of his early success took its toll in 1999-2000, with a series of hamstring injuries, leading to criticism that Liverpool had not given him enough time to recover.

Michael Owen

>

PAAS, David

Forward, Belgian, 185cm, 83kg
Born: 24.02.71, Belgium
Clubs: Eendracht Aalst (1995-97), Vitoria Guimaraes (Por) (1997-98), Harelbeke (Bel) (1998-99), Vitoria Guimaraes (Por) (1998-99), Harelbeke (1999-)
• Modest player from Harelbeke, but dangerous in the penalty area. Was part of the Eendracht Aalst team that reached European football in their first season at the highest level in 1995.
• Linked with a move to English football in summer 2000.

PLAYER
PAAUWE, Patrick

Midfielder, Dutch, 183cm, 74kg
Born: 27.12.75, 't Harde, Holland
Clubs: PSV (1993-95), De Graafschap (1995-96), Fortuna Sittard (1996-98), Feyenoord (1998-)
• Highly promising midfielder or left-back who has pushed himself to the brink of international recognition after switching from Fortuna Sittard to Feyenoord in 1998.
• Intelligent player with good technique and a powerful shot from set-pieces.

PLAYER
PABLO

Full name: Pablo Jose Diaz Stalla
Defender, Argentinian, 178cm, 77kg
Born: 05.08.71, Buenos Aires, Argentina
Clubs: Sporting Gijon (Spa) (1990-1998), Zaragoza (Spa) (1998-)
• Solid Argentinian defender who spent eight years at Sporting Gijon, before joining Zaragoza when the Asturians were relegated in 1998.

PLAYER
PABLO SANZ

Full name: Pablo Sanz Iniesta
Midfielder, Spanish, 190cm, 76kg
Born: 30.08.73, Barcelona, Spain
Clubs: Barcelona B (1993-97), Tarragona (1994-95), Rayo Vallecano (1997-)
• Utility player who can play in central defence or midfield.
• Started out at Barcelona, playing for the youth team and Barcelona B, before trying his luck with the first team and failing to make the breakthrough.
• A key member of Vallecano's midfield in their successful push for promotion in the 1998-99 season.

COACH
PACHECO, Jaime Moreira

Portuguese
Born: 22.07.58
• Intelligent, busy and precise midfielder for Portugal, Sporting Lisbon, FC Porto and Vitoria Setubal who has developed into an equally outstanding coach, realising the considerable achievement of taking unfashionable Boavista into the Champions League in 1999.
• Feisty, bristling with enthusiasm and very flexible tactically. His first instinct is to use an attacking 4-3-3, but on their travels, Boavista do sometimes employ a prudent 4-5-1.
• 'On paper, the likes of Boavista should never beat a giant like Benfica. Fortunately, football is not an exact science and the poor can sometimes rub shoulders with the rich.'

PLAYER
PACHETA

Full name: Jose Rojo Martin Pacheta
Midfielder, Spanish, 184cm, 75kg
Born: 23.03.68, Sabas Infantes, Spain
Clubs: Burgos (1990-91), Atletico Marbella (1991-93), Merida (1993-94), Espanyol (1994-99), Numancia (1999-)

• Highly effective central midfield pivot who made a name for himself in Numancia's first season in the Spanish top flight in 1999-2000.
• Was out-of-contract and was expected to move on in summer 2000.

PLAYER
PACIOREK, Jarda
Midfielder, Czech, 186cm, 86kg
Born: 11.07.79, Krameriz, Czech Rep
Clubs: FC Zlim, Feyenoord (Hol), Excelsior (Hol) (1997-98), Fortuna Sittard (Hol) (1998-)
• Czech midfielder who came through the youth ranks at Feyenoord and went on loan to Fortuna Sittard. Was a big part of Fortuna's success in 1998-99, but spent much of 1999-2000 on the bench as his team fought against relegation.
• A free-kick specialist.

PLAYER
PACO
Full name: Francisco Jemez Martin
Defender, Spanish, 180cm, 80kg
Born: 18.04.70, Las Palmas, Spain
Clubs: Cordoba (1990-91), Murcia (1991-92), Rayo Vallecano (1992-93), Deportivo La Coruna (1993-98), Zaragoza (1998-)
Full international (Spain) 16 caps/0 goals
• Tough man-marking centre-back who broke into the Spanish national team under **Jose Antonio Camacho**, his former coach at Rayo Vallecano.
• Born in the Canary Islands and joined Zaragoza in the summer of 1999 after failing to win a regular place at Deportivo.
• One of the surprise stars of Zaragoza's impressive form in the 1999-2000 season.

COACH
PACO FLORES
Spanish
• An Espanyol stalwart who has been caretaker coach four times. Stepped in during the 1999-

2000 season and led Espanyol to triumph in the Spanish Cup, their first trophy since 1940.

PLAYER
PADALINO, Pasquale
Defender, Italian, 180cm, 74kg
Born: 26.07.72, Foggia, Italy
Clubs: Foggia (1988-92), Bologna (1992-93), Lecce (1993-94), Foggia (1994-95), Fiorentina (1995-)
• Talented, experienced ex-Foggia centre-back who has been an invaluable member of the Fiorentina defence in recent seasons.

COACH
PAGELSDORF, Frank
German
Born: 05.02.58
• Coach of Hamburg since July 1997.
• Made 236 Bundesliga appearances for Hannover 96, Arminia Bielefeld and Borussia Dortmund before taking up a coaching post in charge of the amateurs at Hannover in 1991.
• Moved on to Union Berlin (1992-94) and Hansa Rostock (1994-97) before the switch to Hamburg
• His good work over the last five years with Hansa Rostock and Hamburg has propelled him into the top tier of coaching brains in Germany.
• Adventurous and an admirer of the Dutch style of play, he has enjoyed great success at Hamburg with a three-man defence and trio of attackers.

PLAYER
PAGANIN, Massimo
Defender, Italian, 185cm, 80kg
Born: 19.07.70, Vicenza, Italy
Clubs: Bassano (1986-87), Fiorentina (1987-89), Reggiana (1989-92), Brescia (1992-93), Internazionale (1993-97), Bologna (1997-)
• Strong centre-back and a tough man-marker. Eased out of Inter by the strong competition for places, and headed to Bologna, where he is now well established.

Marian Pahars

PLAYER
PAGLIUCA, Gianluca
Goalkeeper, Italian, 190cm, 87kg
Born: 18.12.66, Bologna, Italy
Clubs: Bologna (1985-86), Sampdoria (1986-94), Internazionale (1994-99), Bologna (1999-)
Full international (Italy) 38 caps/0 goals
• Talented keeper who played in all of Italy's games at the 1998 World Cup in France.
• Signed by Inter from Sampdoria in 1993 to replace Walter Zenga and won everybody over with some stunning reflex saves.
• A penalty specialist who won the League title and European Cup-winners Cup with Sampdoria.
• Moved to home-town club Bologna in 1999 after Inter signed **Angelo Peruzzi**.

PLAYER
PAHARS, Marian
Forward, Latvian, 174cm, 67kg
Born: 05.08.76, Latvia
Clubs: Skonto Riga (1995-98), Southampton (Eng) (1999-)
Full international (Latvia)
• Livewire striker dubbed the 'Latvian **Michael Owen**' because of his size and pace.
• Signed by Southampton in March 1999 for £800,000 after twice being rejected for a work permit.

PLAYER
PAIVA
Full name: Marco Paulo Paiva Rocha
Midfielder, Portuguese, 172cm, 80kg
Born: 07.02.73 Funchal, Portugal
Clubs: Maritimo (1990-94), Benfica (1994-95), Farense (1995-97), Vitoria Guimaraes (1997-)
Full international (Portugal) 1 cap/0 goals
• Experienced campaigner who has helped Guimaraes remain among the contenders in the chasing pack behind Portugal's big three clubs.
• Spent the 1994-95 season at Benfica, but did not play.

Christian Panucci

PLAYER
PALLISTER, Gary
Defender, English, 194cm, 191kg
Born: 30.06.65, Ramsgate, England
Clubs: Middlesbrough (1984-89), Darlington (1985, loan), Manchester United (1989-98), Middlesbrough (1998-)
Full international (England) 22 caps/0 goals
• Experienced centre-back who won a host of honours at Manchester United as one half of the 'Dolly and Daisy' defensive partnership with Steve Bruce.

PLAYER
PALOP, Andreas
Full name: Andres Palop Cervera
Goalkeeper, Spanish, 185cm, 80kg
Born: 22.10.73, Valencia
Clubs: Valencia (1995-), Villarreal (1997-99)
• Promising young keeper who came through the youth ranks at Valencia before going on loan to Villarreal.
• Helped Villarreal win promotion to the Spanish Liga, but returned to Valencia as number two to **Jose Canizares** following Villarreal's relegation to the second division.
• Injury to Canizares gave him valuable experience in the Champions League in the 1999-2000 season.

PLAYER
PAMIC, Igor
Forward, Croatian, 191cm, 93kg
Born: 30.09.69, Pula, Croatia
Clubs: FC Croatia (1993-95), Osijek (1995-96), Sochaux (Fra) (1996-97), Hansa Rostock (Ger) (1997-99), Grazer AK (Aut) (1999-)
Full international (Croatia) 5 caps/1 goal
• Striker who has yet to repay Grazer's heavy investment in him since his move to Austria in 1999.

PLAYER
PANADIC, Andrej
Defender, Yugoslav, 188cm, 84kg
Born: 09.03.69, Zagreb, Croatia
Clubs: Dinamo Zagreb (1988-91), HASK
Gradjanski (1991-92), Croatia Zagreb (1992-94),
Chemnitzer (Ger) (1994-96), Bayer Uerdingen
(Ger) (1996-97), Hamburg (Ger) (1997-)
Full international (Yugoslavia) 5 caps/0 goals
• Tough and effective Croat defensive man-
marker who is equally comfortable on the right
or the left. Played for the old Yugoslavia but has
been surprisingly ignored by the current Croat
national team management.
• Surname pronounced Pan ah deetch.

PLAYER
PANCARO, Giuseppe
Defender, Italian, 186cm, 84kg
Born: 26.08.71, Cosenza, Italy.
Clubs: Acri (1988-89), Torino (1989-91), Avezzano
(1991-92), Cagliari (1992-97), Lazio (1997-)
Full international (Italy) 4 cap/0 goals
• Tough-tackling right-back and an honest Serie
A journeyman who spent five seasons at Cagliari
before joining Lazio in 1997. Had also received
offers from Milan, Juventus and Bayern Munich.
• International debut against Croatia, April 1999.

PLAYER
PANOV, Alexander
Forward, Russian, 170cm, 60kg
Born: 21.09.75, Russia
Clubs: Zeniit St Petersburg (1993-2000), Baokang
Baochan (Chi) (1996), Saint Etienne (Fra) (2000-)
Full international (Russia) 13 goals/3 goals
• Striker who scored two goals in Russia's 3-2
win over France in Paris in a Euro 2000 qualifier
in June 1999 to fully live up to his billing as the
'Russian Jean-Pierre Papin'.
• Has great speed, ball control and aerial ability
despite his small size.
• Had a short 12-game spell in China in 1996

where he scored 19 goals.
• 'The football in China is really tough. There, I
became stronger physically and mentally and I
returned to Russia a more complete player.'
• Joined St Etienne in summer 2000.

PLAYER
PANTIC, Milinko
Midfielder, Yugoslav, 178cm, 75kg
Born: 05.06.66, Loznica, Yugoslavia
Clubs: Partizan Belgrade (1987-91), Panionios
(Gre) (1991-95), Atletico Madrid (Spa) (1995-98),
Le Havre (Fra) (1998-99), Panionios (Gre) (1999-)
Full international (Yugoslavia) 2 caps/0 goals
• Classy left-footed Serb playmaker who first
came to prominence as the architect of Atletico
Madrid's Spanish championship success in the
1995-96 season. Subsequently flopped in France
with Le Havre, but now enjoying a productive
second spell with Panionos – he previously
starred for them between 1991 and 1995.
• Surname pronounced Pan teetch.

PLAYER
PANUCCI, Christian
Defender, Italian, 180cm, 75kg
Born: 12.04.73, Savona, Italy
Clubs: Genoa (1991-93), Milan (1993-97), Real
Madrid (Spa) (1997-99), Internazionale (1999-
2000), Chelsea (Eng) (2000-)
Full international (Italy) 19 caps/1 goal
• Tough, uncompromising right-back who is an
accomplished defender but who likes attack
whenever possible.
• A European Cup-winner with two different
clubs (Milan, 1994, and Real Madrid, 1998).
• Ongoing feud with **Arrigo Sacchi** resulted in
his exclusion from Italy's Euro 96 squad and his
£3million transfer from Milan to Real Madrid after
Sacchi arrived at Milan in late 1996.
• Was linked with a move to Roma to reunite him
with former coach **Fabio Capello** in summer
2000, but instead moved to Chelsea on loan.

COACH
PAPADOPOULOS, Stavros
Cypriot
• National coach of Cyprus for the second time, having also coached AEK Larnaca, Omonia Nicosia, Ethnikos Akhna, Aris Limassol and Paralimni.

PLAYER
PAQUITO
Forward, Brazilian, 187cm, 81kg
Born: 26.08.77, Recife, Brazil
Clubs: Inter Limeir, Salgueiros (Por) (1999-)
• Promising young Brazilian striker who has impressed many in Portugal with his displays for Salgueiros.

PLAYER
PARAMATTI, Michele
Defender, Italian, 181cm, 78kg
Born: 10.03.68, Salara, Italy
Clubs: Spal (1986-87), Russi (1987-89), Spal (1989-95), Bologna (1995-)
• Centre-back and cornerstone of the Bologna defence. A whole-hearted player whose no-nonsense approach to defending has made him a huge favourite with fans in Bologna.

PLAYER
PARFYONOV, Dmitry
Defender, Ukrainian, 170cm, 68kg
Born: 11.09.74, Ukraine
Clubs: Chernomorets (1990-97), Dnipro (1997-98), Spartak Moscow (1998-)
Full international (Ukraine) 6 caps/0 goals
• Several years ago he was considered one of the most talented defenders in Ukraine.
• Was surprisingly called up by Ukraine for the Euro 2000 play-off matches against Slovenia, but was sent-off in the first match.
• Small and fast, a strong performer on the flank – in either defence or attack.

Ray Parlour

PLAYER
PARLOUR, Ray
Midfielder, English, 179cm, 75kg
Born: 07.03.73, Romford, England.
Clubs: Arsenal (1991-)
Full international (England) 7 caps/0 goals
• Right-sided midfielder who has developed under **Arsene Wenger** into a potential international star.
• Linked with a move to Sunderland in summer 2000, but the sale of **Marc Overmars** and **Emmanuel Petit** to Barcelona meant Arsenal insisted that he stay at Highbury.
• International debut: March 1999, v Poland.

ADMINISTRATOR
PARRY, Rick
• Chief executive of Liverpool, formerly with the English Premier League, where he played an instrumental role in negotiating lucrative TV deals with BSkyB.
• Since his arrival at Anfield, Liverpool have formed a strategic media alliance with Granada TV, who have taken a stake in the club, and been one of the first clubs to look seriously at screening matches via the Internet.

AGENT
PASQUALIN, Claudio
• One of Italy's leading agents, whose clients include **Alessandro Del Piero, Oliver Bierhoff, Ciriaco Sforza, Maurizio Ganz, Paolo Montero**.
• **Contact:** Avvocato Pasqualin Management, Viale Roma 3, I-36100 Vicenza, Italy. Tel: 0039-0444 32 30 97.

PLAYER
PASSLACK, Stephan
Defender, German, 183cm, 77kg
Born: 24.08.70, Moers, Germany
Clubs: VfB Homberg, Bayer Uerdingen (1989-93), Koln (1993-94), Eintracht Frankfurt (1994-95), KFC Uerdingen (1994-96), Borussia Monchengladbach (1996-99), Munich 1860 (1999-)

Full international (Germany) 4 caps/1 goal
• Right-sided defensive marker or wing-back who won full caps for Germany while with Borussia Monchengladbach in 1996, only to fade from the international scene as quickly as he arrived.

PLAYER
PASZULEWICZ, Jacek
Defender, Polish, 197cm, 91kg
Born: 15.01.77, Poland
Clubs: LKS Lodz, Polonia Warsaw
• Defender who is dangerous in the air because of his height. Made his name with LKS Lodz and joined Polonia in time to help them win the 1999-2000 Polish championship.

PLAYER
PATSATZOGLOU, Christos
Midfielder, Greek, 180cm, 75kg
Born: 19.03.79, Greece
Clubs: Skoda Xanthi (1996-)
• Talented young midfielder who is one of the hottest properties in Greek football, with Olympiakos and a number of Italian sides said to be at the head of the queue for his signature.
• Missed the early part of the 1999-2000 season through injury but came back strongly and was particularly impressive with the Greek Under-21s. Senior national team coach **Vassilis Daniil** has made it clear that Patsatzoglou is very much in his plans for the World Cup qualifiers.

PLAYER
PAULETA
Full name: Pedro Miguel Correia Resende
Forward, Portuguese, 180cm, 75kg
Born: 28.04.73, Ponta de Algada, Azores
Clubs: Estoril (1995-96), Salamanca (Spa) (1996-98), Deportivo La Coruna (Spa) (1998-)
Full international (Portugal) 14 caps/3 goals
• Striker who played a big part in Deportivo's successful League campaign in 1999-2000.
• Spent two seasons at Salamanca in Spain,

Paulo Sousa

helping the club win promotion to the Spanish first division. But suffered from bouts of home-sickness and never fully settled.

• Joined Deportivo for a reported £3.75million in 1998, but appearances in his first season were restricted by injuries. His goals helped Deportivo win their first Spanish league title in May 2000.

• Member of the Portuguese squad at Euro 2000.

PLAYER
PAULINHO SANTOS

Full name: Joao Paulo Maio dos Santos
Midfielder, Portuguese, 170cm, 66kg
Born: 21.11.70, Vila do Conde, Portugal
Clubs: Rio Ave (1990-92), FC Porto (1992-)
Full international (Portugal) 30 caps/2 goals

• Versatile, hard-working and powerful player who can operate in defence (left-back) or in midfield.

• A regular in the Portuguese national team since making his debut in January 1994 against Spain.

• Started out in the youth section at Varzim, making his League debut with Rio Ave before being picked up by Porto in 1992.

• Won the national championship with Porto in 1993, 1995, 1996, 1997, 1998 and 1999 and the Portuguese Cup in 1994.

• Considered by many at Porto to be the natural successor to Andre, the captain of Porto's 1987 European Cup-winning side.

COACH
PAULO AUTUORI

Brazilian
Born: 25.08.56

• Brazilian coach of Vitoria Guimaraes.

• Attack-conscious and arguably enjoyed his best period of stewardship in charge of Maritimo in the 1992-93 season, qualifying the Madeira club for Europe for the first time ever. 'We're here to excite and entertain,' he said then. 'I'm proud we have not been involved in a goalless draw all season. The aim at this club is simple – to score more than the opposition.'

PLAYER
PAULO BENTO
Full name: Paulo Jorge Gomes Bento
Midfielder, Portuguese, 175cm, 74kg
Born: 20.06.69, Lisbon, Portugal
Clubs: Estrela Amadora (1989-91), Vitoria
Guimaraes (1991-94), Benfica (1994-96), Oviedo
(Spa) (1996-)
Full international (Portugal) 26 caps/0 goals
• Hard-working Portuguese international
midfielder with good technique.
• Member of Portugal's squad at Euro 2000.
Started three of their four games in the holding
midfield role, providing the perfect foil for the
more creative midfield stars of the team.
• Spent his early career with Vitoria Guimaraes
and Benfica, but his career really took off
following a move to Spain's Oviedo.

PLAYER
PAULO MADEIRA
Full name: Paulo Sergio Braga Madeira
Defender, Portuguese, 177cm, 70kg
Born: 06.09.70, Luanda, Angola
Clubs: Benfica (1989-93), Maritimo (1993-94),
Benfica (1994-95), Belenenses (1995-97), Benfica
(1997-)
Full international (Portugal) 24 caps/3 goals
• Central defender who has been the scapegoat
for many followers of Benfica, blaming him for
mistakes which they claim have cost the club the
Portuguese League title in 1999 and 2000.
• Born in Angola but now a Portuguese citizen.

PLAYER
PAULO SERGIO
Midfielder, Brazilian, 180cm, 72kg
Born: 02.06.69, Sao Paulo Brazil
Clubs: Aclimacao, Gremio, Corinthians (1988-92),
Bayer Leverkusen (Ger) (1992-97), Roma (Ita)
(1997-99), Bayern Munich (Ger) (1999-)
Full international (Brazil)
• The long-striding Brazilian winger or attacking

midfielder enjoyed a magnificent first season at
Bayern following a move in the summer of 1999
from Roma, scoring 13 goals and creating seven
others.
• Pacy, inventive and an assured finisher.

PLAYER
PAULO SOUSA
Full name: Paulo Manuel Carvalho Sousa
Midfielder, Portuguese, 177cm, 73kg
Born: 30.08.70, Viseu, Portugal.
Clubs: Benfica (1989-93), Sporting (1993-94),
Juventus (Ita) (1994-96), Borussia Dortmund (Ger)
(1996-1998), Internazionale (Ita) (1998-99),
Parma (Ita) (1999-2000), Panathinaikos (Gre)
(2000-)
Full international (Portugal) 45 caps/0 goals
• Committed, tough-tackling midfielder with
excellent distribution and tactical awareness.
Now approaching the end of his career.
• Twice a European Cup winner, in 1996
(Juventus) and 1997 (Dortmund) and was 1995
Player of the Year in Italy after helping Juve to
the League and Cup double.
• 'I'm basically on the pitch to get hold of the ball
and create. As long as I do my job in the middle
of the field and the team win, I'm happy.'
• Deserted Benfica for Sporting Lisbon in summer
1994, claiming he was owed unpaid wages by
Benfica. After a lengthy legal battle, FIFA ordered
Sporting to pay £3.5million in compensation.
• Spent the 1999-2000 season on loan to Parma
from Inter before a £4million transfer to
Panathinaikos.
• Son of a car mechanic, he planned to become a
teacher until football took over his life.

PLAYER
PAUNOVIC, Veljko
Midfielder, Yugoslav, 182cm, 78kg
Born: 21.08.77, Strumica, Yugoslavia
Clubs: Partizan Belgrade (1994-95), Marbella
(Spa) (1995-96), Atletico Madrid (Spa) (1996-98),

Mallorca (Spa) (1998-99), Atletico Madrid (Spa) (1999-)
• Versatile midfielder who spent the 1998-99 season on loan at Mallorca, where his performances in the run to the 1999 Cup-winners Cup Final earned him a return to Atletico.
• Can play anywhere across midfield, but prefers the anchorman role. Was also used as a striker by Mallorca.

PLAYER
PAVLIN, Miran
Midfielder, Slovenia, 187cm, 79kg
Born: 08.10.71, Kranj, Slovenia
Clubs: Olimpia Ljubljana, Dynamo Dresden (Ger), Freiburg (Ger), Karlsruhe (Ger)
Full international (Slovenia) 29 caps/4 goals
• Defensive midfielder who is a neat, controlled passer of the ball, and rarely ventures forward.
• Played for Slovenia at Euro 2000 having scored the vital equaliser in the second leg of the qualifying play-off against Ukraine.
• Moved to German second division Karlsruhe to gain first-team football.

PLAYER
PAVLOVIC, Zeljko
Goalkeeper, Croatia, 186cm, 80kg
Born: 02.03.71, Sarajevo, Yugoslavia
Clubs: FC Croatia/Croatia Zagreb (1993-96), Linz ASK (Aut) (1996-)
Full international (Croatia) 4 cap/0 goals
• Keeper who has been a regular for Linz after a move from Croatia Zagreb in 1996. Has been on the fringes of the Croatian national team after making his international debut as a second-half substitute against Israel in March 1996.

PLAYER
PAVLOVIC, Zoran
Midfielder, Slovenian, 190cm, 76kg
Born: 27.06.76, Tuzla, Bosnia
Clubs: Rudar Velenje, Dinamo Zagreb (1999-)

Full international (Slovenia) 5 caps/0 goals
• Midfielder who played his way into Slovenia's Euro 2000 squad after a series of good performances for his club, Dinamo (formerly Croatia) Zagreb.
• Born in Bosnia but his parents moved to Velenje, Slovenia, when he was two months old.
• Has a terrific workrate, covers a lot of ground and has a thunderous right-foot shot.

PLAYER
PAVON, Michel
Midfielder, French, 180cm 78kg
Born: 07.11.68, La Ciotat, France
Clubs: Toulouse (1986-94), Montpellier (1994-96), Bordeaux (1996-)
• Comes from the old shipbuilding town of La Ciotat near Marseille and has the same blue-collar approach to his football. The Bordeaux skipper leads by example, churning out 90 minutes of sheer vitality, ball-winning and solid support play.
• Surname pronounced Pah von.

PLAYER
PAWLAK, Mariusz
Defender Polish, 176cm, 68kg
Born: 19.01.72, Poland
Clubs: Lechia Gdansk, Polonia Warsaw (1996-)
• A very solid stopper and a key man in Warsaw's 1999-2000 Polish championship-winning defence.

PLAYER
PAWLOWSKI, Peter
Forward, Polish/Austrian, 186cm, 79kg
Born: 18.03.77, Breslau, Poland
Clubs: Lustenau (1996-97), LASK (1997-99), Tirol (1999)
• Promising young forward who is close to playing for the senior Austrian national team, having been a regular at Under-21 level.

ECCHIA, Fabio
Midfielder, Italian, 171cm, 68kg
Born: 24.08.73, Formia, Italy
Clubs: Avellino (1991-93), Napoli (1993-97),
Juventus (1997-98), Sampdoria (1998-99), Torino
1999-).
• Combative midfielder who joined Juventus in
summer 1997, teaming up with his former Napoli
coach **Marcello Lippi.**
• Found the competition for places in central
midfield tough at Juventus, and joined Sampdoria
in September 1998, moving on to Torino in 1999
following Samp's relegation.

PEDAT, Eric
Goalkeeper, Swiss, 180cm, 82kg
Born: 23.07.67, Switzerland
Clubs: Servette (1989-93), St Gallen (1993-96),
Servette (1996-)
• Reliable, unpretentious keeper with good
reflexes and a solid appreciation of angles. Better
on his line than when coming for crosses.

PEDERSEN, Henrik
Forward, Danish, 180cm, 78kg
Born: 10.06.75, Denmark
Clubs: Silkeborg (1995-)
Full international (Denmark) 2 caps/0 goals
• Powerful, pacy forward whose goals for
Silkeborg have resurrected his career after
serious (season-long) injury problems.
• On the brink of a call-up to Danish squad in the
run-in to Euro 2000, but just missed out.

PEDERSEN, Rune
Norwegian
Born: 19.05.63
• Works as a clerk.
• Awarded his FIFA badge in 1989.

PEDERSEN, Steinar
Defender, Norwegian, 180cm, 78kg
Born: 06.06.75, Norway
Clubs: Start (1994-96), Borussia Dortmund (Ger)
(1996-99), IFK Gothenburg (Swe) (1999-)
• Norwegian Under-21 international who
normally plays at right-back.

PEDERSEN, Tore
Defender, Norwegian, 185cm, 79kg
Born: 29.09.69, Frederikstad, Norway
Clubs: IFK Gothenburg (Swe) (1990-92), Brann
(1993), Oldham (Eng) (1993-94), Brann (1994),
Sanfrecce Hiroshima (Jap) (1995), St Pauli (Ger)
(1995-97), Blackburn (Eng) (1997-99), Wimbledon
(Eng) (1999-)
Full international (Norway) 45 caps/0 goals
• Much-travelled defender who joined **Egil Olsen**
at Wimbledon in summer 1999 after sufferring
relegation with Blackburn, only to suffer the
same fate again 12 months later. Also relegated
from the German Bundesliga with St Pauli in 1997.

PEDONE, Francesco
Midfielder, Italian, 176cm, 69kg
Born: 06.06.68, Milan, Italy
Clubs: Como (1987-88), Centese (1988-89),
Barletta (1989-90), Como (1990-93), Bari (1993-
96), Reggiana (1996), Venezia (1996-)
• Experienced campaigner who has been a key
figure in the resurgence of Venezia in recent
seasons.

PEDRO BARBOSA
Full name: Pedro Alexandre dos Santos Barbosa
Midfielder, Portuguese, 182cm, 80kg
Born: 06.08.70, Gondomar, Portugal
Clubs: Vitoria Guimaraes (1991-95), Sporting
Lisbon (1995-)

Full international (Portugal) 17 caps/3 goals
• Versatile midfield all-rounder and captain of the Sporting Lisbon side which won the 1999-2000 Portuguese League title.

PLAYER
PEDRO ESPINHA
Full name: Pedro Manuel Espinha, Ferreira
Goalkeeper, Portuguese, 180cm, 76kg
Born: 25.09.65, Mafra, Portugal
Clubs: Torreense (1985-86), Academica (1986-87), Sacavenense (1987-89), Belenenses (1989-94), Salgueiros (1994-97), Vitoria Guimaraes (1997-)
Full international (Portugal) 5 caps/0 goals
• Experienced keeper, with 10 seasons with a number of middle-ranking Portuguese clubs, who was Portugal's number two at Euro 2000, having been a capable to **Vitor Baia** down the years.
• International debut as a half-time substitute against Israel in November 1998.

PLAYER
PEDRO SANTOS
Full name: Pedro Jorge Santos dos Santos
Midfielder, Portuguese, 172cm, 77kg
Born: 28.06.75, Venezuela
Clubs: Feirense (1995-98), Gil Vicente (1998-)
• Young midfielder who was instrumental in Gil Vicente's brilliant 1999-2000 campaign, when they finished in fifth place in the Portuguese League.

PLAYER
PEDRON, Stephan
Midfielder, French, 176cm, 72kg
Born: 22.02.71, Redon, France
Clubs: Ancenis, Laval, Lorient (1998-99), St Etienne (1999-)
• Brilliant left-sided midfielder and one of the stars of the French Championship in the 1999-2000 season, excelling in both goalscoring and creative categories.
• Took his time to break into the professional

game. At the age of 22, he was still playing non-league football and working in an air conditioning factory.
• Surname pronounced Pay dron.

PLAYER
PEERSMAN, Tristan
Goalkeeper, Belgian, 193cm, 76kg
Born: 28.09.79, Belgium
Clubs: Beveren (1996-2000), Anderlecht (2000-)
• Another example of the long-standing Beveren goalkeeping tradition. Jean Marie Pfaff, **Filip De Wilde** and **Gert De Vlieger** were his predecessors.
• Probably the most talented goalie in the Belgian League, who was set to join champions Anderlecht for the 2000-2001 season. Definitely one for the future.

PLAYER
PEETERS, Bob
Forward, Dutch, 196cm, 90kg
Born: 10.01.74, Lierse, Belgium
Clubs: Lierse (Bel) (1992-97), Roda JC (1997-)
Full international (Belgium) 2 caps/0 goals
• Very tall, awkward-looking striker who is surprisingly effective – hence his call-up to the Belgian national squad in 1999.

PLAYER
PEETERS, Jacky
Defender, Belgian, 184cm, 82kg
Born: 13.12.69, Belgium
Clubs: Lozen, Overpelt, Genk (1995-98), Arminia Bielefeld (Ger) (1998-)
Full international (Belgium) 6 caps/0 goals
• Implacable Belgian defender capable of operating at right-back or as a central defensive marker. Broke into his country's national team set-up in the 1999-2000 season at the grand old age of 30.
• Surname pronounced Pay ters.

PEIREMANS, Frederic
Midfielder, Belgian, 177cm, 71kg
Born: 03.09.73, Nijvel, Belgium
Clubs: Anderlecht (1994-98), Charleroi (1998-99), FC Twente (Hol) (1999-2000), Real Sociedad (Spa) (2000-)
Full international (Belgium) 3 caps/0 goals
• Combative midfielder with great vision. Came through the youth ranks of Anderlecht but was never highly rated in Brussels, despite playing a couple of matches for the Belgian national team.
• Despite the language barrier (French is his first language) he took command of the midfield in Twente's successful run in the 1999-2000 season. Good in the air, and has a blistering shot.

PEIXE
Full name: Emilio Manuel Delgado Peixe
Midfielder, Portuguese, 177cm, 68kg
Born: 16.01.73, Nazare, Portugal
Clubs: Sporting Lisbon (1990-95), Sevilla (Spa) (1995-96), Sporting Lisbon (1996-97), FC Porto (1997-)
Full international (Portugal) 13 caps/0 goals
• Hard, uncompromising player who has played a key role in central midfield for Porto.
• Moved to Porto in 1997 after a short spell in Spain with Sevilla.
• Made his international debut for Portugal against Luxembourg in October 1991.

PELLEGRINO, Maurizio
Defender, Argentinian, 195cm, 83kg
Born: 05.10.71, Cordoba, Argentina
Clubs: Velez Sarsfield (1992-98), Barcelona (Spa) (1998-99), Velez Sarsfield (1999), Valencia (Spa) (1999-)
Full international (Argentina) 36 games/5 goals
• Strong but clean-tackling left-footed centre-back who spent the 1998-99 season on loan at

Barcelona, but the Catalan club declined to exercise their option to buy, and he returned to Velez.
• Signed by Valencia in summer 1999, three minutes before the close of the transfer deadline.
• Nicknamed 'Sausage' because of his height.

PEMBRIDGE, Mark
Midfielder, Welsh, 170cm, 70kg
Born: 29.11.70, Merthyr Tydfil, Wales
Clubs: Luton (1990-92), Derby (1992-95), Sheffield Wednesday (1995-98), Benfica (Por) (1988-99), Everton (1999-)
Full international (Wales)
• Left-sided midfielder and set-piece specialist who returned to England, to Everton, after failing to settle in Lisbon after being signed by **Graeme Souness** at Benfica.

PENA, Juan Manuel
Full name: Juan Manuel Pena Montano
Defender, Bolivian, 183cm, 74kg
Born: 17.01.73, La Paz, Bolivia
Clubs: Independiente (Col) (1995), Valladolid (Spa) (1995-)
Full international (Bolivia)
• Centre-back who operates as a sweeper, putting his positional sense and ball skills to good use.

PENEV, Dimitar
Bulgarian
Born: 12.07.45
• Coach of CSKA Sofia who was previously in charge of the Bulgarian national side, overseeing qualification for the 1994 World Cup and Euro 96.
• A hugely distinguished player who won 90 caps for Bulgaria and played in three World Cup finals (1966, 1970 and 1974). Won the Bulgarian League seven times with CSKA as a player and five more times as a coach.
• Uncle of **Luboslav Penev**.

ADMINISTRATOR
PENEV, Luboslav
Bulgarian
Born: 31.08.66
• Former national team striker who took the unusual step in 1999 of retiring as a player to become president of CSKA Sofia.
• A big, bustling centre-forward who scored goals throughout his time in Spain with Valencia, Atletico Madrid, Compostela and Celta Vigo. Scored 13 goals in 62 appearances for Bulgaria.
• Survived a testicular cancer scare in 1994. Missed the 1994 World Cup, but continued his playing career at Euro 96 and France 98.

ADMINISTRATOR
PEREZ, Florentino
Spanish
• President of Real Madrid since July 2000, when he was the surprise victor over the incumbant **Lorenzo Sanz**. Victory was achieved by mobilising a postal vote of club members, which took Sanz by surprise.
• During the election campaign, he promised that **Luis Figo** would join Real, and offered season ticket-holders their money back if the transfer did not go through. It later transpired that Perez had signed a contract with **Antonio Veiga**, Figo's agent, who appeared to have signed in the belief that Perez would not be elected.

PLAYER
PEREZ, Kenneth
Forward, Danish, 182cm, 74kg
Born: 29.08.74, Copenhagen, Denmark
Clubs: FC Copenhagen (1995-97), MVV (1997-99), AZ (1999-)
• Danish striker with Spanish blood and protagonist in a major row in the 1999-2000 season. As a player with MVV Maastricht at the beginning of the season, both Roda and AZ wanted to sign him. Perez at first decided to sign for Roda but changed his mind and opted for AZ,

Sebastien Perez

here there was more money on offer. Roda
ent to court claiming he was theirs, but lost.
Ironically AZ didn't benefit much from his
)alscoring reputation as he was ruled out with
a injury for most of the campaign.
Strong in the air and difficult to mark.

LAYER
EREZ, Sebastien
Midfielder, French, 178cm, 74kg
orn: 24.11.73, Saint-Chamond, France
Clubs: Saint-Etienne (1993-95), Rennes (1995-
6), Bastia (1996-97), Blackburn (Eng) (1997-98),
astia (1998-99), Marseille (1999-)
This former French Under-21 left-back is
xcellent in attacking mode, but does lack some
efensive rigour. Although Marseille fans turned
n him with a vengeance in the 1999-2000
eason, it is to his credit that he never let his
ead drop and continued to battle on.
Surname pronounced Pay rez.

OACH
ERRIN, Alain
rench
orn: 07.10.56
Young coach who confounded the critics in the
999-2000 season by keeping Troyes in the
rench first division despite a meagre budget.
Came to Troyes in 1992 after five years in
harge of Nancy youth set-up (1988-93), where
e developed the talents of would-be Moroccan
nd French internationals, **Mustapha Hadji** and
ony Vairelles.
He combines his first-team coaching duties
with those of a general manager, never signs a
ontract for longer than a year and rules with rod
f iron.
• Has no professional playing experience and is a
ormer schoolteacher.

PLAYER
PERROTTA, Simone
Midfielder, Italian, 180cm, 71kg
Born: 17.09.77, Ashton-under-Lynne, England
Clubs: Reggina (1995-98), Juventus (1998-99),
Bari (1998-)
• Defensive midfielder who was born and raised
in England, but returned to Italy to try to his luck
with Reggina, hometown club of his parents.
Signed by Juventus in 1998 and subsequently
loaned out to Bari.

PLAYER
PERRY, Chris
Defender, English, 172cm, 70kg
Born: 26.04.73, Carshalton, England
Clubs: Wimbledon (1991-99), Tottenham (1999-)
• Quick and agile central defender who left
Wimbledon, the team he supported as a boy, for
Spurs in a £4million transfer in July 1999.
• Touted as a possible England international, but
his size has counted against him.

PLAYER
PERUZZI, Angelo
Goalkeeper, Italian, 181cm, 88kg
Born: 16.02.70, Viterbo, Italy
Clubs: Roma (1987-89), Verona (1989-90), Roma
(1990-91), Juventus (1991-9), Internazionale
(1999-2000), Lazio (2000-)
Full international (Italy) 26 caps/0 goals
• Solid, experienced and occasionally inspired
keeper who was Italy's number one at Euro 96,
second choice at France 98, but declined the
offer of third-choice keeper at Euro 2000 behind
Gianluigi Buffon and **Francesco Toldo**.
• A Champions League winner with Juventus in
1996 when he was the hero of the penalty shoot-
out in Rome's Olympic Stadium, coincidentally
the stadium where he was a ballboy at the 1984
Final, when Liverpool beat Roma on penalties.
• Banned for one year in October 1990 when
traces of the amphetamine Fentermine showed

Emmanuel Petit

up in a routine dope test following a Roma-Bologna League match.

• He was transferred to Juventus in summer of 1991 when he still had two months of his suspension to serve.

• Capped 12 times at Under-21 level.

• Joined Lazio for £10million in summer 2000, a transfer which made him the world's most expensive goalkeeper.

COACH
PESICE, Josef
Czech
Born: 12.02.50

• Coach of Teplice who guided them to second in the Czech League in 1998-99 after fashioning a young side on a slender budget and playing attractive football.

PLAYER
PESSOTTO, Gianluca
Defender, Italian, 173cm, 67kg
Born: 11.08.70, Latisana
Clubs: Milan (1988-89), Varese (1989-91), Massese (1991-92), Bologna (1992-93), Verona (1993-94), Torino (1994-95), Juventus (1995-)
Full international (Italy) 19 caps/0 goals

• Product of the Milan youth system who joined Juventus in 1995 from cross-town rivals Torino.

• Can play left-back, left midfield or as a man-to-man marker, as he did against **Zinedine Zidane** in the 1998 World Cup quarter-final. His versatility makes him popular with coaches, but less so with the fans.

• Nicknamed 'Il Professore' (The Professor).

• International debut against Georgia in October 1996.

PLAYER
PETERNAC, Alen
Forward, Croatian, 180cm, 75kg
Born: 16.01.72, Zagreb, Croatia
Clubs: Dinamo/Croatia Zagreb (1990-93),

egesta (1993-95), Croatia Zagreb (1995),
alladolid (Spa) (1995-2000), Zaragoza (Spa)
?000-)
ull international (Croatia) 2 caps/0 goals
Croatian striker with a natural eye for goal.
Has been a prolific scorer for Valladolid in the
panish League but looks to be nearing the end
f his career there.

ETERSEN, Dan
orward, Danish, 186cm, 80kg
orn: 06.05.772, Odense
lubs: Odense, Ajax (Hol), Monaco (Fra) (1994-
7), Anderlecht (Bel) (1997-98), Standard Liege
1998-99), Bastia (Fra) (1999-)
Former Danish Olympic international who has
roved a useful target man for Bastia since
oining from Standard Liege in 1999.

PETIT, Emmanuel
Midfielder, French, 185cm, 79kg
orn: 22.09.70, Dieppe, France.
lubs: Arques, Monaco (1988-97), Arsenal (Eng)
1997-2000), Barcelona (Spa) (2000-)
Full international (France) 41 caps/3 goals
• Highly accomplished all-rounder who developed
under **Arsene Wenger at** Monaco and Arsenal
nto a world-class midfielder.
• One of the stars of the 1998 World Cup, scoring
the third goal in France's 3-0 win in the Final
over Brazil.
• Began as a defender, and his shaky performance
at left-back made him one of the scapegoats
when France lost to Bulgaria and missed out on
qualification for the 1994 World Cup.
• International debut: 15.08.90, v Poland (0-0).
• Joined Barcelona in July 2000 with **Marc
Overmars** in a joint deal worth some £32million,
which valued Petit at £7million.

PETKOV, Ivailo
Defender, Bulgarian, 179cm, 73kg
Born: 07.12.75, Bulgaria
Clubs: Spartak Pleven, Litex Lovech (1997-99),
Istanbulspor (Tur) (1999-)
Full international (Bulgaria) 26 caps/3 goals
• Left-back who is a regular for club and country.
• Made his international debut for Bulgaria
against Saudi Arabia in November 1996 and
made the left-back position his own after a
series of impressive displays in Litex's League
title-winning season in 1997-98.
• Seen as one of the key young players to
revitalise the Bulgarian national side following
the retirement of **Hristo Stoichkov**.

PETKOV, Milen
Midfielder, Bulgarian, 174cm, 65kg
Born: 12.01.74, Bulgaria
Clubs: CSKA Sofia
Full international (Bulgaria) 16 caps/0 goals
• Midfielder who is seen as one of the key men
in the rebuilding of the Bulgarian national side.
• A member of the Bulgarian squad at the 1998
World Cup, but did not play. Featured regularly in
the qualifying campaign for Euro 2000.
• Seen as the long-term replacement for
Krassimir Balakov in the Bulgarian national side.

PETRE, Florentin
Midfielder, Romanian, 166cm, 61kg
Born: 15.01.76, Bucharest, Romania
Clubs: Dinamo Bucharest (1994-)
Full international (Romania) 19 caps/2 goals
• Diminutive midfielder who has been a regular
in the Romanian national team over the past two
seasons.
• Has spent nine seasons with Dinamo Bucharest.
• Made his international debut for Romania
against Norway in a friendly in August 1998,

Dan Petrescu

going on to start in eight of his country's qualifying matches for Euro 2000.
• Member of Romania's squad at Euro 2000.
• Former Under-21 international.

PLAYER
PETRESCU, Dan
Midfielder, Romanian, 175cm, 74kg
Born: 22.12.67, Bucharest, Romania
Clubs: Steaua Bucharest (1985-91), Foggia (Ita) (1991-93), Genoa (Ita) (1993-94), Sheffield Wednesday (Eng) (1994-95), Chelsea (Eng) (1995-2000), Bradford City (Eng) (2000-)
Full international (Romania) 92 caps/12 goals
• Highly skilled, mobile right-sided wing-back who has been a key member of the Romanian national squad at the last two World Cups and European Championships.
• Played in the 1989 European Cup Final for Steaua, who he captained until leaving for Serie B side Foggia in 1991, moving on Serie A and Genoa.
• Missed the 1990 World Cup, but played and scored in 1994 and 1998, a Romanian record.
• Missed the penalty which cost Romania defeat in the USA 94 quarter-final shoot-out against Sweden.
• Demonstrated his commitment to the London club by naming his newborn daughter Chelsea, but joined Bradford in July 2000 after falling out with **Gianluca Vialli** and losing out to **Albert Ferrer**.
• International debut: 29.03.89, v Italy (won 1-0).

PLAYER
PETROUS, Adam
Defender, Czech, 192cm, 80kg
Born: 19.09.77, Czech Republic
Clubs: Slavia Prague
• Young and talented defender who, after featuring in the Czech Under-21 squad, seems set to be a future member of the full national team set-up.
• A key part of the Slavia defence that was the best in the Czech League in 1999-2000.

PLAYER
PETROV, Martin
Forward, Bulgarian, 178cm, 72kg
Born: 15.01.79, Bulgaria
Clubs: CSKA Sofia (1998), Servette (Swi) (1999-)
Full international (Bulgaria) 6 caps/0 goals
• Striker who after a slow start has established himself in the Swiss League. Was dubbed the 'new Stoichkov' because of his moody and tactiturn attitude.

PLAYER
PETROV, Yuri
Forward, Russian, 175cm, 74kg
Born: 18.07.74, Ukraine
Clubs: Dnepr Dnepropetr. (1991), Spartak Moscow (1992), Lokomotiv Moscow (1992-94), RKC (Hol) (1994-95), FC Twente (Hol) (1995-97), RKC Waalwijk (Hol) (1998-)
• Right-footed winger who can also play on the left. Was fired at FC Twente for drunkedness and drink driving along with his friend Sergei Yuran (playing at Bochum in those days). Got a second chance at RKC, but often starts on the bench.

PLAYER
PETTERSSON, Jorgen
Forward, Swedish, 179cm, 79kg
Born: 29.09.75, Lund, Sweden
Clubs: Dosjebro IF, Malmo (1993-95), Borussia Monchengladbach (Ger) (1995-99), Kaiserslautern (Ger) (1999-)
Full international (Sweden) 26 caps/7 goals
• Speedy, determined little striker who shoots powerfully with both feet and who enjoyed something of a renaissance at Kaiserslautern in the 1999-2000 season, performing sufficiently well to earn a recall to the Swedish national team for Euro 2000.

COACH
PETURSSON, Petur
Icelandic
Born: 1958
• Ex-Iceland striker who played in Holland, Belgium and Spain. Took over at reigning champions KR at the end of the 1999 season. Given the resources at his disposal, he will be under considerable pressure to maintain winning ways.

PLAYER
PHILIPAUSKAS, Leonel
Defender, Uruguayan, 180cm, 73kg
Born: 18.05.75, Montevideo, Uruguay
Clubs: Bella Vista (1997-99), Atletico Madrid (Spa) (1999-)
Full international (Uruguay) 4 caps/0 goals
• Defender who was signed by Atletico Madrid after impressing in the Uruguayan team which reached the Final of the 1999 Copa America.
• Struggled to settle down at Atletico, and was likely to be sold following Atletico's relegation from the Spanish Liga in May 2000.

COACH
PHILIPP, Paul
Born: 21.10.51
• Coach of Luxembourg since 1985, making him Europe's longest-serving national coach.

PLAYER
PHILLIPS, Kevin
Forward, English, 172cm, 70kg
Born: 25.07.73, Hitchin, England
Clubs: Watford (1994-97), Sunderland (1997-)
Full international (England) 5 caps/0 goals
• Striker who began as a trainee at Southampton, where he cleaned **Alan Shearer**'s boots, but was rejected for being too small.
• Played for non-League Baldock while working in a factory, before being taken on by Watford, where he scored 24 goals in 59 League games.
• Signed for Sunderland in July 1997 for

£325,000 and has so far rewarded the Wearsiders with goals galore.
• Was the Premier League's top scorer in the 1999-2000 season, when his 30 League goals also made him Europe's leading goalscorer.

PLAYER
PHIRI, Alfred
Forward, South African
Born: 22.06.74, Alexandra, South Africa
Clubs: Jomo Cosmos, Genclerbirligi (Tur)
Full international (South Africa)
• South African striker who earned notoriety at the 1998 France World Cup after being sent off for elbowing Denmark's **Thomas Helveg**, having entered the match as a half-time substitute.
• Made his name at Johannesburg side Jomo Cosmos, before heading for Turkey.
• At Genclerbirligi, he became a key player, scoring vital goals as his team finished fifth in the Turkish League.

PLAYER
PIANGERELLI, Luigi
Midfielder, Italian, 175cm, 70kg
Born: 19.1.0.73, Porto Recanati, Italy
Clubs: Cesana (1991-97), Lecce (1997-)
• Accomplished midfield all-rounder who played a key role in Lecce's promotion to Serie A.

PLAYER
PIERINI, Alessandro
Defender, Italian, 185cm, 86kg
Born: 22.03.73, Bozzano, Italy
Clubs: Udinese (1991-95), Fidelis Andria (1995-96), Udinese (1996-99), Fiorentina (1999-)
• Powerful central defender who spent almost a decade at Udinese before a switch to Fiorentina in 1999, but has made little impression in Florence.
• Made his Serie A debut at San Siro stadium, against Milan in December 1992.

Kevin Phillips

PIERRE, Frederic
Midfielder, Belgian, 178cm, 75kg
Born: 23.02.74, Namur, Belgium
Clubs: Ekeren (1992-95), RWDM (1995-97), Mouscron (1997-99), Standard Liege (1999-)
Full international (Belgium) 8 caps/0 goals
• Powerful striker who has done the rounds of a number of clubs in Belgium. At Standard, he has developed a good partnership with **Michael Goossens.**
• Not the most talented of players but has great determination. Was a member of the Belgian national team under **Georges Leekens.**

PLAYER
PIERRE-FANFAN, Jose
Defender, French, 187cm, 87kg
Born: 26.07.75, Saint-Pol-sur-Mer, France
Clubs: Dunkerque, Lens (1997-)
• Exotically-named central defender with plenty of determination and heading ability. In his element when marking a big, physical striker, but considerably less at ease if facing a forward of the nippy, diminutive variety. Almost moved to Bayern Munich in summer 2000.
• Surname pronounced Ho zay Pee err Fon fon.

PLAYER
PIKABEA, Jose Antonio
Full name: Jose Antonio Pikabea Larrarte
Defender, Spanish, 180cm, 75kg
Born: 26.09.70, San Sebastien, Spain
Clubs: Real Sociedad (1991-)
• Tough-tackling defender who has been a reliable regular since 1996, covering all defensive options.

PLAYER
PINTAC, Djorde
Defender, Yugoslav, 184cm, 77kg
Born: 11.12.66, Yugoslavia
Clubs: Birkirkara
• Solid centre-back in his fourth season in Malta.

ADMINISTRATOR
PINTO DA COSTA, Jorge Nuno
Portuguese
• President of FC Porto.

PLAYER
PIOCELLE, Sebastien
Midfielder, French, 180cm, 72kg
Born: 10.11.75, Gouvieux, France
Clubs: Nantes (1998-), Bastia (2000-)
• His frail physique suggests otherwise. But he is an all-action warrior in the centre of midfield, full of running and excelling in ball-winning duties.
• Was sent on loan to Bastia for the 2000-2001 season.
• Surname pronounced Pee oh sell.

COACH
PIONTEK, Sepp
Polish/German
Born: 05.03.40
• Won international acclaim with Denmark in the 1980s coaching the so-called Danish Dynamite side to the semi-finals of the 1984 European Championships and the second round of the 1986 World Cup.
• Born in what is now Wrockow, Poland, but brought up in Germany, he played for Werder Breman and six times for West Germany before coaching spells with Fortuna Dusseldorf and Haiti.
• Coached in Turkey in the 1990s and, most recently, was a coaching advisor to the newly-formed national side of Greenland.

REFEREE
PIRAUX, Michel
Belgian
Born: 15.10.55
• Professor of mathematics.
• Awarded his FIFA badge his 1990.

Robert Pires

PLAYER
PIRES, Robert
Forward, French, 180cm, 74kg
Born: 29.01.73, Reims, France
Clubs: Metz (1992-98), Marseille (1998-2000), Arsenal (Eng) (2000-)
Full international (France) 38 caps/5 goals
• Whether used as a winger on either flank or in a roaming role just behind the strikers, his quick feet, searing acceleration and imagination make him an attacking-third creator of the highest order. The 1999-2000 season, however, was anything but one of his best. For Marseille his form was patchy, the fans there made him a whipping boy and he lost the club captaincy.
• 'At every level, it was a black period for me. Blows seemed to be raining down on me from everywhere. It seemed as though I had parachuted into a nightmare.'
• A member of France's victorious World Cup 98 squad and played in the Final of Euro 2000, supplying the cross for **David Trezeguet**'s winning golden goal.
• Joined Arsenal in June 2000.
• Pronounced Ro ber Pee rez.

PLAYER
PIRLO, Andrea
Midfielder, Italian, 177cm, 68kg
Born: 19.05.79, Brescia, Italy
Clubs: Brescia (1994-98), Internazionale (1998-99), Reggina (1999-2000, loan)
• Hugely promising talent who was forced to go on loan to Reggina in the 1999-2000 season after failing to get regular first-team action at Internazionale following a high-profile transfer from Brescia in summer 1998.
• Is most effective playing behind the main strikers, where his great vision, passing range and set-piece skills have earned comparisons with **Roberto Baggio**.
• Member of the Italian side which won the European Under-21 title in Slovakia in May 2000.

PLAYER
PIRRI, David
Midfielder, Spanish, 175cm, 65kg
Born: 12.02.74, Barcelona, Spain
Clubs: Barcelona B (1993-95), Merida (1995-99), Deportivo La Coruna (1999-)
• Signed from Merida in 1999, a midfielder who spends longer on the bench than on the pitch.

PLAYER
PISTONE, Alessandro
Defender, Italian, 177cm, 76kg
Born: 27.07.75, Milan, Italy
Clubs: Vicenza (1992-93), Solbiatese (1993-94), Crevacore (1994-95), Vicenza (1995-96), Internazionale (1995-97), Newcastle (Eng) (1997-2000), Venezia (1999, loan), Everton (Eng) (2000-)
• Accomplished left-back who can also play in the centre of defence.
• Joined Newcastle in a £4.3m transfer in July 1997, but lost his first-team place under **Ruud Gullit** and went back to Italy on loan. Joined Everton in summer 2000.
• Italian Under-21 international.

PLAYER
PISZ, Lesek
Midfielder, Polish, 168cm, 62kg
Born: 18.12.66, Poland
Clubs: Legia Warsaw, Kavala (Gre) (1996-)
Full international (Poland) 15 caps/1 goal
• Diminutive schemer who played a key part in Legia Warsaw's Polish championship success in the 1994-95 season and has proved very influential since arriving at Greek club Kavala. An outstanding director of midfield traffic and deadly at free-kicks.

PLAYER
PITAK, Karel
Midfielder, Czech, 184cm, 77kg
Born: 28.01.80, Czech Republic
Clubs: Hradec Kralove

• Midfielder who has represented his country at Under-21 level. Following the relegation of Hradec Kralove at the end of the 1999-2000 season this well-developed young talent was a likely transfer target for bigger clubs.

COACH
PITURCA, Victor
Romanian
Born: 12.04.56
• Coach of Romania in the Euro 2000 qualifying campaign, but was sacked by the Romanian FA following a public row with **Gheorghe Hagi**.
• Has since taken charge of Steaua Bucharest.

PLAYER
PIVOTTO, Matteo
Defender, Italian, 179cm, 72kg
Born: 05.09.74, Montecchio Maggiore, Italy
Clubs: Verona (1992-94), Massese (1994-95), Carpi (1995-97), Roma (1997-98), Chievo (1998-99), Lecce (1999-)
• Much-travelled defender who settled well in his first season with Lecce, helping the club to avoid relegation from Serie A.

PLAYER
PIZARRO, Claudio
Forward, Peruvian, 184cm, 77kg
Born: 03.10.78, Lima, Peru
Clubs: Deportivo Pesquero (1996-98), Alianza Lima (1998-99), Werder Bremen (Ger) (1999-)
Full international (Peru)
• No wonder the Werder management were unhappy that the gifted Peruvian international forward had to miss several Bundesliga games in the 1999-2000 season because of World Cup qualifying commitments with his South American nation. The scorer of 10 German League goals in 1999-2000, he is bright as a button technically, has bags of flair and a strong shot in either foot.

Michel Platini

PLAYER
PJANOVIC, Mihajlo
Forward, Yugoslav, 182cm, 76kg
Born: 13.02.77, Prijepolje Yugoslavia
Clubs: OFK Belgrade, Red Star Belgrade (1999-)
• One the great young hopes of Yugoslav football.
Joined Red Star from OFK Belgrade in January 1999.
• Scored twice for Red Star in the 2000 Yugoslav
Cup Final.

PLAYER
PLASSNEGGER, Gernot
Midfielder, Austrian, 180cm, 72kg
Born: 23.03.78, Leoben, Austria
Clubs: Salzburg (1995-98), Austria Vienna (1998-)
• Promising young midfielder on the fringes of
the Austrian national side after playing for the
Under-21s.

ADMINISTRATOR
PLATINI, Michel
French
Born: 21.06.55
• The greatest French footballer of all time, a
living legend in France and one of the biggest
personalities in world football.
• Captain of the 1984 European Championship-
winning side who also won extensive club
honours with Juventus. Voted European
Footballer of the Year in 1983, 1984 and 1985.
• Had mixed success as a coach, guiding France
to the 1992 European Championship finals.
• Played an influential role in France's hosting of
the 1998 World Cup, as co-president of the
organising committee, and then joined forces
with **Sepp Blatter** to take a role as footballing
director of FIFA. So far, his most notable
achievement has been to oversee a restructuring
of the international footballing calendar, but only
with mixed success.
• Surname pronounced Platt inee.

PLAYER
LETIKOSA, Stipe

Goalkeeper, Croatian, 192cm, 87kg
Born: 08.01.79, Croatia
Clubs: Hajduk Split
Full international (Croatia) 6 caps/0 goals
• Hugely promising young keeper who was
Croatia's best player at the 1999 World Under-20
Youth Cup in Nigeria.
• Fast and strong with good reflexes, he has
been coached at Hajduk by former national team
keeper Tonci Gabric.

PLAYER
POBORSKY, Karel

Forward, Czech, 174cm, 72kg
Born: 30.05.72, Trebon, Czech Republic
Clubs: Ceske Budejovice (1991-94), Viktoria
Zizkov (1994-95), Slavia Prague (1995-96),
Manchester United (Eng) (1996-97), Benfica (Por)
(1998-)
Full international (Czech Republic) 58 caps/3
goals
• Long-haired wideman forever remembered for
the cheeky chipped goal which won the Euro 96
quarter-final for the Czech Republic against
Portugal and was voted goal of the tournament.
• His goal in Euro 96 capped a brilliant year, in
which he also won the Czech League with Slavia
Prague, reached a UEFA Cup semi-final, and
secured a lucrative transfer to Manchester
United.
• His greatest strength is his dribbling skills, but
he failed to secure a regular place at Old Trafford,
and moved on to Benfica.
• Has been more successful in Portugal, and
continued to play a key role for the Czech
national team, but he has been criticised in the
Portuguese press for only showing his true
qualities in high-profile games.
• Nicknamed 'Express Train'.

PLAYER
POCHETTINO, Mauricio

Full name: Mauricio Pochettino Trossero
Defender, Argentina, 80cm, 70kg
Born: 02.03.72, Santa Fe, Argentina
Clubs: Newell's Old Boys (1988-94), Espanyol
(Spa) (1994-)
Full international (Argentina)
• Central defender who has been seen as a great
prospect ever since captaining Argentina at the
1991 World Youth Cup.
• Compared to former Argentina captain Daniel
Passerella because of his aggressive but highly
intelligent play. But was ironically overlooked by
Passerella as national coach.
• Had to wait until the appointment of Marcelo
Bielsa as Argentina national coach before
winning his first international cap, against
Holland in March 1999.
• Was coached by Bielsa at Newell's Old Boys,
where he won the Argentinian League title, and
briefly at Espanyol.
• 'I grew up in a village where there were no
more than 500 people. Now I live in Barcelona,
one of the most important cities in the world. It
hardly seems right.'

PLAYER
PODBROZNY, Jerzy

Forward, Polish
Born: 17.12.66
Clubs: Lech Poznan, Legia Warsaw, Merida (Spa),
Toledo (Spa), Chicago Fire (USA), Zaglebie Lubin
Full international (Poland) 6 caps/0 goals
• Expert finisher who has been in outstanding
form for Lubin since returning to Poland in
January 2000.
• Top scorer in the Polish League while with Lech
Poznan in 1992 and 1993, before joining Legia
Warsaw.
• Spent a year in the United States with Chicago
Fire, the MLS side with a sizeable Polish support.

PLAYER
POGGI, Paolo
Forward, Italian, 181cm, 79kg
Born: 16.02.71, Venice, Italy.
Clubs: Venezia (1989-92), Torino (1992-94), Udinese (1994-99), Roma (1999-)
• Combative but skilful striker who made little impact at Roma following a transfer from Udinese in January 1999.

PLAYER
POLAK, Jan
Midfielder, Czech, 181cm, 78kg
Born: 14.03.81, Czech Republic
Clubs: Stavo Artikel Brno
Full international (Czech Republic) 2 caps/0 goals
• Defensive midfielder who grabbed the headlines when he became the youngest player ever to represent the Czechs in a full international, in a friendly against Poland in 1999.
• A prime target for Prague giants Sparta and Slavia – if he doesn't move abroad first.

REFEREE
POLL, Graham
English
Born: 29.07.63
• Sales manager.
• Awarded his FIFA badge in 1996.

PLAYER
POLSTER, Toni
Forward, Austrian, 188cm, 86kg
Born: 10.03.64, Vienna, Austria
Clubs: Austria Vienna (1981-87), Torino (Aut) (1987-88), Sevilla (Spa) (1988-91), Logrones (Spa) (1991-92), Rayo Vallecano (Spa) (1992-93), Koln (Ger) (1993-99)
• Veteran striker who announced his retirement as a player in summer 2000.
• Played in Germany and Spain in a career in which he won a record 94 caps (44 goals) for Austria.

PLAYER
POLTAVETS, Valentin
Midfielder, Ukrainian, 169cm, 60kg
Born: 18.04.75, Ukraine
Clubs: Metalurg Zaporizha
• Attacking midfielder whose speed and control on the ball has made him one of the stars of the Ukrainian League.
• Was invited by **Valerii Lobanovsky** to join a Ukraine national team training camp in 2000 and a full debut does not seem far away.

PLAYER
POMPEI, Roberto
Midfielder, Argentinian, 176cm, 78kg
Born: 14.03.70, Buenos Aires, Argentina
Clubs: Velez Sarsfield (1990-95), Racing (1995-96), Boca (1996-97), Oviedo (Spa) (1997-)
• Argentinian midfielder with excellent technique and a powerful shot.
• Made his name at Velez Sarsfield, winning the Libertadores Cup and the World Club Cup in 1994.
• Moved to Spain's Oviedo in a £1.5million transfer from Boca Juniors.

PLAYER
PONTE, Robson
Midfielder, Brazilian, 174cm, 66kg
Born: 06.11.76, Brazil
Clubs: Juventude (Sao Paulo), Guarani (1999), Bayer Leverkusen (Ger) (1999-)
• The 1999-2000 season was the young Brazilian's first in Europe and at times he found the going tough. But the attacking midfielder or right-sided forward does have much potential: briliant dribbling skills, a nice touch on the ball and a fair sprinkling of invention.
• Surname pronounced Pohn tay.

PLAYER
POOM, Mart
Goalkeeper, Estonian, 194cm, 85kg
Born: 03.02.72, Tallinn, Estonia

Clubs: Flora Tallinn (1992-94), Portsmouth (1994-96), Flora Tallinn (1996), Derby (1996-)
Full international (Estonia) 70 caps/0 goals
• The most high-profile Estonian player in Europe, with more than three seasons of Premier League football under his belt.
• Signed by Derby for £500,000 from Flora Tallinn after work permit problems had ended his first spell in English football, at Portsmouth.

PLAYER
POPESCU, Gheorghe
Midfielder, Romanian, 188cm, 83kg
Born: 10.09.67, Calafat, Romania
Clubs: Steaua Bucharest (1987), Univ. Craoiv (1988-90), PSV Eindhoven (Hol) (1990-94), Tottenham Hotspur (Eng) (1994-95), Barcelona (Spa) (1995-97), Galatasaray (Tur) (1997-)
Full international (Romania) 101 caps/15 goals
• Arguably Romania's second greatest player after his brother-in-law **Gheorghe Hagi**.
• Defensive midfielder or sweeper who has been voted Romania's Player of the Year six times.
• Played for Romania at three World Cup finals, making 13 appearances. Announced his international retirement in summer 2000.
• Won League titles at Steaua Bucharest, PSV and Galatasaray, as well as two European titles: the 1997 European Cup-winners Cup with Barcelona and the 2000 UEFA Cup with Galatasaray, scoring the decisive penalty in the shoot-out in the Final in Copenhagen.
• Switched to defence in latter years of his career, compensating for declining pace with techinical ability and an exceptional footballing brain.
• Nicknamed 'Baciul' (The Leader).

PLAYER
POPOV, Sergiy
Defender, Ukrainian, 180cm, 75kg
Born: 22.04.71, Ukraine
Clubs: Zenit St Petersburg (Rus), Shakhtar
Full international (Ukraine)

• A regular for Ukraine, a consistent and reliable performer who is particularly dangerous at set-pieces.

PLAYER
POPOVIC, Alexandr
Forward, Moldovan, 184cm, 71kg
Born: 09.04.77, Moldova
Clubs: Tiligul Tiraspol, Duisburg (Ger), Dinamo Moscow (Rus), Torpedo Moscow (Rus)
Full international (Moldova) 16 caps/2 goals
• Left-sided attacker who made his debut for the Moldovan national team at the age of 19 and has gone on to play for a number of leading clubs in the former Soviet Union.

PLAYER
POPOVICH, Valery
Forward, Russian, 185cm, 80kg
Born: 18.05.70, Russia
Clubs: Moscow Spartak (1990-91), TPV Tampere (Fin) (1993), Ilves (Fin) (1994), Haka (Fin) (1995-), Heerenveen (Hol) (1999-2000, loan)
• Russian goalscorer who has been in Finland since 1993 and whose goals have helped FC Haka to three League titles (1995, 1998, 1999).
• Transferred to Finland from Spartak Moscow along with midfielder Oleg Ivanov.
• Not the quickest of players, but has impressive technique and a sharp eye for goal.
• Spent some time in 1999 on loan at Heerenveen, and turned out to be the hero of their Dutch League campaign. He arrived as a stand in for injury-prone **Dennis de Nooijer** and his goals in the latter stages of the competition were vital in securing Heerenveen's first-ever appearance in the Champions League.
• Returned to Haka to for the start of the Finnish League, but Heerenveen wanted to borrow him again for the 2000-2001 Champions League.

PLAYER
PORATO, Stephane
Goalkeeper, French, 183cm, 75kg
Born: 19.09.73, Colombes, France
Clubs: Toulon, Monaco (1992-98), Marseille
(1998-2000), Monaco (2000-)
Full international (France) 1 cap/0 goals
• His bravery and wonderful relexes propelled
him into the full French squad in the 1998-99
season, but in 1999-2000 he went backwards,
making a number of unforced errors and often
looking edgy. In his defence, however, it has to be
said that it is not easy to perform when your own
supporters are jeering you.
• Returned to Monaco for the 2000-2001 season
as a replacement for the Old Trafford-bound
Fabien Barthez.
• Surname pronounced Po rah toe.

PLAYER
POSCHNER, Gerhard
Midfielder, German, 182cm, 78kg
Born: 23.09.69, Mettersdorf, Germany
Clubs: Stuttgart (1987-90), Borussia Dortmund
(1990-94), Stuttgart (1994-98), Venezia (Ita)
(1999), Rayo Vallecano (Spa) (1999-)
• Veteran German midfield general who has been
winding down his career in Spain with Vallecano.
• Former Germany Under-21 international.
• Played in the 1998 European Cup-winners Cup
Final for Stuttgart, which they lost to Chelsea,
before moving to Venezia, where he struggled to
hold down a regular place.

PLAYER
POSKUS, Robertas
Forward, Lithuanian
Born: 05.05.79, Lithuania
Clubs: Atlantas Klaipeda, Hamburg (Ger), Zalgiris
Vilnius, Widzew Lodz (Pol) (2000-)
Full international (Lithuania) 2 caps/0 goals
• Striker who made a big impact in the Polish
League during the second half of the 1999-2000

Gica Popescu

season following a move from his native Lithuania.
• Had a spell in Hamburg, but played only for the reserve team in the Regional League and returned to Lithuania.

PLAYER
POSSANZINI, Davide
Forward, Italian, 181cm, 72kg
Born: 09.02.76, Loreto, Italy
Clubs: Torino (1994-95), Lecco (1995-96), Varese (1996-98), Reggina (1998-)
• Talented striker, nicknamed 'The Brazilian', who starred in Reggina's 1999 promotion-winning side.

PLAYER
POSSE, Martin
Forward, Argentinian, 170cm, 68kg
Born: 20.08.75, Buenos Aires, Argentina
Clubs: Velez Sarsfield (1993-98), Espanyol (Spa) (1998-)
Full international (Argentina)
• Right-sided forward or attacking midfielder who is most effective in the right-hand channel.
• Another of the Argentinian contingent at Espanyol.
• Member of the Argentinian squad at the 1997 Copa America.

PLAYER
POSTULKA, Tomas
Goalkeeper, Czech, 189cm, 82kg
Born: 02.02.74, Czech Republic
Clubs: Sparta Prague
Full international (Czech Republic)
• Talented and experienced keeper with consistency problems that have seen him struggle to keep his place in the Sparta first team and, inevitably, in the Czech national squad.
• Faces fierce competition from **Jaromir Blazek** for the goalkeeper's jersey at Sparta.

PLAYER
POTILLON, Lionel
Defender, French, 178cm, 77kg
Born: 10.02.74, Cluny, France
Clubs: Louhans-Cuiseaux, St Etienne (1994-)
• Solid left-back and model professional who rarely has an off-day. Especially effective when advancing down his flank and putting in accurate crosses.
• Pronounced Lee oh nel Pot tee on.

PLAYER
POUGET, Cyrille
Forward, French, 176cm, 76kg
Born: 06.12.72, Metz, France
Clubs: Metz, Servette, PSG, Le Havre, Marseille
Full international (France) 3 capa/0 goals
• Livewire, spirited frontrunner who has made a commendable return to top-flight action after serving a six-month ban for a failed drugs test – his sample was found to have unacceptable levels of the controversial steroid, nandrolone.
• When he first burst onto the first division scene at Metz, he was labelled the 'new Papin', but he has not lived up to the tag.
• Pronounced See reel Poo jay.

PLAYER
POULSEN, Morten
Midfielder, Danish, 182cm, 72kg
Born: 09.03.71, Denmark
Clubs: Viborg (1996-)
Full international (Denmark) 2 caps/0 goals
• One of the best midfielders in the Danish League, a versatile and energetic player who can operate on either the left or right.
• Called up to a Danish national team squad session made up of domestic players in late 1999 and is now on the fringes of the full squad.

Gustavo Poyet

POURSANIDIS, Ilias

Defender, Greek, 182cm, 78kg
Born: 13.04.72, Greece
Clubs: OFI Crete, Olympiakos (1997-)
Full international (Greece) 30 caps/0 goals
• Dynamic and industrious, the Greek international is often asked to mark the opposition's midfield danger man and can play full-back too. Began his career at OFI Crete, but now a stalwart at Olympiakos.

POWELL, Darryl

Midfielder, English/Jamaican, 183cm, 80kg
Born: 15.11.71, London Lambeth, England
Clubs: Portsmouth (1988-95), Derby (1995-)
Full international (Jamaica)
• Strong running left-sided midfielder who was a late inclusion in Jamaica's 1998 World Cup squad.
• Played in two games at France 98, but was sent off against Argentina following two bookable offences, both late tackles on **Ariel Ortega**.

POYET, Gustavo

Full name: Gustavo Poyet Dominguez
Midfielder, Uruguayan, 187cm, 83kg
Born: 15.11.67, Montevideo, Uruguay
Clubs: River Plate Montevideo (1985-88), Grenoble (Spa) (1988-90), Bellavista (1990), Real Zaragoza (Spa) (1990-97), Chelsea (Eng) (1997-)
Full international (Uruguay)
• Outstanding all-round midfielder who combines box-to-box workrate with skill, passing ability and goalscoring panache.
• Signed by then Chelsea manager **Ruud Gullit** on a free transfer from Zaragoza in July 1997.
• Twice a European Cup-winners Cup medal winners (Zaragoza, 1995 and Chelsea, 1998).

PLAYER
PRAGER, Roy
Forward, German, 172cm, 63kg
Born: 22.09.71, Zossen, Germany
Clubs: Stahl Brandenburg (1990-92), Fortuna Koln (1992-95), Wolfsburg (1995-99), Hamburg (1999-)
• Livewire attacker who is close to a call-up for Germany. A bundle of skill, boundless energy and commitment, he can play anywhere up front, and is just as dangerous through the middle as when flying on the flanks. Good counter-attacker and his finishing is improving all the time.
• Surname pronounced Pray ger.

COACH
PRAHL, Tom
Swedish
Born: 05.01.49
• Highly respected and experienced coach who guided Halmstad to the Swedish League title in 1997, having previously been in charge of Trelleborg.

PLAYER
PRALIJA, Nenad
Midfielder, Croatian, 175cm, 73kg
Born: 11.12.70, Spalato, Croatia
Clubs: Hajduk Split (1993-96), Espanyol (Spa) (1996-98), Hajduk Split (1999), Reggina (Ita) (1999-)
Full international (Croatia) 11 caps/1goal
• Utility player who can operate in defence, midfield or attack. Noted for his extra large lung capacity, shown in tests to be the biggest in the Croatian squad.
• Croatian footballer of the year in 1995.
• Member of Croatia squad at Euro 96.
• Brother Denis was killed during the war in the former Yugoslavia when he stepped on a landmine.

COACH
PRANDELLI, Claudio
Italian
Born: 19.05.57
• Coach of Verona since 1998.
• A successful midfielder with Juventus, winning two Italian League titles and the European Cup.
• Began his coaching career with the Atalanta youth section, before taking charge of newly-promoted Lecce in 1997-98 but was fired halfway through the Serie A campaign.
• Won promotion to Serie A with Verona in 1999.

COACH
PRASNIKAR, Bojan
Slovenian
Born: 03.02.53
• Coach of Slovenian champions Maribor since 1996, having previously coached Mura, Olimpia Ljubljana and Rudar Velenje.

PLAYER
PRATS, Antoni
Goalkeeper, Spanish, 185cm, 84g
Born: 09.09.71, Mallorca, Spain
Clubs: Mallorca (1991-95), Celta Vigo (1995-96), Real Betis (1996-)
• Capable, confident keeper who has aspirations to emulate the goalscoring feats of Paraguayan Jose Luis Chilavert.
• Sold by Celta to Betis in summer 1996 for a reported £1.8million.
• A product of Mallorca's youth scheme.

BUSINESS
PREBBLE, Stuart
• Chief executive of digital TV provider ONdigital, who have entered the TV rights arena in the past two years, bidding successfully for live UK rights to the Champions League and the Premiership.

Michael Preetz

PREETZ, Michael

Forward, German, 192cm, 84kg
Born: 17.08.67, Dusseldorf, Germany
Clubs: Fortuna Dusseldorf (1986-90),
Saarbrucken (1990-92), Duisburg (1992-94),
Wattenscheid (1994-96), Hertha Berlin (1996-)
Full international (Germany) 7 caps/3 goals
• The archetypal late-developer, a hard-running,
opportunistic striker who had to wait until he had
turned 30 to make an impact in German football.
• Was Bundesliga top scorer with 23 goals in
1998-99, when he also made his debut for
Germany – aged 31.

PREKO, Yew

Forward, Ghanaian, 173cm, 70kg
Born: 08.09.74, Ghana
Clubs: Anderlecht (Bel), Gazientepspor (Tur),
(1997-99), Fenerbahce (Tur) (1999-)
Full international (Ghana)
• Striker who has considerable success at Under-
17, Under-20 and Under-23 level with Ghana, but
was badly injured playing for his country at the
1996 African Nations Cup finals.
• Spent most of his career in Belgium with
Anderlecht, but joined the growing band of
Ghanaians playing in Turkey when he moved to
Gazientepspor in 1997.
• Missed the 1998 African Nations Cup finals in
Burkina Faso after a fall-out with the Ghanaian FA.
• Moved to Fenerbahce with **Samuel Johnson** in
summer 1999, but did not entirely convince.

PRIHA, Ville

Forward, Finnish, 180cm, 75kg
Born: 19.09.75, Finland
Clubs: JJK (1996), VPS (1997-)
• One of the best young forwards in the Finnish
League who had a trial at Millwall in 1999.
• Quick but a little unpredictable.

PLAYER
PRILASNIG, Gilbert
Midfielder, Austrian, 183cm, 73kg
Born: 01.04.73, Klagenfurt, Austria
Clubs: Sturm Graz (1992-)
Full international (Austria) 8 caps/0 goals
• Left-sided midfielder who missed out on Austria's 1998 World Cup finals squad but played a major role in his club's Austrian title challenge in 1999, attracting continued interest from foreign scouts.

PLAYER
PRINCE Daye
Forward, Liberian, 172cm, 72kg
Born: 14.04.78, Monrovia. Liberia
Clubs: Bastia
Full international (Liberia)
• Highly-talented and highly-rated young Liberian forward whose the mobility, trickery and sheer explosiveness makes him a most slippery of customers. Definitely one for the future.
• Pronounced Pranse Dai.

PLAYER
PRISKE, Brian
Defender, Danish, 185cm, 74kg
Born: 14.05.77, Horsens, Denmark
Clubs: Horsens (1996-97), Fremad (1997-98), AaB (1999-)
• Promising young right-back who is widely tipped to become a full Danish international having starred at Under-21 level. A strong defender who likes to get forward.
• Joined AaB in 1998 after Aarhus Fremad were relegated.

COACH
PROHASKA, Herbert
Austrian
Born: 08.08.55
• Coach of the Austrian national side at the 1998 World Cup who is now back at Austria Vienna.

• One of Austria's greatest players who won four League titles in Austria before moving to Italy where he helped Roma become champions in 1982-83. Played 84 times (10 goals) for his country and appeared at two World Cup finals.
• Turned to coaching shortly before his 35th birthday, he led Austria Vienna to three League titles. He then took on responsibility for the Austrian Under-21 side, before becoming coach of the senior side in January 1993.

PLAYER
PROKOPENKO, Dmitri
Forward, Russian, 183cm, 73kg
Born: 24.05.72, Russia
Clubs: Torpedo Moscow (1993-96), Chernomorets (1997), Sporting Braga (Por) (1997-98), Santa Clara (Por) (1998-)
• Striker who helped Santa Clara earn promotion to the Portuguese first division in 1998, but was injured for much of the 1999-2000 campaign, which ended in relegation.

COACH
PROKOPENKO, Victor
Ukrainian
Born: 24.10.44
• Coach of Shakhtar Donetsk who returned to Ukraine in early 2000 after coaching spells in Russia.
• Famous for his ability to make provincial clubs strong challengers for the title but has yet to win a League title.

PLAYER
PROMENT, Gregory
Midfielder, French, 178cm, 70kg
Born: 12.10.78, Paris, France
Clubs: Metz (1997-)
• Promising French Under-21 international who is expected to move on to another club before his contract expires in 2002 if he fails to make the Metz first team.

PROSENIK, Christian
Midfielder, Austrian, 180cm, 72kg
Born: 07.06.68, Vienna, Austria
Clubs: Austria Vienna (1990-95), Casino Salzburg (1995-97), Rapid Vienna (1997-99), Munich 1860 (Ger) (1999-)
Full international (Austria) 24 caps/1 goal
• Experienced midfielder who has established himself in the 1860 first team following a move from Rapid Vienna in 1999.

PROSINECKI, Robert
Midfielder, Croatian, 182cm, 83kg
Born: 12.01.69, Schwenningen, Germany
Clubs: Dinamo Zagreb, Red Star Belgrade, Real Madrid (Spa), Real Oviedo (Spa), Barcelona (Spa), Sevilla (Spa), Dinamo Zagreb, Hrvatski dragovoljac
Full international (Croatia) 34 cap/8 goals
• Highly talented midfielder who won the World Youth Cup in 1987 with Yugoslavia and looked liked becoming one of the great players of his generation. But a series of injuries affected his form through the years, and he has never quite realised his potential.
• Was voted player of the tournament at the 1987 World Youth Cup, though he missed Yugoslavia's Final win over West Germany through suspension.
• Was released by Dinamo Zagreb, whose coach **Miroslav Blazevic** did not believe he would make it as a professional. He won three League titles plus the 1991 European Cup with Red Star Belgrade before a move to Spain.
• Played 125 League games in six injury-plagued seasons in Spain, and became one of a handful of players to have moved between eternal rivals Real Madrid and Barcelona.
• Of mixed Croatian and Serbian parentage, he opted to play for Croatia, and played at Euro 96 and France 98.
• The only man to have scored for two nations at the World Cup (Yugoslavia, 1990, and Croatia, 1998).

PRSO, Dado
Forward, French, 187cm, 77kg
Born: 05.11.74, Zader, Croatia
Clubs: Stade Raphaelais, Monaco, Ajaccio, Monaco
• Pony-tailed Croat attacker with high levels of skill, physical presence and finishing ability. Usually a substitute for Monaco in the 1999-2000 season. But did underline his ability by scoring four goals in the French Cup, as well as the injury-time equaliser in a 2-2 draw with Nancy which clinched the title for the Monte Carlo outfit.
• Surname pronounced Per soh.

PRUNEA, Florin
Goalkeeper, Romanian, 184cm, 83kg
Born: 08.08.68, Bucharest, Romania
Clubs: Dinamo Bucharest (1985-88), Univ. Cluj (1988- 90), Univ. Craoiva (1990-92), Dinamo Bucharest (1992-98), Erzurumspor (Tur) (1998-99), Univ. Craiova (1999-)
Full international (Romania) 38 caps/0 goals
• Much-travelled keeper who returned to Romania in 1999 after a season in Turkey, but has been unable to win back his place in the Romanian national side from **Bogdan Stelea**.
• A League and Cup winner with Univ. Craiova in 1990-91 and made his international debut in December 1990 against San Marino.

PUEL, Claude
French
Born: 02.09.61
• In his first full season in charge of a professional club, he guided Monaco to the League title in May 2000 and it should be the first of many honours for this remarkable young coach.
• An assistant to former Monaco boss **Jean Tigana** for two years, Puel's big break came when Tigana resigned early in 1999. He has

hardly put a foot wrong since. Rarely shows any emotion, is tactically very aware and places great importance on discipline and physical fitness. A one-club man, he played 488 league games for Monaco between 1979 and 1996, turning out at right-back, stopper, libero or in defensive midfield.

PLAYER
PURK, Marcus
Midfielder, Austrian, 174cm, 79kg
Born: 21.09.74, Vienna, Austria
Club: Sturm Graz, Rapid Vienna, Munich 1860 (Ger) (1999-)
Full international (Austria) 1 cap/1 goal
• One of four Austrians playing at Munich 1860, where he has established himself on the left side of midfield.
• Scored on his international debut, against Liechtenstein in April 1994, but has not played for his country since then.

PLAYER
PUYOL, Carlos
Defender, Spanish, 178cm, 78kg
Born: 13.04.78, Spain
Clubs: Barcelona (1999-)
• One of the revelations of the 1999-2000 season, filling in at right-back after **Michael Reiziger** was shifted into the centre of defence.
• Showed few nerves when he made his League debut against Real Madrid in front of 100,000 at Camp Nou.
• Promoted from Barcelona B at the start of the 1999-2000 season.

Robert Prosinecki

Q

PLAYER
QUIM
Full name: Joaquim Manuel Sampaio Silva
Goalkeeper, Portuguese, 184cm, 78kg
Born: 13.11.75, Famalicao, Portugal
Clubs: Braga
Full international (Portugal) 3 caps/0 goals
• Portugal's third-choice keeper at Euro 2000 who is favoured as the long-term successor to Vitor Baia.

PLAYER
QUINN, Barry
Midfielder, Irish, 182cm, 80kg
Born: 09.05.79, Dublin, Ireland
Clubs: Coventry City (1999-)
Full international (Rep. Ireland) 4 caps/0 goals
• Talented young Irish midfielder who played 11 times in the English Premiership in 1999-2000, often as a substitute, but will play more often in the future.
• Made his international debut in April 2000 against Greece.

QUINN, Niall
Forward, Irish, 194cm, 96kg
Born: 06.10.66, Dublin, Ireland
Clubs: Arsenal (1983-90), Manchester City (1990-96), Sunderland (1996-)
Full international (Rep. Ireland) 79 caps/20 goals
• Veteran striker whose height makes him an incredibly difficult opponent in the air.

PLAYER
QUINT, Olivier
Midfielder, French, 182cm, 75kg
Born: 18.01.73, Desertines, France
Clubs: Troyes, Sedan (1998-)
• Accomplished left-sided attacking midfielder.

Just four years ago, he was off-loaded by non-league Epernay. Now he's tormenting French top-flight defenders with his sweet left-footed probing and goalscoring.
• Pronounced OI lee vee ay Kwant.

PLAYER
QUIROGA, Facundo Hernan
Defender, Argentinian, 178cm, 76kg
Born: 10.01.78, San Luis, Argentina
Clubs: Newell's Old Boys (1997-98), Sporting Lisbon (1998-99)
• Useful centre-back who has been playing the best football of his career following Sporting Lisbon's 1999-2000 League title triumph.
• Argentinian Under-21 international.

R

PLAYER
RABARIVONY, Franck
Defender, French, 172cm, 70kg
Born: 15.11.70, Tours, France
Clubs: Auxerre (1992-98), Oviedo (Spa) (1998-)
• Solid left-back who likes to attack.
• Moved to Spain's Oviedo in summer 1998 in a £500,000 transfer from Auxerre.
• Won the French League and Cup double with Auxerre in 1996.

PLAYER
RABESANDRATANA, Eric
Defender, French, 185cm, 84kg
Born: 18.09.72, Epinay-sur-Seine
Clubs: Nancy (1990-97), Paris Saint-Germain (1997-)
• The longest surname in the French top-flight. Started his career at Nancy as an attacking midfielder – indeed he scored no less than 16 goals for them in the Second Division in 1995-96. But since moving to Paris Saint-Germain, he has invariably been used as a tough-tackling centre-back.
• A former French Under-21 international.

PLAYER
RADA, Karel
Defender, Czech, 188cm, 83kg
Born: 02.03.71, Czech Republic
Clubs: Skoda Plzen, Dukla Prague, Sigma Olomouc, Trabzonspor (Tur), Slavia Prague
Full international (Czech Republic) 37 caps/4 goals
• Dependable sweeper who returned to the Czech Republic after a spell in Turkey to bolster the Slavia defence.
• Following injury to **Jan Suchoparek** Rada became the obvious starter for the Czech team at Euro 2000, but was sent off in the Czechs' opening match against Holland.

PLAYER
RADEBE, Lucas
Defender, South African, 185cm, 73kg
Born: 12.04.69, Johannesburg, South Africa
Clubs: Kaizer Chiefs (1990-94), Leeds (Eng) (1994-)
Full international (South Africa)
• One of the best African exports to Europe, a central defender with strength and vision in abundance.
• A regular for South Africa, with many games as captain, since the country return from apartheid-enforced isolation.
• Can also operate in midfield, and does so highly effectively for South Africa.

PLAYER
RADIMOV, Vladislav
Midfielder, Russian, 184cm, 78kg
Born: 26.11.75, St Petersburg, Russia
Clubs: CSKA Moscow (1992-95), Zaragoza (Spa) (1996-), Dinamo Moscow (1999)
Full international (Russia) 24 caps/2 goals
• Elegant Russian playmaker who is struggling to regain form after two injury-ruined years.

PLAYER
RADZINSKI, Tomasz
Forward, Polish/Canadian, 174cm, 73kg
Born: 14.12.73, Poland
Clubs: Toronto Rockets, St Catherines Roma, Ekeren (Bel) (1994-98), Anderlecht (Bel) (1998-)
Full international (Canada)
• Fast, free-scoring striker who has been tracked by a number of big clubs.
• Born in Poland but acquired Canadian citizenship while playing for Toronto Rockets.

PLAYER
RAFAEL, Pires Vieira
Forward, Brazilian, 187cm, 81kg
Born: 01.08.78, Brazil
Clubs: HJK Helsinki (Fin) (1997), FC Jazz (Fin) (1998-)

• Striker who was the top scorer in the Finnish League in 1997 aged 19 and despite only playing in half of the matches.

• Posesses a superb touch and technique, but has yet to be totally consistent.

• Back at HJK Helsinki after a spell at FC Jazz.

AGENT
RAIOLA, Carmine

• Holland-based agent whose clients include **Pavel Nedved** and **Regis Genaux**.

• **Contact:** Laan Van Dick Laan 83, NL-2101 PP Heemstede, Holland.

PLAYER
RAMCIC, Edin
Defender, Bosnian, 185cm, 78kg
Born: 01.08.70, Bosnia
Clubs: Istra (Cro) (1992-93), Gent (Bel) (1993-)
Full international (Bosnia)

• Bosnian defender who has served Belgian side Gent well for a number of years. Is a tight marker and good in the air, but lacks pace. But still a key player in a multinational side (like Chelsea, Gent often play with only one local player) that finished third in the League in 1999-2000.

PLAYER
RAMDENE, Abder
Forward, French, 179cm, 71kg
Born: 23.02.74, Nimes, France
Clubs: Le Havre (1996-97), Nimes (1997-98), Hansa Rostock (Ger) (1998-)

• The rangy French striker first came to prominence in 1996 when his goals helped Second Division Nimes reach the French Cup Final, where they narrowly lost to Auxerre. A very strong runner with the ball and a player with lots of intricate footwork.

• Surname pronounced Ram dan.

PLAYER
RAME, Ulrich
Goalkeeper, French, 187cm, 85kg
Born: 19.09.72, Nantes, France
Clubs: Challans, Angers (1993-97), Bordeaux (1997-)
Full international (France) 2 caps/0 goals

• He was turned down as a youngster by the usually sharp-eyed talent spotters at the renowned Auxerre and Nantes academies, but later developed into the French second division's top keeper at Angers. After moving to Bordeaux, he stepped successfully into the breach when Dutch first-choice Stanley Menzo boobed once too often.

• An unpretentious, steady and phlegmatic keeper.

• France's third-choice keeper at Euro 2000.

• Surname pronounced Rah may.

PLAYER
RAMELOW, Carsten
Midfielder, Germany, 185cm, 80kg
Born: 20.03.74, Germany
Clubs: Tasmania 73 Berlin, Tennis Borussia Berlin, Herthe Zehlendorf, Siemensstadt, Hertha Berlin (1991-95), Bayer Leverkusen (1996-)
Full international (Germany) 9 caps/0 goals

Hard-working and intensely competitive defensive midfielder who can also line up at sweeper if need be. A member of the Hertha Berlin amateur side who sensationally reached the Final of the German Cup in 1993 – where they lost to Leverkusen.

COACH
RAMOS, Juande
Spanish
Born: 25.09.54

• Did well to keep Rayo in the top flight in the 1999-2000 season, and in summer 2000 agreed to stay on for another difficult year.

• A modest player who previously coached Logrones, Barcelona B and Lleida.

PLAYER
RAMPULLA, Michelangelo
Goalkeeper, Italian, 188cm, 74kg
Born: 10.08.62, Patti, Italy
Clubs: Pattese (1979-80), Varese (1980-83), Cesena (1983-85), Cremonese (1985-92), Juventus (1992-)
• Reserve goalkeeper at Juventus since 1992, playing only a handful of games.

PLAYER
RAMZY, Adil
Midfielder, Moroccan, 176cm, 73kg
Born: 14.07.77, Marrakesh, Morocco
Clubs: Kawkab, Udinese (Ita) (1997), Willem II (Hol) (1998-2000), PSV Eindhoven (2000-)
Full international (Morocco) 17 caps/1 goal
• Midfield playmaker at Willem II who often plays on the right flank.
• Opted to move to PSV in 2000 despite that fact that Willem II coach **Co Adriaanse** has joined Ajax. Says that he wants to play in Holland one more season before he is ready for Serie A.
• Morocco's captain when they won the African Under-20 title in 1997. Spotted by Udinese, but he failed to make the first team, moving to Willem on loan.
• Started his professional career in Egypt.

PLAYER
RAMZY, Hani
Defender, Egyptian, 185cm, 79kg
Born: 10.03.69, Cairo, Egypt
Clubs: Al Ahly, Neuchatel Xamax (Swi), Werder Bremen (Ger) (1994-98), Kaiserslautern (Ger) (1998-)
Full international (Egypt)
• Kaiserslautern coach Otto Rehhagel says the Egyptian defender is one of the best professionals he has ever worked with and that is some reference. A rare combination of toughness and comfort on the ball, he can play stopper or libero.
• Surname pronounced Ram see.

COACH
RANGNICK, Ralf
German
Born: 29.06.58
• Coach of Stuttgart since May 1999.
• As a player, he never made it past the amateur ranks of Stuttgart before launching his coaching career at Viktoria Backnang in 1983.
• Took charge of the Stuttgart amateur side in 1985, going on to become the youth coach and youth director. Took the part-timers of Ulm to the verge of the Bundesliga, and he was headhunted by Stuttgart in the spring of 1999.
• An academic type whose forte is as a training ground teacher. A German **Roy Hodgson**.

COACH
RANIERI, Claudio
Italian
Born: 20.10.51
• Won the Italian Cup and Supercup with Fiorentina before heading for Spain and spells with Valencia and Atletico Madrid.
• A central defender with Roma, Catanzaro and Catania who began his coaching career in 1987 with C1 side Campania, moving on to Cagliari and Napoli.
• Success at Fiorentina, where he won promotion to Serie A in 1994 and the Coppa Italia two years later, led to a move to Spain's Valencia, where he oversaw their most successful season in almost a decade. They won the Spanish Cup and qualified for the Champions League, before Ranieri was lured away to Madrid.
• Things did not go quite so well at Atletico, and he left before they were relegated in May 2000.

PLAYER
RANKOVIC, Ljubisa
Forward, Yugoslav
Born: 10.12.73, Yugoslav
Clubs: Rad Belgrade, Partizan Belgrade
• Striker whose form in the mid-1990s made him

a candidate for the Yugoslav national team. But he failed to make the breakthrough, and for some time was the forgotten man of Yugoslav football. Now, after a period playing in Korea, he is trying to recapture his old form at Partizan.

PLAYER
RAPAIC, Milan
Forward, Croatian, 183cm, 83kg
Born: 16.08.73, Nuova Gradisca, Croatia
Clubs: Hajduk Split (1991-96), Perugia (Ita) (1996-)
Full international (Croatia) 13 caps/0 goals
• Croatian who is now well established as the creative force in Perugia's attack following the sale of **Hidetoshi Nakata** to Roma in January 2000.

PLAYER
RASMUSSEN, Peter
Forward, Danish, 180cm, 74kg
Born: 16.05.67, Hobro, Denmark
Clubs: Viborg, Stuttgart (Ger), AaB, Viborg (1998-)
Full international (Denmark) 13 caps/2 goals
• Veteran attacker whose spell in Germany did not work out after a combination of a knee injury and homesickness took its toll. Formed a highly effective partnership with **Erik Bo Andersen** in 1995 when his hometown club AaB won the Danish League title.
• Not to be confused with Peter Rasmussen, attacking midfielder of AB.

PLAYER
RAT, Razvan
Midfielder, Romanian
Born: 26.05.81, Slatina, Romania
Clubs: Rapid Bucharest (1998-)
Full international (Romania) 1 cap/0 goals
• Highly promising young midfielder who won the Romanian League with Rapid in 1999-2000 and his first international cap for Romania against Mexico in January 2000.

PLAYER
RATINHO
Full name: Everson Rodrigues
Midfielder, Brazilian, 171cm, 68kg
Born: 08.06.71, Santa Inacio, Brazil
Clubs: FC Matsubara, Atletico Paraense, St Gallen (Ger) (1992-93), Aarau (Swi) (1993-96), Kaiserslautern (Ger) (1996-)
• Neat and clever right-sided Brazilian midfielder who is an outstanding crosser of the ball and taker of set-pieces. Nicknamed 'Little Mouse' because as a child he loved to eat cheese.
• Pronounced Rat teen yo.

PLAYER
RASOVIC, Vuk
Defender, Yugoslav, 182cm, 81kg
Born: 03.01.73, Dortmund, Germany
Clubs: Partizan Belgrade, Slavia Sofia (Bul) (1997-98), Partizan Belgrade (1998-)
Full international (Yugoslavia) 2 caps/0 goals
• Solid centre-back and a great fighter. Returned home to Yugoslavia in summer 1998, after one season in Bulgaria.

PLAYER
RASTELLI, Massimo
Forward, Italian, 175cm, 68kg
Born: 27.12.68, Torre del Graco, Italy
Clubs: Catanzaro (1988-89), Mantova (1989-90), Lucchese (1990-97), Piacenza (1997-)
• Journeyman striker who has spent much of his career in Italy's Serie B, getting a chance to impress when he moved to Piacenza in 1997.

PLAYER
RATAJCZYK, Krrzysztof
Midfielder, Polish, 185cm, 78kg
Born: 09.11.73, Poznan, Poland
Clubs: Legia Warsaw (1991-96), Rapid Vienna (1996-)
Full international (Poland) 12 caps/2 goals
• Hard-working, tough-tackling defender who

often gets into trouble with referees. Played in the Champions League for both Legia and Rapid Vienna.

PLAYER
RAUFFMANN, Rainer
Forward, German, 189cm, 74kg
Born: 26.02.67, Berlin, Germany
Clubs: Meppen (1994-95), Eintracht Frankfurt (1995-96), Arminia Bielefeld (1996-97), Omonia Nicosia (Cyp) (1997-)
• The leading goalscorer in the Cypriot League in recent seasons, and one of the most prolific marksman in Europe, having scored 108 goals in three League campaigns in Cyprus.
• Played in the German first division for Eintracht, but scored just four goals and was sold to Arminia, where he failed to settle.
• Once scored eight goals for Omonia in one game.

PLAYER
RAUL
Full name: Raul Gonzalez Blanco
Forward, Spanish, 180cm, 68kg
Born: 27.06.77, Madrid, Spain
Clubs: Real Madrid (1994-)
Full international (Spain) 35 caps/17 goals
• The undisputed Golden Boy of Spanish soccer and already a vastly experienced international despite only being 23.
• The bow-legged youngster from Madrid is an instinctively intelligent footballer who boasts an uncanny eye for goal and, above all, is a born winner. Looks frail and slightly built, but is remarkably resilient.
• Exploded onto the scene in 1994 as a 17-year-old, becoming Real's youngest ever player.
• Started out in the youth section of rivals Atletico, but the club's youth teams were scrapped by Atletico presdent **Jesus Gil** to save money, and Raul moved across town to Real.
• Has won two Champions League titles, in 1998 and 2000, when he scored an exceptional solo goal against Valencia in the Final in Paris.
• Finished the 1998-99 season as the top scorer in Spain, the first Spanish player to win the award for seven years.
• Scored 11 goals in the qualifiers for Euro 2000.
• 'People always ask me about going to Italy, but I have always found it very hard to think of leaving Madrid. This is home. How could I play for anyone else?'

COACH
RAUSCH, Friedel
German
Born: 17.02.40
• Much-travelled coach who, apart from several stints in the Bundesliga, has also worked in Turkey, Holland, Switzerland and Austria. The sort of boss who can be throwing a tantrum one moment and be putting an arm round a player the next.
• Made headlines as a Schalke player back in 1969 when a police dog bit him during a crowd disturbance in a derby with Dortmund. 'For years opponents were coming up to me and going "Woof, woof".'

PLAYER
RAVANELLI, Fabrizio
Forward, Italian, 188cm, 80kg
Born: 11.12.68, Perugia, Italy
Clubs: Perugia (1986-89), Avellino (1989), Casertana (1990), Reggiana (1991-92), Juventus (1992-96), Middlesbrough (Eng) (1996-97), Marseille (Fra) (1997-1999), Lazio (2000-)
Full international (Italy) 22 caps/8 goals
• Silver-haired striker, dubbed the White Feather, whose career peaked in 1996, winning the European Cup with Juventus and leading Italy's attack at Euro 96.
• Spent most of his career with middle-ranking Serie B sides before a move to Juve in 1992.
• Surprisingly sold by Juventus to Middlesbrough for £7million in 1996, but failed to settle on

Raul Gonzalez

Teesside and was offloaded to Marseille a year later.
• Returned to Italy in January 2000 to help Lazio's title bid and to try to regain his national team place.

PLAYER
REBEJA, Radu
Defender, Moldovan, 184cm, 74kg
Born: 08.06.73, Moldova
Clubs: Zimbru Chisinau, Uralan Elista (Rus)
Full international (Moldova) 37 caps/1 goal
• Reliable central defender or defensive midfielder who a key figure in the Moldovan national side.

PLAYER
REBROV, Sergiy
Forward, Ukrainian, 171cm, 60kg
Born: 03.06.74, Donetsk, Ukraine
Clubs: Shakhtar Donetsk, Kyiv Dynamo (1992-2000), Tottenham Hotspur (Eng) (2000-)
Full international (Ukraine)
• Prolific striker who started his career with Shakhtar Donetsk and then broke all scoring records in Ukraine while with Kyiv Dynamo.
• A natural goal scorer with excellent speed, vision and a precise shot. Especially dangerous in the penalty area in reaching rebounds. Expert penalty-taker.
• Ukrainian Footballer of the Year in 1996 and 1998.
• Joined Tottenham in June 2000 in a £11million transfer from Dynamo.
• Nicknamed 'Radiohead' because of his passion for amateur 'ham' radio.

PLAYER
RECK, Oliver
Goalkeeper, German, 193cm, 95kg
Born: 27.02.65, Frankfurt, Germany
Clubs: Kickers Offenbach (1983-85), Werder Bremen (1985-98), Schalke (1998-)

full international (Germany) 1 cap/0 goals
• Although capped only once for Germany – a friendly with Liechtenstein in 1996 – his lack of international honours does not at all reflect his ability. His acrobatic stops, fine ball-handling and coolness were key factors in a string of trophies for Werder Bremen in the late 1980s and early 1990s.

BUSINESS
REDING, Viviane
• European Union minister with responsibility for EU competition law, and thus directly responsible for the implications of the Bosman ruling. Has resisted, and will continue to resist, attempts by UEFA and FIFA to introduce legislation to restrict transfers, or make football exempt from the Treaty of Rome.

PLAYER
REDKNAPP, Jamie
Midfielder, English, 183cm, 80kg
Born: 25.06.73, Barton on Sea, England
Clubs: Bournemouth (1990-91), Liverpool (1991-)
Full international (England) 16 caps/1 goal
• Elegant, but injury-prone midfielder with wide passing range and a fierce shot.
• Father is West Ham manager **Harry Redknapp**, who introduced him while in charge at Bournemouth.
• Married to pop singer Louise, but has worked hard to shake off the Spice Boy tag applied by the media to a number of young Liverpool players who enjoy all the trappings of their fame.
• Kenny Dalglish's last signing for Liverpool, £350,000 in January 1991.
• Missed France 98 and Euro 2000 because of injury. Was forced to undergo ground-breaking surgery in the United States in the summer of 2000 on his knee in a bid to avoid a potential career-threatening situation.
• International debut: 06.09.95, v Colombia (0-0).

COACH
REDKNAPP, Harry
English
Born: 02.03.47
• Manager of West Ham United since 1992 and the main force behind establishing the London club in the English Premier League in the 1990s.
• An astute manager who has not been afraid to sign foreign players, some of which have been successes (Eyal Berkovic, Paolo Di Canio) while others have not (Paulo Futre, Florin Raducioiu).
• Father of Liverpool midfielder **Jamie Redknapp**.
• 'A lot of people are happy being the number two, the assistant or the coach. They look at the manager's job and think 'I can do that'. Then suddenly they get there, with absolute control, and with the buck stopping with them. Then they understand the pressure.'

PLAYER
REDONDO, Fernando
Full name: Fernando Carlos Redondo Neri
Midfielder, Argentinian, 186cm, 75kg
Born: 06.07.69, Buenos Aires, Argentina
Clubs: Argentina Juniors (1985-90), Tenerife (Spa) (1990-94), Real Madrid (Spa) (1994-2000), Milan (Ita) (2000-)
Full international (Argentina)
• Hugely talented midfielder and a brilliant link between defence and attack for Real Madrid and Argentina.
• Famously fell out with Argentinian national team, coach Daniel Passarella after refusing to cut his shoulder length hair. Passarella had insisted on a new standards of dress (no earings, no long hair) in a bid to introduce discipline into the Argentina team after Maradona's positive drug test at the 1994 World Cup.
• Twice a winner of the European Cup with Real Madrid, in 1998 and 2000.
• Sparked protests in Madrid when Real sold him to Milan in July 2000 for £11million.

Fernando Redondo

PLAYER
REGGI, Enrique
Forward, Argentinian, 188cm, 77kg
Born: 28.05.73, San Martin de Mendoza, Argentina
Clubs: Ferrocarril (1996-97), Independiente (1997-98), Gimnasia Plata (1998-99), Reggina (Ita) (1999-)
• Striker who arrived in Italy in 1999 amid great expectations, but has yet to justify the hype.

COACH
REHHAGEL, Otto
German
Born: 09.08.38
• Coach of Kaiserslautern since July 1996, guiding them to a unique double of German second division and Bundesliga titles in successive seasons.
• A wonderful motivator and canny builder of competitive sides despite limited financial resources, 'King Otto' is one of the most successful German club bosses of the past 15 years. With Werder Bremen he twice won the League (1987-88 and 1992-93) and the Cup-winners Cup in 1992.
• Conventional wisdom has it that he prefers working at smaller clubs and with a minimum of big-name players. A spell in charge of the star-studded ranks of Bayern Munich ended in the sack after less than a season.
• Always controversial, says what he thinks and has an equal number of friends and enemies.

PLAYER
REHN, Stefan
Midfielder, Swedish, 178cm, 75kg
Born: 22.09.66, Stockholm, Sweden
Clubs: Djurgardens (1986-89), Everton (Eng) (1989-90), IFK Gothenburg (1990-95), Lauusanne (Swi) (1995-2000)
Full international (Sweden) 43 caps/6 goals
• Once a misfit at Everton, but for the Swedish national team, IFK Gothenburg and Lausanne, he proved himself to be a top-ranking midfield general of no little intelligence and craft.
• Released by Lausanne in summer 2000.

PLAYER
REHMER, Marco

Defender, German, 187cm, 85kg
Born: 29.04.72, Berlin, Germany
Clubs: TZ Prenzl, Union Berlin, Hansa Rostock (1996-99), Hertha Berlin (1999-)
Full international (Germany) 13 caps/1 goal
• Living proof that you do not have to be a Neanderthal to be a man-marker. An intelligent and tenacious central defender whose passing is sufficiently assured to fill in at right wing-back if required. Coming on strong again following a severe knee injury.
• Surname pronounced Ray mer.

PLAYER
REICH, Marco

Forward, German, 184cm, 76kg
Born: 30.12.77, Meisenreich, Germany
Clubs: Viktoria Merxhaim, Kaiserslautern (1992-)
Full international (Germany) 1 cap/0 goals
• One of Germany's one-hit wonders, players who have fallen out of the national team reckoning after just one appearance. On his day, he is a speedy, skilful and incisive presence on the left-wing, but he is not at full-throttle often enough.
• Surname pronounced Rike.

COACH
REID, Peter

English
Born: 20.06.56
• A tenacious midfielder for Everton and England in his playing days, Reid has adapted well to management with Sunderland, winning promotion to the English Premier League and then more than holding their own in the top flight.
• A hard taskmaster and no mean motivator, Reid has not been afraid to mix playing styles, using the long and short ball game.

PLAYER
REIM, Martin

Midfielder, Estonian, 168cm, 68kg
Born: 14.05.71, Estonia
Clubs: Flora Tallinn, Kotka (Fin)
Full international (Estonia)
• Seasoned Estonian international, one of four Estonians at Finnish club Kotka, having previously played for Estonia's leading club Flora.
• Small, skilful and combative.

PLAYER
REINA, Giuseppe

Forward, Italian/German, 178cm, 75kg
Born: 15.04.72, Unna, Italy
Clubs: Rot-Weiss Unna, Konigsborner SV, Wattenscheid, Arminia Bielefeld (1996-99), Borussia Dortmund (1999)
• The pacy attacker was one of the rare satisfactions of an under-achieving Dortmund in 1999-2000, settling in well following a move from Arminia Bielefeld and winning over fans with his never-say-die attitude and forceful play in a deep-lying role on the right of the front-line.
• Celebrated his transfer to Dortmund by wearing just a Borussia scarf in a risque photo-shoot.
• Known as 'Billy'.
• Surname pronounced Ray na.

PLAYER
REINI, Juha

Defender, Finnish, 188cm, 88kg
Born: 19.03.75, Finland
Clubs: KPV (1995), VPS (1996-98), Genk (Bel) (1998)
Full international (Finland) 3 caps/0 goals
• Technically accomplished defender who can also play in midfield. Not the quickest of players.

REINKE, Andreas

Goalkeeper, German, 190cm, 93kg
Born: 10.01.69, Gustrow, Germany
Clubs: PSV Schwerin, Hamburg (1991-93), St Pauli (1993-94), Kaiserslautern (1994-)
• No longer the gaffe-prone keeper who initially looked out of his depth after moving from St Pauli to Kaiserslautern in 1994. Super reflexes, good ball-handling and generally plays with a lot of authority.
• Surname pronounced Rine ker.

REINMAYR, Hannes

Midfielder, Austrian, 180cm, 76kg
Born: 23.08.69, Vienna, Austria
Clubs: Linz (1991-92), Salzburg (1992-93), Duisburg (Ger) (1993-94), Bayer Uerdingen (Ger) (1994-95), Sturm Graz (1995-)
Full international (Austria) 14 caps/4 goals
• Accomplished midfielder playmaker who played a leading role in Sturm Graz's Austrian title successes in 1998 and 1999, their first League championships.
• Austrian player of the year in 1998.
• Played once, against Italy, at the 1998 World Cup.

REIZIGER, Michael

Defender, Dutch, 178cm, 75kg
Born: 03.05.73, Amsterdam, Holland
Clubs: Ajax (1990-96), Volendam (1992-93, loan), Groningen (193-94, loan), Milan (Ita) (1996-97), Barcelona (Spa) (1997-)
Full international (Holland) 42 caps/1 goal
• Right-back who came through the Ajax youth system, spending time on loan at Volendam and Groningen before establishing himself in Amsterdam.
• Played in midfield at Groningen but was converted to right-back by then Ajax coach **Louis Van Gaal**.
• With Ajax, won the 1995 European Cup, 1995 World Club Cup, 1995 European Supercup and two Dutch League titles.
• Moved to Milan on a free transfer after Euro 96, but failed to establish himself in Serie A.
• The news of his transfer to Barcelona, which leaked out in March 1997, as a replacement for Sergi, was the first sure sign that **Louis Van Gaal** was set to succeed **Bobby Robson** at Camp Nou.
• Faced great hostility from fans in Barcelona, especially as he replaced local boy **Albert Ferrer**, but he quickly impressed with his pace and technique, also filling in at centre-back when required.
• International debut v Norway, 12.10.94.

REKDAL, Kjetil

Midfielder, Norwegian, 186cm, 81kg
Born: 06.11.68, Molde, Norway
Clubs: Molde, Borussia Monchengladbach (Ger), Lierse (Bel) (1990-96), Rennes (Fra) (1996-97), Hertha Berlin (Ger) (1997-)
Full international (Norway) 83 caps/17 goals
• Much-travelled former Norwegian national team captain who fills the libero role at German club Hertha Berlin, but was expected to move on in the summer of 2000.
• Broke a leg early in the 1999-2000 season but recovered in time to make Norway's squad for Euro 2000, although he did not play.
• Played all four games for Norway at the 1998 World Cup, scoring the late winner from the penalty spot against Brazil.

REMY, Patrick

French
Born: 25.08.54
• Sacked by Sedan in summer 2000 for services rendered. He worked wonders on a shoestring in a whirlwind three-year stint at Sedan, leading them to promotion to the First Division for the first time in 25 years, runners-up spot in the

999 French Cup Final and then to a magnificent seventh-place finish in May 2000, only to fall out with his board and be sensationally fired a month later.

• Both at Sedan and at previous club, Beauvais, he assembled teams worth far more than the sum of their individual parts and proved an expert at rotating his first team personnel without any drop in standards.

• A former winger with Metz and Auxerre.

PLAYER
RENFURM, Maikel
Forward, Dutch, 184cm, 80kg
Born: 08.07.76, Paramaribo, Surinam
Clubs: Sparta Rotterdam (1994-98), NEC (1998-)
• Left winger of Surinam origin. Came close to playing for the Dutch national team when playing for Sparta, where problems with extending his contract prompted him to move to
• Can play on both flanks although he is right-footed. Not that skilful, but is physically very strong.

PLAYER
REPKA, Tomas
Defender, Czech, 184cm, 78kg
Born: 02.01.74, Slavicin Zlin, Czech Republic.
Clubs: Banik Ostrava (1990-95), Sparta Prague (1995-98), Fiorentina (Ita) (1998-).
Full international (Czech Republic) 39 caps/1 goal
• Centre-back who been a key performer for club and country since making his international debut for the Czechs against Faroe Islands in June 1993.
• An accomplished defender, particularly as a man-marker, who has acquited himself well in Serie A following his transfer in 1998.
• Missed out on Euro 96 thorugh suspension after being sent off in a European Under-21 championship quarter-final, but was in the squad four years later.
• Made the breakthrough at Sparta Prague under current Czech national coach **Jozef Chovanec**.

PLAYER
REUTER, Stefan
Defender, German, 181cm, 75kg
Born: 16.10.66, Dinkelsbuhl, Germany
Clubs: TSV Dinkelsbuhl, Nurnberg (1984-88), Bayern Munich (1988-91), Juventus (Ita) (1991-92), Borussia Dortmund (1992-)
Full international (Germany) 69 caps/2 goals
• During a wonderful career, he has played all over the park: full-back, stopper, sweeper and in midfield. But the common denominator was always his great tactical awareness, appetite for hard-work and speed off the mark.
• These days, the former German international invariably lines up as sweeper and though his pace has naturally diminished, he remains an above-average performer, a libero of much intelligence and competitiveness.
• Surname prounounced Roy ter.

PLAYER
REVAULT, Christoph
Goalkeeper, French, 190cm, 90kg
Born: 22.03.72, Paris, France
Clubs: Le Havre (1992-97), Paris Saint-Germain (1997-98), Rennes (1998-)
• Three years ago, he looked to have hit the jackpot when Paris Saint-Germain signed him to keep goal for them. But a number of dreadful errors meant his dream move to the capital lasted only one season. Now rebuilding his career at Rennes, but bad luck still dogs him – he missed five months of the 1999-2000 season because of damaged knee ligaments.
• Pronounced Chris tof Ray voh.

PLAYER
REVIVO, Haim
Midfielder, Israeli, 177cm, 65kg
Born: 22.02.772, Asdod, Israel
Clubs: Bnei Yhoda Tel Aviv (1990-93), Hapoel Tel Aviv (1993-94), Maccabi Tel Aviv (1994-96), Celta Vigo (Spa) (1996-2000), Fenerbahce (Tur) (2000-)

Full international (Israel) 48 caps/10 goals
• Hugely skilful midfielder and Israeli football's major star alongside **Eyal Berkovic**.
• Has made a name for himself in Europe for Celta and for Israel with some outstanding performances.
• Plays mainly as a midfielder-forward and is one of the best takers of free-kicks in the side.
• Threatened to quit the national team after the 8-0 aggregate loss to Denmark in Euro 2000 qualifying and the ensuing call-girl scandal, but relented.
• Nicknamed 'El Mago' (The Magician).
• Linked with a move to Barcelona throughout the 1999-2000 season, but joined Turkey's Fenerbahce in summer 2000

PLAYER
REY, Alexandre
Forward, Swiss, 176cm, 78kg
Born: 22.09.77, Switzerland
Clubs: Sion (1990-94), Basle (1994-96), Sion (1996-97), Servette (1997-)
Full international (Switzerland) 11 caps/2 goals
• The Servette front-man was the top scorer in the Swiss First Division in 1998-99 with 19 goals. The Swiss international is one of the game's natural predators, rarely to be found outside the box and scoring most of his goals from close quarters.

PLAYER
REYES, Pedro Antonio
Defender, Chilean, 181cm, 77kg
Born: 13.11.72, Antofagasta, Chile
Clubs: Antofagasta (1991-92), Colo Colo (1993-98), Auxerre (Fra) (1998-)
Full international (Chile)
• Accomplished Chilean World Cup stopper or libero whose strength in the air, sound positional play and comfort on the ball have proved a hit in France. Chile's Player of the Year in 1997, Pedro is the son of an army officer and is a qualified accountant.

Claudio Reyna

REYNA, Claudio
Midfielder, American, 173cm, 71kg
Born: 20.07.73, New Jersey, USA
Clubs: US national team selection (USA), Bayer Leverkusen (Ger) (1995-97), Wolfsburg (Ger) (1997-99), Rangers (Sco) (1998-)
Full international (United States) 76 caps/8 goals
● Captain of the United States national side, Reyna joined Rangers from German Bundesliga side Wolfsburg and injected a degree of class and subtlety into the Ibrox midfield. Highly regarded by the Rangers fans, who have appreciated his influential touches.

PLAYER
REYNDERS, Martin
Forward, Dutch
Born: 15.04.74, Holland
Clubs: Zwolle, FC Jokerit (Fin), FC Haka (Fin)
● Pacy striker who failed to settle at FC Jokerit following a move from FC Zwolle in his native Holland.
● Has done well at FC Haka, scoring the title-winning goal against HJK Helsinki.

COACH
RIBBECK, Erich
German
Born: 13.06.37
● National coach of Germany during Euro 2000 who was brought out of retirement following the resignation of **Berti Vogts** but struggled to come to terms with the problems facing German football. Resigned and became the fall guy for Germany's failure to progress beyond the group stage of Euro 2000. Although he may have contributed to his own downfall with his continual chopping and changing of players and formations, he cannot be blamed for the lack of top-quality players at his disposal.
● Dubbed 'Sir' because of his dapper, English-style dress sense.

● Has been well-travelled during a 35-year career which has seen him at the helm of Eintracht Frankfurt, Kaiserslautern, Borussia Dortmund, Bayer Leverkusen, Hamburg and Bayern Munich.
● Spent six years (1978-84) as assistant to national coach Jupp Derwall.
● Only trophy won was the 1988 UEFA Cup with Leverkusen, but is still considered one of Germany's leading coaches.

PLAYER
RICARD, Hamilton
Forward, Colombian, 188cm, 90kg
Born: 12.01.74, Quibdo Choco Colombia
Clubs: Deportivo Cali, Middlesbrough (Eng) (1998-)
Full international (Colombia)
● Big, strong striker who has adapted well to English football.
● Member of Colombia's 1998 World Cup squad.

PLAYER
RICARDO Carvalho
Full name: Ricardo Alberto Silveira Carvalho
Defender, Portuguese, 186cm, 79kg
Born: 18.05.78, Amarante, Portugal
Clubs: FC Porto, Leca (1996-98), FC Porto (1998-), Vitoria Setubal (2000-)
● Defender who came through the youth ranks at FC Porto but left to gain first-team experience at Leca, returning to the club in summer 1998.
● Left Porto again during the 1999-2000 season, but despite some assured performances, could not prevent Vitoria Setubal being relegated.
● Capped 11 times at Under-21 level by Portugal.

PLAYER
RICHARDS, Dean
Defender, English, 188cm, 186kg
Born: 09.06.74, Bradford, England
Clubs: Bradford (1992-95), Wolverhampton (1995-99), Southampton (1999-)
● Central defender who, thanks to injuries, has

Frank Rijkaard

never quite fulfilled the potential which saw him touted as a future England centre-half.
• Former England Under-21 international.

PLAYER
RICKEN, Lars
Midfielder, German, 178cm, 72kg
Born: 10.07.76, Dortmund, Germany
Clubs: TuS Eving-Lindenhorst, Eintracht Dortmund, Borussia Dortmund (1990-)
Full international (Germany) 8 caps/0 goals
• Early in his career, he was the great white hope of German football, a precocious attacking-third all-rounder who never looked out of place among all the big-name elder statesmen at Dortmund and who struck a marvellous clipped goal in the club's Champions League victory over Juventus in 1997.
• But since then he has struggled to rediscover his magic touch for both Dortmund and Germany.

ADMINISTRATOR
RIDSDALE, Peter
• Chairman of Leeds United and a growing influence within English football.

PLAYER
RIEDL, Thomas
Midfielder, German, 174cm, 69kg
Born: 18.06.76, Germany
Clubs: Phonix Otterbach, Kaiserslautern (1994-99), Munich 1860 (1999-)
• Slightly-built schemer of no little skill and awareness, but needs to work on his goalscoring – in the 1999-2000 season he only scored once but at least he can say it was an important goal, the late winner in 1860's derby victory over Bayern Munich.
• He is the son of Hannes Riedl, who played for Duisburg and Kaiserslautern in the 1970s.
• Surname pronounce Ree dul.

PLAYER
RIISE, John Arne
Defender, Norwegian, 185cm, 77kg
Born: 24.09.80, Molde, Norway
Clubs: Aalesund, Monaco (Fra) (1999-)
Full international (Norway) 6 caps/1 goal
• Left-sided defender or midfielder who was one of the revelations of the French championship in 1999-2000, using a string of five-star performances as a springboard to full international honours.
• A feisty competitor, technically-assured and amazingly mature for his tender years, he has also developed a flair for vital goals.

COACH
RIJKAARD, Frank
Dutch
Born: 30.09.62
• National coach of Holland from July 1998 until Euro 2000, his first coaching position.
• A legendary player who won the European Championship in 1988 and was a member of the Dutch trio alongside **Ruud Gullit** and **Marco Van Basten** who multiple honours at Milan.
• Three times a winner of the European Cup (1989, 1990 and 1995). Also won the European Cup-winners Cup (1987), European Supercup (1989 and 1990), World Club Cup (1989 and 1990), Dutch League (1982, 1983, 1985, 1994 and 1995), Dutch Cup (1983, 1986 and 1987), Italian League (1992 and 1993).
• Made his international debut for Holland aged 18 and played 73 times for Holland, scoring 10 goals.
• Retired as a player after winning the European Cup with Ajax in 1995.
• Set up his own underwear business but returned to football for the 1998 World Cup as a member of the coaching staff of the Dutch national team at France 98.
• Had a difficult time in charge of Holland, winning only one of his first 12 matches in charge. Resigned within minutes of Holland's defeat on penalties by Italy in the semi-final of Euro 2000.

PLAYER
RINALDI, Alessandro
Defender, Italian, 183cm, 73kg
Born: 23.11.74, Rome, Italy
Clubs: Lazio (1992-93), Nola (1993-94), Verona (1994-95), Ravenna (1995-98), Bologna (1998-99), Roma (1999-)
• Right-sided defender who has found competition for places tough since moving to Roma from Bologna in 1999. Started out at Lazio before embarking on a tour of clubs in the lower leagues.

PLAYER
RINK, Paulo Roberto
Forward, German/Brazilian, 184cm, 83kg
Born: Curitiba, Brazil
Clubs: Atletico Parananse (Bra) (1995-97), Bayer Leverkusen (1997-), Santos (Bra) (1998, loan)
Full international (Germany) 11 caps/0 goals
• Striker who immediately clicked into top gear on returning to Leverkusen midway through last season from a loan spell at Brazilian club Santos. His marvellous finishing – with right and left foot and head – helped his club to within a whisker of the Bundesliga title and as an interesting bonus, he earned a recall to the German squad.
• He is Brazilian-born but qualifies for the 'Nationalmannschaft' because his great-grandfather Hermann hailed from the German university city of Heidelberg.

PLAYER
RIOU, Rudy
Goalkeeper, French, 184cm, 72kg
Born: 22.01.80, Beziers, France
Clubs: Montpellier (1999-)
• Highly-rated young keeper with the potential to challenge for full international honours over the next three or four years. Good reflexes, plays with plenty of authority and his distribution is above-average.
• Surname pronounced Ree oo.

PLAYER
RISETH, Vidar
Midfielder, Norwegian, 187cm, 79kg
Born: 21.04.72, Frosta, Norway
Clubs: Rosenborg (1992-93), Kongsvinger (1994-96), LASK (Aut) (1996-98), Celtic (Sco) (1998-)
Full international (Norway) 27 caps/2 goals
- Highly versatile player who played as a striker for Kongsvinger, but often lines up as part of a three-man defence at Celtic. Can also play as a defensive midfielder or a raiding full-back.
- A member of Norway's squad at Euro 2000, but did not play.

PLAYER
RISOM, Henrik
Defender, Danish, 180cm, 76kg
Born: 24.07.73, Denmark
Clubs: VB (1990), Lyngby (1991-93), Dynamo Dresden (Ger) (1994), OB (1994-95), Silkeborg (1995-97), Vejle (1997-)
Full international (Denmark) 9 caps/0 goals
- Veteran defender who is winding down his career back at Vejle after travels in Germany and Denmark.
- Made his international debut for Denmark against England in June 1989.

AGENT
RISPOLI, Vincenzo
- Italian agent who represents **Gianluca Pagliuca**.
- Contact: Piazza Matteotti, 2/8 A-B, I-16123 Genoa, Italy.

PLAYER
RIVALDO
Full name: Vitor Ferreira Barbosa, 'Rivaldo'
Midfielder, Brazilian, 186cm, 75 kg
Born: 19.04.74, Recife, Brazil
Clubs: Corinthians (1993-94), Palmeiras (1994-96), Deportivo La Coruna (Spa) (1996-1997), Barcelona (Spa) (1997-)
Full international (Brazil) 43 caps /23 goals

- Oustandingly gifted Brazilian forward whose performances for Barcelona and Brazil earned him 1999 accolades as *World Soccer* World Player of the Year, European Footballer of the Year and FIFA World Footballer of the Year.
- Often compared to 1950s winger Garrincha because of his bow-legged stance. But despite the frail figure Rivaldo has an outstanding footballing brain and a steely determination born of having to make the 20km round trip to training as a boy on foot. 'People who criticise me for thinking too much about money obviously don't know what it means to be poor.'
- Dedicated his 1999 awards to his father, who was killed in a road accident when he was 16. 'He was my first real coach.'
- Made his League debut for Corinthians in 1993, joining Palmeiras a year later, winning the national championship and Sao Paulo state title.
- International debut: Mexico v Brazil, Guadalajara, December 1993.
- Blamed by many in Brazil for the country's failure in the 1996 Olympics. Brazil were leading Nigeria 3-1 in the semi-final when Rivaldo appeared as a substitute. They lost 4-3 in extra time.
- Scored 21 goals in 41 games for Spain's Deportivo before joining Barcelona in August 1997 for £17million as a replacement for Inter-bound **Ronaldo**.
- Inspirational for Barcelona as they won Spanish League titles in 1998 and 1999 and was voted Spanish Player of the Year in 1998.
- A key member of the Brazilian team which lost the 1998 World Cup Final to France. Helped to restore confidence by inspiring Brazil to victory in the 1999 Copa America.
- Clashed with Barça coach **Louis Van Gaal** in December 1999 because he wanted a free role in attacking midfield, not the left-sided forward role which Van Gaal demanded. Negotiated to stay at Barcelona during the summer of 2000, winning a new deal worth more than £70,000 a week after tax.
- Four-year old son stars in Spanish TV adverts.

Roberto Carlos

PLAYER
RIVAS, David
Full name: David Rivas Rodriguez
Defender, Spanish, 190cm, 79kg
Born: 02.12.78, Sevilla, Spain
Clubs: Real Betis B (1998-99), Real Betis (1999-)
• Left-sided defender for whom everyone at Betis has high hopes. Solid with good technical skills.

COACH
RIX, Graham
English
Born: 23.10.57
• Former Arsenal star who has become a key figure behind the scenes at Chelsea, as number two to first **Ruud Gullit** and now **Gianluca Vialli**.

AGENT
RIZZATO, Gastone
• Italian whose clients include **Francesco Toldo**.
• **Contact:** Via Galileo Galilei 4, 35020 Albignasego, Italy.

PLAYER
RIZZITELLI, Ruggiero
Forward, Italian, 177cm, 68kg
Born: 02.09.67, Margherita di Savoia
Clubs: Cesena (1985-88), Roma (1988-94), Torino (1994-96), Bayern Munich (Ger) (1996-98), Piacenza (1998-)
Full international (Italy) 9 caps/2 goals
• Veteran striker and one of the few Italians to have tried their luck in the German Bundesliga, at Bayern Munich under **Giovane Trapattoni**.
• Had his best spell at Torino in 1994-95 and 1995-96 when he scored 30 League goals in 60 games.

AGENT
ROACH, Dennis
• Businessman who has been closely associated with the career of **Glenn Hoddle**.
• **Contact:** Mudeford House, Christchurch, Dorset BH23 3NJ, England. Tel: 00 44 (0) 1202 47 48 86.

ROBERTO

Full name: Roberto Fresnedoso Prieto
Midfielder, Spanish, 186cm, 84kg
Born: 15.01.73, Toledo, Spain
Clubs: Girona (1991-92), Hospitalet (1992-93), Espanyol (1993-95), Atletico Madrid (1995-97), Espanyol (1998), Atletico Madrid (1998-)
• Lanky, hard-working inside-right who returned for a second spell at Atletico Madrid in 1998.
• First arrived in Madrid in 1995 for £875,000 in an exchange deal which saw striker **Miguel Benitez** moving the other way to Espanyol.
• Born in Toledo but reared in Catalonia, where he joined Espanyol in 1992 after spells with local sides Hospitalet and Girona.
• Won the Spanish League and Cup double with Atletico in 1996, but lost his place after injury and returned to Espanyol. Brought back to Madrid by **Arrigo Sacchi**.
• Former Spanish Under-21 international.

ROBBEMOND, Reinier

Midfielder, Dutch, 180cm, 73kg
Born: 31.01.72, Dordrecht, Holland
Clubs: Dordrecht (1990-96), Utrecht (1996-)
• Midfielder who is getting better and better. Played at Dordrecht in the Dutch second division, but now a regular at Utrecht. Has great pace and plays in either central defence or on the right flank. Takes all penalties.

ROBER, Jurgen

German
Born: 25.12.53
• Coach of Hertha Berlin since January 1996, overseeing a remarkable transformation in the club's fortunes, from the German second division to the UEFA Champions League.
• A solid career as a player, with 303 Bundeliga appearances (75 goals) for Werder Bremen,

Bayern Munich and Bayer Leverkusen, with short spells in England (at Nottingham Forest) and Canada (Calgary Bloomers).
• Began his coaching career as player-coach Rot-Weiss Essen in 1987, becoming head coach in 1991 and moving on for an 15-month spell at Stuttgart in 1993.
• Once played under Brian Clough at Nottingham Forest and seems to have the inherited the Cloughie flair for producing well-organised teams with lots of counter-attacking capability.
• Is a firm believer in a big squad and lots of competition for places. 'Some players might not like it. But the greater the strength in depth, the better your chance of success. I want players who don't get all theatrical if they end up on the bench or in the stand.'

ROBERT, Laurent

Midfielder, French, 176cm, 69kg
Born: May 21, 1975, Saint Benoit, Reunion
Clubs: Montpellier (1995-1999), Paris Saint-Germain (1999-present)
Full international (France) 2 caps/0 goals
• Highly promising left-sided forward or midfielder. Hard-working, quick and with an eye for goal.
• Joined PSG from Montpellier for £4million in summer of 1999.
• International debut: v N. Ireland, August 1999.
• National triple-jump champion at schoolboy level.

ROBERTO CARLOS

Full name: Roberto Carlos da Silva
Defender, Brazilian, 168cm, 70kg
Born: 10.04.73, Garca, Brazil
Clubs: Uniao Sao Joao (1990-92), Palmeiras (1993-95), Internazionale (Ita) (1995-96), Real Madrid (Spa) (1996-)
Full international (Brazil) 72 caps/5 goals

- One of the world's best left-backs, with explosive pace and a famously fierce shot.
- Began his career as a forward at Uniao Sao Joao aged 16 and represented Brazil for the first time at 18 in the 1992 Olympic qualifying tournament, after which he joined Sao Paulo club Palmeiras.
- First came to prominence at the 1995 Umbro Cup tournament in England, where his performances earned him a £4.5million transfer to Internazionale. His time in Italy was not an entirely happy one: he was played out of position in midfield by **Roy Hodgson** and seized the chance to be a 'proper' left-back at Real Madrid under new coach **Fabio Capello**.
- Won the Champions League in his second season in Madrid and again two years later.
- 'When I was a kid, my mother said to me that I must have been born with a silver spoon in my mouth because I was always lucky. I had three sisters and we all had to sleep in the one room. We were poor but we were happy.'

PLAYER
ROBERTO RIOS

Full name: Roberto Rios Patus
Defender, Spanish, 192cm, 84kg
Born: 08.10.71, Bilbao, Spain
Clubs: Real Betis (1992-97), Athletic Bilbao (1997-)
Full international (Spain) 11 caps/0 goals
- Powerful if a little ungainly centre-back who was used by former Spanish national coach **Javier Clemente** in a midfield holding role.
- Became Bilbao's most expensive player when they paid Betis £9million for his services in 1997.
- Son of former international Eusebio Rios.
- International debut v Czech Republic, 1996.

COACH
ROBSON, Bobby
English
Born: 18.02.33
- The most successful English coach of the 1990s, a man with an insatiable appetite and relentless enthusiasm for the game.
- An international player in his own right, winning caps as an inside forward and member of England's squad at the 1958 and 1962 World Cups.
- Made his name as a manager with provincial Ipswich Town, winning the 1978 FA Cup, 1981 UEFA Cup and finishing as League runners-up in 1981 and 1982. Left to take charge of England in summer of 1982.
- His greatest achievement as England coach – fourth place at the 1990 World Cup after losing on penalties to Germany in the semi-final – took place after he had announced his departure in order to take over at PSV Eindhoven. By then, mounting criticism had taken its toll.
- Won the Dutch League title in each of his two seasons at PSV, moving to Sporting Lisbon of Portugal, where he stayed to win two League titles with FC Porto.
- Was appointed head coach of Barcelona in 1996 and, after signing **Ronaldo** from PSV, won the Cup-winners Cup and Spanish Cup before being marginalised by the arrival of **Louis Van Gaal**.
- Returned to PSV in 1998 for a brief caretaker spell before being wooed by Newcastle, his hometown team, to replace **Ruud Gullit**.

COACH
ROBSON, Bryan
English
Born: 11.01.57
- Manager of Middlesbrough since 1995, showing the same battling qualities as a coach that he displayed as a dynamic midfielder for Manchester United and England.
- Won 90 caps for England, often as captain, despite a career in which he was dogged by injury, earning him the nickname Captain Marvel.
- His time at Boro has been characterised by high-profile transfers (**Juninho, Fabrizio Ravanelli, Emerson**) which have not all proved successful. Boro were relegated in 1998 and lost the 1997 FA Cup Final to Chelsea.

PLAYER
ROBSON Luis Pereira
Full name: Robson Luis Pereira da Silva
Born: 21.09.74, Brazil
Clubs: Sorrizo, Paraguacuense, Mogi Mirim, Corinthians, Goias, Uniao Leiria (Por), Ferroviario, Moscow Spartak (Rus) (1997-)
• Highly-skilled Brazilian striker who is one of the few successful foreigners in the Russian League.
• Was initially dismissed by the Russian media as a 'beach footballer' but has won many over with some wholehearted performances, including a hat-trick against rivals Torpedo Moscow.
• His form led Spartak and Russia coach **Oleg Romantsev** to offer him a place in the Russian national side if he adopted dual Brazilian-Russian citizenship. Romantsev said: 'Robson jumps higher and runs faster than any other player in my team.'

PLAYER
ROCHE, Alain
Defender, French, 182cm, 80kg
Born: 14.10.67, Brive, France
Clubs: Bordeaux (1985-89), Marseille (1989-90), Auxerre (1990-92), Paris Saint-Germain (1992-98), Valencia (Spa) (1998-)
Full international (France) 25 caps/1 goal
• Accomplished central defender who is approaching the end of his career.
• Won the Cup-winners Cup with PSG in 1996 and decided to move abroad, to Spain's Valencia, in 1998.
• Was ruled out through injury for much of the 1999-2000 season, but still seen as a key member of the Valencia squad.

PLAYER
RODRIGO Fabri
Forward, Brazilian, 181cm, 74kg
Born: 15.01.76, Sao Paulo, Brazil
Clubs: Portuguesa (1995-97), Real Madrid (Spa) (1997-), Flamengo (1997-99), Real Valladolid (Spa) (1999-2000)

• Brazilian attacker who has never quite fulfilled the potential that many expected of him as a teenager.
• Signed by Real Madrid, but loaned out to Valladolid after a loan spell back in Brazil with Flamengo.
• Most effective when running at defences from a deep-lying attacking position.

COACH
RODRIGO, David
Spanish
Born: 08.05.68
• National coach of Andorra since 1999 after a brief coaching career in the Spanish second division.

PLAYER
RODRIGUEZ, Bruno
Forward, French, 180cm, 80kg
Born: 25.12.72, Bastia, France
Clubs: Monaco (1992-93), Bastia (1993-96), Strasbourg (1996), Metz (1997-98), PSG (1999), Bradford (2000-loan), Lens (2000), Guingamp (2000-)
• Desperately needs to get his career back on track after disappointing spells at Paris Saint-Germain and Bradford City. Has every appearance of a bulldozer-type of frontrunner, but actually has a great touch on the ball and in his heyday at Bastia and Metz hit many a spectacular goal.
• His wife shaves his head before every game.

PLAYER
RODRIGUEZ, Michel
Defender, French, 186cm, 76kg
Born: 25.11.78, Montpellier, France
Clubs: Montpellier (1997-)
• Highly promising French Under-18 defender who was tipped to leave Montpellier in summer of 2000 after relegation to the French second division.

ROEST, Robert

Defender, Dutch, 182cm, 82kg
Born: 30.10.69, Holland
Clubs: Utrecht (1988-94), Beveren (Bel) (1994-95), Fortuna Sittard (Bel) (1995-)
• No-nonsense centre-back with a powerful shot.

PLAYER
ROGACIOV, Serghey

Forward, Moldovan, 183cm, 76kg
Born: 20.05.77, Glodeni, Moldova
Clubs: Olimpia Balti, Constructorul, Serif Tiraspol
Full international (Moldova)
• A consistent scorer in the Moldovan League and a key player in the national side.
• 1996 Moldovan footballer of the year.

PLAYER
ROGER

Full name: Roger Garcia Junyent
Midfielder, Spanish, 175cm, 70kg
Born: 17.11.74, Madrid, Spain
Clubs: Barcelona (1994-99), Espanyol (1999-)
• Talented young midfielder who was a product of the youth system at Barcelona but a victim of **Louis Van Gaal**'s preference for all things Dutch.
• Moved across town to Espanyol in summer 1999 after being squeezed out at Barcelona.
• One of three brothers who at one stage were all at Barcelona. **Oscar** is also now at Espanyol.
• Member of the Spanish team at the 1995 world youth championships in Qatar.

PLAYER
ROGERIO

Full name: Jose Rogerio de Melo
Forward, Brazilian/Portuguese, 179cm, 75kg
Born: 13.10.74, Brazil
Clubs: Boavista (1998-)
• Young striker who has been one of the great prospects at Boavista in the last couple of years, but has been unlucky with injuries.

PLAYER
ROJAS, Ricardo

Full name: Ricardo Ismael Rojas Mendoza
Defender, Argentinian/Paraguayan, 176cm, 76kg
Born: 26.01.71 Posadas, Argentina
Clubs: Libertad (Par) (1991-95), Estudiantes (1995-99), Benfica (Por) (1999-)
Full international (Paraguay)
• Left-sided Argentinian defender who has impressed everyone at Benfica with his honesty, commitment and workrate.
• Born in Argentina, but played for Paraguay at the 1998 World Cup.

PLAYER
ROJAS, Roberto

Defender, Spanish, 175cm, 70kg
Born: 17.11.74, Madrid, Spain
Clubs: Real Madrid (1995-99), Malaga (1999-)
• Versatile flank defender who has established himself at Malaga after getting few opportunities at Real Madrid.
• Played for Real in the 1998 World Club Cup Final win over Vasco da Gama, but played only four League games in Madrid.

COACH
ROLLAND, Daniel

French
Born: 27.11.44
• Former youth team boss at Auxerre who suceeded **Guy Roux** in the summer of 2000 when Roux decided to move upstairs to become general manager.
• Certainly knows all about the Burgundy club; he has been the director of their youth academy for the past 27 years and was the man who discovered and nurtured such talents as Eric Cantona, Basile Boli, Jean-Marc Ferreri and **Bernard Diomede**.
• Trained as a surveyor.

PLAYER
ROMA, Flavio
Goalkeeper, Italian, 191cm, 83kg
Born: 21.06.74, Rome, Italy
Clubs: Lazio (1991-93), Mantova (1993-94), Lazio (1994-95), Venezia (1995-96), Fiorenzuola (1996-97), Foggia (1997-98), Chievo (1998-99), Piacenza (1999-)
• Journeyman keeper who was relegated with Piacenza in summer 2000.

COACH
ROMAO, Jose
Portuguese
Born: 13.04.52.
• Much-travelled coach who has worked at Famalicao, Belenenses, Tirsense, Academica Coimbra, Chaves and Alverca.
• Not unsurprisingly for a coach whose destiny seems to be a life of struggle with cash-strapped clubs in the lower reaches of the top-flight, his gameplans are generally high on damage-limitation and low on adventure.

COACH
ROMANTSEV, Oleg
Russian
Born: 04.01.54
• Coach and president of Spartak Moscow, and also national coach of Russia.
• A defender for Moscow Spartak from 1976 to 1983 and the USSR national team from 1980 to 1982 (15 caps, 1 goal). Rejoined Spartak as a manager in 1989 to lead the team to Russian League seven times and the European Champions Cup semi-final in 1990-91. Combines his role of coach with the position of Spartak president, to which he was appointed in 1993.
• Was Russian national team coach from 1994 to 1996, including Euro 96. Took the position on again in December 1998, combining it with his duties at Spartak.

Ronaldo

ROMASCHENKO, Maxim

Forward, Belarussian, 182cm, 75kg
Born: 31.07.76, Belarus
Clubs: Dinamo Moscow (1997-)
Full international (Belarus)
• Striker whose has become a key figure in the Belarus national side following a move to the Russian League. Scored within 15 minutes of his international debut against Lithuania, with a penalty.

ROMASCHENKO, Myroslav

Midfielder, Belarussian, 187cm, 80kg
Born: 16.12.73, Belarus
Clubs: Moscow Spartak (1997-)
Full international (Belarus)
• Left-sided midfielder and the older of two footballing brothers. Made his international debut against Poland August 1994.

ROMERO

Full name: Enrique Fernandz Romero
Defender, Spanish, 183cm, 79kg
Born: 23.06.71, Cadiz, Spain
Clubs: Logrones (1991-94), Valencia (1994-97), Mallorca (1997-98), Deportivo La Coruna (1998-)
Full international (Spain) 1 cap/0 goals
• Aggressive, ambitious attacking full-back whose form for Deportivo in their 1999-2000 title-winning season brought him into contention for a place in the Spanish national team.
• Played every game for Mallorca in the 1997-98 season, before joining Deportivo that summer.
• Made his only international appearance for Spain against Croatia.

RONALDO

Full name: Ronaldo Luis Nazario de Lima
Forward, Brazilian, 180cm, 75kg
Born: 22.09.76, Bento Ribeiro, Brazil.
Clubs: Cruzeiro (1993-94), PSV Eindhoven (Hol) (1994-96), Barcelona (Spa) (1996-97), Internazionale (Ita) (1997-)
Full international (Brazil) 54 caps/36 goals
• The most explosive talent in world football whose career has been threatened by injuries over the past three years.
• Born into a poor family in Rio de Janeiro and brought up by his mother after his parents split.
• Supported Flamengo as a boy but could not afford the bus fare to train with them on a regular basis, and opted to carry on playing for local side Sao Cristovao.
• Joined Cruzeiro for £30,000 in March 1993 after playing for Brazil in the South American Under-17 championships in Colombia. Made his debut for Cruzeiro, still aged 16, in May 1993 and went on to score 58 goals in his 60 games for the Belo Horizonte club.
• Made his international debut for Brazil as a substitute against Argentina in March 1994 and booked his place in Brazil's 1994 World Cup squad with a breathtaking performance in a friendly against Iceland in May 1994. 'Pay attention to this kid. He's going to be the next Pele,' said coach Mario Zagallo.
• Did not play in the 1994 World Cup, but still earned a £4million transfer to PSV Eindhoven. He scored 30 goals in 34 games in Holland before a £12million transfer to Barcelona. By then he had already been sidelined by a serious knee injury which kept him out of action for the first six months of 1996.
• A sensational year in Barcelona followed his appearance in the 1996 Olympics and he was voted European and World Footballer of the Year. He went on to score the winning goal from the penalty spot in the 1997 European Cup-winners Cup Final.
• Transferred to Inter for £19million in summer 1997 and earned rave reviews for his performances in Serie A, where he scored 25

goals in his first season.

• He went into the 1998 World Cup as the world's most recognisable footballer, but the pressure of being favourites proved too much for Brazil. Ronaldo cut a sorry figure in the final, amid accusations that he had overdosed on painkillers.

• Since France 98, has suffered two serious injuries to the same knee, leading to speculation that he may never be the same player. **Gerald Saillant**, the surgeon who operated on Ronaldo in April 2000 said he may need to change his style of play to carry on. 'He's 23, he's not old, but it's hard to change. If he changed, he might no longer be Ronaldo.'

• Former coach **Bobby Robson**: 'Go anywhere in the world and you won't find a player who can score goals like Ronaldo. He's simply sensational.'

• 'I have prepared myself for the pressure of being in the spotlight. It doesn't bother me one instant. Football is a universal phenomenon and today's football is moved by commercial interests. It encourages the overall spectacle and I'm all for that.'

PLAYER
RONALDO GUIARO
Defender, Brazilian, 186cm, 76kg
Born: 18.02.74, Piracicaba, Brazil
Clubs: Guarani (1993-94), Atletico Mineiro (1994-96), Benfica (Por) (1996-)

• Brazilian centre-back who has played his way into the first team at Benfica.

• No relation of Inter striker **Ronaldo**.

PLAYER
ROOL, Cyril
Midfielder, French, 177cm, 77kg
Born: 15.04.75, Perthuis, France
Clubs: Aix-en-Provence, Bastia (1994-98), Lens (1998-)

• Every big club in France rates the left-footed defensive midfielder's capacity for winning the ball, tactical nous and appetite for hard graft. Yet too often he lives up to his shaven-headed persona, allowing the red mist to descend and getting sent off for violent play.

• Pronounced See reel Roo ll.

PLAYER
ROOS, Axel
Defender, German, 176cm, 70kg
Born: 19.08.64, Pirmasens, Germany
Clubs: TuS Thaleischweiler-Froschen, Kaiserslautern (1979-)

• Underrated, gutsy performer who has spent his entire professional career at Kaiserslautern. A very versatile right-footer, he can operate as a tenacious man-marker, in a wing-back slot or screening centrally in front of the defence.

PLAYER
ROSICKY, Tomas
Midfielder, Czech, 178cm, 65kg
Born: 04.10.80, Prague, Czech Republic
Clubs: Sparta Prague
Full international (Czech Republic) 6 caps/0 goals

• Although only due to turn 20 in October 2000, Rosicky had a sensational 1999-2000 season and was catapulted into the Czech team for Euro 2000.

• Named Czech player of the season for 1999-2000 by the Czech daily *Sport*, and one of the players most highly sought-after by foreign teams.

PLAYER
ROSLER, Sacha
Midfielder, German, 183cm, 82kg
Born: 28.10.77, Germany
Clubs: Friedrichshafen, Ulm (1994-)

• German Under-21 striker or left-sided attacking midfielder. A great prospect who is direct, pacy and boasts superior technique. The weak point of his game is the one shared by so many creative players – he does not like tracking back.

• Surname pronounced Rurs ler.

Sebastian Rozental

PLAYER
ROSSI, Sebastiano
Goalkeeper, Italian, 194cm, 89kg
Born: 20.07.64, Cesana, Italy
Clubs: Cesana (1981-90), Fori (1982-83), Empoli (1984-85), Firenze (1985-86), Milan (1990-)
• Veteran keeper who has won nine domestic and European titles with Milan.
• Holds the Serie A record for going 929 minutes unbeaten (1993-94 season).
• Number one spot at Milan threatened by the arrival of **Jens Lehmann**, then lost out to Christian **Abbiati** after serving a six-match suspension in January 1999.

PLAYER
ROSSI, Youssef
Defender, Moroccan, 181cm, 80kg
Born: 28.06.73, Casablanca, Morocco
Clubs: Raja Casablanca, Rennes (Fra) (1997-99), NEC (Hol) (1999-)
Full international (Morocco)
• Moroccan defender who played at France 98. Was signed by NEC to help boost their fight against relegation. However, his contribution was small as he got injured during the warm-up of one of his first matches in Nijmegen.

PLAYER
ROSSITTO, Fabio
Midfielder, Italian, 178cm, 75kg
Born: 21.09.71, Aviano, Italy
Clubs: Udinese (1989-97), Napoli (1997-99), Fiorentina (1999-)
• Midfield all-rounder who was called up to Italy's squad for Euro 96 following an injury to **Antonio Conte**.
• Made his League debut for Udinese as an 18-year-old.

ROST, Frank
Goalkeeper, German, 194cm, 90kg
Born: 30.06.73, Germany
Clubs: FC Markkleeberg, VfB Leipzig, Werder Bremen (1992-)
• Keeper who has stayed loyal to Werder Bremen down the years, and was rewarded with a starring role in their 1999 German Cup triumph.

ROSU, Laurentin
Midfielder, Romanian, 174cm, 68kg
Born: 26.10.75, Iasi, Romania
Clubs: Politehnica Iasi, Steaua Bucharest (1993-)
Full international (Romania) 16 caps/3 goals
• International midfielder who enjoyed five back-to-back title successes with Steaua Bucharest between 1993 and 1998.
• Began with his hometown club Politehnica Iasi, before moving to Steaua in 1993.
• Made his international debut for Romania away to Portugal in Porto in October 1998. Romania won 1-0 but he was sent off in the 68th minute.
• Member of Romania's squad at Euro 2000.

ROTCHEN, Pablo
Full name: Pablo Oscar Rotchen
Defender, Argentinian, 182cm, 80kg
Born: 23.04.73, Buenos Aires Argentina
Clubs: Independiente (1992-99), Espanyol (Spa) (1999-)
Full international (Argentina)
• Central defender who is comfortable on the ball and highly effective in the air.
• Joined Espanyol from Independiente of Buenos Aires, where he earned rave reviews for his performances in the Argentinian League.

ROUSSEL, Cedric
Forward, Belgian, 190cm, 85kg
Born: 06.01.78, Belgium
Clubs: Standard Liege, La Louviere, Gent (1998-99), Coventry (Eng) (1999-)
• Big, strong striker who joined Coventry on loan from Gent and quickly made an impact.
• Belgian Under-21 international.

ROUVIERE, Jean-Christoph
Midfielder, French, 188cm, 80kg
Born: 04.08.74, Montpellier, France
Clubs: Montpellier (1993-99), Bordeaux (1999-)
• Ex-captain of his hometown club Montpellier and at his most effective in a midfield anchor role. Another of the French side which won the world military title in 1995.
• Pronounced Jon Chris toff Roo vee er.

ROUX, Guy
French
Born: 18.10.38
• One of the great characters of French football who almost single-handedly dragged Auxerre from the amateur ranks to the upper echelons of the French First Division and made them a competitive force in Europe. He served not only as first team coach for an incredible 39 years before stepping aside in summer 2000 to become the club's general manager, but also by being totally involved in every aspect of the life of the club.
• The original control freak, no coach ever had as much power or influence. Renowned for his faith in youth and a 4-3-3 system with flying wingers; infamous for his authoritariansm. No wonder he is a regular on television and on the airwaves. He has an opinion on everything, football-related or otherwise. Says his biggest regret is being prevented by his Auxerre president from taking on the French national team job in 1998.

OXBURGH, Andy

Scottish

• Head of UEFA's technical department and a former national coach of Scotland.

PLAYER
ROZENTAL, Sebastian

Forward, Chilean, 179cm, 82kg
Born: 01.09.76, Santiago, Chile
Clubs: Univ. de Chile (1996), Rangers (Sco) (1996-)
Full international (Chile)

• Originally signed for Rangers by **Walter Smith** three years ago, the striker was afflicted by a prolonged knee injury but after extensive surgery has now made a remarkable comeback.

PLAYER
RRAKLLI, Altin

Forward, Albanian, 174cm, 73kg
Born: 17.07.70, Albania
Clubs: Besa Kavaje (1991-92, Freiburg (1992-96), Hertha Berlin (1996-97), Unterhaching (1997-)
Full international (Albania) 40 caps/8 goals

• The livewire little Albanian forward whose speed, low centre of gravity and dribbling skills makes him a most elusive customer. In the past he has not been particularly known for producing the goods week in and week out, but it was certainly not the case in 1999-2000.

• Surname pronounced Rack lee.

PLAYER
RUBEN NAVARRO

Full name: Ruben Navarro Mendez
Forward, Spanish, 180cm, 78kg
Born: 06.06.78, Barcelona, Spain
Clubs: Valencia (1996-99), Numancia (1999-)

• Promising young striker who made a name for himself with Numancia as a penalty-box predator.

• Moved to Numancia after failing to make the leap from the Valencia youth team to the first team.

Rui Costa

RUDI, Petter

Midfielder, Norwegian, 188cm, 76kg
Born: 17.09.73, Kristiansund, Norway
Clubs: Molde (1991-97), Sheffield Wednesday (Eng) (1997-)
Full international (Norway) 27 caps/3 goals
• Lanky but effective midfielder who had loan/ trial spells in Belgium and Italy before signing for Wednesday in October 1997 for £800,000.
• A good passer of the ball who occasionally tries his luck with long-range shots.
• Missed the 1998 World Cup through injury.

RUDONJA, Mladen

Forward, Slovenia, 175cm, 73kg
Born: 26.07.71, Slovenia
Clubs: Belvedur Izola (Yug) (1992-93), Izola (Cro) (1993-94), Zagreb (Cro) (1993-94), Koper (1994-95), Olimpia Ljubjana (1994-96), Marsonia (Cro) (1995-96), HIT (1996-97), Lugano (Swi) (1997-98), Primorje (1997-98), St Truiden (Bel) (1998-)
Full international (Slovenia) 42 caps/0 goals
• Very quick, left-sided attacking midfielder who played in all of Slovenia's games at Euro 2000. Dubbed the 'Croatian **Robert Jarni**'. Can also play as a second striker.

RUFETE, Francisco Joaquin

Midfielder, Spanish, 178cm, 72kg
Born: 20.11.76, Alicante, Spain
Clubs: Barcelona (1994-97), Toledo (1997-98), Mallorca (1998), Malaga (1998-)
• Quick-witted creative midfielder who has made excellent progress at Malaga since arriving on loan in December 1998.
• A product of the Barcelona youth system, but played only one game for the first team before moving on to Mallorca in 1998.
• Won promotion to the Spanish first division in 1999.

RUI BENTO

Full name: Rui Fernando da Silva Calapez Pereira Bento
Defender, Portuguese, 176cm, 68kg
Born: 14.01.72, Silves, Portugal
Clubs: Benfica (1991-92), Boavista (1992-)
Full international (Portugal) 5 caps/0 goals
• Midfielder who has a regular for Benfica during the last eight seasons, making it to the fringes of the Portuguese national squad.

RUI CORREIA

Full name: Rui Manuel da Silva Correia
Goalkeeper, Portuguese, 177cm, 72kg
Born: 22.10.67, Sao Joao da Madeiro, Portugal
Clubs: Sporting Lisbon (1987-88), Vitoria Setubal (1988-91), Chaves (1991-92), Sporting Braga (1992-97), FC Porto (1997-)
Full international (Portugal) 2 caps/0 goals
• Experienced keeper who was pushed back into third place in the pecking order FC Porto behind **Hilario** and **Vitor Baia**.

RUI COSTA

Full name: Rui Manuel Cesar Costa
Midfielder, Portuguese, 180cm, 74kg
Born: 29.03.72, Lisbon, Portugal
Clubs: Benfica (1991-94), Fiorentina (Ita) (1994-)
Full international (Portugal) 56 caps/18 goals
• Midfield playmaker and one of the most talented players to come out of Portugal in recent years.
• A member of the 1991 Under-20 World Youth Cup-winning side.
• Joined Fiorentina in 1994 from Benfica for £5million.
• **Eusebio** on Rui Costa: 'In Rui Costa and his acceleration, his ability to dribble and his vision, Portugal have a creator of the highest order.'
• International debut: 31.03.93, v Switzerland.

RUI JORGE

Full name: Rui Jorge de Sousa Dias Marcelo de Oliveira

Defender, Portuguese, 170cm, 67kg

Born: 27.03.73, Vila Nova da Gaia, Portugal

Clubs: Rio Ave (1991-92), FC Porto (1992-98), Sporting Lisbon (1998-)

Full international (Portugal) 7 caps/0 goals

• Left-sided defender who won many honours with FC Porto before making the switch to Lisbon in time to play a major role in Sporting's 1999-2000 title triumph.

• A member of Portugal's squad at Euro 2000, starting one group game and appearing as a substitute in the semi-final against France.

• Made his international debut against Norway in 1994, but made only three more appearance before Euro 2000.

RUI OSCAR

Full name: Rui Oscar Neves de Sousa Viana

Defender, Portuguese, 166cm, 61kg

Born: 17.12.75, Gondomar, Portugal

Clubs: FC Porto (1993-94), Uniao Lamas (1994-95), FC Porto (1995-97), Maritimo (1997-2000), Boavista (2000-)

• Defender who joined Boavista in summer 2000 after impressing for Maritimo. Started his career at FC Porto.

RUNJE, Vedran

Goalkeeper, Croatian, 184cm, 85kg

Born: 09.02.76, Croatia

Clubs: Hajduk Split (1995-98), Standard Liege (Bel) (1998-)

• Keeper who has adapted well to life in Belgium and is pushing hard for a regular place in the Croatian national side.

RUSHFELDT, Sigurd

Forward, Norwegian, 188cm, 86kg

Born: 11.12.72, Tromso, Norway

Clubs: Tromso (1992-95), Birmingham City (Eng) (1995-96), Tromso (1996), Rosenborg (1997-99), Racing Santander (Spa) (1999-)

Full international (Norway) 9 caps/0 goals

• Tall, powerful striker who is most effective in the air.

• Moved to Spain's Racing Santander in late 1999 after a deal with Benfica fell through following a financial dispute between Benfica and Rosenborg.

• Won League titles with Rosenborg in 1997 and 1998 after moving back to Norway following a six-month spell in England with Birmingham City in 1995.

• Made his international debut for Norway against Denmark in February 1994.

• Rosenborg director and former international Rune Bratseth on Rushfeldt: 'Sigurd is sharp in the box, courageous and a good runner off the ball. But despite his record, he is not given the credit he deserves. Critics seem to prefer to focus on the shots and headers that do not end up in the net. No striker hits the target every time and to call Sigurd wasteful is much too harsh.'

RUSTU Recber

Goalkeeper, Turkish, 186cm, 76kg

Born: 10.05.73, Antalya, Turkey

Clubs: Antalyspor, Fenerbahce (1994-)

Full international (Turkey) 46 caps/0 goals

• Courageous, agile and confident keeper who has been a key player for club and country over the last three seasons.

• Signed by Fenerbahce from Antalyspor in 1994 as cover for Engin Ipekoglu, who then broke a leg, giving Rustu his chance.

• Won the Turkish league title with Fenerbahce in 1996, having made his international debut in

October 1994 against Iceland.

• Fenerbahce defender Uche Okechukwa on Rustu: 'What reflexes he's got! When its one-on-one with an attacker, he regularly wins the duel.'

• Impressed everyone with his performances as Turkey reached the quarter-finals of Euro 2000.

COACH
RUTTEN, Fred
Dutch
Born: 05.12.62

• A former FC Twente player who took over from Hans Meyer, who moved to Borussia Monchengladbach in autumn 1999. Under his guidance Twente set a club record of 16 games unbeaten and at one stage they reached second spot in the Dutch League, although they finished 1999-2000 just outside of the Uefa Cup places. He began as caretaker, but has since been appointed head coach.

PLAYER
RYTTER, Thomas
Defender, Danish, 180cm, 73kg
Born: 06.01.74, Copenhagen, Denmark
Clubs: Lyngby (1992-96), Sevilla (Spa) (1997-98), FC Copenhagen (1998-)
Full international (Denmark) 1 cap/0 goals

• Reliable rather than outstanding defender who won his only international cap for Denmark against Sweden in 1996.

• Capped 23 times at under-21 level, but has never managed to establish himself at senior level.

S

SA PINTO

Full name: Ricardo Manuel da Silva Sa Pinto
Forward, Portuguese, 177cm, 74kg
Born: 10.10.72, Oporto, Portugal
Clubs: Salgeuiros (1992-94), Sporting Lisbon (1994-97), Real Sociedad (Spa) (1997-)
Full international (Portugal) 40 caps/9 goals
• Tough, determined striker who moved to Spain in 1997 after being banned In Portugal following an attack on the then assistant national coach Rui Aguas. Sa Pinto punched him after learning that he had been dropped from the national team.
• Made his international debut for Portugal against Northern Ireland but only became a regular in the national team following his move to Spain.
• Had been expected to be Portugal's first choice striker at Euro 2000, but lost out to **Nuno Gomes**.
• Tipped for a return to Sporting Lisbon in summer 2000.

PLAYER

SAARENPAA, Kleber

Defender, Swedish, 179cm, 78kg
Born: 14.12.75 Sweden
Clubs: Djurgardens (1995-96), Norrkoping (1997-)
• Skilful Swedish Under-21 central defender with aerial strength who made his international debut against Denmark in January 2000.
• Exotic surname derives from his Finnish-born mother.

PLAYER

SAASTAMOINEN, Jarmo

Defender, Finnish, 188cm, 87kg
Born: 20.09.67, Finland
Clubs: Reipas (1987-88), Kuusysi (1989-94), AIK Stockholm (Swe) (1995), Jaro (1996), HJK Helsinki (1997-)
Full international (Finland) 18 caps/0 goals
• A rugged stopper who has followed coach **Antti Muurinen** from Kuusysi Lahti to FF Jaro, and then to HJK Helsinki. Muurinen continues to pick him for the Finnish national team, too.
• Has slowed down in recent years, but his nickname 'Lumberjack' says a lot about his style.

PLAYER

SABER, Abdelilam

Defender, Moroccan, 181cm, 73kg
Born: 21.04.74, Casablanca, Morocco
Clubs: Wydad Casablanca (1993-96), Sporting Lisbon (Por) (1996-)
Full international (Morocco)
• Right-sided Moroccan defender, a genuine fighter.
• Won the Portuguese League title with Sporting in 1999-2000, but looked set to leave the club in summer 2000.

PLAYER

SABIC, Nermin

Midfielder, Bosnian, 170cm, 70kg
Born: 21.12.73, Zenica, Bosnia
Clubs: Celik Zenica (1989-92), Red Star Belgrade (1993), Dubrava (1994), Inker Zapresic (1995), Osijek (1995-96), Zadarkomerc (1997-98), Croatia Zagreb (1998-)
Full international (Bosnia)
• Bosnian international whose career, like most of his generation, has been affected by the war in the former Yugoslavia. He was with Red Star for only three months before the war broke out and he slipped into Croatia, moving between a number of clubs before joining Croatia (now Dinamo) Zagreb in February 1998.

PLAYER

SABLE, Julien

Midfielder, French, 181cm, 73kg
Born: 11.09.80, Marseille, France
Clubs: St Etienne
• Hard-working former French Under-18

international whose principal task to sit in front of the defence. Forceful and full of stamina, he will on occasion break forward, but he needs to work on his final ball.

• Surname pronounced Sab lay.

PLAYER
SABRY, Abdelsatar
Midfielder, Egyptian, 178cm, 68kg
Born: 19.06.74, Egypt
Clubs: Arab Contractors, FC Tirol (Aut) (1997-99), PAOK (Gre) (1999-2000) Benfica (Por) (2000-)
Full international (Egypt)

• Promising Egyptian bought by Benfica from Greece, with great expectations from everyone in Lisbon.

PLAYER
SACCHETTI, Stefano
Defender, Italian, 180cm, 73kg
Born: 10.08.72, Modena, Italy
Clubs: Modena (1991-92), Sampdoria (1992-97), Piacenza (1997-)

• Accomplished central defender who played several seasons for Sampdoria before a move to Piacenza in 1997, suffering relegation in May 2000.

COACH
SACCHI, Arrigo
Italian
Born: 01.04.46

• Considered to have changed the face of Italian soccer with his attack-orientated Milan side of 1987 to 1991.
• After making his name at Parma in the 1980s, having not played professional football, he won one Italian League title, two European Champions Cups and two World Club Cups with Milan before accepting an offer to become Italian national coach in October 1991.
• Guided Italy to the 1994 World Cup Final, losing on penalties to Brazil, but failed to get past the opening round of Euro 96, and resigned in the face of mounting criticism in the autumn of 1996.

One of the biggest criticisms was that he ignored flair players such as **Roberto Baggio** in favour of more pedestrian players who followed his instructions. In all Sacchi called up 93 players.
• Returned to Milan in December 1996 to replace Oscar Washington Tabarez, but found success much harder second time around.
• Had an unsuccessful spell in Spain at Atletico Madrid in 1998-99, but left in mid-season, vowing to give up coaching. Has since been busy as a media columnist.

PLAYER
SACHY, Nicolas
Goalkeeper, French, 183cm, 76kg
Born: 23.10.67, Dunkerque, France
Clubs: Alencon, Dunkerque, Angers, Sedan (1998-)

• Apart from **Bernard Lama**, no other keeper in the French League had a better 1999-2000 than the experienced Sachy, who proved himself a model of consistency.
• He likes to chat with spectators during matches and once pulled out a newspaper while his team were on the attack.
• Surname pronounced Sash ee.

PLAYER
SAFAR, Szabolcs
Goalkeeper, Hungarian, 189cm, 83kg
Born: 20.08.74, Budapest, Hungary
Clubs: Vasas (1990-97), Salzburg (Aut) (1997-)
Full international (Hungary) 17 caps/0 goals

• Keeper who has successfully replaced Otto Konrad at Salzburg, becoming one of the best in the Austrian League, although he is reluctant to agree to the club's request that he adopt Austrian citizenship.

PLAYER
SAGANOWSKI, Marek
Forward, Polish
Born: 31.10.78
Clubs: LKS Lodz, Feyenoord (Hol), Hamburg (Ger),

KS Lodz
ull international (Poland) 7 caps
  One of the biggest talents in Polish football
who made his international debut as a
7-year-old in 1996.
  Was badly injured in a motorcycle accident in
1998 and has been trying to rediscover his form
since then.

PLAYER
SAGNOL, Willy
Defender, French, 180cm, 78kg
Born: 18.03.77, Saint-Etienne, France
Clubs: Saint-Etienne (1995-97), Monaco (1997-2000), Bayern Munich (Ger) (2000-)
• French Under-21 right-back who joined Bayern
in a £3.5million deal in summer 2000. A polished
performer, both a good marker and coverer, and
supports the attack well. Intends to be a manager
at the end of his playing days and has already
passed the first stage of his coaching exams.
• Surname pronounced Vee lee San yol.

PLAYER
SAHA, Louis
Forward, French, 184cm, 75kg
Born: 08.08.78, Paris, France
Clubs: Metz (1997-99), Newcastle (Eng) (1999,
loan), Metz (1999-2000), Fulham (Eng) (2000-)
• The young Paris-born frontrunner has many
attributes, notably his pace, good first touch and
determination. However, there remain a few
rough edges to his game, especially the way he
sometimes snatches at chances.
• French Under-21 international who scored the
winner when France captured the European
youth title in 1997.

PLAYER
SAILETI, Zeddy
Midfielder, Zambian, 181cm, 76kg
Born: 01.01.69, Zambia
Clubs: RoPS (1994-)

Full international (Zambia)
• A quick attacking player who has spent six
seasons on the Arctic Circle with Rovanimei.

PLAYER
SAKHO, Lamine
Forward, French/Senegal, 178cm, 70kg
Born: 28.09.77, Louga, Senegal
Clubs: Nimes (1996-99), Lens (1999-)
• Forward who made light work in the 1999-
2000 season of the leap from Second Division
Nimes to Lens, impressing both on the domestic
scene and in the UEFA Cup. A most dangerous
attacker thanks to his good technque and power.
• Pronounced Lah mee nay Sack oo.

PLAYER
SALA, Luigi
Defender, Italian, 188cm, 80kg
Born: 21.02.74, Mariano Comense.
Clubs: Como (1993-95), Bari (1995-98), Milan (1998-)
• Confident, composed, right-sided defender who
has established himself at Milan despite stiff
competition from more recognised names. Can
operate as a full-back or in a back three.

PLAYER
SALAS, Marcelo
Full name: Jose Marcelo Salas Meilnao
Forward, Chilean, 173cm, 73kg
Born: 24.12.74, Temuco, Italy.
Clubs: Universidad de Chile (1994-96), River
Plate (Arg) (1996-98), Lazio (Ita) (1998-)
Full international (Chile)
• One of the sharpest finishers in world football
who has already justified the £12million paid by
Lazio to River Plate in June 1998.
• Nicknamed 'El Matador' (the killer) for his
predatory and highly successful approach to
goalscoring.
• Came to worldwide attention during Chile's
successful campaign to qualify for the 1998
World Cup, scoring 11 goals in 13 games as the

Marcelo Salas

Chileans finished as top scorers in the South American qualifying section.

• Signed for £1.9million by River Plate from Universidad de Chile as a replacement for the Parma-bound **Hernan Crespo**.

• Linked with a move away from Lazio in summer 2000, but turned down a switch to Parma as a makeweight in the Hernan Crespo deal, hoping instead for a transfer to Internazionale.

PLAYER
SALER, Jurgen
Midfielder, Austrian, 173cm, 69kg
Born: 04.10.77, Knittelfeld, Austria
Clubs: Leoben (1997-98), Rapid Vienna (1998-)
• Promising young right-sided midfielder who has begun to make his mark at Rapid Vienna.

PLAYER
SALIHAMIDZIC, Hasan
Forward, Bosnian, 176cm, 71kg
Born: 01.01.77, Mostar, Bosnia
Clubs: Velez Mostar, Hamburg (Ger), Bayern Munich (Ger) (1998-)
Full international (Bosnia-Herzegovina)
• Bayern boss **Ottmar Hitzfeld** certainly appreciates the work ethic, skill levels and, above all, the versatility of the Bosnian international. During his time at Bayern, he has played full-back, on the right side of midfield, in the hole behind the forwards, winger and second attacker.
• Pronounced Salee ham eed zeetch.

PLAYER
SALLI, Janne
Defender, Finnish, 188cm, 76kg
Born: 14.12.77, Finland
Clubs: TP-Sjoki (1996-97), FC Haka (1997-)
Full international (Finland) 6 caps/1 goal
• Solid and thoroughly dependable stopper who is strong in the air and composed on the ground.
• Seen in Finland as having a bright future.

MEDICAL
SALLIANT, Gerard
• Paris-based surgeon who is one of the world's leading sports physicians. Has twice operated on the damaged left knee of **Ronaldo**.

PLAYER
SALOU, Bachirou
Forward, Togo, 190cm, 89kg
Born: 15.09.70, Lome, Togo
Clubs: Omnisport Lome, Panthere Sportive de Bangante, Borussia Monchengladbach (Ger) (1990-95), Duisburg (Ger) (1995-98), Borussia Dortmund (Ger) (1998-99), Eintracht Frankfurt (Ger) (1999-)
Full international (Togo)
• Muscular British-style target man who hails from the African state of Togo.
• Has the power and aerial game to worry any stopper, but also has a surprisingly good touch for a big man. Was a target for bigots at Borussia Monchengladbach, where neo-Nazis daubed racist slogans on the walls of his house.
• In April 1993, he scored the 29,000th goal in the history of the Bundesliga (for Monchengladbach against Bayern Munich).

PLAYER
SALVA
Full name: Salvador Ballesta Vialco
Forward, Spanish, 180cm, 79kg
Born: 22.05.75, Seville, Spain
Clubs: Sevilla B (1994-95), Ecija (1996), Sevilla (1996-98), Racing Santander (1998-)
Full international (Spain) 2 caps/0 goals
• Striker whose sensational goalscoring exploits for Racing Santander forced him into the reckoning for Spain's Euro 2000 squad.
• Started out at Sevilla, where he played alongside **Davor Suker** before being farmed out on loan to Third Division Ecija for a year.
• Played alongside **Jose Mari** at Sevilla in 1996-97, but then was struck down by injury.

• Sold to Santander in June 1998 and got hs chance when **Vladimir Beschastnych** was injured.
• Only began playing football aged 17 and says he would have preferred to have been a fighter pilot rather than a footballer.
• International debut against Poland, 16.01.2000.
• Linked with a move to Real Madrid in summer 2000.

PLAYER
SAMARDZIC, Radoslav
Forward, Yugoslav, 175cm, 72kg
Born: 17.10.70, Novi Sad, Yugoslavia
Clubs: Vojvodina Novi Sad (1991-95), Volendam (1995-97), Heerenveen (Hol) (1997-99), Feyenoord (Hol) (1999-)
Full international (Yugoslavia) 1 caps/0 goals
• Gifted Yugoslav winger who plays on the left flank but has rarely featured in the starting line-up at Feyenoord, having previously been a regular at Heerenveen. When he has played for Feyenoord, he has shown great passing ability.

PLAYER
SAMORUKOV, Andrei
Goalkeeper, Russian, 188cm, 81kg
Born: 30.05.70, Russia
Clubs: Tekstilshik (1992-93), Rotor Volgograd (1994-96), Metallurg (1997), Urulan (1998), Dinamo Moscow (1999), Saturn Ramenskoye (2000-)
• One of the Russian League's most experienced goalkeepers, who is exceptionally good on his line.

COACH
SAMMER, Matthias
German
Born: 05.09.67
• World-class attacking sweeper who packed a lot of honours into a short period at the top: Bundesliga titles and Champions League honours with Borussia Dortmund, first prize with Germany at Euro 96 and the European Footballer of the

Matthias Sammer

Year award the same year. But in 1997 he picked up a severe knee injury and after fighting a two-year losing battle to regain full fitness, he turned to coaching.

• In spring 2000, he and veteran Udo Lattek were jointly given the task of reviving struggling Dortmund and after a successful anti-relegation mission, he is now in sole charge.

PLAYER
SAMUEL, Walter
Defender, Argentinian, 184cm, 81kg
Born: 23.03.78, Argentina
Clubs: Newell's Old Boys (1996-97), Boca Juniors (1997-2000), Roma (Ita) (2000-)
Full international (Argentina)
• One of the most promising defenders to have come out of Argentina in recent years and tipped for a long international career after early performances earned comparisons with Daniel Passarella.
• Joined Roma in August 2000 in a £13million transfer from Boca Juniors, a deal which had been agreed a year earlier.
• First came to prominence in Argentina's winning side at the 1997 World Youth Cup.
• Played for Argentina in the 1999 Copa America.

PLAYER
SANCHEZ, Erwin
Forward, Bolivian
Born: 19.10.69, Bolivia
Clubs: Boavista, Benfica, Boavista
• Attacking midfielder who has been in great form since his return to Boavista following two anonymous seasons at Benfica.

PLAYER
SANCHEZ, Juan
Full name: Juan Gines Sanchez Moreno
Forward, Spanish, 172cm, 72kg
Born: 15.05.72, Valencia, Spain
Clubs: Valencia (1992-93), Mallorca (1993-94),

Celta Vigo (1994-99), Valencia (1999-)
Full international (Spain) 1 cap/0 goals
• Striker who came to the fore in the 1998-99 season in Celta Vigo's UEFA Cup run.
• Moved back to Valencia in summer 1999 and made his international debut against Italy in February 2000.

PLAYER
SANCHIS, Manuel
Defender, Spanish, 177cm, 72kg
Born: 23.05.65, Madrid, Italy
Clubs: Real Madrid (1983-)
Full international (Spain) 48 caps/1 goal
• Veteran central defender and the longest serving player at Real Madrid. He made an emotional appearance in the 2000 Champions League Final, equalling Paco Gento's record of 97 European appearances and lifting the trophy for the second time in three seasons.
• His father Manolo Sanchis senior played in Real's 1966 Champions Cup victory.

PLAYER
SAND, Ebbe
Forward, Danish, 183cm, 78kg
Born: 19.07.72, Denmark
Clubs: Hadsund (1991-92), Brondby (1992-99), Schalke (Ger) (1999-)
Full international (Denmark) 26 caps/5 goals
• The Danish international striker enjoyed a magnificent first season in the Bundesliga in 1999-2000, finishing the campaign in the German scoring charts with 14 goals.
• Some think he lacks killer instinct, but this supposed failing was not so apparent for Schalke. Excellent first touch, athletic and an innate flair for goalscoring.

PLAYER
SANDER, Marcelo
Midfielder, Brazilian
Born: 28.12.72, Brazil

Clubs: Lucerne (Swi) (1999-)
• Gifted but impulsive Brazilian midfielder, whose lack of discipline has led to his name featuring strongly in the notebook of Swiss referees.

PLAYER
SANDRO
Full name: Carlos Alejandro Sierra Fumero
Midfielder, Spanish, 170cm, 65kg
Born: 14.10.74, Tenerife, Spain
Clubs: Real Madrid (1993-96), Las Palmas (1996-97), Malaga (1997-)
• Another component of the Malaga miracle. A tiny midfielder who was first given his chance by Jorge Valdano at Real Madrid, then sold off to Las Palmas.

ADMINISTRATOR
SANDU, Mircea
• President of the Romanian Football Federation.

PLAYER
SANOU, Ousmane
Forward, Burkina Faso, 176cm, 74kg
Born: 11.03.78, Bobo Dioulasso, Burkina Faso
Clubs: Bobo Dioulasso, Willem II (Hol) (1996-)
Full international (Burkina Faso)
• Young striker who played a starring role for Burkina Faso in the 1998 African Nations Cup.

PLAYER
SANTA CRUZ, Roque
Forward, Paraguayan, 189cm, 80kg
Born: 16.08.81, 16.08.81, Paraguay
Clubs: Olimpia Asuncion, Bayern Munich (Ger) (1999-)
Full international (Paraguay)
• Bought from Olimpia Asuncion for £4 million in 1999, the Paraguayan attacking boy wonder showed up reasonably well in his inaugural season as a footballing migrant, scoring five times in the League and becoming the youngest-ever Bayern player to score in European club competition

thanks to a goal in the Champions League against PSV Eindhoven. Tall, lively and never fazed by his new and demanding sporting environment.
• Surname pronounced Cruise.

PLAYER
SANTAMARIA, Jose Luis
Defender, Spanish, 181cm, 78kg
Born: 14.01.73, Madrid, Spain
Clubs: Real Madrid (1993-95), Valladolid (1995-)
• Tough but technically accomplished centre-back.
• Another product of the Real Madrid youth system who is now playing at Valladolid.

PLAYER
SANTI
Full name: Santiago Denia Sanchez
Defender, Spanish, 180cm, 73kg
Born: 09.03.74, Albacete, Spain
Clubs: Albacete (1992-95), Atletico Madrid (1995-)
Full international (Spain) 2 caps/0 goals
• Outstandingly talented but impetuous central defender and a key figure for Atletico Madrid for five seasons.
• Former captain of Spain's Under-21 side.
• Signed by Atletico for £500,000 in the summer of 1995.

COACH
SANTINI, Jacques
French
Born: 25.04.52
• Guaranteed a place in French soccer folklore as a midfielder with the all-conquering Saint-Etienne side of the 1970s and as the man who hit the bar with a header in their unlucky 1-0 defeat to Bayern Munich in the 1976 Champions Cup Final at Hampden Park.
• A coach who sets great store by organisation and counter-attacks, he was in charge at Lille, Toulouse, Sant-Etienne and Sochaux before succeding **Bernard Lacombe** at Lyon.

PLAYER
SAPOUNTZIS, Antonis
Midfielder, Greek, 185cm, 83kg
Born: 19.11.71, Greece
Clubs: Panionos (1997-)
• Skipper and standard-bearer at Panionos, where he started his professional career. But the skilful Greek schemer's days at the club may be numbered. He has been a transfer target for many clubs and naturally he was less than overjoyed in the 1999-2000 season when his car was torched by disgruntled Panionos fans.

PLAYER
SARAC, Dragan
Midfielder, Yugoslav, 185cm, 75kg
Born: 27.09.75, Ruma, Yugoslavia
Clubs: Obilic Belgrade
Full international (Yugoslavia) 2 caps/0 goals
• Talented left-footer. Useful wide on the left and in attacking midfield.

PLAYER
SARIC, Daniel
Forward, Croatian, 178cm, 70kg
Born: 04.08.72
Clubs: Rijeka, Sporting Gijon (Spa) (1993-96), Croatia Zagreb (1996-)
Full international (Croatia) 17 caps/0 goals
• Attacking midfielder who returned to Croatia in January 1996 after a disappointing time in Spain with Sporting. Performances on the right hand side of midfield earned him a debut for Croatia against Slovenia in October 1997.

PLAYER
SARR, Pape
Midfielder, Senegal, 180cm, 74kg
Born: 07.12.77, Merina, Senegal
Clubs: St Etienne (1995-)
Full international (Ivory Coast)
• Talented, consistent central midfielder equally comfortable in defensive or attacking mode.

• Pronounced Pap pay Sar.

REFEREE
SARS, Alain
French
Born: 30.04.61
• Works as an importer.
• Awarded his FIFA badge in 1993.

PLAYER
SARTOR, Luigi
Defender, Italian, 182cm, 76kg
Born: 30.01.75, Treviso, Italy
Clubs: Juventus (1991-93), Reggiana (1993-94), Juventus (1994), Vicenza (1994-97), Internazionale (1997-98), Parma (1998-)
Full international (Italy) 1 cap/0 goals
• Accomplished central defender with excellent distribution skills.
• Made his Serie A debut aged 18 with Juventus, but was farmed out to Reggiana for a year. Returned to Juve in 1994 but failed to play once for the Italian title-winning side.
• Rebuilt his career at Vicenza, gaining promotion to Serie A and winning the 1997 Italian Cup.
• Joined Parma from Inter for £3.5million in summer 1998.

PLAYER
SATORRA, Luis
Defender, French, 186cm, 82kg
Born: 15.09.69, Rennes, France
Clubs: Saint-Brieuc, Sedan (1998-)
• A tower of strength in central defence, he is a master in the air and rarely caught of position.
• As captain of Sedan, he led a players' strike during the 1999-2000 season against poor training facilities. 'Every good worker needs decent tools.'
• Pronounced Loo ees Sat tour rah.

PLAYER
SAUNDERS, Dean
Forward, Welsh, 172cm, 68kg
Born: 21.06.64, Swansea, Wales
Clubs: Swansea City (1982-85), Cardiff (1985, loan), Brighton (1985-87), Oxford (1987-88), Derby (1988-91), Liverpool (1991-92), Aston Villa (1992-95), Galatasaray (Tur) (1995-96), Nottingham Forest (1996-97), Sheffield Utd (1997-98), Benfica (Por) (1998-99), Bradford (1999-)
Full international (Wales) 73 caps/22 goals
• Much-travelled veteran striker who joined Bradford the 1999-2000 season after a frustrating time in Portugal at Benfica.

PLAYER
SAUZEE, Franck
Midfielder, French, 187cm, 85kg
Born: 28.10.65, Aubenas, France
Clubs: Sochaux (1983-88) Marseille (1988-90), Monaco (1990-91), Marseille (1991-93), Atalanta (Ita) (1993-94), Strasbourg (1994-96), Montpellier (1996-98), Hibernian (Sco) (1999-)
Full international (France) 39 caps/9 goals
• Hibs manager **Alex McLeish** pulled off a major signing coup when he enticed former French international midfielder Franck Sauzee to Easter Road from Montpelier. The 34-year-old, who won the European Cup with Marseille, became an immediate favourite with the Hibs fans, largely as a result of his exceptional long-range shooting skills.

COACH
SAVA, Kfar
Israeli
• Former coach of Maccabi Haifa who will be in charge of Maccabi Tel Aviv for the 2000-2001 season. Has won three Israeli championships and four Israeli Cups, including the double with Maccabi Haifa in 1991.

PLAYER
SAVAGE, Robbie
Midfielder, Welsh, 185cm, 74kg
Born: 18.10.74, Wrexham, Wales
Clubs: Manchester United (1993-94), Crewe Alexandra (1994-97), Leicester (1997-
Full international (Wales) 16 caps/1 goal
• Hard-working, occasionally fiery, right-sided midfielder or wing-back who failed to make the grade as a trainee at Manchester Utd, where he was a member of the FA Youth Cup-winning side
alongside **David Beckham** and **Paul Scholes**.
• Dropped down two divisions to Crewe and returned to the Premier League following a £400,000 move to Leicester in July 1997.

PLAYER
SAVELJIC, Nisa
Defender, Yugoslav, 187cm, 82kg
Born: 27.03.70, Podgorica, Yugoslavia
Clubs: Buducnost Titograd, Hajduk Kula, Partizan Belgrade (1995-97), Bordeaux (Fra) (1997-)
Full international (Yugoslavia) 30 caps/1 goal
• Physical and highly competitive Yugoslav international centre-back with more than a hint of refinement when on the ball.
• Has a distinct tendency to be outspoken. 'A Yugoslavia not led by such a bad coach as [Slobodan] Santrac would have been world champions in France.'
• Pronounced Nee sa Sav el jeech.

PLAYER
SAVIC, Robert
Goalkeeper, Yugoslav,
Born: 13.09.1968
Clubs: Birkirkara (Mlt)
• A commanding figure in his side's first-ever Maltese League title victory.

PLAYER
SAVICEVIC, Dejan
Midfielder, Yugoslav, 180cm, 77kg
Born: 15.09.66, Podgorica, Yugoslavia
Clubs: Buducnost (1982-88), Red Star Belgrade (1999-92), Milan (Ita) (1992-99), Red Star Belgrade (1999), Rapid Vienna (Aut) (1999-)
Full international (Yugoslavia) 56 caps/20 goals
• Hugely talented attacking midfielder who was one of the stars when Milan beat Barcelona 4-0 in the 1994 European Cup Final. He become one of a select band of players who have won the European Cup with two different clubs; he had already won the Cup with Red Star in 1991.
• A native of Montenegro, he escaped the Yugoslav civil war after a £3.5million transfer to Milan in 1992. Early days at Milan were affected by foreign player restrictions and injuries, but he fought for and won a regular place.
• Nicknamed 'Il Genio' (The Genius).
• Scored on his international debut against Turkey in October 1986, he helped Yugoslavia qualify for the 1998 World Cup before a brief move back home to Red Star, and then a surprise move to Austria.

PLAYER
SAVINAUD, Nicolas
Midfielder, French, 183cm, 69kg
Born: 20.11.75, Fontenay-le-Comte, France
Clubs: Nantes (1995-)
• Fast-improving utility man who can play full-back, stopper, sweeper or in midfield. Tactically disciplined, flawless technique and very consistent
• Pronounced Nee co la Sav ee no.

PLAYER
SAVINO, Matteo
Defender, Italian, 180cm, 73kg
Born: 01.09.73, Pompei
Clubs: Savoia (1990-95), Brescia (1995-99), Lecce (1999-
• Strong, accomplished centre-back who likes to bring the ball out of defence and assist the midfield

PLAYER
SAVIO
Full name: Savio Bortolini Pimentel
Forward, Brazilian, 165cm, 69kg
Born: 09.01.74, Sao Torquato, Brazil
Clubs: Flamengo (1992-97), Real Madrid (Spa) (1998-)
Full international (Brazil)
　Talented left-sided attacker whose form has been inconsistent since joining Real Madrid in January 1998 in an £8million transfer from Flamengo of Rio.
• His time in Spain has been troubled by injury and he has not become the star many believe he can.

COACH
SCALA, Nevio
Italian
Born: 21.11.47
• One of the biggest names in Italian coaching after performing miracles with Parma in the early 1990s.
• Began his coaching career with the Vicenza youth section, moving to Reggina for two seasons in the late 1990s.
• Moved to Parma in 1989 and won promotion to Serie A in his first season in charge. Went on to win the UEFA Cup and Cup-winners Cup, European Supercup and the Italian Cup.
• Was less successful in his subsequent appointments, at Perugia and Borussia Dortmund, but Besiktas had no hesitation in agreeing a two-year contract worth £1million a season, starting in summer 2000.

PLAYER
SCALONI, Lionel
Midfielder, Argentinian, 178cm, 79kg
Born: 16.05.78, Santa Fe, Argentina
Clubs: Newell's Old Boys (1995-96), Estudiantes (1996-98), Deportivo La Coruna (Spa) (1998-)
• Versatile, committed midfielder who won the Spanish League title with Deportivo in May 2000.
• Can play in central midfield, right midfield or right-back.

• Member of the Argentinian side who won the World Under-20 Youth Cup in Malaysia, scoring a memorable goal in the quarter-finals against Brazil.
• Nicknamed 'The Bull'.

PLAYER
SCARCHILI, Alessio
Midfielder, Italian, 180cm, 74kg
Born: 10.09.72, Rome, Italy
Clubs: Roma (1990-92), Lecce (1992-93), Roma (1993-94), Udinese (1994-95), Roma (1995-96), Torino (1996-97), Sampdoria (1997-98), Torino (1998-)
• Elegant midfielder who compansates for his lack of pace with thoughtful passing and intelligent positioning.

COACH
SCHAAF, Thomas
German
Born: 30.04.61
• Werder Bremen through and through. A former full-back, he played 262 Bundesliga games for them, his only professional club, and now that he is their coach, his *modus operandi* is just the same – total dedication and an unassuming nature.
• A number of coaches have come and gone since the legendary **Otto Rehhagel** left the bridge in 1995. But Schaaf certainly seems the best qualified to maintain the high standards of the Rehhagel era. A more than astute tactician and a good man-manager with both old hands and youngsters alike.

COACH
SCHAFER, Winfried
German
Born: 10.01.50
• Charismatic, animated and attack-conscious coach whose heyday was during an 11-year spell in charge of Karlsruhe, whom he transformed from top-flight new boys into a more than respectable Bundesliga force and led to the UEFA Cup semis in 1993-94. However, with the club

Savio

looking doomed for relegation in the spring of 1998, he was sacked and in subsequent engagements with Stuttgart and Tennis Borussia Berlin his star has waned.

• Always has much to say for himself and had a very public row with **Andy Moller** a few years ago, accusing the German international of diving.

COACH
SCHARF, Shlomo
Israeli
Born: 01.01.43
• Former national team coach who spent a record eight years in charge, leading Israel into Europe. A former Israeli League player with Hapoel

PLAYER
SCARPI, Alessio
Goalkeeper, Italian, 188cm, 81kg
Born: 19.04.73, Jesolo, Italy
Clubs: Cagliari (1993-95), Reggina (1995-97), Cagliari (1997-)
• Promising keeper who performed competently for Caglieri until relegation from Serie A in 2000.

PLAYER
SCHARRER, Markus
Midfielder, Austrian, 183cm, 74kg
Born: 03.07.74, Modling, Austria
Clubs: Admira Wacker (1992-96), LASK (1996-98), SV Ried (1998-99), FC Tirol (1998-)
• Midfielder who has good technique and a strong work ethic. Weighs in with a few goals, too.

PLAYER
SCHEIDT, Rafael
Defender, Brazilian, 185cm, 181kg
Born: 10.02.76 Porto Alegre, Brazil
Clubs: Gremio, Celtic (Sco) (2000-)
Full international (Brazil) 3 caps/0 goals
• Ball-playing centre-back who broke through at Gremio after spending a year on loan in Japan.
• Tested positive for the steroid DHEA in 1999

nd was dropped from Brazil's Copa America
quad. Subsequent tests cast doubt on the
original result and a suspension was lifted.
  Made his international debut against Japan in
March 1999.
  Has made little impact in Scotland since a
move to Celtic midway through the 1999-2000
season from Gremio. His prolonged absence in
the first team has been the result of an ongoing
injury problem and Celtic fans are hopeful for a
more tangible contribution in 2000-2001.

PLAYER
SCHEMMEL, Sebastien
Defender, French, 177cm, 76kg
Born: 02.06.75, Nancy, France
Clubs: Nancy (1996-98), Metz (1998-)
• Right-back who found competition at Metz
tough at first, but gradually established himself.

PLAYER
SCHEPENS, Gunther
Midfielder, Belgian, 175cm, 73kg
Born: 04.05.73, Masseman, Belgium
Clubs: Standard Liege (1993-97), Karlsruhe (Ger)
1997-99), Gent (1999-)
Full international (Belgium) 13 caps/3 goals
• Talented striker who should have won more
international caps during his career, but all too
often has fallen out with his coaches. Injury ruled
him out of Euro 2000.

PLAYER
SCHIESSWALD, Gunter
Defender, Austrian, 188cm, 80kg
Born: 25.09.73, Vienna, Austria
Clubs: Austria Vienna (1994-2000), Rapid Vienna
(2000-)
Full international (Austria) 1 cap/0 goals
• Attack-minded defender who made the
controversial switch across town to Rapid Vienna,
a transfer which he hopes will aid his fledgling
international career.

PLAYER
SCHJONBERG, Michael
Defender, Danish, 191cm, 86kg
Born: 19.01.67, Esbjerg, Denmark
Clubs: Esbjerg, Hannover 96 (Ger) (1992-93), OB
Odense (1993-96), Kaiserslautern (Ger) (1996-)
Full international (Denmark) 44 caps/3 goals
• Dependable stopper or left-sided defensive
midfielder. A full Danish international, he used to
earn a living in his homeland as a fishing-net
repairer and was, therefore, just the man to fix
the broken goal nets at his former club OB
Odense.

PLAYER
SCHMEICHEL, Peter
Goalkeeper, Danish, 191cm, 98kg
Born: 18.11.63, Gladsaxe, Denmark
Clubs: Hvidore (1984-86), Brondby (1986-91),
Manchester United (Eng) (1991-2000), Sporting
Lisbon (Por) (2000-)
Full international (Denmark) 124 goals/1 goal
• A world-class keeper who has been, arguably,
the world's number one for much of the 1990s.
A fiercesome competitor and an outstanding
goalkeeping talent.
• A national champion in three different countries
following his 1999-2000 triumph in Portugal with
Sporting Lisbon.
• Had huge success with Manchester United and
was outstanding for Denmark when they won the
1992 European Championship Final.
• Won his 124th cap when Denmark lost to Czech
Republic at Euro 2000, but vowed to carry on his
international career, no doubt with **Lothar
Matthaus**'s record in his sights.
• Scored his first international goal – a penalty –
for Denmark against Belgium in a 2-2 draw
during the run-up to Euro 2000.

Peter Schmeichel

PLAYER
SCHMIDT, Andreas
Midfielder, German, 182cm, 72kg
Born: 14.09.73, Berlin, Germany
Clubs: Siemensstadt, Hertha Berlin (1991-)
• Herr Universal. Utility man of great application
and poise who can play anywhere in the
back-line, as a central midfield enforcer or on the
right side.

PLAYER
SCHNEIDER, Bernd
Midfielder, German, 176cm, 74kg
Born: 17.11.73, Germany
Clubs: Aufbau Jena, Carl Jeiss Jena (1997-98),
Eintracht Frankfurt (1998-99), Bayer Leverkusen
(1999-)
Full international (Germany) 5 caps/0 goals
• The sort of unsung player whose value is only
recognised when he is not out on the pitch. A
dynamic and unselfish midfielder who tirelessly
shuttles up and down the right flank, is a good
crosser of the ball and very tactically aware.
• He was born and raised in the former DDR.

PLAYER
SCHOLES, Paul
Midfielder, English, 168cm, 74kg
Born: 16.11.74, Salford, England
Clubs: Manchester United (1993-)
Full international (England) 27 caps/10 goals
• A hugely influential when operating 'in the hole'
and a regular goalscorer for club and country.
• Missed Manchester United's 1999 Champions
League Final win over Bayern because of
suspension.
• Softly spoken off the pitch and rarely gives
interviews to the media.
• Described by his manager **Alex Ferguson** as
'the best midfielder in England'.
• International debut: 24..05.96, v South Africa
(won 2-1).

PLAYER
SCHOLL, Mehmet
Midfielder, German, 176cm, 69kg
Born: 16.10.70, Karlsruhe, Germany
Clubs: Nordwest Karlsruhe, Karlsruhe, Bayern Munich (1992-)
Full international (Germany) 29 caps/5 goals
  Attacking midfielder whose return to the fray in the spring of 1999 after a year on the sidelines with knee and ankle problems represented a godsend to Bayern and Germany, especially since there is more consistency to his game these days.
● A player of exquisite touch and wonderful vision, he can line up anywhere in the attacking third.
● Born in Germany to Turkish parents.

PLAYER
SCHOLTEN, Arnold
Midfielder, Dutch, 186cm, 72kg
Born: 05.12.62, 's Hertogenbosch, Holland
Clubs: Den Bosch (1983-86), Ajax (1986-89), Feyenoord (1990-95), Ajax Amsterdam (1995-97), JEF United (Jap) (1997-99), Den Bosch (1999-)
● Veteran playmaker who has returned home after a long career. A hard-working player with great vision and tackling.
● Was a very useful stand-in at Ajax in **Louis Van Gaal**'s days. Before his move to Amsterdam he was a key player at Feyenoord. He almost made it to the national team, being called up once.
● His absence through long-term injury in the 1999-2000 season was one of the reasons Den Bosch were relegated.

PLAYER
SCHOPP, Markus
Midfielder, Austrian, 188cm, 76kg
Born: 22.02.74, Graz, Austria
Clubs: Sturm Graz (1992-96), Hamburg (Ger) (1996-97), Sturm Graz (1998-)
Full international (Austria) 24 caps/1 goal
● Midfielder who was a member of Austria's squad at the 1998 World Cup, making one appearance as a substitute against Chile.
● Now established back in Austria after a spell in Germany, where he played 40 games, scoring three goals, for Hamburg.

PLAYER
SCHOTTEL, Peter
Defender, Austrian, 191cm, 77kg
Born: 26.03.67, Vienna, Austria
Clubs: Rapid Vienna (1990-)
Full international (Austria) 56 caps/1 goal
● Veteran central defender who has been the heart and soul of Rapid Vienna's defence for the best part of a decade.
● Played all three games for Austria at the 1998 World Cup in France.

PLAYER
SCHROTH, Markus
Forward, German, 193cm, 85kg
Born: 25.01.75, Karlsruhe, Germany
Clubs: TSV Reichenbach, Karlsruher, Munich 1860 (1998-)
● The former German Under-21 striker puts everything into a first-team appearance, lots of physical presence and unselfish running. Yet the bottom line is that he does not score enough goals – six in 1998-99, three in 1999-2000.
● Surname pronounced Sch rerth.

PLAYER
SCHULP, Dennis
Forward, Dutch, 177cm, 67kg
Born: 18.01.78, Amsterdam, Holland
Clubs: Ajax (1995-97), Volendam (1997-98), Willem II (1998-)
● **Dennis Bergkamp** lookalike who came through the ranks at Ajax but failed to make it to the first team. Moved to Willem II after being signed by his former coach **Co Adriaanse**.
● An important supersub and a strong finisher.

COACH
SCHURMANN, Pierre-Andre
Swiss
Born: 05.07.60
• Coach of Lausanne who took his side to the 2000 Swiss Cup Final, only to lose on penalties to FC Zurich. Was in dispute with the club over funds for new players and looked set to leave the club in summer 2000.

PLAYER
SCHURRER, Gabriel
Full name: Gabriel Schurrer Peralta
Defender, Argentinian, 184cm, 78kg
Born: 16.08.71, Santa Fe, Argentina
Clubs: Lanus (1990-96), Racing (1996-98), Deportivo La Coruna (Spa) (1998-)
Full international (Argentina)
• Central defender who is a useful man-marker with good technique and a powerful shot.
• Won the Spanish title with Deportivo in May 2000.
• Played for Argentina at the 1995 Copa America.

PLAYER
SCHWARZ, Danny
Midfielder, German, 180cm, 73kg
Born: 11.05.75, Goppingen, Germany
Clubs: FC Eislingen, Stuttgart (1995-98), Karlsruher (1998-99), Unterhaching (1999-)
• Very consistent and obdurate left-sided defensive midfielder. Rated one of the best in his position in the Bundesliga.
• Pronounced Sh warts.

PLAYER
SCHWARZ, Stefan
Midfielder, Swedish, 180cm, 74kg
Born: 18.04.69, Malmo, Sweden
Clubs: Malmo (1987-1990), Benfica (Por) (1990-1994), Arsenal (Eng) (1994-1995), Fiorentina (Ita) (1995-1998), Valencia (Spa) (1998-99), Sunderland (Eng) (1999-)
Full international (Sweden) 66 caps/6 goals

Stefan Schwarz

Much-travelled midfield tiger and a crucial figure for Sweden in holding role in midfield.
- Discovered by **Roy Hodgson** at Malmo.
- Was voted Swedish player of the year in 1999 after an impressive season for newly-promoted Sunderland, but missed Euro 2000 through injury.

PLAYER
SCHWARZER, Mark
Goalkeeper, Australian, 197cm, 85kg
Born: 06.10.72, Sydney, Australia
Clubs: Blacktown, Sydney Marconi, Dynamo Dresden (Ger) (1994-95), Kaiserslautern (Ger) (1995-96), Bradford (Eng) (1996-97) Middlesbrough (Eng) (1997-
Full international (Australia)
- Keeper who much such an impression in three months at Bradford in last 1996/early 1997, following a transfer from Germany, that Middlesbrough snapped him up for £1.5million.
- Has won no honours, but already has published an autobiography.

PLAYER/ADMINISTRATOR
SCIFO, Enzo
Midfielder, Belgian, 179cm, 72kg
Born: 19.02.66, Haine-Saint-Paul, Belgium
Clubs: Anderlecht (1982-87), Internazionale (Ita) (1987-88), Bordeaux (Fra) (1988-89), Auxerre (Fra) (1989-91), Torino (Ita) (1991-93), Monaco (Fra) (1993-97), Anderlecht (1997-2000), Charleroi (2000-)
Full international (Belgium) 84 caps/18 goals
- One of the most celebrated Belgian footballers of the late 1980s and 1990s. A brilliant playmaker with great technique and vision.
- Born to Italian parents in Belgium.
- A boy wonder at Anderlecht in the mid-1980s, but spells at Inter, Bordeaux and Torino proved frustrating and it was only at Monaco that his talent came to the fore. Won the French League with Monaco in 1997 to add to a trio of Belgian League titles won with Anderlecht in 1985, 1986 and 1987.

- Returned to Anderlecht in 1997 and was in Belgium's squad for France 98 after making up with coach **Georges Leekens**.
- Moved to Charleroi in summer 2000 to become a player/president.

COACH
SCOGLIO, Francesco
Italian
Born: 02.05.41
- Veteran coach who has had brief spells with a host of Serie A and Serie B clubs since time spent with Messina and Genoa in the 1980s. In eight years between 1990 and 1998, he was in charge of Bologna (6 matches), Udinese (24), Lucchese (18), Pescara (3), Genoa (10), Torino (14), Cosenza (12) and Ancona (4).
- Took over from Henry Kasperczak as coach of Tunisia in July 2000.

PLAYER
SEAMAN, David
Goalkeeper, English, 194cm, 88kg
Born: 19.09.63, Rotherham, England
Clubs: Leeds United (1981-82), Peterborough United (1982-84), Birmingham City (1984-86), QPR (1986-90), Arsenal (1990-)
Full international (England) 59 caps/0 goals
- Vastly experienced keeper with more than 800 senior appearances in various competitions, but is actually a late developer whose career did not take off until a £1.3million move to Arsenal in 1990.
- Began his career at Leeds, but spent a year as a teenager in the reserves before working his way around the the lower leagues.
- Has won the League, FA Cup, League Cup and Cup-winners Cup with Arsenal.
- Made his international debut on 16.11.88 for England against Saudi Arabia (1-1), having previously won 10 under-21 caps for England. Had to wait a further two years as understudy to Chris Woods and Peter Shilton before becoming England's number one.

PLAYER
SEBA

Full name: Jesus Seba Fernandez
Midfielder, Spanish, 166cm, 63kg
Born: 11.04.74, Zaragoza, Spain
Clubs: Zaragoza (1992-94), Villarreal (1994-95),
Wigan (Eng) (1995-96), Burnley (Eng) (1996),
Zaragoza (1996-98), Chaves (Por) (1998-99),
Belenenses (Por) (1999-)
• Much-travelled midfielder or attacker who has
struck it lucky in Portugal, discovering goalscoring
talents that went unnoticed in spells at home
town club Zaragoza and in England.
• His goals proved crucial in keeping Belenenses
in the Portuguese top flight in 1999-2000.

PLAYER
SEBESCEN, Zoltan

Midfielder, German, 189cm, 83kg
Born: 01.10.75, Hungary
Clubs: Stuttgart Kickers (1998-99), Wolfsburg (1999-)
Full international (Germany) 1 cap/0 goals
• The young right-sided midfielder of Hungarian
stock had a nightmarish debut for Germany
against Holland in February 2000 season,
constantly appearing ill-at-ease and at fault for
both Dutch goals. But what did anyone really
expect? Sebescen may have shown good form at
club level last season, but the fact remains that
he had only been a Bundesliga player for a few
months, having only signed for Wolfsburg from
second division Stuttgart Kickers in summer 1999.
• Surname pronounced Zeb esh kan.

PLAYER
SECRETARIO

Full name: Carlos Alberto Secretario
Defender, Portuguese, 174cm, 68kg
Born: 12.05.70, Sao Joao de Madeira, Portugal
Clubs: Penafiel (1989-91), Famalicao (1991-92),
Sporting Braga (1992-93), FC Porto (1993-96),
Real Madrid (Spa) (1996-97), FC Porto (1997-)
Full international (Portugal) 30 caps/1 goal

Clarence Seedo

Attacking right-back who has rebuilt his career ack at Porto after an unsuccessful spell in Madrid. Made his name at Porto, winning the ortuguese Cup in 1994 and the League title in 995, and establishing himself as a key member f the Portuguese national side.

One of Portugal's best players at Euro 96, he ioved to Real Madrid after the tournament, but ailed to establish himself in the first team and eturned to Porto.

A non-playing member of the Portuguese squad t Euro 2000.

PLAYER
5EDLODSKI, Goce
efender, Macedonian, 188cm, 84kg
orn: 10.04.74
:lubs: Pobeda Prilep (1993-96), Hajduk Split (96-8), Sheffield Wednesday (Eng) (1998-99), iinamo (formerly Croatia) Zagreb (1999-)
ull international (Macedonia) 1 cap/0 goals
Central defender who has enjoyed success ack in Croatia with Dinamo after a short-lived pell in England at Sheffield Wednesday during ie made just four appearances.

PLAYER
5EEDORF, Clarence
Midfielder, Dutch, 176cm, 76kg
3orn: 01.04.76, Paramaribo, Surinam
:lubs: Ajax (1992-95), Sampdoria (Ita) (1995-96), Real Madrid (Spa) (1996-99), Inter (Ita) (2000-)
Full international (Holland) 50 caps/7 goals
• Talented and hugely confident midfielder who was one of the pick of the crop of Ajax youngsters who won the 1995 Champions League Final.
• Made his debut for Ajax aged 16 and won the European Cup at 19, before moving to Sampdoria and then catching the eye of Real Madrid.
• Has been accused of causing internal conflicts n dressing rooms, first at Holland during Euro 96, when the young Surinamese black players from Ajax were resentful at the perceived preference

given to the older and better-paid white players. Then at Real Madrid, he fell out with **John Toshack** over tactics ('He [Toshack] didn't appreciate my playing style').
• Twice a European Cup winner (Ajax 1995 and Real Madrid 1998).
• Sold by Real Madrid to Inter in January 2000 for almost £15million, to help clear Real's debts, but also because he has become a disruptive influence.
• 'I am a playmaker. It's said that a playmaker has to use his intelligence to figure out when and how to pass, but I go a lot on instinct. You have to know how to blend intuition with reason without losing any pace. It's a role that combines lots of hard work with imagination.'
• His father acts as his agent.

PLAYER
SELAKOVIC, Stefan
Forward, Swedish/Bosnian, 184cm, 74kg
Born: 09.11.77, Bosnia
Clubs: Halmstad (1996-)
• One of the young lions of **Tom Prahl**'s Halmstad side. Quick, skilful and already a star for Sweden at Under-21 level.

PLAYER
SELLAMI, Jamal
Defender, Moroccan
Born: 06.10.70, Morocco
Clubs: Besiktas (Tur)
• Moroccan international defender who was signed by **John Toshack** for Besiktas.
• Quick and alert, but does tend to disappear from games and was not a regular first choice in the 1999-2000 season.

PLAYER
SELLEMI, Adel
Forward, Tunisian, 180cm, 73kg
Born: 16.11.72, Mahdia, Tunisia
Clubs: Club Africain, Nantes (Fra) (1996-98), Real Jaen (Spa) (1997-98) Freiburg (Ger) (1998-)

Sergen Yalcin

Full international (Tunisia)
• The Tunisian international attacker enjoyed the finest season of his career in 1999-2000, not only scoring 11 goals but often pulling deep to instigate attacks with his incisive passing.
• Surname pronounced Sel lee mee.

PLAYER
SELYMES, Tibor
Midfielder, Romanian, 184cm, 78kg
Born: 14.05.70, Balan, Romania
Clubs: Dinamo Bucharest (1990-93) Cercle Bruges (Bel) (1993-96) Anderlecht (Bel) (1996-99), Standard Liege (Bel) (1999-)
Full international (Romania) 46 caps/0 goals
• Defensive midfielder of Hungarian family origin
• Established an impressive defensive midfield partnership with **Ioan Lupescu** in the Romanian national team.
• A Romanian League runner-up with Dinamo in 1992-93 before moving to Belgium.

PLAYER
SEMAK, Sergei
Midfielder, Russia, 170cm, 66kg
Born: 27.02.76, Russia
Clubs: Asmaral (1993-94), CSKA Moscow (1994-)
Full international (Russia) 19 caps/0 goals
• Unquestionably the team leader at CSKA, a skilful midfield organiser who is equally adept in attack.

COACH
SEMB, Nils Johan
Norwegian
Born: 24.02.59
• National coach of Norway since August 1998.
• Was previously in charge of Norway's Under-20, Under-21 and Under-23 teams and is credited as one of the architects of the coaching structure which has resulted in great improvement in the level of Norwegian football.
• A modest player with Orn-Horten, 1976 to 1985.

PLAYER
SEBWE, Kelvin
Forward, Liberian, 171cm, 65kg
Born: 17.01.65, Monrovia, Liberia
Clubs: Monaco (Fra) (1993), Standard (Bel) (1993-94), Toulouse (Fra) (1994-96), Xanthi (1996-98), AEK (Athens) (1998-99), Iraklis (Gre) (1999-2000), Panahaki (Gre) (2000-)
Full international (Liberia)
• A Liberian attacking midfielder or forward blessed with nimble footwork and much physical power. Very impressive for Iraklis last season and Panahaki came along in the summer of 2000 to make him an offer he could not refuse. A mainstay of the Liberian national team.

PLAYER
SENE, David
Defender, French, 184cm, 78kg
Born: 24.12.67, France
Clubs: Mulhouse, Epinal, Ales, Kriens (Swi) (1996-97), St Gallen (Swi) (1997-99), Neuchatel Xamax (Swi) (1999-)
• Lithe French central defender who is a good reader of the game.

PLAYER
SENSINI, Roberto
Defender, Argentinian, 178cm, 77kg
Born: 12.10.66, Arroya Seco, Argentina
Clubs: Newell's Old Boys (1986-89), Udinese (Ita) (1989-93), Parma (Ita) (1993-99), Lazio (Ita) (1999-)
Full international (Argentina) 56 caps/0 goals
• Experienced centre-back who played for Argentina at the 1994 and 1998 World Cups and has spent 12 seasons in Serie A.
• A key figure at Parma, where coaches as diverse as **Nevio Scala**, **Carlo Ancelotti** and **Alberto Malesani** realised that when he was in the teams, they played better.
• Twice a UEFA Cup winner with Parma (1995 and 1999); Italian champion with Lazio in 2000 and Argentinian champion with Newell's Old Boys.

PLAYER
SERAFIMOVSKI, Zarko
Midfielder, Macedonian
Born: 13.02.71
Clubs: Ljuboten Tetovo (1989-92), Vardar (1992-96), Young Boys (Swi) (1996-98), FCU (1998-99), Makedonija (1999-2000), Trabzonspor (Tur) (2000-)
Full international (Macedonia) 6 caps/0 goals
• Tiny but quick midfielder with good vision and passing skills. Won the League and Cup with Vardar before a two-year spell in Switzerland.

PLAYER
SERENA, Michele
Defender, Italian, 178cm, 76kg
Born: 10.03.70, Venice, Italy
Clubs: Venezia (1987-90), Juventus (1989-90), Monza (1990-91), Verona (1991-92), Sampdoria (1992-95), Fiorentina (1995-98), Atletico Madrid (Spa) (1998-99), Parma (1999-2000), Internazionale (2000-)
Full international (Italy) 1 cap/0 goals
• Experienced left-sided defender who joined Inter in the transfer window in the 1999-2000 season from Parma, having returned from a frustrating season in Spain.

PLAYER
SERBAN, Denis
Midfielder, Romanian, 174cm, 72kg
Born: 05.01.76, Pitetsti, Romania
Clubs: Farul Constanta (1994-96), Steaua Bucharest (1996-98), Valencia (Spa) (1998-)
Full international (Romania) 10 caps/0 goals
• Left-sided midfielder who has long been seen as one of the long-term successors to **Gheorghe Hagi** in the Romanian national team.
• Started at the Farul club in Constanta, Hagi's home town, and joined Steaua in 1996.
• Won two Romanian League championship medals at Steaua, before being signed by Valencia halfway through the 1998-99 season.
• Missed the 1998 World Cup through injury.

Ciriaco Sforza

PLAYER
SERGEN Yalcin
Midfielder, Turkish, 174cm, 70kg
Born: 05.10.72, Istanbul, Turkey
Clubs: Besiktas, Instanbulspor, Fenerbahce, Galatasaray
Full international (Turkey) 32 caps/5 goals
• Talented midfield playmaker who has had a controversial club career in Turkey.
• Began at Besiktas, where he played a key role in their 1995 Turkish League title triumph, having made his international debut against Iceland in October 1994.
• Set a Turkish transfer record when he moved to Instanbulspor for £5.5million in 1998, but was offloaded to Fenerbahce in early 1999 to help alleviate Instanbulspor's financial problems.
• He did not last long at Fenerbahce, where disgreemeents with coach **Zdenek Zemen** led to a move to Galatasaray.
• Performed well at Galatasaray, helping them win the Turkish League and a historic first European title, the UEFA Cup.
• Has been accused of laziness and individualism on the pitch, and indulging in a playboy lifestyle and addiction to gambling off it.
• In Turkey's squad for Euro 2000, but was only used as a substitute.
• 'I'm used to being attacked. I'm criticised for lack of fitneess, for not doing enough defensive work, for all sorts of so-called faults. It doesn't bother me any more. I've answered my critics on the pitch. People should take me as I am. I am not a destroyer. I am a creator.'

PLAYER
SERGI
Full name: Sergi Barjuan Esclusa
Defender, Spanish, 174cm, 68kg
Born: 28.12.71, Barcelona, Spain
Clubs: Barcelona (1992-)
Full international (Spain) 47 caps/1 goal
• Dimunitive but highly effective left-back. Loves

to use his pace to attack down the flank, but is also a highly accomplished defender.
• Has spent his entire career at Barcelona, beginning as a left-winger.
• Thrown into Barcelona's side by **Johan Cruyff** for the Champions League match against Galatasaray in 1993 and a regular ever since.
• Member of the Spanish squads at USA 94, Euro 96 and France 98.
• Scored after only 18 minutes of his international debut, against Poland in February 1994.

PLAYER
SERGINHO
Defender, Brazilian, 180cm, 73kg
Born: 27.06.71, Nilopolis, Brazil
Clubs: Itaperuna (1993), Flamengo (1995-96), Sao Paulo (1997-99), Milan (Ita) (1999-)
Full international (Brazil) 5 caps/0 goals
• Left-sided wing-back or midfielder who broke in the Brazilian national squad while at Sao Paulo and earned an £8million move to Milan.
• Played less than 100 Brazilian League games before the transfer to Italy.
• Adopted by the Milan fans after a series of impressive displays on the left flank. **Silvio Berlusconi:** 'I've heard our supporters sing that Serginho is one of us, and I couldn't agree more.'
• International debut: September 1998, v Yugoslavia.

PLAYER
SERGIO Fernandez Gonzalez
Defender, Spanish, 188cm, 80kg
Born: 23.05.77, Aviles, Spain
Clubs: Sporting Gijon (1995-99), Celta Vigo (1999-)
• Highly-rated young central defender who has been tipped as a future Spanish international.
• Came through the ranks at Sporting Gijon, playing for Spain at the 1997 world youth championships in Malaysia and earning Spanish Under-21 honours.

• Signed by Celta Vigo in summer 1998 but went back to Gijon on loan.
• Has yet to claim a regular first-team place at Celta, but remains a promising talent.

PLAYER
SERGIO Gonzalez Soriano
Midfielder, Spanish, 178cm, 79kg
Born: 10.11.76, Barcelona, Spain
Clubs: Espanyol (1995-)
• Hugely influential player at Espanyol, where his leadership in midfield is vital to the team's success.
• Product of Espanyol's youth system.

PLAYER
SERGIO CONCEICAO
Full name: Sergio Paulo Marceneiro da Conceicao
Midfielder, Portuguese, 177cm, 82kg
Born: 15.11.74, Coimbra, Portugal.
Clubs: Falgueiras (1996), FC Porto (1996-98), Lazio (Ita) (1998-2000), Parma (Ita) (2000-)
Full international (Portugal) 29 caps/5 goals
• Right-sided midfielder who has quickly developed into one of the best midfielders in Europe. An all-purpose player who is equally adept at ball-winning as creating.
• Twice a Portuguese League title winner with FC Porto before his £6.4million transfer to Lazio.
• Signed by Lazio coach **Sven Goran Eriksson** as a replacement for the Parma-bound **Diego Fuser**.
• Twice a Portuguese League title-winner with FC Porto and a European Cup-winners Cup winner with Lazio in 1999.
• Switched to Parma in July 2000 as a makeweight in the (then) world-record transfer of **Hernan Crespo** to Lazio. He was not at all happy with the move: 'I am disappointed. I deserved more respect after all I have given the team. No one warned me I could be sold and I'll be sorry to leave Rome.'

Andrii Shevchenko

PLAYER
SERGIO NUNES
Full name: Sergio Manuel Ferreira Nunes
Defender, Portuguese, 181cm, 74kg
Born: 21.07.74, Matosinhhos, Portugal
Clubs: Leixoes (1992-94), Alves (1994-97), Uniao Leiria (1997-99), Benfica (1999-)
• Central defender who replaced **Paulo Madeira** at Benfica during the 1999-2000 season and helped to tighten up things at the back.

PLAYER
SERKAN Aykut
Forward, Turkish, 175cm, 65kg
Born: 24.02.75, Ankara, Turkey
Clubs: Samsunspor
Full international (Turkey) 1 cap/0 goals
• Striker who has consistently scored goals in the Turkish League, but has yet to break into the national side on a regular basis.

PLAYER
SERRANO, Manuel
Full name: Manuel Serrano Pulido
Forward, Spanish, 173cm, 67kg
Born: 10.09.72, Barcelona, Spain
Clubs: Alaves (1994-98), Espanyol (1998-)
• Striker whose time at Espanyol has been affected by injuries.
• Spent four seasons in the Spanish second division with Alaves, scoring 53 goals in 131 games.

PLAYER
SERRIZUELA, Juan Jose
Defender, Argentinian, 185cm, 88kg
Born: 25.01.77, Lanus, Argentina
Clubs: Lanus (1994-99), Mallorca (Spa) (1999-)
• Versatile defender who has impressed since arriving at Mallorca from Argentinian club Lanus.
• One of a number of players who followed coach **Hector Cuper** from Lanus to Mallorca.
• Can play in central defence or full-back.
• Argentinian Under-21 international.

LAYER

ESA, Davide

orward, Swiss, 174cm, 71kg

orn: 10.07.73, Zurich, Switzerland

lubs: FC Zurich (1991-93), Baden (1993-94), ervette (1994-98), Lecce (Ita) (1999-2000), Japoli (Ita) (2000-)

ull international (Switzerland) 25 caps/1 goal

Technically-accomplished striker who has mpressed in Italy as a maker rather than taker of goals.

PLAYER

SETERNES, Bengt

Forward, Norwegian, 185cm, 90kg

Born: 01.01.75, Norway

Clubs: Odd (1997), Bodo/Glimt (1998-)

• Strong, direct striker who has scored 25 goals in 75 Norwegian League matches.

PLAYER

SFORZA, Ciriaco

Midfielder, Swiss, 180cm, 76kg

Born: 02.03.70, Aarau, Switzerland

Clubs: FC Wohlen, Aarau, Grasshopper, Kaiserslautern (Ger), Bayern Munich (Ger), Internazionale (Ita) (1996-97), Kaiserslautern (Ger) (1998-2000), Bayern Munich (Ger) (2000-)

Full international (Switzerland) 69 caps/6 goals

• The debate rages on whether the Swiss star is better suited to a playmaking or sweeper role. But whatever his brief, Ciri does it with style. His passing is excellent, he has an eye for goal, delivers fine set-pieces and, above all, is a winner. The one drawback is his outspoken nature; he says what he thinks about coaches and team-mates and it does not always make for a calm dressing room.

• A key man for Switzerland throughout the 1990s, as **Roy Hodgson** explained: 'Terry Venables had a choice of Gascoigne, Platt, Beardsley and **Paul Ince**. Any of those would be in the Swiss side. I've got to pick between

Sforza, Sforza and Sforza. I usually pick Sforza.'

• Surname pronounced Ss forts sah.

PLAYER

SHAQIRI, Artim

Midfielder, Macedonian

Born: 23.09.73, Macedonia

Clubs: Karaorman Struga (1991-94), Vardar Skopje (1994-97), Halmstad (Swe) (1997-99), Vardar (1999-00), Tennis Borussia Berlin (Ger) (2000-)

Full international (Macedonia) 28 caps/5 goals

• Quick left-footed midfielder who won the Macedonian tittle in 1994 and 1995 and the Swedish tittle in 1997.

• Linked with a transfer to several English clubs (reportedly Charlton, Nottingham Forest and Ipswich) during the 1999-2000 season, but opted for Tennis Borussia.

PLAYER

SHEARER, Alan

Forward, English, 180cm, 76kg

Born: 13.08.70, Newcastle, England

Clubs: Southampton (1987-92), Blackburn (1992-96), Newcastle (1996-)

Full international (England) 63 caps/30 goals

• Striker who retired from international football after Euro 2000, closing an England career which had peaked four years earlier when he finished as top scorer at Euro 96 and moved from Blackburn to hometown club Newcastle in a world-record £15million transfer.

• Despite his best assurances, the suspicion remains that Shearer may be persuaded out of retirement. Either way, he remains a powerfully effective goalscorer who has topped the scoring charts on a regular basis.

• Born and bred in Newcastle but spotted by Southampton, who took him down south to be a trainee. Became the youngest player ever to score a Football League hat-trick when, aged 17 and 240 days and in only his fourth appearance,

he scored three goals against Arsenal.
- Joined Blackburn for a then record £3.3million in July 1992 and won the Premier League title in the 1994-95 season.
- At Newcastle, he has been much happier since the arrival of **Bobby Robson**. Relations with previous manager **Ruud Gullit** had become extremely strained, but there is now talk that Shearer will be the next manager of Newcastle.
- Is criticised for his boring interview style and his salt-of-the-earth image ('I'm just the son of a sheet metal worker') but he remains one of the most talented footballers of his generation.

PLAYER
SHEKILADZE, Gela
Defender, Georgian, 178cm, 73kg
Born: 14.09.70, Georgia
Clubs: Dynamo Batumi (1990-98), Lierse (Bel) (1998-)
Full international (Georgia) 17 caps/0 goals
- Accomplished defender who has struggled to win a first-team place at Lierse since a move from Dynamo Batumi in 1998.

PLAYER
SHELACH, Amir
Defender, Israeli, 182cm, 79kg
Born: 11.7.70, Israel
Clubs: Hapoel Haifa
Full international (Israel) 75 caps/0 goals
- Is the most-capped among Israel's active players and his experience, often when playing in a central defender's role has seen off many dangerous situations for Israel. Is the regular stand-in captain when **Tal Banin** is unavailable.

PLAYER
SHERINGHAM, Teddy
Forward, English, 183cm, 78kg
Born: 02.04.66, Highams Park, England
Clubs: Millwall (1983-91), Nottingham Forest (1991-93), Tottenham (1993-97), Manchester

Giuseppe Signori

Jnited (1997-)
Full international (England) 38 caps/9 goals
• Striker who has compensated for a lack of
pace with a clever footballing brain and a playing
style which has seen him accused of being lazy,
flash and arrogant.
• A favourite of **Terry Venables**, who signed him
for Tottenham and then paired him with **Alan
Shearer** for England.
• Spent seven years at Millwall, becoming the
club's all-time top scorer with 93 League goals.
Joined Nottingham Forest in 1991 for £2million,
with a move to Spurs a year later.
• Became a highly popular figure at White Hart
Lane, but switched to Old Trafford in summer
1997. He is guaranteed a place in United's
folklore after scoring the equaliser and setting
up the winner in the 1999 Champions League
Final against Bayern Munich.

PLAYER
SHERWOOD, Tim
Midfielder, English, 185cm, 80kg
Born: 02.02.69, St Albans, England
Clubs: Watford (1987-89), Norwich (1990-92),
Blackburn (1991-98), Tottenham (1998-)
Full international (England) 3 caps/0 goals
• Combative midfielder who is a dynamic
presence in central midfield for Spurs and, very
occasionally, for **Kevin Keegan**'s England.
• Was captain of Blackburn's 1995 League
title-winning side but fell out with coach **Roy
Hodgson** and was sold to Spurs in 1998.

PLAYER
SHEVCHENKO, Andrii
Forward, Ukrainian, 183cm, 73kg
Born: 29.09.76, Kiev, Ukraine
Clubs: Kyiv Dynamo (1994-99), Milan (Ita) (1999-)
Full international (Ukraine) 29 caps/9 goals
• One of the most exciting strikers in world
football, who combines brilliant technique with
lightning pace and a sharp eye for goal.

• Finished as top scorer in his first season in
Serie A following a £16million move from Kyiv
Dynamo to Milan.
• Ukrainian footballer of the year in 1997.
• Nicknamed 'Sheva' by Milan fans.
• Made his debut aged 18 for Ukraine against
Croatia in April 1995, having broken into the Kiev
first team less than a year earlier.
• Finished third in the 1999 FIFA World Player of
the Year poll.

PLAYER
SHIRKO, Aleksandar
Forward, Russian, 179cm, 69kg
Born: 24.11.76, Moscow, Russia
Clubs: Moscow Spartak
Full international (Russia) 4 caps/0 goals
• Striker who has graduated from the youth
ranks at Spartak and is now well established in
the first team.
• Has good positioning and speed, but does have
a tendency to fluff chances in front of goal.

PLAYER
SHKAPENKO, Pavel
Forward, Russian, 179cm, 68kg
Born: 16.12.72
Clubs: Metalurg Zaporizha, Kyiv Dynamo, Torpedo
Moscow (1998-)
• Product of Metalurg Zaporizha youth school
who played three seasons for Kyiv Dynamo.
• Very strong in the air, competitive and a tireless
runner between the penalty areas.

PLAYER
SHOUKOV, Dmitri
Midfielder, Russian, 181cm, 82kg
Born: 26.09.75, Samara, Russia
Clubs: CSKA Moscow (1993-95), Vitesse Arnhem
(Hol) (1995-98), NAC (Hol) (1998-99), Willem II
(Hol) 1999-)
• Lively winger from Russia who is two-footed
and has great determination. Moved to Willem

Diego Simeone

after somehow not making it at Vitesse.
• A little underrated although he needs to promote himself better.

PLAYER
SHOVKOVSKY, Olexander
Goalkeeper, Ukrainian, 191cm, 87kg
Born: 02.01.75, Ukraine
Clubs: Kyiv Dynamo
Full international (Ukraine) 26 caps/0 goals
• The best goalkeeper in Ukraine who made his debut in the national team at the age of 20. Has been irreplaceable for both club and country over the past five seasons

PLAYER
SIADACZKA, Rafal
Midfielder, Polish, 180cm, 80kg
Born: 21.02.72, Poland
Clubs: Legia Warsaw, Widzew Lodz (1995-98), Austria Vienna (Aut) (1998-99) Legia Warsaw (1998-)
Full international (Poland) 17 caps/2 goals
• Can play as a left-midfielder or a left-back. Won two championships with Widzew Lodz (1996, 1997) before a move to Austria Vienna. Recently returned to Legia, with whom he made his first division debut in 1991.

PLAYER
SIBIERSKI, Antoine
Midfielder, French, 187cm, 80kg
Born: 05.08.74, Lille, France
Clubs: Lille (1992-96), Auxerre (1996-98), Nantes (1998-2000), Lens (2000-)
• This elegant, incisive attacking midfielder was in outstanding form for Nantes in the 1999-2000 season, scoring 13 goals and having a hand in many more. A French Under -1 international, he has come back even stronger after serving a ban for a failed drugs test – nandrolone again.
• One of the few players in French football to have passed the French equivalent of A levels.
• Surname pronounced See bee er ski.

PLAYER
IBON, Gerald
Forward, Dutch,196cm, 85kg
Born: 19.04.74, Dalen, Holland
Clubs: Twent (1993-94), VVV (1994-96), Roda (1996-97), Ajax (1998-99), Sheffield Wednesday (Eng) (1999-)
• Striker who biggest asset is his height, but has found competition tough at Ajax and Wednesday.

PLAYER
SIEGL, Horst
Forward, Czech, 182cm, 78kg
Born: 15.02.69, Czech Republic
Clubs: Sparta Prague, Kaiserslautern (Ger), Sparta Prague (1996-)
Full international (Czech Republic) 23 caps/7 goals
• Prolific goalscorer and former Sparta captain who fell out of favour early in the 1999-2000 season only to fight his way back into the team looking hungrier and sharper than ever.
• Despite his domestic league record (he was League top scorer in 1998-99), Siegl has never looked convincing on an international stage.

PLAYER
SIETES
Full name: Jose Manuel Suarez Rivas
Defender, Spanish, 174cm, 72kg
Born: 18.02.74, Sietes, Spain
Clubs: Oviedo (1993-95), Valencia (1995-97), Racing Santander (1997-)
• Pacy left-back who started out at Oviedo, before spending two seasons at Valencia, moving on to Racing Santander in 1997.
• Former Spanish Under-21 international.

PLAYER
SIGNORI, Giuseppe
Forward, Italian, 171cm, 68kg
Born: 17.02.68, Alzano Lombardo, Italy
Clubs: Leffe (1984-86), Piacenza (1986-87), Trento (1987-88), Piacenza (1988-89), Foggia (1989-92), Lazio (1992-97), Sampdoria (1998), Bologna (1998-)
Full international (Italy) 28 caps/7 goals
• Striker who played for Italy at the 1994 World Cup and was top scorer in the Italian League in 1992-93 (26 goals), 1993-94 (23 goals) and 1995-96 (24 goals).
• Was one of a number of creative 'thinking' forwards who were discarded by Italian coach **Arrigo Sacchi.**
• Has continued his impressive scoring rate for Bologna after falling out of favour at Lazio.

PLAYER
SIGURDSSON, Helgi
Forward, Icelandic, 186cm, 81kg
Born: 17.09.74, Iceland
Clubs: Vikingur (1990-92), Fram (1993-94), Tennis Borussia Berlin (Ger) (1995-96), Stuttgart (Ger) (1996-97), Stabaek (Nor) (1997-99), Panathanaikos (Gre) (1999-)
Full international (Iceland) 30 caps/4 goals
• Quick-thinking forward, much travelled and now established in Iceland's international squad.

PLAYER
SIGURDSSON, Larus Orri
Defender, Icelandic
Born: 04.06.73, Iceland
Clubs: Stoke City (Eng), West Brom (Eng)
Full international (Iceland) 31 caps/3 goals
• Highly experienced international defender whose 1999-2000 season was cut short by injury shortly after joining West Brom from Stoke.

PLAYER
SIKORA, Eric
Defender, French, 182cm, 77kg
Born: 04.02.68, Courrieres, France
Clubs: Lens (1984-)
• A quick and purposeful right-back, he joined Lens at the age of 12 and is easily the club's

longest-serving player. A thigh injury kept him on the sidelines for much of the 1999-2000 season, but when he does return, many think it will be in the sweeper position.
• Pronounced Ay reek See koor rah.

SIKORA, Victor
Forward, Dutch, 170cm, 63kg
Born: 11.04.78, Deventer, Holland
Clubs: Go Ahead Eagles (1994-99), Vitesse Arnhem (1999-)
• Quick, strong, Under-21 international striker who game has improved since playing alongside **Pierre Van Hooijdonk** in Arnhem.

SILENZI, Andrea
Forward, Italian, 191cm, 86kg
Born: 10.02.66, Rome, Italy
Clubs: Lodogliani (1984-87), Arezzo (1987-88), Reggiana (1988-90), Napoli (1990-92), Torino (1992-95), Nottingham Forest (Eng) (1995-96), Venezia (1996), Reggiana (1997-98), Ravenna (1998-99), Torino (1999-)
Full international (Italy) 1 cap/0 goals
• Tall, cumbersome striker whose best spell of his career came at Torino in the 1993-94 season, scoring 17 League goals. A disastrous spell in England at Nottingham Forest followed.
• Made his one and only international appearance against France in Napoli in February 1994.

SILJAK, Ermin
Forward, Slovenian, 180cm, 79kg
Born: 11.05.73, Ljubljana, Slovenia
Clubs: Svoboda Ljubljana, Olimpia Ljubljana, Bastia (Fra) (1997), Servette (Swi) (1998-)
Full international (Slovenia) 20 caps/4 goals
• Striker who started one game for Slovenia at Euro 2000 after being a late addition to the squad.
• Dangerous in front of goal and skilful on the

ball, but his career has been dogged by injuries, the latest being an achilles injury which kept him out for much of the 1999-2000 campaign.

SILVESTRE, Frank
Defender, French, 180cm, 76kg
Born: 05.04.67, Paris, France
Clubs: Sochaux (1985-93), Auxerre (1993-98), Montpellier (1998-)
Full international (France) 11 caps/0 goals
• Wise old stopper or libero who is the cousin of Manchester United defender **Mickael Silvestre**. In 1988, he helped France capture the European Under-21 title – alongside one Eric Cantona.
• Surname pronounced Seel vest rah.

SILVESTRE, Mickael
Defender, French, 184cm, 82 kg
Born: 09.08.77. Chambray Les Tours France
Clubs: Rennes (1995-1998), Internazionale (Ita) (1998-99), Manchester United (Eng) (1999-)
• Left-sided central defender who left France to join Internazionale after playing just 49 French League games for Rennes. Silvestre and his team-mate **Ousmane Dabo** were offered such derisory terms after graduating from the youth team that they refused to sign the contracts, and moved to Inter on Bosman-style free transfers.
• Dubbed the '**Lilian Thuram** of the next century' by Inter great Sandro Mazzola, but was played out of position and then sidelined by new boss **Marcello Lippi** at the start of the 1999-2000 season.
• Joined Manchester United in September 1999.
• 'The atmosphere in England is much more relaxed than in Italy.'

SILVINHO
Full name: Sylvio Mendes Campos Junior
Defender, Brazilian, 173cm, 67kg

orn: 12.04.74, Sao Paulo, Brazil
lubs: Corinthians (1995-99), Arsenal (Eng) (1999-)
ull international (Brazil)
Left-sided defender who joined Arsenal in a
4million transfer from Corinthians in summer
999. Can also play in midfield.
Seen as the long-term replacement to veteran
•ft-back **Nigel Winterburn**, who left Highbury in
ummer 2000.

LAYER
IMAK, Jan
lidfielder, Czech, 182cm, 73kg
orn: 13.10.78, Czech Republic
lubs: Chmel Blsany
Another product of village team Chmel Blsany's
outh policy, this young midfield prospect has
•een a first-team regular for some time.
A member of the Czech Under-21 team that lost
•ut to Italy in the Final of the 2000 European
hampionships.

PLAYER
SIMANIC, Jovo
lefender, Yugoslav, 194cm, 90kg
orn: 08.08.65, Lazarevo, Yugoslavia
lubs: VfB Stuttgart (Ger), Proleter Zrenjanin,
• Tall, experienced sweeper who made headlines
•n the 1992-93 season when, while at Stuttgart,
:oach **Christoph Daum** sent him on as the fourth
foreigner in a Champions League match against
Leeds. Eventually the Germans paid a heavy price
for that error: the match had to be replayed and
they were eliminated.

PLAYER
SIMAO SABROSA
Full name: Simao Pedro Fonseca Sabrosa
Forward, Portuguese, 170cm, 64kg
Born: 30.10.79, Constatim, Portugal
Clubs: Sporting Lisbon (1996-99), Barcelona
(Spa) (1999-)
Full international (Portugal) 1 cap/1 goal

• Portuguese whizzkid whose £9.2million transfer
from Sporting to Barça in the summer of 1999
led to the inevitable comparisons with **Luis Figo.**
• Like Figo he plays on the right side of attack,
but, as understudy to Figo, had few opportunities
in the 1999-2000 season to demonstrate his
potential. Figo's move to Real Madrid may now
give him more opportunities.

PLAYER
SIMEONE, Diego
Midfielder, Argentinian, 177cm, 70kg
Born: 28.04.70, Buenos Aires, Argentina
Clubs: Velez Sarsfield (1987-90), Pisa (Ita) (1990-
92), Sevilla (Spa) (1992-94), Atletico Madrid (Spa)
(1994-97), Internazionale (Ita) (1997-99), Lazio
(Ita) (1999-)
Full international (Argentina) 92 caps/11 goals
• Tough, uncompromising midfielder who has
won League titles in Spain (Atletico Madrid) and
Italy (Lazio).
• Famous for being the recipient of **David
Beckham's** boot, a foul which resulted in the
Englishman's red card in the 1998 World Cup.
• Cut his teeth in Italy with relegated Pisa, before
moving to Spain, where he established his
reputation as a tough defensive central defender
with playmaker potential.
• Joined Lazio in June 1999, as a makeweight in
the world-record transfer of **Christian Vieri** to
Inter; he was rated as £6million.

PLAYER
SIMEUNOVIC, Marko
Goalkeeper, Slovenia, 190cm, 76kg
Born: 06.12.67, Maribor, Slovenia
Clubs: Red Star Belgrade (Yug), Olimpia
Ljubljana, Sakaryaspor (Tur), Maribor
Full international (Slovenia) 28 caps/0 goals
• Agile, confident keeper who is an excellent
shot-stopper. Was first-choice keeper for
Slovenia until injury forced him out of the Euro
2000 play-off against Ukraine.

PLAYER
SIMIC, Dario
Defender, Croatian, 180cm, 77kg
Born: 12.11.75, Zagreb, Croata.
Clubs: Croatia Zagreb (1992-99), Internazionale (Ita) (1999-)
Full international (Croatia) 36 caps/1 goal
• Powerful central defender who played in all of Croatia's matches in the 1998 World Cup except the third-place play-off.
• Nicknamed 'Pitball' because he owns two.
• Was linked to a host of Italian clubs in 1998, including Milan and Juventus, but eventually joined Inter in January 1999.

PLAYER
SIMIC, Josip
Forward, Croatian, 177cm, 76kg
Born: 16.09.77, Croatia
Clubs: Croatia Zagreb (1994-)
Full international (Croatia) 6 caps/1 goal
• Striker whose career has was slowed by a rare muscle spasm condition which was eventually cured following of specialist treatment in Switzerland.
• Younger brother of **Dario Simic**.
• Made his international debut against South Korea in Seoul in June 1999.

PLAYER
SIMO, Augustine
Midfielder, Cameroonian, 174cm, 82kg
Born: 18.09.78, Cameroon
Clubs: Torino (Ita), Lugano (Swi), Neuchatel Xamax (Swi) (1999-)
• Chunky and explosive Cameroon international striker with Neuchatel Xamax, who, in addition, can play on the shoulder of the strikers. Once on the books of Torino and Lugano, he helped his country's Under 20-side win the African championship in 1995.

PLAYER
SIMONE, Marco
Forward, Italian, 170cm, 68kg
Born: 07.01.69, Castellanza, Italy
Clubs: Como (1986-87), Virescit (1987-88), Como (1988-89), Milan (1989-97), PSG (Fra) (1997-99), Monaco (Fra) (1999-)
Full international (Italy) 4 caps/0 goals
• He was off-colour for most of the 1998-99 campaign at Paris Saint-Germain and many considered the Italian frontrunner as past his sell-by date. But he has bounced back with a vengeance following a move to Monaco and proved a highly influential figure in their conquest of the French League title last season, scoring 21 goals and making 12 more. A brilliant dribbler, very mobile and full of inventiveness, he represents the perfect compliment to a more physical central striker.
• 'Some journalists wrote that I came to Monaco as a pre-retirement exercise, to take the money and run. I think I've put the record straight.'
• Surname pronounced See mo nay.

ADMINISTRATOR
SIMONET, Claude
• President of the French Football Federation.

COACH
SIMONI, Luigi
Italian
Born: 22.01.39
• Respected coach who made his name at Cremonese and Napoli, earning a move to Internazionale in the summer of 1997.
• Sacked by Inter midway through the 1998-99 season, and moved on to Piacenza, but could not prevent relegation in May 2000.
• Known as Gigi.

COACH
SIMONSEN, Allan
Danish
Born: 15.11.52
• Former European Footballer of the year who has been national coach of the Faroe Islands since 1995.
• Won 56 caps for Denmark, scoring 21 goals.

PLAYER
SIMPSON, Pascal
Forward, Swedish, 193cm, 93kg
Born: 04.05.71, Sweden
Clubs: AIK (1991-97), Valerenga (Nor) (1998-)
• Swede who joined Valerenga from AIK two seasons ago. Struggled with injuries in his first season but seemed fitter and lighter in 1999. Strong in the air and a natural finisher.

PLAYER
SINCLAIR, Frank
Defender, Jamaican, 176cm, 80kg
Born: 03.12.71, Lambeth, England
Clubs: Chelsea (1989-98), West Brom (1991-92, loan), Leicester (1998-)
Full international (Jamaica)
• Central defender who was squeezed out of Chelsea by the arrival of **Frank Leboeuf** and **Marcel Desailly**, joining Leicester in autumn 1998.
• Accepted an invitation to play for Jamaica at the 1998 World Cup, but only after the Reggae Boyz had qualified for the finals. Played all three matches at France 98.

PLAYER
SINCLAIR, Trevor
Forward, English, 179cm, 81kg
Born: 02.03.73, Dulwich, England
Clubs: Blackpool (1989-93), QPR (1993-1998), West Ham (1998-)
• Attacker who began as a winger but can also play in a more central attacking role for West Ham.
• A former England Under-21 international who

has been on the fringes of the senior squad for some time, but has yet to win his first cap.

PLAYER
SIONKO, Libor
Midfielder, Czech, 176cm, 70kg
Born: 01.02.77, Czech Republic
Clubs: Banik Ostrava, Sparta Prague (1999-)
Full international (Czech Republic) 1 cap/0 goals
• Young attacking midfielder who moved to Prague from hated rivals Banik Ostrava before the 1999-2000 season as part of Sparta's attempts to build a squad capable of competing in the Champions League.
• Sionko can play as an out-and-out striker, providing Sparta with an extra attacking option.
• Member of the Czech squad that won silver at the 2000 Under-21 European Championships.

PLAYER
SISCHIN, Oleg
Midfielder, Moldovan, 178cm, 72kg
Born: 07.01.75, Moldova
Clubs: Spumante Cricovo, Constructorul Chisinau, CSKA Moscow (Rus)
Full international (Moldova) 21 caps/0 goals
• One of the leading figures in the Moldovan national team who has impressed since a move to Russia.

PLAYER
SIVIERO, Gustavo Lionel
Defender, Argentinian, 182cm, 80kg
Born: 13.09.69, Sante Fe, Argentina
Clubs: San Lorenzo (1992-93), Newell's Old Boys (1993-96), Lanus (1996-98), Mallorca (Spa) (1998-)
• Solid, disciplined centre-back who formed a strong partnership with **Marcelino Elena** when Mallorca reached the 1999 European Cup-winners Cup Final.
• Signed in summer 1998 by then Mallorca coach **Hector Cuper** from Cuper's old club Lanus as a replacement for Real Madrid-bound **Ivan Campo**.

Alexei Smertin

PLAYER
SIVILIA, Nir
Forward, Israeli, 164cm, 66kg
Born: 26.5.75
Clubs: Betar Jerusalem
Full international (Israel) 13 caps/1 goal
• A tall and fast striker, Sivilia has never lived up to his full potential. Athough he scores frequently, he should do much better given the amount of times he get in front of goal. But he is always a danger man and as a substitute has seen Betar Jerusalem out of trouble on many occasions.

PLAYER
SKACEL, Jindrich
Goalkeeper, Czech, 202cm, 90kg
Born: 03.11.77, Czech Republic
Clubs: Sigma Olomouc
• Giant, unsettled goalkeeper who lost his place at both club level and Under-21 team level to team-mate Tomas Bures but who still has time to make his mark at a high level.

PLAYER
SKACHENKO, Serhii
Forward, Ukrainian, 185cm, 72kg
Born: 18.11.72, Kaz, Ukraine
Clubs: Metallist Kharkov, Torpedo Moscow, Cheloka, Dynamo Kiev (1994-96), Lucky Gold Stars (Kor) (1996-97), Torpedo Moscow (1998-99), Metz (Fra) (1999-)
Full international (Ukraine) 15 caps/3 goals
• A hard-working and brave Ukraine national team forward blessed with the speed of an Olympic sprinter. The problem, though, is his lack of durability. He does seem injury-prone. Signed by Metz for the 1999-2000 season after spells in Ukraine, South Korea and Russia.

PLAYER
SKAMMELSRUD, Bent
Midfielder, Norwegian, 178cm, 76kg
Born: 18.05.66, Sarpsborg, Norway

Clubs: Malmo (Swe) (1990), Rosenborg (1991-97), Bayer Leverkusen (Ger) (1997-98), Rosenborg (1998-)
Full international (Norway) 37 caps/6 goals
• Experienced international midfielder who returned for family reasons to Rosenborg after a spell in the German Bundesliga. Has won eight Norwegian League titles and played over 200 League matches for his club, many as captain.

PLAYER
SKERLA, Andrius
Defender, Lithuanian, 185cm, 74kg
Born: 29.04.77, Vilnius, Lithuania
Clubs: Zalgiris Vilnius (1995-97), PSV Eindhoven (Hol) (1997-2000), Dunfermline (Sco) (2000-)
Full international (Lithuania)
• Lithuanian international and a member of the national team despite being a regular on the bench at PSV.
• Had been waiting for his breakthrough ever since **Bobby Robson** bought him. Even with many key defenders injured for a long time he didn't get a chance at PSV. Moved to Scotland in summer 2000.
• Can play at right-back or in central defence. A modest but reliable defender.

COACH
SKIBBE, Michael
German
Born: 04.08.65
• Became the youngest coach in the history of the Bundesliga when, aged just 32, he was appointed first-team boss at Borussia Dortmund in the summer of 1998. He had previously spent the previous 11 years working with the youth teams of Schalke and Dortmund, but despite his lack of experience, he enjoyed a good first season with the pros, steering the 'Dortmunder' to a Champions League qualifying place.
• But the 1999-2000 season was a nightmare for him and with the team plummeting down the

League, he was sent back to the youth set-up.
• He remains well-respected in Germany and was announced as an assistant to new German national team coach **Rudi Voller**.

COACH
SKOVDAHL, Ebbe
Danish
• Recruited from Brondby at the end of the 1999-2000 season, Skovdahl was charged with the task of rejuvenating an Aberdeen side which appeared to have lost its way, and promptly led them to the worst series of results in the club's history.
• A mid-season surge in form was not enough to prevent the Dons finishing bottom of the Premier League, but they avoided the ignominy of relegation due to a technicality. On the bright side, Skovdahl led Aberdeen to both domestic cup finals and has freshened up the side with the signings of talented players such as **Arild Stavrum** and **Hakim Zerouali**.

PLAYER
SKRYPNIK, Victor
Defender, Ukrainian, 183cm, 78kg
Born: 19.11.69, Novomoskvsk, Ukraine
Clubs: Metalurg (1991-94), Dnipro (1994-96), Werder Bremen (Ger) (1996-)
Full international (Ukraine) 16 caps/2 goals
• Steely stopper who transferred from Dnipro to German club Werder Bremen three years ago. Vastly experienced. He is hardly visible on the field but is always in the right part of the field at the time he is most needed.

PLAYER
SLONCIK, Radek
Midfielder, Czech, 174cm, 73kg
Born: 29.05.73, Czech Republic
Clubs: Banik Ostrava, Sparta Prague (2000-)
Full international (Czech Republic) 17 caps/0 goals
• Finally joined Sparta shortly after the winter break in the 1999-2000 season following years of

Nolberto Solano

rumours and months of negotiations.

• This creative midfielder is generally considered to be one of the best in the Czech League but serious injury has prevented him making an appearance for Sparta or challenging for a spot in the Euro 2000 squad.

COACH
SMAIJOVIC, Dragan
• National coach of Bosnia-Herzegovina since 2000.

PLAYER
SMERTIN, Alexei
Midfielder, Russian, 174cm, 63kg
Born: 01.05.75, Russia
Clubs: Zarya (1994-97), Urulan (1997-98), Lokomotiv Moscow (1999-)
Full international (Russia) 12 caps/0 goals
• One of the stars of the Russian League and the Russian national team. A hugely versatile player who is good at the back and in midfield, with great dribbling and shooting ability.

PLAYER
SMETANIN, Andrei
Goalkeeper, Russian, 195cm, 95kg
Born: 21.06.69, Russia
Clubs: Dinamo Moscow (1988-98), Moscow Spartak (1998-)
• Spartak's reserve goalkeeper, a tall and strong player who is close to challenging **Alexander Filimonov** for the number one spot at club and country level.

PLAYER
SMICER, Vladimir
Midfielder, Czech, 180cm, 71kg
Born: 24.05.73, Decin, Czech Republic
Clubs: Slavia Prague (1992-96), Lens (Fra) (1996-1999), Liverpool (Eng) (1999-)
Full international (Czech Republic) 44 caps/18 goals
• Attacker who has come on leaps and bounds at Liverpool after coming to prominence in 1996,

first with Slavia Prague's run to the UEFA Cup semi-finals, and then in the Czech Republic's surprise appearance in the Euro 96 Final.
• Came through the youth ranks at Slavia, rebuilding his career after a serious knee injury and earning a transfer to Lens in 1996. He won the French League title two years later.
• Had to leave the Czech camp before the Final Euro 96…to get married. He not planned on the Czechs getting that far in the competition and planned his wedding accordingly.

PLAYER
SMITH, Alan
Forward, English, 176cm, 66kg
Born: 28.10.80, Wakefield, England
Clubs: Leeds United (1998-)
• One of the brighest prospects to have come through the Leeds youth system in recent years. A precocious young striker with potent mix of confidence and good technique.

COACH
SMITH, Jim
English
Born: 17.10.40
• Veteran manager who has been in charge of Derby since 1994. Has proved himself to be a canny operator in the transfer market, particularly in spotting and signing players from overseas.
• Nicknamed 'the Bald Eagle'.

AGENT
SMITH, Jon
• London-based agent who runs the First Artist group with his brother Phil Smith. Clients include **Kevin Phillips**, **Les Ferdinand** and **Darren Huckerby**.
• **Contact:** First Artist House, 87 Wembley Hill Road, Wembley, Middlesex, HA9 8BU, England. Tel: 44 (0) 20 8900 18 18.

COACH
SMITH, Walter
Scottish
Born: 24.02.48
• Manager of Everton since 1999, who has produced good results despite limited resources at the Merseyside club.
• At Rangers, first as assistant to Graeme Souness and then as manager in his own right, he oversaw the most successful period in the club's history in which they won nine successful Scottish League titles.

BUSINESS
SMITH, Roland
• Former chairman of British Aerospace who is chairman of Manchester United plc, and a crucial figure in United becoming the world's richest club.

PLAYER
SMITS, Rudy
Defender, Belgian, 178cm, 73kg
Born: 12.08.63, Deurne, Belgium
Clubs: Antwerp (1990-97), Charleroi (1997-98), Ekeren (1998-99), GBA (1999-2000), Mechelen (2000-)
Full international (Belgium) 33 caps/1 goals
• Veteran defender with a total of 472 League matches.
• Has played for Antwerp nearly all his life, even now that his former team has fused with Beerschot and Germinal Ekeren. But was allowed to leave in summer 2000 to join Mechelen.
• Played for Belgium at the World Cup finals in 1994 and lost the European Cup-winners Cup Final against Parma while with Antwerp.
• Played for Charleroi during 1997-98, but returned home after an difficult spell there.
• Started as a tight-marking and tough-tackling left-back but is now a libero with good vision and remains a determined character.

COACH
SMUDA, Franciszek
Polish
Born: 22.06.48
• Coach of Legia Warsaw who began his coaching career in 1983 with German amateur VfB Coburg, before going to Turkey, with Altay and Konyaspor. In 1993 he returned to Poland, joining Stal Mielec and then Widzew Lodz, taking them to the League title in 1996 and 1997.
• In 1999 he was a champion again with Wisla Krakow, before moving to Legia in October that year.
• Voted Poland's Manager of the Year in 1996, 1997 and 1999.

COACH
SODERBERG, Tommy
Swedish
Born: 19.08.48
• National coach of Sweden since 1997.
• A modest player with Angby and Continental who began his coaching career as a 24-year-old in 1972 at BK Vaster while also working as a PE teacher.
• Spent a number of years as coach of Brommapojkarna, before making the step up to Stockholm side Djurgardens.
• Coached AIK Stockholm to the 1992 Swedish League title and became coach of the Swedish Under-21 side in 1994 before succeeding Tommy Svensson in charge of the senior side.

PLAYER
SOKOLOWSKI, Tomasz
Midfielder, Polish, 177cm, 71kg
Born: 21.09.70, Poland
Clubs: Stomil Olszty, Legia Warsaw
Full international (Poland) 12 caps/1 goal
• Creative left-sided midfielder who has rediscovered his form after being injured for most of 1999.

PLAYER
SOKOTA, Tomislav
Forward, Croatian, 187cm, 84kg
Born: 08.04.77, Croatia
Clubs: Samobor, Croatia Zagreb
• Croatian youth international who has been a regular in the Zagreb first-team since making his debut in July 1995.

PLAYER
SOLANO, Nolberto
Midfielder, Peruvian, 174cm, 64kg
Born: 12.12.74. Callao, Peru
Clubs: Alianza Lima, Sporting Cristal (1995-97), Boca Juniors (Arg) (1997-98), Newcastle (Eng) (1998-)
Full international (Peru)
• Winger who has had mixed success in England, where managerial changes at Newcastle have unsettled him, but he remains a huge talent.
• Made his name in Sporting Cristal's run to the 1997 Libertadores Cup Final, before moving to Boca Juniors, where he was dubbed 'the little maestro' by Diego Maradona.
• Captain of Peru at the 1999 Copa America and the national team's most influential player.

PLAYER
SOLARI, Santiago
Midfielder, Argentinian, 180cm, 75kg
Born: 07.10.76, Sante Fe, Argentina
Clubs: Newell's Old Boys (1994-95), Renato Cesarini (1995-96), River Plate (1996-98), Atletico Madrid (Spa) (1999-)
Full international (Argentina)
• Gifted left-sided midfielder of whom big things were expected, but whose form suffered in Atletico Madrid's relegation at the end of the 1999-2000 season.
• Comes from a famous footballing family in Argentina. His uncle played for Argentina against England in the 1996 World Cup, while his cousin is midfielder **Fernando Redondo**.

PLAYER
SOLBAKKEN, Stale

Midfielder, Norwegian, 190cm, 81kg
Born: 27.02.68, Kirkenaer, Norway
Clubs: Ham-Kam (1992-93), Lillestrom (1994-97), Wimbledon (Eng) (1997-98), AaB Aalborg (Den) (1998-)
Full international (Norway) 58 caps/9 goals
• Midfielder who left Wimbledon after a mediocre spell in the English Premiership only to become Player of the Year in Denmark following some excellent performances for AaB.
• Highly effective at set-pieces, he has the ability to make well-timed runs forward.
• Played three times for Norway at the 1998 World Cup.

PLAYER
SOLDO, Zvonimir

Midfielder, Croatian, 189cm, 85kg
Born: 02.11.67, Zagreb, Croatia
Clubs: Dinamo Zagreb, Inker Zapresic, Croatia Zagreb, Stuttgart (Ger) (1996-)
Full international (Croatia) 47 caps/2 goals
• Trusty Croat who can line up at centre-back or as a defensive midfielder. Gritty, consistent and follows his coach's instructions to the letter. A more than decent touch on the ball too.
• Played in six of Croatia's seven games at the 1998 World Cup in France.

PLAYER
SOLER, Francisco

Full name: Francisco Soler Atencia
Midfielder, Spanish, 171cm, 69kg
Born: 05.03.70, Palma de Mallorca, Spain
Clubs: Mallorca (1990-)
• Local-born central midfielder who has spent a decade with Mallorca, the club he joined as a boy.
• Not always a regular, but performs admirably when called upon.

Ole Gunnar Solskjaer

Rigobert Song

COACH
SOLLIED, Trond
Norwegian
Born: 29.04.59
• A Norwegian coach who surprisingly steered Gent to a third place finish in the Belgian League in 1999-2000. However, he was criticised for not using local talent, instead transforming the team into 'the Chelsea of Belgium', often with 10 or 11 foreigners on the pitch.
• Because of his success he became a wanted coach, the Gent board couldn't hold on to him and he moved to Club Brugge in summer 2000.

PLAYER
SOLOMATIN, Andrei
Defender, Russian, 183cm, 80kg
Born: 09.09.75, Russia
Clubs: Lokomotiv Moscow (1995-)
Full international (Russia) 2 caps/0 goals
• Strong, versatile and brave defender who can also play in midfield.

PLAYER
SOLSKJAER, Ole Gunnar
Forward, Norwegian, 178cm, 75kg
Born: 26.02.73, Kristiandsund, Norway
Clubs: Molde (1995-96), Manchester United (Eng) (1996-)
Full international (Norway) 34 caps/14 goals
• Striker with pace, technique and a great eye for goal. His career at Manchester United has seen him mostly confined to the bench, but has acquired a reputation as a highly effective supersub, most notably when scoring the last-minute winner in the 1999 Champions League Final against Bayern Munich.
• Has been linked with a move away from Old Trafford in order to gain regular first-team football, but United have resisted any such move.
• Known as the 'Baby-faced Assassin'.

SOLTVEDT, Trond Egil

Midfielder, Norwegian, 186cm, 81kg
Born: 15.12.67, Voss, Norway
Clubs: Viking Stavanger (1988-91), Brann (1992-1994), Rosenborg (1995-97), Coventry (Eng) 1997-99), Southampton (Eng) (1999-)
Full international (Norway) 4 caps/0 goals
• Combative midfielder who has had more luck at Southampton than at Coventry, where he struggled to establish himself.

SOMA, Ragnvald

Midfielder, Norwegian
Born: 10.11.78, Norway
Clubs: Bryne
• Norwegian under-21 international who can play midfield or defence. A strong fighter who has been targeted by a number of foreign clubs.

SOMALIA

Full name: Wanderson de Paula Sabino
Forward, Brazilian, 192cm, 71kg
Born: 22.06.76, Nova Vencia, Brazil
Clubs: America (1997-99), Feyenoord (Hol) (1999-)
• Tall Brazilian striker who came on loan from America MG. Was the hero of Rotterdam when scoring a vital goal against Rosenborg to clinch Feyenoord's second round ticket in the Champions League. Promptly his contract was renewed. Often used as a supersub although that isn't quite his style. Good in the air.

SOMERS, Hans

Midfielder, Belgian, 183cm, 78kg
Born: 09.03.78, Belgium
Clubs: Lierse (1996-)
• Promising Under-21 international midfielder who played a major role in Lierse's 1999 Belgian Cup triumph.

SOMMEIL, David

Defender, French, 179cm, 73kg
Born: 10.08.74, Pointe-a-Pitre, France
Clubs: Saint-Lo, Caen (1993-98), Rennes (1999-)
• Classy stopper or libero, who was a member of **Roger Lemerre**'s side which clinched the world military title in 1995 and helped Caen win the French second division a year later. One of three Rennes players recently in trouble with the law for a bar brawl.
• Dah veed Som may.

SONG, Rigobert

Defender, Cameroonian, 183cm, 75kg
Born: 01.07.76, Nkanglicock, Cameroon
Clubs: Tonerre Yaounde (1993-94), Metz (Fra) (1994-98), Salernitana (Ita) (1998-99), Liverpool (Eng) (1998-)
Full international (Cameroon)
• Left-sided defender who holds the dubious distinction of being the first player sent off in successive World Cup finals, as well as the youngest player to be shown a red card at a World Cup.
• Was a surprise inclusion in Cameroon's squad for the 1994 World Cup finals, aged just 17. But against Brazil he was sent off, although it did not put off Metz, who signed him after the tournament.
• Four years later in France he was sent off again, for elbowing **Marcelo Salas**.
• Was sickly as a child, but was encouraged to play football by his father. His idol was **Ronald Koeman** and he went on to captain Cameroon at the 1993 World Youth Cup in Australia.
• Has set up his own club in Yaounde, Noctambule.

SONGO'O, Jacques

Goalkeeper, Cameroon, 182cm, 80kg
Born: 17.03.64, Sakbeyenne, Cameroon
Clubs: Toulon (Fra) (1989-92), Le Mans (Fra) (1992-93), Metz (Fra) (1993-96), Deportivo La

Coruna (Spa) (1999-)
Full international (Cameroon)
• Cameroon national team goalkeeper and captain who played second fiddle for years to Thomas Nkono and Joseph Antoine Bell before finally become the number one.
• A surprise out-of-contract signing by Deportivo from Metz in 1996, having played only 122 French League games since arriving in France from Canon Yaounde in 1989.
• Named best keeper in the Spanish Liga in 1997 after conceding only 30 goals in 37 matches.
• Played as a striker as a teenager, becoming a goalkeeper by accident when his team's regular keeper was unavailable.
• Won the African Nations Cup with Cameroon in 1988 and again in 2000.
• Captain of Cameroon at the 1998 World Cup, having been in goal for the 6-1 thrashing by Russia at the 1994 World Cup.

PLAYER
SORENSEN, Jan Derek
Forward, Norwegian, 177cm, 75kg
Born: 28.12.71, Norway
Clubs: Lyn (1992-94), Bodo/Glimt (1995-97), Rosenborg (1998-)
Full international (Norway) 6 caps/0 goals
• Winger with explosive pace who was signed by Rosenborg in 1998 to replace Harald Brattbakk.
• Can outpace most defenders and is a lethal weapon down the right flank. Had hoped to get into the Euro 2000 squad. Used to be a striker and has carried on scoring goals.

PLAYER
SORENSEN, Palle
Midfielder, Danish, 177cm, 68kg
Born: 04.04.72, Denmark
Clubs: Viborg (1996-)
• Right-sided defender who was originally a goalscoring midfielder at Danish club AGF. Scored a memorable goal in the 1992 Danish Cup Final.

PLAYER
SORENSEN, Thomas
Goalkeeper, Danish, 193cm, 82kg
Born: 12.06.76, Denmark
Clubs: Odense (1997-98), Sunderland (Eng) (1998-)
Full international (Denmark) 1 cap/0 goals
• Talented young keeper who has been earmarked as the long-term successor to **Peter Schmeichel** in the Danish national side.
• Good in the air and capable of outstanding saves, he make a belated international debut in the Euro 2000 play-off against Israel.

PLAYER
SOSA, Roberto
Forward, Argentinian, 189cm, 86kg
Born: 24.01.75, Buenos Aires, Argentina
Clubs: Gimnasia del Plata (1995-98), Udinese (Ita) (1998-)
• Strong, powerful striker who was signed by Udinese in 1998 to replace the Milan-bound **Oliver Bierhoff.**

PLAYER
SOTTIL, Andrea
Defender, Italian, 185cm, 73kg
Born: 04.01.74, Venaria, Italy
Clubs: Torino (1992-94), Fiorentina (1994-96), Atalanta (1996-99), Udinese (1999-)
• Central defender who has gained a reputation in Italy for being one of the most aggressive players in Serie A, although he appears to have calmed down at Udinese.

PLAYER
SOUMAH, Morlaye
Defender, French/Guinean, 177cm, 70kg
Born: 04.11.71, Conakry, Guinea
Clubs: Bastia (1992-93), Valenciennes (1993-94), Bastia (1994-)
Full international (Guinea)
• He may be one of the French League's least demonstrative players, but the Guinean libero is

Gareth Southgate

nevertheless one of the most influential. His composure, astute positioning and sound distribution form the bedrock of Bastia's competiveness. His younger brother Ousmane is a forward on Bastia's books.

COACH
SOUNESS, Graeme
Scottish
Born: 06.05.53
• Coach of Blackburn Rovers since spring 2000, his first job in England since returning from a spell in Portugal in charge of Benfica.
• A world-class midfielder for Middlesbrough, Liverpool, Sampdoria and Scotland who ended his playing career with Rangers as player-manager. In Glasgow he reversed a traditional transfer trend by importing English players, and won a string of League titles as a result. Was unable to repeat the success at Liverpool after succeeding Kenny Dalglish.
• Has since had mixed success with Galatasaray, Southampton, Torino and Benfica.

COACH
SOUSA, Antonio
Portuguese
Born: 28.04.57
• One of the most promising young coaches in Portugal who guided Beira-Mar to a totally unexpected Cup success in 1999 and though they were relegated from the First Division the same season, he quickly repaired the damage by masterminding promotion in 1999-2000 .
• Favours a 4-1-3-2 formation and is famous for scoring FC Porto's goal in their 2-1 European Cup-winners Cup Final defeat by Juventus in 1984.

PLAYER
SOUTHGATE, Gareth
Defender, English, 184cm, 78kg
Born: 03.09.70, Watford, England
Clubs: Crystal Palace (1989-95), Aston Villa

Dejan Stankovic

(1995-2000)

Full international (England) 37 caps/1 goal

• Central defender who will always be remembered for the penalty miss in England's defeat by Germany in the semi-final of Euro 96.

• An accomplished defender who is comfortable on the ball – as you would expect from a former midfielder. Converted to a centre-back by Brian Little after a £2million transfer to Aston Villa from Crystal Palace in 1995.

• Eloquent and intelligent off the pitch, he wrote his own column for a local newspaper when captain of Palace in the 1994-95 season.

PLAYER
SPEED, Gary
Midfielder, Welsh, 180cm, 80kg
Born: 08.09.69, Mancot, Wales
Clubs: Leeds (1988-96), Everton (1996-98), Newcastle (1998-)
Full international (Wales) 58 caps/3 goals

• Central or left-sided midfielder who won the English League title with Leeds in 1991. A good athlete, he covers a lot of ground, and scores more than his fair share of goals.

PLAYER
SPEHAR, Robert
Forward, Croatian, 184cm, 81kg
Born: 13.05.70, Osijek, Croatia
Clubs: Osijek (1992-93), Croatia Zagreb (1993-94), Osijek (1994-95), Club Brugge (Bel) (1995-97), Monaco (Fra) (1997-99), Verona (Ita) (1999-2000), Sporting Lisbon (Por) (2000-)
Full international (Croatia) 5 caps/0 goals

• Striker who enjoyed the best spell of his career in Belgium, where he was League top scorer in the 1996-97 season with 26 goals for Club Brugge. He had struggled initially to establish himself at first in Belgium after finishing as top scorer in the Croatian League in 1994-95.

• Moved to Monaco in 1997, but did not enjoy the same sort of success and moved on for spells in

aly and Portugal, where he arrived midway
through the 1999-2000 season and helped
Sporting win the League title.

PLAYER
SPENCER, John
Forward, Scottish, 169cm, 73kg
Born: 11.09.70, Glasgow, Scotland
Clubs: Greenock Morton (1988-89), Rangers
(1990-92), Chelsea (1992-96), QPR (1996-98),
Everton (1998), Motherwell (1998-)
Full international (Scotland) 14 caps/0 goals
• After initially turning out for Motherwell on loan
from Everton, the former Rangers and Chelsea
striker finally secured a move from Goodison to
Fir Park where he has, possibly for the first time
in his career, enjoyed a prolonged run at first-
team level. Spencer has been a prolific scorer
and committed performer for 'Well during his
time at the Lanarkshire club.

PLAYER
SPILACEK, Radek
Midfielder, Czech, 181cm, 74kg
Born: 10.01.80, Czech Republic
Clubs: Opava
• Young defender or defensive midfielder who
has been a first team regular with Opava for some
time. Was one of the few first-team regulars to
figure in an Under-20 international friendly
against Israel designed to give Under-21s coach
Karel Bruckner a chance to look at the next
generation in the spring of 2000.

PLAYER
SRNICEK, Pavel
Goalkeeper, Czech, 189cm, 92 kg
Born: 10.03.68, Ostrava, Czech Republic
Clubs: Banik Ostrava (1989-90), Newcastle (Eng)
(1990-98), Banik Ostrava (1998-99), Sheffield Wed
(Eng) (1998-2000), Brescia (Ita) (2000-)
Full international (Czech Republic) 34 caps/0 goals
• Keeper who was first choice for the Czech

Republic at Euro 2000 after winning his place
following a return to form at Sheffield
Wednesday, despite being relegated in May 2000.
• An excellent shot-stopper, he fell out of favour
at Newcastle and returned home to Banik
Ostrava, only to be offered another chance in
England by Wednesday in November 1998.
• Joined newly-promoted Brescia in summer 2000.

PLAYER
SRUTWA, Mariusz
Forward, Polish, 183cm, 73kg
Born: 15.07.71, Poland
Clubs: Ruch Chorzow, Legia Warsaw, Ruch
Chorzow (2000-)
Full international (Poland) 5 caps/0 goals
• Experienced striker who had an unsuccessful
year at Legia Warsaw before rejoining Ruch in
January 2000.

PLAYER
STAELENS, Lorenzo
Defender, Belgian, 185cm, 91kg
Born: 30.04.64, Kortrijk, Belgium
Clubs: Kortrijk, Club Brugge (1989-98),
Anderlecht (1998-)
Full international (Belgium) 71 caps/8 goals
• Veteran defender and former midfielder who
now operates as a tough-tackling, ball-playing
libero.
• Despite his age, he is one of the best players in
the Belgian League, winning then 1999 Player of
the Year award.
• Made the controversial switch from Club
Brugge to Anderlecht in 1998 after nine seasons
with Club Brugge, winning the Belgian League
and Cup double in 1996.
• Played for Belgium at the 1990, 1994 and 1998
World Cups, and at Euro 2000.
• Made his international debut for Belgium
against Romania in May 1990. Announced his
retirement from international football after Euro
2000.

Gintaras Stauce

PLAYER
STAM, Jaap

Defender, Dutch, 188cm, 85kg
Born: 17.07.72, Kampen, Holland
Clubs: Zwolle (1992-93), Cambuur (1993-95)
Willem II (1995-96), PSV (1995-98), Manchester
United (Eng) (1998-)
Full international (Holland) 36 caps/3 goals
• Generally considered to be one of the world's
best defenders. A speedy and powerful centre-back
who has made a huge impression at Old Trafford
since since his move from PSV in May 1988.
• Played all seven games for Holland at France
98, having made his international debut against
Germany in April 1996. Was a late replacement
for the injured **Frank De Boer** at Euro 96, but did
not play.
• Started his career as a midfielder, but switched
to central defence and set a world record fee for a
defender, £10.75million, when he joined United.
• Won the treble in his first season at Old Trafford.

PLAYER
STANDFEST, Joachim

Defender, Austrian, 180cm, 70kg
Born: 30.05.80, Austria
Clubs: Grazer AK (1998-)
• Austrian Under-21 international who established
himself at Grazer AK in the 1998-99 season.

PLAYER
STANIC, Mario

Midfielder, Croatian, 187cm, 82kg
Born: 10.04.72, Sarajevo, Bosnia
Clubs: Zeljeznicar (1988-92), Croatia Zagreb
(1992-93), Sporting Gijon (Spa) (1993-94), Benfica
(Por) (1994-95), Club Brugge (Bel) (1995-96),
Parma (Ita) (1997-2000), Chelsea (Eng) (2000-)
Full international (Croatia) 35 caps/7 goals
• Gutsy, right-sided midfielder who can double
up as a striker. Is very effective in the air, and
his combative attitude makes him a useful option
as a substitute.

At Club Brugge, he earned a reputation as a goal scorer, scoring 20 goals in the 1995-96 season. Started with Zeljeznicar in Sarejevo but had to leave when Serb forces began bombing the city. Everything he owned in Sarajevo was destroyed when a tank crashed into his house. Moved to Chelsea in a £5.6million deal.

PLAYER
STANKOVIC, Dejan
Midfielder, Yugoslav, 181cm, 75kg
Born: 11.09.78, Belgrade, Yugoslavia
Clubs: Red Star Belgrade (1994-98), Lazio (Ita) 1998-)
Full international (Yugoslavia) 20 caps/6 goals
• Ex-Red Star wunderkind who joined Lazio in a £8million transfer aged 19 in spring 1998.
• A powerful ball-winner but also a skilful playmaker with an eye for goal.
• Scored twice on his international debut, against South Korea (22.04.98).
• Enjoyed a fruitful first season in Italy, holding down a regular first-team place and scoring nine goals in 40 matches.
• Comes from a footballing family: father Borislav was a winger with OFK Belgrade and mother Dragica played centre-forward for leading women's side Sloga Zemun.
• Played libero as a youngster, has featured as a right wing-back for Yugoslavia and has played in attacking midfield for Lazio.
• **Sven Goran Eriksson**: 'Stankovic is the most complete player at Lazio. If he continues playing like he does, in two years time he will be the best midfielder in world football.'

PLAYER
STANKOVIC, Jovan
Midfielder, Yugoslav, 184cm, 78kg
Born: 04.03.71, Belgrade, Yugoslavia
Clubs: Red Star Belgrade (1992-95), Mallorca (Spa) (1996-)
Full international (Yugoslavia) 9 caps/0 goals

• Hard-working left-winger whose pinpoint crosses have been a crucial weapon in Real Mallorca's success in recent seasons.
• Free-kick specialist who has become one of the most sought after players in Spain since his 1995 transfer from Red Star Belgrade.
• International debut for Yugoslavia, v Brazil (23.09.98).

PLAYER
STAROSTYAK, Mykhailo
Defender, Ukrainian, 182cm, 72kg
Born: 13.10.73, Ukraine
Clubs: Shakhtar
Full international (Ukraine) 6 caps/0 goals
• Highly versatile player who can operate either on the right or centre of defence, or as a supporting player in midfield. He also likes to attack.

PLAYER
STATUTO, Francesco
Midfielder, Italian, 174cm, 67kg
Born: 13.07.71, Rome, Italy
Clubs: Casertana (1990-92), Cosenza (1992-93), Udinese (1993-94), Roma (1994-97), Piacenza (1999-)
Full international (Italy) 3 caps/0 goals
• Midfielder who enjoyed a good spell at Roma before moving to Piacenza, who were relegated in May 2000.

PLAYER
STAUCE, Gintaras
Goalkeeper, Lithuanian, 187cm, 80kg
Born: 24.12.69, Lithuania
Clubs: Spartak Moscow, Galatasaray, Karsiyaka (Tur), Sariyer (Tur), Duisburg (Ger) (1997-)
Full international (Lithuania) 45 caps/0 goals
• Talented Lithuanian who was rated the best keeper in the Bundesliga in the 1998-99 campaign. Amazingly quick reflexes, a good catcher of the ball under pressure and a very cool customer.
• Surname pronounced St ow ser.

Ernie Stewart

PLAYER
STAURVIK, Tom Kare
Midfielder, Norwegian, 184cm, 81kg
Born: 13.02.70, Norway
Clubs: Rosenborg (1996), NAC (Hol) (1996-97), Bodo/Glimt (1997-)
Full international (Norway) 2 caps/0 goals
• Probably the player in Norway with the hardest shot. Originally a midfielder but can also play as a central defender.

PLAYER
STAVRUM, Arnvil
Forward, Norwegian, 183cm, 83kg
Born: 16.04.72, Norway
Clubs: Brann (1991-93), Molde (1993-96), Stabaek (1997), Helsingborg (Swe) (1998-2000), Aberdeen (Sco) (2000-)
Full international (Norway) 2 caps/0 goals
• Like team mate **Zerouali**, the Norwegian helped raise the spirits of the Aberdeen supporters when he arrived at Pittodrie midway through the 1999-2000 season from Helsingborg. A series of goals and a refreshingly positive attitude which seemed to spread throughout his under-achieving team mates who, despite poor form in the league, took the club to both domestic cup finals.

PLAYER
STAUNTON, Steve
Defender, Irish, 183cm, 81kg
Born: 19.01.69. Drogheda Republic of Ireland
Clubs: Liverpool (1987-91), Bradford (1987-88, loan), Aston Villa (1991-98), Liverpool (1998-)
Full international (Republic of Ireland) 84 caps/6 goals
• Veteran left-sided defender who has been a regular for the Republic of Ireland for more than a decade.
• Was sold by **Graeme Souness** to Aston Villa in 1991 only to be bought back by Liverpool seven years later.

STEEN NIELSEN, Brian
Midfielder, Danish, 180cm, 73kg
Born: 28.12.68, Vejle, Denmark
Clubs: OB (1992-93), Fenerbahce (Tur) (1993-95), OB (1995-96), Urawa Red Diamonds (Jap) (1996), OB (1996-98), AB (1998-)
Full international (Denmark) 55 caps/2 goals
  Veteran central midfielder who is now playing his football back home in Denmark with AB Copenhagen.
• Dubbed the 'grey man' of the Danish national side, an essential mopper-up of trouble who rarely wins any plaudits.
• Has had spells in Turkey and Japan, but is best known for owning and cooking in his own pizzeria in his home town of Vejle.
• International debut v Egypt in February 1990.

PLAYER
STEFANOVIC, Dejan
Defender, Yugoslav, 187cm, 81kg
Born: 28.10.74, Yugoslavia
Clubs: Red Star Belgrade (1992-95), Sheffield Wednesday (Eng) (1995-99), Vitesse Arnhem (Hol) (1999-)
Full international (Yugoslavia) 10 caps/0 goals
• Central defender who won the Yugoslav League with Red Star but had an inconsistent time in England with Sheffield Wednesday, whom he joined with Darko Kovacevic, and was offloaded to Holland.

PLAYER
STELEA, Bogdan
Goalkeeper, Romanian, 182cm, 81kg
Born: 05.12.67, Bucharest, Romania
Clubs: Dinamo Bucharest (1987-91), Mallorca (Spa) (1991-94), Rapid Bucharest (1994-95), Steaua Bucharest (1995-97), Salamanca (Spa) (1997-)
Full international (Romania) 69 caps/0 goals
• Much-travelled, shaven-headed keeper whose

international career has been dogged by criticism from those who say his shot-stopping skills are undermined by lapses of concentration.
• Has won the Romanian League and Cup double twice, with Dinamo in 1990 and Steaua in 1996.
• Made his international debut v Bulgaria in 1989.

PLAYER
STENSGAARD, Michael
Goalkeeper, Danish, 191cm, 87kg
Born: 01.09.74, Denmark
Clubs: Hvidore, Liverpool (Eng), Hvidore, Southampton (Eng), FC Copenhagen
• Keeper who has recovered from an injury which looked like ending his career.
• Was long seen as a future Danish team goalkeeper and was well established as the reserve team keeper at Liverpool when a shoulder injury was thought to have ended his career. He returned to former club Hvidore with a view to becoming goalkeeping coach, but made a remarkable recovery.
• Was signed by Southampton, but has since returned to Denmark, where he is first choice at FC Copenhagen.

AGENT
STEPHENS, Tony
• Midlands-based agent who made his name representing David Platt and has gone to represent **Alan Shearer**, **David Beckham** and **Michael Owen**.
• **Contact:** The Chantry, Leymer, West Midlands, CV7 7SB, England. Tel: 0044 (0)1676 523 602.

PLAYER
STEVANOVIC, Dragan
Forward, Yugoslav, 184cm, 81kg
Born: 16.08.71, Yugoslavia
Clubs: VfL Wolfsburg (Ger), Red Star Belgrade
• Striker with a good touch, who is strong in one-on-one challenges and physically very tough. Scored important goals in Red Star's successful run in spring 2000.

• Moved to the German Bundesliga in 1997, where he had a good start, but didn't manage to make the breakthrough.

COACH
STEVENS, Huub
Dutch
Born: 29.11.53
• Former PSV Eindhoven and Holland defender who was elevated to cult hero status by Schalke fans when he led a well-organised team of battlers to an against-the-odds triumph in the 1997 UEFA Cup. But the honeymoon is well and truly over now. Schalke are struggling and Stevens has been unable to shed his reputation as a safety-first coach whose team plays unattractive football. He is under pressure, but Schalke general manager Rudi Assauer has constantly backed him till now.

PLAYER
STEVIC Miroslav
Midfielder, Yugoslav, 179cm, 73kg
Born: 07.01.70, Ljubovija, Yugoslavia
Clubs: Bratsvo Bratunac, Partizan Belgrade, Rad Belgrade (1990-92), Grasshopper (Swi) (1992), Dynamo Dresden (Ger) (1992-94), Munich 1860 (Ger) (1994-98), Borussia Dortmund (Ger) (1998-)
Full international (Yugoslavia) 6 caps/0 goals
• Inventive Yugoslav central midfielder who provides a thoughtful and stylish link between defence and attack, but also works hard for the team and can certainly tackle.
• Nicknamed 'Mickey'.
• Surname pronounced Stay veetch.

PLAYER
STEWART, Ernie
Midfielder, American, 178cm, 70kg
Born: 28.03.69, Veghel, Holland
Clubs: VVV (Hol) (1988-90), Willem II (Hol) (1990-96), NAC (Hol) (1996-)
Full international (United States)

• Speedy winger and a Holland-born American international. Played at two World Cups, scoring at USA 94 against Colombia.
• Made a sudden switch from Willem II to rivals NAC Breda in 1996, because he was offered better financial terms. NAC were relegated in 1999 but he stayed with the club to try to earn promotion a year later.

PLAYER
STIMAC, Igor
Defender, Croatian, 186cm, 82kg
Born: 06.09.67, Metkovic, Bosnia
Clubs: Hadjuk (1992-93), Cadiz (Spa) (1992-94), Hadjuk (1994-95), Derby (Eng) (1995-99), West Ham (Eng) (1999-)
Full Internternational (Croatia) 47 caps/2 goals
• Central defender who has been one of the mainstays of the Croatian national team, having been one of the members of the Yugoslav team that won the World Youth Cup in 1987.
• Had a playboy reputation in Croatia until he married a former Miss Yugoslavia.
• Won two League championships and a Croatian Cup with Hajduk before heading for Western Europe.

PLAYER
STINGA, Ovidiu
Midfielder, Romanian, 172cm, 71kg
Born: 05.12.72, Craiova, Romania
Clubs: Univ Craoiva (1990-95), Salamanca (1995-96), PSV Eindhoven (Hol) (1996-)
Full international (Romania) 24 caps/0 goals
• Reserve for club and country in a career which has been troubled by injury.

PLAYER
STINGACIU, Dimitriu
Goalkeeper, Romanian, 194cm, 95kg
Born: 09.08.64, Brasov, Romania
Clubs: Kocaelispor (Tur) (1995-)
Full international (Romania) 5 caps/0 goals

Keeper whose size and agility have made him a
ficult opponent for forwards in the Turkish
ague to play against since his move there in
395.

PLAYER
TOGER, Peter

Midfielder, Austrian, 176cm, 67kg
Born: 11.04.66, Vienna, Austria
Clubs: Austria Vienna (1987-94), Tirol (1994-95),
apid Vienna (1995-98), LASK (1997-99), Austria
enna (1999-)
Full international (Austria) 65 caps/15 goals
• Veteran midfielder and a long-time pillar of the
ustrian national team.
• Played once for Austria at the 1998 World Cup.

PLAYER
STOICA, Alin

Midfielder, Romania, 174cm, 65kg
Born: 10.12.79, Bucharest, Romania
Clubs: Steaua Bucharest, (1995-97), Anderlecht
Bel) (1997-)
Full international (Romania) 2 caps/0 goals
• Highly gifted midfielder who took time to settle
n at Anderlecht but was expected to replace **Par**
etterberg as the team's playmaker.

PLAYER
STOICHKOV, Hristo

Forward, Bulgarian
Born: 08.02.66
Clubs: CSKA Sofia, Barcelona (Spa), Parma (Ita),
Barcelona (Spa), Major League Soccer
Full international (Bulgaria) 74 caps/36 goals
• The greatest Bulgarian footballer of all time, an
explosive personality who led Bulgaria to the
semi-finals of the 1994 World Cup and was voted
European Footballer of the Year in 1994.
• Expects to take over as national coach of
Bulgaria when he returns from a spell playing in
Major League Soccer.

PLAYER
STOJKOVIC, Dragan

Midfielder, Yugoslav, 175cm, 73kg
Born: 03.03.65, Nis, Yugoslavia
Clubs: Radnicki Nis, Red Star Belgrade, Marseille
(Fra), Hellas Verona (Ita), Nagoya Grampus Eight
(Jap)
Full international (Yugoslavia) 80 caps/15 goals
• Veteran playmaker and captain of Yugoslavia
who announced his retirement from international
football after Euro 2000 and was expected to
take up a coaching position with the Yugoslav FA
with a view to becoming national coach.
• One of Yugoslavia's greatest ever players, he
did not do himself justice in spells at Marseille
(after a £5million transfer) and Verona, and he
headed off to Japan, where the J.League has
benefitted from his elegant skills.

PLAYER
STOJANOVSKI, Milan

Midfielder, Macedonian, 183cm, 79kg
Born: 16.09.73, Vrsac, Yugoslavia
Clubs: Proleter Zrenjanin (1993-97), Partizan
Belgrade (1997-)
Full international (Macedonia) 10 caps/1 goal
• Former striker who was signed by Partizan
from Proleter Zrenjanin with a reputation as one
of the Yugoslav League's leading scorers.
• In 1998-99, when all his defenders were
injured, former Partizan coach Ljubisa
Tumbakovic put Stojanovski in the libero position.
He did so well that he has remained as sweeper
ever since.

PLAYER
STOLICA, Ilija

Midfielder, Yugoslav, 186cm, 80kg
Born: 07.07.78, Belgrade, Yugoslavia
Clubs: Lleida (Spa) (1998-99), Zemun (1999-)
• Promising midfield playmaker who spent one
season at Lleida in the Spanish second division.
• A member of Yugoslavia's Under-21 side.

PLAYER
STONE, Steve
Midfielder, English, 175cm, 78kg
Born: 20.08.71, Gateshead, England
Clubs: Nottingham (1990-99), Aston Villa (1999-)
Full International (England) 9 caps/2 goals
• Midfielder who broke into the England team under **Terry Venables** and played at Euro 96, but has struggled to establish himself at Aston Villa following a serious knee injury and relegation at Nottingham Forest.
• Most effective when playing wide on the right.

PLAYER
STOVINI, Lorenzo
Defender, Italian, 186cm, 80kg
Born: 24.11.76, Firenze, Italy
Clubs: Roma (1994-97), Vicenza (1997-99), Reggina (1999-)
• Versatile right-sided central defender who impressed at Reggina after failing to break through at Roma.

COACH
STRACHAN, Gordon
Scottish
Born: 09.02.57
• Tenacious midfielder with Aberdeen, Manchester United, Leeds and Scotland who has gone on to impress everyone during his time as manager of Coventry, with some suggesting him as a successor to **Alex Ferguson** at Old Trafford.
• Moved to Coventry from Leeds in 1995 and continued playing while also working as assistant to Ron Atkinson, eventually taking over as manager.

PLAYER
STRAND, Pal
Midfielder, Norwegian, 179cm, 80kg
Born: 03.04.74, Norway
Clubs: Raufoss, Lillestrom (1999-)
• An immediate success at Lillestrom following a transfer from Raufoss. Has a very strong left foot and enjoys attacking down the flank.

Thomas Strunz

PLAYER
STRAND, Roar
Midfielder, Norwegian, 179cm, 76kg
Born: 02.02.70, Trondheim, Norway
Clubs: Rosenborg (1989-92), Molde (1993), Rosenborg (1994-)
Full international (Norway) 25 caps/4 goals
• Midfield dynamo who loves to have a shot at goal. Covers an enormous amount of distance and is versatile. Has won eight Norwegian League titles with Rosenborg.

PLAYER
STRASSER, Jeff
Defender, Luxembourg, 190cm, 80kg
Born: 05.10.74, Luxembourg
Clubs: Metz (Fra) (1993-99), Kaiserslautern (Ger) (1999-)
Full international (Luxembourg) 30 caps/0 goals
• Luxembourg's only quality defender who moved to the Bundesliga in 1999 after six seasons with Metz.

PLAYER
STRATOS, Thomas
Defender, Greek/German, 181cm, 75kg
Born: 09.10.66, Ionnina, Greece
Clubs: Arminia Bielefeld, Hamburg (1990-92), Saarbrucken (1992-94), Arminia Bielefeld (1994-)
• Very underrated sweeper of Greek stock. Reads the game well, has good distribution skills and a tough streak in his defensive game.

PLAYER
STREHMEL, Alexander
Defender, German, 184cm, 72kg
Born: 20.03.68, Germany
Clubs: TSV Birkach, SV Hoffeld, SV Bonlanden, Stuttgart (1986-94), Wattenscheid (1994-96), Unterhaching (1996-)
• Flexible modern sweeper who can play either behind or in front of his defence. A good user of the ball and master of the last-ditch tackle.
• Surname pronounced Stray mel.

AGENT
STRETFORD, Paul
• Leading English agent whose clients include **Dion Dublin** and **Mikael Forssell**.
• **Contact:** 11-13 Manchester Road, Wilmslow, Cheshire SK8 1BQ, England. Tel: 0044 (0) 1625 536 411.

PLAYER
STROENCO, Serghey
Defedner, Moldovan, 180cm, 75kg
Born: 22.02.67
Clubs: Tiligul Tiraspol
Full international (Moldova) 37 caps/0 goals
• Central defender and the most experienced player in the Moldovan League. Has played for Tiligul since 1984, with a short break for compulsory army service.

PLAYER
STRUNZ, Thomas
Defender, German, 183cm, 75kg
Born: 25.04.68, Duisburg, Germany
Clubs: TuRa Duisburg, MSV Duisburg, Bayern Munich (1989-92), Stuttgart, Bayern Munich (1995-)
Full international (Germany) 4 caps/1 goal
• Missed most of the 1999-2000 season through injury and it is not the first time that the utility man's career has been blighted by spells in the hospital or treatment room.
• Forceful and versatile, he can play any number of variations on a defensive or midfield theme, but it is at right-wing-back that he appears the most comfortable.

PLAYER
STRUPAR, Branko
Forward, Belgian, 190cm, 86kg
Born: 09.02.70, Zagreb, Croatia
Clubs: Genk (Bel) (1994-2000), Derby (Eng) (2000-)
Full international (Belgium) 11 caps/5 goals

• Striker who was born in Croatia but made his name as a professional player in Belgium, with Genk, and adopted Belgian nationality after being ignored for selection by Croatia.
• Belgian Footballer of the Year in 1999 after finishing as top scorer in the Belgian League in 1997-98 with 22 goals.

PLAYER
STUBBS, Alan
Defender, English, 187cm, 86kg
Born: 06.10.71, Merseyside, England
Clubs: Bolton (1990-96), Celtic (1996-)
• Hit by a cancer scare during the 1999 close season, Stubbs made a remarakble recovery and remains a favourite with the Celtic fans, who appreciate his strength and resolve in defence.
• During his time with Celtic he has been the subject of numerous transfer rumours.

PLAYER
STURRIDGE, Dean
Forward, Jamaican, 173cm, 76kg
Born: 27.07.73, Birmingham, England
Clubs: Derby (1991-), Torquay (1994-95, loan)
Full International (Jamaica)
• Pacy striker who excelled for Derby in the 1996-97 season, scoring 11 goals to finish as the club's top scorer. He was linked with a move to Arsenal as a replacement for Ian Wright, but injuries and a subsequent loss of form have meant his star has waned.

PLAYER
SUAT Kaya
Midfielder, Turkish, 169cm, 62kg
Born: 26.02.67, Istanbul, Turkey
Clubs: Galatasaray
Full international (Turkey) 10 caps/1 goal
• Industrious, dynamic midfielder who has spent his entire career at Galatasaray. Plays just in front of the defence, where his passing skills make him the starting point of any Galatasaray attack.

• Notorious for undergoing hair replacement surgery, so that he now sports a full head of hair.
• Made his international debut for Turkey against Norway in November 1993.

PLAYER
SUAZO, David
Forward, Honduran, 182cm, 75kg
Born: 05.11.79, Tegucigalpa, Honduras
Clubs: Olimpia Tegucigalpa (1998-99), Cagliari (Ita) (1999-)
Full international (Honduras)
• Promising young strong striker who became the first Honduran to play in Italy.
• Spotted by Cagliari while playing in 1999 World Under-20 Youth Cup.

PLAYER
SUKER, Davor
Forward, Croatian, 183cm, 78kg
Born: 01.01.68, Osijek, Croatia
Clubs: Osijek (1985-89), Dinamo Zagreb (1989-91), Sevilla (Spa) (1991-96), Real Madrid (Spa) (1996-1999), Arsenal (Eng) (1999-2000), West Ham (Eng) (2000-)
Full International (Croatia) 57 caps/42 goals
• One of the leading strikers of the 1990s who helped establish Croatia as a major force within world football and was the top scorer at the 1998 World Cup with six goals.
• Was a member of the Yugoslavia side which won 1987 World Youth Championship in Chile, and made his full international debut for Yugoslavia in December 1990 against Romania.
• Transferred to Sevilla in 1991, playing alongside Diego Maradona and establishing himself as a prolific goalscorer in the Spanish League.
• Scored twice on his debut for independent Croatia against Mexico in 1992.
• Won the Spanish League with Real Madrid in 1997, but was on the bench a year later when Real won the European Cup, having fallen out with coach **Jupp Heynckes**.

PLAYER
SULLIVAN, Neil

Goalkeeper, Scottish, 190cm, 80kg
Born: 24.02.70, Sutton, England
Clubs: Wimbledon (1990-91), Crystal Palace
(1991-92), Wimbledon (1992-2000), Tottenham
(2000-)
Full international (Scotland) 6 caps/0 goals
• Highly capable keeper who opted to play for
Scotland after being ignored by England.
• Joined Tottenham after relegation with
Wimbledon in May 1999.

PLAYER
SUMIALA, Antti

Forward, Finnish, 180cm, 76kg
Born: 20.02.74, Pori, Finland
Clubs: FC Jazz (1993), Ikast (1994-95), Emmen
(1995), NEC (Hol) (1995-97), Twente (Hol) (1997-
99), FC Jokerit (1999-)
Full international (Finland) 33 caps/8 goals
• One of Finland's best-known goalscorers who
is now back home after a spell in Holland.
• Top scorer in Finland in 1993 while playing for
FC Jazz and a strong penalty-box player.

PLAYER
SUNDGOT, Arild

Midfielder, Norwegian, 190cm, 87kg
Born: 17.04.78, Norway
Clubs: Hodd (1995-96), Lillestrom (1997-)
• Midfielder, originally from Hodd, who has
scored regularly for Lillestrom despite struggling
with injuries.

PLAYER
SUNDGREN, Gary

Defender, Swedish, 187cm, 83kg
Born: 25.10.67, Vammla, Finland
Clubs: IK Franke (1986-87), AIK Stockholm (1988-
96), Zaragoza (Spa) (1997-)
Full international (Sweden) 30 caps/1 goal
• Versatile defender who has spent the last two

Davor Suker

seasons in Spain with Zaragoza after playing for AIK Stockholm for the bulk of his career.
• Can play at full-back or centre-back, as he demonstated during Euro 2000, when he stepped in to cover both positions for Sweden following various injuries and suspensions.

PLAYER
SURMA, Lukasz
Midfielder, Polish, 173cm, 70kg
Born: 28.06.77, Poland
Clubs: Wisla Krakow, Ruch Chorzow (1998-)
• Midfielder who can read the game well, pass and shoot. Has largely rediscovered the form after joining Ruch from Wisla Krakow two years ago that made him one of the best player in Chorzow's team.

PLAYER
SUSLOV, Oleg
Goalkeeper, Ukrainian
Born: 02.01.69, Ukraine
Clubs: Chornomorets, Salzburg (Aut), St Polten (Aut)
Full international (Ukraine) 12 caps/0 goals
• Experienced shot stopper who started with Chornomorets and had spells with Salzburg in Austria. Lost his place in the Ukrainian national team after a move to Austrian second division club St Polten.

PLAYER
SUTTON, Chris
Forward, England, 190cm, 86kg
Born: 10.03.73, Nottingham, England
Clubs: Norwich (1990-94), Blackburn (1994-99), Chelsea (1999-2000), Celtic (Sco) (2000)
Full international (England) 1 caps/0 goals
• Striker whose £10million move to Chelsea from Blackburn was a spectacular flop. He scored one League goal in the whole of the 1999-2000 season and was offloaded to Celtic in summer 2000 for £6million.

• Made his name at Norwich, earning a £5million transfer to Blackburn, where his partnership with **Alan Shearer** became known as the SAS (Shearer and Sutton).
• Fell out with then England manager **Glenn Hoddle** after refusing to play for England B, believing instead that he should be in the A team.
• Strong in the air, he has also been used as a makeshift centre-back.

ADMINISTRATOR
SURKIS, Grigory
• President of Kyiv Dynamo since July 1997 and the man responsible for negotiating the sale of **Andrii Shevchenko** and **Sergii Rebrov**.

PLAYER
SVENSSON, Anders
Midfielder, Swedish, 177cm, 82kg
Born: 17.07.76, Sweden
Clubs: Elfsborg (1996-)
Full international (Sweden) 3 caps/0 goals
• One of the brightest, most inventive midfielder creators in the Swedish League and the big hope of everyone at Elfsborg.
• At one stage he looked like leaving the club, then decided to stay, unlike his former partner **Tobias Linderoth**, signed by Norway's Stabaek.
• A little on the frail side, but a target for foreign buyers in 2000.

PLAYER
SVENSSON, Hakan
Goalkeeper, Swedish, 192cm, 85lg
Born: 20.01.70, Sweden
Clubs: Halmstads (1994-)
Full international (Sweden) 2 caps/0 goals
• Respected keeper, even though his international career was cut short by a nightmarish 4-0 defeat by Spain in March 1998. Reliable rather than eye-catching. Swedish League champion in 1997.

VENSSON, Magnus

Midfielder, Swedish, 172cm, 77kg
Born: 10.03.69, Norway
Clubs: Vinbergs (1992-93), Halmstad (1994-97), Viking Stavangar (Nor) (1998-99), Brondby (Den) (2000-)
Full international (Sweden) 14 caps/0 goals
• Dynamic Swedish international who was voted Player of the 1999 season in Norway and was then transferred to Denmark.
• A Swedish League champion with Halmstad in 1997.

SVERISSON, Eyolfur

Defender, Icelandic, 186cm, 77kg
Born: 03.08.68, Iceland
Clubs: UMF Tindastoll, Stuttgart (Ger) (1989-99), Besiktas (Tur) (1994-95), Hertha Berlin (Ger) (1995-)
Full international (Iceland) 52 caps/6 goals
• Experienced Icelandic international who usually lines up on the left-side of Hertha's three-man defence. Great anticipation, a robust tackler and as a former midfielder, his distribution skills are very much up to the mark.

SVINDAL-LARSEN, Tommy

Midfielder, Norwegian, 172cm, 73kg
Born: 11.08.73, Norway
Clubs: Start (1991-94), Stabaek (1995-)
Full international (Norway) 5 caps/0 goals
• Midfielder who originally comes from Odd but joined Stabaek after three seasons with Start. Has great skills and is strong with both feet.

SWIERCZEWSKI, Piotr

Midfielder, Polish, 180cm, 79kg
Born: 08.04.72, Nowy Sacz, Poland
Clubs: GKS Katowice, Saint Etienne (Fra), Bastia (Fra) (1999-)
Full international (Poland) 48 caps/1 goal

• Now in his second spell at Bastia after a short interim in the Japanese J.League. Very experienced Polish international midfielder whose stock-in-trade is seek-and-destroy missions on opposing playmakers. Curiously for someone who relishes the physical side of the game, chess is one of his pastimes.
• Pronounced Pee otrr Sver ches key.

SYOMIN, Yuri

Russian
Born: 11.05.47
• Coach of Lokomotiv Moscow since 1992, his second spell at the club.
• A midfielder for a number of Soviet League teams, including Moscow Spartak, Dynamo and Lokomotiv, from 1964 to 1980.
• His coaching career started in 198 and includes one year (1991) as a consultant for the Olympic team of New Zealand.
• Won the Russian Cup in 1996 and 1997 and reached the Cup-winners Cup semi-finals in 1997-98 and 1998-99.

SZABO, Josef

Ukrainian
Born: 01.03.40
• Former Soviet international midfielder (41 caps, 8 goals between 1960 and 1972) who spent most of his club career at Kyiv Dynamo.
• Moved into coaching with Dynamo, before suceeding **Valerii Lobanovsky** as coach of Ukraine in 1996. Stepped down in late 1999 after Ukraine's defeat by Slovenia in the Euro 2000 play-offs.

SZCZESNY, Maciej

Goalkeeper, Polish, 191cm, 84kg
Born: 28.06.65, Poland
Clubs: Polonia Warsaw

Full international (Poland) 7 caps/0 goals
• Hugely experienced keeper who missed the whole of the 1997-98 season through injury but has since become only the second player in the history of Polish football to win the League title with three different clubs (twice with Legia in 1994 and 1995, then with Widzew in 1997 and with Polonia in 2000).

PLAYER
SZULIK, Marcin
Midfielder, Poland, 178cm, 83kg
Born: 10.01.77
Clubs: Dozamet Nowa Sol, Saint Etienne (Fra), Polonia Warsaw, Stomil Olsztyn (1997)
• Midfielder who scored the golden goal that gave Poland victory in the Final of the Under-16 European Championship and then spent some time in France with St Etienne's youth system.

PLAYER
SZYMKOWIAK, Miroslaw
Midfielder, Polish, 179cm, 71kg
Born: 01.02.76
Clubs: Widzew Lodz
Full international (Poland) 3 caps/0 goals
• Can play in any position except goal, a hard worker who has returned to action after a serious knee injury. Never misses an opportunity to go forward in support of the attack.

T

PLAYER
TACCHINARDI, Alessio
Midfielder, Italian, 187cm, 80kg
Born: 23.07.75, Crema, Italy
Clubs: Atalanta (1992-94), Juventus (1994-)
Full international (Italy) 3 caps/0 goals
• Product of the Juventus youth team who made his first-team debut for Atalanta aged 17.
• Was once hailed as the new Franco Baresi, but played badly in his international debut, against Slovenia in September 1995.
• His versatility took him back into contention for a national team place before Euro 2000.

PLAYER
TAFFAREL, Claudio Andre
Goalkeeper, Brazilian, 182cm, 80kg
Born: 08.05.66, Santa Rosa, Brazil
Clubs: Internacional, Parma (Ita), Reggiana (Ita), Atletico Mineiro, Galatasaray (Tur)
Full international (Brazil) 101 caps/0 goals
• Keeper who won the World Cup with Brazil in 1994.
• Solid but unexceptional, but the best Brazil had to offer for most of the 1990s.
• Winner of the World Youth Cup with Brazil in 1985 before moving to Italy, where he won the Italian Cup with Parma in 1992.
• Was criticised after Brazil lost the 1995 Copa America on penalties to Uruguay, but responded with some excellent perfomances at the 1998 World Cup in France.
• Devout Christian who had a prayer published in his honour in a Rio newspaper after his performances for Brazil at France 98.
• Returned to Europe from Brazil in summer 1998, joining Turkey's Galatasaray for £440,000. Won the Turkish League in 1999 and then the UEFA Cup in May 2000.
• 'Fans in Turkey are intense in their desire to see their team win. I've had the same pressure with the Brazil and Parma. I'm a calm person and know how to keep all the hype and expectations at arm's length and just concentrate on my game.'

PLAYER
TAGGART, Gerry
Defender, Northern Irish, 185cm, 78kg
Born: 18.10.70, Belfast, Northern Ireland
Clubs: Manchester City (1988-90), Barnsley (1989-95), Bolton (1995-98), Leicester City (1998-)
Full international (N. Ireland) 46 caps/7 goals
• Rugged, left-sided centre-back who joined Leicester on a free transfer in July 1998.

PLAYER
TAGLIALATELA, Giuseppe
Goalkeeper, Italian, 182cm, 72kg
Born: 02.01.69, Ischia, Italy
Clubs: Napoli (1987-99), Palermo (1988-89), Avellino (1989-90), Palermo (1991-92), Bari (1992-93) Napoli (1993-99), Fiorentina (1999-)
• Capable keeper who has had to make do as understudy to **Francesco Toldo** at Fiorentina after six seasons as number one at Napoli.

PLAYER
TAIBI, Massimo
Goalkeeper, Italian, 190cm, 82kg
Born: 18.02.70, Palermo, Italy
Clubs: Licarta (1988-89), Trento (1989-90), Milan (1990-91, (1997-98), Como (1991-92), Piacenza (1992-7), Venezia (1998-99), Manchester United (Eng) (1999-2000), Reggina (2000-)
• Keeper who had a terrible time at Manchester United, having moved from Venezia to Old Trafford in autumn 1999 after **Marc Bosnich** failed to impress as the successor to **Peter Schmeichel**.
• A series of poor performances and calamitous mistakes led to him being dubbed the 'Blind Venetian'.
• He returned to Italy, on loan to Reggina, and the move was made permanent in summer 2000.

PLAYER
TAINIO, Teemu
Midfielder, Finnish, 175cm, 69kg
Born: 27.11.79, Tornio, Finland
Clubs: FC Haka, Auxerre (Fra) (1997-)
Full international (Finland) 3 caps/0 goals
• Since leaving his native Finland for Auxerre in the autumn of 1997, he has had more than his share of injuries. But there were unmistakeable signs in the 1999-2000 season that the young Scandinavian was finally coming good, demonstrating a nice line in nimble creativity on the right side of midfield.
• Turned down an offer from PSV Eindhoven after relegation with FC Haka in 1996, but signed for Auxerre for £400,000 in autumn 1997.
• International debut: February 1998, v Cyprus.
• Pronounced Tee moo Tie nn no.

PLAYER
TAIS, Washington
Defender, Uruguayan, 179cm, 75kg
Born: 21.12.72, Montevideo, Uruguay
Clubs: Penarol (1994-97), Racing Santander (Spa) (1997-)
Full international (Uruguay)
• Uruguayan right-back who likes to get forward.

PLAYER
TAL, Idan
Midfielder, Israeli
Born: 07.03.71, Israell
Clubs: Brescia (Ita)
Full international (Israel) 17 caps/1 goal
• A committed and influential midfielder, he is the natural leader in the Israel national squad and was the obvious choice for captain.
• He has improved greatly since going to the Italian League, to second division Brescia.
• Is unquestionably the most fearless player in the Israeli national side, and is a crunching tackler who plays fair, but very tough.

PLAYER
TALAN, Jefrey
Forward, Dutch, 175cm, 73kg
Born: 29.09.71, Katwijk, Holland
Clubs: Den Haag (1990-92), ADO Den Haag (1992-94), Den Haag (1994-95), Heerenveen (1995-)
Full international (Holland) 3 caps/0 goals
• Speedy, skilful winger whose performances for Heerenveen have earned him international recognition.

PLAYER
TALKER, Ofer
Forward, Israeli, 183cm, 69kg
Born: 22.04.73, Israel
Clubs: Hapoel Haifa
Full international (Israel) 10 caps/0 goals
• Has his sights set on a career abroad, and has been the subject of interest by more than one Scottish club. As a winger, Talker is naturally fast with good ball control. He scores often in the Israeli league, but is yet to get on an international scoresheet.

PLAYER
TAMUDO, Raul
Full name: Raul Tamudo Montero
Forward, Spanish, 180cm, 74kg
Born: 19.10.77, Barcelona, Spain
Clubs: Espanyol (1996-), Alaves (1997-98, loan) Lleida (1998-99, loan)
• Pacy striker who returned to Espanyol in 1999 after loan spells at Lleida and Alves.

PLAYER
TANASIJEVIC, Jovan
Defender, Yugoslav, 180cm
Born: 20.01.78, Yugoslavia
Clubs: Vojvodina Novi Sad
• A great prospect in central defence. A regular in Yugoslavia's Under-21 side.

PLAYER
TANGEN, Rune

Defender, Norwegian, 187cm, 88kg

Born: 16.12.64, Norway

Clubs: Moss (1990), Rosenborg (1991-93), Strindheim (1994), Moss (1996), FC Tirol (1996-7), LASK (1998-99), Moss (1999-)

Full international (Norway) 3 caps/0 goals
  Veteran central defender who is back with Moss after a spell in Austria.

PLAYER
TANGHE, Stefan

Midfielder, Belgian, 175cm, 69kg

Born: 15.01.72, Kortrijk, Belgium

Clubs: Kortrijk, Mouscron (1997-2000), Utrecht (Hol) (2000-)

Full international (Belgium) 7 caps/1 goal
  Attacking midfielder who moved to Holland in the summer of 2000 after three seasons at Mouscron.
  Broke into the Belgian national side after the 1998 World Cup, making his international debut against the Czech Republic in February 1999, but fell out with new national coach **Robert Waseige** after declaring that he wanted to play in a central attacking role, rather than the right-sided, more defensive role Waseige had in mind.

ADMINISTRATOR
TANZI, Stefano

Born: 23.07.68

• President of Parma since July 1996 and the youngest club owner in Serie A.

PLAYER
TAPALOVIC, Filip

Defender, Croatian/German, 183cm, 81kg

Born: 22.10.76, Croatia

Clubs: Fortuna Gelsenkirchen, Bochum (1996-97), Schalke (1997-99), Munich 1860 (1999-)

• Central defender or sweeper who moved to Munich on a free transfer in summer 1999 after rarely getting a game at Schalke.

Stefan Tanghe

PLAYER
TAPIA, Hector Urdile
Forward, Chilean, 175cm, 73kg
Born: 30.09.77, Santiago, Chile
Clubs: Colo Colo (1994-98), Universidad de Chile (1999), Perugia (Ita) (1999-)
Full international (Chile)
• Powerful young striker who has played for Chile at Under-21 and senior level and is tipped as a future star.

PLAYER
TARANTINO, Massimo
Defender, Italian, 180cm, 72kg
Born: 20.05.71, Palermo, Italy
Clubs: Catania (1986-89), Napoli (1989), Monza (1989-90), Barletta (1990-91), Napoli (1991-96), Internazionale (1996-97), Bologna (1997-)
• Strong, capable centre-back who established himself in Serie A during five seasons at Napoli. But he failed to make the most of a big-money move to Internazionale and moved on after a season to Bologna.

COACH
TARDELLI, Marco
Italian
Born: 24.09.54
• Former Italian international – a hero in Italy after scoring the winning goal in the 1982 World Cup Final — who is earning a great reputation in charge of the Italian Under-21 and Olympic side.
• Oversaw the Italian victory in the European Under-21 championships in May 2000.

PLAYER
TARE, Igli
Forward, Albanian, 191cm, 85kg
Born: 25.07.73, Albania
Clubs: Karlsruhe (Ger), Fortuna Dusseldorf (Ger) (1998-99), Kaiserslautern (Ger) (1999-)
Full international (Albania) 22 caps/3 goals
• Striker who compensates for a lack of technique with hard work and application in the penalty area, although he has found it tough establishing himself in the Kaiserslautern first team.

PLAYER
TARNAT, Michael
Midfielder, German, 186cm, 67kg
Born: 27.10.69, Hilden, Germany
Clubs: Hilden-Nord, Duisburg (1990-94), Karlsruhe (1994-97), Bayern Munich (1997-)
Full international (Germany) 19 caps/0 goals
• Consummate professional and much more than just a left-sided back-up to **Bixente Lizarazu**. Very consistent, disciplined and a fine left-foot, which he uses to whip in great crosses and blast long-range free kicks.
• A late-developer, who had to wait until he was 28 to make his debut for Germany.

PLAYER
TAROZZI, Andrea
Defender, Italian, 178cm, 68kg
Born: 17.10.73, St. Giovanni Periceto, Italy
Clubs: Bologna (1991-97), Fiorentina (1997-)
• Defender who helped hometown team Bologna win promotion from the Italian third division to the first in successive seasons before joining Fiorentina in 1997.
• Struggled initially as a centre-back in Florence, but things improved when he was switched to attacking wing-back.

PLAYER
TAYFUN Korkut
Defender, Turkish, 184cm, 75kg
Born: 02.04.74, Germany
Clubs: Stuttgarter Kickers (Ger), Fenerbahce
Full international (Turkey) 27 caps/0 goals
• Disciplined campaigner who can be used on either side of defence or in midfield, but is most likely to be used at left-back.
• Born in Germany of Turkish parents and joined the youth section of Stuttgarter Kickers, where he

ayed alongside **Fredi Bobic**.
Moved to Turkey in 1995 when Stuttgarter
•ckers were relegated from the German second
•vision, and made such rapid progress with
•enerbahce that he won an international debut in
•ovember 1995 against Sweden.
Played in all of Turkey's games at Euro 2000.

AYER

AYFUR Havutcu

•idfielder, Turkish, 180cm, 75kg
•orn: 23.04.70, Turkey
•orn: Kocaelispor, Fenerbahce, Besiktas
•ull international (Turkey) 25 caps/5 goals
Versatile player who played a crucial role in
•urkey's qualification for the finals of Euro 2000.
Moved to Germany as a boy and started at
armstad before move to Fenerbahce in 1993
•nder German coach Holger Osieck.
Followed Osieck to Kocaelispor in 1995 and
•en signed by Besiktas.
Nicknamed the Icebox for his cool attitude.
International debut: Turkey v Macedonia,
•ugust 1994.

•DMINISTRATOR

•AYLOR, Gordon

Secretary of the English Professional
•ootballers' Association and the spokesman
•r more than 2,500 players throughout the
•nglish Leagues.
Former player with Bolton and Birmingham
•ity.

•LAYER

•AYLOR, Ian

•idfielder, English, 185cm, 76kg
•orn: 04.06.68, Birmingham, England
•lubs: Port Vale (1992-4), Sheffield Wednesday
1994-95), Aston Villa (1995-)
• Tall, tough, combative central midfielder who
•overs lots of ground and has a useful shot from
•ong-range.

Tayfur Havutcu

Fatih Terim

PLAYER
TCHEREVCHENKO, Igor
Defender, Russian, 188cm, 84kg
Born: 21.08.74, Russia
Clubs: Lokomotiv Moscow (1996-)
Full international (Russia)
• Powerful central defender who is strong in the air.
• Surname also spelt Cherevchenko.

PLAYER
TCHOUGA, Jean-Michel
Forward, Cameroonian
Born: 20.12.78
Clubs: Olympic Yaounde, Yverdon (Swi), Basel (Swi) (2000-)
• Great things are expected of this promising young Cameroon striker. Physically powerful, direct and keeps a cool head in front of goal.
• He was linked with a move to Spain in the 2000 close season, but instead left Yverdon for Basel and he is shaping up well at his new club.

PLAYER
TCHOUTANG, Bernard
Forward, Cameroonian, 177cm, 75kg
Born: 02.09.76, Yaounde, Cameroon
Clubs: Vanspor (Tur) (1994-97), Genk (Bel) (1997), Roda JC (Hol) (1998-)
Full international (Cameroon)
• Fleet-footed striker or winger who has done well at Roda after spells in Turkey and Belgium. A member of the Cameroon side which won the African Nations Cup in February 2000.

PLAYER
TCHUGAINOV, Igor
Defender, Russian, 187cm, 81kg
Born: 06.04.70, Russia
Clubs: Torpedo Moscow (1986-89), Lokomotiv Moscow (1990), Torpedo Moscow (1991-93), Lokomotiv Moscow (1994-)
Full international (Russia) 16 caps/0 goals

Probably Russia's most reliable libero: experienced, good in attack and often scores match-winning goals.
• Surname also spelt Chugaynov.

PLAYER
TEDESCO, Giovanni
Midfielder, Italian, 168cm, 64kg
Born: 13.05.72, Palermo, Italy
Clubs: Reggina (1990-93), Fiorentina (1993-95), Foggia (1995-97), Salernitana (1997-98), Perugia (1998-)
• Energetic all-purpose campaigner who is one of the best midfield dynamos in Serie A.

PLAYER
TELESNIKOV, Jan
Midfielder, Russian/Israeli
Born: 11.12.74, Torinsk, Russia
Clubs: Beitar Jerusalem (1996-99), Dundee United (Sco) (1999-2000)
Full international (Israel) 20 caps/4 goals
• One of the most serious players in the Israeli national squad, Telesnikov is a playmaker who can turn a game with a deft pass or dinking run.
• He is unfortunate to be playing at the same time as **Eyal Berkovic**, and for this reason he is often overlooked, as the two play in a similar role.

PLAYER
TELFER, Paul
Midfielder, Scottish, 175cm, 72kg
Born: 21.10.71, Edinburgh, Scotland
Clubs: Luton (1990-95), Coventry (1995-)
Full international (Scotland)
• Versatile midfielder who can also play at full-back.
• Joined Coventry in a £1.5million transfer from Luton in 1995 and has so far proved great value for money.
• Made his international debut for Scotland against France in March 2000.

PLAYER
TEN HAG, Eric
Defender, Dutch, 180cm, 73kg
Born: 02.02.70, Haaksbergen, Holland
Clubs: FC Twente (1989-), De Graafschap (1990-91), RKC (1994-95), Utrecht (1995-96), Twente (1996-)
• Libero or central midfielder who has arguably his best season in 1999-2000. Good shot and great vision.

PLAYER
TENGSTEDT, Thomas
Defender, Danish, 185cm, 84kg
Born: 15.05.75, Denmark
Clubs: Dundee United, Viborg (1997-)
• Left-back who is back in Denmark after a spell in Scotland with Dundee United. Solid defender but lacks ball skills and attacking ideas.

PLAYER
TER AVEST, Berthil
Midfielder, Dutch, 186cm, 75kg
Born: 19.11.70, Wierden, Holland
Clubs: FC Twente (1989-91), Roda JC (1991-93), Groningen (1993-94), FC Twente (1994-2000)
• Former left winger who now plays in midfield where he is a tireless worker, takes on more responsibility than he used to and is more consistent as a result.
• Was set to follow former coach Hans Meyer to Borussia Monchengladbach to earn more money in the summer of 2000.

PLAYER
TERYOKHIN, Oleg
Forward, Russian, 175cm, 79kg
Born: 12.08.70
Clubs: Sokol Saratov (1990-94), Dinamo Moscow (1996-99), Lokomotiv Moscow (2000-)
Full international (Russia) 1 caps/0 goals
• Excellent finisher and one of the Russian League's most consistent strikers.

PLAYER
TESSEM, Jo
Forward, Norwegian, 190cm, 82kg
Born: 28.02.72, Norway
Clubs: Lyn (1996-97), Molde (1998-1999), Southampton (Eng) (2000-)
• Attacker whose versatility has made him a huge asset to Southampton since a moved from Norway, where he was a regular scorer, midway through 1999-2000.
• Once worked as a policeman.

PLAYER
TESTIMITANU, Ivan
Defender, Moldovan, 178cm, 76kg
Born: 27.04.74
Clubs: Zimbru Chisinau, Bristol City (Eng)
• Versatile player who play can play anywhere in defence or midfield.
• The first Moldovan to play in England and voted footballer of the year in Moldova in 1995 and 1997.

PLAYER
TETRATZE, Omar
Defender, Georgian, 176cm, 71kg
Born: 13.10.69, Tbilisi, Georgia
Clubs: PAOK Salonika (Gre)
Full international (Russia) 3 caps/1 goal
• A Russian with Georgian roots who can operate as a defensive marker or in a midfield holding role for PAOK Salonika. Tenacious, full of stamina and selfless, he always goes out of his way to make new signings feel welcome at the club.

PLAYER
THATCHER, Ben
Defender, English, 180cm, 79kg
Born: 30.11.75, Swindon, England
Clubs: Millwall (1993-96), Wimbledon (1996-2000), Tottenham (2000-)
• Left-back who probably would have played for England in the run-up to Euro 2000 had he not been caught by TV cameras elbowing

Sunderland's Nicky Summerbee during a League match. In the resulting bad publicity **Kevin Keegan** felt it necessary to drop Thatcher from his plans.
• England Under-21 international who joined Spurs in summer of 2000 after being relegated with Wimbledon.

PLAYER
THIAM, Pablo
Midfielder, Guinean, 186cm, 78kg
Born: 03.01.74, Conakry, Guinea
Clubs: Stuttgart (Ger)
Full international (Guinea) 9 caps/0 goals
• Talented defensive midfielder who is well established in the Bundesliga and has been tipped to move to a bigger club.
• Son of a diplomat.

PLAYER
THOMSEN, Claus
Midfielder, Danish, 193cm, 89kg
Born: 31.05.70, Aarhus, Denmark
Clubs: Aarhus, Ipswich (Eng), Everton (Eng), FC Copenhagen, Wolfsburg (Ger)
Full international (Denmark) 20 caps/0 goals
• Danish international who can be very effective in a midfield holding role, but whose best position is as a left-sided defensive marker. Spent four years playing in England with Ipswich Town and Everton and it was during his time at Goodison Park that he revealed a spectacular side to his game, scoring with an acrobatic overhead kick in a game with Derby County in February 1998.

PLAYER
THOMPSON, Alan
Midfielder, England, 183cm, 80kg
Born: 22.12.73. Newcastle, England
Clubs: Newcastle (1991-93), Bolton (1993-98), Aston Villa (1998-)
• Left-footed midfielder who joined Villa after

elegation with Bolton in 1998. He had been one
f the best performers in Bolton's midfield,
mpressing with his passing and running, despite
he poor results.
  Made a promising start at Villa, but injuries and
competition for places conspired to restrict his
progress and inhibit his confidence.

PLAYER
THOMPSON, David
Midfielder, English, 171cm, 64kg
Born: 12.09.77 Birkenhead, England
Clubs: Liverpool (1996-2000), Swindon (1997-98,
oan), Coventry (2000-)
• Young midfielder who was sold by Liverpool in
August 2000 after being edged out following the
arrival of **Nicky Barmby** and **Gary McAllister**.
• Won the FA Youth Cup in 1996 and went on to
win a place in the Liverpool first team with his
hard-tackling and often fiery style.

ADMINISTRATOR
THOMPSON, Geoff
English
• Chairman of the Football Association since 1999.
• Voted on to the executive of UEFA in June 2000.

PLAYER
THON, Olaf
Defender, German, 170cm, 68kg
Born: 01.05.66, Gelsenkirchen, Germany
Clubs: Schalke (1985-88), Bayern Munich (1988-
94), Schalke (1994-)
Full international (Germany) 52 caps/3 goals
• No active Bundesliga professional has
appeared in more German First Division games
than the Schalke libero, who in 16 seasons has
played in 434 games.
• Began his career as a stylish playmaker before
making a successful switch to the sweeper
position during a spell at Bayern Munich.
• Played in three World Cups (1986, 1990 and 1998).
• Surname pronounced Tohn.

COACH
THORDARSON, Olafur
Icelandic
Born: 1965
• With Reykjavik side Fylkir, he won on the
Icelandic first division title at a canter in 1999,
his first full season as player/coach. Now back at
IA Akranes, the club he served so well for much
of the 1990s, he will be looking to transfer his
uncompromising style as a player to put IA back
among the honours.

COACH
THORDARSON, Teitur
Icelandic
Born: 14.01.52
• National coach of Estonia.

COACH
THORDASSON, Gudjon
Icelandic
• Coach who steered Iceland to within a whisker
of qualifying for the finals Euro 2000 from a
tough qualifying group that also included France,
Ukraine and Russia. Was previously a highly
successful club coach in Iceland.
• Left the Iceland job to take charge of Stoke
City in early 2000 following the club's takeover
by an Icelandic businessman.

PLAYER
THORNINGER, Thomas
Midfielder, Danish, 181cm, 73kg
Born: 20.12.72, Denmark
Clubs: FC Copenhagen (1997-)
• Attacking midfielder or striker who has found
competition for places at FC Copenhagen tough
after returning to Denmark following a spell in
Italy.
• Inconsistency is his main problem, and he has
still to recapture the form which once led to him
finishing as Danish League top scorer.

Lilian Thuram

PLAYER
THURAM, Lilian
Defender, French, 185cm, 78kg
Born: 01.01.72, Pointe-a-Poitre, Guadaloupe.
Clubs: Monaco (1990-96), Parma (Ita) (1996-)
Full international (France) 62 caps/2 goals
• One of the world's most accomplished defenders who never misses the opportunity to attack.
• A World Cup winner in 1998 who sensationally scored France's two goals against Croatia in the semi-final.
• Plays right-back for the national side, having played at centre-back throughout his club career.
• Voted best defender in Serie A in 1997.
• A UEFA Cup winner with Parma in 1999.
• Born in Guadaloupe and moved to Paris at the age of nine.
• Wear glasses and adopts a studious manner off the pitch. Flirted with taking up the priesthood as a teenager.

PLAYER
THURRE, Leonard
Forward, Swiss, 178cm, 71kg
Born: 09.09.77, Switzerland
Clubs: Lausanne (1995-99), Servette (1999-)
Full international (Switzerland) 2 caps/0 goals
• Livewire young attacker who left Lausanne for Servette in the summer of 1999. Forceful and quick.

COACH
TIGANA, Jean
French
Born: 23.06.55
• Former international midfielder and a key member of the 1984 European Championship-winning side.
• Made his name as a coach at Monaco, whom he guided to the 1997 French League title before resigning in 1999.
• Has been touted as a future coach of the French national side, but amazed everyone in France by accepting an offer from English first division club Fulham to be their coach.

PLAYER
TIKHONOV, Andrei
Forward, Russian, 180cm, 73kg
Born: 16.10.70, Russia
Clubs: Moscow Spartak (1992-)
Full international (Russia) 29 caps/1 goal
  Spartak's captain and leader, a great team
player who controls the left wing and often
scores from this position – not surprising given
that he began his career as a striker, switching to
midfield in 1995.
• Russian Footballer of the Year in 1996, but was
left out of the squad for Euro 96, having made his
international debut against Malta in February 1996.

PLAYER
TIKO, Roberto
Full name: Roberto Martinez Ripodas
Midfielder, Spanish, 178cm, 74kg
Born: 15.09.76, Pamplona
Clubs: Osasuna (1996-99), Athletic Bilbao (2000-)
• Elegant left-sided midfielder signed from
Osasuna in January 2000. A fine prospect.

PLAYER
TIKVA, Avraham
Midfielder, Israeli, 182cm, 76kg
Born: 228.06.76
Clubs: Grasshopper (Swi), Hapoel Tel Aviv (2000-)
Full international (Israel) 11 caps/1 goal
• The Israeli attacking midfielder left
Grasshopper when his contract expired in the
summer of 2000 to return to Hapoel Tel Aviv in
his homeland.
• Scored 11 goals in the 1998-99 season to
finish joint-third in the national scoring charts,
but went off the boil in 1999-2000.

PLAYER
TIMOFTE, Ion
Midfielder, Romanian, 177cm, 72kg
Born: 16.02.67, Anina, Romania
Clubs: Politehnica (1990-92), FC Porto (Por)

(1992-94), Boavista (Por) (1994-)
Full international (Romania) 10 caps/1 goal
• Experienced, goalscoring midfielder whose
performances for Boavista in the Portuguese
League have not earned him the international
recognition he deserves.

PLAYER
TITOV, Yegor
Midfielder, Russian, 190cm, 77kg
Born: 29.05.76, Russia
Clubs: Moscow Spartak (1995-)
Full international (Russia) 17 caps/2 goals
• Young attacking star who plays a crucial role in
controlling Spartak's midfield.

PLAYER
TJIKUZU, Razundara
Midfielder, Namibia, 173cm, 68kg
Born: 12.12.79, Namibia
Clubs: Werder Bremen (Ger)
Full international (Namibia) 18 caps/0 goals
• Elegant attacking midfielder who has come
through the youth ranks at Werder, playing 25
Bundesliga matches up to the start of the
2000-2001 season.

PLAYER
TOBIASEN, Ole
Defender, Danish, 189cm, 86kg
Born: 08.07.75, Copenhagen, Denmark
Clubs: FC Copenhagen (1992-96), Heerenveen
(Hol) (1996-97), Ajax (Hol) (1997-)
Full international (Denmark) 6 caps/1 goal
• Young full-back who missed France 98 with a
cruciate knee ligament injury and Euro 2000 with
a long-term ankle injury.
• Seen as a star of the future and often compared
to **Morten Olsen**, who signed him for Ajax.
• Can play anywhere in defence, but his speed
and technique are best used at full-back.

Ole Tobiesen

TOCHILIN, Alexander
Defender, Russian, 179cm, 74kg
Born: 27.04.74, Russia
Clubs: Dynamo Moscow (1995-)
• Defender with good ball control who often creates opportunities in attack.

PLAYER
TODOROV, Svetoslav
Forward, Bulgarian, 183cm, 75kg
Born: 30.08.78, Bulgaria
Clubs: Liteks Lovech
Full international (Bulgaria) 15 caps/1 goal
• Promising young striker who is already established in the rebuilt Bulgarian national side.

PLAYER
TOEDTLI, Mariano Ramon
Forward, Argentinian, 182cm, 76kg
Born: 23.03.76, Leones, Argentina
Clubs: Hurucan (1998-99), Maritimo (Por) (1999-)
• Young striker who performed well for Maritimo early in the 1999-2000 season, but was unsettled by speculation linking him with a move to Benfica.

PLAYER
TOFTING, Stig
Midfielder, Danish, 173cm, 70kg
Born: 14.08.69, Denmark
Clubs: Aarhus, Hamburg, OB Odense, Duisburg (Ger) (1997-)
Full international (Denmark) 22 caps/2 goals
• A sort of Danish Gazza but without the slice of genius. A chunky midfield gladiator who will run, chase and tackle all day and is no mean passer of the ball either.

PLAYER
TOKENE, Bertin
Defender, Cameroonian, 178cm, 75kg
Born: 10.05.75, Cameroon
Clubs: Electsport, Ascot N'Djamena, Unisport

afang, Charleroi (Bel) (1997-)
Full international (Cameroon) 2 caps/0 goals
• Talented but at times frustrating central
defender or defensive midfielder. Can appear to
ack concentration, but he is a clever player who
uses to ball well to initiate attacks.

TOKIC, Mario
Defender, Croatian, 179cm, 74kg
Born: 23.07.75, Derventa, Bosnia-Herzegovina
Clubs: Rijeka, Croatia Zagreb (1998-)
Full international (Croatia) 4 caps/0 goals
• Young full-back or wide midfielder who played
for Croatia Zagreb in the Champions League after
making his international debut for Croatia against
the Republic of Ireland in September 1998.

TOLDO, Francesco
Goalkeeper, Italian, 196cm, 90kg
Born: 01.12.71, Padova, Italy
Clubs: Milan (1988-90), Verona (1990-91), Trento
(1991-92), Ravenna (1992-93), Fiorentina (1993-)
Full international (Italy) 14 caps/0 goals
• Very tall but remarkably agile keeper who has
established himself as the number one national
team keeper for Italy.
• Made his international debut in October 1995
against Croatia, appearing a substitute after **Luca
Bucci** was sent off.
• Started out at Milan, but did not get a game
and moved on to Trento and Ravenna, with Milan
retaining a share of him.
• Performances in Fiorentina's promotion-
winning season in 1993-94 persuaded the
Florence club to pay Milan £2.5million to buy
their 50 per cent ownership of the player.
• Italy's number one keeper at Euro 2000 after an
injury to **Gianluigi Buffon** before the tournament,
and he performed heroics as Italy reached the
Final.
• Capped eight times at Under-21 level.

TOLEDO, Adelio
Defender, Paraguayan, 179cm, 73kg
Born: 02.10.76, Cecilio Baez, Paraguay
Clubs: Atletico Colegiales (1996-98), Cerro
Porteno (1999), Udinese (Ita) (1999), Espanyol
(Spa) (2000-)
Full international (Paraguay)
• Paraguayan defender who is now trying his
luck in Spain after failing to settle in Italy with
Udinese following a transfer in summer 1999.

TOMAS
Full name: Tomas Alberto Hervas Giron
Midfielder, Spanish, 184cm, 80kg
Born: 25.11.70, Ponferrada, Spain
Clubs: Sporting Gijon (1991-98), Celta Vigo (1998-)
• Left-sided midfielder and another product of
Sporting Gijon's famed youth system.
• Joined Celta after relegation with Sporting in 1998.

TOMAS, Stjepan
Defender, Croatian, 186cm, 82kg
Born: 06.03.76, Croatia
Clubs: Istra, Croatia (now Dinamo) Zagreb (1993-),
Istra Pula, Hrvatski dragovoljac
Full international (Croatia) 8 caps/1 goal
• Defender who has been loaned out twice since
joining Dinamo Zagreb in spring 1993.
• Made his international debut against Poland in
April 1998, but missed the 1998 World Cup
through injury.

TOMASCHEK, Robert
Midfielder, Slovakian, 187cm, 79kg
Born: 25.08.72, Slovakia
Clubs: Slovan Bratislava, Nitra, Slovan Bratislava,
Partizan Belgrade (Yug), Hearts (Sco) (2000-)
Full international (Slovakia) 43 caps/3 goals
• Hearts created a major surprise when they

Jon Dahl Tomasson

Tomaschek from Partizan Belgrade shortly after the New Year but his appearances in the Tynecastl first team have been few and far between.

PLAYER
TOMASSI, Damiano

Midfielder, Italian, 180cm, 75kg
Born: 17.05.74, Negrar, Italy
Clubs: Verona (1992-96), Roma (1996-)
Full international (Italy) 2 caps/0 goals

• Quietly-spoken hard-working right-sided midfielder who has established himself at the highest level in Serie A.

• Spent four seasons with local club Verona in Serie B, before winning promotion in 1996 and immediately joining Roma.

• A member of Italy's side at the 1996 Atlanta Olympics.

• Has been on the fringes of the Italian national squad for the past two seasons, having made his international debut against Spain in November 1998.

PLAYER
TOMASSON, Jon Dahl

Forward, Danish, 182cm, 74kg
Born: 29.08.76, Roskilde, Denmark
Clubs: Koge BK, Heerenveen (Hol) (1994-97), Newcastle (Eng) (1997-98), Feyenoord (Hol) (1998-)
Full international (Denmark) 21 caps/8 goals

• Top scorer for Hereenveen in 1995-96 (14 goals) and 1996-97 (18 goals) who earned a transfer to Newcastle (despite interest from Barcelona and Ajax) in summer 1997.

• Sank without a trace in a failing side at St James' Park, missing the cut for Denmark's World Cup squad.

• Revived his form at Feyenoord, scoring five goals in successive matches to help Denmark qualify for Euro 2000.

• Can fade from a game, but when on form is most effective playing behind the main strikers.

LAYER
OMIC, Djordje

Midfielder, Yugoslav, 180cm, 73kg
Born: 11.11.72, Slovenigradecv, Yugoslavia
Clubs: Guingamp (Fra), Atletico Madrid (Spa),
Partizan Belgrade
Full international (Yugoslavia) 1 cap/0 goals
Playmaker with an attractive style of play, a
good left-foot shot, and a dangerous free-kick.
Not so strong in one-on-one duels.

LAYER
OMIC, Tomas

Goalkeeper, Croatian, 189cm, 82kg
Born: 10.01.77, Croatia
Clubs: Bayern Munich (Ger) (1997-98), Grazer AK
(Aut) (1998-)
• Young keeper signed to replace the Arsenal-bound
Alex Manninger. So far he has not disappointed.

PLAYER
TONI

Full name: Antonio Jimenez Sistachs
Goalkeeper, Spanish, 181cm, 80kg
Born: 12.10.70, Barcelona, Spain
Clubs: Figueres (1990-92), Rayo Vallecano (1992-
93), Espanyol (1993-1999) Atletico Madrid (1999-)
Full international (Spain) 3 caps/0 goal
• Experienced keeper who was a rival for **Jose
Molina** at club and international level in 1999-
2000, but failed to displace the more experienced
Molina and seemed likely to stay at Atletico
following relegation.

PLAYER
TONI

Full name: Antonio Munoz Gomez
Defender, Spanish, 176cm, 73kg
Born: 04.02.68 Cordoba, Spain
Clubs: Atletico Madrid (1989-)
Full international (Spain) 10 caps/2 goals
• Skilful, attacking, hard-shooting left-back
who has been an institution at Atletico Madrid

for 11 seasons since joining the B squad from
Cordoba in 1989.

PLAYER
TONITO

Full name: Antonio Jesus Garcia Gonzalez
Forward, Spanish, 170cm, 65kg
Born: 24.02.77, Spain
Clubs: Tenerife (1996-97), Vitoria Setubal (Por)
(1997-99), Sporting Lisbon (Por) (1999-)
• One of the next big stars of Portuguese football
and the subject of a controversial transfer after
Sporting lured him from Vitoria Setubal in 1999.

COACH
TOPPMOLLER, Klaus

German
Born: 12.08.51
• Not surprisingly for an ex-forward – he starred
for Kaiserslautern and made three apperances
for Germany – he has always been a coach who
places the emphasis on creative and attacking
football and for the first-half the 1993-94 season,
it looked as though his Eintracht Frankfurt side
were going to romp to the Bundesliga title in
style. But after the winter break goalscorer-in-
chief **Tony Yeboah** was injured, the team fell
apart and Toppmoller was fired.
• Took Bochum to the Second Division title in
1995-96 and Saarbrucken hope he can do the
same for them in 2000-2001.

PLAYER
TORRAO

Full name: Pedro Miguel Silva Torrao
Defender, Portuguese, 175cm, 68kg
Born: 12.03.77, Lisbon, Portugal
Clubs: Lourihanense (1997-98), Sporting Lisbon
(1998-99), Uniao Lama (1998-99),
Campomaiorense (1999-)
• Defender who played a key role in
Campomaiorense's successful fight against
relegation in 1999-2000.

TORRES GOMEZ, Javier
Midfielder, Spanish, 178cm, 72kg
Born: 09.01.70, Madrid, Spain
Clubs: Real Madrid B (1991-93), Valladolid (1993-99)
• Competent right-sided defender who is accomplished on the ball and likes to get forward.
• Has spent seven seasons at Valladolid, making him the club's longest-serving player.

TORRICELLI, Moreno
Defender, Italian, 183cm, 78kg
Born: 23.01.70, Erba, Italy
Clubs: Caratese (1990-92), Juventus (1992-98), Fiorentina (1998-)
Full international (Italy) 8 caps/0 goals
• Long-haired former carpenter who was discovered by Juventus as an amateur in 1992 and proved to be the revelation of the 1992-93 season.
• Tough and versatile – can play as a centre-back, right-back or midfielder. Greatest strength is his ability to attack down the right.
• Won the Champions Cup, the UEFA Cup and three Italian League titles while with Juventus.
• Made his international debut for Italy against Wales in January 1996.

TORRISI, Stefano
Defender, Italian, 184cm, 77kg
Born: 07.05.71, Ravenna, Italy
Clubs: Modena (1987-91), Ravenna (1991-93), Reggiana (1993-94), Torino (1994-95), Bologna (1995-98), Atletico Madrid (Spa) (1998-99), Parma (1999-)
Full international (Italy) 1 cap/0 goals
• Fearsome, tough-tackling centre-back who is one of the hardest defenders in Serie A.
• Made his reputation at Bologna and won his only cap for Italy against France in June 1997.
• Spent an unhappy season in Spain with Atletico Madrid, having been signed by **Arrigo Sacchi**, but returned to play for Parma.

TOSHACK, John
Welsh
Born: 22.03.49
• Much-travelled coach who has worked in Spain, Portugal, Turkey and Wales. A clever tactician with a sharp eye for a player but also a coach who demands maximum effort from his players.
• Was a powerful centre-forward who formed a strong partnership with **Kevin Keegan** at Liverpool, winning three League championships, the FA Cup and two UEFA Cups. Scored 95 goals in over 200 games for Liverpool and also won 40 caps (13 goals for Wales).
• Became player-manager of Swansea in 1979 and famously took them from the fourth division to the first division before leaving to join Sporting Lisbon.
• Moved on to Real Sociedad in 1985, winning the Spanish Cup in 1987 and finishing second in the League a year later.
• Was appointed coach of Real Madrid in 1989 and won the Spanish title in his first season, scoring a record 108 goals. Was sacked the following season after three successive defeats. 'I admit that I'm to blame for our performances this season, just as I was to blame for the 108 goals we scored last season.'
• Returned for a second spell spell at Real Sociedad where, in 1994, he briefly tried to combine the job with that of part-time coach of Wales but resigned after just one game, a defeat by Norway.
• Had further jobs at Deportivo La Coruna and Besiktas of Turkey before being reappointed at Real Madrid in February 1999. He lasted until the following November, when he was sacked after falling out with Real president **Lorenzo Sanz**.

OTTI, Francesco

orward, Italian, 180cm, 80kg
orn: 27.09.76, Rome, Italy
lubs: Roma (1992-)
ull international (Italy) 17 caps/3 goals
The great young hope of Italian soccer who is
een by many in Italy as the talented playmaker
he national side has lacked since the days of
iancarlo Antognoni.
• Extremely gifted, with excellent vision and
echnique and the ability to hit accurate long
asses. A formidable free-kick expert, to boot.
• Has already spent eight seasons at Roma,
aving made his debut aged 16, in March 1993,
n a 2-0 win for Roma against Brescia.
• Used to support Roma from the terraces and
nodels himself on the former 'Prince of Roma',
iuseppe Giannini.
• Has thrived at Roma under coach **Fabio
Capello**, who has played him in a midfield playmaking role behind strikers **Marco Delvecchio**
and **Vincenzo Montella**, rather than the striking
position favoured by previous coaches.
• In the run-up to Euro 2000, national coach **Dino
Zoff** resisted the growing bandwagon calls to
play Totti as the national team playmaker, instead
playing him as a second striker.
• A hero and pin-up with the Roma fans, but he
has said he will change clubs if he has to in
order to win some silverware. 'I want to win
something because when your career is over, the
greatest satisfaction is to look back on the
League titles and Cups you have won.'

PLAYER
TOYES, Geoffray

Defender, French, 176cm, 76kg
Born: 18.05.73, Bordeaux, France
Clubs: Bordeaux, Metz
• Former Under-21 and Olympic cap who can line
up at left-back, right-back or stopper. A tough-
tackler, quick, with above-average distribution.

PLAYER
TOZE

Full name: Antonio Jose Ferreira Cerdeira
Goalkeeper, Portuguese, 183cm, 79kg
Born: 14.01.71, Serta, Portugal
Clubs: National (1996-98), Rio Ave (1998-)
• Keeper who impressed in the 1999-2000 season
in Portugal, despite being relegated with Rio Ave.

COACH
TRAPATTONI, Giovanni
Italian
Born: 17.03.39
• The most successful coach in the history of
Italian football.
• Has won seven Italian League titles, one
German League title, two Italian Cups, one
European Champions Cup, one European Cup-
winners Cup, three UEFA Cups, one European
Supercup, one World Club Cup and one German Cup.
• Won 17 caps for Italy in a playing career spent
with Milan and Varese. Won the European Cup
twice with Milan, in 1963 and 1969.
• Guided Milan to the Italian League title in 1976,
his first season in charge.
• Achieved most of his great successes at
Juventus, winning the League in 1977, 1978,
1981, 1982, 1984 and 1986, the Cup-winners Cup
in 1984 and the European Cup at Heysel in 1985.
• Moved to Milan in 1986 and won a record
seventh League title with Inter in 1989, adding
the UEFA Cup a year later.
• Returned to Juventus in 1992 and won the
UEFA Cup in 1993 before resigning and taking up
an offer from Bayern Munich, but he quit at the
end of the season, citing the language barrier as
a problem.
• Was sacked for the first time in his career in
1996, after 21 matches in charge of Cagliari.
Returned to Germany in 1997, where this time
there were fewer language problems and Bayern
won the League title.
• Joined Fiorentina in 1998 and guided them into

Giovane Trapattoni

the Champions League before resigning in October 1999.

• Appointed Italian national coach in July 2000 following the surprise resignation of **Dino Zoff**.

PLAYER
TREZEGUET, David
Forward, French/Argentinian, 187cm, 75kg
Born: 15.10.77, Rouen, France
Clubs: Platense, Monaco
Full international (France) 21 caps/8 goals

• Prolific young marksman, who was runner-up in the French League scoring charts in the 1999-2000 season with 22 goals. A full French international since the age of 20 and a member his country's World Cup and European Championship-winning squads, he is a born penalty box predator, renowned for his ability to lose markers and his composed finishing with hi deadly right-foot.

• Born in France but raised in Argentina, he was once turned down by Paris Saint-Germain.

• Scored the extra time Golden Goal in France's Final victory over Italy at Euro 2000. Joined Juventus after the tournament for £15million.

• Pronounced Dah veed Tray zay gay.

PLAYER
TROBOK, Goran
Midfielder, Bosnian, 180cm, 70kg
Born: 06.09.74, Pale, Bosnia
Clubs: Partizan Belgrade

• Ballwinner with a good touch. Due to his consistent form, he is a player on whom his coach always can count.

COACH
TROSSERO, Enzo
Argentinian

• National coach of Switzerland since July 2000.

• A former Argentinian international who played for his country in the 1986 World Cup qualifiers, but did not make the squad for the finals.

SARTAS, Vassilis

Midfielder, Greek, 185cm, 75kg
Born: 12.11.72, Alexandria, Greece
Clubs: AEK Athens (1992-96), Sevilla (Spa) (1996-2000), AEK Athens (2000-)
Full international (Greece) 33 caps/5 goals

One of the Greek national side's most influential players, a talented midfielder with an eye for goal.

Moved to Sevilla in 1996 and scored the two goals in a 1999 promotion play-off which secured the club's return to the Spanish first division. Returned to Greece in summer 2000.

SYKHMEISTRUK, Edward

Forward, Ukrainian, 172cm, 69kg
Born: 08.07.77, Ukraine
Clubs: CSKA Kyiv
Full international (Ukraine) 7 caps/0 goals

One of the best playmakers in the Ukrainian national championship, a skilful, accurate passer. However, he has failed to reproduce his club form for the national team.

TSYMBALAR, Ilya

Midfielder, Russian, 176cm, 71kg
Born: 17.06.69, Kiev, Ukraine
Clubs: Chernomorets (1989-1994), Moscow Spartak (1994-1999), Lokomotiv Moscow (2000-)
Full international (Russia) 28 caps/4 goals

• Former Spartak captain and a charismatic leader, an excellent passer with good ball control.
• Played two unofficial internationals for Ukraine before opting to play for Russia and played at Euro 96.
• Voted Russian Footballer of the Year in 1995.

TUDOR, Igor

Defender, Croatian, 193cm, 90kg
Born: 16.04.78, Spalato, Croatia.
Clubs: Hajduk Split (1995-98), Juventus (Ita) (1998-)
Full international (Croatia) 15 caps/0 goals

• Tall, powerful centre-back who has been likened by **Tomislav Ivic** to a combination of **Frank Rijkaard** and **Marcel Desailly**.
• A non-playing member of Croatia's 1998 World Cup squad.
• Joined Juventus in summer 1998 after receiving offers from a number of big clubs.

TUGAY Kerimoglu

Midfielder, Turkish, 175cm, 72kg
Born: 24.08.70, Istanbul, Turkey
Clubs: Galatasaray (1987-1999), Rangers (Sco) (2000-)
Full international (Turkey) 59 caps/2 goals

• Experienced left-sided midfielder who has tried with limited success to curtail his 'wild man' reputation in recent years.
• A strong and effective player in midfield holding positions but has been criticised for not venturing forward more often.
• A member of team, coach by **Fatih Terim**, which won the gold medal at the 1993 Mediterranean Games.
• A veteran of Euro 96, he played two games as a substitute at Euro 2000, before starting the group game against Belgium. But he reacted angrily to being substituted before half-time by throwing a water bottle at coach **Mustapha Denizli**, and was sent home in disgrace.
• Joined Rangers in January 2000.

PLAYER
TUMA, Vitezslav

Forward, Czech, 190cm, 92kg
Born: 04.07.71, Czech Republic
Clubs: Karvina, Petra Drnovice
• Prolific marksman, latterly with Karvina and now with the village club Drnovice. Tuma is a regular fixture on the Czech League's top goalscorers chart but has never forced his way into the national team.

PLAYER
TUMBA, Zico

Forward, DR Congo, 186cm, 86kg
Born: 29.04.77, Kinshasa, DR Congo
Clubs: Mulhouse (Fra), Metz (Fra) (1996-97), Mulhouse (Fra) (1997-98), De Graafschap (Hol) (1998-)
• Attacker from DR Congo with great pace and strong work rate. One of those exotic surprises De Graafschap has a habit of introducing. Started on the bench but later kept star man Eric Viscaal out of the team.

PLAYER
TUR, Diego

Defender, Danish, 186cm, 77kg
Born: 03.10.71, Denmark
Clubs: FC Copenhagen
• Hugely promising youth talent whose career was derailed when he broke a leg in the 1992 Danish Cup Final, and he missed the Olympic Games. Has suffered from injuries ever since.
• Danish mother and a Spanish father, but opted to play for Denmark.

PLAYER
TURCI, Luigi

Goalkeeper, Italian, 188cm, 87kg
Born: 27.01.70, Cremona, Italy
Clubs: Cremonese (1988-90), Treviso (1990-91), Alessandria (1991-92), Cremonese (1992-96), Udinese (1996-)

• Experienced keeper whose performances helped to keep Cremonese in the top flight against the odds.

PLAYER
TURDO, Mario

Forward, Argentinian,185cm, 82kg
Born: 01.01.79, Armstrong, Argentina
Clubs: Independiente (1997-99), Celta Vigo (1999-)
• Highly promising young winger and a product of the Independiente youth system in Buenos Aires.
• Very quick, but has yet to develop the finishing ability to match his pace.
• Argentinian Under-21 international.

PLAYER
TURIEL, Jesus Angel

Full name: Jesus Angel Turiel de la Cruz
Defender, Spanish, 180cm, 74kg
Born: 06.10.73, Malaga, Spain
Clubs: Valladolid (1993-)
• Defensive midfielder with useful shot who can also play in central defence.
• Now well-established at Valladolid after several seasons in Spain's lower divisions.

PLAYER
TYCE, Roman

Midfielder, Czech, 177cm, 70kg
Born: 07.05.77, Roudnice, Czech Republic
Clubs: Sparta Prague, Slovan Liberec, Munich 1860 (Ger) (1998-)
Full international (Czech Republic) 1 cap/0 goals
• Promising young Czech midfield destroyer with all the usual attributes of the ball-winner breed: good timing in the tackle, physical strength, application and lack of ego. However, there is also a strong element of flair in his game, an interesting trick or two with the ball.

PLAYER
DOVIC, Saso
Forward, Slovenian, 180cm, 75kg
Born: 12.12.68, Slovenia
Clubs: Beveren (Bel) (1993-96), Lausanne (Swi) (1996-99), LASK (Aut) (1999-)
Full international (Slovenia) 41 caps/17 goals
Striker who played for Slovenia at Euro 2000, having played in all 12 qualifying matches. His height and good first touch make him an effective target man, but he is also a useful penalty-box poacher.
Made his international debut against Estonia in 1993.

PLAYER
UJFALUSI, Tomas
Defender, Czech, 182cm, 72kg
Born: 24.03.78, Czech Republic
Clubs: Sigma Olomouc
Young midfielder who figured prominently in both the qualification stages and the finals of the 2000 European Under-21 Championships, at which the Czechs were runners-up.

PLAYER
ULICH, Ivo
Midfielder, Czech, 174cm, 70kg
Born: 05.09.74, Czech Republic
Clubs: Slavia Prague
Full international (Czech Republic) 8 caps/1 goal
• Young flair midfielder who was cruelly one of the four Czech squad members culled from the original 26 before the team travelled to Euro 2000.
• Ulich is impressive on the ball but can over-elaborate and is erratic in front of goal.

COACH
ULIVIERI, Renzo
Italian
Born: 02.02.41
• One of Italy's leading coaches after his success in reviving the fortunes of Bologna, taking the former Italian champions from Serie C to Serie A and into the UEFA Cup.
• Has since had less successful spells at Napoli, where he was sacked in mid-season with the club in mid-table in Serie B, and Cagliari, who were relegated from Serie A in 1999-2000.
• Was previously in charge of Perugia, Sampdoria, Modena and Vicenza.

PLAYER
UMIT Davala
Defender, Turkish, 186cm, 74kg
Born: 30.07.73, Germany
Clubs: Waldhof Mannheim, Apyonspor, Istanbulspor, Diyarbakirspor, Genclerbirligi, Galatasaray
Full international (Turkey) 8 caps/0 goals
• The ultimate utility player, having lined up in every position for Galatasaray except goalkeeper. However, his favoured position is right-back for his club and for the Turkish national team.
• Has a knack of scoring important goals; he scored both goals in Galatasaray's Turkish Cup Final victory over Besiktas.
• International debut against Azerbaijan in April 1996.

PLAYER
UPSON, Matthew
Defender, English, 186cm, 72kg
Born: 18.04.79, Eye, England
Clubs: Luton Town (1996-97), Arsenal (1997-)
• Young English centre-back who was signed by Arsenal for £1million as a long-term replacement for the ageing back four at Highbury, but has yet to establish himself as first-choice under **Arsene Wenger**.
• England Under-21 international.

PLAYER
URIBE, Christian
Midfielder, Chilean, 182cm, 70kg
Born: 01.08.76, Concepcion, Chile
Clubs: Huachipato (1995-99) Benfica (Por) (2000-)
Full international (Chile)
• Chilean midfielder with a fiery temperament. Joined Benfica in January 2000, on loan from Huachipato.

PLAYER
URRUTIA, Josu
Full name: Jose Urrutia Telleria
Midfielder, Spanish, 177cm, 70kg
Born: 10.04.68, Bilbao, Spain
• Attacking midfielder who has been fiercely loyal to Athletic Bilbao, staying at the club for 15 seasons and becoming a key player, valued for his ball skills and passing ability.

PLAYER
URZAIZ, Ismael
Full name: Ismael Ursaiz Aranda
Forward, Spanish, 188cm, 83kg
Born: 07.10.71, Tudela, Spain
Clubs: Albacete (1991-92), Real Madrid B (1992), Celta Vigo (1993), Rayo Vallecano (1993-94), Salamanca (1994-95), Espanyol (1995-96), Athletic Bilbao (1996-)
Full international (Spain) 20 caps/8 goals
• Tall, commanding striker with good ball skills who is favoured by Spain coach **Jose Antonio Camacho** as a partner for Raul in the national team.
• A product of the Real Madrid youth system who has spent the past four seasons at Athletic Bilbao after spells at a number of different clubs.
• Signed by Bilbao from Espanyol in summer 1996 for £2million.
• International debut against the Czech Republic on 09.10.96.
• Made a big impact in the Euro 2000 qualifying campaign, scoring six times and helping to dispel the myth of him as a simple target man who just creates chances for others. Member of the Spanish squad for the finals.

PLAYER
AIRELLES, Tony
Forward, French, 186cm, 76kg
Born: 10.04.73, Nancy, France
Clubs: Nancy, Lens, Lyon
Full international (France) 8 caps/1 goal
  At Nancy and Lens, he was rightly considered among the most dangerous forwards in France; whether playing through the middle or out wide, his pace, close control, directness and goals made him a defender's nightmare. But he struggled to settle following a move to Lyon in 1999 and, for his pains, found himself cut from the French Euro 2000 squad.
• An all-round good guy, he was the choice of the French players union to front an anti-violence campaign.
• Surname pronounced Vah rell.

PLAYER
VALCARCE, Vincente
Full name: Vincente Valcarce Cano
Defender, Spanish, 171cm, 66kg
Born: 19.10.74, Lanzarote, Spain
Clubs: Real Madrid C (1995-96), Real Madrid B (1996-98), Malaga (1998-)
• Hard-working left-back with a powerful shot who established himself at Malaga after coming through the youth system at Real Madrid.

ADMINISTRATOR
VALE E AZEVADO, Jose Antonio
Portuguese
• President of Benfica since late 1997. A lawyer by profession, he was seen as the man to save the Lisbon club, but has so far struggled to deal with the club's mounting debts.
• 'Every day, there were new debts. I really thought Benfica could not survive. But the balance sheet is not so terrifying now.'

PLAYER
VALENCIA, Juan Jose
Full name: Juan Jose Valencia de la Serna
Goalkeeper, Spanish, 179cm, 76kg
Born: 18.09.71, San Sebastian, Spain
Clubs: Athletic Bilbao (1991-99), Sevilla (1999-)
• Reliable keeper with good positional sense.
• Had the unenviable task of succeeding the great Andoni Zubizarretta at Athletic Bilbao.
• Moved on to Sevilla, where he was a regular first-choice during their first season back in the Spanish top flight.

PLAYER
VALERON, Juan Carlos
Full name: Juan Carlos Valeron Santana
Midfielder, Spanish, 184cm, 71kg
Born: 17.06.75, Gran Canaria, Spain
Full international (Spain) 14 caps/0 goals
• Playmaker who starred for Mallorca in the 1997-98 season and was subsequently picked by Atletico Madrid, where his performances persuaded national coach Jose Camacho to give him an international debut as a second-half substitute against Italy in November 1998.
• Is most efffective playing behind two strikers, where his vision and passing range can unhinge any defence.
• Compared by some in Spain to Zinedine Zidane.
• Played for Spain at Euro 2000 and joined Deportivo after the tournament in a package alongside Juan Capdevila and Jose Molina.

PLAYER
VALGAEREN, Joos
Midfielder, Belgian, 187cm, 82kg
Born: 03.03.76, Leuven, Belgium
Clubs: Mechelen (1994-97), Roda JC (Hol) (1997-2000), Celtic (Sco) (2000-)
Full international (Belgium) 6 caps/0 goals
• Midfielder or centre-back who kept a low profile while with Mechelen, but came to the fore in Holland at Roda JC.

Giovanni Van Bronckhorst

• Made a surprise international debut in Februar 2000 against Portugal, and his assured performance catapaulted him into contention for a starting place at Euro 2000.
• Used his height to good effect in central defence alongside **Lorenzo Staelens** in the Belgian national side at Euro 2000.
• Moved to Scotland, to Celtic, after Euro 2000.

PLAYER
VALTOLINA, Fabian
Midfielder, Italian, 170cm, 62kg
Born: 10.06.71, Limbiate, Italy
Clubs: Milan (1990-91), Pro Sesto (1991-93), Monza (1993-94), Bologna (1994), Chievo V. (1994-95), Bologna (1995-96), Piacenza (1996-98), Venezia (1998-)
• Diminutive striker who started out at Milan but was crowded out by the stars and was forced to do the rounds of the lower leagues before moving to Piacenza in 1996.

PLAYER
VAN BASTEN, Marco
Dutch
Born: 31.10.64
• One of the greatest strikers of the modern era, a complete forward who was voted European Footballer of the Year in 1988 and 1999. His volleyed goal for Holland in the Final of the 1988 European Championship will be remembered as one of the greatest goals scored in a major Final.
• Won multiple honours with Milan in the late 1980s and early 1990s, but his career was cruelly cut short by an ankle injury which forced him to retire in 1995.
• Now lives in Monte Carlo, where he plays golf, and rarely, if ever, speaks to the media.

PLAYER
VAN BOMMEL, Mark
Midfielder, Dutch, 187cm, 85kg
Born: 22.04.77, Maasbracht, Holland

ubs: Fortuna Sittard, (1992-99), PSV (1999-)
Rugged midfielder who impressed in PSV's
999-2000 Champions League campaign.
Spent seven seasons at Fortuna Sittard where
ther-in-law **Bert Van Marwijk** was coach.
Former Under-21 and Olympic international
oped for future honours.

LAYER
AN BRONCKHORST, Giovanni
idfielder, Dutch, 178cm, 776kg
orn: 05.02.75, Rotterdam, Holland
lubs: Feyenoord (1992-93), RKC (1993-94),
eyenoord (1994-98), Rangers (Sco) (1998-)
ull international (Holland) 19 caps/1 goal
One of **Dick Advocaat's** first signings at Ibrox,
ne Dutch midfielder has brought a touch of class
) Rangers' midfield and has fought his way
nto contention for a place in Holland's Euro
'000 squad.
A versatile player, he plays at left-back for the
utch national side.

PLAYER
AN DEN BERGH, Dave
orward, Dutch, 190cm, 80kg
Born: 07.05.776, Amsterdam, Holland
Clubs: Ajax Amsterdam (1996-97), Rayo
Vallecano (Spa) (1997-)
• Right-sided midfielder or forward who has
excellent technique and a powerful shot.
• A product of the Ajax Amsterdam youth system
who was once tipped as the 'Next Big Thing' but
failed to live up to expectations.
• Moved to Vallecano in 1997, but has been used
mostly as a substitute.

AGENT
VAN DEN BOSSCHE, Dirk
• Belgian agent who represents **Aliyu
Mohamed**.
• **Contact:** Vossenberg 7, B-8340 Damme-Susele,
Belgium. Tel: 00 32 50 35 66 98.

PLAYER
VAN DEN BROM, John
Midfielder, Dutch, 187cm, 78kg
Born: 04.10.66, Amersfoort, Holland
Clubs: Vitesse Arnhem (1986-93), Ajax (1993-95),
Istanbuspor (Tur) (1995-96), Vitesse Arnhem (1996-)
Full international (Holland) 2 caps/1 goal
• Veteran who was in the Vitesse side which won
promotion to the Dutch first division and was then
transferred to Ajax, but failed to win a regular place.
• Now back at Vitesse and a key man for **Ronald
Koeman**.
• A midfielder with good skills and vision.

PLAYER
VAN DER DOELEN, Bjorn
Midfielder, Dutch, 179cm, 70kg
Born: 24.08.76, Goirle, Holland
Clubs: PSV Eindhoven (1994-97), Standard Liege
(1997-98), PSV Eindhoven (1998-)
• Strong central midfielder who graduated from
the PSV youth ranks under **Bobby Robson**, but
has struggled under **Eric Gerets**.

COACH
VAN DER ELST, Franky
Belgian
Born: 30.04.61
• Spent nearly all his playing career (16 seasons)
at Club Brugge. Was a highly effective midfielder
in the Belgian national team, playing in four
World Cups.
• Had been expected to get a coaching job at
Club Brugge, but surprisingly went to newly-
merged club Germinal Beerschot Antwerp, where
he had a solid first year as coach in 1999-2000.

REFEREE
VAN DER ENDE, Mario
Dutch
Born: 28.03.56
• Works full-time as a teacher.
• Awarded his FIFA in badge 1990.

PLAYER
VAN DER GAAG, Mitchell
Forward, Dutch, 188cm, 81kg
Born: 22.10.71, Zutphen, Holland
Clubs: PSV Eindhoven (1989), NEC (1990), Sparta Rotterdam (1990-92), PSV (1992-94), Motherwell (Sco) (1995-97), Utrecht (1997-)
• Skipper of Utrecht and a powerful defender who is particularly strong in the air and is a regular scorer. Learned his skills at PSV but was injured too often to make it in Eindhoven.

PLAYER
VAN DER GOUW, Raimond
Goalkeeper, Dutch, 191cm, 83kg
Born: 24.03.63. Oldenzaal Holland
Clubs: Go Ahead Eagles (1985-88), Vitesse Arnhem (1988-96), Manchester United (Eng) (1996-)
• Keeper who moved to Old Traffford in 1996 after eight seasons as number one at Vitesse. Was number two to **Peter Schmeichel** and looked set to concentrate on his coaching role in Manchester following the signing of **Mark Bosnich** and **Massimo Taibi**. But with both two faltering in 1999-2000, he was named by **Alex Ferguson** as his preferred number two to new arrival **Fabien Barthez** in August 2000.

PLAYER
VAN DER HAAR, Hans
Forward, Dutch, 186cm, 87kg
Born: 01.02.75, Amersfoort, Holland
Clubs: Ajax, Haarlem, De Graafschap, KFC Uerdingen (Ger), Ulm (Ger) (1999-)
• Striker and **Dennis Bergkamp** lookalike who was Ulm's top scorer in 1999-2000 with 10 goals.
• Learnt his football at Ajax, where his reserve team coach for six years was **Louis Van Gaal**, who once told him: 'You have no future up front. You'd be better off trying your luck as a defender.'

PLAYER
VAN DER HOORN, Freddy
Defender, Dutch, 180cm, 78kg
Born: 12.10.63, Den Bosch, Holland
Clubs: Den Bosch (1984-89), Dundee United (Sc (1989-94), Eendracht Aalst (Bel) (1994-96), Den Bosch (1997-)
• Experienced defender with spells in Scotland and Belgium who has now returned to his forme club.
• Has a good shot but lacks pace due to his age Has had to live with people reminding him abou a particularly nasty foul on Danny Hesp, brother of **Ruud Hesp** and then a promising left-back at Ajax. The foul broke Hesp's leg.

PLAYER
VAN DER LAAN, Harry
Forward, Dutch, 173cm, 72kg
Born: 24.02.64, Gouda, Holland
Clubs: Den Haag (1988-90), Feyenoord (1990-91), Den Haag (1991-95), Dordrecht (1995-96), Cambuur (1996-98), Den Bosch (1998-)
• Another veteran who didn't quite hit the big time. He lacks consistency and is often blamed for being too arrogant. But a good penalty-taker.

COACH
VAN DER LEM, Gerard
Dutch
Born: 15.11.52
• Coach of AZ Alkmaar since July 1999.
• Close associate of **Louis Van Gaal**, for whom he was assistant at Ajax from 1989 to 1997 and Barcelona from 1997 to 1999, and was linked to a move to the Dutch national team to link up as Van Gaal's number two for a third time.
• Modest player with Roda, Feyenoord, Sparta Rotterdam and Utrecht who began his coaching career in 1984 as assistant coach at AZ, moving on to Haarlem and then to Ajax.

PLAYER
VAN DER LUER, Eric

Midfielder, Dutch, 179cm, 70kg
Born: 16.08.65, Maastricht, Holland
Clubs: MVV (1982-87), Assent (1987-88), Roda JC (1988-)
Full international (Holland) 2 caps/0 goals
Influential skipper of Roda JC who is a tireless worker for the team. Has a good left foot and takes a great free-kick. Has been on the fringes of the Dutch national team in the past, but never managed to add to his couple of caps.

PLAYER
VAN DER MEYDE, Andy

Forward, Dutch, 175cm, 74kg
Born: 30.09.79, Arnhem, Holland
Clubs: Ajax Amsterdam (1997-99), FC Twente (1999-2000), Ajax Amsterdam (2000-)
• Another talent from the famed Ajax school who was sent on loan lent to FC Twente, where he had a brilliant season, both scoring goals and providing assists from the right wing.
• Due to return to Ajax for the 2000-2001 season, although he said that he would prefer to stay in Enschede for another year if going back to Amsterdam meant being on the bench.

PLAYER
VAN DER SAR, Edwin

Goalkeeper, Dutch, 197cm, 85kg
Born: 29.1070, Voorhout, Holland
Clubs: Ajax (1990-99), Juventus (Ita) (1999-)
Full international (Holland) 51 caps/0 goals.
• One of the world's best goalkeepers who won a host of honours – Dutch League, Champions League, World Club Cup – with Ajax before joining Juventus in the summer of 1999.
• An excellent 'footballing' keeper with great reflexes who likes to play the ball out of defence.
• 'In Holland the beauty of the game is as important as the result. In Italy the only thing that matters is winning.'

Edwin Van der Sar

Louis Van Gaal

PLAYER
VAN DER STRAETEN, Yves
Goalkeeper, Belgian, 187cm, 78kg
Born: 08.08.71, Dendersmondts, Belgium
Clubs: Antwerp (1993-96), Maritimo (Por) (1997-2000), Lierse (2000-)
• Keeper who is back in Belgium after a three-year spell in Portugal with Maritimo.

PLAYER
VAN DER VEGT, Hendrik
Midfielder, Dutch, 185cm, 75kg
Born: 18.02.72, Kampen, Holland
Clubs: Zwolle (1991-95), Willem II (1995-98), Udinese (Ita) (1998-)
• Central midfielder who impressed many in Italy with his performances for Udinese following a free transfer from Willem II in 1998. But since showing that early promise, he has been hit by injuries and found it difficult to win his place back in the side.

PLAYER
VAN DIEMEN, Patrick
Midfielder, Dutch, 185cm, 82kg
Born: 12.06.72, Woerden, Holland
Clubs: Utrecht (1990-94), AZ (1994-95), NEC (1995-96), RKC (1996-98), Anderlecht (Bel) (1998-)
• Talented right-sided midfielder who came into his own during Anderlecht's title-winning season in 1999-2000.

COACH
VAN GAAL, Louis
Dutch
Born: 08.08.51
• Highly-respected figure in Dutch and European football who succeeded **Frank Rijkaard** as Holland coach in July 2000 after resigning from Barcelona at the end of the 1999-2000 season.
• An accomplished player – a creative midfielder – who came close to playing for Holland but found opportunities at Ajax restricted by the

resence of **Johan Cruyff**, and he moved to AZ. Made his name as a coach with Ajax, where he ecame first-team boss in September 1991 and ained a reputation for playing fast, attacking ootball featuring young talent from the club's outh system. Under Van Gaal, Ajax won the UEFA Cup in 1992 and the European Cup in 1995 plus ive Dutch League titles and the World Club Cup.

Was approached by Barcelona, but saw out his ontract in Amsterdam, joining the Catalan club n summer 1997. He guided them to successive Spanish League titles, but faced growing criticism for his signing of Dutch players at the expense of local Catalan talent such as **Gerard**, **Oscar** and **Roger.**

• In typically forthright style – some would say arrogant – he refused to acknowledge his critics, and continued only with the support of club president **Josep Nunez**. When Nunez announced his intention to step down in summer 2000, Van Gaal lost his last remaining supporter and resigned as coach.

• **Jari Litmanen**: 'Louis Van Gaal is a tough man but at this level you don't get by with just a smile and a few kind words.'

PLAYER
VAN GALEN, Barry
Midfielder, Dutch, 180cm, 73kg
Born: 04.04.70, Haarlem, Holland
Clubs: Haarlem (1991-93), Roda JC (1993-96), NAC (1996-97), AZ (1997-)
• Midfielder who is just short of international class. Nevertheless he is a little underrated, with a good left foot and great work-rate, although he gets too many bookings. Should be playing at a top club.

PLAYER
VAN GASTEL, Jean-Paul
Midfielder, Dutch, 178cm, 78kg
Born: 28.04.72, Breda, Holland
Clubs: Willem II (1990-96), Feyenoord (1996-)

Full international (Holland) 5 caps/2 goals
• Midfield playmaker at Feyenoord who missed out on Euro 2000 because of injuries.
• A busy player in the midfield engine room who hits a good long pass and packs a powerful shot at free-kicks. Succeeded **Ronald Koeman** at Feyenoord.
• Also plays in central defence.
• Scored with a penalty on his debut for Holland, against Brazil in 1996.
• Stayed at Feyenoord for the 1999-2000 season after a transfer to Roma broke down. 'If money was the only thing that mattered to me I would have gone abroad earlier in my career. I could have gone to court and let the judge decide what Roma had to pay. But I didn't want to because Feyenoord are too precious to me.'

PLAYER
VAN GOBBEL, Ulrich
Defender, Dutch, 182cm, 91kg
Born: 16.01.71, Paramaribo, Surinam
Clubs: Baval, NEC (1982-88), Willem II (1988-90), Feyenoord (1990-96), Galatasaray ((Tur) (1996), Southampton (Eng) (1996-97), Feyenoord (1997-)
Full international (Holland) 8 caps/0 goals
• Solid centre-back with lashings of power and commitment (sometimes too much). Returned to Feyenoord after spells in England and Turkey.

PLAYER
VAN HALST, Jan
Defender, Dutch, 177cm, 77kg
Born: 20.04.69, Utrecht, Holland
Clubs: Utrecht (1988-89), Wageningen (1989-90), FC Twente (1990-99), Ajax (1999-)
• Bald-headed defender cum midfielder who had a bad season at Ajax in 1999-2000. Can play centre-back, marker or holding midfielder. Not a great technician, a hard man.
• Played several years for FC Twente, where he was a key player.

Ruud Van Nistelrooy

PLAYER
VAN HINTUM, Marc
Midfielder, Dutch, 174cm, 64kg
Born: 22.06.67, Oss, Holland
Clubs: Helmond Sport (1987-88), RKC (1988-92), Willem II (1992-97), Vitesse Arnhem (1997-)
Full international (Holland) 1 cap/0 goals
• Left-back who reached the national team in the autumn of his career, making his debut under **Frank Rijkaard** against Germany in November 1998. Loves to come forward. Has great pace and is skipper of Vitesse.
• Made his name in the national team thanks the brilliant run of Vitesse in the Dutch League and injuries to **Winston Bogarde** and **Arthur Numan**.

PLAYER
VAN HOOIJDONK, Pierre
Forward, Dutch, 194cm, 86kg
Born: 29.11.69, Steenbergen,Holland
Clubs: RBC (1989-91), NAC (1991-95), Celtic (Sco) (1995-97), Nottingham Forest (Eng) (1997-99), Vitesse Arnhem (1999-2000) Benfica (Por) (2000-)
Full international (Holland) 20 caps/7 goals
• Tall, strong striker who has not been without his personal problems. Went on strike in 1998 in a bid to earn a transfer to a bigger club after relegation with Nottingham Forest.

PLAYER
VAN HOUDT, Peter
Forward, Belgian, 176cm, 70kg
Born: 04.11.76, Hasselt, Belgium
Clubs: St Truiden (1994-96), Roda JC (1996-)
Full international (Belgium) 2 caps/0 goals
• Belgian striking partner of **Bob Peeters** who has benefitted from the close attention paid by defenders to Peeters.
• Had to go into hiding for a couple of weeks in 1999-2000 after receiving anonymous death threats.

PLAYER
AN KERCKHOVEN, Nico
Midfielder, Belgian, 190cm, 80kg
Born: 14.12.70, Lier, Belgium
Clubs: Lint, Lierse, Schalke (1998-)
Full international (Belgium) 26 caps/2 goals
Lanky Belgian international left-sided midfielder
or full-back who may lack a little defensive steel
but is excellent when moving forward to support
the attack. Very influential when his former club
Lierse took the Belgian title in 1996-97.
Surname pronounced Kirk hoven.

COACH
VAN MARWIJK, Bert
Dutch
Born: 19.05.52
A former defender who performed miracles at
lowly Fortuna Sittard in the 1997-98 season: not
only did they finish eighth in the Dutch League,
Fortuna were also runners-up in the Cup Final. It
was only a question of time before Van Marwijk
left and he eventually succeeded Leo Beenhakker
at Feyenoord in the summer of 2000.
• Father-in-law of PSV's **Mark Van Bommel**.

PLAYER
VAN MEIR, Eric
Defender, Belgian, 185cm, 85kg
Born: 28.02.68, Deurne, Belgium
Clubs: Charleroi (1991-96), Lierse (1996-)
Full international (Belgium) 17 caps/1 goal
• Imposing defender who can operate in the
centre or as a full-back. Has a reputation in
Belgium for being a hard man who is strong in
the air and in the tackle.
• Made his international debut in October 1993
against Gabon, but has never established himself
in the starting eleven, despite being a member of
the squad at the 1994 and 1998 World Cups and
at Euro 2000.
• Path at international level has usually been
blocked by **Lorenzo Staelens**, although critics

have suggested he lacks the necessary flair.
• Possesses a powerful shot from long range.
• Won the Belgian League title in 1997 with
Lierse, a year after moving from Charleroi.

PLAYER
VAN NISTELROOY, Ruud
Forward, Dutch, 188cm, 80kg
Born: 01.07.76, Oss, Holland
Clubs: Den Bosch (1993-97), Heerenveen (1997-
98), PSV Eindhoven (1998-)
Full international (Holland) 10 caps/1 goal
• The great white hope of Dutch soccer whose
£19million transfer to PSV from Manchester
United was scuppered after he refused to
undergo extensive medical tests. Within days of
the transfer breaking down, he himself broke
down with a serious knee injury.
• The leading scorer in the Dutch League for two
successive seasons with PSV.
• Began at amateur club Nooit Gedacht, which
translates as Never Thought Of, in his native
region of Brabant.
• Appears to be the complete striker, with no
obvious faults. 'I'm in motion for 90 minutes,
always trying to lose my markers, and defenders
never know what I'm going to do.'
• Cites **Marco Van Basten** as his hero, leading
to the inevitable comparisons.
• Made his international debut against Germany
in November 1998.

ADMINISTRATOR
VAN PRAAG, Michael
Dutch
• President of Ajax Amsterdam and a leading fig-
ure in the G-14 group of leading European clubs.

ADMINISTRATOR
VAN RAAY, Harry
Dutch
• President of PSV Eindhoven.

Yves Vanderhaeghe

PLAYER
VAN UTRECHT, Leonard
Forward, Dutch, 182cm, 77kg
Born: 25.02.69, Noordwijk, Holland
Clubs: Excelsior (1992-95), Padova (Ita) (1996), Cambuur (1997-)
• Lively, skilful winger who returned to Cambuur after a spell at Padova in Italy. Has a good shot, but as one of the key players at Cambuur, couldn't prevent them from relegation in May 2000.

PLAYER
VAN VOSSEN, Peter
Forward, Dutch, 182cm, 79kg
Born: 21.04.68, Zieriksee, Holland
Clubs: Beveren (1989-92), Anderlecht (Bel) (1992-93), Ajax (1993-95), Istanbulspor (Tur) (1995-96), Rangers (Sco) (1996-98), Feyenoord (1998-)
Full international (Holland) 31 caps/9 goals
• Striker who spent three years in Turkey and Scotland before returning to Holland in 1998, and earning a recall against Peru in October 1988, when he scored.
• A member of the Ajax squad which won the Champions League in May 1995.
• Moderate technique but very high work-rate.
• Was a surprise inclusion in the Dutch squad at Euro 2000, when **Frank Rijkaard** was criticised for playing a former team-mate in crucial matches.
• Has won championship medals in Scotland, Holland and Belgium.

PLAYER
VAN WONDEREN, Kees
Defender, Dutch, 185cm, 75kg
Born: 04.01.69, Bergen, Holland
Clubs: NEC (1991-94), NAC (1994-96), Feyenoord (1996-)
Full international (Holland) 5 caps/0 goals
• Former midfielder turned centre-back who reads the game well and is composed on the ball. Plays full-back at international level.
• Late developer who surprised many, including

ouis Van Gaal, when he broke into the Dutch ational side under **Frank Rijkaard**, making his ebut against Ghana, 13.10.98 (0-0).

DMINISTRATOR
ANDEN STOCK, Roger
President of Anderlecht.

PLAYER
ANDERHAEGHE, Yves
Midfielder, Belgian, 180cm, 82kg
Born: 01.30.70, Roeselare, Belgium
Clubs: Roeselare, Cercle Bruges, Eendracht Aalst 1994-98), Mouscron (1998-2000), Anderlecht 2000-)
Full international (Belgium) 15 caps/0 goals
• Holding midfielder who made a belated arrival on the international scene aged 29.
• Made his international debut for Belgium against Peru in May 1999 and went on to establish himself in the eyes of coach **Robert Waseige** as the long-term successor to **Franky Van der Elst** in the centre of Belgium's midfield.
• Spent the majority of his career with Belgium's less fashionable clubs after making a remarkable recovery after being struck down by a virus at the age of 18 which left him with a five per cent chance of survival. He was in a coma and one newspaper even published his obituary.
• 'I considered suicide, thinking 'what would my life be like if I couldn't play sport again?' I didn't want to live like a vegetable for the rest of my life. During my time in hospital I lost 44 lb and couldn't eat, speak or walk. But deep down I was convinced that if you don't want to die, you're not going to. My character has pulled me through.'
• Has yet to win any silverware, something a move to Anderlecht in summer 2000 was designed to change.

PLAYER
VANENBURG, Gerald
Defender, Dutch, 172cm, 69kg

Born: 05.03.64, Utrecht, Holland
Clubs: Munich 1860 (Ger)
Full international (Holland) 42 caps/1 goals
• The Dutch golden oldie thought he had played his last game as 1860's sweeper at the end of the 1998-99 season. But when his replacement, the Czech **Tomas Votava**, broke his leg in summer 1999, Vanenburg was persuaded out of retirement to step into the breach and played with his customary style and foresight.
• Began his career as a midfield whizzkid with Ajax, earning the nickname of 'Geraldinho' for his Brazilian-like skill. Member of the Dutch 1988 European Championship-winning squad.

PLAYER
VANOLI, Paolo
Defender, Italian, 184cm, 79kg
Born: 12.08.72, Varese, Italy
Clubs: Varese (1989-91), Bellinzago (1991-92), Corsico (1992-93), Venezia (1993-95), Verona (1995-98), Parma (1998-2000), Fiorentina (2000-)
Full international (Italy) 2 caps/1 goal
• Left-sided midfielder was a useful squad player at Parma for the past two years, playing in the team which beat Marseille in Moscow to win the 1999 UEFA Cup. Moved to Fiorentina in July 2000.
• Made his Serie A debut for Verona against Bologna in September 1996.

PLAYER
VAREILLE, Jerome
Forward, French, 181cm, 82kg
Born: 01.06.74, Vernoux, Belgium
Clubs: Metz (1992-95), Mulhouse (1995-97), Kilmarnock (Sco) (1997-)
• The Frenchman made a dramatic impression when he joined Kilmarnock from Mulhouse three years ago and the strong-running striker has become a great favourite with the Rugby Park fans, even although his form dipped sharply during 1999-2000.

Ivica Vastic

PLAYER
VARESANOVIC, Mirsad
Midfielder, Bosnian, 184cm, 72kg
Born: 31.05.72, Sarajevo, Bosnia
Clubs: Bursaspor (Tur)
Full international (Bosnia)
• Versatile Bosnian international who can play o
the right side of midfield or in attack.
• Moved to Turkey after a season in Greece with
Olympiakos, where he won the League title and
played in the Champions League.

PLAYER
VARGA, Stanislav
Defender, Slovakian, 193cm, 93kg
Born: 08.10.72, Slovakia
Clubs: Tatran Presov (1995-98), Slovan Bratislava
(1998-2000), Sunderland (Eng) (2000-)
Full international (Slovakia)
• Tall, imposing centre-back who joined
Sunderland in summer 2000.

PLAYER
VASARA, Vesa
Midfielder, Finnish, 183cm, 73kg
Born: 16.08.76, Finland
Clubs: HJK Helsinki (1995-)
Full international (Finland) 7 caps/2 goals
• A quick winger known for his excellent crosses.
• Not the strongest of players physically, and has
struggled with injuries.
• Finnish Under-21 international.

PLAYER
VASCHUK, Vladyslav
Defender, Ukrainian, 180cm, 72kg
Born: 02.01.75
Clubs: Kyiv Dynamo, Ukraine
Full international (Ukraine) 28 caps/1 goal
• Product of Kyiv Dynamo youth school who has
developed over several seasons from an
inexperienced rookie into one of the best
central defenders in Ukraine.

ASSELL, Darius

Forward, English, 171cm, 76kg
Born: 13.06.80. Birmingham England
Clubs: Aston Villa (1998-2000)
Young striker who broke into the Villa first team in the 1999-2000 season and is seen as having a bright future. Pacy and stocky, his impact has so far been restricted to substitute appearances. England Under-21 international.

VASTIC, Ivica

Forward, Croatian/Austrian, 182cm, 78kg
Born: 29.09.69, Split, Croatia
Clubs: Hajduk Split (1990-91), Austria Vienna (1991-92), St Polten (1992-93), Admira Wacker (1993-94), Duisburg (Ger) (1993-94), Sturm Graz (1994-)
Full international (Austria) 28 caps/11 goals
Croatian-born striker who has established himself as a leading marksman for Sturm Graz and his adopted national team Austria.
Became an Austrian citizen in 1996 and was one of Austria's most impressive players at the 1998 World Cup in France.

VEIGA, Antonio da Silva

• Portuguese agent who is best known for his role as agent for **Luis Figo**, but also represents **Emerson Moises Costa, Fernando Couto, Sa Pinto** and **Simao Sabrosa**.
• **Contact:** Av. Conde Valbom, 67-1°. Esq., P-1000, Lisbon, Portugal. Tel:00 351 1797 1440.

VEKIC, ZORAN

• Spanish-based Yugoslav agent who represents **Predrag Mijatovic**.
• **Contact:** Maria de Molina 5, E-47001, Valladolid, Spain.

VELAMAZAN

Full name: Antonio Velamazan Tejedor
Midfielder, Spanish, 173cm, 70kg
Born: 22.01.77, Barcelona, Spain
Clubs: Barcelona (1994-96), Real Oviedo (1996-97), Albacete (1997-98), Extremadura (1998-99), Espanyol (1999-)
• Versatile defender or midfielder who does most of his best work as an anchorman at the back of midfield.

VELASCO, Juan

Defender, Spanish, 179cm, 75kg
Born: 17.05.77, Seville, Spain
Clubs: Sevilla (1996-99), Celta Vigo (1999-)
Full international (Spain) 4 caps/0 goals
• Pacy right-back and former winger who came to the fore during Celta Vigo's recent successes, earning an international debut for Spain against Poland on 26.01.2000.
• Came through the youth ranks at Sevilla, joinng Celta for £3.75million in summer 1999.

VELLISCA, Martin

Full name: Martin Vellisca Gonzalez
Midfielder, Spanish, 172cm, 64kg
Born: 22.08.71, Madrid, Spain
Clubs: Getafe (1992-93), Salamanca (1993-99), Zaragoza (1999-)
• Frail left-winger signed from Salamanca when they suffered their latest relegation, in 1999. Has done a good job covering up for the departure of both **Gustavo Lopez** and **Kili Gonzalez**.

VENABLES, Terry

English
Born: 06.01.43
• Coach of England at Euro 96 who has not worked as a coach since leaving Crystal Palace

in early 2000.

• Continues to be high-profile in the UK thanks to his media work, and is occasionally touted for a return to the England manager's job, though it is highly unlikely that the Football Association would ever consider such a move.

• Nicknamed 'El Tel' after a successful spell at Barcelona in the 1980s, when he won the Spanish League and lost the European Cup Final on penalties to Steaua Bucharest.

PLAYER
VENCEL, Alexander
Goalkeeper, Slovakian, 189cm, 80kg
Born: 02.03.67, Bratislava, Slovakia
Clubs: Slovan Bratislava (1989-94), Strasbourg (Fra) (1994-2000), Le Havre (Fra) (2000-)
Full international (Slovakia) 19 caps/0 goals

• Tall, experienced keeper who moved to Le Havre in summer 2000 after losing his place in the Strasbourg first team.

PLAYER
VENETIDIS, Stelios
Defender, Greek, 170cm, 62kg
Born: 15.10.76, Greece
Clubs: Skoda Xanthia (1998-99), PAOK (1999-)
Full international (Greece) 10 caps/0 goals

• The versatile and combative PAOK man can play full-back, centre-back or as a defensive midfielder and as one of the most-improved players in the country, he fully deserved his breakthrough into the Greek national squad in 1999.

COACH
VENGLOS, Jozef Dr
Slovakian

• Highly respected coach who has been in charge of five different national teams: Czechoslovakia, who he guided to victory on penalties in the 1976 European Championship Final, Australia, Malaysia, Oman and Slovakia.

• At club level, he twice won the old Czech League with Slovan Bratislava and was a runner-up in the European Cup-winners Cup. Has also coached Sporting Lisbon, Aston Villa, Fenerbahce and Celtic.

• Has worked for FIFA as a technical advisor at World Cups, and was a member of UEFA's technical study group at Euro 2000.

PLAYER
VENNEGOR OF HESSELINK, Jan
Forward, Dutch, 188cm, 85kg
Born: 07.11.78, Oldenzahl, Holland
Clubs: FC Twente (1996-)

• Dutch Under-21 international striker with an excellent eye for goal.

• One of Holland's biggest talents at the moment. Tall and powerful striker who is extremely dangerous in the penalty area and in the air. Might go to a top club soon and would be well suited for the English Premier League.

• Has the longest name in Dutch football. Vennegoor and Hesselink used to be the names of two separate farms in the area of Enschede. Both farms were merged but kept their name. (Of means or in Dutch). He prefers to use his entire name, even when signing autographs.

PLAYER
VENTOLA, Nicola
Forward, Italian, 185cm, 80kg
Born: 24.05.78, Grumo Appula, Italy
Clubs: Bari (1994-98), Internazionale (1998-99), Bologna (1999-), Atalanta (2000-)

• Young striker who showed great promise at Bari and then in a season at Inter, but found competition for places in Milan too strong following the arrival of **Christian Vieri** and was sold to Bologna for £7.5million in summer 1999.

• Italian Under-21 international and a member of Italy's victorious squad at the 2000 European Under-21 championship.

ENTURIN, Giorgio

idfielder, Italian, 170cm, 68kg
orn: 09.07.68, Bollate, Italy
lubs: Torino (1987-88), Cosenza (1988-89), rino (1989-90), Napoli (1990-91), Torino (1991- l), Lazio (1994-99), Atletico Madrid (1999-)
ll international (Italy) 1 cap/0 goals
One of **Arrigo Sacchi**'s failed signings at Atletico adrid, a midfield worker who failed to adapt to panish football and was tipped for a return home.

ERBIR, Pavel

orward, Czech, 176cm, 76kg
orn: 13.11.72, Czech Republic
lubs: Teplice
ull international (Czech Republic) 9 caps/2 goals
Prolific and talented striker who appears oomed to remain on the fringes of the Czech ational team set-up, despite looking relatively omfortable on the few occasions when he has gured in the team.
Considered for Euro 2000 but ultimately discarded y national team coach **Jozef Chovanec**.

ERGOOSSEN, Sef

utch
orn: 05.08.47
A local hero in Limburg, the southern province f Holland, where he impressed at MVV before noving to neighbours Roda JC. There, he omehow managed to guide his team into uropean competition.

ERHEYEN, Gert

Midfielder, Belgian, 189cm, 86kg
Born: 20.09.70, Hoogstraten, Belgium
Clubs: Anderlecht (1990-92), Club Brugge (1992-)
Full international (Belgium) 31 caps/5 goals
• Hard-working, extremely determined right-sided midfielder who has been in and out of the Belgian national side over the past six seasons.
• A tireless worker for his team-mates who likes to get forward into goalscoring positions.
• International debut v Denmark in October 1994.
• Played his way into the Belgian team for Euro 2000 with a series of goalscoring performances in the warm-ups.

VERLAAT, Frank

Defender, Dutch, 184cm, 78kg
Born: 05.03.68, Haarlem, Holland
Clubs: Ajax (1986-89), Lausanne (Swi) (1989-92), Auxerre (Fra) (1992-95), Stuttgart (Ger) (1995-99), Ajax (1999-2000), Werder Bremen (Ger) (2000-)
Full international (Holland) 1 caps/0 goals
• Veteran defender who played most of his best football away from Holland after playing as a teenager in the 1987 European Cup-winners Cup Final for Ajax.
• Returned to Ajax for the 1999-2000 season, but was a disappointment and he returned to Germany in the summer of 2000.

VERLINDEN, Danny

Goalkeeper, Belgian, 176cm, 82kg
Born: 15.08.63, Belgium
Clubs: Lierse (1987-88), Club Brugge (1988-)
Full international (Belgium) 1 cap/0 goals
• Athletic and agile keeper who comes off his line well, but sometimes lacks authority.
• Belgium's third choice keeper at the 1994 and 1998 World Cups.

VERLINDEN, Jan

Defender, Belgian, 170cm, 72kg
Born: 08.03.77, Mechelen, Belgium
Clubs: Mechelen (1996-99), Twente (Hol) (1999-)
• Intelligent defender who moved to Holland in 1999 after completing a teaching degree in Belgium.

Juan Sebastien Veron

PLAYER
VERMANT, Sven

Midfielder, Belgian, 183cm, 79kg
Born: 04.04.73, Mechelen, Belgium
Clubs: Mechelen (1991-93), Club Brugge (1993-
Full international (Belgium) 2 caps/0 goals
• Attacking left-sided midfielder who has shone i
fits and starts in the Belgian League since joinir
Club Brugge in 1993 as a promising 20-year-old
• Made his international debut for Belgium
against Armenia in October 1995, but has never
managed to win a regular place in the national
squad and has been ignored by **Robert Waseig**

PLAYER
VERNAZZA, Paolo

Midfielder, English, 175cm, 70kg
Born: 01.11.79, London Islington, England
Clubs: Arsenal (1996-), Ipswich (1998, loan),
Portsmouth (2000, loan)
• Young central or right-sided midfielder who
is one of the few home-grown players to have
broken into the Arsenal first team under **Arsene
Wenger**.

PLAYER
VERON, Juan Sebastien

Midfielder, Argentinian, 186cm, 80kg
Born: 09.03.75, Buenos Aires, Argentina
Clubs: Estudiantes (1993-96), Boca Juniors
(1996), Sampdoria (Ita) (1996-97), Parma (Ita)
(1997-99), Lazio (Ita) (1999-)
Full international (Argentina)
• One of the few players in world football who
deserve the label of 'playmaker'. A mover and
shaker on the pitch, a tireless runner with great
vision and intelligence.
• Joined Lazio in a £20million transfer from
Parma in June 1999, a year after Parma had paid
Sampdoria £13million for his services.
• Father – also Juan Veron – was a
uncompromising striker (nicknamed The Witch)
for Estudiantes de la Plata in the 1960s.

UEFA Cup winner with Parma in 1999 and an
alian League champion with Lazio in 2000.
Sports a large tattoo of Che Guevara on his
est.

REFEREE
ESSIERE, Gilles
rench
orn: 18.09.59
Lists his occupation as a manager.
Awarded his FIFA badge in 1992

PLAYER
IALI, William
efender, Italian, 185cm, 79kg
orn: 16.11.74, Vaprio d'Adda, Italy
lubs: Atalanta (1991-93), Fiorenzuola (1993-94),
avenna (1994-95), Cesena (1995), Monza (1995-
6), Ascoli (1996-97), Lecce (1997-)
• Invaluable and trusted member of the Lecce
efence, a centre-back who captains the team
vith authority and determination.

COACH
IALLI, Gianluca
talian
orn: 09.07.64
• Coach of Chelsea since February 1998, when
he replaced **Ruud Gullit**, though he had joined
the club in July 1996 as a player.
• Has used his reputation as a player – a
European Cup winner with Juventus, 59 caps and
16 goals for Italy, 1995 *World Soccer* Player of
the Year – to attract world-class players to
Stamford Bridge.
• Retired as a player during the 1999-2000
season to concentrate on being coach, and he
is widely expected to return to a high-profile
position in Italy at some stage.

PLAYER
VIANDER, Jani
Goalkeeper, Finnish, 190cm, 86kg

Born: 18.08.75, Finland
Clubs: TuPS, FinnPa (1994-95), Ilves (1995), Jaro
(1996), Jazz (1997), Kortrijk (Bel) (1997-98), HJK
Helsinki (1998-)
Full international (Finland) 7 caps/0 goals
• Has worked hard to become one of Finland's
top goalkeepers, serving a number of clubs at
home and abroad.
• Won a first-team place at HJK Helsinki only in
1999, but is now a regular for Finland.
• A powerful keeper with a good reach.

PLAYER
VICTOR
Full name: Victor Manuel Fernandez Gutierrez
Midfielder, Spanish, 165cm, 66kg
Born: 17.04.74, Merida, Spain
Clubs: Real Madrid B (1993-95), Tenerife (1995-
96), Toledo (1996), Valladolid (1996-2000),
Villarreal (2000-)
Full international (Spain) 1 cap/0 goals
• Tiny playmaker capped by **Jose Antonio
Camacho**, but overlooked for Euro 2000. He
signed, surprisingly, for newly-promoted Villarreal
in summer 2000.

PLAYER
VICTOR
Full name: Victor Sanchez del Amo
Midfielder, Spanish, 183cm, 74kg
Born: 23.02.76, Madrid, Spain
Clubs: Real Madrid (1994-98), Racing Santander
(1998-99), Deportivo La Coruna (1999-)
• Right-sided midfielder who played an important
role in Deportivo's Spanish League title-triumph
in May 2000.
• Came through the ranks at Real Madrid, but
was surprisingly sold to Racing Santander,
despite claiming a regular spot in the Real
Madrid first team.
• Impressed at Santander and was sold on to
Deportivo.

Christian Vieri

VICTOR FERNANDEZ
Spanish
Born: 28.11.60
• Affable and upwardly-mobile, the heir apparen
for the Spain national team job should the pressure overwhelm **Jose Antonio Camacho**. Came
to prominence by building an attractive Zaragoz;
side between 1990 and 1997, winning the Cup-
winners Cup in 1995. Failed at Tenerife, but has
turned Celta Vigo into an
attractive, albeit brittle, side.

PLAYER
VIDAKOVIC, Hristo
Defender, Yugoslav, 183cm, 76kg
Born: 05.01.69, Sekovici, Bosnia
Clubs: FK Sarajevo (1989-92), Red Star Belgrade
(1992-94), Real Betis (Spa) (1994-)
Full international (Yugoslavia) 8 caps/0 goals
• Central defender who was born in Bosnia but
opted to make himself available for Yugoslavia
after moving from FK Sarajevo to Red Star in 1992.
• A hard-tackling centre-back or libero who
believes in playing football from the back.
• Missed the 1998-99 season following a serious
knee injury.

PLAYER
VIDARSSON, Arnar
Midfielder, Icelandic, 179cm, 77kg
Born: 15.03.78, Iceland
Clubs: FH, Lokeren (Bel) (1997-)
Full international (Iceland) 4 caps/0 goals
• Highly promising young midfielder who is set to
move on from Lokeren at some stage after
impressing many with his passing ability.

PLAYER
VIDIGAL
Full name: Jose Luis da Cruz Vidigal
Defender, Portuguese, 184cm, 83kg
Born: 15.03.73, Sa da Bandeira, Angola

lubs: Elvas (1990-94), Estoril (1994-95), porting Lisbon (1995-)
ull international (Portugal) 8 caps/0 goals
A hard-working midfielder and one of the most eliable players in any team. Versatile and can lso play in defence.
Member of the Sporting Lisbon side which won e 1999-2000 Portuguese League title.
Elder brother Lito is an international for Angola. Made his international debut for Portugal gainst Belgium in February 2000.

LAYER
IDOVIC, Gordan
efender, Belgian/Croatian, 189cm, 87kg
orn: 23.06.68, Sarajevo, Bosnia
lubs: Mouscron (1996-)
ull international (Belgium) 16 caps/0 goals
• Left-back who was born in the former Yugoslavia, but is now a naturalised Belgian, having made his international debut for Belgium against San Marino in 1997.
• A good man-to-man marker who reads the game well, and has pace, too.
• Made his name during Mouscron's surprise Belgian League title challenge under **Georges Leekens**.

PLAYER
VIDUKA, Mark
Forward, Australian, 188cm, 86kg
Born: 09.10.75, Melbourne, Australia
Clubs: Croatia Zagreb (Cro), Celtic (1998-2000) (Sco), Leeds (Eng) (2000-)
Full international (Australia) 16 caps/2 goals
• Powerful but temperamental striker who was never far from the headlines during an 18-month spell in Scotland with Celtic, whom he left to join Leeds for £7million in summer 2000.
• Born in Australia to Croatian parents, but got his professional break in Croatia, before a £3million transfer from Croatia Zagreb to Celtic in December 1998. But the pressure of a high-

profile move after a difficult final few months in Zagreb, got the better of him, and he deserted Glasgow for Australia, before returning in a better frame of mind a few weeks later.
• Despite his problems, he finally settled at Celtic and displayed a remarakable scoring ability, finishing the 1999-2000 season as top scorer in the Scottish League on 25 goals.

PLAYER
VIEIRA, Patrick
Midfielder, French, 191cm, 82kg
Born: 23.06.76, Senegal
Clubs: Cannes (1993-96), Milan (Ita) (1995-96), Arsenal (Eng) (1996-)
Full international (France) 30 caps/0 goals
• Stylish, powerful central midfielder who established himself as first-choice in the French national side in the period between winning the World Cup in 1998 and triumphing at Euro 2000.
• Was signed by Arsenal in early 1996 for £3million after **Arsene Wenger**, who had first spotted Vieira playing for Cannes against Monaco in July 1994, took advantage of the player's unhappy spell at Milan.
• He played only four times in 14 months for Milan and jumped at the chance to move to Highbury.
• Played a key role for Arsenal when they won the League and Cup double in 1998. **Dennis Bergkamp**: 'Patrick has the ability to attack and defend, and that gives us so much more power.'

PLAYER
VIERCHOWOD, Pietro
Defender, Italian, 180cm, 76kg
Born: 06.04.59, Calcinate, Italy
Clubs: Como (1977-81), Fiorentina (1981-82), Roma (1982-83), Sampdoria (1983-95), Juventus (1995-96), Milan (1996-97), Piacenza (1997-2000)
Full international (Italy) 45 caps/2 goals
• Veteran centre-back who refuses to retire. In August 2000, he vowed to play on until he has beaten **Dino Zoff**'s Serie A appearances record.

'I've played 562 times in the top flight and Zoff played 570 times. It would be a shame to stop now. That's why I've decided to play on.'
• Was looking for a new Serie A club to join after being relegated with Piacenza in May 2000.

PLAYER
VIERI, Christian
Forward, Italian, 185cm, 82kg
Born: 12.07.73, Bologna, Italy
Clubs: Prato (1989-90), Torino (1990-92), Pisa (1992-93), Ravenna (1993-94), Venezia (1994-95), Atalanta (1995-96), Juventus (1996-97), Atletico Madrid (Spa) (1997-98), Lazio (1998-99), Internazionale (1999-).
Full international (Italy) 20 caps/10 goals
• Australian-raised striker who became the world's most expensive striker following a £31million transfer from Lazio to Inter in July, Inter paying Lazio £25million plus the £6million-rated Diego Simeone.
• An outstanding striker who combines pace and power with good technique and hard work.
• Father Bob played professional football in Italy before emigrating to Australia.
• Scored Italy's 1000th goal on his international debut, against Moldova on March 1997.
• 'Is my son really worth that much?' Bob Vieri after his son's £12.5m transfer to Atletico Madrid.
• Has spent the past nine seasons with nine clubs, and attracting combined transfer fees in excess of £65million.
• Made the breakthrough in 1995 at Atalanta, scoring seven goals in 19 League games and joining Juventus at the end of the season.
• Played a starring role for Juventus in the 1996-97 Champions League after an injury to **Alen Boksic**. Was then surprisingly sold to Atletico Madrid, a move described by Juve president **Giovanni Agnelli** as 'foolishness'.
• Scored 24 goals in 24 games for Atletico before being sold for £19million in the summer of 1998.
• Claims not to be worried about money. 'At this level, a million more or less makes no difference to your lifestyle.'
• Finished as the second highest top scorer at the World Cup, with five goals for Italy. Missed Euro 2000 with a hamstring injury.
• Former Italy coach **Dino Zoff**: 'Vieri may be big and strong and good in the air but he is surprisingly nimble on the ground, as plenty of defenders have found out to their cost!'

PLAYER
VILJUGREIN, Bjorn
Midfielder, Norwegian, 180cm, 75kg
Born: 24.11.69, Norway
Clubs: Strommen (1991), Valerenga (1992), Lorenskog (1993-94), Stabaek (1995-96), Valerenga (1997-)
Full international (Norway) 1 cap/0 goals
• Injuries ruined the 1999 season but he bounced back in 2000. A midfielder with an enormous workrate who loves to have a crack at goal.

PLAYER
VILLA, Matteo
Defender, Italian, 181cm, 71kg
Born: 23.01.70, Vimercate, Italy
Clubs: Trento (1989-90), Reggiana (1990-91), Cagliari (1991-)
• Former Italian Under-21 defender who has been Cagliari's longest-serving player, serving them well for nearly a decade.

ADMINISTRATOR
VILLAR LLONA, Angel Maria
Born: 21.01.50
• President of the Spanish Football Federation and a member of the FIFA executive committee since 1998. Also a member of the UEFA executive.
• A lawyer by profession.
• He led Spain's campaign to host the 2004 European Championships, but did not have the influence to prevent smaller European countries backing Portugal.

VILNROTTER, Andras
Defender, Finnish, 188cm, 86kg
Born: 219.05.67, Finland
Clubs: TPS (1990-94), Jaro (1994-95), Inter Turku (1995-)
• Solid keeper whose consistent performances helped FC Haka to the Finnish League title in 1999.
• Good shot-stopper who often stays on his line.

VIOLEAU, Philippe
Midfielder, French, 178cm, 71kg
Born: 19.08.70, Challans, France
Clubs: Niort, Auxerre, Lyon
• An unsung hero in the middle of the field. Vastly experienced midfield workhorse who harries and tackles as though his life depended on it and who keeps the play ticking over with his uncomplicated but assured distribution.
• A skipper of the lead-by-example variety and a French double winner with Auxerre in 1995-96.

VIRT, Yuri
Goalkeeper, Ukrainian,
Born: 04.05.74, Ukraine
Clubs: Shakhtar
• Quick reactions, acrobatics and determination are his strongest characteristics. Impressed in 1999-2000 when he emerged as a clear challenger to **Alexander Shovkovsky** as Ukrainian number one.

VITAKIC, Milivoje
Defender, Yugoslav, 184cm, 80kg
Born: 16.05.77, Cacak, Yugoslavia
Clubs: Red Star Belgrade
• Left full-back who can also play in central defence. A similar player to one of his predecessors at Red Star, **Goran Djorovic**, but is more confident going forward.
• A regular in Yugoslavia's Under-21 side.

VITOR BAIA
Full name: Vitor Manuel Martins Baia
Goalkeeper, Portuguese, 186cm, 80kg
Born: 15.10.69, Vila Nova de Gaia, Portugal
Clubs: FC Porto (1988-96), Barcelona (Spa) (1996-2000), FC Porto (1998-99, loan), FC Porto (2000-)
Full international (Portugal) 74 caps/0 goals
• Portugal's leading keeper, a flamboyant showman who is close to breaking the all-time Portuguese caps record set by Joao Silva Pinto.
• Established himself as one of Europe's leading goalkeepers in the mid-1990s, winning a prize from ESM (European Sports Magazines) as the best goalkeeper in Europe in 1996.
• Grew up in a family of Benfica fans, but went along for a trial with FC Porto just to keep a friend company.
• Made his debut for Porto in 1988-89 season after an injury and suspension crisis.
• Winner of Portuguese League title in 1990, 1992, 1993 and 1995.
• Portuguese player of the year in 1992, having set a domestic record for not conceding a goal in more than 1000 minutes of play.
• Joined Barcelona in 1996 after playing for Portugal at Euro 96, but lost his place following a knee injury in 1997 and then fell out with coach **Louis Van Gaal** after criticising his rotation policy.
• Returned to Porto in 1999 and helped to win the League title again, but then suffered further knee trouble which put his participation at Euro 2000 in doubt.

VIVAR DORADO
Midfielder, Spanish, 182cm, 77kg
Born: 12.02.74, Madrid, Spain
Clubs: Leganes (1992-94), Tenerife (1994-98), Racing Santander (1998-)
• Elegant midfielder signed from Tenerife in 1998. Has linked up well with **Salva** and **Pedro Munitis** at Racing Santander.

PLAYER
VIVAS, Nelson
Defender, Argentinian, 170cm, 65kg
Born: 18.10.69, San Nicolas, Argentina
Clubs: Quilmes, Boca Juniors (1995-97), Lugano (Swi) (1998), Arsenal (Eng) (1998-), Celta Vigo (Spa) (1999, loan)
Full international (Argentina)
• Tough utility defender who has struggled to establish himself in Europe after playing for Argentina in the 1998 World Cup.
• Failed to win a first-team place at Arsenal and went on loan to Celta.

PLAYER
VIZCAINO, Juan
Midfielder, Spanish, 181cm, 77kg
Born: 06.08.66, Pobla de Mafumey, Spain
Clubs: Zaragoza (1987-90), Atletico Madrid (1990-98), Valladolid (1998-)
Full international (Spain) 15 caps/0 goals
• Hard-working anchor man who spent eight seasons at Atletico Madrid, winning the League and Cup double in 1996.
• Now winding down his career at Vallodolid but still finds the time and energy for attacking runs into the opposing half, where his solid right foot shot is put to good use.

PLAYER
VLCEK, Petr
Defender, Czech, 190cm, 83kg
Born: 18.10.73
Clubs: Slavia Prague, Standard Liege (Bel) (2000-)
Full international (Czech Republic) 15 caps/0 goals
• Defender who played a key part in the Slavia defence that was the best in the Czech League in 1999-2000.
• Occasional member of the Czech national team.
• Signed a contract with Standard Liege in the summer of 2000.

PLAYER
VLCEK, Stanislav
Forward, Czech, 182cm, 80kg
Born: 26.02.76, Czech Republic
Clubs: Sigma Olomouc
Full international (Czech Republic) 1 cap/0 goals
• Striker who made his international debut in February 2000 at the Carlsberg Cup friendly tournament in Hong Kong as part of a Czech national team drawn entirely from the domestic League.

PLAYER
VLAOVIC, Goran
Forward, Croatian, 178cm, 75kg
Born: 07.08.72, Nova Graasjska, Croatia
Clubs: Osijek (1989-91), Hask Grandjanski (1991-92), Croatia Zagreb (1992-94), Padova (Ita) (1994-97), Valencia (Spa) (1997-2000), Panathinaikos (Gre) (2000-)
Full international (Croatia) 40 caps/13 goals
• Lively striker with good technique.
• Famous for scoring goals for Croatia at Euro 96 and the 1998 World Cup.
• Dedicated his goal against Turkey at Euro 96 to the surgeon who performed a life-saving operation on him following a serious head injury.

PLAYER
VOGEL, Johann
Midfielder, Swiss, 177cm, 71kg
Born: 08.03.77, Geneva, Switzerland
Clubs: Grasshopper (1992-99), PSV (Hol) (1999-)
Full international (Switzerland) 34 caps/1 goal
• Talented midfielder of whom big things were expected at Grasshopper.
• A rare example of a French-Swiss player making a name for himself at Grasshopper, the German-Swiss flagship club.
• Made his debut for Grasshopper aged 15.
• Favourite position is central midfield, but can also play on the wing.
• Played in all of Switzerland's games at Euro 96.

COACH
VOGTS, Berti
German
Born: 30.12.46
• National coach of Germany for most of the
1990s, winning the 1996 European Championship
and reaching the quarter-finals of the 1994 and
1998 World Cups, but ultimately paid the price for
a lack of quality players.
• Played 96 times for Germany and spent his
entire playing career at Borussia
Monchengladbach before joining the German FA's
coaching set-up. He was in charge of the Under-
16s and Under-21s and was assistant to **Franz
Beckenbauer** at Italia 90, before taking charge
of the senior side in August 1990.

COACH
VOLLER, Rudi
German
Born: 13.04.60
• Former German international (47 goals in 90
appearances) and World Cup winner who was a
surprise appointment as German national coach
in the aftermath of Euro 2000.
• Has never coached a club side since retiring
as a player in 1996, instead working as sports
director at Bayer Leverkusen.
• Will be succeeded by Leverkusen coach
Christoph Daum in summer 2001.

PLAYER
VOLPI, Sergio
Midfielder, Italian, 175cm, 69kg
Born: 02.02.74, Orzinuovi, Italy
Clubs: Brescia (1992-94), Carrarese (1994-95),
Brescia (1995-96), Bari (1996-98), Venezia (1999-)
• Midfielder who is well established in Serie A
after an excellent spell at Bari, where he
attracted interest from a number of top clubs.

PLAYER
VONK, Hans
Goalkeeper, Dutch/South African, 196cm, 80kg
Born: 30.01.70, Alberton, South Africa
Clubs: RKC (1988-91), Wageningen (1991-92), Den
Bosch (1992-93), RKC (1993-96), Heerenveen (1996-)
Full international (South Africa) 13 caps/0 goals
• Experienced keeper who played in all of South
Africa's matches at the 1998 World Cup after
excellent form for Heerenveen in the Dutch League.

PLAYER
VOROBEI, Andrii
Forward, Ukrainian, 179cm, 65kg
Born: 29.11.78, Ukraine
Clubs: Shakhtar
Full international (Ukraine) 1 cap/0 goals
• Recent product of the Shakhtar youth school and
one of the great new hopes of Ukrainian football
after greatly improving his game in 1999-2000.
• An inventive, stylish forward with a bright
future and a regular Ukraine youth international.

PLAYER
VOROBYOV, Valeriy
Goalkeeper, Russian, 182cm, 75kg
Born: 14.01.70, Ukraine
Clubs: Krivbas (1992-94), Kyiv Dinamo (1995-95),
Krivbas (1995-97), Torpedo Moscow (Rus) (1997-)
Full international (Ukraine) 6 caps/0 goals
• Simple, reliable keeper who avoids showing off.
Famous for his ability to take penalty kicks.

PLAYER
VOS, Henk
Forward, Dutch, 187cm, 85kg
Born: 05.06.68, Wouw, Holland
Clubs: PSV Eindhoven (1985), Willem II (1985-87),
RBC (1987), Eindhoven (1987-88), Germinal
Ekeren (Bel) (1988-89), Standard Liege (Bel)
(1990), Metz (Fra) (1991), Standard Liege (1991-
93), Sochaux (Fra) (1993-96), Feyenoord (1996-
99), Den Bosch (1999-)

- Striker who has long been regarded as the enfant terrible of Dutch football, having made his debut at 15. Played for numerous clubs in Holland, Belgium and France, having been forced to go abroad after kicking a referee. Certainly wasn't a favourite at Feyenoord, where he played second fiddle to **Peter Van Vossen** and **Julio Cruz** at Feyenoord before going on loan to FC Den Bosch for the 1999-2000 season.

PLAYER
VOTAVA, Tomas
Defender, Czech, 186cm, 79kg
Born: 21.02.74, Czech Republic
Clubs: Dukla Prague, Sparta Prague, Munich 1860 (Ger) (1999-)
Full international (Czech Republic) 8 caps/0 goals
- Czech international sweeper who broke a leg shortly after signing for 1860 from Sparta Prague in the summer of 1999. A time-and-motion libero, more efficient than flash.

PLAYER
VRANJES, Mica
Midfielder, Yugoslav, 185cm
Born: 08.09.75, Yugoslavia
Clubs: Vojvodina Novi Sad
- Technically strong left wing-back who was captain and a key player for Vojvodina until he and several other players fell out with the club's management and went on strike for three weeks.

PLAYER
VREDE, Regillio
Defender, Dutch, 198cm, 90kg
Born: 18.01.73, Paramaribo, Surinam
Clubs: RKC (1995-96), Roda JC (1996-)
- Extremely tall defender who has great pace, tackles well and is good in the air. Scores a lot of goals from set-pieces and was nominated by several pundits to be part of **Frank Rijkaard**'s plans for the Dutch national team.
- His surname means peace.

PLAYER
VUGRINEC, Davor
Forward, Croatian, 179cm, 76kg
Born: 24.03.75, Varazdin, Croatia
Clubs: Trabzonspor (Tur), Lecce (Ita) (2000-)
Full international (Croatia) 7 caps/1 goals
- Promising striker who moved to Italy in June 2000 after impressing in Turkey with Trabzonspor.
- Scored twice on his international debut for Croatia against Malta in October 1998.

PLAYER
VURAL Korkmaz
Midfielder, Turkish, 180cm, 70kg
Born: 23.12.72, Samsun
Clubs: Samsunspor
Full international (Turkey) 4 caps/0 goals
- Midfielder who is most effective when using his pace on the flanks.
- Would probably have won more caps if he had been playing for a bigger club than Samsunspor.

PLAYER
VURENS, Edwin
Forward, Dutch, 188cm, 80kg
Born: 06.06.68, Leidschendam, Holland
Clubs: Sparta Rotterdam, FC Twente, Roda JC, St Gallen (Swi) (1996-98), Servette (Swi) (1999-)
Full international (Holland) 1 cap/0 goals
- Former Dutch Under-21 striker currently with Servette. Intelligent, a good mover off the ball and usually finishes with aplomb. Both hero and villain as his St Gallen side lost the 1998 Swiss Cup final to Lausanne. He scored twice but also missed a penalty in normal time and Lausanne fought back from 2-0 down to equalise and win in a shoot-out.

W

WAKELING, Vic
• Managing director of pay-TV company Sky Sports and a key figure in BSkyB's bids for English Premiership TV rights.

PLAYER
WAGNER, Martin
Midfielder, German, 174cm, 70kg
Born: 24.02.68, Offenburg, Germany
Clubs: Offenburger, Nurnberg, Kaiserslautern (1992-)
Full international (Germany) 6 goals/0 caps
Powerful, industrious left-sided midfielder and striker of a mean free-kick. Hit the winner when Kaiserslautern beat Karlsruhe in the Final of the 1996 German Cup.
Surname pronounces Vag ner.

PLAYER
WAGNER, Rene
Forward, Czech, 184cm, 70kg
Born: 31.10.72, Brno, Czech Rep
Clubs: Boby Brno (1992-96), Rapid Vienna (Aut) 1996-)
Full international (Czech Rep) 10 caps/3 goals
• Highly capable forward who has been a regular scorer in Austria since a move from his native Czech Republic.
• Top scorer in the Austrian League in 1996-97 with 21 goals.

PLAYER
WAHLSTEDT, Erik
Forward, Swedish, 179cm, 76kg
Born: 16.04.76, Sweden
Clubs: IFK Gothenburg (1994-96), Helsingborg (1997-)
• Dubbed a supersub while at IFK Gothenburg after he headed in a memorable winner against Milan in the Champions League in 1997. At Helsingborg, has added weight and workrate to midfield, helping them to the Swedish League title in 1999.

PLAYER
WALDOCH, Tomasz
Defender, Polish, 187cm, 83kg
Born: 10.05.71, Gdansk, Poland
Clubs: Stoczniowiec Gdansk, Gornik Zabrze, Bochum (Ger), Schalke (Ger) (1999-)
Full international (Poland) 59 caps/2 goals
• Centre-back of great aerial and tackling ability and who is extremely reliable. Looks comfortable when bringing the ball out of defence.

PLAYER
WALEM, Johan
Midfielder, Belgian, 170cm, 68kg
Born: 02.01.72, Soignies, Belgium
Clubs: RWDM, Anderlecht, Udinese (Ita), Parma (Ita), Udinese (Ita) (2000-)
Full international (Belgium) 20 caps/1 goal
• Arguably one of the most talented Belgian players of his generation and one of the few Belgians to have succeeded in Italy's Serie A.
• Made his debut for Anderlecht aged 18 and then capped at international while a still a teenager, making his debut for Belgium in November 1991 against Germany.
• Helped Anderlecht win three League titles in a row from 1993-95, including a League and Cup double in 1994.
• Moved to Udinese in 1997 and was granted a licence to roam in central midfield. His playmaking skills were crucial in creating goals for striker **Oliver Bierhoff**, who tried unsuccessfully to persuade Milan to sign Walem when he moved to Milan in 1998. Moved to Parma a year later, doing well to get a regular game in a fiercely competitive squad.
• Plays mostly on the left of midfield, but he has

Johan Walem

been unsuccessful in holding a regular place in the Belgian national side, missing out on France 98 completely, but making the squad for Euro 2000.

PLAYER
WALKER, Des
Defender, English, 180cm, 75kg
Born: 26.11.65, Hackney, England
Clubs: Nottingham (1983-92), Sampdoria (Ita) (1992-93), Sheffield Wednesday (1993-)
Full international (England) 59 caps/0 goals
• Central defender who was an England regular while with Nottingham Forest and earned a lucrative move to Italy, where he had an unhappy time at Sampdoria because he was played out of position at left-back.
• Returned to England in a £2.7million transfer to Sheffield Wednesday, but lost his England place as Graham Taylor's side failed to qualify for the 1990 World Cup.
• He has slowly regained his confidence, and his pace and intuitive reading of the game still make him a formidable opponent.

PLAYER
WALKER, Ian
Goalkeeper, English, 188cm, 83kg
Born: 31.10.71, Watford, England
Clubs: Tottenham (1990-), Oxford (1990-91, loan) Ipswich (1990-91, loan)
Full international (England) 3 caps/0 goals
• Keeper whose future at Spurs was placed in doubt by the summer 2000 signing of **Neil Sullivan**.
• Former Under-21 international who has not played for the full England side since his mistake let in a shot from Italy's **Gianfranco Zola** in a World Cup qualifier at Wembley in November 1996.
• Son of former Norwich and Everton manager Mike Walker.

WALLACE, Rod

Forward, English, 170cm, 73kg
Born: 02.10.69, Lewisham, England
Clubs: Southampton (1987-91), Leeds (1991-97), Rangers (Sco) (1998-)
Arguably **Dick Advocaat**'s most valuable signing, Wallace arrived at Ibrox from Leeds on a free transfer and scored over 20 goals in his first season as Rangers progressed to the domestic treble.
One of three footballing brothers: elder brother Danny played for Manchester United in the late 1980s, Ray played for Southampton.

PLAYER

WALLEMME, Jean-Guy

Defender, French, 186cm, 81kg
Born: 10.08.67, Maubeuge, France
Clubs: Lens, Coventry (Eng), Sochaux, St Etienne
Highly-experienced stopper or libero renowned for his consistency. Enjoyed his heyday during an excellent 10-year spell with Lens and many French football writers rate him as the best uncapped player of recent times.
Pronounced Jon-Gee Val em.

PLAYER

WALLERSTEDT, Jonas

Forward, Swedish, 180cm, 79kg
Born: 18.03.78, Sweden
Clubs: Norrkoping (1995-)
Full international (Sweden) 3 caps/0 goals
• Combative midfielder with an eye for goals. One of **Olle Nordin**'s favourite players who always gives 100 per cent. Made his international debut against South Africa in November 1999.

PLAYER

WALLINDER, Johan

Forward, Swedish, 185cm, 83kg
Born: 19.08.75 Sweden
Clubs: Orebro (1996-)
• Former left-back who has been converted to a striker. Started at Orebro, where he impressed and frustrated fans with his skilful but sometime irrational style.
• An economics student.

PLAYER

WAMBERTO

Full name: Wamberto Sousa Campos
Midfielder, Brazilian, 168cm, 67kg
Born: 13.12.74, Sao Luis Maranhao, Brazil
Clubs: Seraing (Bel) (1991-96), Standard Liege (Bel) (1996-98), Ajax (Hol) (1998-)
• Lightweight Brazilian winger who was in and out the Ajax team in 1999-2000. Came from Standard Liege, but was looking for another club for the 2000-2001 next season because he was unlikely to feature in **Co Adriaanse**'s plans.
• Has great pace but is not very creative and is only right-footed.
• Was a member of the Brazilian Under-17 team at the world youth championship in 1991, after which he signed a contract at Seraing.

PLAYER

WANCHOPE, Paulo

Forward, Costa Rican, 190cm, 78kg
Born: 31.07.76, Costa Rica
Clubs: Herediano (1996), Derby (Eng) (1996-99), West Ham (Eng) (1999-2000), Manchester City (Eng) (2000-)
Full international (Costa Rica)
• Unpredictable but talented striker whose career England has fluctuated from the brilliant to the mundane over the last four years.
• Burst onto the scene in autumn 1996 when he scored a brilliant solo goal for Derby against Manchester United at Old Trafford. But a move to West Ham did not work out and he joined Manchester City in August 2000.

PLAYER
WAPENAAR, Harald
Goalkeeper, Dutch, 185cm, 76kg
Born: 10.04.70, Vlaardingen, Holland
Clubs: RBC (1993-94), Helmond (1994-97, Utrecht (1997-98), Udinese (Ita) (1998-99), Utrecht (1999-)
• Keeper who is back at Utrecht after playing just two games for Udinese in 1998-99.

PLAYER
WARMUZ, Guillaume
Goalkeeper, French, 186cm, 83kg
Born: 22.05.70, Saint-Vallier, France
Clubs: Marseille, Louhans-Cuiseaux, Lens
• One of France's most consistent keepers for the best part of a decade. Started his career at INF Clairefontaine, the French national school of excellence and played a key role in Lens' League title victory in 1997-98.
• Gee oh mm Var mooz

PLAYER
WARZYCHA, Krzysztof
Forward, Polish,174cm, 69kg
Born: 17.11.64, Poland
Clubs: Ruch (1987-89), Panathinaikos (Gre) (1989-)
Full international (Poland) 50 caps/9 goals
• Never mind that the veteran ex-Polish international striker only managed nine goals in the 1999-2000 season. In 11 years up front for Panathinaikos, he has amassed no less than 222 League goals, making him the club's top all-time scorer.
• The original penalty box predator, he is always looking for a half-chance and is adept at finding space for himself in the box.
• Brother Robert was also a Polish international.
• Surname pronounced Wah shee ka.

PLAYER
WARLEY
Full name: Warley Silva dos Santos
Forward, Braziliam, 174cm, 68kg
Born: 13.02.78, Brasilia, Brazil
Clubs: Atletico Paraense (1998), Sao Paulo (1999), Udinese (Ita) (1999-)
Full international (Brazil)
• Stocky but skilful striker who has a similar playing style to Romario, but has yet to develop the same ruthlessness in front of goal.

COACH
WASEIGE, Robert
Belgian
Born: 26.08.39
• The first Walloon (French-speaking) national coach of Belgium who succeeded **Georges Leekens** in August 1999 and was credited for turning round the fortunes of the national side.
• Has had a long but for the most part undistiguished career as a club coach in Belgium over the past 30 years.
• Started out at Winterslag, taking them from the third division to the first. Moved on Standard Liege for three years, then returned to Winterslag
• Spent eight years at FC Liege (1983-92), before spells at Charleroi and Standard Liege. Also had a brief, unsuccessful spell in Portugal with Sporting.
• Was voted's Belgium manager of the year in 1986, 1994 and 1995, with his only notable silverware being the 1990 Belgian Cup with Liege.
• A League runner-up with Standard Liege in 1995 and a Cup finalist with FC Liege in 1987 and 1993.

PLAYER
WATERREUS, Ronald
Goalkeeper, Dutch, 185cm, 85kg
Born: 25.08.70, Lemiers, Holland
Clubs: Roda JC (1992-94), PSV (1994-)
• Keeper who took over from Stanley Menzo at PSV in 1994, but lost out following the signing of **Ivica Kralj**.

...ATSON, Steve

...efender, English, 183cm, 79kg
...orn: 01.04.74. North Shields, England
...ubs: Newcastle (1990-99), Aston Villa (1998-
...00), Everton (2000-)
Versatile campaigner who can play in defence
...' midfield but is most effective as a right-wing
...ack. He can appear a little cumbersome at
...mes, but is solid defensively and works hard.
   Moved to Everton in summer 2000 for £2.5
...illion in a bid to get into the England squad. He
...ad left Newcastle for Villa in a £4million transfer
...fter falling out of favour with **Ruud Gullit**.

...OACH
...VDOWCZYK, Dariusz

...olish
...orn: 25.09.62
   Coach of Polonia Warsaw and a former player
...ith Gwardia and Legia Warsaw. In 1989 he
...oved to Celtic and five years later to Reading
...efore returning to Poland in 1998 and earning
... reputation as one of the country's most
...romising coaches.
... Took over Polonia in 1998, and completed a
...emarkable treble in 1999-2000, winning the
...olish League, FA Cup and League Cup.

...PLAYER
...VEAH, George

...rward, Liberian, 185cm, 82kg
...orn: 01.10.66, Monrovia, Liberia
...lubs: Young Survivors (1981-84), Bongrange
...1984-85), Mighty Barolle (1985-86), Invicible
...leven (1986-87), Tonerre Yaounde (Cam) (1987-
...88), Monaco (Fra) (1988-92), Paris Saint-Germain
...Fra) (1992-95), Milan (Ita) (1995-2000), Chelsea
...Eng) (2000, loan), Manchester City (Eng)
...ull international (Liberia)
● One of the greatest African foobailers of all
time who is winding down his career in England.
● A powerful, strong-running striker with

Arsène Wenger

Taribo West

excellent technique and control, he has won League titles with Monaco, Paris Saint-Germain and Milan and was voted FIFA Footballer of the Year in 1995, when he also become the first African to win the European Footballer of the Year award.

• Born into poverty in Liberia, he has singlehandedly supported the Liberian national team, often paying the team's expenses and travel costs, and acting as a national figure of reconciliation in a country ravaged by civil war. Appointed as a UNICEF ambassador.

• Dedicated his 1995 FIFA award to **Arsene Wenger**, who spotted and developed him while at Monaco.

• His wife and children live in New York, away from the civil war in Liberia.

COACH
WEBER, Heribert
Austrian
Born: 28.06.55

• Coach of Rapid Vienna since 1998. As a player he won 68 caps for Austria, and played for Sturm Graz, Rapid Vienna and Salzburg. As a coach he won the League with Salzburg before joining Rapid.

PLAYER
WEBER, Ralf
Midfielder, German, 191cm, 81kg
Born: 31.05.69, Germany
Clubs: SpVgg Hainstadt, Kickers Offenbach, Eintracht Frankfurt (1989-)
Full international (Germany) 9 caps/0 goals

• Eintracht skipper and left-back or wing-back who has shown great character to fight back to full fitness after spending two years out in the mid-1990s with knee trouble. Always ready to raid down his flank and an accurate crosser of the ball, he would surely have made many more international appearances if he had not been jinxed by injury.

• Surname pronounced Vay ber.

PLAYER
WEISER, Patrick
Midfielder, German, 181cm, 72kg
Born: 25.12.71, Germany
Clubs: Koln, Rennes (Fra) (1997-1999), Wolfsburg (1999-)
Very capable left-sided wing-back. Always has been dynamic and very competitive, but a two-year spell in France with Rennes has sharpened up his technique and awareness no end.
Surname pronounced Vie zer.

PLAYER
WEIR, David
Defender, Scottish, 188cm, 86kg
Born: 10.05.70, Falkirk, Scotland
Clubs: Falkirk (1992-96), Hearts (1996-99), Everton (1999-)
Full international (Scotland) 13 caps/ 0 goals
• Central defender who won an international call-up after achieving success with Hearts and played at the 1998 World Cup finals before joining Everton in early 1999.

COACH
WENGER, Arsene
French
Born: 22.10.49
• Manager of Arsenal since September 1996 who has been a profound influence at Highbury and on English football in general. His thoughtful approach to the game, in particular fitness and physical preparation, has helped to prolong the career of a number of players who had been thought to be past their best. In addition, his scouting network and knowledge of world football have reaped huge value in the transfer market.
• Obtained an economics degree from Strasbourg University in 1974, and after an undistinguished playing career with Mulhouse and Strasbourg, he became youth coach at Strasbourg in 1983, moving on to become head coach at Nancy in 1984, and Monaco in 1987.

• Made his name at Monaco, where he won the French League title in 1991 and was a strong influence on the future careers of **George Weah** ('Arsene made me the man I am today') and **Glenn Hoddle** ('He opened my eyes to coaching').
• Moved to Japan in 1994 to coach Nagoya Grampus Eight, returning to Europe in September 1996, to Arsenal.

PLAYER
WEST, Taribo
Defender, Nigerian, 186cm, 80kg
Born: 26.03.73, Lagos, Nigeria
Clubs: Julius Berger (1993), Auxerre (Fra) (1993-97), Internazionale (Ita) (1997-99), Milan (Ita) (1999-)
Full international (Nigeria) 22 caps/2 goals
• Tough, uncompromising, centre-back who made the switch across town from Inter to Milan in the 1999-2000 transfer window after falling out of favour at Inter.
• Established regular for Nigeria who played at France 98 and was a member of the 1996 Olympic gold medal-winning side.
• Had blue and black beads woven into his dreadlocks when he joined Inter ('Inter is in my head').
• Grew up in poverty in Lagos and once saw a friend stabbed to death in front of him. 'When you have come through something like that, playing football in front of a big crowd isn't such a big deal.'

COACH
WESTERHOF, Hans
Dutch
• A former teacher who moved to Willem II for the 2000-2001 season. Made his name at Groningen before moving on to PSV, where the board thought he was the only coach who could control Romario (he couldn't).
• He returned to Groningen before being appointed as director of the famous Ajax youth scheme.

WESTERVELD, Sander

Goalkeeper, Dutch, 190cm, 88kg
Born: 23.10.74, Enschede, Holland
Clubs: Twente (1994-96), Vitesse (1996-99),
Liverpool (Eng) (1999-)
Full international (Holland) 5 caps/0 goals
• Keeper whose transfer to Liverpool in summer
1999 has improved his international prospects:
he is now number two to **Edwin Van der Sar** in
the Dutch goal.
• Joined Liverpool for £4million, a UK record for a
goalkeeper.

WETL, Arnold

Midfielder, Austrian, 178cm, 81kg
Born: 02.02.70, Eibiswald, Austria
Clubs: Sturm Graz (1990-96), FC Porto (Por)
(1996-97), Rapid Vienna (1997-)
Full international (Austria) 21 caps/4 goals
• Left-sided attacking midfielder who was a
member of the Austrian squad at the 1998 World
Cup. He has played himself back into contention
following a disappointing time in Portugal with FC
Porto.

WHELAN, Noel

Forward, English, 187cm, 77kg
Born: 30.12.74, Leeds, England
Clubs: Leeds (1992-96), Coventry (1996-2000),
Middlesbrough (2000-)
• Striker who joined Middlesbrough in July 2000
in a £2.5million transfer after losing his place in
the Coventry starting line-up to **Cedric Roussel**.
• Came through the youth ranks at Leeds and
was a member of the 1993 FA Youth Cup-winning
side before joining Coventry for a club record
£2million in 1996.

Sylvain Wil

PLAYER
WHELLITON
full name: Whelliton Augusto da Silva
Forward, Brazilian, 185cm, 80kg
Born: 23.07.75, Sao Paulo, Brazil
Clubs: Corinthians, Boavista (Por) (1999-)
 Forward who was signed by Boavista in the summer of 1999 to provide more attacking options for the Champions League campaign.
 He had an impressive first season in Portugal, scoring 11 goals in 23 matches and finishing as Boavista's top scorer.

PLAYER
WIBRAN, Peter
Midfielder, Swedish, 179cm, 79kg
Born: 23.03.69, Sweden
Club: Osters, Helsingborg, Hansa Rostock (Ger)
Full international (Sweden) 10 caps/0 goals
 Defensive midfielder who has been praised for his performances for Rostock since a 1998 move from his native Sweden.

PLAYER
WICKY, Rafael
Defender, Swiss, 178cm, 75kg
Born: 26.04.77, Leuggern
Clubs: Steg, Sion (1993-97), Werder Bremen (Ger) (1997-)
Full international (Switzerland) 27 caps/0 goals
 Highly promising Swiss international midfielder who has adapted well to life in the German Bundesliga. A versatile campaigner, he has good technique and can play in a number of positions in defence or midfield.

PLAYER
WIEDENER, Andree
Defender, German, 175cm, 70kg
Born: 14.03.70, Helmstedt, Germany
Clubs: TSV Bahrdof, SV Velpke, Werder Bremen (1987-)
 Ever-dependable and versatile defensive bulwark

who can play full-back, wing-back or as a defensive midfielder. With Werder since 1987 and very much part of the furniture there.
 Surname pronounced Vee der er.

PLAYER
WIESZCZYCKI, Tomasz
Midfielder, Polish, 181cm, 78kg
Born: 21.12.71, Lodz, Poland
Clubs: LKS Lodz, Legia Warsaw, Le Havre (Fra), LKS Lodz, Polonia Warsaw (2000-)
Full international (Poland) 11 caps/3 goals
 Attacking midfielder with great technique who is dangerous when running from deep. Started his career with LKS Lodz, then moved to Legia Warsaw and spent one and half years with Le Havre in France. On his return to LKS he won the championship in 1998. Joined Polonia in January 2000.

PLAYER
WIJKER, Peter
Defender, Dutch, 185cm, 83kg
Born: 20.07.71, Heerhugowaard, Holland
Clubs: AZ (1993-)
 A hugely important player in defence for AZ, a big threat at set-pieces and a powerful tackler.
 Linked with a move to PSV, but has so far stayed loyal to AZ.

PLAYER
WILCOX, Jason
Midfielder, English, 182cm, 179cm
Born: 15.07.71, Bolton, England
Clubs: Blackburn (1989-99), Leeds (1999-)
Full International (England) 3 caps/ goals
 Left-sided midfielder or winger who joined Leeds in a £3million transfer in December 1999, having spent his entire career until then with Blackburn.
 League winner with Blackburn in 1995 when his crosses were the main supply line for **Alan Shearer**.

• He won a surprise call-up to the England squad in the run-up to Euro 2000, but injury forced him out of the reckoning.

ADMINISTRATOR
WILL, David
Born: 20.11.36
• Scottish member of the FIFA executive committee since 1990, and one of the few to back England's bid to stage the 2006 World Cup.
• A lawyer by profession.

PLAYER
WILLI, Tobias
Midfielder, German, 177cm, 71kg
Born: 14.12.79, Germany
Clubs: VfL Pfaffenweiler, Freiburg (1992-)
• Dynamic right-wing flyer who burst upon the Bundesliga scene in the 1999-2000 season. With the German national team in some disarray, some thought he might be worth a try at the highest level. It did not happen for the youngster, but with his uncommon pace, energy and crossing ability, a first full cap ought not be far away.
• Surname pronounced Vili.

PLAYER
WILLIAM
Full name: Bassey William Andem
Goalkeeper, Cameroonian, 186cm, 90kg
Born: 14.06.68, Yaounde, Cameroon
Clubs: Union Douala (1989-93), Cruzeiro (Bra) (1994-96), Bahia (Bra) (1997), Boavista (Por) (1997-)
Full international (Cameroon)
• Keeper whose performances were crucial in helping Boavita qualify for the 1999-2000 Champions League.
• An experienced, agile performer who is well established as Boavista's number one.

PLAYER
WILMOTS, Marc
Midfielder, Belgian, 184cm, 86kg
Born: 22.02.69, Dongelberg, Belgium
Clubs: St Truiden, Mechelen, Standard Liege, Schalke (Ger) (1996-)
Full international (Belgium) 49 caps/17 goals
• The Belgian international started his career as a bullish central striker in Belgium with Mechelen. But in recent years he has proved far more effective as an attacking midfielder. Makes great late runs into the box, has a powerful shot and is strong in the air too.
• A farmer's son.
• Starred for Schalke when they won the 1997 UEFA Cup and was captain of Belgium at Euro 2000.
• A member of Belgium's squads at the 1990, 1994 and 1998 World Cups.
• Surname pronounced Vil mots.

PLAYER
WILTORD, Sylvain
Forward, French, 174cm, 73kg
Born: 10.05.74, Neuilly-sur-Marne, France
Clubs: Rennes, Deportivo La Coruna (Spa), Rennes, Bordeaux (1997-2000), Arsenal (Eng) (2000-)
Full international (France) 18 caps/6 goals
• France's top marksman in the 1998-99 season and though the goals did not flow quite as freely in 1999-2000, he compensated by excelling in the creative department. Formerly a right-sided midfielder or winger; now an outstanding all-round frontrunner with explosive pace, well judged runs and ice cool finishing.
• A Parisian by birth and a member of the senior French squad since early 1999.
• 'The last two-and-a-half years have been a tremendous adventure and I've been delighted with my progress. But there are even more good things to come from me.'
• Joined Deportivo but did not play a game in Spain and was loaned back to Rennes before

oining Bordeaux in 1997.
• Joined Arsenal in August 2000 after Bordeaux and Arsenal finally agreed a fee of £13million.
• Pronounced Sil van Vil tord.

PLAYER
WINKLER, Bernhard
Forward, German, 183cm, 80kg
Born: 24.06.66, Wurzburg, Germany
Clubs: Schweinfurt 05, Wattenscheid, Kaiserslautern, Fortuna Koln, Munich 1860 (1993-)
• The years seem to be catching up with the veteran goalpoacher. In 1999-2000 he was on the score-sheet only three times, while in the previous three campaigns he racked up 40 goals.
• A member of the Kaiserslautern squad which won the Bundesliga in 1990-91 and second in the all-time list of 1860 goalscorers (63 goals).
• Surname pronounced Vink ler.

PLAYER
WINTER, Aron
Midfielder, Dutch, 176cm, 74kg
Born: 01.03.67, Paramaribo, Surinam
Clubs: Ajax (1985-1992), Lazio (Ita) (1992-96), Internazionale (Ita) (1996-99), Ajax (1999-)
Full international (Holland) 84 caps/6 goals
• One of the most experienced players in the Dutch League, having spent seven years in Italy and, recently, breaking Ruud Krol's Dutch record of 83 caps despite never having been a regular.
• Euro 2000 was his seventh major tournament, having made his international debut in March 1987 against Greece (1-1). Used mainly as a subsitutute in the Dutch national side.
• Plays in defensive midfield nowadays.

PLAYER
WINTERBURN, Nigel
Defender, English, 173cm, 72kg
Born: 11.12.63, Coventry, England
Clubs: Birmingham City (1982-83) Oxford United (1983-84), Wimbledon (1983-87), Arsenal (1987-

2000), West Ham (2000-)
Full international (England) 2 caps/0 goals
• Veteran left-back who finally left Highbury in the summer of 2000 after 13 seasons with Arsenal.
• Won a host of honours at Arsenal – three League titles, the European Cup-winners Cup, two FA Cups – but did not win as many England caps as his solid, no-nonsense play deserved.

PLAYER
WISE, Dennis
Midfielder, English, 168cm, 64kg
Born: 16.12.66, Kensington, England
Clubs: Wimbledon (1984-90), Chelsea (1990-)
Full international (England) 19 caps/1 goal
• Tiny midfielder whose creative play for Chelsea has been overshadowed by the darker side of his game. On his day, he is one of the best midfielders in England, as his performances in the 1999-2000 Champions League testify, but he tends to spend too much time trying to wind up the opposition.
• Won the FA Cup with Wimbledon in 1988 and Chelsea in 1997 and 2000.
• Played for England at Euro 2000, but seemed out of his depth.

PLAYER
WISS, Jarkko
Midfielder, Finnish, 182cm, 80kg
Born: 12.04.72, Finland
Clubs: TPV Tampere (1993-95), Jaro (1996), HJK Helsinki (1997-98), Molde (Nor) (1999), Lillestrom (Nor) (1999-)
Full international (Finland) 28 caps/2 goals
• Finnish midfielder who played for several clubs in his mother country before joining Molde. Unable to establish himself there, he moved on to Lillestrom, only to sign for Moss prior to the 1999 season.

WITSCHGE, Richard
Midfielder, Dutch, 184cm, 77kg
Born: 20.09.69, Amsterdam, Holland
Clubs: Ajax (1986-1991), Barcelona (Spa) (1991-1993), Bordeaux (Fra) (1993-95), Blackburn (Eng) (1995), Bordeaux (Fra) (1995-96), Ajax (1996-)
Full international (Holland) 30 caps/1 goal
• Talented all-round midfielder who never quite fulfilled his potential after leaving Ajax for Barcelona in 1991.
• Became more of a team player with Bordeaux but returned home to Ajax in 1996, after playing in all four of Holland's matches at Euro 96.
• Older brother Rob played for Feyenoord.

WITTL, Charles
Midfielder, Ghanaian/Austrian, 174cm, 67kg
Born: 05.10.71, Ghana
Clubs: Neuchatel (Swi) (1991-93), St Gallen (Swi) (1994), Neuchatel (Swi) (1994-)
• Effervescent Neuchatel Xamax attacking midfielder or forward who does not score nearly enough goals but is not nearly so shy on the creative front.
• Holds dual Ghanaian-Austrian nationality.

WOLF, Stefan
Defender, Swiss, 190cm, 83kg
Born: 31.01.71, Switzerland
Clubs: Lucerne (1990-97), Sion (1997-98), Servette (1998-)
Full international (Switzerland) 14 caps/0 goals
• Commanding Servette stopper and inspirational skipper. Full Swiss international who, while with Lucerne, played most competently as a midfielder.

WOLF, Wolfgang
German
Born: 24.09.57
• It was generally thought to a risky move when Wolfsburg lured him away from Second Division Stuttgarter Kickers and put him in charge of the first team coach in March 1998, with the critics pointing to the fact that he had no Bundesliga coaching experience. But he would conclusively prove that it was not only his surname which made him suitable for the job, qualifying Wolfsburg for the UEFA Cup in 1998-99 and steering them to a good seventh place in 1999-2000.
• An old-school disciplinarian but a thoroughly modern and flexible tactician.

WOJCIK, Ryszard
Polish
Born: 06.06.56
• Works as a company manager.
• Awarded his FIFA badge in 1990.

WOME, Pierre
Midfielder, Cameroon, 178cm, 78kg
Born: 26.03.79, Doula, Cameroon
Clubs: Fogape (1993-94), Canon Yaounde (1994-96), Vicenza (Ita) (1996-97), Lucchese (Ita) (1997-98), Roma (Ita) (1998-99), Bologna (Ita) (1999-)
Full international (Cameroon)
• Utility defender who played for his country aged 16 and three months, holding the record for being the youngest player to play at the African Nations Cup before it was broken one day later by **Mohammed Kallon**.
• Made his Serie A debut a year later at Vicenza, playing two matches before being farmed out to Lucchese in Serie B.
• A strong-tackling defender with a powerful left-foot shot who has been sent off a number of times playing for Cameroon.

• Moved to Bologna in summer 1999 after going absent without leave at Roma.

WOODGATE, Jonathon
Defender, English, 189cm, 80kg
Born: 22.01.80, Middlesborough, England
Clubs: Leeds (1998-)
Full international (England) 1 cap/0 goals
• Highly-rated young centre-back who was one of the most impressive newcomers in the 1998-99 season, making his international debut for England against Bulgaria in June 1999.
• But his game went off the boil in 1999-2000, possibly as a result of his involvement in a much-publicised court case following an incident in a Leeds nightclub.

PLAYER
WOOTER, Nordin
Forward, Dutch, 172cm, 70kg
Born: 24.08.76, Breda, Holland
Clubs: Ajax Amsterdam (1994-97), Zaragoza (Spa) (1997-99), Watford (Eng) (1999-)
• Diminutive but pacy striker signed by Watford for just under £1million in late 1999 but could not add much to Watford's fight against relegation.
• Broke into the Ajax first team in the 1995-96 season, but was not in the same class as some of his contemporaries.

PLAYER
WORNS, Christian
Defender, German, 184cm, 80kg
Born: 10.05.72, Mannheim, Germany
Clubs: Phonix Mannheim, Waldhof Mannheim, Bayer Leverkusen, Paris Saint-Germain (Fra), Borussia Dortmund (1999-)
Full international (Germany) 33 caps/0 goals
• Strong-tackling, purposeful right-sided marker or wing-back, who has had nothing but bad luck in recent times: a red card in Germany's World Cup 98 quarter-final defeat against Croatia, an

unhappy spell during the 1998-99 season at Paris Saint-Germain, Dortmund's near-miss with relegation and a knee injury which put him out of Euro 2000.
• Surname pronounced Verns.

PLAYER
WOSZ, Dariusz
Midfielder, German, 169cm, 65kg
Born: 08.06.69, Katowice, Poland
Clubs: Hallescher, Bochum, Hertha Berlin (1998-)
Full international (East Germany) 7 caps/0 goals, (Germany) 15 caps/1 goal
• This tiny Polish-born German international is not a classic playmaker, a midfield general who elegantly strokes passes around. Operating just behind the main strikers, he is a non-stop bundle of energy, a man capable of punching holes in any defence with his searing pace and mazy dribbling.
• Surname pronounced Vosh.

COACH
WOTTE, Mark
Dutch
Born: 16.12.60
• Known as the crown prince of Dutch football and was expected to get a big coaching job one day, but so far hasn't lived up to the expectations.
• Started as a coach at Den Haag in the second division before joining highly ambitious Utrecht. But he failed to achieve the club's ambition dream of joining Holland's big three and moved to Den Bosch halfway through the 1999-2000 season, but couldn't prevent them from relegation.

PLAYER
WREH, Christopher
Forward, French/Liberian, 181cm, 73kg
Born: 14.05.75, Monrovia, Liberia
Clubs: Monaco, Guingamp (loan), Arsenal (Eng) (1997-99), AEK Athens (Gre) (1999, loan), Den Bosch (Hol) (1999-)

Full international (Liberia)
- Striker who is more famous for being a cousin of **George Weah** than any exploits on the football pitch.
- Has twice played for **Arsene Wenger**, at Monaco and at Arsenal, where he failed to establish himself ahead of **Dennis Bergkamp** and **Nicolas Anelka**.

PLAYER
WRIGHT, Alan
Defender, English, 164cm, 59kg
Born: 28.09.71, Ashton-under-Lyme, England
Clubs: Blackpool (1987-92), Blackburn (1992-95), Aston Villa (1994-)
- One of the smallest players in the English League but a highly effective left-back who was close to England recognition before Euro 96, but has never had the call.

PLAYER
WRIGHT, Paul
Forward, Scotland, 173cm, 73kg
Born: 17.08.67, East Kilbride, Scotland
Clubs: Aberdeen (1983-89), QPR (1989-90), Hibernian (1989-91), St Johnstone (1991-95), Kilmarnock (1995-)
- Wright arrived at Rugby Park with experience in abundance. He achieved immortality at Kilmarnock by scoring the only goal of the 1997 Scottish Cup Final against Falkirk. His consistency has been a major failing since then and he has spent considerable periods of time on the substitutes bench.

PLAYER
WRIGHT, Richard
Goalkeeper, English, 185cm, 82kg
Born: 05.11.77, Ipswich, England
Clubs: Ipswich
Full international (England) 1 cap/0 goals
- The most promising young keeper in England and the heir apparent to **David Seaman** at international level. Ipswich have resisted all attempts to sell him, and persuaded him to sign new contract in summer 2000.
- Was England's third-choice keeper at Euro 2000 after making his international debut against Malta in a pre-tournament friendly, in which he scored an own goal and then conceded and saved a penalty.

X

Y

PLAYER
XAVI
Full name: Xavier Hernandez Creus
Midfielder, Spanish, 168cm, 66kg
Born: 25.01.80, Barcelona, Spain
Clubs: Barcelona (1997-)
  Midfield general, likened to his team-mate **Pep Guardiola**, and one of the rising stars of Spanish football.
• Product of the Barcelona youth system who was promoted to the A squad at the start of the 1998-99 season, having been called into the 1997-98 Champions League squad, playing all six matches for Barça in the competition.
• One of the stars of Spain's 1999 World Under-20 triumph in Nigeria.

PLAYER
YAKIN, Hakan
Forward, Swiss, 180cm, 78kg
Born: 22.02.77, Basle, Switzerland
Clubs: Basle (1994-97), Grasshopper (1997), St Gallen (1998-99), Grasshopper (1999-)
Full international (Switzerland) 4 caps/2 goals
• Up-and-coming Swiss international front-man who is the younger brother of national team midfield stalwart **Murat Yakin**. Slightly-built, instinctive goalscorer. Widely-regarded as one of the best young players in the country.

PLAYER
YAKIN, Murat
Midfielder, Swiss, 183cm, 83kg
Born: 15.09.74, Basle, Switzerland
Clubs: Stuttgart (Ger), Fenerbahce (Tur), Basel, Kaiserslautern (Ger) (2000-)
Full international (Switzerland) 20 caps/3 goals
• Accomplished defensive midfielder who become the subject of a strange dispute with Turkish club Fenerbahce. He had not been happy in Istanbul following a move from the Bundesliga in 1998. Following the Turkish earthquakes in 1999, he fled to Switzerland and refused to return to Istanbul, claiming he was too frightened. He then surfaced at Basel, with Fenerbahce claiming compensation, before a move back to the Bundesliga with Kaiserslautern.

PLAYER
YANKOV, Zlatko
Defender, Bulgarian, 184cm, 80kg
Born: 07.06.66, Bourgas, Bulgaria
Clubs: Chernomerets, Levski Sofia, Valladolid (Spa), Levski Sofia, KFC Uerdingen (Ger), Besiktas (Tur), Adanaspor (Tur), Nefchi Bourgas
Full international (Bulgaria) 79 caps/4 goals
• Experienced and much-travelled defender or

Tony Yeboah

defensive midfielder who is now back in Bulgaria after a career spent moving around the Continent.
• Veteran of two World Cup campaigns and a reliable team man.
• Returned home to Levski Sofia after suffering relegation with KFC Uerdingen, but then was on the move again, to Besiktas of Turkey, moving on to Adanaspor, before another return home, to Nefchi Bourgas.

PLAYER
YANOVSKY, Igor
Midfielder, Russian, 187cm, 80kg
Born: 03.08.74, Vladikavkaz, Russia
Clubs: Alania Vladikavkaz, Paris Saint-Germain (Fra)
Full international (Russia) 25 caps/1 goal
• Showed up well in the latter part of the 1999-2000 season as a raiding left-back, but the Russian international can also play in virtually any position in midfield. There are many strings to his bow: good distribution skills, industry and strength in the air.
• Pronounced Ee gor Jan off ski.

PLAYER
YANG, Chen
Midfielder, Chinese, 185cm, 79kg
Born: 17.01.74, China
Clubs: Gvoan Peking, Eintracht Frankfurt (Ger) (1998-)
Full international (China)
• The first Chinese to play in the German Bundesliga, were he has more than held his own.

PLAYER
YAPI, Cyril
Forward, French, 175cm, 67kg
Born: 18.02.80, Lorient, France
Clubs: Rennes (1998-), Laval (2000, loan)
• Young midfielder who was used mostly as a substitute at Rennes and was sent on loan to

aval for the 2000-2001 season.

ARTSEV, Georgi
Born: 11.04.48.

Coach of Rotor Volgograd since 2000 who played as a striker for a number of lower league teams before joining Moscow Spartak at the age of 30. Was the Soviet League's top scorer in 1979, winning five caps.

Became Moscow Spartak manager for one year in 1996, replacing **Oleg Romantsev** and the Russian League title. Left Spartak for Moscow Dynamo after Romantsev's return from the national team in 1997.

PLAYER
YASHCHUK, Oleg
Forward, Ukrainian, 181cm, 71kg
Born: 26.10.77, Ukraine
Clubs: Nyva Ternopil (1994-96), Anderlecht (Bel) (1996-)

• Came from the youth ranks of Anderlecht but failed to clinch a regular starting place, despite being a regular scorer. Was tipped to leave Anderlecht in summer 2000.
• Ukrainian Under-21 international.

PLAYER
YASHKIN, Artem
Midfielder, Ukrainian, 174cm, 68kg
Born: 29.04.75, Russia
Clubs: Kyiv Dynamo

• Adroit, mobile and very quick, Yashkin is the 'new Zavarov' according to national coach **Valerii Lobanovsky**. He is of Russian origin but recently received Ukrainian citizenship and is eligible for the Ukraine national team.

PLAYER
YASIN Sulun
Midfielder, Turkish
Born: 17.12.77, Turkey
Clubs: Besiktas

• One of the bright young stars of Turkish football, a skilful midfielder who was given his chance in the Besiktas first team by **John Toshack**.
• Turkish Under-21 international.

PLAYER
YASSER, Radwan
Midfielder, Egyptian, 176cm, 72kg
Born: 22.04.71, Mehalla, Egypt
Clubs: Beladeli Mehalla, Hansa Rostock (Ger) (1996-)
Full international (Egypt)

• Gifted midfielder whose talents have not always been appreciated in the Bundesliga. Played for Egypt at the 2000 Nations Cup.

PLAYER
YEBOAH, Anthony
Forward, Ghanaian, 181cm, 77kg
Born: 06.06.66, Kumasi, Ghana
Clubs: Corner Stores Kumasi, Okwahu Stores United, Saarbrucken (Ger), Eintracht Frankfurt (Ger), Leeds United (Eng), Hamburg (Ger) (1997-)
Full international (Ghana)

• Some in England claimed the Ghanaian striker was over the hill when he quit Leeds United in 1997 after falling out with his manager **George Graham**. Not so. The African front-man may have lost a little speed but thanks to his muscle, penalty box guile and outstanding technique, he continues to prosper in the Bundesliga, both taking and making chances.
• Former West Germany and Hamburg attacking idol Uwe Seeler has no doubts about his quality: 'For me Tony Yeboah is still one of the most dangerous strikers in Europe. He's skilful, a great competitor and has untold influence on the

Dwight Yorke

Hamburg team. Without him, we wouldn't have qualified for the Champions League.'

PLAYER
YESIPOV, Valeri
Forward, Russian, 170cm, 69kg
Born: 04.10.71, Russia
Clubs: Rotor Volgograd (1992-)
Full international (Russia) 4 caps/0 goals
• Agile and fast, one of the Russian League's most experienced players.

PLAYER
YEVSEYEV, Vadim
Defender, Russian, 176cm, 70kg
Born: 08.01.76, Russia
Clubs: Moscow Spartak (1996-98), Torpedo Moscow (1998), Moscow Spartak (1999), Lokomotiv Moscow (2000)
Full international (Russia) 1 cap/0 goals
• Good on the wing, fast and active in attack.

PLAYER
YEVTUSHOK, Olexander
Defender, Ukrainian, 184cm, 79kg
Born: 11.01.70, Ukraine
Clubs: Karpaty Lviv, CSKA Kyiv
Full international (Ukraine) 7 caps/0 goals
• Had a brief spell in England with Coventry but moved to CSKA after financial problems with his club Karpaty. Dangerous when going forward, he has been in and out of the Ukrainian national side.

PLAYER
YEZERSKY, Vladimir
Defender, Ukrainian, 182cm, 73kg
Born: 15.11.76, Ukraine
Clubs: Kyiv Dynamo, Kryvbas
Full international (Ukraine) 1 cap/0 goals
• After several years on the bench at Kyiv Dynamo, he moved to ambitious Kryvbas. Safe at the back and is a potential candidate for the Ukrainian national side.

PLAYER
IANNAKOPOULOS, Stelios

Midfielder, Greek, 172cm, 70kg
Born: 12.07.74, Greece
Clubs: Olympiakos (1996-)
Full international (Greece) 11 caps/3 goals
  Diligent and tactically-aware Olympiakos
all-rounder, noted for his solid defensive work
but also with an eye for goal – he scored 10
times in 1999-2000. A player who improves
season on season, he has been a member of
the full Greek squad for the past four years.

PLAYER
YORDANOV, Ivailo

Midfielder, Bulgarian, 179cm, 75kg
Born: 22.04.68, Samokov, Bulgaria
Clubs: Sporting Lisbon (Por) (1991-)
Full internatonal (Bulgaria) 49 caps/ goals
  Veteran Bulgarian midfielder who has struggled
in the final years of his career with the news that
he has multiple sclerosis.
• Spent many years at Sporting Lisbon, finally
winning the Portuguese League title in 1999-
2000 season.
  Made his name in Bulgaria by finishing as
the League top scorer in 1989-90 with 21 goals
in 29 games.
  Joined Sporting in 1991, but injuries have
restricted his performances.
• Appeared as substitute four times for Bulgaria
in the 1994 World Cup in the USA.
• Scored both goals in Sporting's 1995
Portuguese Cup Final victory.
• Surprised doctors with the speed of his
recovery from a back injury suffered in a car
crash in Bulgaria in summer 1995.

PLAYER
YORDI

Full name: Jorge Gonzalez Diaz
Forward, Spanish, 182cm, 83kg
Born: 14.09.74, San Fernando, Spain
Clubs: Sevilla B (1993-96), Sevilla (1996-97),
Atletico Madrid (1996-97), Zaragoza (1997-)
• Striker who struggled to establish himself at
Sevilla after coming through the youth ranks, and
fared little better at Atletico. But he has had more
luck at Zaragoza, where his physical game is
appreciated.

PLAYER
YORKE, Dwight

Forward, Trinidad & Tobago, 179cm, 76kg
Born: 03.11.71. Trinidad & Tobago
Clubs: Aston Villa (1989-99), Manchester United
(1998-)
Full International (Trinidad & Tobago)
• Striker who joined Manchester United for a
club record £12.5million in summer 1998 and
quickly established himself at Old Trafford, forming a highly effective partnership with **Andy Cole**
and finishing as the joint Premier League top
scorer in 1998-99 with 18 goals.
• A positive personality who never stops smiling.
• A regular international for Trinidad and Tobago,
which causes friction with United manager **Alex
Ferguson**.
• Was signed by Villa for £10,000 from Tobago
side St St Clair's.

PLAYER
YOUNG, Luke

Defender, English, 182cm, 79kg
Born: 19.07.79, Harlow, England
Clubs: Tottenham (1998-)
• Young centre-back who has broken through at
Spurs under **George Graham** and is highly rated
by the coaching staff at Tottenham.
• England Under-21 international.
• Can also play at right-back.

YOUSEF, Mohamed

Defender, Egyptian, 183cm, 71kg

Born: 09.10.70, Egypt

Clubs: Al Ahly, Denizlispor

• Egyptian defender who has adapted well to life in Turkey, proving to be one of the most capable defenders in the League.

• A non-playing member of the Egyptian squad at the 2000 African Nations Cup finals.

ACCHERONI, Alberto

Italian
Born: 01.04.53

Coach of Milan since 1998, who guided the club to the Italian League title in his first season in charge.
Made his name during three seasons at Udinese, whom he steered to third place in the Italian League, their highest ever finish.
He favours bold attacking tactics and both Udinese and Milan have fielded 3-4-3 formations.
Shares a birthday with his predecessor **Arrigo Sacchi**.

PLAYER
AFARIN, Davy

Midfielder, Dutch, 175cm, 73kg
Born: 22.05.78, Kerkrade, Holland
Clubs: Roda JC (1995-)

Right winger or attacking midfielder who broke through in the 1999-2000 season. A good dribbler with a keen eye for goal. Scored the golden goal that secured Roda a place in the Dutch Cup Final, but was only a substitute for the Final.

PLAYER
AGORAKIS, Theo

Midfielder, Greek, 176cm, 73kg
Born: 27.10.71, Kavala, Greece
Clubs: PAOK (Gre) (1992-98), Leicester (Eng) (1997-2000), AEK Athens (2000-)
Full international (Greece) 50 caps/0 goals
Experienced international who returned home to Greece in summer 2000 after failing to hold down a regular place in Leicester's midfield.

PLAYER
ZAHOVIC, Zlatko

Forward, 01.02.71, 180cm, 76kg
Born: 01.02.71, Maribor, Slovenia
Clubs: Vitoria Guimaraes (Por) (1993-96), FC Porto (Por) (1996-99), Olympiakos (Gre) (1999-2000), Valencia (Spa) (2000-)
Full international (Slovenia) 51 caps/26 goals
• Talented attacking midfielder and the undoubted star of the Slovenian national team at Euro 2000.
• An outstanding playmaker and valuable goalscorer – his strike rate of a goal every other game is one of the best in world football.
• Has never played in the Slovenian League, having begun his career in Yugoslavia with Partizan before a move to Portugal.
• Won three League titles with FC Porto and was one of the stars of the 1998-99 Champions League after scoring seven goals in six group matches.
• Was sold by Porto to Olympiakos for £6.5million in summer 1999, but the move was problematic from the outset. Zahovic never settled and he went on strike in autumn 1999 for two months, claiming that the Greek League was staffed by 'jealous, lazy and unprofessional' players.
• He returned in the new year, only to fall out with coach **Alberto Bigon** when he was substituted in a crucial League match. He hurled a volley of abuse at Bigon and was banned for two months by Olympiakos.
• Joined Valencia after Euro 2000, in which he scored three times for Slovenia.

PLAYER
ZAJAC, Bogdan

Defender, Polish, 188cm, 75kg
Born: 16.11.72, Poland
Clubs: Wisla Krakow (1995-)
Full international (Poland) 1 cap/0 goals
• Experienced sweeper who played for amateur JKS Jaroslaw and Kamax Kanczuga before joining Wisla in 1995. Since then, he has been the key man for Wisla.

Gianluca Zambrotta

ZAJAC Marcin
Forward, Polish, 180cm, 74kg
Born: 19.05.75, Poland
Clubs: Start Lodz, Widzew Lodz (1996-)
Full international (Poland) 3 caps/0 goals
• Started with third division Start Lodz and moved to Widzew in 1996 and won the Polish championship a year later.
• Quick striker but plagued by injury for the pas two years.

ZAJAC, Marek
Defender, Polish, 186cm, 80kg
Born: 17.09.73, Poland
Clubs: Hutnik Krakow, Wisla Krakow (1997-)
Full international (Poland) 1 cap/0 goals
• Solid right-back who has made steady progres since moving from Hutnik Krakow to Wisla in 199. Won his first cap against Spain in January 2000
• Not related to another Wisla defender, **Bogdan Zajac**.

ZALAYETA, Marcelo
Forward, Uruguayan, 186cm, 91kg
Born: 05.12.78, Montevideo, Uruguay
Clubs: Danubio (1996), Penarol (1997), Juventus (Ita) (1997-99), Empoli (Ita) (1998-99), Sevilla (Spa) (1999-2000)
• Big, strong athletic striker who made the breakthrough at the 1997 World Under-20 Youth Cup in Malaysia.
• Was signed by Juventus after the Malaysia tournament, but failed to make an impact in Turi and was loaned to Empoli.
• Spent 1999-2000 on loan at Sevilla, where his physical presence and powerful shot were put to good use.
• Played in the Uruguay side which surprisingly reached the Final of the 1999 Copa America, where they lost to Brazil.

ZAMBROTTA, Gianluca
Midfielder, Italian, 181cm, 76kg
Born: 19.02.77, Como, Italy
Clubs: Como (1994-97), Bari (1997-98)
Full international (Italy) 10 cap/0 goals
Versatile, combative player whose performances his first season for Juve earned him a regular place in the Italian national side.
Juventus coach **Carlo Ancelotti**: 'Zambrotta has the ability to play anywhere.'
Most effective as a right-wing raider.
Preferred to **Diego Fuser** in Italy's squad for Euro 2000.
International debut: February 1999, v Norway.

AMORANO, Ivan
Forward, Chilean, 178cm, 72kg
Born: 18.01.67, Maipu, Chile.
Clubs: Cobre Sal (1987-88), St Gallen (Swi) (1989-90), Sevilla (Spa) (1990-92), Real Madrid (Spa) (1992-96), Internazionale (Ita) (1996-)
Full international (Chile)
• Veteran striker who has been a prolific scorer during his time in Europe.
• Was due to move to the Italian League in 1989, but was farmed out by Bologna to Switzerland, from where he moved to Spain.
• A Spanish League winner with Real Madrid in 1995, when he finished as the League top scorer with 28 goals from 38 games.
• Nicknamed Bam Bam because of his danger anywhere near goal.
• Injuries affected his time in Italy, as well as competition from **Ronaldo** and **Christian Vieri**.
• Top scorer in 1998 World Cup qualifiers, hitting 12 goals in 10 games, when he formed a prolific partnership with **Marcelo Salas**, dubbed the 'Za-Sa connection.'
• A national hero in Chile, where Inter matches have been screened live.

ZANCHI, Marco
Defender, Italian, 178cm, 76kg
Born: 15.04.77, San Giovanni Bianco, Italy
Clubs: Atalanta (1994-96), Chievo (1996), Bari (1996-97), Udinese (1997-)
• Promising young defender who has the ability to become a first-class sweeper or libero but his career has been troubled by injury and a failure to win a first-team place at Bari. But things have improved for him at Udinese.

ZANETTI, Cristiano
Midfielder, Italian, 180cm, 75kg
Born: 14.04.77, Carrara, Italy
Clubs: Fiorentina (1994-96), Venezia (1996-97), Reggiana (1997-98), Internazionale (1998), Cagliari (1998-99), Roma (1999-)
• Hard-working midfielder and an Italian Under-21 international.
• No relation to **Javier Zanetti**.

ZANETTI, Javier
Midfielder, Argentinian, 178cm, 73kg
Born: 10.08.73, Buenos Aires, Argentina
Clubs: Talleres (1992-93), Banfield (1993-95), Internazionale (Ita) (1995-)
Full international (Argentina) 53 caps/3 goals
• A stalwart of Inter's midfield for the past five seasons.
• A dynamic all-rounder who never shirks responsibility. **Abel Balbo**: 'Javier is the sort of player you can always rely upon. No matter what the circumstances, he will always give total commitment. Supporters love players like him, those who dig in and fight.'
• As a teenager, he was thought unlikely to make it as a professional because of his slight frame, but he made substantial gains in height and weight thanks to a diet of beans, lentils and milk. 'They were difficult times but thankfully I came

through them with the help of good medical advice and the support of my family.'
• Member of Argentina's silver medal-winning side at the 1996 Olympics and started all five of Argentina's games at the 1998 World Cup.
• Quiet, soft-spoken man and a fervant Catholic who described an audience with the Pope as the most important day of his life.

PLAYER
ZDEBEL, Thomas
Midfielder, German, 178cm, 76kg
Born: 25.05.73, Germany
Clubs: Rot-Weiss Essen (1990-92), Koln (1992-97), Lierse (Bel) (1997-2000), Genclerbirligi (Tur) (2000-)
• Hard-working midfielder who was a key player for Lierse before a surprise move to Turkey in summer 2000.

PLAYER
ZDRILIC, David
Forward, Australian, 183cm, 80kg
Born: 13.04.74, Australia
Clubs: Sydney United (1996-97), Aarau (Swi) (1997-99), Ulm (Ger) (1999-2000), Unterhaching (Ger) (2000-)
Full international (Australia) 11 caps/3 goals
• Australian striker who was relegated with Ulm in 1999-2000 but impressed enough to earn a transfer to Unterhaching.

PLAYER
ZDRAVKOV, Zdravko
Goalkeeper, Bulgarian, 186cm, 86kg
Born: 04.10.70, Bulgaria
Clubs: Adanaspor (Tur) (1999-)
Full international (Bulgaria) 33 caps/0 goals
• Experienced goalkeeper who is well-established as the Bulgarian national team number one, winning the battle to succeed veteran Bobby Mikhailov.
• Moved to Turkey after playing in all three of Bulgaria's games at France 98, moving on to Adanaspor in 1999.

PLAYER
ZE ELIAS
Full name: Jose Elias Moedin Junior
Midfielder, Brazilian, 178cm, 76kg
Born: 25.00.76, Sao Paulo
Clubs: Corinthians (1993-96), Bayer Leverkuser (Ger) (1996-97), Internazionale (Ita) (1997-99), Bologna (Ita) (1999-2000), Olympiakos (Gre) (200C
• Tough-tackling Brazilian midfielder who mode himself on the 1994 World Cup-winning captain Dunga.
• Signed by Internazionale in summer 1997 to replace **Paul Ince** in the midfield holding role.
• Nicknamed 'Alemao' because of his blond hair

PLAYER
ZE ROBERTO
Full name: Jose Roberto da Silva Junior
Midfielder, Brazilian, 172cm, 71kg
Born: 06.07.74, Sao Paulo, Brazil
Clubs: Portuguesa, Real Madrid (Spa) (1996-98) Flamengo (1998), Bayer Leverkusen (Ger) (1998-
Full international (Brazil)
• Began his career at left-back, but Leverkusen had the good sense to use his sublime attacking talents in a much more advanced position, effectively employing him as a left-winger.
• Has thrilled legions of German fans with his uncommon athleticism and electrifying touchline bursts, though he is prone to individualism; Leverkusen striker **Ulf Kirsten** has complained that Ze Roberto hardly ever passes to him.

PLAYER
ZELIC, Ned
Defender, Australian, 187cm, 83kg
Born: 04.07.71, Sydney, Australia
Clubs: Sydney Croatia, Borussia Dortmund (Ger) (1992-95), QPR (Eng) (1995), Eintracht Frankfurt (Ger) (1996), Auxerre (Fra) (1996-97), Munich 1860 (Ger) (1997-)
Full international (Australia) 33 caps/3 goals
• An Australian international of Croat extraction,

e can do a good job as a sweeper or as a defensive midfielder. Captained the Aussie side which came ourth at the 1992 Olympics.

Surname pronouced Zel leetch.

EMEN, Zdenek
Czech

Born: 12.05.47

• Chain-smoking Czech who has been one of the most high-profile coaches in Italy over the past decade.

• Made his name with Foggia, who he guided to promotion to Serie A, before moving on to Lazio, who finished as runners-up in Serie A in 1995.

• Left Lazio midway through the 1996-97 season after indifferent results and he made the controversial move across town to Roma.

• He caused a storm in Italy in 1998 when he implied in a magazine interview that Juventus players had been using drugs to improve their physical condition.

• Had a brief, unsuccessful spell in Turkey in 1999, and took charge of newly-promoted Napoli in the summer of 2000.

ADMINISTRATOR
ZEN RUFFINEN, Michel
Swiss

Born: 24.04.59

• General secretary of FIFA since December 1998, when he succeeded **Sepp Blatter**.

• A former international referee (1993-95) who is responsible for the day-to-day running of FIFA.

• A lawyer by profession, he began working at FIFA as head of the legal department, becoming deputy general secretary in 1995.

PLAYER
ZENDEN, Boudewijn
Midfielder, Dutch, 174cm, 70kg
Born: 15.08.76, Maastricht, Holland
Clubs: PSV (1994-98), Barcelona (Spa) (1998-2000)

Full international (Holland) 26 caps/5 goals

• Speedy left winger who rose to prominence at PSV, being named Holland's Young Player of the Year and earning a transfer to Barcelona.

• Took time to adapt to life in La Liga, but was successfully converted to a left-back and kept local hero **Sergi** out of the side with some impressive performances.

• A member of the Dutch squads at France 98 and Euro 2000.

• Nicknamed Bolo.

• Excelled at judo as a youth.

• International debut v San Marino, 30.04.97.

• Linked with a move to Lazio in summer 2000.

PLAYER
ZEROUALI
Midfielder, Moroccan, 174cm, 70kg
Born: 17.01.77, Morocco
Clubs: Rabat, Aberdeen (Sco) (1999-)
Full international (Morocco)

• The Moroccan international brought hope to the downcast Aberdeen fans when his arrival at Pittodrie in December 1999 heralded a brief revival in the team's fortunes. Injury forced him to miss the closing weeks of the season, however, with the team ending up bottom of the Premier League, avoiding relegation on a technicality.

PLAYER
ZEWLAKOW, Marcin
Forward, Polish, 183cm, 77kg
Born: 22.04.76, Poland
Clubs: Polonia Warsaw (1995-98), Beveren (Bel), (1998-99), Mouscron (Bel) (1999-)
Full international (Poland) 3 caps/0 goals

• Strong, powerful striker who looks to have a bright future after scoring regularly in the Belgian League.

• Twin brother of **Michal Zewlakow**.

Boudewijn Zenden

PLAYER
ZEWLAKOW, Michal
Defender, Polish, 183cm, 77kg
Born: 22.04.76, Poland
Clubs: Polonia Warsaw (1995-98), Beveren (Bel), (1998-99), Mouscron (Bel) (1999-)
Full international (Poland) 7 caps/0 goals
• Twin brother of **Marcin Zewlakow**. Right-footed left-back with a good workrate. Can play on the left side in midfield as well. Made his debut for the Polish national team a few games earlier than his brother.

PLAYER
ZETTERBERG, Par
Midfielder, Swedish, 174cm, 74kg
Born: 14.10.70, Sweden
Clubs: Anderlecht (Bel) (1990-91), Charleroi (Bel) (1991-92), Anderlecht (Bel) (1992-2000), Olympiakos (Gre) (2000-)
Full international (Sweden) 30 caps/6 goals
• Accomplished creative midfielder who left Anderlecht in summer 2000 to sign a lucrative contract with Olympiakos.
• Was hugely successful in Belgium, winning the 2000 League title and twice being named footballer of the year. Was never booked in eight seasons with Anderlecht.
• Fell out with Swedish national **Tommy Soderberg** and refused to play at Euro 2000 in a dispute over the national team's long-ball tactics. 'I won't return as long as Soderberg is the national coach.'

PLAYER
ZHARINOV, Mikhail
Defender, Russian, 192cm, 84kg
Born: 25.01.75, Russia
Clubs: Dinamo Moscow, Uralan Elista
• Tall sweeper, reliable and a strong, clean, tackler.

IANI, Stephane

Midfielder, French, 171cm, 68kg
Born: 09.12.71, Nantes, France
Clubs: Nantes, Bastia, Rennes, Bordeaux, Lens, Deportivo La Coruna (Spa)

Pocket-sized schemer with quick feet and superior vision. A footballing gypsy, he changes clubs like he changes his boots. 'People call me a mercenary, but they forget I spent 15 years at my first club Nantes.'

Surname pronouced Zee ann nee.

ICKLER, Alexander

Forward, German, 188cm, 84kg
Born: 28.02.74, Bad Salzungen, Germany
Clubs: Dynamo Dresden, Bayern Munich (1993-)
Full international (Germany) 3 caps/0 goals

Although injury problems towards the end of the 1999-2000 season scuppered his chances of going to Euro 2000 with Germany, there were unmistakeable signs that this rangy attacker was finally coming of age after years of false promises.

A muscular forward of rip-roaring speed, he used to be infamous for snatching at goal chances. But not any more, it seems.

Goes by the nickname of 'Zico'. Whether it'a compliment or derogatory is debatable.

ZIDANE, Zinedine

Midfielder, French, 185cm, 80kg
Born: 23.06.72, Marseille, France
Clubs: Cannes (1988-92), Bordeaux (1992-96), Juventus (Ita) (1996-)
Full international (France) 59 caps/16 goals

• Brilliant midfield visionary who was voted World Player of the Year by *World Soccer* and FIFA in 1998 after scoring two headed goals in the World Cup Final. Was the inspiration behind France's success two years later at Euro 2000.

• Last of the great playmakers, according to Michel Platini.

• Scored twice on his international debut, against the Czech Republic in August 1994, the year he was voted Best Young Player in France.

• Big things were expected of him at Euro 96, but he suffered from fatigue after playing non-stop for the previous 12 months with Bordeaux reaching the UEFA Cup after qualifying through the InterToto Cup.

• Escaped unhurt from a car crash just before Euro 96.

• Won the Italian League in his first season in Serie A and finished on the losing side in the 1997 and 1998 Champions League Finals.

• Was the hero of France's 1998 World Cup triumph, despite being sent off for stamping on a Saudi Arabia player in a group match.

• Born in Marseille to Algerian immigrants.

• Nicknamed Zizou.

• 'Winning the World Cup has given me a remarkable feeling of self-confidence. It is not easy to keep pushing at this level, but when you're used to winning, it's a great feeling. You want it to go on forever.'

PLAYER

ZIEGE, Christian

Defender German 186cm 82kg
Born: 01.02.72 Berlin Germany
Clubs: Bayern (Ger) (1990-97), Milan (Ita) (1997-99), Middlesborough (Eng) (1999-2000), Liverpool (Eng) (2000-)
Full International (Germany) 52 caps/8 goals

• Has largely rediscovered the form which made him one of the world's best wing-backs when he won Euro 96 with Germany.

• Was set to move on from Middlesbrough in the summer of 2000, to Liverpool, after a season in which he had put his time with Milan behind him.

• Began as a goalkeeper before making his name at Bayern as a left-back.

• Missed the 1994 World Cup finals through

injury after making his international debut against Brazil in June 1996.

• Was one of Germany's stars at Euro 96, and he was expected to continue his success following a move to Milan in 1997. But he failed to find his best position amid the tactical straitjacket of Italian football, and was happy to move to Middlesbrough in 1999.

PLAYER
ZIELINSKI, Jacek
Defender, Polish, 184cm, 80kg
Born: 10.10.67
Clubs: Legia Warsaw
Full international (Poland) 39 caps/1 goal
• A rock in the centre of defence for Legia. Voted Polish player of the year in 1999. Made his national team debut in 1995 and has become the country's undisputed first choice.

PLAYER
ZILIC, Dragan
Goalkeeper, Yugoslav, 197cm, 90kg
Born: 14.12.74, Yugoslavia
Clubs: Vojvodina
Full international (Yugoslavaia) 1 cap/0 goals
• Solid keeper who has made it into Yugoslavia's full national squad, making his debut against Brazil in 1998.

PLAYER
ZITELLI, David
Forward, French, 180cm, 76kg
Born: 30.10.68, Longwy, France
Clubs: Nancy (1986-92), Metz (1992-95), Strasbourg (1995-98), Karlsruhe (Ger) (1998-99), Strasbourg (1999-)
• Veteran striker and free-kick specialist who returned to Strasbourg in January 1999 after a brief spell in the German second division with Karlsruhe.
• His best season was in 1996-97, when he scored 19 goals in 35 League games for Strasbourg.

Zinedine Zi

VKOVIC, Boris
Defender, Croatian, 182cm, 80kg
Born: 15.11.75, Zivinice, Croatia.
Clubs: FK Sarajevo, Marsonia Slavonski Brod, Hrvatski Dragovalac Zagreb, Bayer Leverkusen

Rugged right-sided Croat defender who is a capable man-marker and strong in the air. But he has been known to undo his good work by impulsively diving in for challenges which he has no chance of winning.

Surname pronounced Zeev ko veetch.

OFF, Dino
Born: 28.02.42

National coach of Italy since July 1998 until his surprise resignation in July 2000.

A distinguished career as a player: was Italy's goalkeeper and captain at the 1982 World Cup, aged 40. Is still Italy's most capped player, with 112 appearances (59 as captain), although **Paolo Maldini** is close to overtaking him.

• Won the Italian League six times with Juventus, having previously played for Udinese, Mantova and Napoli. Also a UEFA Cup winner (1977) and Italian Cup-winner (1979 and 1983).

• Spent two years as coach of Juventus (1988-90), moving on to Lazio (1990-94), before stepping aside to become club president.

ZOLA, Gianfranco
Forward Italian,168cm, 65kg
Born: 05.07.66, Oliena, Italy
Clubs: Nuorese (Ita) (1983-86), Torres (1986-89), Napoli (1989-93), Parma (1993-96), Chelsea (Eng) (1996-)
Full international (Italy) 35 caps/9 goals

• Diminutive striker who has been Chelsea's most creative player in recent seasons, scoring the winning goal in the 1998 Cup-winners Cup Final and proving that he remains a world-class player.

• Came to the game relatively late in his career, joining Napoli in 1989 where he eventually replaced Diego Maradona.

• Says that he would like to finish his career with Cagliari in his native Sardinia.

ZONGO, Mamadou
Forward, Burkina Faso, 179cm, 65kg
Born: 08.10.80, Bobo Dioulasso, Burkina Faso
Clubs: RC Bobo Dioulasso (1995-96), ASEC Abidjan (1996-97) Vitesse Arnhem (Hol) (1997-)
Full international (Burkina Faso)

• Forward who began early, playing League football aged 15, scoring 22 goals in his season and moving to ASEC Abidjan a year later.

• One of 22 children, his father having four wives. Half-brother Boureima is a Burkina international too.

• International debut aged 16, v Gabon, October 1996.

ZORIC, Sasa
Midfielder, Yugoslavia, 170cm, 66kg
Born: 02.09.74
Clubs: Obilic Belgrade

• Captain of Obilic and a hard-working midfielder with useful ball skills.

ZUBERBUHLER, Pascal
Goalkeeper, Swiss, 196cm, 99kg
Born: 08.01.71, Frauenfeld, Switzerland
Clubs: Grasshopper (1991-99), Basle (1999-2000), Bayer Leverkusen (Ger) (2000-)
Full international (Switzerland) 9 caps/0 goals

• Keeper who has been a stalwart of the Swiss League for a decade. Joined Leverkusen in summer of 2000 on loan for a year after Leverkusen signed **Hans-Jorg Butt** but could not persuade Hamburg to release him before the start of the 2001-2002 season.

Dino Zoff

PLAYER
ZUBOV, Hennadiy
Midfielder, Ukrainian, 162cm, 58kg
Born: 12.09.77, Ukraine
Clubs: Shakhtar Donetsk
Full international (Ukraine) 8 caps/0 goals
• Product of Shakhtar's youth system, a small utility player who can lead the attack and create from midfield. Unstoppable when at his best, he is a bright prospect both for Shakhtar and Ukraine.

PLAYER
ZURAWSKI, Maciej
Forward, Polish, 180cm, 74kg
Born: 12.09.76, Poland
Clubs: Warta Poznan, Lech Posznan, Wisla Krakow
Full international (Poland) 7 caps/0 goals
• One of the best young prospects in Poland who showed his potential shortly after joining Lech from second division Warta Poznan two years ago. Moved to Wisla in October 1999.

PLAYER
ZWAANSWIJK, Patrick
Defender, Dutch, 190cm, 86kg
Born: 17.01.75, Haarlem, Holland
Clubs: Ajax, Utrecht (1998-)
• Central defender who was still playing amateur football until recently. Was spotted by Ajax and is now making name at Utrecht. One for the future. Strong in the air and a regular scorer.

PLAYER
ZWYSSIG, Marco
Defender, Swiss, 190cm, 86kg
Born: 24.10.71, Switzerland
Clubs: Gossau (1993-96), St Gallen (1996-)
Full international (Switzerland) 5 caps/0 goals
• Lanky right-sided defender or midfield enforcer. A strong character who will fight to the last.

COACHES

ADMINISTRATORS

BUSINESS

AGENTS

OTHERS

REFEREES